URBAN
AMERICA

URBAN AMERICA

A HISTORY
WITH DOCUMENTS

Bayrd Still
New York University

LITTLE, BROWN AND COMPANY
Boston

Thanks are due the following persons and publishers for permission to
reprint material for which they hold the copyright:

The Belknap Press of Harvard University Press for an excerpt from L. H.
Butterfield, ed., *Diary and Autobiography of John Adams.*

Dover Publications, Inc., New York, for an excerpt from *Peter Kalm's
Travels in North America* by Peter Kalm. Reprinted through permission of the
publisher.

Harvard University Press, for an excerpt from W. T. Baxter, *The House
of Hancock: Business in Boston* © 1945.

The Massachusetts Historical Society, for an excerpt from "Journal of
Josiah Quincy, Junior, 1773," *Proceedings*, XLIX (1915–1916).

The University of California Press, for an excerpt from *The Autobiography of Benjamin Franklin*, ed. by Leonard Labaree et al., reprinted by permission of The Regents of the University of California.

The New England Historic Genealogical Society, for an excerpt from
[John Boyle], "Boyle's Journal of Occurrences in Boston, 1759–1778," re-
printed by permission of the New England Historic Genealogical Society from
The New England Historical and Genealogical Register, LXXXIV (1930).

The Macmillan Company, for an excerpt from *The Diary of George*

Credits

The American Academy of Political and Social Science, for permission to reprint excerpts from the foreword and five articles in *The Automobile: Its Province and Its Problems*, in The American Academy of Political and Social Science, *The Annals*, CXVI (November, 1924).

Franklin M. Garrett, for an excerpt from *Atlanta and Environs*, by Franklin M. Garrett, reprinted by permission of the author and Bruce M. Lewis, of the Lewis Historical Publishing Co.

The Nation, Inc., for an excerpt from Mauritz Hallgren, "Chicago Goes Tammany," *The Nation*, CXXXII (April 22, 1931), reprinted by permission of The Nation, Inc.

Wallace E. Maciejewski, for permission to reprint excerpts from Thaddeus Borun, compiler, *We, the Milwaukee Poles: the History of Milwaukeeans of Polish Descent and a Record of Their Contributions to the Greatness of Milwaukee* (Milwaukee: Nowiny Publishing Co., 1946).

The Macmillan Co., for an excerpt reprinted with permission from *The Urban Villagers* by Herbert J. Gans, © 1962 by The Free Press of Glencoe, a Division of The Macmillan Co.

Albert Boni, for an excerpt from Alain Locke, *The New Negro: an Interpretation*, reprinted by permission of Albert and Charles Boni, Inc.

James E. Burns, Director, The Chicago Commission on Human Relations, for permission to reprint excerpts from report, *Solving the Problems of Chicago's Population Growth*, May 29, 1957.

Time, Inc., for an excerpt from "The Black and the Jew: A Falling Out of Allies," *Time*, January 31, 1969, reprinted by permission from *Time, The Weekly Newsmagazine*; © Time, Inc., 1969.

The New York Times Co., for excerpts from the issues of November 23, 1969, June 14, 1970, April 22, 1971, February 3, 1972. © 1969, 1970, 1971, 1972 by The New York Times Co. Reprinted by permission.

Random House, Inc., for an excerpt from *A Study of Slum Culture*, by Oscar Lewis. Copyright © 1968 by Oscar Lewis. Reprinted by permission of Random House, Inc.

National Municipal League, for an excerpt from Frank Bane, "Feeding the Hungry," *National Municipal Review*, XXI (November, 1932). Reprinted by permission of the National Municipal League.

Curtis R. Buttenheim, for an excerpt from Herbert Hoover, "A Statement from Secretary Hoover to Readers of *The American City*," reprinted from *The American City*, XXXVII (November, 1927), permission of Buttenheim Publishing Corp.

Curtis R. Buttenheim, for an excerpt from "What the Cities Want from Washington," reprinted from *The American City*, LII (January, 1937), permission of Buttenheim Publishing Corp.

Columbia University Press, for an excerpt from Fiorello H. LaGuardia, "Making Democracy Work in the Modern Industrial City," *Proceedings of the National Conference of Social Work: Selected Papers, Sixty-sixth Annual Conference . . . 1939*, reprinted by permission of Columbia University Press.

Robert C. Weaver, for an excerpt from "Rebuilding American Cities: an Overview," *Current History*, LV (December, 1968), reprinted by permission of *Current History* and the author.

Michael Tabor, for an excerpt from "Forest Hills Report," reprinted from *Te'chiyat Hanefesh*, February 23, 1972, quoting *Genesis* 2, Boston, with permission of the author and consent of the publisher.

The North American Review, for an excerpt from Oliver McKee, Jr.,

"Washington as a Boom Town," *North American Review*, CCXXXIX (February, 1935), reprinted by permission of *The North American Review*.

The American Mercury Co., for an excerpt from Donald Wilhelm, "America's Biggest Boom Town," *American Mercury*, LIII (September, 1941), reprinted by permission of American Mercury, Torrance, Cal., 90505.

U.S. News & World Report, for excerpts from a copyrighted article, "Tragedy of Nation's Capital: A Story of Crime and Fear," *U.S. News & World Report*, July 29, 1968.

The New York Times Co., for an excerpt from Richard Reeves, "The Impossible Takes a Little Longer," *The New York Times Magazine*, January 28, 1968. © 1968 by The New York Times Co. Reprinted by permission.

E. P. Dutton & Co., Inc., for an excerpt from the book *BOSS: Richard J. Daley of Chicago* by Mike Royko. Copyright, © 1971 by Mike Royko. Published by E. P. Dutton & Co., Inc. and used with their permission.

John L. Cobbs, editor, *Business Week*, for permission to use excerpts from "Greater Miami Gets a Chance," *Business Week*, November 17, 1956, copyright 1956, by McGraw-Hill, Inc.

The Rotarian, for an excerpt from John Kay Adams, "Miami's Mighty Metro," reprinted from *The Rotarian*, April, 1959.

The Bobbs-Merrill Co., for an excerpt from Milton Kotler, *Neighborhood Government: the Local Foundations of Political Life*, copyright, 1969, reprinted by permission of the Bobbs-Merrill Co., Inc.

The Citizens League, Twin Cities, Minnesota, for permission to reprint an excerpt from Citizens League Report, *Sub-Urbs in The City*, Minneapolis, May 13, 1970.

Robert F. Wagner, for permission to reprint an excerpt from "Open Letter to Governor Rockefeller and Mayor Lindsay: The Danger of Decentralization."

Curtis R. Buttenheim, for an excerpt from Wallace L. Braun, "Are Business Streets for Parking — or Motoring?" reprinted from *The American City*, LV (August, 1940), permission of Buttenheim Publishing Corp.

Time, Inc., for an excerpt from Francis Bello, "The City and the Car," in *The Exploding Metropolis*, copyright, 1958, reprinted by permission of Time, Inc.

The New York Times Co., for an excerpt from Norman Mailer, "Why Are We In New York?" *The New York Times Magazine*, May 18, 1969. © 1969 by The New York Times Co. Reprinted by permission.

The Macmillan Co., for an excerpt reprinted with permission of The Macmillan Co. from Michael Harrington, *The Other America: Poverty in the United States*. © Michael Harrington, 1962, 1969.

Sterling Lord Agency, for an excerpt from Jimmy Breslin, "Paying Our Dues," *Daily News*, June 16, 1969. Copyright © 1969 by Jimmy Breslin. Reprinted by permission of The Sterling Lord Agency.

The Center for the Study of Democratic Institutions / The Fund for the Republic, Inc., for an excerpt from Hallock Hoffman, "Policing the Police," reprinted, with permission, from the May, 1968 issue of *The Center Magazine*, a publication of the Center for the Study of Democratic Institutions in Santa Barbara, California.

The New York Times Co., for excerpts from Eugene Raskin, Samuel Tenenbaum, and Richard Reeves, "Are Our Cities Doomed?" *The New York Times*, May 2, 1971. © 1971 by The New York Times Co. Reprinted by permission.

Credits

National Affairs, Inc. and Daniel P. Moynihan, for an excerpt from "Toward a National Urban Policy," *The Public Interest* (Fall, 1969), reprinted by permission of the author and *The Public Interest*. © National Affairs, Inc., 1969.

Illustrations

Cover: Gravure, "View North on Dearborn Street, Chicago, 1892," from *Chicago* (1892), courtesy Chicago Historical Society.

Part I, page 8: Etching by William Birch, "Arch Street," from *The City of Philadelphia . . . as it appeared in . . . 1800*, courtesy Prints Division, The New York Public Library, Astor, Lenox and Tilden Foundations.

Part II, page 74: Aquatint by Henry Papprill, "New York from the Steeple of St. Paul's Church, looking East, South, and West, after J. H. Hill," 1849, courtesy Prints Division, The New York Public Library, Astor, Lenox and Tilden Foundations.

Part III, page 204: Gravure, "View North on Dearborn Street, Chicago, 1892," from *Chicago* (1892), courtesy Chicago Historical Society.

Part IV, page 350; Photograph by J. R. Eyerman, "Los Angeles Freeway," 1967, courtesy J. R. Eyerman, Time-Life Picture Agency.

To Helen and Donald

CONTENTS

INTRODUCTION   3

PART ONE   10

      THE CITY
      IN EARLY
      AMERICA

1. *Emerging Urbanism*   10

Excerpt from an Inventory of New England Towns:
    1660   13
Town Lots in Philadelphia — a Good Investment: 1684   16
Virginia Needs Towns — a Colonists' Plea: 1697   19
Arguments for Towns and "Cohabitation" in Maryland
    and Virginia: 1705   20
A Planned Capital — Williamsburg: 1724   21
City Planning in Georgia — Savannah: 1735/1736   23
A New Jerseyman's Argument in Support of Cities and
    Urban Growth: 1753   25
Urban Concentration Opposed — a Counter View:
    1753   26
The City Criticized and Admired — John Adams: 1758   27

2. *Commerce and Industry*   28

Sweden's Peter Kalm Describes New York's
    Commerce: 1748   29

Contents

A Boston-Based Trading Venture: 1743   30
Urban Specialization — Wares and Services — New
  York: 1754   31

3. People   33

Problems of Scotch-Irish Migrants in Eighteenth-
  Century Boston: 1717–1736   33
Charles Town, Philadelphia, and New York — the
  Social Scene: 1773   36
Dogs in New York City: 1753   38

4. Government and Politics   39

Municipal Controls — New York City Ordinances:
  1731   40
Benjamin Franklin and the Evolution of Urban
  Services in Colonial Philadelphia   44
Support for a "Reform" Council — New York City
  Politics: 1735   47

5. The Break with England   49

"Mob" Activity in New York City: 1765   50
The Boston Tea Party: 1773   52
Grievances of the Workingmen: 1767   54
Governor Colden on Resistance in New York City:
  1774   55
Wartime New York City: 1775–1783   56

6. Urbanism in the New Nation   57

Burgeoning Baltimore: 1797   59
Town Making on the Illinois Frontier: 1820   61
Dr. Daniel Drake's Cincinnati: 1815   63
New Orleans — Seaport of the West: 1823   64

De Witt Clinton on the Obligations of City
   Government: 1815   67
Yellow Fever in Philadelphia: 1793   68
Poverty and Pauperism — Growing Problems in Growing
   Cities: 1815–1820   70
The Nation's Urban Prospects: 1819   72

PART TWO   76

URBAN
GROWTH:
1820-1870

1. *Transportation*   80

Railroads and Urban Rivalry: 1840's   81
New York City — National Metropolis: 1865   83
The Omnibus, the Railroad, and the Escape from the
   "Walking" City: 1850   85
Horsecar vs. Omnibus — Philadelphia: 1859   87

2. *Manufacturing*   88

Lowell — "Miniature Manchester" — with a Difference:
   1834   89
Pittsburgh — "Birmingham of America": 1862   92

3. *Town Making in the Middle West*   92

Jesup Scott on the Urban Potential of the Central
   Plain: 1853   93
James Fenimore Cooper on Townsite Speculation: 1835   94
A Paper City in Illinois: 1830's   97
Townsite Speculation — the Sober Afterview: 1840   98

Contents

Railroads and the Chicago-St. Louis Rivalry: 1860's   100
"Serene" St. Louis — Mirror of "Comfortable"
    Philadelphia: 1867   101

4. Urbanism and the Self-Conscious South   103

Northern Cities Criticized — a Defense of Southern
    Institutions: 1850's   104
The City Disdained — a Southerner's Reaction: 1857   107
New Orleans and the Trade of the West (and the
    World?): 1847   109
Hinton Helper Blames Slavery for the South's Lack of
    Cities: 1857   111
Baltimore — Metropolis for an Independent South:
    1860   113
Denial of Urban Ambitions Triggers Anti-Southern
    Sentiment — Buffalo: 1856   114
Charleston's Future — an Argument for Southern
    Independence: 1860   115

5. Immigrants   116

Living Conditions of Boston's Irish-Born Residents:
    1860's   120
The Foreign Born and the Urban Culture of the Middle
    West: 1850   121
New York's "Kleindeutschland": 1850's   123
The Immigrant and Urban Tensions: 1840's and 1850's   125

6. Blacks   127

European Views of New York City's Black Community:
    1820's and 1830's   128
The Black Community of Philadelphia: Late 1840's   130
Slavery in the City — "City Air Makes Free": 1852   132
Black Newcomers in Post-Civil War Atlanta: 1865   135
The Blacks of New York City: 1867   137

7. *The Urban Scene*   139

The B'hoys and G'hals of New York: 1849–1850   141
The Bowery B'hoys and the Tricks of the City: 1848   143
Fires and Fire Fighting: 1850's   146
Retail Stores — Attraction of the Big City — Philadelphia's Wanamaker and Brown: 1867   149
Anthony Trollope on American Hotels: 1860's   151
Hotels of the 1860's — "Palace Homes" for Residents and Travelers   153
The Ways of the Rich — New York City: 1865   155
Club Life in New York City: 1868   156
Mansions in the Middle West — Cleveland: 1858   157
The Modern Apartment House Anticipated: 1860   158
A Visit to Philadelphia's Suburbs: 1859   159
Suburban Growth in the Chicago Area: 1869   161
Tenement Conditions — New York: 1853   162
The Ways of the Poor — New York: 1868   163
Vagrant Street Children: 1850–1870   165

8. *Government*   165

Ward Autonomy vs. Citywide Communication — Milwaukee: 1852   167
New York's Mayor Fernando Wood — Spokesman for "No Mean City": 1856   168
James Parton on Municipal Corruption in New York City: 1866   170
A New Approach to the Government of Large Cities: 1867   173

9. *Urban Services*   175

Clean Streets—a Municipal Obligation: 1851   176
Urban Disorder and the Need for Improved Police Protection   179
Efforts to Achieve a Paid Fire-Fighting Force — Cincinnati: 1850's   181

Municipal Responsibility for the Public Health — New
    York: 1860's   183
Private Rights vs. Municipal Regulation — Housing
    and Pollution: 1868   184
Locking San Francisco into a Gridiron Street Plan:
    1840's   187
Trees to Grow in Brooklyn: 1830   189
A. J. Downing on Public Parks and Gardens: 1848   190
"Lungs" for St. Louis: 1852   191
Frederick Law Olmsted on Parks and Parkways as a
    Palliative for Urban Ills: 1870   192

10. *City vs. Country*   *194*

City Living Criticized: 1836   195
City Living Praised: 1855   196
Contrasting Views of the Large City: Mark Twain and
    Walt Whitman   197
The City of the Future — an 1870 View   201

PART THREE   206

URBAN
EXPANSION:
1870-1920

1. *Front Runners in Urban Growth*   *209*

Chicago, "Metropolis of the Prairies": 1880   209
Atlanta, "Chicago of the South": 1879   215
Urbanism on the Plains: 1888   218
Mushroom Towns of the Plains and Mountain West:
    1868   219
Dodge City — Kansas Cattle Town: 1877   221

Cosmopolitan San Francisco: 1882   223
The Difficulty of Defining Urbanism: 1880   224
Front Runners in Population Growth: 1920   226

2. *Why Cities Grew*   228

Material Reasons for the Urban Drift   229
Concentration of Production and Exchange, a Cause
   of Large-City Growth   230
Promoting Indianapolis: 1870's and 1880's   232
The Advantages of City Living: 1895   235
Ragged Dick Shows a Country Boy the Big City   238
A Playwright's View of the Lure of the City: 1909   239
Cultural Attractions and the Appeal of the City: 1904   241

3. *Technology*   243

The Operation of the New York "L": 1879   244
Richmond, Virginia — Pioneer in Electric Traction:
   1888   245
Reactions to the Opening of New York's Subway:
   1904   246
Wabash, Indiana — Pioneer in Electric Street Lighting:
   1880   248
Gas Company Derogation of Electric Light — Milwaukee:
   1881   248
Chicago's Towers: 1892   250
New York — "City of Giants": 1920   252

4. *Spatial Patterns: Segmentation,*
Mobility, and Suburbanization   253

Edward Everett Hale on Suburbs: 1880's   254
Adna Weber on Rapid Transit and Urban Decongestion:
   1902   256
Annexation — Legal Adjustment to Suburban Growth   258
The Suburbanite — an Emerging Type: 1902   259

Contents

5. The "New" Immigration   261

The Large City an Alleged Deterrent to Absorption of
    the Foreign Born: 1904   263
The Italian Immigrant in the American City: 1903   270
Russian and Polish Jews in New York City: 1902   273
The "Huddled Poles" of Buffalo: 1911   275
The Mood of the Ghetto — the Impact of the City on
    the Jewish Migrants: 1902   276

6. Blacks   277

The "Black Belt" of Chicago: 1905   278
Negro Housing in Newark: 1918   280
Race Riots in Chicago: 1919   281

7. The Tenement Problem   282

The Tenement Scene — New York: 1890   283
Human Breakdown in Stephen Crane's Rum Alley:
    Early 1890's   284
Theodore Roosevelt Assesses Tenement Reform —
    Brooklyn: 1911   288
Lawrence Veiller and Housing Reform through
    Regulatory Legislation: 1913   291

8. The Contributions of the Settlements
and the Urban Church   293

Jane Addams Describes Chicago's Hull House: 1892   293
Settlement Workers and Improved Conditions on New
    York's East Side: 1908   296
The Church and the City — a "Social Gospel" View:
    1907   297
The Salvation Army — Efforts to Reach the "Submerged
    Tenth": 1894   299
Transforming the "City Wilderness" — Boston: 1898   301

9. *Machine Politics* 303

The Mismanagement of American Cities: 1890   304
How to Build a Political Machine: 1880   306
The Lexow Investigation — Police "Payoffs": the 1890's   309
Lincoln Steffens on Municipal Corruption — St. Louis:
    1902   311
Countering a Franchise "Steal" — Detroit: 1891   313
The Political Machine as Welfare Agency: 1905   314

10. *Civic Reform* 316

City Clubs as Generators of Municipal Reform: 1912   318
Activities of Women in Civic Reform — Denver: 1898   320
"Civic Interest" Among the Working People — New
    York: 1907   322
The National Municipal League and Structural Changes
    in City Government: 1894–1916   324
"Business Government" in Houston: 1908   326
"Wards Must Go" — an Argument for City Manager
    Government: 1915   327
Statehood Proposed for Large Cities: 1913   328
An Active City — "The Hope of Democracy": 1905   330
Seth Low on Municipal Control of Public Utilities:
    1889   333
Hazen Pingree and Benefits for the People — Detroit:
    1890–1897   335
Tom Johnson, Reform Mayor of Cleveland: 1901–
    1909   336
Campaigning with "Golden Rule" Jones — Toledo:
    1901–1903   338
Planning for a "Better, Bigger and Brighter Milwaukee":
    1918   340

11. *City Planning* 341

Achieving the "City Beautiful" in Kansas City: 1892–
    1910   342

Burnham's "Chicago Plan" — Landmark in Comprehensive
  City Planning: 1908   343
Benjamin C. Marsh and Social Goals for City Planning:
  1908   345
John Nolen on City Making — a Scientific Art: 1909   346
The American City "Comes of Age": 1909   347
The New City and the New Democracy: 1916   348

PART FOUR   352

THE METROPOLITAN ERA:
1920-1970's

1. *Suburbs and New Cities*   354

Metropolitanism — the Twentieth-Century Feature of
  American Urbanism: 1960   354
Frederick Lewis Allen on the Evolution of Suburbia:
  1920–1950   361
Speculation in Subdivisions — Florida: 1925   363
Shopping Center — Symbol of Suburbia: 1951   365
New Regional Cities, not Suburbs — the Hope of an
  Urban Society — Lewis Mumford: 1926   368
Radburn — Twentieth-Century Experiment in Planned
  Urbanism: 1928   371
"Reston: A New Town for a New Kind of Life":
  1966   374
Suburbia — New American Norm: 1958   376
The Suburb Monotonous: 1960's   377
An Argument for Compact, Centralized Cities — Jane
  Jacobs: 1963   380
Robert Moses on the Virtues of the Central City:
  1956   382
A Case for the Central City — New York: 1967   383

2. *Urban Regions* 385

An Emerging Megalopolitan Regionalism: the 1960's   385
Urban Regions — Pattern of the Future   387
The Automobile and the City — Reactions: 1920's   390
The Automobile and the Central City — Atlanta: 1926   391

3. *Ethnic Elements* 392

A Czech Mayor for Chicago: 1931   397
The Polish-Americans of Milwaukee: 1946   398
Ethnic Enclaves as "Urban Villages" — Boston's West
   End: 1958   400
The City and the "New" Negro — Alain Locke: 1925   405
The Iron Ring of the Black Ghetto — Chicago: 1957   409
"Burn, Baby, Burn!" — Black Protest in American Cities:
   1967   412
The Black and the Jew — New York City: 1969   415
Italians and Blacks — Mayoral Politics in Newark: 1970   416
Puerto Ricans and the American City: 1964   418

4. *Federal Involvement: Relief* 419

How to Feed the Hungry? 1931–1932   420
When Local Relief Dried Up — Philadelphia: 1932   422
What Washington Does for Cities — Herbert Hoover:
   1927   424
What the Cities Want from Washington: 1937   425
La Guardia on Federal Aid for Distressed Cities: 1939   426
A Credo of Federal Responsibility for the City: 1937   427

5. *Housing and Urban Rehabilitation* 430

The Pros and Cons of Public Housing — Senate Hearings:
   1945   431
John F. Kennedy on the Challenge of the City: 1962   434
Secretary Weaver on the Federal Commitment to
   Urban Rehabilitation: 1968   435

Contents

"Model Cities" Accomplishments in Atlanta: 1969   437

The Complications of City Planning with Social Goals
— Forest Hills: 1971   439

A Call for Fiscal Aid from the Federal Government:
1971   441

6. Capital City   442

New Deal Washington — Boom Town of the 1930's:
1935   442

Wartime Washington — Boom Town of the 1940's:
1941   444

Washington — American City: 1968   446

7. City Management: New Style   447

Lindsay — Mid-Twentieth-Century Mayor: 1968   448

Chicago's Daley — Mid-Twentieth-Century Boss and
Mayor   452

8. Metropolitan Government   455

Metropolitan Government — Challenge of the 1960's   456

Metro Government for Greater Miami: 1956   457

Miami's "Metro" Has Its Difficulties: 1959   460

A Neighborhood in Charge of Its Destiny — Columbus,
Ohio's ECCO: 1969   462

"Sub-Urbs" in the City — Twin Cities, Minnesota: 1970   463

Two-Tier Government — "Metro" and Neighborhood
Reconciled — New York: 1972   465

The Dangers of Decentralization — New York: 1972   466

9. Urban Problems   467

Parking — Early Problem of the "Automobile Age" —
Baltimore: 1920–1940   468

The Automobile and the City: Late 1950's   470
Norman Mailer on Air Pollution — New York City
   "Etherized": 1969   472
Michael Harrington on the City and the "Other Amer-
   icans": 1960's   474
Jimmy Breslin on Drugs and the Insecurity of City
   Life: 1969   476
"Law and Order" in the City — the Dilemma of the
   Police: 1968   478

10. *The Urban Prospect*   480

Are Our Cities Doomed? "Yes," Says Raskin   481
Are Our Cities Doomed? "No," Says Tenenbaum   482
Are Our Cities Doomed? "Not Necessarily," Says
   Reeves   482
"Toward a National Urban Policy": 1969   486

Notes   489

Suggestions for Further Reading   543

Index to Special Topics and Selected Cities   563

LIST OF TABLES

Table 1.1   Urban Population in Colonial America   12
Table 2.1   Urbanism by State and Section: 1820 and 1870   77
Table 2.2   Population Growth of Representative Cities by
            Section: 1820–1870   79
Table 2.3   Foreign Born and Blacks in Populations of
            Selected Cities: 1860   118
Table 3.1   Urban Growth by State and Section: 1870–1920 207
Table 3.2   Population Growth of Representative Cities by
            Section: 1870–1920   210
Table 3.3   Foreign-born Elements in Populations of
            Selected Cities: 1900   264
Table 3.4   Foreign-born Elements in Populations of
            Selected Cities: 1920   266
Table 4.1   Population Growth of Representative Cities
            and Metropolitan Areas: 1920–1970   356
Table 4.2   Foreign Born and Foreign Stock in Selected
            Cities and Metropolitan Areas: 1970   394
Table 4.3   Number and Percentage of Blacks in Selected
            Central Cities: 1900–1970   406

ACKNOWLEDGMENTS

I have benefited from the work of so many people in the years since I began to think about the history of the American city — scholars whose views I respect and students of whom I am proud — that their number precludes individual mention. One I would single out, and that is Blake McKelvey, whose accomplishments during a long career of dedication to the study of urban history have been a source of inspiration as well as information. I am grateful to historians Glen E. Holt and Stanley K. Schultz and to Charles H. Christensen, of Little, Brown and Company, for suggestions made in connection with reading the manuscript, to Sally Carson, the designer, and to Deborah G. Otaguro, who had the responsibility of carrying the book through production.

Without great libraries — one of the ornaments of urban civilization — this book would not have been possible; hence I am much indebted to those who have assembled these rich collections and to the librarians who make them available to the public. I have made use especially of the New York Public Library, the library of the New-York Historical Society, the New York University Library, the library of the New York Genealogical and Biographical Society, and the Newberry Library, in Chicago. Xerox copying facilities are a boon to the author of a book of this kind. I thus acknowledge this contribution of technology to research, as well as the support from the Arts and Science Research Fund of New York University, which underwrote the cost of xeroxing. I appreciate, too, the cooperation of the many persons who have given me permission to use excerpts from their writing.

The preparation of many of the tables was the work of Marlyn Dalsimer. I greatly appreciate her help in this, as in other ways, as I do the assistance of Dr. Diana Klebanow, in the early days of the project. Along the way, I have benefited from the helpfulness of Elizabeth H. Dudley, of the New York University

Acknowledgments

Library, Dr. David Konig, Dr. Marilyn Thornton Williams, Peter E. Derrick, Liza Fields, Robert B. Fisher, Esther Katz, Diane Margulies, Andrea Miller, Judy Siegel, Evelyn Tondettar, Wanda Ward, and Rochelle Wolf. The typing of the manuscript was largely the work of Jane Butler, Sheila Macauley, and Lorraine Wolfson, and for assistance in the final stages of production I am much indebted to Emilie M. Adam. To all of these, my heartiest thanks.

URBAN
AMERICA

INTRODUCTON

No aspect of the American experience has had more influence on the pattern and problems of life in the United States today than the growth of cities. The overwhelming majority of Americans are now an urban — or suburban — people. No area of the economy or of the society, from production to politics, is unaffected by the aspirations and needs of cities and city dwellers. The attitudes and behavior of millions of Americans are conditioned by their experience and that of their forebears in the urban environment. This book is designed to put today's preponderant urbanism in historical perspective by tracing the nation's urban growth and the evolution of its urban society from the early seventeenth century to the present. Three centuries ago, the urban component of American society was limited to the residents of a few tiny clumps of urbanism hugging the Atlantic coast. Today, nearly three-fourths of the people of the United States are identified as urban dwellers, and the huge metropolitan agglomerations in which more than two-thirds of the total population are clustered can be found in all parts of the country. If the existence and settlement of the open West provided the nation with a significant behavioral experience in the course of its growth, so, too, did the existence of cities, their increase in size and number, and the problems they presented as the United States became predominantly urban.

What constituted "urban America" and how "urban" America was at any given time in its history depend upon how one identifies an urban community and an urban dweller and indeed upon the facilities of communication that affect the impact of cities beyond their borders. The census of 1970, upon which the statistics of urbanism in this book are based, designated as urban all residents of incorporated communities of 2,500 or more people and all persons living on the fringes of metropolitan clusters, whether or not in incorporated communities. This arbitrary criterion for identifying an urban community does not satisfy all interpreters of the American urban scene; in fact, the prerequisite population figure used by the census has varied from census to census over the years. Some critics of current census practice in this regard argue that a community is not truly urban unless it has a population of at least 50,000 people. At the other extreme are those who insist that a community and its residents are urban from the moment they aspire to urban status, regardless of population size. Occupational and ethnic diversity is often posited as a manifestation of urbanism; but the degree of urbanism this reflects depends upon the extent to which residents and outsiders view such occupations and such ethnic variety as contributing to an image of urbanism. Attitudes are often more significant than numbers as indices of urban status, and I have taken both into account in delineating the development of the nation's urbanism over the years.

The history of urbanism in American life can be seen to fall into four broad periods, at least when viewed in terms of the movement of population toward cities or within urban clusters and in terms of contemporary perceptions as to the place and potential of urbanism in the society and the economy. From the early seventeenth century to the early nineteenth century — an era of slow moving settlement — conditions in America gave life on the land a much stronger appeal for most Americans than city living. These years saw little perceptible increase in the small proportion of the population identified with urban centers, and as late as the 1820's most of the residents of the United States believed that the destiny of the young nation lay far less with cities than with farms.

A new tempo in city life, an evident acceleration of urban growth, and a much heightened interest in city promotion and in the nature of city living make the period extending from the 1820's to the turn of the 1870's markedly different from previous years. The surge of population westward following the close of the War of 1812 produced cities as well as farms; in the East new cities emerged to exploit the industrial potential of water power; immigrants from Europe, arriving in unprecedented numbers, supplemented native sources of urban population growth; and the railroad, an innovation of the 1820's that by 1869 had spanned the continent, facilitated the outward-reaching commercial activities that caused cities to grow large, both east and west. After two centuries in which urban dwellers had constituted less than 10 per cent of the total population, the proportion soared, by 1870, to 25 per cent. Between 1820 and 1870, there was a tenfold increase in the number of urban communities; those exceeding 100,000 in population rose from one to 14, and one of the 14 approached a million in population. By the late 1860's, contemporaries viewed the "rush" to cities, and especially to large cities, as heralding a revolution in national behavior.

The half century between the turn of the 1870's and the close of World War I constitutes an identifiable period in the nation's urbanism, in terms of popular attitudes and behavior, because in these years cities, and especially large cities, had a greater appeal and prestige, despite admitted shortcomings, than they had known before or were to enjoy thereafter. Large cities emerged in all parts of the nation, even in the traditionally rural South, as focal points of a developing economic regionalism that was fostered by the employment of new business and industrial techniques and by the extension of the nation's railroad network, which reached its maximum mileage in these years. During this half century, the number of cities exceeding 100,000 in population rose from 14 to 68, three of them with more than a million residents by 1920. At the same time, the proportion of urban dwellers in the total population increased from 25 to more than 50 per cent, with the result that the census, in 1920, disclosed for the first time that the nation was predominantly urban. Though this large-scale urbanism rested primarily on economic foundations, it also was encouraged by the residential inclinations of immigrants from Europe, whose numbers reached a peak in these years, and by technological developments that not only made possible the accommodation of large numbers of people in limited space, for business and residence, but provided for comforts of living and recreational opportunities in the city that could not as yet be matched in the small town or rural setting. In this era of manifest nationalism, flourishing cities were viewed as symbols of the nation's commercial and industrial achievement, and as late as 1920 many Americans looked optimistically upon the potential of large urban concentrations, when honestly and scientifically managed and supplied with publicly funded facilities and social amenities, to provide the best possible way of life in the modern era.

Disenchantment with life in the central city and an intensified identification of city dwellers with suburbs, becoming evident by the 1920's, differentiate this and the succeeding decades of the twentieth century from earlier periods in the nation's urbanism. Americans had been taking up residence in suburban communities for many years, but until 1920 the total population in the central cities had increased more rapidly than that in the communities that surrounded them. From the 1920's onward, however, the suburban fringes grew at a faster rate than the central cities, creating ever widening metropolitan complexes; and by 1970 the nation's suburban population actually exceeded the total in central cities as well as on farms. The motor car and the improved highway made possible the deconcentration that characterized this metropolitan phase of American urbanism; and here, too, the 1920's mark a turning point. By 1920, an automobile was registered for one in every 13 persons in the population, by contrast with one in 200, only 10 years earlier. By the 1920's, also, the federal government had begun to increase highway construction in ways that encouraged population dispersal. At about the same time, the advent of radio, talking motion pictures, and suburban shopping centers provided suburbanites with amenities of living formerly identified only with the central city.

As the century progressed, the mood of most city dwellers became increasingly critical of large cities as overcrowded, unhealthful, physically dangerous, unduly expensive, and politically unmanageable. The image of the city also suffered as the outward migration of the middle class left many central cities predominantly in the possession of the poor, many of them Blacks and Puerto Ricans. These years saw an increasing involvement of the federal government in the problems of the cities, but this belated recognition of urbanism as a national responsibility did not dispel the prevailing frustration over the dilemma of the large city, even among those who were convinced of its importance for the advancement of civilization. On the eve of the 1920's, American progressives had viewed the city as "the hope of democracy." By the 1970's the problems of many of the nation's cities were posing a challenge that the world's most experienced democracy was finding itself hard put to meet.

In tracing the growth of the urban segment of American society I have woven into the narrative excerpts from many contemporaneous commentators on the developing urban scene. These include not only such well known Americans as William Penn,

Benjamin Franklin, John Adams, Theodore Roosevelt, Herbert Hoover, John F. Kennedy, Fiorello La Guardia, Robert C. Weaver, James Fenimore Cooper, Horatio Alger, Frederick Law Olmsted, Stephen Crane, Jacob Riis, Jane Addams, Lewis Mumford, Frederick Lewis Allen, Michael Harrington, and Norman Mailer, but scores of others — merchants, townsite promoters, travelers, physicians, clergymen, mayors, city managers, policemen, legislative investigators, planners, municipal reformers, playwrights, magazine editors, and newspaper reporters — whose observations disclose the quality of urban life and the problems it presented in their day. In reproducing these excerpts I have adhered to the spelling, capitalization, and punctuation of the document, even though these deviate from stylistic practices elsewhere in the book. I also have provided a series of tables based on a wide variety of census figures, from which the nature, if not the attitudes, of the less articulate elements in the evolving urban society can be perceived.

The testimony of eye witnesses is offered not only to provide what seems to me convincing corroboration of the text, but also to give the reader an immediate sense of the tone and character of the urban side of American society as it evolved over the years and of the contemporaneous reaction to its development. This documentary evidence provides reinforcing proof that from the beginning of settlement urbanism has been a fact of American life with significant effect on the nature of the society and the economy, that Americans traditionally have exhibited an ambivalence of attitude and behavior toward cities that has complicated the adjustment to the nation's inevitable urbanization, and that because of the essentially timeless nature of urbanism the dilemmas of cities in the past, albeit less in the forefront of national attention, were strikingly similar to the problems — many still unsolved — of cities of the present day. This does not mean that these problems never can be solved, but that their solution will be hastened if the history of the nation's urban development, the ambivalence of its traditional reaction to city living, and the deep-rooted nature of its urban problems are better understood.

PART ONE

THE CITY
IN EARLY
AMERICA

The roots of the urbanism that dominates American society today extend deep into the nation's past, indeed to the days of the earliest permanent European settlements along the Atlantic coast. Urban centers were necessary to the flow and control of trade, in the opinion of the mercantile-minded joint stock companies and profit-seeking proprietors to whom European governments gave the responsibility for exploiting the New World. The settlers they recruited, though predominantly rural in background, were products of a society that knew cities and associated them with economic achievement and the advancement of civilization. By the early seventeenth century, when the first permanent settlements took shape along the North Atlantic coast, there were thirteen or fourteen cities in Europe with populations exceeding 100,000; by 1700, according to estimates, one-fourth of the inhabitants of England and Wales were living in cities and market towns. It could be expected, then, that from the earliest days of colonization the migration from Europe to America should have produced cities as well as farms.

1. EMERGING URBANISM

Many factors, besides tradition, encouraged urbanism in an environment where agricultural abundance was conducive to rural dispersion. Along the coast, towns were needed to implement the mercantile relations between the American plantations and their European sponsors; inland, towns arose at points where the products of the soil could be collected, processed, and exchanged. The insecurity of the wilderness dictated compact settlement for purposes of protection; centers of local administration inevitably attracted population. Urbanism was fostered, too, by its recognized relationship to economic growth and public order; and the prospect of profit from real estate speculation was present in the promotion of towns, even in colonial days.

Though the society of colonial America remained overwhelmingly rural, urban centers took shape from the beginning of settlement, and by the eve of the American Revolution the colonies had as many as 20 communities with populations in excess of 3,000 people. Some of these approached in size the larger cities of England, other than London. Most of them, like the "big three" —

Philadelphia, New York, and Boston — hugged the Atlantic coast: Portsmouth, Salem, Marblehead, Providence, Newport, New London, New Haven, Baltimore, Annapolis, Norfolk, Charles Town, and Savannah. The most populous inland towns (with populations of 4,000 to 8,000) were Norwich, Middletown, and Hartford, Connecticut; Albany, New York; and Lancaster, Pennsylvania. Many smaller clusters had a quasi-urban quality, to judge from the reaction of contemporaneous writers to their appearance and economy.

This quasi-urban quality followed from the nature of the original occupation of New England, which entailed settlement by groups of families to create a going community based upon the tradition of the English medieval village. The settlers were allocated parcels of workable land in the surrounding neighborhood, which they sometimes worked in common, but the home lots were so placed as to bind the residents into the social unity of an English village. The towns were relatively self-contained economically and subject to corporate self-government, the corporate allocation of land, and the ministration of a congregational church. The social life of the town dwellers represented what anthropologists would call a dense collective experience through the daily contacts of neighbors and townsfolk, the expectation of regular church attendance, and the continuous association of young people among themselves as they were growing up.

In time, the populations of some of these towns became less cohesive, as settlers moved onto more isolated farms; on the other hand, some of the towns, although they remained small, functioned increasingly as local social and economic centers, like Springfield or Braintree, Massachusetts, or, like Dedham and Brookline, near Boston, as suburbs or suppliers of larger cities. To a lesser degree, similar activities and a similar quasi-urban quality prevailed in the small inland towns of the Middle Colonies and in an occasional county town in the South, with its courthouse, shops, and lawyers' establishments.[1] These communities, together with the larger centers, constituted a segment of colonial society — probably never more than 10 per cent of the total population — that early was distinguishable not only in physical appearance but in social behavior from the society of farm and frontier.

The figures, based predominantly on estimates, in Table 1.1 exhibit the population growth of the major cities, those with pop-

Table 1.1[a]

URBAN POPULATION IN COLONIAL AMERICA[2]

	MAJOR CITIES				
	NEW AMSTERDAM (NEW YORK)	BOSTON	NEWPORT	PHILADELPHIA	CHARLES TOWN
1630	300				
1640	400	1,200	96		
1650	1,000	2,000	300		
1660	2,400	3,000	700		
1680	3,200	4,500	2,500		700
1685				2,500	900
1690	3,900	7,000	2,600	4,000	1,100
1700	5,000	6,700	2,600	5,000	2,000
1710	5,700	9,000	2,800	6,500	3,000
1720	7,000	12,000	3,800	10,000	3,500
1730	8,622[b]	13,000	4,640[b]	11,500	4,500
1742	11,000	16,382[b]	6,200	13,000	6,800
1760	18,000	15,631[b]	7,500	23,750	8,000
1775	25,000	16,000	11,000	40,000[c]	12,000
1776	5,000	3,500	5,299	21,767	12,000

SECONDARY CITIES ABOUT 1775

New Haven	(1771)	8,295[b]	Hartford	(1774)	4,881
Norwich	(1774)	7,032[b]	Middletown	(1775)	4,680
Norfolk	(1775)	6,250	Portsmouth	(1775)	4,590
Baltimore	(1775)	5,934	Marblehead	(1776)	4,386
New London	(1774)	5,366[b]	Providence	(1774)	4,361
Salem, Mass.	(1776)	5,337	Albany	(1776)	4,000
Lancaster, Pa.	(1776)	5/6,000	Annapolis	(1775)	3,700
			Savannah	(1775)	3,200

[a] This table reproduces the figures given in Bridenbaugh, *Cities in the Wilderness*, 6n, 143, 303n; *Cities in Revolt*, 5, 216–17. Bridenbaugh compiled these figures from a wide variety of sources; he points out that except for those taken from an actual census they represent estimates only.

[b] Actual census.

[c] This estimate of the population of Philadelphia differs from that of Sam B. Warner, Jr., who estimates that in 1775 not more than 23,739 people lived in Philadelphia—16,560 in the city proper and 7,179 in the adjacent districts of Northern Liberties and Southwark. *The Private City* (Philadelphia: University of Pennsylvania Press, 1968), 11.

ulations that exceeded 10,000 by 1775, and the populations of about that date in what might be called the secondary urban centers. As the figures for the major urban centers reveal, urban growth was slow and fluctuating in colonial days. The sharp decline in numbers that some of the cities showed in 1776 reflects the flight from the city at the outset of the American Revolution.

New England was early set upon its path toward urbanization by the manner in which towns were established and settled in that area. In the founding of Boston in 1630, John Winthrop envisioned his "Citty upon a Hill" as a centralized community whose residents would be "knitt together . . . as one man" in a physical as well as a religious sense. The founders of New Haven in 1638 staked out a town plot in the form of nine squares, reserved the central section for a market place, and assigned lots for home building in the remaining eight. With the increase in population, towns, based upon the authorization of a church and the promulgation of a covenant, spread inland, associating settlement of a mixed urban-rural sort with the utopian ideal that figured so significantly in the original occupation of New England.[3]

The semiurban, semirural quality of the early New England town is reflected in the "Briefe Discription of New England and the Severall Townes" that was written by a resident New Englander in about 1660. Its author was Samuel Maverick, an early migrant to New England, who, in marveling at "the handsome Houses & Churches in so many Townes . . . in a place so late a wilderness," anticipated contemporary reactions in the next two hundred years to the speed with which urbanism emerged in a frontier environment.[4]

EXCERPT FROM AN INVENTORY OF NEW ENGLAND TOWNS: 1660

Newbury — At the mouth on the southside of Meromack . . . is seated the Towne of Newbury, the Houses stand at a good distance each from other a feild and Garden between each house, and so on both sides the street. . . . In this Towne and old Newbury adjoining are 2 Meeting Houses.

Rowley — Three Miles beyound this Old Newbury is a large and populous Towne called Rowley. . . . the Inhabitants are most Yorkshiremen very laborious people and drive a pretty trade, makeing Cloath and Ruggs of Cotton Wool, and also Sheeps wooll . . . not only to supply themselves but also to send abroad. This Towne aboundeth with Corne, and Cattle, and have a great number of Sheep.

Ipswich — Three Miles beyond Rowley lyeth Ipswich at the head of Agawame River, as farr up as Vessells cane come. It hath many Inhabitants, and there farmes lye farr abroad, some of them severall miles from the Towne. So also they do about other Townes. . . .

Salem — . . . is very commodious for fishing, and many Vessells have been built there and (except Boston) it hath as much Trade as any place in New England both inland and abroad. . . .

Charles Towne — . . . hath some considerable Merchants in it and many usefull handicraftsmen and many good farmers belonging to it.

Cambridge — . . . in which there is a Colledge a Master and some Number of Students. . . . The Towne hath many great ffarmes belonging to it. . . .

Boston — the Metrapolis of New England . . . is large and very populous. It hath two handsome Churches in it, a handsome market place, and in the midest of it a Statehouse. In the Towne are fouer full companys of ffoote and a Troope of horse. . . . The Towne is full of good shopps well furnished with all kind of Merchandize and many Artificers, and Trad'smen of all sorts. In this Towne are kept the Courts of Election ye Generall quarter Court besids the Country Courts. . . .

Dedham — . . . In this Towne leiveth many Bisquett makers and Butchers and have Vent enough for their Commodities in Boston. . . .

Newhaven — . . . This Towne is the Metropolis of that Government . . . which was the first built in those parts, many stately and costly houses were erected the Streete layd out in a Gallant forme, a very stately Church; but ye Harbour proveing not Comodious, the land very barren, the Merchants either dead or come away, the rest gotten to their Farmes, The Towne is not so glorious as once it was.[5]

By 1660, Boston possessed a population of about 3,000 people. Already, within a generation of its founding, its activities as a political and commercial center had shattered the cohesiveness of Winthrop's covenanted community, and had pushed agricultural pursuits to the periphery of the town. Contemporaneous writers like Edward Johnson, author of *The Wonder-working Providence of Sion's Saviour in New England,* saw in this "Metropolis" of New England the promise of a "sumptuous city," with its "buildings beautiful and large," its "comly streets . . . full of Girles and Boys sporting up and downe," and its "continued concourse of people." [6] As the commercial focus of expanding New England, it remained the largest city in the American colonies until the mid-eighteenth century. On the eve of the American Revolution its population numbered close to 16,000.

A fortified trading post at the tip of Manhattan Island, established in 1625 or 1626 by the Dutch West India Company and called New Amsterdam, marked the frankly commercial origins of what was to become New York City. In the early days, the residents were mainly occupied with the fur trade and the processing of undressed pelts, lumber, and wheat for export to the Netherlands. By the 1660's, however, when its population approached 2,500, it was evolving from a wilderness trading post into a busy entrepot of commerce in the New World. "The town . . . hath good air," wrote a visitor to the city in 1661, "and is . . . inhabited with severall sorts of trades men and marchants and mariners." [7] Taken over by the British in 1664 and renamed New York, it grew into a flourishing seaport and provincial capital with a population estimated at 25,000 by 1775.

Philadelphia owes its origins to William Penn's conviction that urban development was essential to a colony's economic growth. This idea, together with the intention to build a city according to a plan, was implicit in Penn's provisions for the Quaker haven that became Pennsylvania. Town making and town design were not new to Penn, for he had been involved as early as 1677 in the founding of Burlington in West Jersey and later in plans for Perth Amboy. Pennsylvania investors were advised that a site would be established for "a large town or city" and that before land was distributed, "great roads" would be laid out "from city to city" as well as "streets in the towns and cities" so that no one would "build irregularly, to the damage of another." Pennsylvania's proposed metropolis — the future Philadelphia — was to be compact but uncrowded, "a green country town," free of the threat of damage that fire had visited upon London 15 years earlier.[8]

Contemporaneous plans for the reconstruction of London

probably influenced Penn and his surveyor general Captain Thomas Holme as they projected regular streets and symmetrically balanced open spaces for the new city. Their city plan, with a gridiron street pattern and a central square, became a model that was to have wide imitation in American cities; in following London's example of allocating squares for recreation purposes, they made the first provision, in a New World city, for public parks.[9] Surrounding the central city were to be "liberty lands," in which the settlers holding town lots were to be entitled to a farm. Philadelphia was founded in 1682; within a year it was so much a reality that a map portraying the plan of the new city (the primordial example of American townsite promotion), revealing its broad streets and tree-shaded squares, was published in London with the intriguing title, *A Portraiture of the City of Philadelphia.*[10]

In 1685, after spending a year and ten months in the province, Penn published a progress report (also largely for promotional purposes) in which he stressed the flourishing growth of Philadelphia — "our intended Metropolis." He recounted the first steps in realizing the physical pattern of the community, described the commercial and industrial activity in the new city, as well as the provisions for guaranteeing public order, and emphasized the already evident increase in the value of town lots.

TOWN LOTS IN PHILADELPHIA —
A GOOD INVESTMENT: 1684

Philadelphia . . . our intended Metropolis . . . is two Miles long, and a Mile broad, and at each end . . . upon a Navigable River. . . . Besides the High Street, that runs in the middle from River to River, and is an hundred foot broad, it has Eight streets more that run the same course, the least of which is fifty foot in breadth. And besides Broad Street, which crosseth the Town in the middle, and is also an hundred foot wide, there are twenty streets more, that run the same course, and are also fifty foot broad. The names of those Streets are mostly taken from the things that Spontaneously grow in the Country. . . . From [August, 1683 to August, 1684], a Year within a few Weeks, the Town advanced [from fourscore] to Three hundred and fifty-seven Houses; divers of them large, well built, with good Cellars, three stories, and some with Balconies. . . . There is also a fair

Key [quay] of about three hundred foot square . . . to which a ship of five hundred Tuns may lay her broadside. . . . We have also a Ropewalk . . . and cordage for shipping already spun at it. . . . There inhabits most sorts of useful Tradesmen, As Carpenters, Joyners, Bricklayers, Masons, Plasterers, Plumers, Smiths, Glasiers, Taylers, Shoemakers, Butchers, Bakers, Brewers, Glovers, Tanners, Felmongers, Wheelrights, Millrights, Shiprights, Boatrights, Ropemakers, Saylmakers, Blockmakers, Turners, etc. . . .

There are Two Markets every Week, and Two Fairs every year. . . . Seven Ordinaries for the Intertainment of Strangers and Workmen, that are not Housekeepers, and a good Meal to be had for sixpence, sterl. . . . The hours for Work and Meals to Labourers are fixt, and known by Ring of Bell. . . . After nine at Night the Officers go the Rounds, and no Person, without very good cause, suffered to be at any Publick House that is not a Lodger. . . . Some Vessels have been here Built, and many Boats; and by that means a ready Conveniency for Passage of People and Goods. . . . Divers Brickerys going on, many Cellars already Ston'd or Brick'd and some Brick Houses going up. . . . The Town is well furnish'd with convenient Mills. . . . The Improvement of the place is best measur'd by the advance of Value upon every man's Lot. . . . the worst Lot in the Town, without any Improvement upon it, is worth four times more than it was when it was lay'd out, and the best forty.[11]

Philadelphia prospered and with it the province of Pennsylvania. As a port of entry, it attracted migrants to the Quaker colony, many of whom remained in the city. Jobs developed as its merchants quickly made it an organizing center for trade within the British mercantile system; in turn the expanding urban market stimulated the agricultural development of the surrounding countryside. In 1690, Penn made an abortive attempt to found another city on the Susquehanna, but one metropolis sufficed for the region until after 1750 when Baltimore (chartered in 1729) began to perform this function in its area. By 1700 Philadelphia's population exceeded 5,000 (perhaps as much as a quarter of the total population of the region); on the eve of the Revolution its residents numbered close to 24,000, of whom about 16,500 lived in the city proper and the remainder in the neighboring suburban "liberties." By 1730 county towns (some founded by the Penn family), emerging in the back country, facilitated internal commerce and performed the nodal function as market towns for their neighborhoods that Philadelphia supplied for a wider area.[12]

In the southern colonies, too, both the desire for towns and a concern for urban planning were evident from the beginnings of settlement, even though the seeds of urbanism took far longer to germinate there than in other parts of the country. For both Virginia and Maryland, the authorities in Britain favored the growth of towns as a means of controlling trade, collecting duties, and discouraging an undue dispersion of the population. The London Company in 1606 instructed the settlers leaving for Virginia not only to establish Jamestown but also to "set your houses even and by a line, that your streets may have a good breadth, and be carried square about your market place." On numerous occasions from 1655 to 1705, laws creating port towns and providing inducements for their settlement were passed in the Virginia Assembly only to be repealed or set aside by the Crown because of pressure from local planters and British traders.[13]

Though presumably it would have been to the planters' advantage to have market towns and ports at which their tobacco could have been collected for shipment, it suited their convenience to trade directly with merchants in England. Moreover, a lack of acquaintance with towns on the part of many long-time residents of the colony may well have made them unaware of the advantages towns might afford. The British merchants, for their part, opposed the growth of towns in the New World in the belief that the gathering of tradesmen and artisans in towns might result in the rise of manufacturing and that towns would encourage the emergence of native importers whose competition they feared. Local advocates of towns also confused the situation by proposing the founding of more towns than at the moment were warranted and by opposing the efforts of the Crown to have port towns the exclusive centers of import and export.

The proponents of towns projected a grim prospect for Virginia if it failed to heed the example of New England in laying the basis for urban growth. This point was made in 1697 by three Virginians — a merchant and planter, a clergyman, and a lawyer — in a publication entitled *Large and True Account of the Present State of Virginia*.

VIRGINIA NEEDS TOWNS —
A COLONISTS' PLEA: 1697

. . . as to . . . natural advantages [Virginia] is one of the best. . . . But . . . if we inquire for well-built towns, for convenient ports and markets [it is] one of the poorest, miserablest, and worst countries in all America. . . . No doubt [this] is chiefly to be imputed to the first wrong measures that were taken *in not seating themselves in towns.* . . .

For want of towns, markets, and money, there is but little encouragement for tradesmen and artificers. . . . A tradesman having no opportunity of a market, where he can buy meat, milk, corn, and all other things, must either make corn, keep cows, and raise stocks himself; or must ride about the country to buy meat and corn where he can find it; and then is puzzled to find carriers, drovers, butchers; [or obtain] salting (for he cannot buy one joint or two) . . . which there would be no occasion for if there were towns and markets. . . . The merchants . . . are subject to great inconveniencies in the way of their trade, which might be avoided if they had towns, markets, and money. . . .

In New-England, they were obliged at their first settlement to settle in towns, and would not permit a single man to take up land, till a certain number of men agreed together, as many as might make a township; then they laid them out a town, with home lots for gardens and orchards, out lots for corn-fields, and meadows and country lots for plantations . . . which would have proved an excellent way in such a country as Virginia is. But this opportunity being lost, they [the Virginians] seated themselves, without any rule or order, in country plantations. . . . Their General Assemblies have made several attempts to bring the people into towns, which have proved all ineffectual.

One error has generally run through all these undertakings, viz. that they always appointed too many towns. . . . Another error . . . in their last law for towns, was, that they made it utterly unlawful to buy or sell any goods exported or imported but at these towns.[14]

Other arguments for towns, especially as stimuli for crop diversification and cultural growth, were advanced by Francis Makemie in his A *Plain & Friendly Perswasive to the Inhabitants of Virginia and Maryland For Promoting Towns and Cohabitation.* The conclusion of his "Perswasive," published in London in 1705, was that the only persons "averse to Towns" were "Fools, who cannot see their own Interest . . . in having Towns, . . . Knaves . . . afraid and ashamed of being exposed at a Publick Market, . . . Sluggards, . . . and . . . Sots, who may be best Cured . . . by a pair of Stocks in Town."

ARGUMENTS FOR TOWNS AND "COHABITATION" IN MARYLAND AND VIRGINIA: 1705

1. [With the promotion of towns and cohabitation] . . . our Woods and Timber, that are at present of little or no value to us, would be a commodity for many uses, as building Houses for Habitations, Stores, and other services; the worst thereof would be bought and transported for Fire-wood. . . . Also all the Product of our Plantations . . . that we can spare . . . should have a ready market at those Towns; so great Encouragement would be given thereby for raising and producing much more. And yet by the multitude of sellers, many things would be sold at easier rates than generally now they are in many places, where no Towns are. . . .

2. Towns . . . would soon fill our Country with people of all sorts, and so add to our strength, and render us more formidable against all Enimies which we lie naked unto. . . .

3. Towns and Cohabitations would render Trade universally more easie, and less expensive, especially to the Trading Part of England . . . if our Trade were reduced and contracted to particular places. . . .

4. Towns and Cohabitation would effectually prevent, and soon regulate a great many Frauds, Irregularities, Abuses, and Imposition on Trade and Trades. . . .

5. Cohabitation would . . . employ thousands of people . . . in transporting Tobacco, Provisions and Timber . . . others employed in promoting Gardens and Orchards to furnish those Towns with Fruit, Herbs, Roots, and Melons of all sorts; others would be employed in Hunting, Fishing and Fouling, and the more diligently if assured of a publick Market. And Tradesmen that a[re] half Tradesmen half Planters would altogether follow their Trades, and raise many Apprentices, which they are now discouraged to do, for want of a full employ . . . and all for want of Towns.

6. Towns and Cohabitations would highly advance Religion . . . for in remote and scattered settlements we can never enjoy so fully, frequently, and certainly, those Priviledges and Oppor-

tunities as are to be had in all Christian Towns and Cities. . . .

7. Cohabitation would highly advance Learning and School-Education: for this flourishes only in such places, for the smallest and meanest of schools cannot be maintained without a competent number of Scholars. . . .[15]

Fewer towns took shape in the southern colonies than their advocates desired, but those that were founded reflected, as had been the situation in Philadelphia, an interest in development according to an orderly plan. This was especially manifest in Annapolis, Williamsburg, Charles Town, and Savannah. Credit for the planned character of Annapolis (1694) and Williamsburg (1699) belongs to Francis Nicholson, who was governor at different times of Maryland and Virginia and who held other important colonial administrative posts. Nicholson, an inveterate advocate of towns, may well have been influenced by the ideas of Christopher Wren in devising a plan for Williamsburg that has been described, with that of Savannah, as "the most successful essay in community layout in colonial America." [16] The Reverend Hugh Jones, in a work on Virginia that was published in 1724, described Nicholson's accomplishments as a city builder and commented at the same time upon the obstacles to urban development in eighteenth-century Virginia.

A PLANNED CAPITAL — WILLIAMSBURG: 1724

The first *Metropolis, James Town*, was built in the most convenient Place for Trade and Security against the *Indians*, but often received much Damage, being twice burnt down; after which it never recovered its Perfection, consisting at present of nothing but Abundance of Brick Rubbish, and three or four good inhabited Houses. . . . When the *State House* and *Prison* were burnt down, *Governor Nicholson* removed the Residence of the *Governor*, with the Meeting of *General Courts* and *General Assemblies to Middle Plantation*, seven Miles from *James Town*, in a healthier and more convenient *Place*, and freer from the Annoyance of *Muskettoes*.

Here he laid out the *City of Williamsburgh* (in the Form of a Cypher, made of W. and M.) on a Ridge at the Head Springs of two great *Creeks* . . . at the Head of which *Creeks* are good *Landings*, and *Lots* laid out, and Dwelling Houses and Ware Houses built . . . . Publick Buildings here of Note, are the Col-

lege, the Capitol, the Governor's House, and the Church. . . .
. . . Neither the Interest nor Inclinations of the *Virginians* induce them to cohabit in Towns; so that they are not forward in
contributing their Assistance towards the making of particular
Places, every Plantation affording the Owner the Provision of a
little Market; wherefore they most commonly build upon some
convenient Spot or Neck of Land in their own Plantation, though
Towns are laid out and establish'd in each County; the best of
which (next *Williamsburgh*) are *York, Glocester, Hampton,
Elizabeth Town*, and *Urbanna*.[17]

The early settlers of Charles Town prided themselves on the formal plan that was adopted when what was to be South Carolina's
"cheeff town" was laid out in 1672 on a peninsula between the
Ashley and Cooper rivers. The town was "run out into four large
streets," wrote Maurice Mathews, describing the city in 1680. He
continued: "The Court house which we are now building is to be
erected in the midle of it, in a Square of two ackers of land upon
which the four great streets of 60 foot wide doe center, and to the
water side there is laid out 60 foot for a publick wharfe as also for
other conveniences as a Church yard, Artillery ground, etc., and
. . . care taken that the front lines be preserved whereby wee shall
avoid the undecent and incommodious irregularities which other
Inglish Collonies are fallen unto for want of ane early care in laying out the Townes." [18] Capitalizing on the merits of its port,
Charles Town attracted a larger population than did the other cities
of the colonial South. By 1775 it was a handsome city of 12,000
people, its regularly disposed streets lined with elegant town houses
and its dock area the scene of vigorous commercial activity.

Urban planning figured even more conspicuously in the beginnings of colonial Georgia. James Oglethorpe's plan for Savannah, which was founded in 1732, in many ways recapitulated the
earlier experience of the New World in town making. Whatever
its origins, the plan embodied features that had characterized both
the New England town and Penn's pattern for Philadelphia, as
well as the design ideas, especially the provision of squares, then
currently popular in England. For Savannah, Oglethorpe projected
a series of neighborhood units that he called wards, each with
uniform streets focusing upon a square and with lots reserved for
public buildings. Surrounding the compact settlement was open

space devoted to garden plots and larger farms.[19] The first steps in the realization of Oglethorpe's plan for Savannah, with its provisions for both orderly compact settlement and access to open space, were described in the journal of Francis Moore, keeper of stores for the new town of Frederica, Georgia.

CITY PLANNING IN GEORGIA — SAVANNAH: 1735/1736

The Town of Savannah is built of Wood; all the Houses of the first 40 Freeholders are of the same Size with that Mr. *Oglethorpe* lives in, but there are great Numbers built since; I believe 100 or 150, many of these are much larger, some of 2 or 3 Stories high, the Boards plained and painted. The Houses stand on large Lotts, 60 Foot in Front by 90 Foot in Depth; each Lott has a fore and back Street to it; the Lotts are fenced in with split Pales; some few People have Pallisades of turned Wood before their Doors, but the Generality have been wise enough not to throw away their Money, which in this Country, laid out in Husbandry, is capable of great Improvements. . . .

Each Freeholder . . . has a Lott . . . beyond the Common, of 5 Acres for a Garden. Every ten Houses make a Tything, and to every Tything there is a Mile Square. . . . Each Free-holder of the Tything has a Lott or Farm of 45 Acres there, and two Lotts are reserved by the Trustees in order to defray the Charge of the Publick. The Town is laid out for two hundred and forty Freeholds; the Quantity of Lands necessary for that Number is 24 Square Miles; every 40 Houses in Town make a Ward, to which 4 Square Miles in the Country belong. . . . Where the Town-Lands end, the Villages begin; four Villages make a Ward without, which depends upon one of the Wards within the Town. . . . There is Ground also kept round about the Town ungranted, in order for the Fortifications, whenever Occasion shall require. Beyond the Villages, commence Lotts of 500 Acres; these are granted upon Terms of keeping 10 Servants. . . .

There is near the Town, to the East, a Garden belonging to the Trustees, consisting of 10 Acres; the situation is delightful. . . . On the North-part of the Garden is left standing a Grove of Part of the old Wood, as it was before the arrival of the Colony there. . . . The Garden is laid out with Cross-walks planted with Orange-trees. . . . in the warmest part of the Garden, there was a Collection of *West-India* Plants and Trees, some Coffee, some Cocoa-nuts, Cotton, Palma-christi, and several *West-Indian* physical Plants, some sent up by Mr. *Eveleigh* a publick-spirited Merchant at Charles-Town, and some by Dr. Houstoun, from the *Spanish West-Indies*, where he was sent at the Expence of a Collection raised by that curious Physician Sir *Hans Sloan*, for to collect and send them to *Georgia*.[20]

Given the controlled character of much of Britain's colonization of the New World as well as the interest in urban design in England and Ireland during the era of settlement, it was natural that as towns were conceived, in implementing the colonization process, concern should have been given to physical planning of communities along European lines. Nevertheless, the local environment also influenced the form of America's nascent urbanism. The pattern of virtually every town from New England to Georgia provided for open space surrounding the clusters of dwellings and public buildings — common lands, liberties, garden plots, or farms. Space was at no premium in this period of beginnings (though it seemed to some to be by the close of the colonial period), and the planning of a community to ensure agreeable living was in the spirit of the idealism that underlay settlement in many of the colonies. In the larger cities, by the mid-eighteenth century population and business had already begun their unremitting encroachment upon open space, but interest in preserving the attributes of the countryside within the city and in having easy access to the country typified the image of the urbanism that was taking shape in America in these early years.

The increased size and complexity of American cities by the 1750's — even though none then exceeded 20,000 people — were already prompting the expression of the conflicting views concerning the merits of urban living that were to become a constant quality of American attitudes toward the city. The chief argument at this time in support of urban development was the continued assertion of the economic benefits to be derived from cities, as set forth in Virginia as early as the late seventeenth century. In 1753 a New Jersey correspondent to the *New-York Gazette* extolled the specialization that cities made possible and argued that, given the existence of cities, farmers could specialize, too, and reap the benefits of supplying an urban market.

A NEW JERSEYMAN'S ARGUMENT IN SUPPORT OF CITIES AND URBAN GROWTH: 1753

It should not be permitted for one Man to carry on the Business of Tanning, Currying, and Shoemaking; much less ought a Farmer to do one or all of those Occupations within himself; but they being all different Handicrafts, ought to be the Business of different Persons, that so Work might be done to Perfection, which would be a considerable Profit to the Country, as well as a comfortable Support, to those who are Proficients in those Handicrafts: For by unexperienced Persons, a considerable Value of Materials are wasted; and such as are good Proficients, are debarr'd of those Benefits which are justly due to them, and may be deemed so much Loss to the publick Interest. . . .

A Farmer also ought to employ himself in his proper Occupation, without meddling with Smiths, Masons, Carpenters, Coopers, or any other mechanical Arts, except making and mending his Plow, Harrow, or any other Utensil for Farming. . . .

Shop-keepers, at present, settling at every 2, 3, or 4 Miles Distance, throughout a considerable Part of the Province hinders Towns from increasing; and at the same Time, such Shop-keepers themselves, get scarce enough to subsist. . . .

It wou'd be no Inconveniency to the Country, for Tradesmen to settle in, or near a Town for Exportation, because the Produce of the Country must be brought by Land-Carriage to such a Town, in order to be exported. Therefore, People cou'd be sure to supply themselves, with all Sorts of Necessaries at such Towns; whereas now they must, oftentimes, spend more Time to and fro for a Pair of Shoes, or other Necessaries than they are worth; not to mention, that many of our Inhabitants are often obliged to go, or send to the neighbouring Provinces for many Things; which, if such Towns were improved, Merchants might be enabled to keep so large an Assortment, that there would not be so great a Need to be beholden to our neighbouring Provinces. . . . Moreover, such Regulations wou'd cause an extraordinary Vent for Provisions of all Kinds; such as Beef, Pork, Mutton, Veal, Poultry, Garden-Roots and Herbs, etc. by the Profits of which, many Families might subsist on small Plantations, and small Stocks of Cattle.

And this, no doubt, wou'd be a great Benefit . . . especially to the rising Generation; for as Land grows scarce, and increases in Value, our Posterity will, in all Probability, be obliged to seek their Subsistence on small Plantations; which is impossible, if there are no populous Towns, where they may vent their Provisions: For instance, Farmers within 10, or 12 Miles of the City of *New-York*, not only get a comfortable Living, but even grow wealthy on 10, 20, 30, or 40 Acres of Land, as effectually as our Farmers do, on one, 2, 3, or 400 Acres.[21]

In the same year the standard ingredients of the negative attitude toward cities were expressed in the comments of New Yorker William Smith, Jr., in a January, 1753 issue of *The Independent Reflector*, a single-essay journal of which he was one of the editors. Urban concentration was contrary to the ideal of self-sufficient husbandry, he argued, and luxury and ostentation were the undesirable results of the specialization that cities encouraged.

URBAN CONCENTRATION OPPOSED —
A COUNTER VIEW: 1753

There is Nothing more common, in *Connecticut* and the *Massachusetts-Bay* Colonies, . . . than for Gentlemen to urge the great Number of their Towns, as a Proof of the Prosperity of their Country; whereas Nothing can be of more mischievous Consequence to all new Settlements. Sound Policy will teach them, that Husbandry calls for their first Attention; erecting Townships being never adviseable, till the Number of Planters can supply their Necessities; nor even then, are they to be encouraged, unless the Rise of Arts and useful Manufactures, render the reciprocal Aids of the Inhabitants indispensibly necessary. Every Town unemployed in these, is a dead weight upon the Public; for when Families collect themselves into Townships, many Tracts of Land, must, of Consequence, lie unimproved: Besides, such persons will always endeavour to support themselves by Barter and Exchange; which can by no Means augment the Riches of the Public. . . . Now, suppose, what really is true, that not a Town in those Provinces, of which there are not less than three Hundred, is, in the least Degree, supported by any kind of Manufacture whatsoever; how vast must be their Consumption! how incredible their Expence! . . .

Another Consequence of their clustering into Towns, is Luxury — a great and mighty Evil, carrying all before it, and crumbling States and Empires, into slow, but inevitable Ruin. . . . It is almost impossible for a Number of People, and absolutely so, if they are idle, to live together, but they will very soon attempt to outvie each other, in Dress, Tables, and the like. This is the Case in the *Massachusetts-Bay*: Let a Man enter one of their Country Churches, and he will be struck with the Gaiety of Ladies, in Silks and Lawn. . . . *Boston* is their pattern, and too, too closely imitated. . . . perhaps it may deserve the serious Consideration, of their *Society for the Promotion of Industry, and Employment of the Poor*, whether the first Step they took, should not be, to dissipate their Towns, and multiply the Number of their Farms.[22]

Ambivalence, which traditionally has characterized the attitude of many Americans toward cities, found early expression in the comments of 23-year-old John Adams, after he had visited Boston in 1758. The future president was offended by the noise, the filth, and the distracting confusion of the city, where he had gone to arrange for his admission to the bar. He nevertheless confessed his pleasure in being able to observe the most distinguished lawyers of the colony and to attend a "Consort" in the "most Spacious and elegant Room," amid the "gayest Company of Gentlemen and the finest Row of Ladies" he had ever seen.[23]

THE CITY CRITICIZED AND ADMIRED — JOHN ADAMS: 1758

Am returned from Boston, and according to my Promise. . . begining to write you a Discription or a History of what I saw, and heard, &c. . . .

My Eyes were entertained with Objects, in every figure and Colour of Deformity, from the Blacksmith in his darksome Shop to the Chimney Sweeper rambling in the Streets. My Ears were ravished with every actual or imaginable sound, except harmonious sounds, from the Hurley burley upon Change, to the Rattling and Grumbling of Coaches and Carts &c. The fragrance of the Streets, were a continual feast to my Nostrils. — Thus Pleasure entered all my senses, and roused in my Imagination, scenes of still greater tumult, Discord, Deformity, and filth.

As for Reason, what Entertainment could that find, among these Crouds? None. . . .

But all this is the dark side. — In reward of this Pain, I had the Pleasure to sit and hear the greatest Lawyers, orators, in short the greatest men, in America, harranging at the Bar, and on the Bench. I had the Pleasure of Spending my Evenings with my friends in the . . . Joys of serene sedate Conversation, and perhaps it is worth my while to add, I had the Pleasure of seeing a great many, and of feeling some very [pretty?] Girls.[24]

2. COMMERCE AND INDUSTRY

Trade and commerce held the center of the stage in the economic life of the major colonial cities, but a sizable proportion of the urban population (at least half of Philadelphia's work force by 1774)[25] was engaged in processing pursuits that today would be labeled manufacturing — spinning, weaving, milling, brewing, baking, sugar refining, shipbuilding, and metal work. The merchants in Boston early traded with the rural hinterland, exchanging furs, grain, timber, and cattle for manufactured goods; this activity, together with seagoing trade, accounted for the early preeminence of Boston in terms of population. The relative size of population and economic position of the cities were changing, however, by the mid-eighteenth century, as New York and Philadelphia benefited from the movement of farmer-settlers into their potentially broader hinterlands and as they caught up with Boston in shipbuilding. By 1760 both New York and Philadelphia exceeded Boston in population. Flour, meat, and livestock, produced on frontier farms, gave the merchants of New York and Philadelphia commodities for trade with the West Indies, England, and southern Europe; the processing of goods both for shipment and for the local market provided employment for increasing numbers of artisans. By the mid-eighteenth century the economy of the major colonial cities exhibited specialization both in retail merchandising and in the production of "manufactured" goods.

The imperatives and the opportunities of trade and commerce made the cities of colonial America the seedbeds of social change, economic growth, and conflict within the British Empire. Merchant operations fostered, indeed necessitated, contacts with the wider world both inside and outside the bounds of British mercantile regulations. In Boston, the activities of local merchants and of the newcomers whom trade brought to the community transformed a town that had been expected to be an isolated Bible Commonwealth into a center of trade and commerce touched by the business spirit of a new age.[26] Similarly, elsewhere, the vigor of merchant activity underwrote increases in population and local wealth. The far-roving character of New York City's trade was described by the Swedish naturalist, Peter Kalm, Professor of Economy in the University of Åbo, who visited New York and Philadelphia in the fall of 1748. He was impressed with the commercial mien of these thriving colonial cities — the waterside dwellings of the leading merchants, the busy wharves, and the "very numerous shipping" in the harbors.

SWEDEN'S PETER KALM DESCRIBES NEW YORK'S COMMERCE: 1748

New York probably carries on a more extensive commerce than any town in the English North American provinces, at least it may be said to equal them. . . . The trade of New York extends to many places, and it is said they send more ships from there to London than they do from Philadelphia. They export to that capital all the various sorts of skins which they buy of the Indians, sugar, logwood, and other dyeing woods, rum, mahogany and many other goods which are the produce of the West Indies, together with all the specie which they get in the course of trade. Every year several ships are built here, which are sent to London and there sold; and of late years a quantity of iron has been shipped to England. . . . New York sends many ships to the West Indies with flour, grain, biscuit, timber, tuns, boards, meat and pork, butter, and other provisions, together with some of the few fruits that grow here. Many ships go to Boston in New England with grain and flour, and take in exchange, meat, butter, timber, different sorts of fish, and other articles, which they carry further to the West Indies. They now and then carry rum from Boston, which is distilled there in great quantities, and sell it here at a considerable advantage. . . . The Hudson River is very convenient for the commerce of this city. . . . During eight months of the year this river is full of greater and lesser vessels, either going to New York or returning from there, laden either with native or foreign goods.[27]

The trade with the West Indies was made necessary because of obstacles, in some types of trade, to a two-way direct exchange between the colonial cities and England. Merchants of the Middle Colonies and New England thus engaged in multilateral trading operations that widened the colonists' horizons and often brought them into conflict with mercantile regulations imposed by the Mother Country. The ships of Thomas Hancock, a successful

Boston merchant of the 1740's, engaged in complicated operations, carrying fish to the West Indies, taking on molasses (sometimes illegally from French possessions) as well as other cargoes, which, after their return to Boston, often were carried to Holland to be exchanged for European merchandise, in violation of British regulations.[28] Hancock's instructions to Captain Simon Gross, concerning a trading venture of 1743, illustrate the international character of the operations in which these urban merchants were engaged.

A BOSTON-BASED TRADING VENTURE: 1743

Capt Simon Gross   Boston Dece[r] 20th 1743
   You having the Command of the *Charming Lydia* Brigantine and She in all Respects fitt for the Sea, My Order to you is that you take the first wind & weather for Sailing and proceed to the West Indies. You have Liberty to go to any of the English Islands, & if you think it Safe to any of the french Islands. . . . You . . . are to procure a Load of Molasses & proceed back to Boston & if you have more Cargo than Loads you, then Ship it on the best Terms you Can in Molasses or bring it in Indigo. I'd have you unload at Nantaskett if no man of War there. You are Interested One eighth in the Cargo & are to have one eighth of the neat proceeds of Returns. . . . Make all possible Dispatch that you may be here early for the Land, See that your Casks be Good, & well Stow'd, bring me some fruit for the officers if any to be had, be prudent & saving of Expences — Should it happen that you Can get bills of Exchange on Holland or England for your Cargo at a good price & a good freight for Holland or England you may take it, advising me thereof that I may Insure, or if you have Oppertunity to Sell Vessell & Cargo for Bills on Holland or London at a price you think may answer you have my Liberty. . . . But if you come back to this place a Load of Molasses will be the best Cargo you can bring here. . . . The Good Lord protect you & our Interests, from all Dangers & Enemies & Give you Conduct & prudence in all things to act for the Best, I wish you a Good Voyage & am your Owner.[29]

Imports from Europe were increasingly supplemented in the seaboard cities by the products of local craftsmen, such as tailors, hatmakers, shoemakers (cordwainers), furniture and cabinetmakers (joiners), and metalworkers (gunsmiths, tinsmiths, and silversmiths). As the cities grew, production in these and other crafts was characterized by an increasing specialization and a refinement of skills that sprang from the magnitude of the demand and the presence of competition in the urban market.[30] Here, as in trading operations, the dynamics of the urban economy brought local activity into potential conflict with British regulations. By the mid-eighteenth century, advertisements in the newspapers of the major cities, as in the following excerpts from *The New-York Gazette: or, the Weekly Post-Boy*, mirrored the variety of products — merchant's imports and craftsmen's handiwork — as well as the specialized services available to the urban dweller.

URBAN SPECIALIZATION — WARES AND SERVICES — NEW YORK: 1754

Just imported in the *Snow* Irene, *Capt.* Garrison, and *Snow* Hull Merchant, Capt. Griffiths, from London, and to be sold by RICHARD VAN DYCK At his Store in *Hanover-Square*, near the *Meal Market* A Large Assortment of *European and India Goods*, for the Season: Also, Looking Glasses, Sconces, Pictures, Florence Oil, and best Bohea Tea.   — July 22, 1754

M. DERHAM, Millener, from London, by Way of Philadelphia, in the *Rachel*, Capt. *Joy*, at her Shop near Alderman Livingston's, in Smith-Street, has brought a genteel and new Assortment of figur'd Ribbons, plain Ducaps, and Sattin ditto, Gauzes, Cat cut, Parisnet, white and colour'd Blond Lace, Silk Edgings, and Thread ditto, Gauze Handkerchiefs, strip'd and plain Dresden Handkerchifs, Aprons, Ruffles both for Gentlemen and Ladies, French Gloves, neat tann'd, glaz'd and Sattin Gloves, Necklaces, Ear-Rings, Fans, Patches, and Court Plaister, Lavender, Hungary, and Honey Waters; Chip Hats; French Silks for Capuchines, black Silk Laces and Fringes, Hollands, Long-Lawns . . . ; likewise an Assortment of Hosery and Haberdashery, fine Green and Bohea Teas, Ladies Shoes; an Assortment of Cutlery, Cards and Ink Powder. . . . Every Thing in the Millenery Way, is made up after the newest Fashion, such as Lappet Heads, Caps, French Handkerchiefs, Ruffles, Stomachers, Ruffs, Sleeve and Glove Knots, Shades, Capuchines, Bonnets, &c. at the very lowest Prices.   — August 26, 1754

To be sold by JACOB REED, Taylor, at his House in William-Street, three doors above Mr. John Dyer's near the Horse and Cart, A Choice Assortment of ready made Cloaths, both for Men and Boys, in full Suits or otherwise, both fine and Corse, of dif-

ferent Sorts, Colour, and Make, from a Superfine to a Bear-skin; Surtout, and new fashion'd Taberwelton Coats and Wais-coats, Scarlet, black Shagg, Plush and Stocking Waistcoats and Breeches, and Working Jackets, all as well made as can be done in England, or for the most constant Customers, at the most reasonable rates, by their humbly Servant   JACOB REED
— December 30, 1754

WILLIAM ANDERSON, Taylor, who lately lived in *Queen-street*, next door to Mr. Robert G. Livingston's, near the Meal-Market; has removed to the House wherein Mr. *Van Dyck*, Cutler, lived, in *Hanover Square*, between the Dwelling Houses of Mr. *Lewis Morris*, Merchant, and *John Brown*, Ironmonger, where he continues his Business to make Clothes, either lac'd or plain, with his usual Care and Expedition.   — May 27, 1754

DANIEL FUETER, Gold and Silver-smith Lately arrived in the Snow *Irene*, Capt. *Garrison* from *London*, living back of Mr. *Hendrick Van De Waters*, Gun-Smith, near the Brew-House of the late Harmanus Rutgers . . . makes all Sorts of Gold and Silver Work, after the newest and neatest Fashion; he also gilds Silver and Metal, and refines Gold and Silver after the best Man-ner . . . all at a reasonable Rate. He buys old Gold and Silver Lace, and Gold-smith's Sweeps.   — July 8, 1754

MARGARET POWELL, living at Mrs. Elbertson's in New-Street, New York, hereby gives Notice that she undertakes the Cure of all Rhumatic Pains, Sore Legs, and Cataracts of the Eyes; but above all the Canker, either in the Nose, Mouth, or Throat, of ever so long standing, or to whatever Height the dis-ease might have run: — She has lately made a Cure of an ob-stinate Canker in the City of New-Brunswick. — August 26, 1754

TO BE SOLD (for no Fault) A LIKELY handy House Wench, about 28 Years Old, with her Child: Enquire of the Printers hereof.   — December 9, 1754

RUN away on the 1st Instant *November*, from Garret Cozine, of this City, a *German* Servant Man, named *George Tele*, by Trade a Joiner, aged about 35 Years, about 5 feet 5 Inches high; he wears his own Hair, and has the middle finger of his Left Hand cut off, and speaks broken *English*. Had on a green close bodied Coat, blue Jacket, one Leather Pair of Breeches, and another of black Cloth, one white and one check Shirt, an old Beaver Hat, and a pair of half worn Shoes, with Brass Buckles. Whoever takes up and secures said Servant, so that his Master may have him again, shall have *Twenty Shillings* Reward, and reasonable Charges, paid by Garret Cozine.

— December 9, 1754 [31]

3. PEOPLE

The variety in occupational activity that characterized the mid-eighteenth-century city was matched by an increasing diversity in the racial and ethnic ingredients of the major cities and by a widening disparity in social status. By 1750, Blacks constituted at least 40 per cent of the population in Charles Town, 16 per cent in New York, and 8 per cent in Boston. Beginning in the second quarter of the eighteenth century, a rising tide of Palatine Germans and migrants from northern Ireland of Scottish and Irish background increased the already considerable cosmopolitanism of New York City, added variety to the population of Charles Town, and contributed a large and as yet generally unassimilated German element to Philadelphia's population. By the early 1730's a German newspaper was being published in the Pennsylvania city, German signs could be seen over shop doors, and local merchants advertised in German in the English press.[32] Though many of the European newcomers moved inland from the ports of entry, a considerable number, with skills as artisans or without resources to go further, remained in the seaboard cities. Because of the demand for their labor they encountered little hostility except in Boston where, in 1729, antagonism in the form of mob resistance to the landing of Scotch-Irish migrants anticipated the nativism of later years.[33] The records of the Boston town government document the local reaction to these Scotch-Irish newcomers and exhibit some of the problems they faced in a community more exclusive than most, where there was strong opposition to migrants — European-born or otherwise — who might become a public charge.

PROBLEMS OF SCOTCH-IRISH MIGRANTS IN
EIGHTEENTH-CENTURY BOSTON: 1717–1736

[October 28, 1717.] At a meeting of ye Select men. . . . Voted. That the Select men will defray ye charge of Sending [out of the city] Severall persons Strangers who have Obtruded into this Town. [Among these] James Goodwin from Ireland who arrived here wth Capt Douglis ab^t a moneth before, was on ye 28th of Septr Last warned to depart.

[May 4, 1723.] The Inhabitants According to Adjornment being Assembled. . . . Whereas great numbers of Persons have very lately bin Transported from Ireland into this Province, many of which . . . Are now Resident in this Town whose Circomstances and Condition are not known, Some of which if due care be not taken may become a Town Charge or be otherwise prejudical to the well fair & Prosperity of the Place. for Remedy whereof Ordered That Every Person now Resident here, that hath within the Space of three years last past bin brought from Ireland, or for the future Shal come from thence hither, Shal come and Enter his name and Occupation with the Town Clerk, and if marryed the number and Age of his Children and Servants. . . .

[September 9, 1730.] William fryland & francis Clinton Joyners from Ireland are admitted to Reside and Inhabit within this Town and have Liberty to Exercise their Callings haveing [given] Security to Indemnifie the Town to the Satisfaction of the Select men according to Law.

[August 16, 1736.] At a meeting of the Select men . . . Mr. James Wimble Informs, That Capt. Benedict Arnold . . . is just arrived from Cork with Passengers. . . . Accordingly the Master Capt. Arnold was sent for Who appear'd and gave Information, That he came from Ireland about Twelve Weeks ago, and that he is Bound to Philadelphia with his Passengers, Who in all, are one Hundred and Twenty, Hopes to Sail in a few days, as soon as he can Recruit with Water and Provissions, and Promises That the Passengers which came ashore Yesterday shall repair aboard again to day. . . .

[September 1, 1736.] John White Cordwainer Informs that he has taken One John Wallace into his Family as a Journey man, Who was lately imported by Capt. Beard from Ireland.[34]

The appearance and attitudes of colonial city dwellers reflected the wide range of status in the society of the larger cities. At one extreme were the merchant aristocracy and the administrative gentry with their splendid homes, fine carriages, and fashionable attire. At the other were the underprivileged and the poor, whose insecurity was heightened, especially in the urban environment, by the consequences of war, depression, and seasonal unemployment. Blacks, many of them slaves, as well as Indians and mulattoes, were a proscribed group in all the cities, although slaves were not numerous in Philadelphia by the mid-eighteenth century.[35] Widows, orphans, and other dependents made continuing demands upon public relief for the poor and upon private charity. The differences between rich and poor became more apparent as wealth was increasingly concentrated. In the major cities, by the eve of the Revolution, the richest 10 per cent of the residents owned about 60 per cent of the wealth.

The manifest affluence of the elite provoked an undercurrent of envy and resentment among the lower ranks of the urban society; however, in this age of deference these feelings rarely took aggressive form. Moreover, despite the prevailing social stratification the economic dynamism of these expanding urban centers made social mobility not only possible but evident as well. Industrious laborers could become artisans and shopkeepers, and now and again thrifty traders advanced to merchant status. It has been estimated that between one-third and two-fifths of the merchants in pre-Revolutionary New York City were self-made men and that more than half of the artisans in Philadelphia and Boston surpassed their fathers' economic status — a rate of advancement, especially in those occupations requiring little venture capital, somewhat greater than that of residents of the older farming communities.[36]

The increase in wealth and population fostered an expansion of public facilities for entertainment, education, and the enjoyment of the arts that widened the differences between city and country. Private entertainment became more and more elaborate as wealth encouraged the gentry to try to duplicate social behavior in the Mother Country. By the mid-eighteenth century, men's social clubs flourished in all the cities and dancing assemblies were in high fashion. Horse racing had an enthusiastic following in New York and Charles Town. The performance of London plays, as early as the 1730's, marked the advent of professional theater, always the most distinctive entertainment feature of urban life. Public and private concerts by small musical ensembles enriched the cultural dimension of the city scene, as did the availability of bookstores and subscription libraries and the provision of increasingly specialized educational opportunities. By the late 1760's, professional medical education was available at the College of Philadelphia and at King's College in New York City. The differences in the nature of the urban amenities and in the local response to them, from city to city, contributed to qualities of urban personality that already were seen to distinguish one city from another — the gentility of Boston, the sobriety of Philadelphia, the elegance of Charles Town, and the "gayety and dissipation" of New York.[37] The urbanity of life in three of the larger colonial cities, as well as the differences of tone in their society, is reflected in the comments of a young Massachusetts patriot, Josiah Quincy, recorded in the journal of his trip to Charles Town in 1773.

CHARLES TOWN, PHILADELPHIA, AND NEW YORK — THE SOCIAL SCENE: 1773

February 28 [*1773*, Charles Town]. On landing, Sunday Evening just before dark, the numbers of inhabitants and appearance of the buildings far exceeded my expectation. I proceeded to the Coffee-house, where was a great resort of company as busy and noisy as was decent. . . .

March 2. . . . Received a ticket from David Deis [Deas], Esquire, for the St. Cecilia Concert, and now quit my journal to go.

March 3. The Concert-house is a large inelegant building. . . . The performers were all at one end of the hall and the company in front and on each side. The musick was good. The two bass-viols and French horns were grand. One Abbercrombie, a Frenchman just arrived, played a first fiddle and solo incomparably, better than any I ever had heard. . . . Abbercrombie can't speak a word of English and has a salary of 500 guineas a year from the St. Cecilia Society. . . . Here was upwards of two hundred fifty ladies, and it was called no great show. . . . In loftiness of head-dress these ladies stoop to the daughters of the North: in richness of dress surpass them. . . . The gentlemen many of them dressed with richness and elegance uncommon with us — many with swords on. . . .

March 7. . . . Dined with considerable company at Miles Brewton, Esqr's, a gentleman of very large fortune: a most superb house said to have cost him 8000£ sterling. The grandest hall I ever beheld, azure blue satin window curtains, rich blue paper with gilt, mashee borders, most elegant pictures, excessive grand and costly looking glasses etc. . . . A most elegant table, three courses, nick-nacks, jellies, preserves, sweetmeats, etc.

March 9. Spent all the morning in viewing the Public library, State house, public offices, etc. . . . The public library is a handsome, square, spacious room, containing a large collection of very valuable books, cuts, globes, etc. . . .

March 12. . . . Spent the evening with the Friday-night Club, consisting of the more elder substantial gentlemen. . . .

March 15. . . . Spent the evening with Monday-night Club; introduced by Mr. Brewton. Cards, feasting, and indifferent wines. N. B. This was at a tavern, and was the first time of my meeting with ordinary wines since my being at Charlestown. . . .

March 16. . . . Am now going to the famous Races. [Later] The races were well performed, but Flimnap beat Little David (who had won the sixteen last races) out and out. . . . 2000£ sterling was won and lost at the Race. . . .

March 17. . . . Feasted with the Sons of St. Patrick. While at dinner six violins, two hautboys and bassoon, with a hand-taber beat excellently well. After dinner six French horns in concert — most surpassing musick! Two solos on the French horn by one who is said to blow the finest horn in the world: he has fifty guineas for the season from the St. Cecilia Society. . . .

[*May* 9, Philadelphia.] This city and province are in a most flourishing state: and if numbers of buildings, men, artificers, and trade is to settle the point, Philadelphia is the metropolis of this Northern region. . . . The Philadelphians in respect of the bounty and decency of table are an example to the world; especially to the American: with the means of profusion, they are not luxurious; with the bounties of earth and sea, they are not riotous; with the riches of commerce and industry, they avoid even the appearance of epicurean splendor and parade. . . .

May 11 [New York]. . . . Went to the playhouse in the evening, saw the Gamester and Padlock performed — the players make but an indifferent figure in tragedy, they make a much better in comedy. Hallam has merit in every character he acts. . . . I was . . . upon the whole much gratified, and believe if I had stayed in town a month should go to the theatre every acting night. . . .

May 12. . . . Attended a public concert which was very full. . . . The ladies sprightly, loquacious, familiar and beautifull: the men not so richly or elegantly dressed as I expected, nor so gallant as the incitements of the night seemed to justify. . . .

May 13. Spent . . . the evening at the playhouse. The Tempest of Shakespear, the Masque of Neptune and Amphitrite, and the Honest Yorkshireman was performed. . . .

May 17. . . . The general character of the inhabitants of this city is much tinctured with gayety and dissipation.[38]

Though hardly an attribute of urban society in a cultural sense, dogs played a role in the urban scene, in early America, similar to that of later times — for protection, for companionship and amusement, and even, perhaps, for imparting to the city the fast disappearing qualities of the countryside. This letter of complaint, which appeared in a January, 1753 issue of *The New York Independent Reflector* documents also the prevalence of the poor in the mid-eighteenth-century city.

DOGS IN NEW YORK CITY: 1753

It appears, *Sir*, from the most accurate Calculation, that we have in this City, at least a Thousand Dogs: I do not mean of the human Kind; for the Extirpation of those, would prove such an *Augean Stable*, as to require a Labour perfectly *Herculean*. The Dogs I intend, are that real canine Species, which, with their dismal Howlings, disturb the Repose of the Healthy, break the interrupted Slumbers of the Sick, add fresh Horrors to the Night and render it perillous to traverse our Streets after the Sun is sunk beneath our Horizon. . . .

I may venture to take it for granted, that our Dogs daily consume as much eatable Provision, as would suffice Five Hundred Men: A monstrous Extravagance, and a Piece of Luxury, that would almost redden the Cheek of a *Lucullus!* The Expence of a Thousand Dogs at a *Penny* a Day, amounts to £1,520.16.8 *per Annum*. . . . What Clamour should we hear, was such a Sum to be annually raised by a Tax on the Inhabitants, for the Maintenance of our Poor! . . .

There is Nothing more common, than daily to behold at our Doors, the shivering pale-visag'd home-born Poor, and the penurious half-clad Stranger, banished by the Rage of Persecution, from his native Soil, imploring with the persuasive Eloquence of flowing Tears, and silent Sorrow, the cold Morsel, and the scanty Boon, which he is inhumanly refused, while Towser, Tray and Mopsy, are pampered with Dainties, and gorged with the Fat of the Land!

It may, indeed, be objected, that to Gentlemen they are useful Animals, in guarding their Yards, and proclaiming the Approach of Robbers: But not One in Fifty . . . is kept for that Purpose; and where it really is the Case, let such Persons be compelled to confine them to their Yards, and prevent them from being a Terror and Disturbance to their Neighbours.[39]

4. GOVERNMENT AND POLITICS

The nature of municipal government in colonial America was affected both by the New World environment and by the aspirations and heritage of those who founded urban centers and resided in them. The ideal of a covenanted community inspired the form of local government where the Puritan influence was strong; but even here, as elsewhere, its details bore a strong resemblance to what the colonists had known in Europe.[40] No uniform pattern prevailed throughout the colonies. The town meeting, with its governing selectmen, was customary in the urban communities of New England. The English borough was often the model elsewhere. Here the officialdom consisted of a mayor (usually an influential public figure) and a recorder, appointed by the governor, and aldermen and councilmen who were self-perpetuating in some cities, popularly elected in others, as in New York City in 1684 and thereafter. These officials, acting together, passed ordinances and meted out local justice. The municipalities frequently owed their authority to charters from the provincial governments, setting the practice whereby cities today depend in many ways upon the will of the state legislature. The provincial assembly of South Carolina kept an unusually tight rein over the municipal government of Charles Town. Lack of confidence in the municipal corporation of Philadelphia led the Pennsylvania assembly to assign the responsibilities of urban management to elected commissioners, such as a board of assessors, city wardens to administer the night watch, street commissioners, and a board of overseers for the poor. This experience with committee government proved useful to the Philadelphians when they faced establishing a new city government during the Revolution.[41]

In their early years the municipal governments exerted extensive social and economic controls. This activity was in part an imitation of European practice in an age of mercantile regulation; it was prompted, too, by the real problems of urban existence in an isolated environment, such as possible shortages of food and firewood, dependency of the unemployed, and dangers of hostile Indians, local disorder, or epidemic disease. Markets were strictly regulated so as to attract country producers but forestall monopoly;

standards were prescribed to prevent fraud in the sale of food and firewood; limitations were placed on the number of persons permitted to work in given occupations; sanitary regulations were imposed; and restrictions were placed upon strangers, lest they become a burden upon the community. Every citizen was expected to participate in fighting fire, preserving order, and repairing the streets.

In time, as physical conditions became more secure, controls were relaxed; the increase in population (with resulting heterogeneity and impersonality) forced municipalities to find more specialized solutions, either subscription or taxation, for such characteristically urban problems as the condition of the streets and sidewalks, fire protection, collection of filth and garbage, and provision of a safe and adequate water supply. Thus, by the early eighteenth century in the older cities, special forces existed for fighting fire, a paid watch replaced the use of the general citizenry for keeping order, and the municipality began to contribute to the cost of paving, street lighting, waste disposal, and welfare.

The laws and ordinances operative in eighteenth-century New York City reveal the broad scope of regulation — of personal behavior, economic pursuits, occupational selection, citizen obligation, and even traffic — accorded municipal government in the cities of colonial America. These particular regulations were published at the City Hall in 1731, "after the Ringing of three Bells and Proclamation made for silence."

MUNICIPAL CONTROLS —
NEW YORK CITY ORDINANCES: 1731

LAWS ORDERS AND ORDINANCES Established by the Mayor Recorder Aldermen and Assistants of the City of New York Convened in Common Council for the good Rule and Government of the Inhabitants. . . .

A LAW FOR THE OBSERVATION OF THE LORDS DAY CALLED SUNDAY. . . . No Children to play on the sabbath. penalty one Shilling or House of Correction. . . . No Publick Housekeepers to Sell Strong Liquors on Sundays. . . . Slaves not above three to meet together . . . on the Lords Day. . . . penalty of being Whip'd at the publick Whipping Post fifteen Lashes, unless the Master or Owner of such slave will pay Six shillings to Excuse the Same. . . .

A LAW TO PREVENT STRANGERS FROM BEING A CHARGE TO THIS CORPORATION. Masters of Vessells and

Boats to give Account of their Passengers. . . . Constables to make A Strict Search and Enquiry after Strangers. . . . Fine on Housekeepers who Entertain Strangers [more than two days] without giving Notice. . . .

A LAW FOR THE BETTER PREVENTING OF FIRE. Viewers of Chimneys and Hearths . . . Shall View the same once in Every Month, and where they find any defective . . . give Notice, that the same may be Swept or mended. . . . Fire Engines Hooks and Ladders. . . . to be kept in Convenient places within this City for Avoiding the Peril of fire. . . . Leather Bucketts to be in Every House. . . .

A LAW FOR MARKING OF BREAD. . . . Every Baker within this City shall put a Mark with the two letters of his Name plainly to be Seen, upon all the Loaf Bread he Shall Expose to sale within the said City. . . . Assize of Bread to be sett Every Three Months or oftner and Viewers of Bread . . . to Inspect the goodness thereof, and see that the same be of full and due Assize. . . .

A LAW FOR REGULATING NEGROES AND SLAVES IN THE NIGHT TIME. Slaves above fourteen years Old not to Appear an hour after Sunsett without A Lanthorn and lighted Candle unless in Company with Some White Person. . . .

A LAW FOR REGULATING OF CARTS AND CARMEN. . . . That there be so many Carmen Lycenced . . . (not Exceeding One hundred) and that no Person do serve in that Capacity for hire or Wages but who shall be . . . Lycenced. . . . Carmen to Mend the Streets & Highways Gratis. . . . each Cart imployed for the Carrying of any goods, Merchandise, Fire Wood or Other things, within this City, shall be two foot Eight Inches wide, and three foot high. . . . No Carman [to] . . . drive his Cart a Trot in the Street, but Patiently. . . . Number of his Licence [to be] fairly Painted upon each side of his Cart with Red Paint. . . . Penalty on Carmen who Refuse to . . . Employ his Horse and Cart for any Person when Required. . . . Carmen are to Cart goods Subject to damage before any Other. . . . Prices and Rates to be taken by Carmen . . . [to] be According to the Rates and Prices hereafter mentioned. . . .

A LAW FOR REGULATING THE OFFICE OF GUAGERS PACKERS AND CULLERS. . . . that they will not put the Packers Mark to any Cask of Beef or Pork but to Such as Shall be good and wholsome Meat, fit for Transportation, and in Cask according to Law. . . .

A LAW RELATING TO MAKING FREEMEN. . . . no Person or Persons whomsoever, within this City and Liberties thereof, do Keep shop, or sell or Expose to Sale any Goods or Wares by Retail, or Exercise any Handy Craft Trade or Occupation, but such as are Freemen thereof, or so Admitted by the Mayor Recorder and Aldermen . . . and all Persons . . . made Free of this Corporation shall pay for the Freedom thereof . . . Every Merchant Trader or shopkeeper the sum of three pounds of Current Money of this Colony, and Every Handy Craft Tradesman the sum of twenty shillings. . . .

A LAW FOR CLEANING THE STREETS LANES AND ALLEYS OF THE SAID CITY. . . . all . . . Citizens, Freeholders, Housekeepers and Inhabitants . . . shall on Every Fryday, Weekly, Either by themselves or servants Rake and sweep together all the Dirt, Filth and soil lying in the Streets before their Respective dwelling Houses upon heaps and on the same day or on the saturday following shall Cause the same to be Carried away and thrown into the River, or some Other Convenient place under the Penalty of six shillings for each Neglect Refusal or Default. . . . No Carrion Guts Garbige &c: to be Cast in the Streets. . . . Streets not to be Encumbred with Beams Timber &c or any Other Lumber without leave of the Mayor. . . . No Tubs of Dung, Close Stools &c: to be Emptied in the Streets. . . . Ordures to be Emptied in the River [but not] to be Emptied or Carried through any Street, till after Eleven of the Clock at Night from the twenty fifth day of March to the twenty Ninth day of September and till after Ten A Clock at Night from the twenty Ninth day of September to the twenty fifth day of March. . . .

A LAW FOR PAVING THE STREETS LANES & ALLEYS WITHIN THE CITY OF NEW YORK. . . . all . . . Citizens, Freeholders and Inhabitants . . . shall . . . Well and sufficiently Pave or Cause to be well and sufficiently Paved with good and sufficient Pibble Stones Suitable for Paving, all, or so much of the Streets Lanes and Alleys, within the . . . City as shall Front the Respective Buildings and Lots of Ground that belong to them Respectively . . . and keep and Maintain the same in good Repair. . . .

A LAW FOR PREVENTING FRAUDS IN FIREWOOD. . . .

A LAW FOR REGULATING THE PUBLICK MARKETTS WITHIN THE CITY OF NEW YORK. Forasmuch as the Marketts of this City of New York are Chiefly Supplyed by the Country People with Provisions and Victuals by Water Carriage from the Neighbouring Counties and Colonies at Different times and seasons, as the Tides, Winds and Weather will permitt, by

Reason whereof no Certain Times or Days Can Conveniently be appointed for holding the said Marketts, without Manifest Hurt and prejudice as well to the Inhabitants of the said City as to the Country People who frequent and supply the said Marketts. . . . Every day in the Week (Sundays Excepted) . . . are hereby Appointed Publick Market Days . . . from sun Rising to sun Setting, where the Country People, and Others Resorting to the said Marketts may stand or Sitt, and Vend their Flesh, Fish, Poultry Herbs, Fruit, Eggs Butter Bacon and Other such like Provisions and Commodities. . . . No Hucksters or Retailers to Enter the Market till afternoon . . . to the End that House Keepers may provide themselves in the Forenoon of Every Day at the first Hand. . . . None to Forestall Regrate or Engross Provisions Comeing to Market. . . . No unholsome Victualls Blown Meat or Leprous Swine to be Exposed to Sale. . . . Butter to be Marked & if wanting weight to be forfeited to the Poor. . . .

A LAW FOR ESTABLISHING AND BETTER ORDER-ING THE NIGHT WATCHES IN THE CITY OF NEW YORK. . . . all . . . Persons able and fitt to Watch or to find an Able and fit Person to Watch . . . in . . . their Stead, do and Ought, by Reason of their Habitation Occupation and dwelling, to keep Watch within the said City, for the Preservation of the Kings Peace and for the Arresting and Apprehending of all Night Walkers Malefactors and suspected Persons which shall be found Passing Wandering and Misbehaving themselves. . . . A Constable & Eight Watchmen to Watch Every Night. . . . Equal Duty to be done by Every Ward. . . . Constables to Warn [notify] the Inhabitants to Watch the day before the Watch Night. . . . And deliver A List of the Names of those who are to Watch and when to the Constables of the Watch and to the Supervisor. . . . Persons Appointed & Warned to Watch Making Default to forfeit Eight Shillings. . . . Supervisor [of the Watch] to be appointed . . . by the Common Council . . . to take Care . . . that the Watch and Watches . . . be . . . duely kept, and that the Constables and Watchmen do their Duties and services therein or Otherwise pay their Forfeitures . . . for their Defaults. . . . AND that no Boys Apprentices or servants be Admitted to be Watchmen, and None but able and sober Men of good Reputation be Received as such.[42]

The communication among city dwellers, induced by urban living, contributed to the solution of some of the community problems of the maturing colonial city. This is nowhere better illustrated than in the activities of Benjamin Franklin, that most urban of early Americans. Franklin furthered communication, not only as printer and newspaper publisher, but through such "civic" organizations as the Junto, a discussion club that he recruited as early as 1727 from "most of his Ingenious Acquaintance." He relied on the members of the Junto and related clubs when in 1731 he organized a subscription library, the first to be established in an American city, and with these club members he discussed many of his practical proposals for improving urban conditions in Philadelphia. In his autobiography he describes his endeavors and the role of the clubs in generating pressure for improvements in police and fire protection, and the paving, cleaning, and lighting of the streets.[43]

BENJAMIN FRANKLIN AND THE EVOLUTION OF URBAN SERVICES IN COLONIAL PHILADELPHIA

I began now to turn my Thoughts a little to public Affairs, beginning however with small Matters. The City Watch was one of the first Things that I conceiv'd to want Regulation. It was managed by the Constables of the respective Wards in Turn. The Constable warn'd a Number of Housekeepers to attend him for the Night. Those who chose never to attend paid him Six Shillings a Year to be excus'd, which was suppos'd to be for hiring Substitutes; but was in reality much more than was necessary for that purpose, and made the Constableship a Place of Profit. And the Constable for a little Drink often got such Ragamuffins about him as a Watch, that reputable Housekeepers did not chuse to mix with. Walking the rounds too was often neglected, and most of the Night spent in Tippling. I thereupon wrote a Paper to be read in Junto, representing these Irregularities, but insisting more particularly on the Inequality of this Six Shilling Tax of the Constables, respecting the Circumstances of those who paid it, since a poor Widow Housekeeper, all whose Property to be guarded by the Watch did not perhaps exceed the Value of Fifty Pounds, paid as much as the wealthiest Merchant who had Thousands of Pounds-worth of Goods in his Stores. On the whole I proposed as a more effectual Watch, the Hiring of proper Men to serve constantly in that Business; and as a more equitable Way of supporting the Charge, the levying a Tax that should be proportion'd to Property. This Idea being approv'd by the Junto, was communicated to the other Clubs, but as arising in each of them. And tho' the Plan was not immediately carried into Execution, yet by preparing the Minds of People for the Change, it paved the Way for the Law obtain'd a few Years after, when the Members of our Clubs were grown into more Influence.

About this time I wrote a Paper, (first to be read in Junto but it was afterwards publish'd) on the different Accidents and Carelessnesses by which Houses were set on fire. . . . This was much spoken of as a useful Piece, and gave rise to a Project . . . of forming a Company for the more ready Extinguishing of Fires, and mutual Assistance in Removing and Securing of Goods when in Danger. Associates in this Scheme were presently found amounting to Thirty. Our Articles of Agreement oblig'd every Member to keep always in good Order and fit for Use, a certain Number of Leather Buckets, with strong Bags and Baskets (for packing and transporting of Goods) which were to be brought to every Fire; and we agreed to meet once a Month and spend a social Evening together, in discoursing and communicating such Ideas as occur'd to us upon the Subject of Fires as might be useful in our Conduct on such Occasions.

The Utility of this Institution soon appear'd, and many more desiring to be admitted than we thought convenient for one Company, they were advised to form another, which was accordingly done. And this went on, one new Company being formed after another, till they became so numerous as to include most of the Inhabitants who were Men of Property. . . . The small Fines . . . paid by Members for Absence at the Monthly Meetings, have been apply'd to the Purchase of Fire Engines, Ladders, Firehooks, and other useful Implements for each Company. . . .

Our City, tho' laid out with a beautifull Regularity, . . . had the Disgrace of suffering [its] Streets to remain long unpav'd, and in wet Weather the Wheels of heavy Carriages plough'd them into a Quagmire, so that it was difficult to cross them. And in dry Weather the Dust was offensive. I had liv'd near the Jersey Market, and saw with Pain the Inhabitants wading in Mud while purchasing their Provisions. . . . By talking and writing on the Subject, I was at length instrumental in getting the Street pav'd with Stone between the Market and the brick'd Foot-Pavement that was on each Side next the Houses. This for some time gave an easy Access to the Market, dry-shod. But the rest of the Street not being pav'd, whenever a Carriage came out of the Mud upon this Pavement, it shook off and left its Dirt upon it, and it was soon cover'd with Mire, which was not remov'd, the City as yet having no Scavengers. After some Enquiry I found a poor industrious Man, who was willing to undertake keeping the Pavement clean, by sweeping it twice a week and carrying off the Dirt from before all the Neighbours Doors, for the Sum of Sixpence per Month, to be paid by each House. I then wrote and printed a Paper, setting forth the Advantages to the Neighbourhood that might be obtain'd by this small Expence; the greater Ease in keeping our Houses clean, so much Dirt not being brought in by People's Feet; the Benefit to the Shops by more Custom, as Buyers could more easily get at them, and by not having in windy Weather the Dust blown in upon their Goods, &c. &c. I sent one of these Papers to each House, and in a Day or two went round to see who would subscribe an Agreement to pay these Sixpences. It was unanimously sign'd, and for a time well executed. All the Inhabitants of the City were delighted with the Cleanliness of the Pavement that surrounded the Market, it being a Convenience to all; and this rais'd a general Desire to have all the Streets paved; and made the People more willing to submit to a Tax for that purpose.

After some time I drew a Bill for Paving the City, and brought it into the Assembly. It was just before I went to England in 1757. and did not pass till I was gone, and then with an Alteration in the Mode of Assessment, which I thought not for the better, but with an additional Provision for lighting as well as Paving the Streets, which was a great Improvement. It was by a private Person, the late Mr. John Clifton, his giving a Sample of the Utility of Lamps by placing one at his Door, that the People were first impress'd with the Idea of enlightning all the City.[44]

Issues of municipal management sometimes prompted heated town or city elections in the urban centers of colonial America, though political activity generally was slow in tempo and often consensual. When such political crises did occur, they pointed up a tension between the gentry and the artisans and workers that became more and more evident as the cities increased in size. In the larger cities, the merchant elite usually controlled the municipal governments and ran them to suit their interests, even though in New England and in New York City the suffrage was relatively broadly based.[45] At times, however, in order to win elections and maintain power, they found it expedient to espouse "reforms" that appealed to the artisan or "middling" ingredient of the community. On occasion a "popular" party would gain control through addressing itself to manifestly urban problems and grievances.

Thus in the municipal election of 1734 in New York City, the "popular" party turned out the "court" party and replaced the

Common Council made up primarily of merchants with one that included three bakers, a painter, a bricklayer, a jeweler, a bolter, and a "laborer." [46] Among the issues in this election were questions of honesty and economy in the administration of the city government and its properties, such as markets and docks; payment for the keeper of the public library; and the demand for a paid watch, in order to ease the burden on those who could not afford to hire substitutes. A broadside, published on the eve of the election of 1734, satirized the extravagance of the "Governour's" party and counseled "Brother Trades-Men in the City," like "Shuttle the Weaver, Steep the Tanner, Vulcan the Smith, Crispin the Shoemaker, Drive the Carter," and other artisans, to "assert their Liberties" if they were dissatisfied with some or all of the magistrates. "You have Numbers sufficient," the author asserted, "and if you *dare* to chuse GOOD MEN, these GOOD MEN will *dare* to stand by you." [47]

In the municipal election of 1735 the issue again was joined. Each faction had its supporting newspaper, appeals were made to ethnic "interest," and the popular party sought to demonstrate the accomplishments of its administration of the city in meeting the complaints and reducing the burdens of the artisans and the common people. As the election approached, a friend of the "reform" Common Council, in a communication to John Peter Zenger's *New-York Weekly Journal*, sought to encourage its reelection by praising its achievements.

SUPPORT FOR A "REFORM" COUNCIL —
NEW YORK CITY POLITICS: 1735

Mr. Zenger: . . . If the Magistrates have behaved well . . . it is our Interest to choose them. . . . For my own Part, I think they have deserved well of the People. . . . No sooner had these Gentlemen entered upon their Offices, but . . . they ordered the *Charter of the City* to be printed, that the People might know their Rights and Privileges, and what Duties were thereby incumbent on their public Officers, to both which (for want of Printing the *Charter*) they were almost utter Strangers. . . . but what has abundantly shewn them to be worthy of the Trust reposed in them, is the great Care they have taken to raise the Revenue[s] of the City . . . and the frugal . . . employment of the public Money rais'd thereby. . . . Particularly they have set to farm the great Dock and Slips of the City for three Years, at £83.10.0.

per Annum, which for eight Years last past, through the Mismanagement or Neglect of their Predecessors, had not brought into
the City Treasury more in the whole than about Ten Pounds.
. . . They have also appropriated the City's Money arising from
the Markets to the City's Use, whereby they have increased the
City Revenue in that single Article near £100 *per Annum;* which
Money had been lost to the City by the Mayor's making his own
private Advantage of that Branch of the City's Revenue. . . .

And as they have been careful to raise the publick Revenue, so
they have been as frugal and discreet in applying it. . . . Among
their first Resolutions that they took upon their entring into their
Offices, They resolved *That no Account should be paid out of the
City Treasury unless the Accomptant would swear to the Truth
of his Accompt;* whereby . . . they have saved the City a good
Deal of Money.

So perfectly disinterested were they, that . . . they resolved,
that the City should be put to no Expence for the Corporation
Committee's, which they have punctually observed . . . whereas
the Expences of former Committees, former Presentments of Free-
doms, Gold Boxes, and great Entertainments, have cost the City
large Sums of Money: And as for breaking Bottles, Decanters and
Glasses, that heretofore unluckily happened upon some such jovial
Occasions, to the no small Cost of the City, the present Magistrates have occasioned no such Expence.

These Gentlemen have given none of their Members any
Wages for their Care annd Trouble in providing Materials and employing Workmen in the Public Business of the City, which formerly cost the City large Sums of Money; but every Member of
the present Corporation has served the Public in these Businesses
generously, without any Fee or Reward. . . . Thus have these
Gentlemen saved the City's Money.

Now, how have they imploy'd it? . . . Besides the ordinary
Repairs of the public Buildings, Long Bridge, and the Payment
of the Keeper of the public Library, Etc. they have at a large
Expence built a Work-House, for the Entertainment of idle and
vagrant Persons and for preventing their becoming a public
Charge. . . . Besides this they have maintained a City Watch
out of the City's Revenue, which heretofore had proved a heavy
Burden upon the poorer Sort of the People, by which two Acts
alone they have done more good to this City than has been done
by the former Magistrates in many Years before.

These Gentlemen have been as tender of the *Liberties* of the
City, as they have been careful of its *Revenues;* they would not
obey the Order of the Governor and Council, to attend the Burn-

ing of *Zenger's Journals*; because they were not satisfied that that Order was lawful; and they thought, that to obey an unlawful Warrant would give a dangerous Example, and that by their Compliance they should betray the Freedom of the City of which they were chosen to be the Guardians.

In order to preserve the City's Liberties, these Gentlemen have also rescued the public Seal out of the Hands of the Mayor, and lodg'd it in the Hands of the Clerk, and have established such Rules and Orders relating thereto, that it cannot be applied without the Consent of the Corporation.

They have not been unmindful of the Trade of this City in its languishing Condition, but have appointed a committee to prepare a Draught of a By-Law, to prohibit the Exportation of Flower [Flour] from this City, till inspected and found Merchantable.

As to the faithful and impartial Administration of justice, their Conduct in that Respect appears not only altogether unblemished, but singularly honourable. . . . As to those Laws which regard Religion, these Gentlemen have it for their Honor, that the Sabbath hath been more strictly observ'd within the Time of their Administration, than has ever been known before.[48]

5. THE BREAK WITH ENGLAND

Political confrontations between "court" and "popular" parties reflected the tension between colonies and Crown that was building up in urban America by the mid-eighteenth century, a tension that was to become more pronounced in the 1760's when the objections of city merchants to the arbitrary exercise of British authority coincided with the increasing frustrations of artisans and mechanics desirous of improving their status. But urbanism fostered in a more general way the movement that resulted in American independence. A century of trading contacts among the coastal cities had promoted a sense of American nationality, self-sufficiency, and potential, as had the integration of seaboard cities and interior settlements through ever increasing commercial ties. Distance and the demands of an urban market had tempted city dwellers to engage in types of manufacturing that were prohibited by imperial policy. Depressed economic conditions in the cities after 1763, affecting laborers, artisans, and tradesmen, as well as the merchant elite, also played a part. Cities, moreover, were the major channels through which the intellectual ferment of the Enlightenment reached the colonies, and where, by means of such urban institutions as newspapers, bookstores, and social clubs, these ideas were disseminated. Urban communities, too, provided the most visible setting for concerted protest that often brought tension into the open.[49]

Action by the mob (a contemporary term), as a means of popular protest, was not limited to cities. Farmers engaged in mob action, too, as a means of redressing their grievances and asserting their rights. But the numbers available in the city — especially seamen, youths, and unemployed — provided ever ready ingredients of demonstrations. Riots of seamen opposing impressment as an infringement of liberty took place in Boston as early as 1747; as these continued they set a pattern for the use of the mob to challenge the Stamp Act of 1765. In all the major cities, opponents of the Stamp Act, many of them lawyers and merchants, encouraged the mob to demonstrate and sometimes themselves took part in the demonstrations. Lawyers were said to have instigated the activities of the mob in New York City, though they ultimately expressed concern lest the people get out of control.[50] The British engineer Lieutenant John Montresor, stationed at Fort George, New York, during the Stamp Act crisis, described the behavior of the mob there. Like most colonial mobs, its actions were directed to specific issues and confined to the destruction of property rather than life.

"MOB" ACTIVITY IN NEW YORK CITY: 1765

23rd [October 1765]. Arrived the vessel with the Stamps. . . . 2000 people (mob) on the Battery expecting the Stamps would be landed, but were disappointed. However they were secretly landed in the night and deposited in the Fort. . . . Many placards put up threatening the Lives, Houses and properties of any one who shall either issue or receive a stamp.

31st October 1765. Several people in mourning for the near Issue of the stamps and the Interment of their liberty. Descended even to the Bag-gammon Boxes at the merchant's Coffee House, being covered with Black and the Dice in Crape. This night a mob in 3 squads went through the Streets crying "Liberty" at the same time breaking the Lamps & threatening particulars that they would the next night pull down their Houses. Some thousands of windows Broke. Major James of the Royal Artillery — threatened to be buried alive by the Populace as Commanding the Troops in the Fort for the protection of the Stamps. Merchants of this place met to Know whether they shall carry on trade or not. Agreed in the negative till the 1st of May.

November 1st. . . . This night the Rabble or rather Rebels assembled again early in the evening & Continued the Riot till 4 this morning, their numbers about 2000 during which time they broke open the Governor's coach house . . . took out his chariot & 2 Sleighs & a chair which they burnt in the Bowling Green with effigies & Gallows &c &c. . . . 300 Carpenters belonging to the mob were collected & prepared to . . . cut down the Fort Gate on the first Shot fired from thence. From thence they proceeded to Major James' House and there after breaking every window, cut down all the window shutters & broke down all the Partitions — then they distroyed 9¼ casks of Wine & distroyed & Stole all his plate, Furniture, apparel Books &c. . . . The Mob got the permission to toll the Bells of the several churches, meetings and other Houses of worship except the churches of England, which they broke into & tolled the bells beginning at ½ after Nine. . . .

5th. . . . At last . . . the Stamps were delivered up to the mayor & Corporation . . . to prevent an effusion of Blood and the Calamities of a civil war which . . . withholding them seemed to threaten. Seven Boxes of Stamps were delivered . . . to the city Hall in Carts and deposited there attended by 5000 people. . . .

6th. Perfect tranquillity (as to appearances) this day: advertisements put up about *Peace proclaimed.* . . . The Lawyers levelled at, by the people, to be at the bottom of this disloyal Insurection and seconded by many people of property of the place and its neighbourhood.[51]

The most storied destruction of property by mob action and the one that had the most irrevocable consequences was the so-called Boston Tea Party. Boston had led the successful opposition to the Stamp Act; but repeal of the act had not put an end to legislation that triggered opposition both in the Massachusetts city and elsewhere in the colonies. In 1768 the quartering of British regulars in the city contributed to an altercation between soldiers and citizenry that was publicized as the Boston Massacre. In the same year duties imposed by the British Parliament on glass, paper, paint, and tea prompted nonimportation agreements on the part of the merchants of Boston and other cities that further unified the urban opponents of British policy. By 1773 the tax on tea, which Parliament refused to repeal, had become symbolic of the growing impasse in the relations between Britain and America. In all the major ports colonists resisted the landing of ships bringing tea. The actual destruction of tea in Boston after unsuccessful efforts to have the cargo returned to England and the punitive measures with which Parliament responded, including the closing of the Boston port until the tea was paid for, brought imperial relations to the "point of no return." With the ensuing call for the First Continental Congress in 1774, the colonists were well along the road to the American Revolution. A Boston bookseller described the local reactions that resulted in the citizens' determination to make Boston harbor "a teapot tonight."

THE BOSTON TEA PARTY: 1773

[*Novr.*] *29* [*1773*]. This Morning the following Notification was posted up thro' the Town,

"*Friends!   Brethren!   Countrymen!*

"That worst of Plagues, the detested Tea, shipped for this port by the East-India Company, is now arrived in this Harbour; the hour of Destruction or manly Opposition to the Machinations of Tyranny stares you in the face; every Friend to his Country, to himself and Posterity, is now called upon . . . to make a united and successful Resistance to this last, worst, and most destructive Measure of Administration." In Consequence . . . the People of Boston and the neighbouring Towns assembled . . . at Faneuil-Hall in great Numbers. . . . A Motion was made . . . Whether it is the firm Resolution of this Body that the Tea shall not only be sent back, but that no duty shall be paid thereon? pass'd in the Affirmative. . . .

Novr. 30. . . . the Town met according to Adjournment. . . . Mr. Sheriff Greenleaf . . . read a Proclamation . . . from Govr. Hutchinson, exhorting . . . the People thus assembled forthwith to disperse and to surcease all further "unlawfull" Proceedings at their utmost peril. After it was read, there was a loud and general Hiss. . . . Voted, That any Person who shall import Tea from Great-Britain, until the unrighteous Act imposing a Duty thereon Shall be repealed, shall be deemed by this Body an Enemy to his Country. Voted, That the Proceedings of this Meeting be transmitted to New-York and Philadelphia. . . .

[*Decr.*] *14* [*1773*]. . . . the People . . . assembled . . . to enquire the Reason of the delay in sending the Ship Dartmouth, with the East-India Tea back to London . . . they enjoin'd [the Owner, Mr. Rotch] to demand of the Collector of the Customs a Clearance of the Ship, and appointed a Committee of Ten to see it performed. . . .

[*Decr.*] *16.* Body met pursuant to Adjournt: And were inform'd by Mr. Rotch, that a Clearance was refus'd him, they enjoined him immediately to enter a Protest. . . . near sunset, Mr. Rotch . . . inform'd them that he had . . . waited on the Govr. for a pass, but his Excy: told him he could not consistent with his duty grant it untill his Vessel was qualified [cleared]. The People finding all their Efforts to preserve the property of the East-India Company, and return it safely to London, frustrated by the Tea Consignees, the Collector of the Customs, and the Govr. of the Province, dissolved their Meeting. But behold! what followed! A Number of brave and resolute Men, determined to do all in their power to save their Country from the ruin which their Enemies had plotted, in less than four hours emptied every Chest of Tea on board the three Ships, commanded by the Capts. Hall, Bruce and Coffin, amounting to 342 Chests, into the Sea! without the least damage being done to the Ships or any other property. . . . Mr. Paul Revere was immediately dispatched express to New-York and Philadelphia with the Glorious Intelligence. . . .

[*Decr.*] *27.* Mr. Paul Revere returned from New-York and Philadelphia. . . . The Inhabitants of those Cities were highly pleased with the Conduct of the People here in destroying the Tea, and they were determined that when the Tea Ships expected there should arrive, they should be immediately returned to the Place from whence they came.[52]

It was apparent by 1774 that resistance to British policy had unleashed forces that threatened to change the balance of political power in the cities of colonial America. In Charles Town (not to be called Charleston officially until its incorporation in 1783), the organization of local mechanics — to protest regulations that forced their products into competition with British wares — strongly advanced the political power of this occupational group in a community once tightly dominated by an aristocracy of merchants and planters. In New York City, the popular reaction to the closing of the Boston Port was such as to cause conservatives to fear that the "people" might get out of control. "The mob begin to reason," wrote the conservative patriot, Gouverneur Morris, in May, 1774.

"Poor reptiles! it is with them a vernal morning, they are struggling to cast off their winter's slough, they bask in the sunshine, and ere noon they will bite, depend upon it. . . . if the disputes with Britain continue, we . . . shall be under the dominion of a riotous mob." [53]

Historians have debated the role of class antagonisms in the behavior of urban dwellers during the Revolutionary crisis. Though the laboring population aired grievances on a number of counts against their superiors, and although the middle class openly sought privileges denied them by the aristocrats, no unified class alignment within the urban population appears to have existed as a force conditioning the resistance movement. British measures aggravated merchant and city laborer alike. Given the implications of external imperial policy the urban community was more conducive to common protest than to the solidification of internal division.

Evidence that British policy and the hard times that followed in its wake affected workingmen as well as merchants is seen in a letter written in November, 1767, to the printer of the *New-York Journal, Or General Advertiser.*

GRIEVANCES OF THE WORKINGMEN: 1767

In this time of great distress and grievous complaining among tradesmen, about dullness of trade, and uncommon scarcity of money, it would be extremely beneficent if the wealthy and money'd men of all denominations, would call for their trades- men's bills and pay those sums which to them are trifling and inconsiderable, but to the poor industrious tradesman, the needy mechanic, and all men of narrow circumstances, are of great consequence. . . . These little payments coming spontaneously from the great, would do the poor man infinite service; yet such may be his condition, that he dare not ask for one of these sums through fear of offending his rich employer, and through him many others connected with him by friendship and interest, conse- quently ruining his trade. Thus are many worthy men circum- stanced at this day; on every side threatened with impending ruin; pressed hard by their creditors on the one side, afraid to demand their own on the other. . . . Hard alternative! either to disoblige his customers or to go to gaol for them! . . .[54]

Lieutenant-Governor Cadwallader Colden, writing to the Earl of Dartmouth concerning the situation in New York in 1774, alluded to the willingness of the merchant gentry to make common cause, within limits, with the plain people and to the resistance movement as primarily an urban phenomenon.

GOVERNOR COLDEN ON RESISTANCE IN NEW YORK CITY: 1774

[*June 1, 1774.*] The Men who . . . call'd themselves the Committee — who dictated, and acted in the name of the People, were many of them, of the lower Rank and all, the warmest zealots of those call'd the Sons of Liberty. — The more considerable Merchants & Citizens seldom or never appeared among them; but I believe were not displeased with the Clamour and Opposition that was shewn against internal Taxation by Parliament. — The Principal Inhabitants being now afraid that these hot headed men might run the City into dangerous measures, appeard in a considerable body, at the first Meeting of the People after the Boston Port Act was publish'd here. — They dissolved the former Committee, and appointed a new one of 51 Persons, in which care was taken to have a number of the most prudent . . . People of the Place [who] . . . were induced to appear . . . from a Consideration that if they did not; the Business would be left in the same rash Hands as before. . . .

[*July 6, 1774.*] The present Political zeal and frenzy is almost entirely confined to the City of New York. The People in the Counties are no ways disposed . . . to bear any Part in what is proposed by the Citizens. I am told all the Counties, but one, have declined an Invitation . . . from New York, to appoint Committees of Correspondence. This Province is every where . . . except in the City of New York, perfectly quiet and in good Order.[55]

As tension moved to the point of armed encounter, it was natural that the major cities, as centers of communication, should be focal points of military action. The Battle of Bunker Hill, the bloodiest engagement of the entire war, took place in June, 1775, on Breed's Hill overlooking Boston, where the British remained until March, 1776, when they turned their attention to New York. Patriot soldiery attempted to hold this crucial port, but General William Howe's troops captured it in September, 1776, and New York remained an occupied city — the center of British operations — until after hostilities ceased and independence was recognized in 1783. In the fall of 1777 the British took over Philadelphia, the patriot capital, and held it until May, 1778. In December of that year a successful attack on Savannah permitted King George's troops to overrun Georgia; Charles Town, after an abortive British effort to take it in 1776, fell in May, 1780. It remained in British hands until the siege of Yorktown in 1781, which settled the conflict in the Americans' favor.

The war affected all aspects of city life. Fear of troop occupation and of the plots and counterplots the conflict generated caused many to flee the urban centers, with the result that all the major cities lost population during the war. Once the cities were evacuated by the British, city industries contributed to the war effort by building privateers and producing supplies. Municipal government was taken over by committees, whose constituencies often reflected the benefits accruing to the middle class from the break with England. During British occupation the loyalist elements in the city came into their own. The diary of a loyalist sympathizer, Ewald G. Schaukirk, minister of New York's Moravian Congregation from 1775 to 1784, reveals the traumatic and dislocative effect of patriot resistance and British occupation upon life in New York City.

WARTIME NEW YORK CITY: 1775–1783

April 29th [*1775*]. . . . The past week has been one of commotion and confusion. . . . Fear and panic seized many of the people, who prepared to move into the country. . . .

August 28th [*1775*]. . . . Moving out of the city continues, and some of the Streets look plague-stricken, so many houses are closed. . . .

September 18th [*1775*]. . . . The Minute men paraded today, with their baggage and provisions. It was thought they were going on an expedition, but they marched but five miles out of the city and returned in the evening. Many of them got drunk, fought together where they had halted, and on their return the Doctors and Surgeons were kept busy. May the Lord have mercy on this poor City!

January 20th [1777 — after occupation]. . . . It appears from the newspapers, that another attempt to destroy the city by fire would be made. The city watch was regulated anew, by which eighty men watched every night in the different wards; and the Light Horse patrol the streets. . . .

November 29th [1777]. . . . A plot was discovered that many here . . . had been enlisted for the rebel service, and intended to fall on the city within or set it on fire, when an attack was made on the island by the rebels. Several were arrested, one Mott and wife, in the Bowery; a shoemaker; a saddler; a milkman; and Skimmey, a tailor, who made his escape.

August 19th [1779]. . . . the military gentlemen amuse themselves with trifles and diversions. . . .

December 16th [1780]. . . . The year is near ended and nothing has been done by the troops here. . . . thro' idleness [they] fall into all manner of the worst of vices, contract illnesses, which take off many. . . .

December 11th [1781]. . . . Weather very cold; great distress for want of wood. . . .

February 1st [1782]. . . . The rents of houses are again raised to extravagant figures. . . .

April 8th [1783]. . . . At noon the King's Proclamation of the cessation of hostilities, was read at the City Hall. . . .

May 3d [1783]. . . . Many of those persons who left the city when the troubles began are returning. . . .

November 25th [1783]. . . . Today all the British left New York, and General Washington with his troops marched in and took possession of the city.[56]

6. URBANISM IN THE NEW NATION

Independence stimulated the recovery of the seaboard cities, even though they suffered from the consequences of war-incurred debt and destruction and from the exclusion of the new United States from trade with the British West Indies. New trade with the Baltic and the Far East gave business to the seaports of New England and to New York City; and the conflict between Britain and France at the end of the eighteenth century greatly invigorated the economies of Boston, New York, Philadelphia, and Baltimore. However, the availability of land gave farming such a widespread appeal that in the early years of nationhood the proportion of urban to rural dwellers exceeded only slightly what it had been in colonial times. Between 1790 and 1820 the number of communities of 2,500 or more people rose from 24 to 61; by 1820 the young country had two cities with populations exceeding 100,000 — New

York City totaling about 125,000 and Philadelphia about 109,000, of whom some 64,000 lived in the city proper and about 45,000 dwelt in the closely adjacent suburbs. However, the proportion of urban to rural dwellers in the nation (that is, persons in communities of 2,500 or over) actually declined slightly in the decade from 1810 to 1820, in part because of the sluggish condition of the eastern seaports, then suffering from the falloff in foreign trade.[57] As late as 1820, urban dwellers still constituted less than 8 per cent of the total population, and nearly half of the urban population of the country was concentrated in Boston, New York, Philadelphia, and fast growing Baltimore. In 1790, contemporaries regarded Philadelphia as the young nation's largest city, with its population of more than 42,000, which included residents of the city and the closely contiguous suburbs. New York then numbered about 33,000; Boston, 18,000; Charleston, 16,000; and Baltimore, 13,500.

What contemporaries called the "prodigious" growth of New York City (from 33,131 in 1790 to 123,706 in 1820) was one of the two most significant features of American urban development during the early national period. The other was the rise of urban communities in connection with the accelerated settlement of the trans-Allegheny West.[58] By 1811, New York had become the most populous city of the country; its population exceeded the combined population of Philadelphia and its contiguous suburbs.[59] From the early 1790's to the period of the Embargo of 1807, New York, like the other seaboard cities, benefited from the carrying trade that was opened to American shippers during the Napoleonic wars. The superiority of its harbor gave the rising "Empire City" a continuing advantage over its seaboard rivals, as did the breadth of its hinterland, by contrast with the hinterlands of Baltimore and Boston. By 1825, when the newly completed Erie Canal further widened its tributary domain, New York had captured a large part of the southern cotton trade and was the major commercial center for imports from Europe. With the possible exception of Philadelphia, wholesale and retail trade was the predominant economic pursuit of all the seaboard cities, most of which served as economic "hinges" in the exchange of goods between the trans-Allegheny West and the Atlantic community. Boston channeled much of its commerce to the textile towns of the Merrimack Valley.[60]

The expansion of domestic manufacturing in response to conditions created by the Embargo of 1807 and the War of 1812 contributed to the growth of existing cities and led to the rise of mill villages and factory towns in the neighborhood of the older cities and at new sites where water power was available. Many of these enterprises were promoted by merchants in the seaport cities, using capital acquired through trade. Boston merchants established the Boston Manufacturing Company at Waltham, Massachusetts, in 1814, and built the industrial town of Lowell on the Merrimack in 1823. The absence of widespread and large-scale industrial activity in this era of the mercantile city is to be explained by the existing shortage of capital and labor, the immobility of water power, the state of technology, and inadequacies of transportation that restricted the accessible market. Such manufacturing as existed was closely related to the mercantile pursuits of the city — the processing of exports, the provision of printed matter, ships, and other commodities related to trading activity, or the production of household goods and construction materials needed in the local urban market.[61]

The growth of New York City was only slightly more newsworthy than that of Baltimore, which was emerging, by the beginning of the nineteenth century, as one of the major Atlantic coast cities. Baltimore increased in population from 13,500 to nearly 63,000 between 1790 and 1820. As early as 1796, *Carey's American Atlas* referred to Baltimore as the fastest growing city on the continent; by 1810 it had overtaken Boston to become the "number-three" city of the young nation. In encouraging road building as well as flour milling, its merchants exploited the potential of wheat production in its neighborhood and for purposes of trade took advantage of being slightly closer to Pittsburgh than was Philadelphia. Its ships, making regular runs to Bremen, invigorated its ocean-going commerce and attracted the migration of German farmers and artisans whose skills supported the city's continuing expansion. The vigor of its growth was already evident by the late 1790's when it was visited and described by the Duke of La Rochefoucauld-Liancourt, the French social reformer.[62]

BURGEONING BALTIMORE: 1797

Baltimore is, after Philadelphia and New-York, the most important trading post in America; at least, it disputes this rank with Charlestown and Boston. Being situated nearer to the rivers Youghiogheny and Monongahel[a], which empty themselves into the Ohio by Pittsburg . . . Baltimore possesses a part of the trade of the back country of Pennsylvania, supplies most of the stores which furnish the western territories with merchandize, and receives in return a part of their produce. It contains at present from four to five thousand houses, and has been almost entirely built since the peace of 1763. It has still more rapidly increased since 1783, and especially since the beginning of the present war [between England and France]. The inn-keeper at Poplar-Spring told me, that in 1749, when he landed in Baltimore on his arrival from Germany, the whole place consisted of nine miserable log houses, and now it is one of the finest towns on the Continent, as it contains no old houses, and most of the present have been constructed of late years . . . mostly of bricks. The numerous churches of all religious persuasions . . . are constructed in a simple and elegant style. The town, which increases in every direction, gains in extent, particularly on the bay, where streets are paved and formed on a ground wrested from the sea. . . . Ships of burthen cannot proceed up the river higher than *Fell's Point*, at which they load and unload. No business, however, is transacted at *Fell's Point*; every thing being done at Baltimore, which is separated from it by a flat and open space of ground about a mile in extent. The merchants' counting-houses and principal warehouses are at Baltimore. . . . If the trade of this city continues to increase as hitherto, the space . . . lying between Baltimore and Fell's Point will be covered with buildings, and the two places will form but one town. At present new houses are building on every street; and the town spreads every day towards the harbour, and on the west side upon the grounds belonging to *Colonel Howard* [owner of the estate, Belvedere] the value of which from this circumstance increases continually.[63]

As the frontier of settlement moved westward in the late eighteenth century and early nineteenth century, especially after the War of 1812, the rise and growth of towns accompanied the advance of farmer settlement. This development was dictated by the need for centers in which to market the produce of profit-minded settlers, the desire for local manufactures, owing to the cost of transporting finished products from the East, and the demand for goods that was generated by newcomers and transients. The grain and livestock economy that developed north of the Ohio River encouraged urbanism to a greater degree than did the economic pursuits of the region to the south, with its increasing emphasis upon the growth of cotton, a commodity that required less processing and less immediate exchange. Pittsburgh, Louisville, and Cincinnati became small-scale replicas of the seaboard cities, especially after the advent of the steamboat on the western rivers in 1811; many small interior towns sprang up in Ohio and Illinois. By 1820, Pittsburgh claimed more than 7,000 residents and Cincinnati more than 9,600. St. Louis, a wilderness outpost when it was founded in 1764, had attracted nearly 4,600 residents by 1820; and the population of New Orleans, focus of exports from the rapidly developing West, grew from about 17,000 in 1810 to more than 27,000, ten years later.[64]

Some of the urban centers of the advancing West developed because of the migration of covenanted communities, especially from New England, but most of them grew by accumulation, for the purpose of facilitating trade and achieving the amenities of urban living in this countryside of dispersed farmer settlement. Such motives for town making underlay the emergence of Albion, Illinois, the urban center of the English Settlement, founded by George Flower and Morris Birkbeck in 1817 and 1818 on the southern Illinois frontier. Flower described its beginnings in his history of the settlement.

TOWN MAKING ON THE ILLINOIS FRONTIER: 1820

In about three years [after the founding of the settlement], a surplus of corn, pork, and beef was obtained, but no market. Before they could derive any benefit from the sale of their surplus produce, the farmers themselves had to quit their farms . . . and convey their produce along until they found a market. . . . One evening . . . we discussed the measures that should be taken to form some village or town, as a centre for those useful arts necessary to agriculture. Every person wanted the services of a carpenter and blacksmith. But every farmer could not build workshops at his own door. . . . Thus the spot for our town in a central situation was decided upon. Now for a name. . . . At last we did what almost all emigrants do, pitched on a name that had its association with the land of our birth. Albion was then and there located, built, and peopled in imagination. . . .

We met the next day in the woods according to appointment. The spot seemed suitable. . . . "Here shall be the centre of our town," we said. . . . Mr. Fordham . . . forthwith went to work, and completed the survey and the plat. One of our number went to Shawneetown, and entered the section of six hundred and forty acres, which was laid off in town lots. The public-square was in the middle. . . .

The first double-cabin built, was designated for a tavern, and a single one for its stable. . . . Another and second double and single cabin were occupied as dwelling and shop by a black-smith. I had brought bellows, anvils, tools, and appliances for three or four blacksmith-shops, from the City of Birmingham, England. There were three brothers that came with Mr. Trimmer, all excellent mechanics. . . . Jacob, the blacksmith, was imme-diately installed, and went to work. There stood Albion, no longer a myth, but a reality, a fixed fact. A log-tavern and a blacksmith-shop.

Two germs of civilization were now planted — one of the use-ful arts, the other a necessary institution of present civilization. Any man could now get his horse shod and get drunk in Albion, privileges which were soon enjoyed, the latter especially. . . . The town-proprietors, at first four, afterward increased to eight (each share five hundred dollars), went to work vigorously. They put up cabin after cabin, which were occupied as soon as put up, by emigrants coming in. The builders of these were the backwoods-men, some from twenty to thirty miles distant.[65]

The growth of Cincinnati reflects the stimulus given to urban development in the West not only by the need for centers of ex-change but by the expediency of manufacturing locally. This wilderness community was founded in 1788, far in advance of the frontier of farmer settlement. In many ways it recapitulated, on the banks of the Ohio River, the experience of the major Atlantic coast cities. Philadelphia was the model for its physical layout as well as for many of its social institutions; its leading citizen, phy-sician Daniel Drake, was reminiscent, in his public-mindedness, of Philadelphia's Benjamin Franklin, to whom he was often likened. His *Natural and Statistical View, or Picture of Cincinnati and the Miami Country*, published in 1815, when Cincinnati's population was 6,000, was undoubtedly inspired by *The Picture of Philadelphia* by James Mease, which had appeared four years earlier. Drake's account attests not only to the imitative character of urban development but to Cincinnati's role as a spearhead of westward advance and to the relationship of manufacturing in the West to comparative urban growth.[66] It reflects also the aspiration to urbanism in connection with the westward moving frontier.

DR. DANIEL DRAKE'S CINCINNATI: 1815

Philadelphia seems to have been the model after which [the first town plat of Cincinnati] . . . was planned. Between Broadway and Western Row there are six streets, each 66 feet wide, running from the river. . . . These are intersected at right angles by others of the same width. . . . Not a single alley, court, or diagonal street, and but one common, was laid out. . . .

As this town is *older* than the surrounding country, it has at no time had a surplus of laboring population or of capital. The former have been required to assist in clearing and improving the wilderness; the latter has been invested in lands, which from their low price and certain rise, have held out to capitalists a powerful inducement. The conditions which are said to constitute the basis of manufacturing establishments, have not, therefore, existed in the same degree as if the town had been *younger* than the adjoining country. Notwithstanding this, some progress has been made [in the manufacture of nails, utensils, firearms, saddlery, furniture, wagons, paint, cotton and woolen goods, liquor, and flour].

In the fine arts we have not anything to boast; but it is worthy of being mentioned, that all kinds of labelling, sign and ornamental painting, together with engraving [of] . . . seals, cards of address, and vignettes, is executed with taste and elegance. . . .

Where will be erected the chief cities of this promising land? It may be answered with certainty — on the borders of the Ohio river. . . . Pittsburgh, Cincinnati and Louisville, are the places which at present have the fairest prospects of future greatness. . . . It is well known . . . that for twenty years, both foreign and Atlantic goods . . . have been annually waggoned to Pittsburgh . . . and shipped in its boats for the country below. . . . Hundreds of [western] merchants were passing . . . through this town; and it was early discovered, that if manufactures were established, it would be possible to dispose of many articles required in the newer settlements below. Hence founderies, glass houses, breweries, and iron manufactories of various kinds, were erected; and the wares of this "Birmingham of America" superadded to the merchandise of the East, soon spread extensively over our country. . . . But a change in the current of our im-

portations — such a change as has already begun — must inevitably reduce the ratio of improvement in that place, just as
much as it will be increased by the same cause, in Cincinnati,
Louisville, and the other towns below. . . . Pittsburgh, therefore,
has not so high a destination as its younger rivals to the westward. . . .

. . . there are reasons for believing that CINCINNATI IS
TO BE THE FUTURE METROPOLIS OF THE OHIO. Its
site is more eligible than that of most towns on the river. It is susceptible of being rendered healthier than Louisville, and is extensive enough for a large city. . . . These are some of the local
advantages of Cincinnati; and if improved with a spirit corresponding to their magnitude, its inhabitants cannot fail to realise
their most glowing anticipations of future greatness.[67]

With the increase in settlement of the Ohio Valley, New
Orleans assumed for the West the role of economic hinge performed by the seaports of the Atlantic coast. Founded by the
French in 1718 and taken over by Spain in 1763, this "Marseilles
of the New World" already was a city of 8,000 people when, with
the purchase of Louisiana in 1803, it became a possession of the
United States. As of that date, its foreign trade was valued at
$5,000,000, and it could boast the manufacture of rum, cordage,
hair powder, vermicelli, and shot. With the migration of planters
into the lower Mississippi Valley, New Orleans had increasing
supplies of sugar, molasses, cotton, and tobacco to ship; soon the
newly garnered abundance of the upper Middle West — hides and
fur, lumber, whiskey, and foodstuffs — was piling up on New
Orleans wharves. In 1821, when its exports had climbed in value
to $16,000,000, Lloyd's of London is said to have prophesied that
New Orleans was destined to be the world's greatest port.[68] Timothy Flint, a New Englander who did missionary work in the West
from 1815 to 1825, described the New Orleans commercial scene
in his *Recollections of the Last Ten Years*, published in 1826.

NEW ORLEANS — SEAPORT OF THE WEST: 1823

One hundred miles from the mouth of the Mississippi, and
something more than a thousand from the mouth of the Ohio
. . . is . . . the city of New Orleans, the great commercial capital of the Mississippi valley. . . . Its regular winter population,
between forty and fifty thousand inhabitants, is five times the

amount . . . it had, when it came under the American government. . . . The street that passes along the leveé, and conforms to the course of the river, is called Leveé street, and is the one in which the greatest and most active business of the city is transacted. The upper part of the city is principally built and inhabited by Americans. . . . The greater number of the houses in this fauxburg are of brick, and built in the American style. In this quarter are the Presbyterian church and the new theatre. The ancient part of the city, as you pass down Leveé street toward the Cathedral, has . . . an imposing and brilliant aspect . . . far more resembling European cities, than any other in the United States. The houses are stuccoed . . . white or yellow, and [this] strikes the eye more pleasantly than the dull and sombre red of brick. . . . The streets are broad, and the plan of the city is perfectly rectangular and uniform. There are in the limits of the city three malls, or parade grounds, of no great extent. . . .

There are sometimes fifty steam-boats lying in the harbour . . . and . . . from twelve to fifteen hundred flatboats lying along the river. . . . More cotton is shipped from this port than from any other in America, or perhaps in the world. I could never have formed a conception of the amount in any other way, than by seeing the immense piles of it that fill the streets, as the crop is coming in. It is well known that the amount of sugar raised and shipped here is great, and increasing. The produce from the upper country has no limits to the extent of which it is capable; and the commerce of this important city goes on steadily increasing.

This city exhibits the greatest variety of costume, and foreigners; French, Spanish, Portuguese, Irish in shoals, in short, samples of the common people of all the European nations, Creoles, all the intermixtures of Negro and Indian blood, the moody and ruminating Indians, the inhabitants of the Spanish provinces, and a goodly woof to this warp, of boatmen, "half horse and half alligator"; and more languages are spoken here, than in any other town in America. . . . In March the town is most filled; the market shows to the greatest advantage; the citizens boast of it, and are impressed. . . that it far surpasses any other. In effect this is the point of union between the North and the South.[69]

North and south (or east and west), the cities of young America were few in number, small by modern standards, compactly settled, and limited in physical extent. As of 1820, more than three-fourths of the communities of 2,500 or more people had fewer than 10,000 residents, and the average "urban" cluster probably numbered fewer than 2,000. These were essentially "walking" cities in which work and residence rarely were separated by any significant distance. Many merchants used their homes for business purposes, and most lived within walking distance of their offices. Frequently they provided a room for an employee above or at the back of the store. Most artisans, even in New York City, labored in their place of residence or in close proximity to it. It was not until the 1830's that improvements in urban transit facilities permitted New Yorkers who could afford the cost of commutation to live more than a mile from their places of business. As late as 1840, only 23 per cent of the industrial workers in New York City were employed outside their homes.[70]

Given the social gradations characteristic of eighteenth-century America, it is hard to say to what extent a sense of community was present in the cities of this period, despite the fact that the size of most of them and the patterns of work and residence were conducive to communication. Even in the largest, a sense of obligation to the community prevailed among the group who assumed responsibility for the administration of the cities during this period of transition from colonial dependence to national status. With the achievement of independence, the state legislatures replaced Parliament and Crown as the sources of ultimate authority for the governance of cities. In form, the new municipal governments reflected the concern for checks and balances that suffused the thinking of the framers of the Federal Constitution. The new charters provided for municipal legislatures elected by all residents who enjoyed the state franchise. But in several instances they were bicameral, in imitation of the practice in most of the states and in the federal government. And the mayor continued to be an appointed official, chosen by the governor or by a council of appointment. Artisans and craftsmen were an influential segment of the urban electorates, as they had been since the eve of the American Revolution. But even in the larger cities the direction of civic affairs continued to be controlled by an identifiable social and cultural elite, though the aspirations of the elite groups for community development were beginning to be affected by the new social and political forces that were signaling the era of Jacksonian democracy.[71]

Typical of these traditional leadership groups and of their philosophy of the role of the municipal government was De Witt Clinton, who resigned his seat in the United States Senate to become mayor of New York City and served in that capacity for most of the period from 1803 to 1815. Clinton not only championed the economic advantage of New York City, as in his advocacy of the Erie Canal, but also urged municipal encouragement of cultural endeavors, such as the New-York Historical Society (1803) and the Literary and Philosophical Society, founded in 1814 to give New York City the counterpart of Philadelphia's American Philosophical Society and Boston's Academy of Arts and Sciences. Clinton's reply to the Common Council, when in 1815 it memorialized his services as mayor, reflects the concern of the leadership elite for the potential of the close-knit city as a "great community." [72]

DE WITT CLINTON ON THE OBLIGATIONS OF CITY GOVERNMENT: 1815

Gentlemen

Having had the honor of receiving a Resolution of your Board, expressing your approbation of my conduct during my official connexion with you, I should do injustice to my feelings, were I not to return my respectful acknowledgements for this signal proof of your regard. . . .

At a time when we were threatened with invasion . . . you appealed to the public spirit of our fellow citizens; you drew forth the resources of the City[;] you supplied ample funds . . . ; and there can be no doubt but that this important section of the Country was, under the blessings of Heaven, indebted for its safety . . . to the wisdom of your counsels and to the energy of your measures — In all other cases I have found you equally solicitous to promote the public prosperity. . . . I feel also satisfied, that you will not consider it obtrusive in me to suggest, that the return of peace and its attendant blessings, has enabled you by patronizing the arts and sciences & encouraging the cultivation of the human mind, to elevate still more the character of this great community, and to erect imperishable monuments of public utility.[73]

The growth of the larger cities, during the first two decades of the nineteenth century, certainly prompted an increasing awareness

of the city's role as an incubator of cultural development; at the
same time city growth made more apparent the traditional shortcomings of urban society — poverty, squalor, epidemic disease,
and the prevalence of crime, vice, and social tension — conditions
that early emphasized the interdependence of city life. Fires and
fevers were the most spectacular urban hazards; by the turn of the
nineteenth century experience with epidemics in American cities
constituted a major count against city living. Yellow fever and
cholera, which periodically (at times, annually) attacked American
cities through the first half of the nineteenth century, were the
most dreaded epidemics. The yellow fever epidemic of 1793 in
Philadelphia took a death toll of more than 5,000 persons in a
population of about 55,000. Called the "most appalling collective
disaster that had ever overtaken an American city," it early jarred
Americans into sensing the darker side of city life.[74] Philadelphia
journalist Mathew Carey's *Short Account* of the epidemic reveals
the community implications of such an urban-aggravated scourge.

YELLOW FEVER IN PHILADELPHIA: 1793

It was some time before the disorder attracted public notice.
. . . The first death that was a subject of general conversation,
was that of Peter Aston, on the 19th of August [1793]. . . .
Mrs. Lemaigre's, on the day following, and Thomas Miller's, on
the 25th, with those of some others . . . spread an universal
terror.

The removals from Philadelphia began about the 25th or 26th
of this month: and so great was the general terror, that, for some
weeks, carts, waggons, coaches, and chairs, were almost constantly transporting families and furniture to the country in every
direction. Many people shut up their houses wholly; others left
servants to take care of them. Business then became extremely
dull. Mechanics and artisans were unemployed; and the streets
wore the appearance of gloom and melancholy. . . .

The first official notice of the disorder, was on the 22d of
August, on which day the mayor of Philadelphia, Matthew Clark-
son, esq. wrote to the commissioners, and . . . gave them the
most peremptory orders, to have the streets properly cleansed
and purified by the scavengers and all the filth immediately
hawled away. . . .

Of those who remained [in the city] many shut themselves
up in their houses, and were afraid to walk in the streets. . . .

Many houses were hardly a moment in the day, free from the smell of [such supposed preventatives as] gunpowder, burned tobacco, nitre, sprinkled vinegar, etc. Some of the churches were almost deserted, and others wholly closed. The coffee-house was shut up, as was the city library, and most of the public offices. . . . Many were almost incessantly employed in purifying, scouring, and whitewashing their rooms. Those who ventured abroad, had handkerchiefs or sponges impregnated with vinegar or camphor at their noses, or smelling-bottles full of the thieves' vinegar. . . . The corpses of the most respectable citizens . . . were carried to the grave, on the shafts of a chair, the horse driven by a Negro. . . . Acquaintances and friends avoided each other in the streets, and only signified their regard, by a cold nod. The old custom of shaking hands, fell into such general disuse, that many shrunk back with affright at even the offer of the hand. . . .

[The epidemic] has been dreadfully destructive among the poor. It is very probable, that at least seven-eighths of . . . the dead, were of that class. The inhabitants of dirty houses have severely expiated their neglect of cleanliness and decency. . . . Whole families, in such houses, have sunk into one silent, undistinguishable grave.

The mortality in confined streets, small allies, and close houses, debarred of a free circulation of air, has exceeded, in a great proportion, that in the large streets and well-aired houses. In some of the allies, a third or fourth of the whole of the inhabitants are no more. . . . The streets in the suburbs, that had the benefit of the country air, especially towards the west part of the city, have suffered little.[75]

Poverty and pauperism became so evident in the seaboard cities by 1820 that the leadership element felt serious concern. The rapid growth of these cities made the dependent poor increasingly numerous and visible. Many of them were immigrants, induced to migrate after 1815 by postwar dislocations in Europe; their arrival in America, in such numbers as to be newsworthy, came at a time when economic conditions were also depressed in the seaboard cities.[76] Though poverty was an accepted attribute of urban living, the recipients of public and private charity in the larger cities were now so numerous as to pose what some contemporaries saw as a threat to "the pillars of the social order." As early as 1805, Mayor Clinton of New York had requested a legislative appropriation to meet the needs of 10,000 residents of the city dependent on public charity during the winter months; by 1820, relief was said to be "administered to one-tenth or twelfth of the whole number of inhabitants." The problem excited concern in all of the nation's largest cities in the years following the War of 1812, and societies were founded in New York (1817), Philadelphia (1817), and Baltimore (1820) for the purpose of countering the apprehended increase in the number of urban dependents.[77]

Most contemporaries viewed pauperism as resulting from a lack of moral fiber in those affected. The New York Society for the Prevention of Pauperism attributed the increase in poverty in part to the availability of relief, which, it held, weakened the recipients' will to provide their own support, and in part to what it viewed as frailties of character as exhibited in idleness, intemperance, extravagance, imprudent and hasty marriages, and the patronage of lotteries, pawnshops, and houses of ill fame. In proposing a system of home visitation, to ascertain eligibility for relief as well as to encourage improved behavior, and in advocating central channeling of relief resources and the provision of work relief, this short-lived organization (1817–1823) anticipated methods that were to be used in succeeding years to cope with the endemic problem of the city poor.[78] The mood of the society was reflected in its Fifth Annual Report, published in 1821, in which it suggested that the prevalence of relief was a reason for the appeal of the city as a place of residence and cited the need for coming to grips with an urban problem that increased in seriousness as cities grew in numbers.

POVERTY AND PAUPERISM — GROWING PROBLEMS IN GROWING CITIES: 1815–1820

It is the willing dependence of the poor upon the public bounty appropriated for them, which warns us to expect that this form of pauperism will advance, and to press upon the means provided for relieving it. . . . This principle of legal maintenance acting upon those who are willing to be maintained, forms, it is believed, the root and germ of the evil. It is this which peoples those towns, where the best accommodations and amplest funds exist, with the vagrants and paupers of the surrounding country, and stimulates the march of hundreds from the interior to the city at the approach of winter, and invites the indigent from foreign countries, or determines them to a city residence after their arrival.

A reference to the most populous towns and districts of this country might suffice to show, that laws designed to relieve the poor by maintaining them, actually cause an increase of pauperism, and add prodigality and vice to poverty. No demonstration can well be stronger than that which we have . . . in this city. . . . It will be enough to state that [in New York City] the annual public expenditure for the support [of the poor] has doubled in ten years, and risen to about one hundred thousand dollars, while that of societies and individuals is estimated at twenty or thirty thousand more; that in the winter season relief is administered to one-tenth or twelfth of the whole number of inhabitants; and that there is an average of about fifteen hundred paupers in the Almshouse, and three hundred to four hundred delinquents in the City Penitentiary, throughout the year. These statements are deemed to be within bounds. If they are substantially correct, they will justify the inference, that relieving poverty, instead of doing it away, increases it, and that the source of this evil must be dried up, its elements destroyed, its germ uprooted, or nothing valuable will be accomplished. The Managers are constrained to ascribe it to the same cause in this city as in England, namely, to the provision made for the relief and maintenance of the poor, that pauperism has increased amongst us in a ratio as great as was ever witnessed in that country.[79]

Apart from the association of cities with epidemic disease, unemployment, and pauperism — conditions that prompted Thomas Jefferson's oft-quoted derogation of city life — it was the image of the manufacturing city with its dependent, volatile population that accounted for the distaste with which most Americans viewed cities in these years. Yet by the end of the War of 1812, serious analysts of American society accepted manufacturing as vital to the nation's recently tested independence, and cities, the customary habitat of manufacturing, as essential to the nation's economic growth as well as to the achievement of its political and cultural potential. Even Jefferson, who in 1803 deplored the "too strong current" then running "from the country to the towns," concluded by 1816 that "manufactures are now as necessary to our independence as to our comfort" and that, as a result, we must "now place the manufacturer by the side of the agriculturist." [80]

As early as 1791, Alexander Hamilton had extolled manufacturing not only for its bearing on economic growth but as an expedient means of coping with the numbers of urban unemployed. A similar view, in an even more nationalistic vein, was expressed by George Tucker, former congressman and professor at the University of Virginia, who saw manufacturing as the only ultimate means of providing employment for a fast-growing population that was destined to spread densely across the continent from the Atlantic to the Pacific. Writing in 1813, he foresaw the day when the "general settlement of this whole continent" would make the West "the seat of extensive manufactures" and when one of the large cities on the "margin" of the Mississippi would become a new seat of government for the nation.[81]

As in colonial days, so during the early years of independence, cities played a significant role in the economy and society of the young nation. Their increasing visibility in the national scene is reflected in the fact that Britisher Isaac Holmes, writing what was essentially an expanded immigrants' guide to the United States, published in the early 1820's, devoted an entire chapter to the "Cities and Towns" of the new country.[82] Contemporaries were sensitive to the fact that increasing urbanism was in the future of the nation and that it already had produced social change. They did not anticipate, however, the marked upsurge in urban growth that was to begin in the 1820's or the magnitude of its expansion in the decades that followed. That the direction and dimensions of the nation's impending urbanism were as yet not fully sensed is seen in the comments of William Tudor, founder and first editor of *The North American Review*, in his *Letters on the Eastern States*, written in 1819. Cities were in the young country's present, in his view, and manufacturing was in its future; but the shape of the nation's urban destiny was not yet clearly discerned, and large cities based on manufacturing as well as commerce were hopefully a long way off.

THE NATION'S URBAN PROSPECTS: 1819

The commercial cities of the United States may be divided into two classes; the first contains those which, situated on rivers at a distance from the coast, are the depots for the sale of the domestic produce of the district, which resorts to them for a market, and also for the supply of the same country, with the foreign merchandise they consume. The second class consists of those cities which, in addition to these branches of trade, are, from their proximity to the ocean, convenient marts for general commerce, where every species of merchandise is placed in depot for subsequent distribution. . . . The fate of some of our cities seems yet undecided. The natural course of events will lessen the number that will be great depots. The small places are drawn into the vortex of the larger ones. This process has been produced by Philadelphia, New-York, and Boston.

It seems probable that some place on the Gulf of Mexico, east of the Mississippi, must become an immense mart of commerce, not only for the countries bordering on that Gulf and the West India islands; but as a seaport for New-Orleans, and through the latter, for the vast commerce that will be borne on the Mississippi. . . . New-York is daily developing a prodigious growth, which its position, both with regard to internal and external commerce, is calculated to give it. . . . The two principal depots of commerce on our Atlantic coast, will be New-York and Boston. . . .

There are several parts of the United States where certain branches of manufactures are permanently fixed, without including those household productions, which are made to a great extent in every state in the Union. . . . There can be no doubt of the practicability of our becoming manufacturers, and the expediency is . . . growing daily more evident. With the fullest belief, however, of the utility and necessity of manufactures, I am not anxious for the growth of large manufacturing towns, and the kind of population that exists in them in Europe; though it will naturally come in the course of things, no wise or benevolent man would wish to advance it. Our manufacturing population is now blended with that of agriculture; the labourers in the former are drawn from the latter, and frequently return to it for a time. This preserves their health and energy. . . . But to have large manufacturing cities, swarming with labourers, who are mere spinning *mules* and *jennies* . . . such a state of things I do not wish to see existing, while there is any land left to give our population the means of subsistence. Indeed, there is no fear that it will happen for many generations to come. . . . A well regulated manufactory, situated in the country, may be made subservient to the promotion of good principles and good habits in those employed in it; while in large towns, and with a straining competition incessantly exerted, the labour is too continuous to admit of any instruction or any relaxation. Health and morals are both disregarded, and too frequently destroyed altogether.[83]

PART TWO

URBAN
GROWTH
1820-1870

Like the settlement of the continent, the urbanization of the United States proceeded far more rapidly than Americans of the early nineteenth century expected. Developments during the 1820's opened the way for urban growth of a speed and magnitude beyond anything the preceding generation could — or wanted to — imagine. In the half century from 1820 to 1870 there was a tenfold increase in the number of urban places, and the proportion of urban dwellers in the total population rose from 8 per cent to 25 per cent. By 1870 an interdependent network of sizable cities, stretching from coast to coast, was playing an important role in organizing the national economy. From the 1830's forward, contemporaries conceded the pull of the city as they had not done earlier, though many deplored the presumed consequences; by 1870 the townward trend made it appear that the whole population was headed for the city. "We cannot all live in cities," wrote Horace Greeley in the *New York Tribune* in 1867; "yet nearly all seem determined to do so. Millions of acres . . . solicit cultivation . . . ; yet hundreds of thousands reject this and rush into the cities." [1]

Census figures document the dramatic increase in urban living in the years from 1820 to 1870 — an increase exhibited not only in the mounting number of cities and in their growing populations, but in the rapid expansion of urbanism across the continent as far west as the Pacific coast. As of 1820, no state or section of the United States was as much as 25 per cent urban. Fifty years later, the populations of Rhode Island, Massachusetts, New York, and the District of Columbia were more than half urban; and in most of the states of the Old Northwest nearly every fourth resident was an urban dweller. In this half century the number of cities exceeding 25,000 in population rose from five to 51; New York, a city of less than 125,000 in 1820, was by 1870 the center of a metropolitan complex that included more than a million. In 1820, no city west of the Alleghenies, other than New Orleans, numbered as many as 10,000 people; by 1870, seven tramontane cities had populations exceeding 100,000 — one of them San Francisco. Indeed, by 1870 the foundations had been laid for virtually every major city of twentieth-century United States, and the growth of regional cities posited a potential challenge to the urban giants of the Atlantic coast. The tables that follow portray these developments in statistical detail.

Table 2.1 shows the increase in the number of urban dwellers,

Table 2.1

URBANISM BY STATE AND SECTION: 1820 AND 1870[2]

	URBAN DWELLERS 1820	URBAN DWELLERS 1870	PER- CENT- AGE URBAN 1820	PER- CENT- AGE URBAN 1870	NUMBER OF "URBAN" PLACES[a] 1820	1870
New England						
Maine	8,581	131,744	2.9	21.0	4	16
New Hampshire	7,327	83,456	3.0	26.2	3	8
Massachusetts	119,187	972,081	22.8	66.7	16	62
Rhode Island	19,086	162,107	23.0	74.6	2	11
Connecticut	20,804	177,153	7.6	33.0	5	23
Vermont	—	22,960	—	6.9	0	6
Middle Atlantic						
New York	160,996	2,189,455	11.7	50.0	7	88
New Jersey	7,457	396,012	2.7	43.7	3	23
Pennsylvania	136,465	1,312,833	13.0	37.3	10	75
South Atlantic						
Delaware	—	30,841	—	24.7	0	1
Maryland	66,378	295,459	16.3	37.8	2	5
Dist. Columbia	28,825	120,583	87.2	91.6	3	2
Virginia	27,235	145,618	2.6	11.9	3	13
West Virginia	—	36,009	—	8.1	0	5
North Carolina	12,502	36,218	2.0	3.4	4	6
South Carolina	24,780	61,011	4.9	8.6	1	3
Georgia	7,523	100,053	2.2	8.4	1	10
Florida	—	15,275	—	8.1	0	3
North Central						
Ohio	9,642	682,922	1.7	25.6	1	59
Indiana	—	247,657	—	14.7	0	32
Illinois	—	596,042	—	23.5	0	45
Missouri	4,598	429,578	6.9	25.0	1	18
Michigan	—	237,985	—	20.1	0	27
Wisconsin	—	207,099	—	19.6	0	27
Iowa	—	156,327	—	13.1	0	22
Minnesota	—	70,754	—	16.1	0	11
Nebraska	—	22,133	—	18.0	0	2
Kansas	—	51,870	—	14.2	0	7
South Central						
Kentucky	9,291	195,896	1.6	14.8	2	15
Tennessee	—	94,237	—	7.5	0	8
Alabama	—	62,700	—	6.3	0	4
Mississippi	—	33,255	—	4.0	0	5
Arkansas	—	12,380	—	2.6	0	1
Louisiana	27,176	202,523	17.7	27.9	1	3
Texas	—	54,521	—	6.7	0	8

Table 2.1 (Cont.)

	URBAN DWELLERS 1820	URBAN DWELLERS 1870	PER-CENT-AGE URBAN 1820	PER-CENT-AGE URBAN 1870	NUMBER OF "URBAN" PLACES[a] 1820	1870
Mountain						
Montana	—	3,106	—	15.1	0	1
Colorado	—	4,759	—	11.9	0	1
New Mexico	—	4,765	—	5.2	0	1
Arizona	—	3,224	—	33.4	0	1
Utah	—	15,981	—	18.4	0	2
Nevada	—	7,048	—	16.6	0	2
Pacific						
California	—	208,438	—	37.2	0	7
Oregon	—	8,293	—	9.1	0	1

[a] The number of urban places must be accepted as only approximate because data in the censuses of 1820 and 1870 make it difficult to identify precisely urban communities in the New England and Middle Atlantic states with a minimum population of 2,500.

by state and section, between 1820 and 1870, as well as the increase during this half century in the percentage of urban dwellers in each of the states. The criteria used in this table for identifying urban dwellers are those used in the censuses of 1930 and 1940. Urban dwellers, according to these criteria, include the residents of cities and other incorporated places having 2,500 or more inhabitants and residents of certain other clusters of population not incorporated as municipalities but having a population density deemed more urban than rural. Table 2.1 also exhibits the increase in the number of urban places during the half century from 1820 to 1870 and, especially, the contrast between the North and South by 1870 in terms of the number of urban places. The censuses of 1820 and 1870 have been used to identify the communities that qualify as urban places. In general, a population cluster of 2,500 persons designated as a city or a town has been used as the prerequisite, but it should be kept in mind that this figure constitutes an arbitrary criterion and that it does not recognize as urban the many communities that were only slightly under 2,500 in population. Table 2.2 documents the fact that this half century of rapid urban growth saw the emergence of large cities in all parts of the nation, some of them approximating the size, at the mid-century,

Table 2.2

POPULATION GROWTH OF REPRESENTATIVE CITIES
BY SECTION: 1820–1870[3]

	1820	1830	1840	1850	1860	1870
New England						
Boston	43,298	61,392	93,383	136,881	177,840	250,526
Lowell	—	6,474	20,796	33,383	36,827	40,928
Providence	11,767	16,833	23,171	41,513	50,666	68,904
New Haven	7,147	10,180	12,960	20,345	39,267	50,840
Middle Atlantic						
New York	123,706	202,589	312,710	515,547	813,669	942,292
Brooklyn	11,187	20,535	47,613	138,882	279,122	419,921
Buffalo	2,095	8,668	18,213	42,261	81,129	117,714
Newark	—	10,953	17,290	38,894	71,941	105,059
Philadelphia	63,802	80,462	93,665	121,376	565,529	674,022
Pittsburgh	7,248	15,369	31,204	67,863	77,923	139,256
South Atlantic						
Baltimore	62,738	80,620	102,313	169,054	212,418	267,354
Washington	13,247	18,826	23,364	40,001	61,122	109,199
Richmond	12,067	16,060	20,153	27,570	37,910	51,038
Charleston	24,780	30,289	29,261	42,985	40,522	48,956
Savannah	7,523	—	11,214	15,312	22,292	28,235
Atlanta	—	—	—	2,572	9,554	21,789
North Central						
Cincinnati	9,642	24,831	46,338	115,435	161,044	216,239
Cleveland	606	1,076	6,071	17,034	43,417	92,829
Detroit	1,422	2,222	9,102	21,019	45,619	79,577
Milwaukee	—	—	1,712	20,061	45,246	71,440
Chicago	—	—	4,470	29,963	112,172	298,977
St. Louis	—	4,977	16,469	77,860	160,773	310,864
Minneapolis	—	—	—	—	2,564	13,066
Omaha	—	—	—	—	1,883	16,083
South Central						
Mobile	—	3,194	12,672	20,515	29,258	32,034
New Orleans	27,176	46,082	102,193	116,375	168,675	191,418
Memphis	—	—	—	8,841	22,623	40,226
Nashville	—	5,566	6,929	10,165	16,988	25,865
Louisville	4,012	10,341	21,210	43,194	68,033	100,753
Houston	—	—	—	2,396	4,845	9,382
Mountain						
Denver	—	—	—·	—	4,749	4,759
Pacific						
Los Angeles	—	—	—	1,610	4,385	5,728
San Francisco	—	—	—	—[a]	56,802	149,473
Portland	—	—	—	—	2,874	8,293

[a] 1850 returns destroyed by fire; 34,776 in 1852 (state census).

of such world cities as Liverpool (376,000), Glasgow (329,000), Birmingham, England (232,000), Berlin (378,000), Hamburg (205,000), Vienna (431,000), St. Petersburg (490,000), Moscow (360,000), Constantinople (400,000), and Calcutta (400,000).

1. TRANSPORTATION

Improvements in transportation, beginning to be evident by the 1820's, laid the basis for the system of sizable cities that had developed across the continent by 1870. A build-up of steamboat tonnage on the Ohio, Mississippi, and Missouri rivers and on the Great Lakes contributed to the growth of ports on the inland waters. The construction of canals and railroads widened the markets of existing cities and gave rise to new urban centers. The Erie Canal, begun in 1817, and completed in 1825, produced both of these results of transportation innovations; the advantage it gave New York City prompted her seaboard rivals to project similar connections, by either canal or railroad, with potential western markets.[4] The efforts of Boston capitalists gave that city rail connections with Worcester in 1835 and with Albany by 1842. At the same time, the merchants of Philadelphia and Baltimore, competing for business advantage in tramontane Maryland, Pennsylvania, and Ohio, were advocating both canal and rail connections as tools of their commercial ambitions. The Pennsylvania Railroad reached Pittsburgh in 1852; the Baltimore and Ohio Railroad touched Wheeling in 1853. A railroad from Charleston to Hamburg, South Carolina, completed in 1833, diverted to Charleston trade that had been going by river to Savannah. Meanwhile, New Yorkers, not content to rely only on their Hudson River–Erie Canal connections with western markets, underwrote railroads that, as early as 1851, tied New York City to Albany on the Hudson and Dunkirk on Lake Erie.

Canal and railroad construction in the rapidly developing Middle West not only implemented urban development there but extended the potential hinterlands of the seaboard cities. Limitations of technology made the rail networks generally tributary to the water transport system, as railroads were built outward from the major ports or to them from concentrations of resources; but in time the consolidation of lines made through connections possible. Rails linked the Mississippi River with the Atlantic seaboard by the late 1850's; and by 1869, with the completion of the first transcontinental railroad, rail connections were available from the Atlantic to the Pacific. These developments gave the United States a national system of transportation, albeit a crude one, that revolutionized the urban pattern of the nation. The author of "The Railroad System," an article published in *The North American Review,* in April, 1867, attributed the growth of great cities in the United States as well as in Europe by that date to "the influence of steam locomotion as applied to trade," a development that he dated as beginning in the early 1830's.[5]

City promotion and urban rivalry were powerful forces behind these transportation achievements. In 1827 eleven Baltimore firms, seeing the advantage of a railroad in the city's rivalry with Philadelphia, took one-fifth of the stock of the Baltimore and Ohio Railroad and induced Wheeling to put up $1,000,000 to assure its selection as the Ohio River terminus. The city of Albany issued $1,000,000 in bonds to support the Western Railroad that linked Albany and Boston. Its completion in 1842 so alarmed New York's business community that the Board of Aldermen urged the citizenry to support proposed rail connections — "the better improvement of the age" — between New York and Albany and thus counter "the stealthy march of our rivals," who have attempted to turn "the channel of our trade in a new direction." [6] The aldermen resolved that the New-York and Albany Railroad was "indispensable to the welfare of the Commercial, Mercantile, and Mechanical interests of our city." In this they were influenced by the arguments of John Delafield, president of the proposed railroad, whose communication to the mayor, written in 1842, reveals both the role of railroads in the rivalry of the seaboard cities and the contemporary recognition of the relationship of transportation facilities to urban growth.

RAILROADS AND URBAN RIVALRY: 1840's

Communication from the President of the New-York and Albany Railroad Company, to Robert H. Morris, Mayor of the city of New-York: Sir — The announcement of the completion of a railroad from Boston to Albany, demands the attention of the people of this city; . . . this new avenue of trade and travel, with such inducements as are offered for its use, must make . . . serious inroads upon the trade and commerce hitherto enjoyed by this city.

This new avenue also opens a continuous line of railroad (nearly completed) from Boston, through Albany and Troy, to Buffalo. It branches off, in the New-England States, by a webb of well constructed railroads, carrying the products of the western country direct to every eastern seaport; inviting the producers of our own State, as well as the hardy sons of Michigan and Ohio, by an uninterrupted channel, to markets beyond the borders of this State — open at all seasons, and therefore offering unquestioned advantages during many months of the year, while our water courses and canals are fast bound by ice.

The facilities of rapid transportation, the ready market for interchange of commodities, in winter or summer; the establishment of steam packets with England, and probably with France, are advantages held out by Boston — a proof of her wealth, and highly honorable to her character for enterprize; at the same time an example is held up to us, and a warning given, that if we omit to improve the natural advantages we so eminently enjoy, we must revert to the position of deriving supplies from Boston and elsewhere, instead of being the great centre of trade and commerce of the Union.

We must not close our eyes to the advantages possessed by our sister cities of Philadelphia and Baltimore, by reason of a mild climate, opening their canals several weeks before our waters are unbound, and keeping their railroads in unceasing action throughout the year. With such formidable rivalry, it behooves the people of this city to be on the alert, not only to secure what is in danger of passing away, but, by well timed efforts, to add to the wealth and prosperity of each and of all. . . .

[This city's] increase of population depends upon the perpetuity of benefits to be offered to, and enjoyed by, the people. If, then, our channels for intercourse with the interior are less in number, or more difficult in use, than those offered by other cities, we have before us disheartening prospects of a decreasing business, increasing taxes and burthens, with the consequent train of depreciated real estate and property, fast sinking our city in the scale of national importance.

In the fruition of prosperity we may have become supine; and the energies of our neighbors, with a generous rivalry, will, we trust, now awaken our people to the danger of delay, and excite them to take effectual and prompt measures to recover what we may have lost, and to counteract our competitors in their efforts to cut off or absorb the fountains of our prosperity. . . . The completion of the New-York and Albany railroad will do more to effect the important objects in view, than any other enterprise. We should not only retain the trade of our own State, hitherto almost exclusively enjoyed by ourselves, but we should create facilities for intercourse with the several eastern States as yet not accessible. The completion of this road would also open a perfect chain of railroads from this city to Lake Erie, by a shorter route, and by far easier grades, than by any other known route; and necessarily more economical in its use.

We deem it unnecessary to detail the many natural advantages possessed by this city, by reason of its geographical position; but would advert to the fact that, in proportion as other cities remove obstacles, and extend their means of intercourse by artificial works, our natural advantages must diminish in relative value, and the streams of our prosperity be diverted from their usual channels.[7]

Feeder railroads, built with Boston capital, held Lowell, Worcester, Providence, and other New England towns within Boston's trading orbit, and this commercial domain, including a ring of thriving suburbs, made the Boston area the prototype of a metropolitan region as early as the mid-nineteenth century. But it was New York City that ultimately benefited most from the network of canals and railroads forged across the continent in the years from 1820 to 1870. With her economic reach now extended into the heart of the continent, as well as to southern markets by way of a flourishing coastal trade, New York became, for the time at least, the national metropolis. The contribution the transportation revolution had made to the growth of New York City, and, indeed, the contribution New York capital had made to the nation's transportation development, were buoyantly extolled in a pamphlet, *The Growth of New York City*, published in 1865 and attributed to Isaac C. Kendall, a New York City merchant.[8]

NEW YORK CITY — NATIONAL METROPOLIS: 1865

Prior to 1820, the city of New York had the ordinary growth of a seaport town, at the mouth of a river giving it 150 miles of navigation into an undeveloped country. . . . [It now is] at the beginning of its . . . advance to metropolitan greatness . . . [when it] stands in relation with the whole country as its commercial and financial capital. . . . From 1820 to 1860, a portion of its wealth was employed in constructing railroads and other works of internal improvement, over the valleys of the Ohio and Mississippi and along the borders of the lakes. . . . The leading lines of railroad across this region, beginning to stretch up the western side of the Mississippi valley, have been so long completed that now the promised results of increase of production and wealth have ripened into a harvest for the city. . . . But westward, beyond that region, lies a new country, which we are now . . . rising up to possess. . . .

In this general growth of the continent, New York will stand as the great heart of the country. . . . The news of the country concentrates and emanates from here. . . . No provincialism or sectionalism can secure a lodgment here. . . . New York will aid this coming development of our broad domain with . . . the energy and ability of its business men, with its money; and the results of this development will converge here. Every new mine opened, every town built up, comes into relations with New York; and every railroad, no matter how short, has one terminus here. . . . We can now do the business of the Mississippi valley better than fifty years ago we could do that of the Hudson. The Pacific coast is quite as near to us now as then were the shores of Long Island sound. The commercial and productive energies of any part of the country can be directed here. The accumulated fortunes tend to settle here. The metropolis will ere long stand in as close business relations with every town in the United States, as, fifty years ago, it did with its own up-town wards. . . . The products of the wheatfields of the prairies, the gold mines of the Pacific coast, the coal fields and oil wells of Pennsylvania, the factories of New England, and the plantations of the South, will heap up a portion of their accumulations here, just as accurately as if all these fields of labor were within the city limits.[9]

Improvements in urban mass transit facilities were another aspect of the transportation revolution that encouraged the accumulation of population in large urban centers, by making it possible for those who could afford to do so to reside beyond walking distance of their places of employment. With the expansion of omnibus service, beginning in the 1830's, and the perfection of horse railways, in the 1850's, city dwellers were able at reasonable cost to ride to work from outlying parts of the city. By the later 1830's steam railroads provided commuter service to and from small communities beyond the city limits.[10] Writing in *The Democratic*

Review in 1850, Thomas Kettell described transportation innovations in New York and Boston that not only allowed these cities to progress, in their urban growth, beyond the phase of the "walking" city, but also made possible the provision of the fresh food needs of their expanding urban populations.

THE OMNIBUS, THE RAILROAD, AND THE
ESCAPE FROM THE "WALKING" CITY: 1850

The business portion of the city is necessarily crowded within a small space, because . . . economy of time requires that all the places to which merchants and dealers are called many times each day . . . should be readily accessible. . . . Where the means of travel between these localities and [places of residence] are few and costly, the utmost economy of room is practised. In European cities, lofty buildings without yards, in narrow streets, contain the family above, and the office below, and until about twenty years since, New-York was cramped in a similar manner. At that time the omnibus system commenced running. By that plan coaches pass every five minutes through the principal avenues, carrying business men to their homes at night, and to their offices in the morning. This immediately permitted an expansion of the surface occupied by dwellings, and houses multiplied rapidly in the upper part of the city, which spreads from the business section in a fan-like form over the island. The Harlem Railroad . . . constructed in 1832, running the length of the island, affords cheap and prompt conveyance to great numbers of citizens. The effect of this improved means of conveyance, has been to enhance the supply of land suitable for city use, dwellings are removed from the lower part of the city, devoting it almost entirely to stores, without imposing loss of time and labor in traveling to and fro. . . .

While the omnibus system has thus expanded the city surface, steam has greatly reduced the cost of fuel and food. . . . Railroads . . . enable the perishable fruits and vegetables of summer to reach the market from considerable distances, and by so doing, not only place within the reach of citizens, fresh and cheap garden stuffs, but . . . confer on a larger number of farmers the profits of garden culture. The article of milk, as an instance, requires to be placed within the reach of the consumers in a very brief period from the time of its yield, necessarily, the circle of country which supports cows for the supply of city milk, must be very contracted; all cities have seriously felt the inconvenience of this fact. New-York dairies were established, in which swill-fed cows, diseased through constant confinement and unnatural food, yielded an abundant but deleterious fluid, having none of the properties of milk, although sold as such to the deluded citizens. The railroads now bring fresh milk every morning from a distance of sixty miles in time for use, and consequently the proportion of healthy milk used, has much increased, while the price at which it is afforded to citizens has been proportionally reduced. . . .

Without these means of communication, one of two things must have happened — viz., the city must have ceased to grow, or its general business must have yielded such profits as would have enabled citizens to pay extravagant prices for food and fuel. The means of obtaining food and fuel now presented are equal to any demand, at moderate prices. . . . The breadth of land that supplies the city with milk, vegetables, and other food, is extended almost indefinitely as compared with former times.

Boston enjoys a greater degree of railroad accommodation than most cities, and its statistics of population indicate [the influence of local railroads in spreading city population over a larger surface]. . . . In the decade ending with 1840 . . . the relative increase of Boston and the surrounding towns was the same . . . but in the decade ending the present year [1850] the pressure upon Boston, and the enhanced facilities for moving dwellings out of it by means of railroads, have produced the vast increase of 81 per cent. in the adjoining towns, which have for the first time exceeded the proportionate increase of Boston, great as that increase [65 per cent] has been. . . .[11]

It was the horsecar, rather than the omnibus or the steam railroad, that provided the first practical means of moving large numbers of people within the nation's now fast-growing cities. Horse railways came into dependable use in the Atlantic coast cities in the early 1850's. By the early 1860's, the principal street railways of New York City were carrying at least 45,000,000 passengers annually, Boston's as many as 6,500,000. New Yorkers, arguing that "street Railroads are a public necessity," were beginning to advocate placing municipal limitations on franchises. By 1860, Philadelphia had nearly 150 miles of street railways, and lines had been spread widely over Brooklyn, which now had become the "number-three" city of the nation in terms of population. The horsecar companies almost always were referred to as "metropolitan" railroads, an apt designation in view of their relationship to the widening boundaries of the large cities in these years.[12]

Like all major urban innovations, when private investment was involved, the introduction of the horsecar met opposition from proponents of existing facilities, in this instance from the omnibus companies. A Philadelphia advocate of the new transportation facility argued the merits of the horsecar over the omnibus in *A Practical Treatise on Street or Horse-power Railways* (1859).

HORSECAR VS. OMNIBUS — PHILADELPHIA: 1859

Popular prejudice is the great enemy . . . which the advocates of innovation have had to combat, and . . . the more useful the measure advocated, the greater has been . . . the opposition brought to bear against it. . . . The street railways have been tested in the cities of New York, Boston, and Philadelphia, and are found to be the "improvement of the age." . . . That increased facilities for commerce and transportation cause greater influx of traffic and travel to the principal streets of large cities, is indisputably recognized, and where the consequent inconvenience of narrow thoroughfares cannot be corrected, it must be modified by economizing time and space.

Time is economized by regularity of transit; the cars being quickly stopped by the application of the brake, the most refractory horses are immediately arrested; while the whole operation becomes so mechanical, that the horses, when accustomed to the signals of the bell, stop or start without any action on the part of the driver, by which means a time table can be effectively used, and business men are not subjected to delays incident to the old — and we trust soon to say obsolete — *omnibus system.*

Space is economized, because omnibuses, . . . surging from side to side of the streets, are abolished, while the work heretofore inadequately performed by three of those vehicles, is easily accomplished by one car, in half the time, notwithstanding it is concentrated and confined to one channel. . . .

Here is a picture. — A wet day — every corner of the side walk crowded with impatient pedestrians, each one anxiously peering up or down the street in search of the particular omnibus among the fifteen or twenty approaching, to carry him home . . . ; the omnibuses crowded to excess, cannot accommodate the vexed crowd on the side-walk, and the sudden halt with imminent risk of collision, with the drivers' "plenty of room, sir," with twenty inside — by no means softens the temper either of those in waiting, or those, who seated — not comfortably — look upon each moment of unnecessary delay, as an infringement on their rights.

Here is another. — Not an *omnibus* is seen in the whole length of the street — carriages, drays and carts move with comparative ease, little strips of iron are laid along the street, upon and across which, vehicles pass without inconvenience, and which, the drivers (particularly of private carriages) evidently seek; there is no crowd, for the little cars glide along rapidly and frequently, accommodating every body; at a slight signal the bell rings, the horses stop, the passenger is comfortably seated, no rain drops in from the roof, the conductor is always ready to take the fare when offered, and the echo, "great improvement, this," is constantly repeated.

There is no accident on record, of injury to any passenger of street railways, whilst occupying a seat in the car; some few have happened to boys and incautious persons, from drunkenness, jumping from the cars whilst in motion, &c., but even these, are few in comparison with omnibus accidents.[13]

2. MANUFACTURING

The expansion of city-based manufacturing, increasingly performed in factories, was another major cause of the sizable increase in the number of urban dwellers between the 1820's and the end of the Civil War. Industrial employment offered job opportunities that drew farm dwellers to the cities or held newcomers there, whether from Canada, Europe, or other parts of the United States. The census of persons employed in manufacturing rose from roughly 350,000 in 1820 to more than 2,000,000 in 1870. In most cities, trade and commerce were still predominant factors in urban growth; but by 1860 many cities of New England and several in the mid-Atlantic area, such as Philadelphia, Troy, Rochester, Utica, Newark, Paterson, and Wilmington, had manufacturing as the mainstay of the urban economy. In the middle West, processing of regional products and local manufacturing to avoid the transportation costs of importing finished goods gave the larger cities a significant industrial dimension, especially Cincinnati, St. Louis, and Louisville. As early as 1841, the editor of *The Missouri Reporter* argued that St. Louis could not "continue to grow without manufactures and extensive mechanical establishments to sustain her increasing population."[14] The nation's chief manufacturing cities in 1860, ranked in the order of the value of the goods produced, were New York and Philadelphia (far ahead of their rivals), Cincinnati, Boston, and Brooklyn (a second major group), and Newark, St. Louis, Baltimore, San Francisco, Lowell, Providence, Louisville, Richmond, Pittsburgh, New Bedford, and Chicago.

As long as manufacturing was dependent primarily upon water power, river sites were sought for manufacturing enterprises; new towns were developed to take advantage of this power source. By the early 1840's, however, when cheap coal became available along the Atlantic coast and improvements were made in the construction and operation of steam engines, factory production expanded tremendously in the seaport cities, where both a market and distribution facilities were more readily available. Nevertheless, the difficulty of transporting coal on railroads with light stock and iron rails induced continued reliance on water power, and as late as 1870 water wheels still produced half of the inanimate energy for manufacturing, thus giving water-power sites a continuing attraction in the location of industrial communities. The textile town of Lowell, Massachusetts, on the Merrimack River, was typical of the cities developed to take advantage of water power. A product of Boston capitalists, it combined, at its inception, the qualities of a model community and a company town. Textile production began there in 1823. The population of Lowell grew from about 2,500 when it was incorporated in 1826 to nearly 18,000 ten years later, and to 41,000 in 1870. The original workers, most of them women, came from the surrounding rural neighborhood, but as labor conditions deteriorated with competition from steam-powered factories, immigrants from Canada or Europe replaced the original labor supply.[15] It was the "extemporaneous" quality of the water-power cities and the nature of their labor supply that most impressed the French economist Michel Chevalier when he visited Lowell in 1834.

LOWELL — "MINIATURE MANCHESTER" —
WITH A DIFFERENCE: 1834

Lowell is a city eleven years old and it now contains fifteen thousand inhabitants, inclusive of the suburb of Belvedere. Twelve years ago it was a barren waste in which the silence was interrupted only by the murmur of the little river of Concord, and the noisy dashings of the clear waters of the Merrimack. . . . At present, it is a pile of factories . . . five, six, or seven stories high . . . [each] capped with a little white belfry, which strongly contrasts with the red masonry of the building. . . . On one side [of the river are] fancy-goods shops and milliners' rooms without number, for the women are the majority in Lowell . . . [on the other side], canals, water-wheels, water-falls, bridges, banks, schools, and libraries, for in Lowell reading is the only recreation and there are no less than seven journals printed here. All around are churches and meeting-houses of every sect. . . . Everywhere is heard the noise of hammers, of spindles, of bells calling the hands to their work or dismissing them from their tasks, . . . of the blowing of rocks to make a mill-race or to level a road; it is the peaceful hum of an industrious population, whose movements are regulated like clockwork; a population not native to the town, and one-half of which at least will die elsewhere, after having aided in founding three or four other towns; for the full-blooded American has this in common with the Tartar, that he is *encamped*, not established, on the soil he treads upon.

Massachusetts and the adjoining small States of New England contain several manufacturing towns similar to Lowell, but none of them on so large a scale. . . . In 1823, the Merrimack corporation began operations at Lowell, where the Merrimack has a fall of 32 feet, creating a vast motive power, and has been followed by the Hamilton, Appleton, Lowell, Suffolk, Tremont, Lawrence, and other companies in succession . . . ; it is one of the speculations of the merchants of Boston. . . . Lowell is a miniature Manchester. About 30,000 bales of cotton . . . are consumed in Lowell, besides which there are several manufactories of broadcloths, cassimeres, and carpets. . . .

The cotton manufacture alone employs six thousand persons . . . ; of this number nearly five thousand are young women from 17 to 24 years of age, the daughters of farmers from the different New England States, and particularly from Massachusetts, New Hampshire, and Vermont. . . . On seeing them pass through the streets in the morning and evening and at their meal-hours, neatly dressed; on finding their scarfs, and shawls, and green silk hoods which they wear as a shelter from the sun and dust (for Lowell is not yet paved), hanging up in the factories amidst the flowers and shrubs, which they cultivate, I said to myself, this, then, is not Manchester; and when I was informed of the rate of their wages, I understood that it was not at all like Manchester. . . .

The manufacturing companies exercise the most careful supervision over these girls. . . . When the manufactories were set up, it also became necessary to provide lodgings for the operatives, and each company has built for this purpose a number of houses within its own limits, to be used exclusively as boarding-houses for them. Here they are under the care of the mistress of the house, who is paid by the company at the rate of one dollar and a quarter a week for each boarder, that sum being stopped out of the weekly wages of the girls. . . . Each company has its rules and regulations, which are not merely paper-laws, but which are carried into execution with all that spirit of vigilant perseverance that characterises the Yankee. . . . Every individual who shall be notoriously dissolute, idle, dishonest, or intemperate, who shall be in the practice of absenting himself from divine service, or shall violate the Sabbath, or shall be addicted to gaming, shall be dismissed from the service of the Company. . . . All ardent spirits are banished from the Company's grounds, except when prescribed by a physician. All games of hazard and cards are prohibited within their limits and in the boarding-houses. There is . . . a special rule relative to boarding-houses. . . . It . . . requires that the keepers of the houses shall . . . give an account of the behaviour of the girls. It also prescribes that the doors shall be shut at ten.[16]

In existing cities, the acceleration of industrial activity caused a wide variety of physical and organizational arrangements. New, heavy industries, devoted to the production of machines, engines, and transportation equipment, grew out from older locations or formed nuclei of population growth along the edges of the city, often where railroad lines terminated, or along the docks when shipbuilding was involved. Production in other trades was often characterized by a mixture of the old and the new, a situation that aggravated the dislocations resulting from the increase in industrial pursuits. In Philadelphia's textile industry, for example, some firms had big, steam-powered mills, while others still relied on domestic industry. Carriage manufacturers concentrated the assembly function, using parts fabricated in small shops located throughout the city.[17]

In many cities, the extent of industrial activity was obscured because of the nature of the manufactures or the attention attracted by other pursuits. But there was no doubt of the predominance of industry in Pittsburgh by the 1850's. Its location near sources of coal and iron, together with the growing demand for steamboat engines, locomotives, and rails, led to a concentration of coal, iron, and machine production that gave it the reputation of being the "Birmingham" of America. As early as 1857, its more than 50 iron-works, employing close to 8,000 men, gave the city a markedly different appearance than it had earlier when boat building and outfitting activities were the chief pursuit of this "Gateway to the West." [18] The English novelist Anthony Trollope found Pittsburgh reminiscent of British industrial cities when he visited there in 1862.

PITTSBURGH — "BIRMINGHAM OF AMERICA": 1862

Pittsburg is . . . an amalgamation of Swansea, Merthyr-Tydvil, and South Shields. It is without exception the blackest place which I ever saw. The three English towns which I have named are very dirty, but all their combined soot and grease and dinginess do not equal that of Pittsburg. . . . The tops of the churches are visible, and some of the larger buildings may be partially traced through the thick, brown, settled smoke. But the city itself is buried in a dense cloud. . . . Pittsburg and Alleghany, which latter is a town similar in its nature to Pittsburg on the other side of the river, . . . are in effect one and the same city. They live under the same blanket of soot, which is woven by the joint efforts of the two places. Their united population is 135,000, of which Alleghany owns about 50,000. The industry of the towns is of that sort which arises from a union of coal and iron in the vicinity. The Pennsylvanian coal-fields are the most prolific in the Union; and Pittsburg is therefore great, exactly as Merthyr-Tydvil and Birmingham are great. But the foundry-work at Pittsburg is more nearly allied to the heavy, rough works of the Welsh coal metropolis than to the finish and polish of Birmingham.[19]

3. TOWN MAKING IN THE MIDDLE WEST

The westward movement of population, which assumed flood proportions from the 1830's to the eve of the Civil War, augmented the urban dimension of American society not only by spawning new cities and swelling the population of those that already existed, but by expanding the agricultural base on which urban communities could grow. The emergence of towns in the trans-Allegheny West accounted for more than half of the increase, between 1820 and 1870, in the number of urban communities with populations of 2,500 or more in the nation as a whole. The cities that had resulted from the original westward thrust of settlement by way of the Ohio River continued to increase in size; but by the 1850's their rate of growth was far exceeded by that of the newer urban communities that had sprung up with the settlement of the region bordering the Great Lakes. By 1870, Pittsburgh and neighboring Allegheny numbered 139,256; Louisville, 100,753; Cincinnati, 216,-239; St. Louis, 310,864; and New Orleans, 191,418. Chicago, however, had grown to a population of 298,977 in much shorter time; Buffalo totaled 117,714; Cleveland, 92,829; Detroit, 79,577; and Milwaukee, 71,440.

Contemporaries marveled at the speed of urban growth in mid-America; and belief in the urban potential of the West was one facet of the ebullient nationalism of the 1840's. In 1846, J. B. D. De Bow, editor of *The Commercial Review of the South and Southwest*, a periodical published in New Orleans and popularly called *De Bow's Review*, predicted that in 50 years there would be "at least twenty cities westward of the Allegheny mountains with a population of half a million. . . each." "If such a thought," he wrote, "does not awake in our bosoms true conceptions of the prospective greatness of our country, we know not what will." [20] Avid exponents of urban development in the West like Chicago promoter John S. Wright and Toledo newspaperman Jesup W. Scott predicted that the cities of the interior plain, and especially those on the Great Lakes ,would become the largest in the nation. In his numerous writings during the 1840's and 1850's, Scott contended that it was in the growth of large cities in the Middle West that the United States would most positively demonstrate its destined achievement. One of his many articles expressing this view was published in *De Bow's Review* in 1853.[21]

JESUP SCOTT ON THE URBAN POTENTIAL OF THE CENTRAL PLAIN: 1853

The West is no longer the west; nor even the *great* west. It is the great centre. It is the body of the American eagle whose wings are on the two oceans. . . . Steam, working on rail-roads, will soon . . . promote the growth of leading centres of commerce and manufacture. . . . Our leading cities will be very populous, and spread over a wide surface. In our central plain will, probably, grow up the hugest aggregations of people in the world. Before it reaches the density of England, it will contain one or more cities numbering ten millions. . . . The imagination can conceive nothing more imposingly grand than this march of humanity westward, to enter into possession of "time's noblest Empire." No logical induction . . . can be clearer to our mind, than that here will come together the greatest aggregations of men in cities — outrivalling in splendor as in magnitude, all which past ages have produced.[22]

Townsite promotion played an important role in the founding of new western towns, as it did, incidentally, in motivating the migration westward. Always to some degree a factor in the establishment of cities, townsite speculation became especially prevalent in the 1830's, with the increased accessibility of the West, the rising interest in city living, and the entrepreneurial spirit of Jacksonian America. In his *Home As Found*, James Fenimore Cooper describes the mania for speculation in western towns, as well as in urban real estate in general, that he observed in 1834 and 1835, on his return from England. He brings this out in a conversation between two of the characters in the novel, Sir George Templemore and Mr. Aristabulus Bragg, an American attorney.

JAMES FENIMORE COOPER
ON TOWNSITE SPECULATION: 1835

"Law is flat with us of late, and many of the attorneys are turning their attention to other callings."

"And pray, sir," asked Sir George, "what is the favorite pursuit with most of them just now?"

"Some our way have gone into the horse-line; but much the greater portion are just now dealing in western cities."

"In western cities!" exclaimed the baronet, looking as if he distrusted a mystification.

"In such articles, and in mill-seats, and railroad lines, and other expectations. . . . There are many profitable occupations in this country, Sir George, that have been overlooked in the eagerness to embark in the town-trade — "

"Mr. Bragg does not mean trade in town, but trade in towns," explained John Effingham.

"Yes, sir, the traffic in cities. I never come this way without casting an eye about me, in order to see if there is anything to be done that is useful; and I confess that several available opportunities have offered, if one had capital. . . ."

[Some days later, Sir George was taken to visit the Exchange, in Wall Street, where he could observe the traffic in cities at first hand.] Effingham led the way up stairs into the office of one of the most considerable auctioneers. The walls were lined with maps, some representing houses, some lots, some streets, some entire towns.

"This is the focus of what Aristabulus Bragg calls the town trade," said John Effingham, when fairly confronted with all these wonders. . . . "Mr. Hammer, do us the favor to step this way. Are you selling to-day?"

"Not much, sir. Only a hundred or two lots on this island [Manhattan] . . . with one western village."

"Can you tell us the history of this particular piece of property, Mr. Hammer?"

"With great pleasure, Mr. Effingham; we know you to have means, and hope you may be induced to purchase. This was the farm of old Volkert Van Brunt, five years since, off of which he and his family had made a livelihood for more than a century, by selling milk. Two years since, the sons sold it to Peter Feeler for a hundred an acre, or for the total sum of five thousand dollars. The next spring Mr. Feeler sold it to John Search, as keen a one as we have, for twenty-five thousand. Search sold it at private sale to Nathan Rise for fifty thousand the next week, and Rise had parted with it to a company, before the purchase, for a hundred and twelve thousand, cash. The map ought to be taken down — for it is now eight months since we sold it out in lots, at auction, for the gross sum of three hundred thousand dollars. As we have received our commission, we look at that land as out of the market for a time."

"Have you other property, sir, that affords the same wonderful history of a rapid advance in value?" asked the baronet.

"These walls are covered with maps of estates in the same predicament. Some have risen two or three thousand per cent. within five years, and some only a few hundred. There is no calculating in the matter — for it is all fancy."

"And on what is this enormous increase in value founded? Does the town [New York] extend to these fields?"

"It goes much further, sir; that is to say, on paper. In the way of houses, it is still some miles short of them. A good deal depends on what you call a thing, in this market. Now, if old Volkert Van Brunt's property had been still called a farm, it would have brought a farm price; but as soon as it was surveyed into lots, and mapped — "

"Mapped!"

"Yes, sir; brought into visible lines, with feet and inches. As soon as it was properly mapped, it rose to its just value. We have a good deal of the bottom of the sea that brings fair prices in consequence of being well mapped." . . .

"We will now go into the sales-room," said John Effingham, "where you shall judge of the spirit, or energy, as it is termed, which at this moment actuates this great nation."

Descending, they entered a crowd, where scores were eagerly bidding against each other, in the fearful delusion of growing rich by pushing a fancied value to a point still higher. One was purchasing ragged rocks, another the bottom of rivers, a third a bog, and all on the credit of maps. Our two observers remained some time silent spectators of the scene. . . .

"And all those persons are hazarding their means of subsistence on the imaginary estimate mentioned by the auctioneer?"

"They are gambling as recklessly as he who places his substance on the cast of the die. So completely has the mania seized every one, that the obvious truth . . . that nothing can be sustained without a foundation, is completely overlooked. . . . I have witnessed many similar excesses in the way of speculation; but never an instance as gross, as widespread, and as alarming as this." [23]

Although speculation in townsites figured in the beginnings of virtually every major city of the Middle West, hundreds of projected cities never developed beyond the paper stage, to the chagrin of many investors and settlers for whom town property and urban business in the newly developing parts of the country represented El Dorado. The consequences of being gulled by townsite speculators were satirized in an account, published in 1839, of the disastrous results of a New Englander's investment in the rising town of "Edensburgh, Illinois." It supposedly was written by Major Walter Wilkey, "an honest Yeoman," who was induced by Squire Samuel Soaper to exchange his farm in Maine for "twenty valuable house-lots in EDENSBURGH! . . . one of the most delightful, prosperous and thriving CITIES in the West, which (in commercial point of view) promised soon to equal, if not outrival the cities of New-York and Philadelphia! and like the former, already boasting of her public squares, her parks, her parade grounds, her 'Change! — Broadway — Wall — Washington — Pearl — Franklin — Grand — Commercial and other streets." [24] Having made his purchase, Wilkey and his family proceeded by farm wagon, canal boat, and lake vessel to the Illinois country to claim their new urban possession. At last they came upon a small log hut labeled "Hotel." After they made one or two thumps at the door, the landlady appeared at the window.

A PAPER CITY IN ILLINOIS: 1830's

Major — "Can you tell us, good lady, whether you ever heard of . . . Edensburgh? And if so, where and in what part of the world it may be found?" . . .

Landlady — "Wha! unbelieving man, . . . this here city is Edensburgh — so named but a-three months ago by Squire Soaper, the lucky good man who bought the land!"

Major — ". . . But where in the name of *gosh*, woman, are its public and private edifices, its increased population, its Park, College, State House, and other squares, its Broadway, Pearl, Washington, Wall, Grand, and other streets?" . . .

The old lady here hastily withdrew . . . and . . . returned with the "Platt" that the Squire had left with her. "Here," said she, "it is, in plain black and white, just as it was staked down by Squire Soaper, (placing her forefinger of the right hand upon the sheet). . . . You now stand Major . . . with one foot in Washington street, and the other in Grand street; your good woman between Pearl and Broadway, your horse in State street, the fore-wheels of your waggon in Wall street, and the hind in Market street."

Major — ". . . And pray tell me, good woman, how long was the Squire himself an inhabitant of Edensburgh, as you call it?"

Landlady — "Just three half days; half a day in making the purchase and staking out the City — half a day in drawing and fixing this here Platt, and another half day, with the assistance of my old man, in logging the house we live in."

Major — "And Landlady, will you now inform me what . . . number of inhabitants Edensburgh now contains?"

Landlady — "Well, let me see, (counting her fingers) there is myself and my old man, are *two*, and there is Bridget Bilkey is *three*, Ebednigo Bilkey is *four*, Epaphrosticus Bilkey is *five*, Askwell Bilkey is *six*, Birchee Bilkey is *seven* and Ruthful Bilkey is *eight*, of these myself and husband are *living* inhabitants, but the Bilkeys (poor souls) are all *dead*, and died with the *Fever* and *Ague* within one week of each other! and lie buried in 'Market Square.' " [25]

Speculation in townsites helped to precipitate the economic crisis of 1837, suggesting the bearing of urbanization upon fluctuations in the business cycle. The promoters of mushroom communities like Chicago and Milwaukee overextended themselves in grading streets and constructing bridges and hotels in order to make the city visible, and this contributed to an economic collapse that canal and railroad construction had helped to instigate. In the wake of the panic, land values in Chicago dropped from $10 million to $1,250,000. Commercial editors of the early 1840's warned against promoting cities before a rural hinterland had been developed to support them. This was the view of a contributor to *Hunt's Merchants' Magazine and Commercial Review* for July, 1840.

TOWNSITE SPECULATION —
THE SOBER AFTERVIEW: 1840

We well know that a feeling of distrust has been thrown around the western character, from the spirit of speculation which, in 1835 and '36, seemed to absorb all other enterprise, and which may be considered, not its silver or golden, but its paper age! But that spirit was kept up and acted on, as much by eastern as by western men. The whole territory was regarded as a sort of lottery-office, to which individuals from all quarters might resort for the accumulation of wealth, and invoke the favors of the capricious and blind goddess. Agriculture, and all those substantial enterprises which contribute to the solid glory of a people, were neglected. The land swarmed with greedy speculators, who cut up the woods into paper villages, and constructed in imagination a chain of compact cities, from the head of the St. Clair to the rapids of the Maumee. This was the period when there was the most immigration to the territory, and the greatest influx of temporary travellers. Thousands were defrauded. The log houses swarmed with buyers and sellers, when there was scarcely food enough in the country to maintain the vast accession to its population; and many erroneous impressions were disseminated of the general condition of the country, from the circumstances of that extraordinary period. It is a matter of the highest congratulation, that the lax spirit which at that time pervaded the portion of the west upon the borders of the lakes, has become discountenanced, and that the energies of the people have quietly sunk down into the accustomed channels of substantial industry.[26]

Cities that weathered the hazards of townsite speculation still had to contest their economic position with ambitious competitors, for it was in the spirit of the place and of the age that every major city of Middle America aspired to be the "Queen City" of the West. A vigorous promotional zeal characterized the behavior of the leadership element in most of these western communities. Here, as in the seaboard cities, the railroad was seen to be the most effective weapon of urban rivalry — not only to implement commercial development but to attract population to the new cities of the West. Typical of the railroad-minded promoters of western cities was William B. Ogden, Chicago's first mayor. Among a host of other activities designed to promote the city's growth and welfare, Ogden mobilized private subscriptions for Chicago's pioneer railroad connecting the city with the traffic of the Mississippi River, took an active part in the development of lines that gave Chicago rail connections with Fort Wayne and Pittsburgh as well as points in Wisconsin and Minnesota, presided in 1850 over the National Railway Convention, and in 1862 became the first president of the first transcontinental line, the Union Pacific.[27]

The rate of Chicago's growth, by contrast to that of St. Louis, her more venerable regional rival, seemed to confirm the view that aggressive personal effort and especially the promotion of railroads provided the key to urban advantage in the contest for business and population supremacy among the cities of the Middle West. Between 1860 and 1870, St. Louis failed to double her population, while Chicago nearly tripled hers. Contemporaries laid the difference in the growth of the two cities to Chicago's greater vigor in promoting railroads, while St. Louis had relied, in conservative complacency, on her resources for river transport. A writer in *The Atchison* [Kansas] *Free Press* described the way Chicago had used the railroad, together with other promotional techniques, as a weapon of urban imperialism in her contest with St. Louis in the 1860's.

RAILROADS AND THE CHICAGO–ST. LOUIS
RIVALRY: 1860's

Chicago and St. Louis — There are two great business centres in the West — Chicago and St. Louis. Each of them is extending its arms to draw to its bosom the trade which otherwise will fall to its rival. There was a time when St. Louis was the centre of all the trade of the West. . . . Its merchants were staid, substantial men. . . . The current of their business flowed on as smoothly as the placid waters upon which all their commerce floated. The nervous, far-sighted, often reckless Yankee was not there, or if he came he could not unloose the purse-strings of those whose wealth was necessary to extend speedily from that point, the arms of [a] railroad system over the West. . . .

Chicago had not begun to spring up till long after St. Louis had become opulent in her quiet wealth and ease. But at length shrewd and active merchants set their stakes at Chicago. At first they bought grain by the wagon-load, and sent it all by schooners down the lakes. Then they commenced the construction of railroads. In all directions they caused them to push their way out over the prairies to bring in the productions of the ten thousand farms. . . . St. Louis merchants clung to the fogyism and the faith of their correspondents away down the Mississippi. . . . Chicago railroads cut St. Louis off on the east, away down to Cairo, long ago; cut across the State of Missouri to the Missouri river, long ago, and penetrated to the heart of Iowa, and cut across Wisconsin to Minnesota. Now they reach across Kansas by two lines — one by the way of Cameron, Kansas City, and the Eastern division, Pacific; the other by the Central branch Pacific, from Atchison. They cross Nebraska by the Pacific Trunk to the Rocky Mountains. They reach the Territory of Dacotah at Sioux City. And everywhere these iron arms are being rapidly lengthened out.

Chicago merchants bought Nebraska grain two years ago, and paid more for it than would St. Louis merchants. . . . And it is not only grain but the beef and the pork of the Northwest that the Chicago merchants monopolize by their superior enterprise. . . . While Chicago has gathered up the produce of the West and marketed it in every eastern city and in Europe, she has kept her exchange accounts even. The grain merchant does not from his sales bring currency to buy more grain with. He gives a bill of exchange. This is transferred to the Chicago dry goods and grocery merchant. To every point from whence comes grain to the Chicago market, Chicago dry goods and grocery merchants

sent bills of goods. Every northwestern town is visited by the
Chicago merchant, and orders solicited. Every newspaper in the
Northwest teems with inducements offered by Chicago merchants
to retail dealers. . . . The Chicago merchant has his arrangements for shipping complete. . . . Every stream is bridged or
being bridged. Not many months hence Chicago will reach the
furthermost confines of every northwestern State without breaking bulk. Modern St. Louis men are working out a railroad system — but at a slow pace. St. Louis merchants, at the spring
rise in the river, manifest much spasmodic life, and then they
sell considerable bills of goods. But the unceasing enterprise, the
unfailing energy of the Chicago merchant is wanting among
the merchants of St. Louis.[28]

The contrast between Chicago and St. Louis impressed James
Parton, journalist and biographer, who visited St. Louis in 1867
while preparing a series of articles for *The Atlantic Monthly* on
the cities of the West. His comments on the Missouri city not only
document the less dynamic tone of its society, in comparison with
Chicago, but suggest the extent to which Philadelphia provided a
model for the physical design of many western cities. Yet despite
its imitative form, the varied sources of its population gave St. Louis
an urban personality distinctively its own.

"SERENE" ST. LOUIS — MIRROR
OF "COMFORTABLE" PHILADELPHIA: 1867

St. Louis is an immense surprise to visitors from the Eastern
States, particularly to those who come round to it from furious
and thundering Chicago. It has stolen into greatness without
our knowing much about it. If Chicago may be styled the New
York, St. Louis is the serene and comfortable Philadelphia, of
the West. . . . Chicago amuses, amazes, bewilders, and exhausts
the traveller; St. Louis rests and restores him. . . .

No daughter is more like her mother than St. Louis is like
Philadelphia. From 1775 to 1800, Philadelphia was the chief
city of the country, to which all eyes were directed, and to which
the leaders of the nation annually repaired. So dazzling was this
plain and staid metropolis to the eyes of Western members and
merchants, that, in laying out the cities of the West, they could
not but copy Philadelphia, even in the minutest particulars. The
streets of Philadelphia running parallel to the river are num-

bered; so are those of St. Louis, Cincinnati, and other Western towns. The cross-streets of Philadelphia were named after the trees, plants, and bushes that grew upon its site, such as Sycamore, Vine, Cherry, Walnut, Chestnut, Pine, and Spruce. Accident changed some of these appellations in the course of years, so that we find such names as "Race" and "Arch" mingled with those of the trees. So infatuated were the Western men of the early day with the charms of Philadelphia . . . that they not only named their streets at home Sycamore and Chestnut, but used also the accidental ones, such as Race and Arch. Nearly every street in Nashville has a Philadelphia name. Half the streets of Cincinnati have Philadelphia names. In St. Louis, too, we are reminded of the Quaker City at every turn, both in the names and the aspect of the streets. Those old-fashioned, square, roomy brick mansions, — the habit of tipping and pointing everything with marble, — the brick pavements, — the chastened splendor of the newer residences, — the absence of any principal thoroughfare, such as Broadway, — the prodigious extent of the city for its population, — the general quiet and neatness, — all call to mind comfortable Philadelphia. They have even adopted, of late, the mode of numbering the houses practised in the Quaker City. . . .

The resemblance of this highly favored city to Philadelphia is only external. It has a character of its own, to which many elements have contributed, and which many influences have modified. The ball-clubs, playing in the fields on Sunday afternoons, the billiard-rooms open on Sunday, the great number of assemblies, balls, and parties, the existence of five elegant and expensively sustained theatres in a town of two hundred and twenty thousand inhabitants, . . . and an indefinable something in the tone and air of the people, notify the stranger that he is in a place which was not the work exclusively of the Puritan, nor even of the Protestant. It is, indeed, a town of highly composite character. The old and wealthy families, descendants of the original French settlers, still speaking the French language and maintaining French customs, give to the place something of the style of New Orleans. . . . The negro, too, has imparted his accent to the tongue of the people. Nearly one half of the population being Catholic, . . . the civilization of the town is essentially Catholic. . . . The city . . . has attracted a few thousands of Northern people. . . . Add to these various elements sixty thousand Germans, whom the secessionists of St. Louis compliment with the title of the "Damned Dutch," — uttering the words with that ferocious emphasis which they usually reserve exclusively for the

"Damned Yankees." Our placid and good-natured German friends . . . have contrived to make themselves most intensely abhorred by the "aristocracy" of the place, nine in ten of whom were Secessionists. . . .

How interesting the spectacle of those rising cities of the West! How cheering to discover that the ruling minds in them all are alive to the fact that posterity, to the remotest ages, will be affected by what the men do who control the cities that they are now forming! [29]

4. URBANISM AND
THE SELF-CONSCIOUS SOUTH

The movement of population into the lower Mississippi Valley generated some new towns and added numbers to existing cities, but urbanism was much less prevalent in the southern half than in the northern half of the region — a fact that was to contribute to the growing difference between the sections. In the upper Mississippi Valley the increase in communities with populations of 2,500 or more was from 1 to 235, in the years from 1820 to 1870; in Kentucky, Tennessee, Alabama, Mississippi, Arkansas, Louisiana, and Texas the increase was from 3 to only 46. By the eve of the Civil War sizable cities existed on the periphery of what had become an increasingly self-conscious South — Memphis, New Orleans, Mobile, Savannah, Charleston, and Richmond; but in the section as a whole the nature of both the society and the economy had tended to discourage the dynamic and pervasive urban growth that by 1860 characterized the upper Mississippi Valley and the North in general.[30]

The large plantation, worked by slave labor, though not the predominant farm unit in the South, was the social ideal of most white Southerners, an ideal bolstered by the rural background of most of the migrants into the lower Mississippi Valley. In terms of the economy, the ability to carry on long-distance trade directly from the large plantations militated against the growth of sizable cities other than ports and their up-river subsidiaries. Moreover, by 1825, Southerners had permitted the carrying trade to be monopolized by New York merchants, thus reducing a source of profit that would have fostered the growth of Charleston, Savannah, Mobile, and New Orleans. The relative self-sufficiency of the large plantation, in providing craft and mechanical services, made it a substitute in this respect for the small town; and the fact that great numbers of small farmers remained at the subsistence level of production reduced the demand for goods that would have caused urban centers to grow. The resultant lack of rural as well as urban purchasing power, together with the absorption of capital in slaves and the rural mindedness of southern political leadership, retarded the growth of manufacturing and the urbanization it would have encouraged, even though a scattering of mill villages and some manufacturing in the larger cities (especially Richmond) reflected the efforts of a small group to encourage local industry.[31] One champion of local manufacturing was William Gregg, who set up a cotton factory at Graniteville, South Carolina, but this textile town had grown to only 900 people by 1859.

The attitude toward urbanism constituted one of the manifest differences between the North and the South as the two sections were growing apart in the pre-Civil War years; the alleged advantages of rural over urban living figured strongly in the argument by which dominant elements in the South attempted to justify their way of life as it came to be threatened by an economy in which urbanism was becoming ascendant. Southern leaders took heart from the statement of Cincinnatian Ellwood Fisher, who tortured census statistics to show the superiority of the more rural South over the more urban North in terms of per-capita wealth (of the white population), health and longevity, working conditions, and rates of poverty and crime. First presented at a meeting of the Mercantile Society of Cincinnati and widely circulated "at the expense of members of Congress," Fisher's conclusions were printed in *De Bow's Review* in 1849 and reprinted there in 1857, with only slight changes based on statistics from the Census of 1850. Fisher's exposition suggests the origins as well as the rationale of the South's rural tradition.

NORTHERN CITIES CRITICIZED — A DEFENSE OF SOUTHERN INSTITUTIONS: 1850's

The progress and prospects of the Northern and Southern sections of this Union involve some of the greatest and gravest questions of the age. Each has a form of civilization peculiar to

itself, and to modern times. . . . I maintain that the South is
greatly the superior of the North in wealth, in proportion to the
number of their citizens. . . .

Rural life . . . has seldom been thought favorable to the accumulation of wealth — the first want of civilization. It is also
usually associated with rudeness of manners. Hence, the votaries
of fortune and society have preferred the city; and, if to these
we add the vast multitude who seek the immediate gratification
of their appetites and passions, which cities afford, at the hazard
of future want, we have a clear solution of the undue tendency
to city at the expense of country life. This great evil, sufficient of
itself to cast a stigma on civilization and even ultimately to destroy it, was for the first time . . . conquered by the institutions
of the South; and . . . Virginia led the way. Amongst the early
white settlers of Virginia were many of the Cavaliers who had
been driven into exile by the . . . Roundheads. . . . The Cavaliers were of the country party in England, the cities and towns
were more generally devoted to the Roundheads. The Cavaliers
. . . seem to have brought over with them . . . a hostility even
to the modes of life of the enemies they left behind. . . .

The soil of Virginia was . . . adapted to the cultivation of
tobacco, and African slave labor to its cultivation. . . . [By] the
introduction of this sort of labor . . . agriculture has been
made . . . so profitable and attractive as to render rural life the
favorite of wealth as well as of the mass of the people, . . .
the country, instead of the towns, the abode of elegant manners
and refined taste. And this system of society has prevailed throughout the other States of the South, owing to the . . . emigration
into them of many Virginians . . . and to the culture of cotton,
which is more favorable to the employment of slave labor than
that of tobacco.

Thus we have fifteen Southern States — one-half the number
belonging to the Union . . . who have . . . given ascendancy
within their borders to country life over city, in social and political power. . . . About one-half the population of the old northern States resides in towns or cities — in the southern about one-
tenth. Even Ohio, a new State, has already a town and city
population estimated at one-fourth of the whole; the single city of
Cincinnati, only fifty years of age, containing more people than
ten of the largest towns of Virginia, the oldest State of the
Union. . . .

. . . The average wealth of the inhabitants of cities . . .
results from the influx into the city of persons who have become
rich in the country, and who resort to the cities, because they

cannot carry on agricultural operations extensively in the country, in free States. This results from the high price of agricultural labor in the free States, and its irregularity. An industrious laborer on a farm, soon acquires enough money to buy a small tract of public land, and emigrates to it. Hence a farmer who acquires some wealth in these States, and finds it difficult to extend his operations in the country, resorts to commercial operations, and settles in town. . . .

Besides the extravagant and speculative habits of cities, . . . we must add the enormous taxation to which they are subject. The city of New York, with its four hundred thousand people, is taxed for the present year, about three millions of dollars, a sum which is about half as much as the taxes of all the fifteen southern States combined. But the most disastrous and appalling consequences of city avocations, is the waste of human life. . . . According to an official statement of the duration of human life . . . the three avocations of city life, merchants, mechanics, and laborers, average about 46½ years, whilst farmers live more than 64½ years, or one-third longer. . . . Thus, then, the superior productiveness of agricultural labor, the great intrinsic value . . . of its products, the extravagant style of living in towns and cities, and finally, the ruinous waste of human life and labor they occasion, are reasons enough to account for . . . the triumph of the agricultural States of the South over the more commercial States of the North. . . .

The South is rural in residence and habits. It does not present the temptation or the opportunity for sensual gratification to be found in city life. It is to cities that the passions and appetites resort for their carnival. The theatre, the gaming house, the drinking house, and places of still more abandoned character abound in them, and to these the dissipated youth goes forth at night from home, along the high road to ruin. In the family of the southern planter or farmer, although wine may be drank, and cards played, all is done at home under parental and feminine observation; and, therefore, excess can never go so far. Of course the sons of planters visit the cities, but those in their neighborhood are trivial in size, and meagre in attractions — those more distant are the more seldom seen.[32]

Many southern publicists were developing an image of the North compounded, in part, of attributes associated with its urbanism, which they viewed with distinct distaste. "Python," writing in *De Bow's Review* in 1857, condemned the North for the ideas generated by its "no-property" urban masses, strengthened in their assertiveness by "the principle of association" that city life fostered and that had given rise to " 'Trades-union' organizations — the 'Sons-of-Temperance' affiliations — the 'Odd-Fellows' societies — the institutions of the 'Druids' — the brotherhoods of 'Red-Men,' the fraternities of 'Orangemen,' and many other kindred *modern* associations," including "Know-Nothingism" and "the political party designated by some as Black Republican." [33] Daniel R. Hundley was offended by the sense of superiority Northerners manifested because of their allegedly more sophisticated urban society. He expressed this view in his *Social Relations in Our Southern States*. He disdained urbanism even in the South, which, he reported, had its woebegone villages smelling of whiskey and hogs and its cities dominated by "Cotton Snobs" and "Southern Yankees" obsessed with the pursuit of the Almighty Dollar.

THE CITY DISDAINED —
A SOUTHERNER'S REACTION: 1857

We remember travelling once on the Mississippi in company with an old gentleman from New-York, (it was in the autumn of '57,) . . . on his first visit Southward. In truth, so long as the bustle and confusion lasted, our bachelor acquaintance seemed pleased with every thing about him. So long had he been used to the continuous hum and noise of a large city — so long had he been accustomed to being jostled about at every turn — that to him *unrest* seemed to be the only species of *rest* of which he knew any thing. . . . For a long time he endured the [quiet on the river; then] says he, "WHERE'S YOUR TOWNS?" The question was so characteristic, and was uttered with such a meaning look and gesture, we could not refrain from turning aside to have a quiet laugh. And yet at least one half of the Northern people, used all their lives to the bustle of cities and towns, and the noisy clatter of mechanical trades, if similarly situated with our earnest New-York acquaintance, would propound just such a question as he did — never once reflecting that cotton, sugar, rice, wheat, corn, tobacco, and all other agricultural products, grow only in the country and very *quietly*, too, at that. Hence, even while they are passing a princely plantation — hid from view though it be by the dense forest on the river's bank — whose proprietor could with a single year's crop buy up half-a-dozen New-England villages, they will whisper confidentially in your ear: "Ah! Sir, how unlike our thrifty Down East villages!" . . .

No matter what may be the Southern Gentleman's avocation, his dearest affections usually centre in the country. He longs to live as his fathers lived before him, in both the Old World and the New; and he ever turns with unfeigned delight from the bustle of cities . . . to the quiet and peaceful scenes of country life. The glare of gas and the glitter of tinsel, the pride, the pomp, the vanity, and all the grace and wit of *la bonne compagnie*, he surrenders without a sigh of regret. . . . Indeed, with all classes in the South the home feeling is much stronger than it is in the North; for the bane of hotel life and the curse of boarding-houses have not as yet extended their pernicious influences to our Southern States, or at best in a very small degree. . . . It may be owing in part to the sparse population of the South, but the fact is indisputable: as a general rule, family ties are much stronger there than in the North, while the parental discipline is more rigid, and Young America is rarely met with save in the large towns and villages; for these are much the same all over the country, except that the Southern villages have a more wo-begone look, and smell stronger of mean whisky and hogs than the trim-villages of New-England. . . .

Nearly all classes of residents in the Southern cities, differ in no essential particulars from the same classes in other cities any where else in the Union. . . . The Cotton Snob does not hail from the city originally, though he may later in life go to the city to live, and when he does so becomes invariably the most disgusting cockney one can find any where in the four quarters of the globe. He is always of country breeding, and his manners more often than otherwise lack that *quasi* polish which the city snob sometimes possesses, despite his toadying mannerisms and want of native manliness of character. . . . Now, the poor white trash are about the only paupers in our Southern States. . . . Moreover, [they] are wholly rural; hence the South will ever remain secure against any species of agrarianism, since such mob violence always originates in towns and cities, wherein are herded together an unthinking rabble.[34]

Other Southerners, far from disdaining cities, argued that the development of them was the only way to compete with the fast-urbanizing North. Proponents of individual cities, as well as southern nationalists, agitated for improvements in transportation that would permit the South to compete for the trade of the West and that would tie the section together as an effective economic unit. From the mid-1840's onward, De Bow, in his *Review,* was goading Southerners to move in this direction.

In 1847 he urged New Orleans to make dock improvements that would strengthen the city's bid for "the growing commerce of the great West" in a contest in which Boston, Philadelphia, Baltimore, and especially New York already were engaged with their "vast expenditure of money in building railroads, digging canals, etc." By 1858, when it appeared evident that New Orleans could not control the trade of the West above the junction of the Missouri River with the Mississippi, the *Review* argued for building up Norfolk, Virginia, as "a third great centre of trade, corresponding with New Orleans and New York." This "emporium of the bay," DeBow predicted, "would give the South two-thirds of the trade of the Union," and unite "the traders and merchants of the world to a greater metropolis than has ever yet been dreamt of." [35] Construction of east-west railroad lines in the South during the 1850's linked the Atlantic coast and the Mississippi; and rails edged northward from Mobile and New Orleans; but New Orleans never generated the drive that animated her northern seaboard rivals or Chicago, the burgeoning metropolis of the Great Lakes. De Bow alluded as early as 1847 to urban rivalries between the Northeast and the South for advantage in the West — rivalries already aggravating the tensions that ultimately brought the North and South to armed conflict.

NEW ORLEANS AND THE TRADE OF THE WEST (AND THE WORLD?): 1847

A contest has been going on between the North and South, not limited to slavery or no slavery — to abolition or no abolition, nor to the politics of either whigs or democrats, as such, but a contest for the wealth and commerce of the great valley of the Mississippi . . . , a contest tendered by our Northern brethren, whether the growing commerce of the great West, shall be thrown upon New Orleans, or given to the Atlantic cities — which shall receive, store, sell and ship the immense products, of that great country, lying between the Appalachian and Rocky Mountains? Shall Boston, New York, Philadelphia and Baltimore do it, or shall our own New Orleans? . . .

In the midst of this grand display of enterprise . . . by our northern brethren, to draw the commerce of the west to them, the question comes up, what have we of the State of Louisiana, and New-Orleans in particular, done to ensure this commerce to ourselves? . . . Possessing, as Louisiana does, the ownership of the Mississippi river . . . , but little exertion *was wanting*, but little exertion is *now wanting* to ensure to New-Orleans . . . the untold millions of its commerce, to be forever carried on through the mouths of the Mississippi. Had a tithe of the exertion been made to retain it, that has distinguished the efforts of the north to draw it off, we should not now be called to look with astonishment at beholding one-half in bulk and value of western produce seeking a market at the northern Atlantic cities, where twenty years ago, not a dollar was sent through the channels now bearing it away from New-Orleans. . . .

A duty now lies before us — . . . we must meet our Northern competitors upon their own ground, and with corresponding weapons. Where they offer one facility, we must offer a better. . . . The disadvantages that New-Orleans now labours under . . . no other commercial city in the United States has to contend with. In Boston, New-York, Philadelphia and Baltimore, vessels come alongside the wharves on which the warehouses are built for the reception of the produce or merchandize. In New-York they have, since the great increase of business from the west to that city, gone to an enormous expense in building what is called the "Atlantic Dock," covering a space of forty acres of ground, where vessels can discharge cargoes right into the warehouses . . . without subjecting the owner to any charge of drayage or risk of damage from wet. . . . The same . . . interests demand for New Orleans the like improvements. . . . The petition . . . now before the Legislature, is intended to effect this object, by clothing . . . this Municipality, with power to authorize the erection of warehouses upon the Levee . . . and collonading over the wharfs . . . so that vessels coming alongside can discharge their cargoes . . . protected from rain, damp and mud. . . .

The supineness with which we of the South have hitherto looked upon the efforts of our Northern brethren to draw away from our port so large a part already of the produce of the great Valley of the Mississippi, should be stopped at once, and our energies aroused to apply quickly and effectually the remedies properly applicable to win for New-Orleans not the second or third rank, but the *front rank* in commercial importance over every other city in the world. . . . The signs of the times indicate clearly, that a change in the course of the trade of Asia and the East Indies must, and soon will be brought about. . . . When this connection with the Pacific is once had, the foreign commerce of New Orleans and the great West will be at once cut loose from the leading strings of New York, and the supplies now purchased in the North for the South and West, will be had direct from the work-shops of Europe, the payments for which will be made in Western produce shipped direct to New Orleans, the great mart for all the nations of the world; and the profits we are now paying to the mercantile gentlemen of New York will be secured to our own city by the enterprise of our own merchants. . . . If it is made the interest of the West to ship their produce to the Northern Atlantic cities through artificial channels, to the North it will go. Make it their interest to ship to New Orleans, and to New Orleans it will come.[36]

The sharpest critic of the South for its failure to encourage urban growth was North Carolinian Hinton R. Helper, who laid the South's lack of cities to the slaveholding planter and the institution of slavery. He expressed this view in *The Impending Crisis of the South: How to Meet It*, which he wrote in 1856 and published a year later in New York. "Without a city," he contended, "a great Southern importing, exporting and manufacturing city," the South could "never develop her commercial resources nor attain to that eminent position to which those vast resources would otherwise exalt her." [37] He reported the decreasing number of slaves in Baltimore and St. Louis, two of the largest cities in the slave states, thus reflecting the fact, though he did not make the point, that urban conditions were not congenial to the institution of slavery.

HINTON HELPER BLAMES SLAVERY
FOR THE SOUTH'S LACK OF CITIES: 1857

Nothing is more evident than the fact, that our people have never entertained a proper opinion of the importance of home cities. Blindly, and greatly to our own injury, we have contributed hundreds of millions of dollars toward the erection of mammoth cities at the North, while our own magnificent bays and harbors have been most shamefully disregarded and neglected. Now, instead of carrying all our money to New York, Philadelphia, Boston and Cincinnati, suppose we had kept it on the south side of Mason and Dixon's line — as we would have done, had it not

111

been for slavery — and had disbursed it in the upbuilding of Norfolk, Beaufort, Charleston or Savannah, how much richer, better, greater would the South have been to-day? How much larger and more intelligent would have been our population? How many hundred thousand natives of the South would now be thriving at home, instead of adding to the wealth and political power of other parts of the Union? How much greater would be the number and length of our railroads, canals, turnpikes and telegraphs? How much greater would be the extent and diversity of our manufactures? How much greater would be the grandeur, and how much larger would be the number of our churches, theatres, schools, colleges, lyceums, banks, hotels, stores and private dwellings? . . .

Almost invariably do we find the bulk of the floating funds, the best talent, and the most vigorous energies of a nation concentrated in its chief cities; and does not this concentration of wealth, energy and talent conduce, in an extraordinary degree, to the growth and prosperity of a nation? Unquestionably. Wealth develops wealth, energy develops energy, talent develops talent. What, then, must be the condition of those countries which do not possess the means or facilities of centralizing their material forces, their energies and their talents? Are they not destined to occupy an inferior rank among the nations of the earth? Let the South answer. And now let us ask . . . what do we so much need as a great Southern metropolis? . . .

It is a remarkable fact . . . that Baltimore and St. Louis, the two most prosperous cities in the slave States, have fewer slaves in proportion to the aggregate population than any other city or cities in the South. While the entire population of the former is now estimated at 250,000 and that of the latter at 140,000 — making a grand total of 390,000 in the two cities, less than 6,000 of this latter number are slaves; indeed neither city is cursed with half the number of 6,000. In 1850, there were only 2,946 slaves in Baltimore, and 2,656 in St. Louis — total in the two cities, 5,602; and in both places, thank heaven, this heathenish class of the population was rapidly decreasing.[38]

As the sectional antipathy hardened, the proponents of southern nationalism looked to the cities of their own region to relieve the South's dependency upon the North. They attempted to hold ambivalent Baltimore within the complex of cities that would implement self-sufficiency for a southern "nation." An article, published in *De Bow's Review* in September, 1860, urged Southerners to woo Baltimore and Baltimorians in the hope of identifying them with the South.

BALTIMORE — METROPOLIS
FOR AN INDEPENDENT SOUTH: 1860

Baltimore possesses in its locality . . . advantages surpassing those of any city in the world. . . . All [the tide-water river navigation of the Chesapeake] is connected with and tributary to Baltimore, its common centre. . . . Besides this, her Ohio railroad makes her the nearest and best market to a large portion of the West. She commands the trade also of the Potomac and Susquehannah valleys in Maryland and Virginia, which is one of the best wheat regions in the world. . . . Her wealth, population, and position make her the most eligible importing city for the whole Southeast. Added to all this, she is slaveholding, in fact and feeling, for she has lately driven away a Black Republican convention that attempted to pollute her territory.

If the South will patronize her properly, she, Richmond, Charleston, Savannah, Mobile, and New-Orleans would very soon be able to supply all goods, foreign and domestic, needed South of Mason and Dixon's line. How easily we might cut off all dependence on the North. We have but to will it, and 'tis done. Now, we are but the slave colonies of the North. We labor, and they get all the profits. We make money at home to spend it among our bitter enemies. Let us of the slaveholding States, from Delaware to Texas, stand by and sustain one another. . . . Why cool the patriotic ardor of Southern cities, by slighting them and passing them by, in order to encourage and enrich our enemies. Are we of the South prepared for the perils of and privations of a long war with the North, and yet are so delicate, effeminate, and luxurious, that the great and wealthy city of Baltimore cannot gratify our fastidious tastes.

Let Baltimore, on the other hand, do her whole duty. Let her suppress and effectually crush out forever the demon spirit which has ruled at her ballot-box, and led to riotous demonstration in her streets. Let her look more to the South, and exhibit greater sympathy in its fortunes. She has not been doing this always, and we understand from the editor that at the present moment not five copies of the *Review*, in which this paper appears, is taken in Baltimore, and that the booksellers there announce that they cannot sell a single copy. Yet this is a work which has been for fifteen years devoting itself to the development of the South in every element of wealth and power. . . . Austin, Texas, has contributed five times as much.[39]

Aspirations of specific cities both north and south helped to bring the tension between the sections to the point of arms.[40] The resulting war, fought between the North and South from 1861 to 1865, immediately furthered urbanization in the North and created conditions that encouraged the wider urbanization of the nation as a whole. On the eve of the conflict, business leaders in cities with intersectional commercial connections, like New Orleans and New York, favored compromise, but in other cities, both north and south, the ambitions of urban business interests and city promoters whetted the growing friction between the sections. The port cities of the Great Lakes blamed the influence of Southerners upon national policy for the failure of the federal government to heed their demands for harbor improvement. Charleston saw in the prospect of southern independence an opportunity to become the New York of the South. The frustrated aspirations of some of the northern cities were reflected in the Buffalo press.

DENIAL OF URBAN AMBITIONS TRIGGERS ANTI-SOUTHERN SENTIMENT — BUFFALO: 1856

The President is determined that the commerce of the western lakes shall not be protected while it is in his power to prevent it. The new doctrine of "state equality" is being rapidly carried into effect by forcing the northern states and northern people into a condition of semi-barbarous "equality" with the south. . . . Twenty-six thousand dollars are taken out of the United States treasury to pay for the capture at Cincinnati and forcible return of a woman to helpless bondage; the army and navy, and the whole power of the federal government are brought into requisition to conquer the prejudices of a free people in Kansas against the lawless rule of Missouri ruffians, but not one cent can be appropriated, with the consent of [President] Pierce, to deepening the channel of the St. Clair Flats, or repairing the dilapidated harbors upon our lakes, in order to insure protection to the lives and property of the whole north. Nay, even while the President is in the act of bullying and browbeating the British Government, which is seeking to restrain the piratical movements of the southern propagandists, our merchants and ship owners are forced to go begging to that very government for pecuniary aid, to enable them to pass in safety with their property over one of the most important highways of nations. Verily is not the humiliation of the North completed?[41]

Charleston's aspirations were verbalized, on the eve of the presidential election of 1860, in *The Charleston Mercury*, which asserted the advantage for Charleston of separation from the Union, a position that caused some apprehension in the New York City business community.[42]

CHARLESTON'S FUTURE — AN ARGUMENT
FOR SOUTHERN INDEPENDENCE: 1860

There are no people in the Southern States who will gain so certainly by a dissolution of the Union as the merchants and mechanics of our cities. At present Norfolk, Charleston, Savannah and Mobile are but suburbs of New York, Philadelphia and Boston. . . . In the Union, with the fixed policy of the federal government, there is no hope of any increase in our cities corresponding to their natural advantages. . . . *When the constitution of the United States was adopted the commerce and shipping of Charleston was greater than that of New York.* Without the partial interference of the government to our disadvantage, Charleston would have flourished and grown as much as New York. . . .

Break up our union with the North — let Charleston and the other Southern cities resume their natural commerce — let Charleston import directly from the great consumers of our agricultural productions throughout the world all those manufactured commodities which they produce and we need — and what a mighty change will come over the prospects of our city. . . . Charleston would not only import for South Carolina but for a vast portion of the South — of which she is the natural emporium. Our now colonial and tributary commerce, with the North would cease; but a mighty free commerce would arise in its stead with all portions of the world. We would have our own, as before the Revolution, with all the proportionate prosperity it then created. Capital would come where it could be used to advantage. The Rothschilds and the Barings would have their agents here. The agents of the great manufacturers of Europe would be here, with their goods in our bonded warehouses. Great jobbing houses would accumulate. The city would be thronged with strangers, and would bound on in the high way of prosperity. Real estate would rise in value. The toil and ventures of a few years, with our merchants, would give them more than now the anxious labor of life. Our banks, disconnected with the North, would no longer be embarrassed by its crazy speculations, or more crazy panics, and would do an immense business in every line. Our railroads would increase their transportation and advance the value of their stocks. Our mechanics and laborers of all kinds would find ample employment. Carpenters, bricklayers, shipwrights, blacksmiths, machinists, would raise the grand hymn of industry with their strong arms, resounding far and near throughout our now voiceless city. How any owner of real estate in Charleston — how any intelligent merchant or mechanic — can be opposed to a dissolution of our union with the North on the score of interest, is one of those incomprehensible marvels our very marvellous nature sometimes produces. Independent of that absolute necessity to all slaveholding countries of ruling themselves — independent of all reference to the great principles of justice and liberty, interest, money — profit should make them the foremost, sternest and most anxious disunionists. Those who have ears to hear, let them hear what a calculation of dollars and cents teaches.[43]

5. IMMIGRANTS

One reason why urban dwellers were more numerous in the North than in the South was the wider appeal of northern cities for European immigrants, whose arrival in unprecedented numbers was a major cause of the spectacular increase in urbanism in these years. Though southern cities drew some of the newcomers, many more tended to settle in the North because most of the major ports of entry were in the Northeast and because accessible transportation westward led more directly into the upper Middle West. More than half a million newcomers entered the United States in the decade of the 1830's; and in the succeeding two decades the number of immigrants swelled to more than four million. Though many of them settled on farms, a substantial number, for both economic and social reasons, remained in the ports of debarkation or took up residence in other cities. Actually, the proportion of foreign born in many of the nation's major cities was larger during this period than at any other time in the nineteenth and twentieth centuries.

This, together with the large number of Blacks, both slave and free, in many southern cities, gave the American city of the mid-nineteenth century an ethnic heterogeneity that was unique in cities of the western world.

The populations of most of the major cities of the nation, as of 1860, were more than a third foreign born. In 1860, when the foreign born constituted only 15 per cent of the nation's total numbers, they made up 48 per cent of the population in New York City, 37 per cent in Newark, and 36 per cent in Boston. In the newly settling Middle West, the proportion of foreign born in the populations of the larger cities was even higher. More than half of the residents of Milwaukee and Chicago were foreign born, and in St. Louis three out of five were natives of foreign countries. To the extent that immigrants settled in the South, there, too, they gravitated to cities. Charleston's population was more than 15 per cent foreign born, and this group represented at least 67 per cent of all the foreign born in the state of South Carolina. Blacks added further variety to the population mixture in most cities, and in many southern cities they made up from 20 to 40 per cent of the population. The bearing of foreign born and Blacks on the population patterns of major mid-nineteenth-century American cities is exhibited in Table 2.3.

Irish and Germans made up the bulk of the foreign-born city dwellers of this period. Though Irish were the most numerous foreign-born group in the nation as a whole, German-born migrants outnumbered them in the major cities of the Mississippi Valley, with the exception of New Orleans. These newcomers, together with migrants from the British Isles, Canada, and Scandinavia, influenced the developing American cities in many ways. The Irish provided Boston with a cheap labor force of such proportions as to turn its economy into unaccustomed industrial channels.[44] The Germans identified Cincinnati, Milwaukee, and St. Louis with particular industries, such as brewing and tanning, and put a Teutonic stamp upon the social life and culture of these cities, as well.[45] The construction of streets, sewers, and other public works owed much to the brawn of immigrant labor, especially Irish; and the growth of political machines was often aided by the ballots of hastily, and often fraudulently, naturalized new citizens. The poverty of many of the newcomers contributed to the development of slums and to the disease, crime, intemperance, and prostitution

Table 2.3a

FOREIGN BORN AND BLACKS IN POPULATIONS OF SELECTED CITIES: 1860[46]

	Total Population Free and Slave	Foreign Born in Total Population	Percentage of Foreign Born in Total Population	Most Numerous Foreign-Born Group		Next Most Numerous Foreign-Born Group		Total Black Population	Percentage of Blacks in Total Population	Free Black Population	Slave Black Population
New England											
Boston	177,840	63,791	36.0	Irish	45,991	British-American	6,807	2,261	1.3	2,261	—
Lowell	36,827	12,107	33.0	Irish	9,460	English	1,128b	41	—	41	—
Providence	50,666	12,570	25.0	Irish	9,534	English	1,387	1,537	3.0	1,537	—
New Haven	39,267	10,645	27.0	Irish	7,391	German	1,842	1,488	3.8	1,488	—
Middle Atlantic											
New York	805,651	383,717	48.0	Irish	203,740	German	119,984	12,472	1.5	12,472	—
Brooklyn	266,661	104,589	39.0	Irish	56,710	German	23,993	4,313	1.6	4,313	—
Buffalo	81,129	—	46.0	German	18,233	Irish	9,279	809	1.0	809	—
Newark	71,941	26,625	37.0	Irish	11,167	German	10,595	1,287	1.8	1,287	—
Philadelphia	565,529	169,430	29.0	Irish	95,548	German	43,643	22,185	3.9	22,185	—
Pittsburgh	49,217	18,063	37.0	Irish	9,297	German	6,049	1,154	2.3	1,154	—
South Atlantic											
Baltimore	212,418	52,497	25.0	German	32,613	Irish	15,536	27,898	13.0	25,680	2,218
Washington	61,122	10,765	18.0	Irish	6,282	German	2,729	10,983	18.0	9,209	1,774
Richmond	37,910	4,956	13.0	Irish	2,244	German	1,623	14,275	37.6	2,576	11,699
Charleston	40,522	6,311	15.5	Irish	3,263	German	1,944	17,146	42.0	3,237	13,909
Savannah	22,292	4,652	21.0	Irish	3,145	German	771	8,417	38.0	705	7,712

North Central											
Cincinnati	161,044	73,614	46.0	German	43,931	Irish	19,375	3,731	2.3	3,731	—
Cleveland	43,417	19,437	45.0	German	9,078	Irish	5,479	799	1.8	799	—
Detroit	45,619	21,349	47.0	German	7,220	Irish	5,994	1,403	3.1	1,403	—
Milwaukee	45,246	22,848	50.5	German	15,981	Irish	3,100	106	0.2	106	—
Chicago	109,260	54,624	50.0	German	22,230	Irish	19,889	955	0.9	955	—
St. Louis	160,773	96,086	60.0	German	50,510	Irish	29,926	1,755	2.0	3,297	1,542
Minneapolis	2,555	—	—	—	—	—	—	8	0.3	8	—
Omaha	1,883	—	—	—	—	—	—	20	1.0	20	—
South Central											
Mobile	29,258	7,061	24.0	Irish	3,307	German	1,276	817	29.0	8,404	7,587
New Orleans	168,675	64,621	38.0	Irish	24,398	German	19,752c	10,689	14.0	24,074	13,385
Memphis	22,623	6,938	31.0	Irish	4,159	German	1,412	198	17.0	3,882	3,684
Nashville	16,988	—	—	—	—	—	—	719	23.0	3,945	3,226
Louisville	68,033	22,948	34.0	German	13,374	Irish	6,653	1,917	10.0	6,820	4,903
Houston	4,845	—	—	—	—	—	—	8	22.0	1,077	1,069
Mountain											
Denver	4,749	—	—	—	—	—	—	23	0.5	23	—
Salt Lake City	8,236	—	—	—	—	—	—	17	0.2	17	—
Pacific											
Los Angeles	4,385	—	—	—	—	—	—	66	1.5	66	—
San Francisco	56,802	28,454	50.0	Irish	9,363	German	6,346	1,176	2.1	1,176	—
Portland, Oregon	2,874	—	—	—	—	—	—	16	0.6	16	—

a These figures, taken from the *Population* volume of the United States Census of 1860, frequently do not square with population totals for 1860 in later census volumes, which reflect corrections. Within this *Population* volume there are contradictory figures; hence all numbers and percentages in this table must be regarded as only approximate.

b The third most numerous foreign-born group was British-American: 1,082. There were, however, only 34 Germans.

c French: 10,564.

to which squalid and congested living conditions give rise. The visibility of the foreign born as a result of their concentration in cities caused popular apprehensions that were reflected in politics, both at the local level, and, at times, even in the nation at large.

Natives of Ireland were especially evident in the cities of the Atlantic seaboard. Many arrived virtually penniless at such ports of entry as Boston or New York and were forced to seek work in the cities where they landed or in nearby factory towns. More than a quarter of the total population of Boston and New York was of Irish origin, according to census figures for 1850 and 1860, and the same was true of Lowell in 1860. Because of their proportionate number, the Irish probably exerted more impact on the economy and society of Boston than on any other American city, though their even greater numbers in New York gave them an evident influence on the personality of that city. The squalid housing to which poverty reduced many of the Boston Irish and conditions resulting from the low pay of labor generally were described in a report of the Massachusetts Bureau of Statistics and Labor in December, 1869.

LIVING CONDITIONS OF BOSTON'S IRISH-BORN RESIDENTS: 1860's

We next passed into Stone's Yard, on Cross Street, between Nos. 100 and 102 Hanover Street. A three-foot passage-way led into the yard, thirty-two feet long by twelve wide, wherein lived fourteen families. There was one privy, too horrible to be described, for the whole tenantry. Some small places partitioned off in the yard, and intended for fuel, were covered with human excrement. The buildings were three stories high, wretched tumble-downs, and not fit for cattle. The . . . room we visited was 14 × 14 feet, and 7 feet post, occupied by four persons, one in bed and sick. The floor was perforated by the gnawing of rats of the hugest proportions, whose mordacious work had been patched up by inpourings of anthracite ashes. . . .

Going, then, up a dark, winding and rickety stairway, we came to a room occupied by a Mrs. R. (Irish). She stood at a tub, washing. In the room was a bedstead, a table, three chairs and a stove. Everything denoted the lowest stage of poverty. The officer attending us said that he once found here a family starving. Mrs. R. appeared cleanly and industrious, but thoroughly disheartened. *In less than a week from our visit she was stabbed and killed, in a quarrel with a neighbor about the loan of five cents!* . . .

We next visited "Young's Court." . . . These buildings are in a worse condition of dilapidation than any we examined: the door-steps gone at one door, the stairways rotten and dangerous, many of the windows destitute of glass. . . . Called on the family of Mr. J. H——, an Irishman, at that time engaged in repairing some tools, being out of work for some weeks. He was thirty-nine years old, with a sick wife and four children. . . . Worked last in South Malden, sixty hours per week, at an average pay, sometimes in wages and sometimes in piece-work, of $14 per week, *paid at the convenience of the employer, a portion being always kept back.* Loses a quarter part of the year from lack of work. Breakfasted at quarter past five o'clock in the morning, started then for Malden, commencing work at seven o'clock; worked till six to seven, P.M., with a half hour for dinner, which he carried from home in a tin pail, as most laborers do, being a member of the large body usually designated as the "Tin-pail Brigade." Got home, when closing work at six, by half past seven o'clock for supper. Walked to and from Malden, rather than live there (he could not afford to ride,) because of the uncertainty of work. By living in town, chance work, when out of steady work, is more readily obtained. This is quite customary with workmen.[47]

The immigrant contribution to both the growth and the culture of the fast-growing cities of the Middle West was of special interest to Fredrika Bremer, the Swedish novelist and humanitarian, who spent a two-year sojourn in the United States, beginning in 1849. Her letters to relatives and friends, published in 1853 in *The Homes of the New World: Impressions of America*, described the German sections of the cities she visited as well as the activities of some of her Swedish compatriots.

THE FOREIGN BORN AND THE URBAN CULTURE OF THE MIDDLE WEST: 1850

[*Chicago*], *September 24th* [*1850*]. I must now tell you of some agreeable Swedes who reside here. . . . These Swedish gentry, who thought of becoming . . . cultivators and colonizers of the wilderness . . . miscalculated their fitness and their powers of labor. Besides this, they had taken with them the Swedish inclination for hospitality and a merry life. . . . Nearly all were unsuccessful as farmers. Some . . . removed from . . . the forest to Chicago. . . . There are a great number of Germans in Chicago, especially among the tradespeople and handcraftsmen. . . .

October 1st. From Chicago I went by steamer . . . to Milwaukee. . . . Nearly half of the inhabitants are Germans, and they occupy a portion of the city to themselves, which is called "German Town." This lies on the other side of the River Milwaukee. Here one sees German houses, German inscriptions over the doors or signs, German physiognomies. Here are published German newspapers; and many Germans live here who never learn English, and seldom go beyond the German town. The Germans in the Western States seem, for the most, to band together in a clan-like manner, to live together, and amuse themselves as in their fatherland. Their music and dances, and other popular pleasures, distinguish them from the Anglo-American people, who, particularly in the West, have no other pleasure than "business." . . .

St. Louis, November 8th. . . . There are a great number of Germans in St. Louis. They have music and dancing parties, which are zealously attended. There are also here French and Spaniards. At the hotels all is in French style, with French names for dishes and wines. The Irish here, as every where else throughout the United States, constitute the laboring population; excepting negro slaves, the greater portion of servants are Irish. Spite of the greatly increasing trade of the city, it is . . . almost impossible for a young emigrant to obtain a situation in any place of business. If, on the contrary, however, he will begin by doing coarse hand-labor, as a miller's man, for instance, or a worker in a manufactory, he can easily find employment and get good wages. And if he lives carefully, he may soon gain sufficient to undertake higher employment. Better still are his prospects if he can superintend some handcraft trade; he is then in a fair way to become the artificer of his own fortune. . . .

Cincinnati, Nov. 29th. . . . Cincinnati . . . is a cosmopolitan city, and embraces in her bosom peoples of all nations and all religious sects. Germans constitute a considerable portion of the population of the city. . . . The Germans live here as in their old Germany. They are *gemüthlich* [convivial], drink beer, practice music, and still ponder here *"über die Weltgeschichte"* [about the state of the world].[48]

Economic considerations affected the residence pattern of the foreign born. Sometimes they dispersed fairly widely throughout the city; but the poor tended increasingly to reside in the vicinity of the central business district where jobs for unskilled workers were most available. Often they rented quarters in or near the homes of their compatriots, with the result that national enclaves developed. In newer cities, like Cincinnati and Milwaukee, Germans arrived early enough and in such numbers as to create virtually distinct national sections. An identifiable German section had developed in New York City by the 1850's. Urban dwellers of German birth joined the ranks of craftsmen, primarily, rather than of heavy labor; and their migration gave a new impulse to the labor movement in American cities. At the same time, the possibility of a hardening along class lines was probably minimized by the tendency of the newcomers to live among their compatriots, where even the poorest saw many of their countrymen "making good." Karl T. Griesinger's *Land und Leute in Amerika: Skizzen aus dem amerikanischen Leben*, written after he spent the years 1852 to 1857 in the United States, reveals the nationality-focused activity that city life made possible and that helped to ease the newcomers' adjustment to their transplanted existence. It reveals, too, the differences in culture which were to engender tension between native and foreign-born residents of many American cities.

NEW YORK'S "*KLEINDEUTSCHLAND*": 1850's

The traveller who passes up Broadway, through Chatham Street, into the Bowery, up Houston Street, and thence right to First Avenue will find himself in a section which has very little in common with the other parts of New York. . . . This is *Kleindeutschland* ["Little Germany"], or *Deutschländle*, as the Germans call this part of the city. . . . New York has about 120,000 German-born inhabitants. Two-thirds of these live in Kleindeutschland. . . . Naturally the Germans were not forced by the authorities . . . to settle in this specific area. It just happened. But the location was favorable because of its proximity to the downtown business district where the Germans are employed. Moreover, the Germans like to live together; this permits them to speak their own language and live according to their own customs. . . . Life in Kleindeutschland is almost the same as in the Old Country. . . . There is not a single business

123

which is not run by Germans. Not only the shoemakers, tailors, barbers, physicians, grocers, and innkeepers are German, but the pastors and priests as well. There is even a German lending library where one can get all kinds of German books. The resident of Kleindeutschland need not even know English in order to make a living, which is a considerable attraction to the immigrant. . . .

One who has not seen the Deutschländle on a Sunday, does not know it at all. What a contrast it presents to the American sections, where the shutters are closed, and the quiet of a cemetery prevails. . . . The Protestant Germans do not indulge in much religious observance. They profess to be freethinkers, and do not go to church very often. On the other hand, the Catholic Church on Third Street is always overcrowded. It was built from the voluntary contributions of the German workingmen. . . . It has a big tower and three bells, and nearby is a school which the German children attend and where classes are conducted in German. . . .

On Sunday the movement in the streets is like that in a dovecote. People go from the tavern to the church and back to the tavern again. Everybody wears his Sunday clothes and is in high spirits. In the afternoon, on days when the weather is good, almost everybody leaves town and goes on a picnic. On Sunday nights there is still more merriment in Kleindeutschland. The taverns are crowded, even with women. There is music, in spite of the laws against making noise on Sunday. The Germans have a *Volkstheater*. . . . At the end of the hall is a small stage; and the performances are not real plays as much as entertainment by comedians whom the proprietor hires to amuse his customers. . . . The people enjoy themselves immensely; the entertainment costs only ten cents, and one gets a free beer now and then. Such is the way Sunday is celebrated in Kleindeutschland.[49]

Tension between natives and the foreign born triggered periodic outbreaks of mob violence in many American cities. These episodes contrasted sharply in motivation and behavior with the mob activity of the Revolutionary era. The outbreaks of the mid-nineteenth century took a less focused and more ruthless turn. Often they were prompted by native resentments toward the foreign born because of the job competition they represented or because of fear of Catholicism, with which many of the newcomers were identified. In the early 1860's, friction developed on the part of the

Irish, especially, toward Blacks, whose impending emancipation was thought to make them competitors in the labor market. These tensions had political as well as economic implications; they reflected, too, the breakdown of community as an increasing ethnic diversity characterized expanding city populations. As early as the 1830's anti-Catholic and nativist sentiments led to open conflict in cities where the foreign born were numerous. In New York City, the American Republican Party, proposing to lengthen the period preceding naturalization to 21 years, carried the municipal elections of 1844. In Philadelphia's nativist expressions of that year, military companies fought in the streets, Catholic churches were burned, and the homes of the foreign born were pillaged by mobs. The augmented immigration of the 1850's heightened urban disorder; in New York City's draft riots of 1863, it was reported that the "mob killed, pillaged, hung Negroes to lamp posts, and mutilated and tortured their prisoners." [50] The intensity of the native reaction to the immigrant newcomers is reflected in the comments New Yorker George Templeton Strong committed to his diary, beginning in 1838, when Strong was 18 years old.

THE IMMIGRANT AND URBAN TENSIONS:
1840's AND 1850's

November 6 [1838]. It was enough to turn a man's stomach — to make a man adjure republicanism forever — to see the way they were naturalizing this morning at the Hall. Wretched, filthy, bestial-looking Italians and Irish, and creations [creatures] that looked as if they had risen from the lazarettos of Naples for this especial object; in short, the very scum and dregs of human nature filled the clerk of C[ommon] P[leas] office so completely that I was almost afraid of being poisoned by going in. A dirty Irishman is bad enough, but he's nothing comparable to a nasty French or Italian loafer. . . .

April 13 [1842]. We had some hard fighting yesterday in the Bloody Sixth, and a grand no-popery riot last night, including a vigorous attack on the Roman Catholic Cathedral with brick bats and howls, and a hostile demonstration on Hughes's episcopal palace, terminating in broken windows and damaged furniture. Also the Spartan Band got into the Sixth Ward Hotel, as the no-popery rioters of old did into "the Maypole," and "made a noise and broke things" in great style. . . .

April 28 [*1848*]. Orders given to commence excavating in Twenty-first Street Wednesday night. . . . Hibernia came to the rescue yesterday morning; twenty "sons of toil" with prehensile paws supplied them by nature with evident reference to the handling of the spade and the wielding of the pickaxe and congenital hollows on the shoulder wonderfully adapted to make the carrying of the hod a luxury instead of a labor commenced the task yesterday morning. . . .

November 13 [*1854*]. Met a prodigious Know-Nothing procession moving uptown, as I omnibussed down Broadway to the vestry meeting; not many banners and little parade of any kind, but a most emphatic and truculent demonstration. Solid column, eight or ten abreast, and numbering some two or three thousand, mostly young men of the butcher-boy and *prentice* type; many a Simon Tappertit among them, no doubt, and many a shoulder-hitter and shortboy beside; marching in quick time, and occasionally indulging in a very earnest kind of hurrah. They looked as if they might have designs on St. Patrick's Cathedral, and I think the Celts of Prince and Mott Streets would have found them ugly customers. . . .

July 7 [*1857*]. Yesterday morning I was spectator of a strange, weird, painful scene. Certain houses of John Watts DePeyster are to be erected on the northwest corner of this street and Fourth Avenue, and the deep excavations therefor are in progress. Seeing a crowd on the corner, I stopped and made my way to a front place. The earth had caved in a few minutes before and crushed the breath out of a pair of ill-starred Celtic laborers. They had just been dragged, or dug, out, and lay white and stark on the ground where they had been working, ten or twelve feet below the level of the street. Around them were a few men who had got them out, I suppose, and fifteen or twenty Irish women, wives, kinfolk or friends, who had got down there in some inexplicable way. The men were listless and inert enough, but not so the women. I suppose they were "keening"; all together were raising a wild, unearthly cry, half shriek and half song, wailing as a score of daylight Banshees, clapping their hands and gesticulating passionately. Now and then one of them would throw herself down on one of the corpses, or wipe some trace of defilement from the face of the dead man with her apron, slowly and carefully, and then resume her lament. It was an uncanny sound to hear, quite new to me. . . . Our Celtic fellow citizens are almost as remote from us in temperament and constitution as the Chinese. . . .[51]

6. BLACKS

Black Americans were much less conspicuous in northern cities in the pre-Civil War years than they were to be a century later; nevertheless, in the North they were urban dwellers to a far greater degree than were Americans as a whole. As Negro editor Frederick Douglass wrote Harriet Beecher Stowe in 1853: "It is almost impossible to get colored men to go on the land. From some cause or other . . . colored people will congregate in large towns and cities; and they will endure any amount of hardship and privation rather than go into the country." Though Blacks had contributed to the population of the major northern cities since colonial times, their proportion in the total population had declined as the nineteenth century progressed; by 1860 they made up not more than 1 to 3 per cent of the population in the larger cities. New York City's more than 3,000 Blacks, in 1790, were 10 per cent of the city's total population; but the proportion had dropped to 1.5 per cent by 1860, and the absolute numbers had dropped from 16,358 to 12,472 between 1840 and 1860.[52] By 1860, Philadelphia had the largest Black community in the North; its 22,185 Blacks made up nearly 4 per cent of the total population. Other sizable Black communities in the free states, in 1860, were Brooklyn's 4,313, Cincinnati's 3,731, and Boston's 2,261. By that date, Newark, San Francisco, Pittsburgh, and Detroit all had Negro communities exceeding 1,000 persons.[53]

Although tradition already had relegated Blacks in northern cities to a position of social inferiority (as reflected in segregation in theaters, restaurants, and public transportation), the coming of large numbers of immigrants posed economic competition that further depressed the Negroes' occupational status and hence their economic and social, if not their legal, position. As late as the 1830's, Blacks managed small stores, ran oyster and fruit stands, and figured prominently in the barbering business. They found ready employment as stevedores, wood sawyers, brick makers, cooks, and house servants. Visitors to American cities in the 1830's commented on the flamboyant finery and "air of consequence" that characterized some members of the Black community in New York City.[54] By the 1850's, however, as white immigrants took jobs once held by Blacks, the Blacks were forced into more menial occupations; and prejudice, exacerbated by competition for employment, worsened the Negroes' social status.[55] Riots involving Blacks and whites, especially the Irish, reflected both the competition and the prejudice. Five major anti-Negro riots occurred in Philadelphia between 1832 and 1849; they were but a prelude to the bloody anti-Negro violence associated with the New York draft riots of July, 1863.[56]

In the years before the arrival of large numbers of immigrants, many European visitors, to whom the Black population of northern cities was something of a novelty, reported a considerable degree of self-possession in the Black residents of New York City. Following are the reactions of Karl Bernhard, the Duke of Saxe-Weimar Eisenach, who visited New York in September, 1825, and of Mrs. Frances Trollope, a visitor in the spring of 1831.

EUROPEAN VIEWS OF NEW YORK CITY'S
BLACK COMMUNITY: 1820's AND 1830's

Karl Bernhard [1825]. Negroes and mulattos are abundant here, but they generally rank low and are labourers. . . . There are public schools . . . for the instruction of coloured children. . . . In the city there are several churches belonging to the coloured population; most of them are Methodists, some Episcopalians. A black minister, who was educated in an Episcopalian seminary, is said to be a good preacher. . . . On the afternoon of the third of October, there was a great procession of negroes, some of them well dressed, parading through the streets, two by two, preceded by music and a flag. An African club, called the Wilberforce Society, thus celebrated the anniversary of the abolition of slavery in New York, and concluded the day by a dinner and a ball. The coloured people of New York, belonging to this society, have a fund of their own, raised by weekly subscription, which is employed in assisting sick and unfortunate blacks. This fund, contained in a sky-blue box, was carried in the procession; the treasurer holding in his hand a large gilt key; the rest of the officers wore ribands of several colours, and badges like the officers of free masons; marshals with long staves walked outside of the procession. During a quarter of an hour, scarcely any but black faces were to be seen in Broadway.

Frances Trollope [1831]. There are a great number of Negroes in New York, all free. . . . Not even in Philadelphia, where the anti-slavery opinions have been the most active and violent, do the blacks appear to wear an air of so much consequence as they do at New York. They have several chapels, in which negro ministers officiate; and a theatre, in which none but negroes perform. At this theatre a gallery is appropriated to such whites as choose to visit it; and here only are they permitted to sit; following in this, with nice etiquette, and equal justice, the arrangement of the white theatres, in all of which is a gallery appropriated solely to the use of the blacks. I have often, particularly on a Sunday, met groups of negroes, elegantly dressed; and have been sometimes amused by observing the very superior air of gallantry assumed by the men, when in attendance on their *belles*, to that of the whites in similar circumstances. On one occasion we met in Broadway a young negress in the extreme of the fashion, and accompanied by a black *beau*, whose toilet was equally studied; eye-glass, guard-chain, nothing was omitted; he walked beside his sable goddess uncovered, and with an air of the most tender devotion. At the window of a handsome house which they were passing, stood a very pretty white girl, with two gentlemen beside her; but alas! both of them had their hats on, and one was smoking! [57]

Like other ethnic groups, urban Blacks in the pre-Civil War North developed institutions that helped in their adjustment to the urban community. Foremost among these was the all-Negro church, initially organized by Negro Methodists of Philadelphia in 1787 in protest against segregation in houses of worship. Subscription schools for Black children, library companies, mutual aid societies ("to support the members in sickness and to bury the dead"), newspapers edited by such leading Black figures as Frederick Douglass of Rochester and Samuel E. Cornish of New York City, and national conventions to promote solutions of their problems paralleled similar agencies and institutions being developed at the same time by city dwellers of Irish and German background.[58] A survey of the Black community of Philadelphia, undertaken in the late 1840's by the Society of Friends, reveals the existence of these institutions that gave cohesiveness to the Black community; at the same time it reflects the relative decline in numbers and deterioration in status (in terms of occupation and residence) that followed the influx of European immigrants. The report refers to the mobs of 1842 in an altercation between whites and Blacks over a Negro parade commemorating the abolition of slavery in the West Indies.

Many Negroes were beaten, several homes destroyed, and the new African Hall and the Colored Presbyterian Church were burned.[59]

THE BLACK COMMUNITY OF PHILADELPHIA: LATE 1840's

It being thought desirable to obtain an accurate account of the number and condition of the coloured population of the city and districts of Philadelphia, means were taken in the autumn of 1847, and the following winter, to obtain it. . . . We find the actual population, as far as this enumeration can be relied on, to be 20,240. . . . Several causes have probably contributed to diminish the rate of increase of this population within our city during the last ten years; the chief of which are the mobs of 1842, which drove away many of the people of colour; and the great increase of poor emigrants from Europe, who have supplanted them in employments, which a few years ago were altogether in their hands. . . .

When we consider the extent to which the free coloured population is constantly augmented from the emancipated and fugitive slaves of the south, we shall see no reason to doubt that their numbers are kept down by the greater number of deaths among them, as well as by checks upon the natural increase. . . . That this decreasing ratio of increase is owing in part to the greater mortality among the blacks, is shown by the returns of the Board of Health, from which, during the 10 years from 1830 to 1840, it appears that the average annual death among the coloured people . . . [was] nearly 40 per cent. greater than among the [whites]. . . .

The returns enable us to state the occupations . . . of . . . about four-fifths of the able bodied population, above 21 years of age. . . . Occupations of the men: Mechanics, 286; Labourers, 1581; Seafaring men, 240; Coachmen, carters, etc., 276; Shop keepers and traders, 166; Waiters, cooks, etc., 557; Hairdressers, 156; Various, 96. . . . Occupations of the women: Washerwomen, 1970; Needle-women, 486; Cooks, 173; Occupied at home, 290; Occupied at day's work, 786; Living in Families, 156; Various, 72; Trades, 213; Raggers and boners, 103. . . .

By the returns it appears that 4904 persons, or nearly one-half the adult population, are members of Mutual Beneficial Societies, the funds of which are appropriated to support the members in sickness, and to bury the dead. Many of these persons belong to two or more Societies at once, with the view of increasing the amount to be received when sick. The names of 106 of these Mutual Beneficial Associations have been received. . . . The contributions are from 25 to 37½ cents per month. . . . The allowance per week to the sick members varies from $1.50 to $3.00 per week. . . . From ten to twenty dollars is usually allowed for funeral expenses. . . .

We have not sufficient returns to enable us to estimate the number of persons that are members of [the 19] religious societies. . . . There are a number of Library Companies and Literary Associations established among the people of colour, several of which appear to be supported with zeal and ability, and which, no doubt, have an important influence upon those who are within the sphere of their operations.

A remarkable feature in the statistics of the coloured population of Philadelphia, is the difference in the character of the different districts. . . . Many . . . are from the adjoining free states, and a large proportion of the remainder have been slaves, who have bought their own freedom, and often that of their nearest relations, and have shown, in freeing themselves from bondage, the energy and industry which have made them useful and respectable citizens. Yet it is equally certain, that this [immigrant] part of the coloured population is the most numerous in those crowded streets and alleys where the destitution and wretchedness is most intense and infectious, and where the evil effects of herding together in crowded courts and miserable buildings, and the indifference to the ordinary comforts and decencies of life, are most apparent. . . . The coloured population show a strong tendency to crowd together in narrow courts and alleys.[60]

Organizations of urban Blacks, supported by white sympathizers, attempted to improve conditions for Negroes in northern cities, but as late as the eve of the Civil War few gains had been made. The Equal School Rights Committee, formed by Boston Negroes, achieved legislation in 1855 opening the public schools of Boston to Blacks; but in most cities public education for Negroes was in separate schools in no sense equal in appearance and facilities to those for white children. At the Colored National Convention, held in Rochester in 1853, Frederick Douglass urged without success the establishment of a manual labor school for Blacks, contending that education for mechanical trades would provide them with the best means of adjusting to the urban living that most Blacks in the North desired. Segregation in public transit continued in New York despite the reform efforts of a Negro "Legal Rights

Association," and not until 1867 was it outlawed in Philadelphia. By 1860, a growing number of urban Negroes had acquired sufficient education and capital to engage in the professions, small business, and mechanical trades within the confines of the Black community, but the majority lived in squalid surroundings and were limited to menial pursuits.[61]

Black Americans — both slave and free — made up a sizable proportion of the city populations of the pre-Civil War South. On the eve of the war, Baltimore had the largest Negro community in the nation, with nearly 28,000 Blacks; New Orleans was a close second with more than 24,000. Though Blacks were less numerous in Charleston (17,146), Richmond (14,275), and Washington (10,983), they represented a much larger proportion of the total population in these cities. In the border cities, such as Baltimore and Washington, free Blacks greatly outnumbered slaves; the reverse was true of Charleston and Richmond. In New Orleans, free and slave were more evenly balanced, about 13,000 slaves to about 10,000 free Blacks. In most southern cities, by 1860, the absolute number of slaves was on the decline; the conditions of urban living tended to relax the bonds of slavery, and the limited use to which slaves could be put in the city (though some were employed in factories) caused an ever smaller proportion of town dwellers to hold slaves. Urban slaves often were permitted to hire themselves out and retain a portion of their wages. Their greater freedom of movement and residence in the city brought them into contact with free Negroes and sympathetic whites, encouraged them to seek their freedom, and made discipline more difficult to maintain.[62] Frederick Law Olmsted, traveling through the South in late 1852 and 1853, sensed the threat that urbanism posed to the institution of slavery.

SLAVERY IN THE CITY —
"CITY AIR MAKES FREE": 1852

[*Washington, D.C., December, 1852.*] The majority of servants . . . are now *free* negroes, which class constitutes one-fifth of the entire population. The slaves are one-fifteenth, but are mostly owned out of the District, and hired annually to those who require their services. . . . The colored population voluntarily sustain several churches, schools, and mutual assistance and improvement societies, and there are evidently persons among them of no inconsiderable cultivation of mind. Among the Police Reports of the City newspapers, there was lately . . . an account of the apprehension of twenty-four "genteel colored men" (so they were described), who had been found by a watchman assembling privately in the evening, and been lodged in the watch-house. . . . On searching their persons, there were found a Bible, a volume of *Seneca's Morals; Life In Earnest;* the printed Constitution of a Society, the object of which was . . . *"to relieve the sick, and bury the dead;"* and a subscription paper *to purchase the freedom of Eliza Howard,* a young woman, whom her owner was willing to sell at $650. . . . One of the prisoners, a slave named Joseph Jones, [was] ordered to be flogged; four others, called in the papers free men . . . were sent to the Work-house, and the remainder, on paying . . . fines, amounting, in the aggregate, to one hundred and eleven dollars, were permitted to range loose again. . . .

[*Richmond, December, 1852.*] I have seen large gangs [of slaves] coming in from the country, and these contrast much in their general appearance with the town negroes. The latter are dressed expensively, and frequently more elegantly than the whites. They seem to be spending money freely. . . . The slaves have a good many ways of obtaining "spending money," which . . . they . . . use for their own gratification, with even less restraint than a wholesome regard for their health and moral condition may be thought to require. A Richmond paper, complaining of the liberty allowed to slaves in this respect, as calculated to foster an insubordinate spirit, speaks of their "champagne suppers." The police broke into a gambling cellar a few nights since, and found about twenty negroes at "high play," with all the usual accessories of a first class "Hell." . . . It is the custom of tobacco manufacturers to hire slaves and free negroes at a certain rate of wages per year. A task of 45 lbs. per day is given them to work up, and all that they choose to do more than this they are paid for — payment being made once a fortnight; and invariably this over-wages is used by the slave for himself. . . . One of the manufacturers offered to show me, by his books, that nearly all gained by overwork $5 a month, many $20, and some as much as $28. . . .

[*New Orleans, 1853.*] As Commerce, or any high form of industry requires intelligence in its laborers, slaves can never be brought together in dense communities, but their intelligence will increase to a degree dangerous to those who enjoy the benefit of their labor. The slave must be kept dependent, day by day, upon his master for his daily bread, or he will . . . declare his independence, in all respects, of him . . . ; every attempt to bring [the slave's] labor into competition with free labor can only be successful at the hazard of insurrection. Hundreds of slaves in New Orleans must be constantly reflecting and saying to one another, "I am as capable of taking care of myself as this Irish hod-carrier, or this German market-gardener; why can't I have the enjoyment of my labor as well as they? I am as capable of taking care of my own family as much as they of theirs; why should I be subject to have them taken from me by those . . . who call themselves our owners? . . . One thing I know, if I can't have my rights, I can have my pleasures; and if they won't give me wages I can take them. . . ."

Similar complaints to the following, which I take from the *New Orleans Crescent*, I have heard, or seen in the journals, at Richmond, Savannah, Louisville, and most other large manufacturing, or commercial towns of the South. "Something must be done to regulate and prescribe the manner in which passes shall be given to slaves. . . . The slave population of this city is already demoralized to a deplorable extent, all owing to the indiscriminate license and indulgence extended them by masters, mistresses, and guardians, and to the practice of *forging passes*, which has now become a regular business in New Orleans. . . . As things now stand, any negro can obtain a pass for four bits or a dollar, from miserable wretches who obtain a living by such infamous practices. The consequence is that hundreds spend their nights drinking, carousing, gambling, and contracting the worst of habits, which not only make them *useless to their owners*, but dangerous pests to society. . . . It has been suggested to us that if the [Common] Council would adopt a form for passes, different each month, to be obtained by masters from the Chief of Police, exclusively, that a great deal of good would be at once accomplished." [63]

One immediate effect of the Civil War was to increase the number of Blacks in southern cities and in cities on the border of the South. Runaway slaves from Maryland and Virginia began to arrive in Washington early in the war, and after emancipation, fugitives augmented the population of many border cities. Once the war was over, many ex-slaves, now detached from their former plantation homes, migrated to urban centers within the South for sustenance, if not as proof of their freedom. The census of 1870 is not noted for its reliability, but according to its returns the Black population more than doubled in New Orleans and Louisville between 1860 and 1870 and increased from about 28,000 to nearly

40,000 in Baltimore, from 11,000 to 35,500 in Washington, and from about 3,300 to more than 22,000 in St. Louis. Blacks accounted for sizable increases in the populations of small towns too. Though some ultimately returned to farming because of the rising demand for agricultural workers, many remained urban dwellers.

These newcomers, generally unaccustomed to urban ways, presented many problems. In Washington, where for a time they had the status of "contraband of war," their often irresponsible behavior threatened the public image of the more established Black community and precipitated problems of urban service and public order.[64] In most cities the new arrivals were segregated in back alleys or on the edge of the city in "Black Centers" or "Dark Towns," where their living conditions duplicated the squalor and congestion in which immigrant newcomers to northern cities were living. In many parts of the South these conditions were aggravated by the general desolation that the war had visited upon southern cities. The journalist-writer John T. Trowbridge, who traveled through the South during the summer of 1865 and the following winter, described this aspect of postwar Atlanta, whose Black population allegedly grew from less than 2,000 in 1860 to nearly 10,000 ten years later.

BLACK NEWCOMERS
IN POST-CIVIL WAR ATLANTA: 1865

I reached Atlanta at seven o'clock in the evening. . . . Everywhere were ruins and rubbish, mud and mortar and misery. The burnt streets were rapidly rebuilding; but in the mean while hundreds of the inhabitants, white and black, rendered homeless by the destruction of the city, were living in wretched hovels, which made the suburbs look like a fantastic encampment of gypsies or Indians. Some of the negro huts were covered entirely with ragged fragments of tin-roofing from the burnt government and railroad buildings. . . . "In dry weather, it's good as anybody's houses. But they leaks right bad when it rains. . . ." So said a colored mother of six children, whose husband was killed "fighting for de Yankees," and who supported her family of little ones by washing. "Sometimes I gits along tolerable; sometimes right slim; but dat's de way wid everybody — times is powerful hard right now."

Every business block in Atlanta was burned, except one. The railroad machine-shops, the founderies, the immense rolling-mill, the . . . shot-and-shell factories, and storehouses, of the late Confederacy, disappeared in flames and explosions. Half a mile of the principal street was destroyed. . . . "When I came back in May," said a refugee, "the city was nothing but piles of brick and ruins. It didn't seem it could ever be cleared. But in six weeks new blocks began to spring up, till now you see more stores actually in operation than we ever had before." The new business blocks were mostly one-story structures, with cheap temporary roofs, designed to be rebuilt and raised in more prosperous times. . . . Here and there, between the new buildings, were rows of shanties used as stores, and gaps containing broken walls and heaps of rubbish. Rents were enormous. Fifteen and twenty dollars a month were charged for huts which a respectable farmer would hardly consider good enough for his swine. . . .

. The destitution among both white and black refugees was very great. Many of the whites had lost everything by the war; and the negroes that were run off by their masters in advance of Sherman's army had returned to a desolate place, with nothing but the rags on their backs. As at nearly every other town of any note in the South which I visited, the small-pox was raging at Atlanta, chiefly among the blacks, and the suffering poor whites. . . . A tide of negro emigration was at that time flowing westward . . . to the rich cotton plantations of the Mississippi. Every day anxious planters from the Great Valley were to be met with, inquiring for unemployed freedmen. . . . As it cost no more to transport able-bodied young men and women than the old and feeble, the former were generally selected and the latter left behind. Thus it happened that an unusually large proportion of poor families remained about Atlanta and other Georgia towns.[65]

The emancipation of southern Blacks as a result of the Civil War drew new attention to the Black element in northern cities. In 1867, when Congress was debating Reconstruction policy, newspapers in both Philadelphia and New York City published surveys of the local Negro population. On March 16, 1867, *The New York World* devoted its entire front page to an article entitled "Our Negro Population," dealing with the city's approximately 10,000 Blacks. Although there is a note of condescension in this account and evidence of the traditional racial discrimination, the reporter depicts the Blacks of New York as an orderly element in the urban society not yet conspicuously ghettoized, widely dependent upon the church and clerical leadership, and exhibiting organizational patterns and class differentiation similar to those of other ethnic groups in the variegated urban scene.

THE BLACKS OF NEW YORK CITY: 1867

The wards or precincts in which the negroes most abound are the Fourth, Fifth, Sixth, Seventh, Eighth, Fifteenth, Sixteenth, Twentieth, Twenty-eighth, and Twenty-ninth, though a few ne-groes are to be found in every ward throughout the city limits. . . . The pursuits followed by . . . the colored population in New-York may be summed up as follows: Barbers, many; 'long-shoremen, a very few; caterers, many; nurses, a few; waiters, public, many; waiters in private families, many; whitewashers, a consider-able percentage; oyster-openers, ditto; laundresses, many; dyers, a certain number; chimney-sweeps, a few; fortune-tellers, a consider-able number; shoe-makers and tailors, a few; carpenters and black-smiths, a few; boot-blacks, a certain number; cooks, many; private coachmen, many; laborers, a few; cart-drivers and porters, a con-siderable number; saloon-keepers, a few; waiters in gambling-houses and houses of ill-fame, a large number; thieves, a consider-able percentage; prostitutes, a considerable number; mercantile agents, a very few; doctors, a very few; ministers, a few; notary publics, two or three; druggists, two or three; school teachers, a few; professional musicians, a few; writers and editors, a very few; orators, a very few; and gentlemen of leisure, a select and envied baker's dozen. . . . Those who judge the New-York negroes by dilapidated individual specimens commit a great mistake. There are not a few "colored" men and women who, if money should command respect, are to be highly respected, for they "own much." . . .

The city schools for the colored children are under the same general management and special regulations as the schools for the whites. There are seven negro schools in New-York [of which one is discontinued]. . . . There are about twelve male teachers em-ployed, and about thirty-six female teachers. . . . Over 1,000 children are educated in the negro schools of this city. . . . The Rev. Mr. [John] Peterson [of St. Phillip's Episcopal Church on Mulberry Street] is, perhaps, the leading colored clergyman of the city, and one of the most influential and respectable men in the metropolis. He is a school teacher, a minister, and a bank director. . . .

The negro has strong domestic instincts where he has enjoyed the opportunity of gratifying them. . . . In the more southern latitudes the ties of kindred have set somewhat loosely upon the colored population, but in New-York and other No[r]thern cities it has been found that negroes make as good husbands or wives, fathers or mothers, as the average whites. . . . As a race, the negroes of New-York, considered from a police point of view, are a better class of citizens than the lower grades of whites. As . . . a class, the negroes give the police comparatively little trouble. This is the almost universal testimony alike of patrolmen, sergeants, captains, and superintendents; and we publish it as at least an approximation to the truth. . . .

There are grades in negrodom as in Japonicadom. There is "good" colored society in New-York; there are black exquisites and woolly belles. As a rule, the fashions for the colored population are set [for] them in their churches — these latter answering the purposes of weekly "balls," "reunions," or "Germans." The Episcopal Church in Mulberry street is especially notable for the "fashion" displayed by its congregation — who are as well dressed as any average white congregation in the city. The families of the rich negroes . . . generally keep themselves aloof from the poorer class, although the heads of these families . . . are personally "plain men," thus presenting a perfect analogy to the corresponding white families of the metropolis. . . . Negro tea-drinkings are not rarely given, sometimes on a quite elaborate scale; while among the educated colored people a social circle exists which is really to be respected and commended. . . .

The negroes are a gregarious race. . . . "Societies" abound among them; "associations" of all kinds are plentiful. About thirty Masonic organizations have originated in their midst, together with five societies of Odd Fellows, and one temperance association. In addition to these there is a "Cooks and Stewards' Benevolent Society," a Coachmen's Protective Union, and a Mutual Relief Society, organized nearly a half century ago. The appellation "Brothers and Sisters of Love and Charity" is given to an association comprising both sexes of the colored population; while under the titles of the Daughters of Esther, the Daughters of Samaria, the Perseverance Association, etc., the colored women of this city have united their forces and their tongues. There is also an African Civilization Society. . . . The negro masons are very much attached to the imposing regalia and ceremonies of their craft; while the various benevolent societies are really deserving institutions. In proportion to the population there is far less vagrancy and pauperism among the blacks than the whites. . . .

In the city of New-York the black man is placed under various irksome restrictions as regards his amusements. Though fond of dramatic representations, the theatres are generally denied to him.

He is, or was, allowed to penetrate the upper tier of "the Academy"; he is also permitted, we believe, to enter Barnum's Museum and the Old Bowery; but the great majority of the places of amusement are closed against him. Though fond of dancing, the negro is not admitted to the masked and public balls of the whites, but must either stay at home or betake himself to a colored dancehouse. Still the negro continues to submit with a good grace to these deprivations, and occasionally he "splurges" on his own account. At the Stuyvesant Institute, for example, a colored musical entertainment was wont to be given, in which the singers, the musicians, the conductor, and the audience were alike black, and all of them well gotten up in the items of handkerchiefs, dresses, kid gloves, and imitation diamonds. Colored concerts have also been given at the Cooper Institute, which have been very successful in point of numbers. An Old Folks Troupe of Negroes, attired in the fashion of the olden time, has been originated under the direction of Mr. J. T. Spelman. . . . Musical parties at the residences of private colored individuals have also become somewhat in vogue. Musical entertainment by the choirs of churches are occasionally given.[66]

7. THE URBAN SCENE

The magnitude of urban growth in the 1840's and 1850's excited an unprecedented interest in the city scene, not only because of the immigrants and Blacks who added diversity to the urban population, but also because of a wide variety of sights and sounds that increasingly differentiated the city from the country. In 1847, *Hunt's Merchants' Magazine* began publishing an extensive series of articles on "The Commercial Cities and Towns of the United States." In 1852, *Phelps' Hundred Cities and Large Towns of America* was published, avowedly designed for readers seeking information concerning "the large and increasing cities of the United States." As early as the late 1830's, writers of popular fiction began to respond to the prevailing interest in city life. From the mid-1840's to the mid-1850's a market flourished for books dealing, often in sensational fashion, with the "mysteries and miseries" of major cities of the nation, especially Boston and New York.[67]

With the introduction of gas lighting by the 1820's — for stores, theaters, and streets — the physical appearance of the city became increasingly different from that of the country, especially at night. Noise, a characteristic of the city noted as early as the mid-eighteenth century, was an even more evident difference between city and country. "Every stranger from the country, who comes to the city, is astonished at the variety of noises which assail his ears on every side," wrote the author of *City Cries: or, a Peep at Scenes in Town*, published in New York in 1850: "the constant rumbling of heavy drays, carts, and carriages over the pavement, and the bawling cries of all sorts of petty traders, and jobbers crying their commodities, or offering their services in the streets." [68] The new books on the city also identified occupational types peculiar to the urban scene, as in a Philadelphia publication of 1851 — newsboys, chimney sweeps, firemen, crab and oyster mongers, fruit hucksters, hot corn women, wood sawyers, whitewashers, watchmen, police, aldermen, carters, omnibus drivers, stevedores, walking advertisers, ragpickers, street sweepers, scavengers, and dandies and swells.[69] In the late 1860's and early 1870's numerous books described the full spectrum of the city scene. They included Matthew H. Smith's *Sunshine and Shadow in New York* (1868), Junius Browne's *The Great Metropolis; a Mirror of New-York* (1868), and James D. McCabe's *Lights and Shadows of New York Life; or, the Sights and Sensations of the Great City* (1872), which purported to acquaint curious readers with the city's "splendors and wretchedness, its high life and low life, its marble palaces and dark dens, its attractions and dangers, its rings and frauds, its leading men and politicians, its adventurers, its charities, its mysteries, and its crimes."[70]

Among the personalities most frequently identified with the urban society of the 1840's and 1850's were the so-called "b'hoys" and "g'hals" of the large cities, whose brash and often unruly behavior reflected both the exuberance of "Young America" and the social and psychological consequences of rapid urban growth. In temperament, they were the urban counterparts of the rough but self-reliant figures who were pushing forward the agricultural frontier. Independent with a "pride and a passion," if uncouth in manner, Mose, Jake, and Sykesey were the Davy Crocketts of mid-nineteenth-century urban America. At their rowdiest, they were problems of public order, apt to organize gangs, such as New York's Bowery Boys, Philadelphia's Dead Rabbits, and Baltimore's Plug-uglies, to participate in riots, to patronize groggeries and "tiger dens," and to take advantage of country greenhorns. But in their often helpful services in fighting fires and in their distaste for pretense and aristocracy, they exhibited attitudes admired by most Americans of their day. By the mid-1860's, the increasing size and changing composition of the nation's large cities made the type virtually extinct.[71] New York journalist George G. Foster described the activities of the b'hoys and g'hals of New York City in his *New York in Slices* (1849) and *New York by Gas-light* (1850).

THE B'HOYS AND G'HALS OF NEW YORK: 1849–1850

There are the great middle classes in all . . . countries — but in none other does any branch of them display any thing like the peculiar and distinguishing attributes of the American b'hoy and g'hal. All through our . . . country . . . the type is found in abundance, but very slightly modified by location and surrounding circumstances. The b'hoy of the Bowery, the rowdy of Philadelphia, the Hoosier of the Mississippi, the trapper of the Rocky Mountains, and the goldhunter of California are so much alike that an unpracticed hand could not distinguish one from the other; while the "Lize" of the Chatham Theater and the belle of a Wisconsin ball-room are absolutely identical, and might change places without any body being the wiser. Not even Mose himself would be likely to suspect the substitution. . . .

The governing sentiment, pride and passion of the b'hoy is independence — that he can do as he pleases and is able, under all circumstances, to take care of himself. He abhors dependence, obligation, and exaggerates the feeling of self-reliance so much as to appear, on the surface, rude and boorish. But the appeal of helplessness or the cry of suffering unlocks his heart at once, whence all manner of good and tender and magnanimous qualities leap out. The b'hoy can stand anything but affectation — on that he has no mercy; and should he even find a fop or a coxcomb in absolute distress, we fear his first impulse would be to laugh at him.

In his amusements, as in his food and clothes, the b'hoy isn't particularly nice as to their quality, so that they are "rich and racy." . . . He is especially fond of the bar-room and the engine-house, always on the look-out for a fire, a fight or a frolic, and seldom long without one or the other of these commodities "on hand." Perhaps, however, if we were called upon to select the one thing in which above all others the b'hoy delights, we should name the target excursion. With his trim-fitting black panties,

141

"sixty inches round the bottom," and his fire-new red flannel shirt, his gun jauntily carried at a "support" and the periphery of his straight-brimmed hat cutting the plane of the ecliptic at an angle of twenty-three degrees twenty-eight minutes — with his spotless white belt across his manly chest, a splendid band of music in front, the inevitable negro with the target behind, and Lize smiling and clapping her hands in admiration from the window — who so proud and happy as he? . . .

If Mose is most perfectly himself at a target-excursion, Lize never feels herself at home but at the theater or the dance. . . . She is perfectly willing to work for a living, works hard and cheerfully, as any day laborer or journeyman mechanic of the other sex. She rises before the sun, tidies up herself and afterward her little room — swallows her frugal breakfast in a hurry, puts a still more frugal dinner in her little tin kettle . . . , and starts off to her daily labor in the press-room, the cap-sewing or the book-folding establishment, as happy and care-free as a bird. Perhaps she deviates a block or two from her direct route to exchange a smile and a word with Sykesey or with Mose, and make an appointment for a steamboat excursion, a sleigh-ride or a visit to the Bowery [Theatre]. . . . From six to six o'clock she works steadily, with little gossip and no interruption, save the hour from twelve to one, devoted to dinner. . . .

The g'hal is as independent in her tastes and habits as Mose himself. Her very walk has a swing of mischief and defiance in it, and the tones of her voice are loud, hearty and free. Her dress is "high," and its various ingredients are gotten together in uttter defiance of those conventional laws of harmony and taste imposed by Madame Lawson and the French mantua-makers of Broadway. The dress and the shawl are not called upon to have any relationship in color — indeed, a light pink contrasting with a deep blue, a bright yellow with a brighter red, and a green with a dashing purple or maroon, are among the startling contrasts which Lize considers "some pumpkins" and Mose swears is "gallus." But the bonnet! — that is the crowning achievement of the out-door adornment of the full-rigged g'hal. . . . The outside is trimmed with a perfect exuberance of flowers and feathers, and gigantic bows and long streamers of tri-colored ribbons give the finishing touch to a hat which, resting on the back of the head, extends its front circumference just round from ear to ear across the top of the forehead, leaving the face entirely exposed, and the eyes at full liberty to see what is going on in every direction.

The newest invention in the costume of the g'hal is a fascinating article of outside gear, termed by some a "polka," but generally known as a "monkey-jacket." It is cut like a gentleman's tight sack to fit the back and shoulders smoothly, and reaches half way down the thigh. When neatly cut and fitting to the figure of a plump, healthy and elastic-limbed g'hal, with the full-skirted dress swelling out voluptuously from beneath it and undulating like a balloon, it certainly has a very exhilarating appearance.[72]

The exploits of the b'hoys and g'hals figured prominently in the popular novels and plays of the 1840's and 1850's, as in Edward Z. C. Judson's pioneer dime novel, *The Mysteries of New York*, published under the pen name Ned Buntline in 1848, and the original "Mose" play, *A Glance at New York*, first produced in New York in February, 1848. Its author was the playwright-actor-manager Benjamin A. Baker. Baker's play deals with the attraction of the city for the rural dweller, the activities of volunteer fireman Mose, Lize, his female counterpart, and the Bowery b'hoys, who reveal their sharper side in outwitting a gullible country cousin.[73]

THE BOWERY B'HOYS AND THE TRICKS OF THE CITY: 1848

ACT I, SCENE I. . . . *Enter* HARRY *and* GEORGE. . . . GEORGE *has a valise.*

Harry. . . . Well, here we are in the great metropolis of the Western World, where . . . you can purchase amusements of all kinds from the Astor Place Opera, to the far famed "Hall of Novelty;" five minutes' walk will take you from the extreme of wealth to the extreme of poverty. . . . How much better it is to live here, than in your stupid village in the backwoods, with no society but that of Bumpkins and old women; to be sure, you have some pretty girls there . . . but what are your country girls, compared to our dashing New York belles? I declare, during the two months I have passed with you there, I have grown almost as verdant as yourself.

George. Well, Harry, you must admit that your visit to our village has somewhat improved your health. Poor father! — it was a long time before he'd give his consent for me to visit New York. The old gentleman has a great regard for my morals, and I believe nothing but your promise to look after me would have induced him to let me come.

Harry. . . . We must now look about us for a conveyance to the Astor House. . . . Remain you here till I find one. I'll not be long. [*Exit* HARRY. . . .]

143

Enter JAKE *and* MIKE. . . .

Mike. I say, Jake, there's a greenhorn. I knew it the minute he stepped ashore. . . .

Jake. [*Advancing and touching* GEORGE *on the shoulder.*] I beg your pardon, sir: if I mistake not, you're from the country?

George. Yes, sir, I am.

Jake. So am I. I belong up the river. I came here about two months ago, in hopes of getting a situation in a store, but I can't make it out. I've spent all the money my father gave me, and have nothing left but this gold watch. [*Shows watch.*] I wouldn't part with it if I could help it, but I've been turned out of my boarding-house, and had nothing to eat these two days. Wouldn't you like to buy it?

George. I don't know as I can afford it! Besides I have a very good silver one, that answers my purpose. [*Shows it.*]

Jake. I will sell it to you cheap, sir. As I am in want of money to take me home, I wouldn't mind trading with you for a little to boot. . . . I'll tell you what I'll do — I'll swop with you, if you give me ten dollars to boot!

George. [*Aside.*] Egad, I'll do it. [*Aloud.*] As you say you're very much in want of money, I'll trade with you. But is it good gold?

Jake. If you have any doubts, you can go with me to the jeweler's and ask him.

George. No, my friend, I will take your word. There! [*Gives him silver watch and money, and receives gilt watch from* JAKE]. . . .

George. [*Puts watch in pocket.*] What a swell I will cut when I get home! Father and mother will open their eyes wider than ever, and all the neighbors will be anxious to see my gold watch! [*Struts about.*]

Jake. I've done it, Mike. Here's your five. [*They divide money.*] I think you can come the drop game there, while I go and sell the silver one. [*They exit.*]

Re-enter HARRY. . . .

Harry. I hope you are not tired of waiting for me, George. I had to go two blocks before I could find a coach; now I'll go and get my valise out of the Captain's office, and be with you in a minute. . . .

George. Stop one minute, Harry! I want to show you what a glorious bargain I've made! [*Shows watch.*] What do you think of that?

Harry. You don't mean to say you've been buying that?

George. Yes, my boy! I got it dirt cheap. I gave my silver lever and ten dollars to boot!

Harry. George, you've been sadly victimized! This watch is not worth ten cents!

George. Nonsense! Don't you see it's gold?

Harry. All is not gold that glitters. You've been the dupe of a scoundrel!

George. Do you really mean to say I have been deceived in this watch?

Harry. I do! Why, my dear George, I thought you too cunning for the watch-stuffers.

George. I tell you, Harry, the poor fellow who sold it to me was from the country, and almost starving.

Harry. Nonsense! this is the old stereotyped tale! But console yourself — you are not the first greenhorn that has been taken in by that manoeuvre. There's about as much gold in that watch as you can put in your eye! . . . Stop here till I return from the boat.   [*Exit* HARRY]. . . .

JAKE *and* MIKE *re-enter . . . dressed as cartmen. Mike drops pocket-book between* GEORGE's *legs, then stoops and picks it up.*

Jake. Let me look at that.

Mike. No you don't! No doubt it belongs to some gentleman who arrived by the Albany boat.

Jake. Maybe it belongs to some of the cartmen about here?

Mike. I tell you it ain't possible! it's full of papers, &c. [JAKE *goes up.* — MIKE *offers it to* GEORGE.] Here's your pocket-book, sir; I've just picked it up, and that man wanted to claim it.

George. [*Feeling pockets.*] You are mistaken, friend; it does not belong to me.

Mike. Indeed, sir! Well, I could have sworn it did [*Opens and shows* GEORGE.] You see, it's full . . . of bank-bills. . . . you'd better take it, and keep it till a reward is offered, which, I dare say, will be something handsome — fifty dollars at the least! then we'll go halves. . . .

• *George.* [*Aside.*] Egad! Here's a speculation. [*Aloud.*] Very well, my friend. I will take it.   [*Offers to take it.*]

Mike. Stop a minute! You see, I'm going to trust you with almost a fortune — as I don't know you, suppose you let me have ten dollars now, and when you get the remainder, you can call at my boarding house and let me have the balance of my share.

George. Well, that's fair enough. [*Takes out pocket-book and gives him a ten-dollar bill.*] There.

Mike. And there's the pocket-book. Good day. . . .

Re-enter HARRY, *with valise.* . . .

Harry. Come, George, let's be off.

George. Now, Harry, laugh if you dare. I think I have fully redeemed myself. . . . See! [*Shows pocket-book.*] This will make up for my loss.

Harry. Where did you get that?

George. A man found it, and placed it in my hands until a reward is offered for it.

Harry. Well?

George. I advanced him ten dollars.

Harry. Ha! ha! ha! duped again! They have initiated you into the drop business! Ha! ha! ha!

George. Don't laugh, Harry. See, here are a number of bank bills — Globe Bank, and Hoboken Banking & Grazing Company.

Harry. Globe Bank bills are as worthless as chaff! Ha! ha! ha! you have been done capitally! . . . if you stay here much longer you'll not have a cent left.[74]

Mose, the prototype of the city b'hoy of the 1840's and 1850's, was usually portrayed as a volunteer fireman, one of the most characteristic personalities of the mid-century urban scene. Certainly, fires and the fire laddies dashing to a fire or parading in colorful regalia were among the occurrences and personalities that most sharply differentiated city from country. At times, fires were an almost daily (and nightly) spectacle, some of such magnitude, like the Great Fire of 1835 in New York and the Chicago Fire of 1871, as to wipe out whole sections of a city. Until the mid-century, the fire-fighting function usually was performed by companies of unpaid volunteers, using equipment provided by the municipality.[75] According to the English journalist Charles Mackay, there was something particularly American about the organization and behavior of the fire companies and the color and excitement they imparted to the city. Mackay observed this aspect of city life in 1857.

FIRES AND FIRE FIGHTING: 1850's

The fire system, in nearly all the principal cities of the Union, is a peculiarity of American life. Nothing like it exists in any European community. As yet the city of Boston appears to be the only one that has had the sense and the courage to organize the fire brigades on a healthier plan, and bring them under the direct guidance and control of the municipality. Everywhere else the firemen are a power in the State, wielding considerable political influence, and uncontrolled by any authority but such as they elect by their own free votes. They are formidable by their numbers, dangerous by their organization, and in many cities, are principally composed of young men at the most reckless and excitable age of life, who glory in a fire as soldiers do in a battle, and who are quite as ready to fight with their fellow-creatures as with the fire which it is more particularly their province to subdue. In New York, Philadelphia, Baltimore, and other large cities, the fire service is entirely voluntary, and is rendered for "the love of the thing," or for "the fun of the thing," whichever it may be. . . .

The firemen are mostly youths engaged during the day in various handicrafts and mechanical trades, with a sprinkling of clerks and shopmen. In New York each candidate for admission into the force must be balloted for, like a member of the London clubs. If elected, he has to serve for five years, during which he is exempt from jury and militia duty. The firemen elect their own superintendents and other officers, by ballot, as they were themselves elected; and are divided into engine companies, hook and ladder companies, and hose companies. The engine and accessories are provided by the municipality; but the firemen are seldom contented with them in the useful but unadorned state in which they receive them, but lavish upon them an amount of ornament, in the shape of painted panels, silver plating, and other finery, more than sufficient to prove their liberality, and the pride they take in their business. . . .

The men — or "boys," as they are more commonly called — not only buy their own costume and accoutrements, and spend large sums in the ornamentation of their favourite engines, or hydrants . . . but in the furnishing of their bunk-rooms and parlours at the fire-stations. The bunk or sleeping rooms, in which the unmarried and sometimes the married, members pass the night, to be ready for duty on the first alarm of fire, are plainly and comfortably furnished; but the parlours are fitted up with a degree of luxury equal to that of the public rooms of the most celebrated hotels. At one of the central stations, which I visited . . . , the walls were hung with portraits of Washington, Franklin, Jefferson, Mason, and other founders of the Republic; the floor was covered with velvet-pile carpeting, a noble chandelier hung from the centre, the crimson curtains were rich and heavy, while the sideboard was spread with silver claret-jugs and pieces of plate, presented by citizens whose houses and property had been preserved from fire by . . . the brigade; or by the fire companies of other cities, in testimony of their admiration for some particular act of gallantry or heroism which the newspapers had recorded.

If the firemen be an "institution," Fire itself is an institution in most American cities. . . . Into whatever city the traveller goes, he sees the traces of recent conflagration; sometimes whole blocks . . . levelled to the ground, or presenting nothing but bare and blackened walls. So constant appears to be the danger that the streets of New York, Boston, and other cities, are traversed in all directions by telegraphic wires, which centre invariably at the City Hall, and convey instantaneously to headquarters, day or night, the slightest alarm of fire. . . .

The assertion is frequently made by Americans . . . that many fires are purposely caused by the "boys" for the sake of a frolic, or a run, or in a spirit of rivalry between two or more companies. . . . In Philadelphia and Baltimore alarms of fire are regularly expected on Saturday nights, when the "boys" have received their week's wages, and are ripe for mischief.[76]

Physical structures, as well as people and occurrences characteristic of the urban scene, were among the sights that gave novelty and interest to American cities in the 1850's and 1860's. Palatial dry-goods stores, symbols of the commercial orientation of the city, were marveled at by visitors and cited in guidebooks as "things to see." Boston had its Jordan, Marsh and Company and Philadelphia its Wanamaker and Brown, among other extensive mercantile establishments.[77] When Lord and Taylor in New York occupied its five-story white marble emporium in August of 1859, the *Times* described the new structure as "more like an Italian palace than a place for the sale of broadcloth"; and travelers to New York City in the 1860's, visiting A. T. Stewart's stores (one for wholesale and one for retail) viewed "in utter amazement" the "successive tiers of showrooms . . . the magnificent staircases . . . the extent of area enclosed by the walls, and the business transacted within them." [78] A Chicago guidebook, published in 1866, called the visitor's attention to "the great dry goods house" of Field, Leiter and Company — "the Stewart's of Chicago" — a "fine five-story edifice of Athens marble, with sales rooms on every floor from the basement to the top," where sales had "exceeded seven millions of dollars" in the twelve months ending May 31, 1866.[79] E. R. Freedley's description of Wanamaker and Brown, in his "handbook" of the "Great Manufactories and Representative Mercantile Houses of Philadelphia," suggests the contribution of the leading retail stores to the glamor of the major cities and to their attraction for rural dwellers. Their cast-iron facades, in the new mode of construction pioneered by James Bogardus in New York City in 1848, gave the business blocks of the growing cities a spacious, monumental quality that enhanced the city's physical appeal.[80]

RETAIL STORES — ATTRACTION OF THE BIG CITY — PHILADELPHIA'S WANAMAKER AND BROWN: 1867

Strangers from afar come and gaze upon the lofty structure as one of the city's peculiar landmarks. Messrs. Wanamaker and Brown have been liberal patrons of the press, and, in turn, newspapers, magazines and books, have furnished wings, with which the fame of their establishment has flown to every city, town and village in the Union. . . . The erection of the new Iron Front [was begun in 1866]. . . ; though extremely massive, the symmetry of the line, and the spaces allowed between the arches, give the whole a light and ornate appearance, that is not probably equalled by any other Iron Front in Philadelphia. . . .

Entering from Market Street through the grand arched doorway, we find ourselves on the threshold of as fine a salesroom as our metropolis affords. On our left, extending to nearly midway, is the Gentlemen's Furnishing Goods Department — a moderate business emporium of itself. . . . At the rear end of the floor is the department for Boy's Clothing, well stocked with garments for boys, youths, and children.

We ascend to the second story by a massive walnut staircase, reminding us of the grand staircase at the Capitol at Washington, and find ourselves in a spacious salesroom, elegantly fitted up and used solely for the Custom Department. In glancing around over the maze of fabrics and busy life which here greet us, we fancy that if two ordinary cloth stores and a dozen old fashioned tailor shops were thrown together into one, the effect produced would be very similar. . . .

The third floor is wholly devoted to overcoats and fine dress coats. Forty-nine counters are here arranged, all loaded with garments — coats enough . . . to dress an empire — made up in every desirable mode and style, to suit people of all sizes, ages, tastes, and occupations. The fourth story brings us to the Whole-sale and Manufacturing Rooms, where a large portion of the garments are cut and sent out to be made up. . . . The fifth story is the Cloth, Cassimere and Trimming Room.

The clerk who sells, never delivers the parcel to his customer. He simply makes his ticket of sale, and another, whose business it is, packs and delivers. The house is provided throughout with speaking tubes and dumb waiters, by which means all parts are brought into direct communication. . . . The number of persons to whom this establishment now gives steady employment . . . is over six hundred. . . . The great majority of these persons have families which are supported from their earnings, so that it is no extravagant estimate to suppose that this establishment affords constant support to no less than twenty-five hundred people — enough to populate a county town.[81]

But more than the abundantly stocked department stores, it was the hotels, especially in the major cities, that epitomized the bustle, excitement, and physical splendor of the urban scene. Hotels were traditional attributes of cities, especially in ever-moving America; but the emergence of the palatial first-class hotel coincided with the acceleration of urban growth that began in the 1820's. Boston's Tremont House, opened in 1829, set a pattern that shortly was imitated in the other larger cities of the country. The architect Isaiah Rogers conceived its monumental design in Greek Revival style with colonnaded portico; and he was called upon to plan comparable structures for many other cities: New York's Astor House (1836), the Charleston Hotel (1839), the Exchange Hotel in Richmond (1841), the Burnet House in Cincinnati (1850), New Orleans's second St. Charles Hotel (1851), the Battle House in Mobile (1852), the Galt House in Louisville (1865), and Nashville's Maxwell House, begun in 1859 but not completed until 1869. "The hotels are among the sights of New York," wrote an English visitor of 1854; a guidebook to New Orleans described the effect of the St. Charles Hotel, with its impressive dome, as "similar to that of St. Paul's, London." [82]

Hotels served a community function in providing space for meetings and conventions and for the balls and receptions that enlivened the urban social scene; at the same time their size and the throng that frequented them contributed to the anonymity of urban life. European travelers found the best of them far more magnificent than the hostelries of England and Western Europe; and they regarded even the average hotels as peculiarly American institutions because of their emphasis on size and space, their appeal to permanent residents (to the extent that anything was permanent in the United States), and the role they played in the promotion of new cities in the West. These aspects impressed the British novelist Anthony Trollope who traveled widely through the United States in 1861 and 1862.

ANTHONY TROLLOPE ON AMERICAN HOTELS: 1860's

. . . in the States the hotels are so large an institution, having so much closer and wider a bearing on social life than they do in any other country, that I feel myself bound to treat them . . . as a great national feature in themselves. They are quite as much thought of in the nation as the legislature, or judicature, or literature of the country; and any falling off in them, or any improvement in the accommodation given, would strike the community as forceably as a change in the constitution or an alteration in the franchise. . . .

Hotels in America are very much larger and more numerous than in other countries. They are to be found in all towns, and I may almost say in all villages. . . . the first sign of an incipient settlement is an hotel five stories high, with an office, a bar, a cloak-room, three gentlemen's parlours, two ladies' parlours, a ladies' entrance, and two hundred bedrooms. . . .

Size and imposing exterior are the first requisitions. . . . They are always built on a plan which to a European seems to be most unnecessarily extravagant in space. . . . The visitor enters a great hall by the front door, and almost invariably finds it full of men who are idling about, sitting round on stationary seats . . . and getting through their time as though the place were a public lounging room. And so it is. The chances are that not half the crowd are guests at the hotel. . . . The price at these hotels throughout the Union is nearly always the same, viz., two and a half dollars a day, for which a bedroom is given, and as many meals as the guest can contrive to eat. This is the price for chance guests. The cost to monthly boarders is, I believe, not more than the half of this. . . . This includes a great deal of eating, a great deal of attendance, the use of reading-rooms and smoking-rooms — which, however, always seem to be open to the public as well as to the guests, — and a bedroom with accommodation which is at any rate as good as the average accommodation of hotels in Europe. In the large Eastern towns baths are attached to many of the rooms.[83]

Not only were the first-class hotels among the "sights" of the city; they also were symbols — with their steam heat, toilet facilities, gas lighting, and elevators — of the comforts and conveniences of city as opposed to rural residence, and of the glamor and conviviality of city life. As journalist Nathaniel P. Willis remarked in 1844, "Going to the Astor and dining with two hundred well dressed people, and sitting in full dress in a splendid drawing room with plenty of company — is the charm of going to the city." [84] Cities took pride in the sumptuous furnishings and novel mechanical appurtenances of such hotels as Boston's Revere House (1847), famed for its statuary, gilt chandeliers, and rich carpeting;[85] New York's Fifth Avenue Hotel (1859) — that "Prince of American caravanserais," which boasted steam heat, eight public and 120 private parlors, and the first effective "vertical railway" to carry its guests from floor to floor;[86] and Philadelphia's six-story, 600-room Continental Hotel (1860), that offered, according to its advertisements, "every feature of a gentleman's private mansion, where retirement may be secured for those who desire it; or the promiscuous gatherings of travelers enjoyed at reasonable expense."[87]

One aspect of the intercity relations that developed with increasing urbanization is illustrated in the career of the famous hotel entrepreneur, Paran Stevens — a mid-nineteenth-century Conrad Hilton — who was involved in the ownership or management of Boston's Revere House, New York's Fifth Avenue Hotel, the Continental Hotel in Philadelphia, and two hotels in Mobile. When Stevens moved from Boston to New York in 1863, his fortune was estimated at $5,000,000, and he continued to augment it through real estate investment in New York City.[88] His identification with the Continental Hotel in Philadelphia was one of its claims to distinction. The Continental, which opened in February, 1860, was said to represent the ultimate in hotel luxury, a quality described for women readers in the May, 1860 issue of *Godey's Lady's Book and Magazine*.

HOTELS OF THE 1860's — "PALACE HOMES" FOR RESIDENTS AND TRAVELERS

In our Great Republic we deck no palaces for our dignitaries; official power is too short-lived to require a gorgeous dwelling place. We are not, however, without magnificent and spacious habitations; but these, under the name of HOTELS (significant here as palaces for the people), are erected . . . not for a few of some exclusive caste or family, but for the travelling public of the whole nation and of all nations; all may find a home in these palaces.

Most of our great cities are handsomely provided with such Hotels, but . . . Philadelphia, in the *Continental*, has surpassed all others, and given a model that will not be rivalled easily. . . . The carpets are . . . of the richest and best texture. . . . the mirrors of many forms and diverse patterns . . . each suited exactly to its place; the chandeliers, candelabras, and gas-fixtures . . . of the most beautiful fashions. . . . Each apartment has the air of an elegant private home. . . .

The whole house is both warmed and ventilated by long and spacious galleries or halls, superbly carpeted and curtained. The dining and tea rooms are all elegant, but the large Dining-room is, in size and finish, unsurpassed in splendor and convenience. The walls and ceiling are tastefully painted in fresco. . . . This spacious Hotel is six stories high, but a vertical railway, on a new and scientific plan, has been contrived, which will take the inhabitants of the upper stories up and down without . . . the fatigue of ascending . . . stairs.[89]

Like the hotels of the major cities, the homes of the rich brought out the contrast between the way of life of the wealthy and that of the poor. This contrast was one of the notable differences between city and country living, and it became increasingly apparent in the decade of the 1860's. A guidebook to Baltimore, published in 1866, cited the mingling of "splendor and squalor" and the extremes of "penury and extravagance" among the sights to be noted in visiting the Maryland metropolis. Descriptions of the newer cities of the Middle West, by the late 1850's, alluded to fashionable streets, such as Cleveland's Euclid Avenue, lined with imposing mansions that contrasted sharply with the living quarters of the average city dweller.[90] New York, because of its numbers, provided the most frequently mentioned example of the differences in standards of living that characterized urban life. It was reported in 1870 that an estimated 5 per cent of New York City's population owned a larger share of the real and personal property (in terms of value) in the city than did the remaining 95 per cent.[91]

By 1860, New York's Fifth Avenue was taking on the quality of the handsome, exclusively residential street that was to be characteristic of the post-Civil War American city. In this respect Fifth Avenue now overshadowed Broadway, once the locale of both fine residences and commercial structures. In 1859, John Jacob Astor III and his brother, William B. Astor (called "the richest man in New York"), erected impressive brick dwellings on the west side of Fifth Avenue between Thirty-third and Thirty-fourth streets. In the same vicinity, in the mid-1860's, A. T. Stewart, New York's leading dry-goods merchant, built a white marble mansion at an estimated cost of $800,000.[92] *Miller's New York As It Is or Stranger's Guide-Book*, which went through several editions in the 1860's, listed among the sights of the city the broad avenues and squares "studded with a succession of splendid mansions . . . in some instances costing from $50,000 to $200,000," and counseled the visitor not to miss "Fifth Avenue, the great centre of wealth and fashion," if he would "form any adequate idea of the progress and opulence" of the city.[93]

The residential specialization apparent on Fifth Avenue by the 1860's was a sign of the transition from a diversified to a segregated pattern of occupational and residential location then taking place in large cities. Though improved transit facilities encouraged the outward movement of residence, diversity still characterized the spatial pattern of most large cities in the 1840's and 1850's. Downtown districts were still a mixed area of offices, financial houses, stores, and factories of all kinds. Two types of increasingly specialized neighborhoods surrounded the downtown area: patches of slums, where immigrant newcomers found housing in structures abandoned by their original residents and awaiting the expansion of commercial activity, and fashionable residential sections, occupied by the most affluent city dwellers who desired a central address. Beyond these specialized enclaves stretched a still highly diversified mixture of residential dwellings and commercial and industrial structures.

The contrasts in the life styles of rich and poor were graphically delineated in *Frank Leslie's Illustrated Newspaper*, in

November, 1865. On facing pages, engravings depicted the rich —
"Yachting," "In Central Park," "At the Opera," "In Fifth Avenue,"
"In the Parlor," "Fancy Dress Ball," "Shopping on Broadway," "At the Academy of Music," "At Greenwood Cemetery" —
and the poor — "Driven from Home," "Sewing for a Living at
Six Cents a Shirt," "Garbage Gatherers," "A Midnight Haul of
Prostitutes and Bums," "Found Dead in the Street," "Bootblacks,"
"Child Beggars," and "Potter's Field." An accompanying article,
entitled "The Rich and Poor of New York," elaborated on the
contrasts as characteristic not only of New York but of cities in
general.[94]

THE WAYS OF THE RICH — NEW YORK CITY: 1865

The people of the country can hardly realize the marked distinction in classes that exists in the town. In the country the poor
man associates with the rich on an equal basis in most cases. . . .
But in the city, the classes are so distinctly marked, that they
exist, as it were, in different worlds.

No city in the world offers greater inducements to the rich,
than New York, or less to the poor. The rich can find in its
pleasures everything that human invention can afford; every
luxury, every privacy in their enjoyment, and every style of
society to enjoy them with. Its streets are admitted by all foreigners to be the most brilliant in the world, and its *salons*, both
private and public, conducted more lavishly than can be found
elsewhere. . . . How far the extravagancies of life are carried in
the homes of our millionaires, can only be realized by actual
contact with their splendors. . . .

It is not the only drain upon the purse of pater-familias that
he supports a magnificent house upon Fifth Avenue or Madison
Square. There are . . . carriages and horses for madam, his fair
wife, a pony chaise for miss, the just budding daughter, that they
may appear well in the Park, to say nothing of saddle horses for
the heir of the house, who must also have a yacht. How could
he weather through the summer, and appear at Newport without
it. Then there is the opera and the theatre, unless, as one New
York millionaire has chosen to do, he chooses to build a theatre
of his own. There are balls, costumes, and otherwise, through
the season; dinner parties, with from ten to a hundred covers,
given at home, at Delmonico's, the Maison Dorée, and elsewhere; and last, though not least, there is shopping at Stewart's,
Lord & Taylor's, Legrain's, and such other economical places,

where really a lady could not expect to get anything to wear short of a morning's bill of two or three thousand dollars. Ah! money may be the root of all evil, but it is a mighty pleasant esculent for the New York market.[95]

In the multiplication of fashionable clubs, "high society" in the American city reflected its conformity to urban patterns then prevailing in the western world. Writing in 1865, the editor of *The Nation* called this development one of the most striking contemporary "symptoms of metropolitanism," one in which "our other chief cities are following the lead of New York." Clubs, he wrote, "may now be considered a recognized feature of American town life." [96] The growth of clubs for the "upper ten" was described by Matthew Hale Smith in his widely read description of life in the metropolis, *Sunshine and Shadow in New York*, published in 1868. His comments reflect, too, the rise of the new, and sometimes transiently rich, during the Civil War era.

CLUB LIFE IN NEW YORK CITY: 1868

After the London fashion, clubs are becoming common among the upper ten. The most elegant buildings on Fifth Avenue are club houses. They are furnished in the most gorgeous manner. . . . Nearly every club-house indicates the brief life of a New York aristocrat. A lucky speculation, a sudden rise in real estate, a new turn of the wheel of fortune, lifts up the man who yesterday could not be trusted for his dinner, and gives him a place among the men of wealth. He buys a lot on Fifth Avenue; puts up a palatial residence, outdoing all who have gone before him; sports his gay team in Central Park, carpets his sidewalk, gives two or three parties, and disappears from society. His family return to the sphere from which they were taken, and his mansion, with its gorgeous furniture, becomes a club-house. These houses are becoming more and more numerous. They are breaking up what little social and domestic life remains in the city. Few homes are known to New York high life. Men go to the club to dine, and spend their evenings amid its fascinations.[97]

The brick row house, with few exceptions, continued to provide the pattern for the homes of the affluent in the seaboard cities. The Greek Revival style, with imposing columned entrances, was popular in the 1830's; by the 1850's, chocolate-colored brownstone had become a fashionable construction material. Stuccoed dwellings in the French style, with open courtyards and rear wings, were characteristic of the homes of the wealthy in New Orleans; the free-standing mansion, of stone, brick, or wood, was usual in the cities of the Middle West. Suburban homes, in both the East and the West, reflected the popularity of the Gothic Revival and Italian villa styles. Since the 1840's, technology had been adding to urban comfort by providing for the heating of buildings by means of hot water and hot air.[98] In the late 1850's, Cleveland industrialists were building expensive houses in an Americanized villa style in exclusive sections of Euclid Avenue. To a writer in the January 28, 1858 issue of *The Cleveland Leader,* these dwellings, with their sumptuous, wood-paneled interiors and their modern plumbing and heating installations, were among the "ornaments" of Cleveland.

MANSIONS IN THE MIDDLE WEST — CLEVELAND: 1858

The most prominent among the costly residences which have made our city, particularly Euclid St., so famous is that of Amasa Stone, Jr. The exterior is a massive structure, with over 700,000 brick being used. . . . The main building is 50 × 60 feet, with two projections, one on each side. The height of its stories is 15 and 13 feet respectively. . . . The ceilings of the parlor and library are of recess, panel, and cornice work, and have a most handsome effect. The staircase in the hall is finished in mahogany. The newel posts, balusters, and railing, and the doors of the parlor, reception room, and library are finished with rose wood; those of the other apartments are of oak. From the hall door is the view of the second hall floor, by means of an oval opening in the ceiling. The roofs are of tin and thoroughly painted. The furnace is fireproof, being solidly encased in brick and stone work, designed to convey, by means of requisite pipes, heated air over the entire building. Attached to the furnace is a capacious boiler for heating water. A supply of hot and cold water is found in nearly every apartment. . . . In the rear of the basement is . . . a model laundry and fuel room. Connected with the laundry is a pipe leading to a large cistern, by means of which soft water can always be had. . . . It is the finest, the most complete and convenient residence west of [the] Hudson.[99]

Many city dwellers who could not afford to own or rent single-family houses resorted to hotel or boarding-house living; it was done to such an extent that Americans were sometimes described as "a boarding people" and New York City as "a vast boarding house." A compromise was suggested, as early as 1860, that anticipated the modern apartment house. This entailed leasing groups of rooms and maintaining individual households under a common roof — a kind of residence popular in Paris in the 1850's and hence called a "French flat." The first such "apartment house" in an American city was built in New York in 1870 from designs by Richard Morris Hunt. Arguing for this kind of multiple living arrangement, in March, 1860, a writer in Frank Leslie's *Illustrated Newspaper* called it the application of the "tenement-house system" to the "wants of respectable people."

THE MODERN APARTMENT HOUSE ANTICIPATED: 1860

Next to the plague of servants, the plague of rents and of residences forms the greatest domestic affliction in our good village of New York, and we regret to see that year by year it manifests itself in cities in every part of the Union. . . . At present the only alternative for those who cannot hire a house is to take lodgings at a boarding-house or hotel. But the very vulgar popular mania for ostentation . . . makes all lodging in such places as expensive as housekeeping. The obvious remedy is, of course, good rooms in good buildings, rented furnished or unfurnished, with or without meals, on the Unitary Home principle. . . . The owner . . . should sublet . . . to the occupants, employing a resident agent to collect the rents. . . . Hitherto the common American feeling that every family to be "respectable" must have a house of his own, has withheld architects from attempting to perfect [moderate-priced apartments] . . . or capitalists from erecting them. But the tremendous rate at which people are being crowded together in our rapidly growing cities will soon bring the improved lodging-house system into notice. People will find, to their amazement, that they may live [as family units] in brown stone-fronted houses, in as good rooms as in the most respectable hotel, and among perfectly respectable fellow-lodgers, for one-third the rent which they now pay. . . . We commend the consideration of this subject not only to the inhabitants of New York, but of other cities.[100]

The cost of living in large cities, especially New York, encouraged people of moderate means, as well as some of the affluent, to take advantage of the steam railroads and the horsecars to move to the outskirts of the city or to communities in its vicinity. This development further contributed to the impression that there were "but two classes in the city — the poor and the rich." James D. McCabe, Jr., writing in 1868, described the pattern of suburban living already taking shape for a distance of 40 miles from New York. "They come into the city, to their business, in crowds, between the hours of seven and nine in the morning," he wrote, "and literally pour out of it between four and seven in the evening. In fair weather the inconvenience of such a life is trifling, but in the winter it is absolutely fearful. A deep snow will sometimes obstruct the railroad tracks, and persons living outside of the city are either unable to leave New York, or are forced to spend the night in the cars. . . . At such times the railroad depots . . . are crowded with persons anxiously awaiting transportation to their homes." [101] In 1859 the lawyer-historian Sydney G. Fisher described the extension of suburban living on the outskirts of Philadelphia, a development that he attributed to the availability of horsecar transportation.

A VISIT TO PHILADELPHIA'S SUBURBS: 1859

Geo. Blight . . . took me thro one or two streets between his place & Germantown, which I had not seen for many years and which are now lined with cottages & villas, surrounded by neat grounds, trees, shrubbery & flowers, many of them costly & handsome, all comfortable and pretty. They are in every variety of taste and size and there are hundreds of them. The same spectacle is to be seen on every lane near Germantown all the way up to Chestnut Hill, and not around Germantown only, but at Frankford, West Philada., Chester, along the Delaware, over in Jersey, everywhere, in short, within ten miles of the city where a railroad runs. They are the result of railroads which enable anyone to enjoy the pleasures of country life and at the same time attend to business in town. They are owned by shopkeepers, manufacturers, merchants, &c, and their beauty and general good taste and the care and attention lavished on them show what sources of enjoyment they are and how superior is the life they promote to that of the streets. Fresh air, space, trees, flowers, privacy, a convenient & tasteful house, can now be had for the same expence as a narrow & confined dwelling on a pavement, surrounded by brick walls & all the unpleasant sights & sounds of a crowded town. The advantages are so obvious that this villa & cottage life has become quite a passion and is producing a complete revolution in our habits. It is dispersing the people of the city over the surrounding country, introducing thus among them, ventilation, cleanliness, space, healthful pursuits, and the influences of natural beauty, the want of which are the sources of so much evil, moral & physical, in large towns.

The . . . horse railroads have given a great impulse to this movement. They are scarcely more than two years old, yet they . . . offer to those who live in the country a pleasant way of going to town at all hours & in any weather at trifling expense. One is now constructing on the Germantown road and will be in running order in a few weeks. It spoils the road for driving, but all the people in Germantown can by it go to town for 10 cents every 10 minutes. One consequence of this is the immense improvement of the country & rise in the value of property. In Germantown, they have now gas & water from water-works in every house. Shops & mechanics follow the rich population of the villas, and soon every luxury of a city can be had in the neighborhood. All the families who own much land here have been enriched, and as the neighborhood was composed of farms only a few years ago, these are very numerous. . . . Blight has 60 acres worth, he told me, $5000 per acre & increasing in value. The same process is going on in every direction around the city.[102]

Some of the newly developing "suburban villages" were carefully planned communities in which the romantic villa style of architecture and naturalistic landscape design practiced by Alexander Davis and Andrew Jackson Downing were employed. One of the earliest of this type was Llewellyn Park, at Orange, New Jersey, developed between 1853 and 1869 by Llewellyn Haskell, a New York businessman, and designed by Alexander Davis. Two communities in the vicinity of Chicago — Lake Forest, projected in the late 1850's, and Riverside, a decade later (the work of Frederick Law Olmsted and Calvert Vaux, designers of New York's Central Park) — are examples of professional suburban planning in the Middle West. Such planned suburbs did not represent a repudiation of the city but rather were thought of as constituting a part of the city in the countryside. The goal of the planners was to develop communities having easy access to the central city and offering the amenities of city living.[103] The suburbs of most cities, however, developed in more haphazard fashion, the result of speculative promotion by real estate companies or of the growth of already existing small communities to which potential commuters were attracted. By the late 1860's, city boosters were taking as much pride in the growth of the city's suburban satellites as in the population increase of the city itself. This is reflected in a brochure published in 1869 by the Western News Company of Chicago, a publication presumably subsidized by real estate dealers.

SUBURBAN GROWTH IN THE CHICAGO AREA: 1869

The possibilities of Chicago can never be estimated justly until one has taken a view of its suburbs, . . . such picturesque spots as Riverside, Hinsdale, Thatcher and Harlem, to the west, and such already populous suburbs as the township of Hyde Park affords to the south. . . . It is probable that comparatively few even of the oldest residents of Chicago are aware that there are *forty* towns, more or less populous, that are strictly suburban to Chicago, where gentlemen doing business and having all of their interests in Chicago live with their families. These towns — and there are others not included in this enumeration, because they have not yet assumed strictly suburban features — are increasing in size very rapidly, and there are few of them where the advantages of improvements are not now recognized. Some of the new locations are retarded considerably, and especially those nearest the city, because of the speculative habits of Chicago men, who buy the property not for the purpose of building and improving, but for the enjoyment of the increase in value, which is sure to result in all cases. This spirit is being overcome in many places, however, by the adoption of a plan to sell no property except upon the condition that the buyer shall build within a year, or some other specified time — a plan that should be universally adopted.[104]

The increasing opulence of the homes of the wealthy heightened the contrasts in life style between the rich and the poor. Immigration augmented the congestion in the inner portions of the older cities, and that part of New York, for example, became

161

more heavily populated than similar areas in London and Paris.[105] Despite the availability of omnibuses and horse railways, most laborers could not afford the cost of commuting to work. Thus the poor sought lodging either in residences on the edges of the business district given up by their original owners, or in structures that came to be known as "tenements," built expressly for the purpose. Some of these were brick structures, especially in New York and Philadelphia, and others were of frame, like Boston's "three-deckers." The results of converting former residences into housing for the poor were described in the 1853 report of the New York Association for Improving the Condition of the Poor, a philanthropic organization founded in 1843. Its 1853 report showed the magnitude of the problem of poverty and demonstrated a sensitivity to the social disorientation caused in newcomers to the city by the congested living arrangements to which they were unaccustomed. Pressure from the AICP prompted the first legislative investigation of tenement conditions in an American city, in 1856.

TENEMENT CONDITIONS — NEW YORK: 1853

In the lower wards, there are thousands of poor persons, but comparatively few buildings suitable for their accommodation. Most of the houses are those which were formerly occupied by the wealthy who have removed up town. . . . Large rooms have been divided by rough partitions, into dwellings for two or three families — each, perhaps, taking boarders, where they wash, cook, eat, sleep and die — many of them prematurely. . . . And *in addition, night lodgers*, consisting of homeless men, women and children, are not unfrequent, who for a trifling sum are allowed temporary shelter. There, huddled together, like cattle in pens, the inmates are subjected to the most debasing influences. . . . The resident poor in the First Ward have doubled since 1846; and . . . there are now . . . of that class needing relief, not less than *fifteen thousand persons*. . . .

When families of five, eight or ten persons . . . live in a contracted apartment, that is applied to every conceivable domestic use, and from fifteen to thirty such families in the same house — having the entry, stairway and yard in common, the last badly drained, perhaps unpaved, and the receptacle of all deleterious and offensive things, it would be truly surprising if the tenants did not become filthy, reckless and debased, whatever might have been their previous habits and character. . . . How should members, often of different families and of different sex, sleep in the same room, nay, often in the same bed, without danger? "I know," says one, "of nothing so demoralizing as the absence of private conveniences, and where there is a community of beds and bedrooms to all ages and both sexes." . . .

Says one witness: "The habits of a family are more depressed and deteriorated by the defect of their habitations, than the greatest pecuniary want to which they are subjected. The most cleanly and orderly female will invariably despond and relax her exertions under the influence of filth, damp and stench; and at length, ceasing to make farther effort, will probably sink into a noisy, discontented, rum-drinking slattern — the wife of a man who has no comfort in his house, the parent of children whose home is the street or the work-house." . . . In regard to the proneness of such persons to *intemperance*, it is said, "That the dreadful depression consequent on ill health (the effect of crowded, filthy, badly ventilated dwellings), tempts these poor creatures with a force we cannot adequately appreciate, to have recourse to stimulating drink." . . . The connection of juvenile depravity which so fearfully abounds, with the wretched conditions of life described, is fully shown by the Chief of Police Reports, and is too obvious and direct to require remark.[106]

The still distressing condition of the poor, by the late 1860's, when "tenements" had been built expressly for their occupancy, was described by James McCabe, Jr., in *The Secrets of the Great City*, published in 1868.

THE WAYS OF THE POOR — NEW YORK: 1868

You will see the extremes of poverty and want in and about the Five Points district [in New York City]. In the day time half-clad, filthy, emaciated creatures pass you on the gloomy streets, and startle you with the air of misery which they carry about them. At night these poor creatures huddle into cellars, so damp, foul, and pestilential that it seems impossible for a human being to exist in them. The walls are lined with "bunks," or "berths," and the woodwork and bedding is alive with vermin; the floors are covered with wretched beds in a similar condition. The place is either as dark as midnight, or dimly lighted with a tallow dip. Sometimes a stove, which only helps to poison the atmosphere, is found in the place, sometimes a pan of coals, and often there is no means of warmth at hand. Men, women, and children crowd into these holes, as many as thirty being found in some of them. . . . The air is . . . heavy with such foul odors that one unaccustomed to it cannot remain five minutes in the place. . . .

The scarcity of land in the city has led to the construction of numbers of buildings known as "Tenement Houses." . . . As pecuniary investments they pay well, the rents sometimes yielding thirty-five percent. on the investment. . . . One of the houses stands on a lot with a front of fifty feet, and a depth of two hundred and fifty feet. It has an alley running the whole depth on each side of it. These alley-ways are excavated to the depth of the cellars, arched over, and covered with flag stones, in which, at intervals, are open gratings to give light below; the whole length of which space is occupied by water closets, without doors, and under which are open drains communicating with the street sewers. The building is five stories high and has a flat roof. The only ventilation is by a window, which opens against a dead wall eight feet distant, and to which rises the vapor from the vault below. There is water on each floor, and gas pipes are laid through the building, so that those who desire it can use gas. The building contains one hundred and twenty-six families, or about seven hundred inhabitants. Each family has a narrow sitting-room, which is used also for working and eating, and a closet called a bed room. Pass these houses on a hot night, and you will see the streets in front . . . filled with the occupants, and every window choked up with human heads, all panting and praying for relief and fresh air. . . . There is a multitude of these squares, any of which contain a larger population than the whole city of Hartford, Connecticut, which covers an area of seven miles. There is one single house in the city which contains twelve hundred inhabitants.[107]

The prevalence of child vagrants gave further proof of the extremes of poverty in the mid-nineteenth-century city. Some 10,000 abandoned, orphaned, or runaway children were roaming the streets of New York City in 1852, according to a police report. By 1868 the number had increased to at least 30,000. The Children's Aid Society was organized in 1853 to procure foster homes in rural districts for vagrant boys and girls. In 1854 its founder, Charles Loring Brace, opened the first lodging house for street boys and newsboys. He described his work with homeless boys in *The Dangerous Classes of New York and Twenty Years' Work Among Them*, published shortly after 1870.

VAGRANT STREET CHILDREN: 1850–1870

. . . My attention had been called to the extraordinarily degraded condition of the children in a district lying on the west side of the city, between Seventeenth and Nineteenth Streets, and the Seventh and Tenth Avenues. . . . The parents were invariably given to hard drinking, and the children were sent out to beg or to steal. Besides them, other children, who were orphans, or who had run away from drunkards' homes, or had been working on the canal-boats that discharged on the docks near by, drifted into the quarter. . . . These slept around the breweries of the ward, or on the hay-barges, or in . . . old sheds. . . . They were mere children, and kept life together by all sorts of street-jobs — helping the brewery laborers, blackening boots, sweeping sidewalks, "smashing baggages" (as they called it), and the like. Herding together, they soon began to form an unconscious society for vagrancy and idleness. Finding that work brought but poor pay, they tried shorter roads to getting money by pettey thefts, in which they were very adroit. . . . The police soon knew them as "street-rats;" but, like the rats, they were too quick and cunning to be often caught in their petty plunderings. . . .

I determined to inaugurate here a regular series of the "moral disinfectants," if I may so call them, for this "crime-nest." . . . These measures, though imitated in some respects from England, were novel in their combination. The first step . . . is to appoint a kind-hearted agent or "Visitor," who shall go around the infected quarter, and win the confidence of, and otherwise befriend the homeless . . . children of the neighborhood. Then we open an informal, simple, religious meeting — the Boys' Meeting . . . ; next we add to it a free Reading-room, then an Industrial School, afterwards a Lodging-house; and . . . our final and most successful treatment is . . . the forwarding of the more hopeful cases to farms in the West.[108]

8. GOVERNMENT

The rapid growth and increasing diversity of city populations between 1820 and 1870 gave rise to changes in the form and function of municipal government, principally in limiting the wide discretionary powers of the aldermen, centralizing authority, and regularizing the provision of basic, though minimal, urban services. Fragmentation characterized municipal government in these years.

This fragmentation, originating in a traditional concern for ward autonomy, was intensified by the influx of immigrants from Europe and by the increasing disparity between rich and poor, which caused the major cities to be less socially homogeneous than they had been. The widening of the suffrage, by the 1820's, made the great mass of male newcomers to the city potential voters, susceptible to political manipulation at the ward level, and led to their participation in local government in ways that often transformed its character. The editor of the *New York Evening Post* noted this change as early as June 10, 1827, complaining that aldermen of the traditional stamp — "men of virtue, character, influence, and wealth," with a "strong feeling for the growth and prosperity" of the city — were being replaced by persons who had "obtruded" themselves into the city council for the purpose of "begging a fat office . . . or of getting a valuable contract under its golden auspices." [109]

One change, designed to induce a less fragmented approach to city problems, was the strengthening of the mayor at the expense of the aldermen and city councilmen, whose customarily wide powers of appointment and administrative authority were a major reason for the political fragmentation. The mayoralty was made an elective office during the 1820's and 1830's, both in the seaboard cities and in the newer cities of the Middle West — in Boston and St. Louis (1822), Detroit (1824), Philadelphia (1826), Baltimore (1833), and New York (1834). In succeeding years, mayors were given wider powers of appointment and a stronger veto upon the acts of the municipal legislature.[110] Bicameral city councils were instituted in the hope of checking hasty legislation; and the replacement of council committees with elected or appointed boards in many areas of municipal administration further reflected the prevailing distrust of self-serving and ward-oriented municipal legislators.

By the late 1850's, criticism (often politically motivated) of the behavior of locally elected officials, as well as popular exasperation at the failure of municipal governments to cope effectively with the multiplying complexities of local problems, inspired appeals to state legislatures to impose responsibility for police protection, fire fighting, public health, parks, and other urban services in state-appointed, citywide (or even metropolitan) commissions. Most large cities were subjected to these controls in the decade of the 1860's. Meanwhile, an informal method of overcoming fragmentation was found in the growing influence of political machines, lubricated by patronage — the awarding of appointments, jobs, and contracts — and run by a new breed of urban specialist, the professional politician or "boss." Boss Tweed of New York City referred to the machine as a means of overcoming fragmentation when he wrote, "This population is too hopelessly split into races and factions to govern it by universal suffrage, except by the bribery of patronage and corruption." [111]

The often impassable condition of the streets symbolized the lack of citywide communication to which the concern for ward autonomy gave rise. Milwaukee of the 1850's had no uniform practice in street construction and repair, services that were the responsibility of the individual alderman. On November 26, 1852, *The Milwaukee Sentinel* despaired of the city's ever achieving proper grades and adequate streets and sidewalks so long as this kind of municipal "states'-rights-ism" prevailed.

WARD AUTONOMY VS. CITYWIDE COMMUNICATION — MILWAUKEE: 1852

Some days since we hinted a wish, that some alderman from the Fifth Ward might be obliged to pass through the mud, between the Menomonee River and Lake Street, hoping that such an adventure might induce him to repair the sidewalks. Well, yesterday, after trudging through a spot in that locality, we encountered one of them, carrying a couple of window sash, just at the spot where the plank walk terminates in a profound abyss. . . . Said our official friend: "See here, when you come into the Fifth Ward you find walks like this [the plank walk]. . . . That [pointing to the abyss] is in the Fourth Ward." We did not lift up our voice and weep, it would have been of no use, but, digging off the mud, we mused upon the unaccountable stupidity which . . . made [the boundary line of the Ward] an imaginary one, so that the aldermen from two Wards would have to agree (an unheard of thing) before any repairs could be made on the street. And as we stood musing, our aldermanic friend with the sash went hurrying, staggering and plowing through the mud, northward, while, at the same time, a man on a gray pony yelled for help, as he sank nearly out of sight in that fathomless abyss of mud and water.[112]

167

Fernando Wood, mayor of New York City in the 1850's, viewed the mayoralty as symbolic of the whole city, and criticized the lack of centralization in the city government. He argued for "home rule" in opposing the creation by the state legislature of commissions that could bypass locally chosen agencies of municipal government, and defied the authority of a "metropolitan police force," established by the state.[113] Carrying his "home rule" ideas to the ultimate, as tension between the North and South threatened New York's business interests and the dominance of the Democratic Party, he proposed in 1861 that New York become a "free city." His concern for home rule and for a strong mayoralty is reflected in his annual message of 1856.

NEW YORK'S MAYOR FERNANDO WOOD — SPOKESMAN FOR "NO MEAN CITY": 1856

The extending area and the increasing population of New York have already surpassed the ability of the [state] law-making power to provide for their interests. . . . Whilst we have progressed in the accumulation of the elements of prosperity, we have retrograded in the means to preserve our power and provide for the necessities of our condition. . . . The government of the city is far more utilitarian and practically perceptible than either [the state or national] governments. It directly involves and affects the comfort, interest or health of every citizen. It is a living, ever present fact; we see and feel it daily. . . . [Yet] our local legislation, and the management of our executive·offices have not fulfilled the requirements of our present wants, to say nothing of our future destiny. . . .

Next to commerce, the principle . . . internal element upon which the city of New York depends, is its government. . . . I look upon the want of concentration of power and absence of sufficient check to the action of the several departments, together with the weak and almost powerless condition of the mis-called Chief Executive Officer, as the main defects in the present government of the city. . . . There must be one head to which the other functionaries should be subordinate, all acting in harmony and concert. The Mayor should be to the city what the President of the United States is to the general government, and the several heads of the departments should be his cabinet, appointed by him, . . . and be liable, for cause, to removal by him. . . . It may be said with truth, when these [needs] are cared for,

. . . a New Yorker [will] be proud of his citizenship in this metropolis; it will bear him honorable reception throughout all civilized lands; for he can say, with Paul of Tarsus, "I am a citizen of no mean city." [114]

More influential, often, than the mayor, was the political boss, whose power and that of his political machine were nourished by the patronage and contracts that the fast growing population and ever expanding physical needs of the city made possible. Throughout the nation, boss and machine politics coincided with the emergence of large cities in the pre-Civil War years. In Philadelphia, Joel B. Sutherland, capitalizing on his association with the local militia, had forged a political machine by the early 1830's. In New York City, William M. Tweed used a closely knit fire company to get himself elevated to the city council in 1851. There his activities in a group of aldermen popularly known as "The Forty Thieves" provided a pale preview of the bribery and political manipulation and favoritism that were to make the "Tweed Ring" notorious in the later 1860's for mulcting New York City of a sum variously estimated at $20,000,000 to $200,000,000. Similar behavior, if on a smaller scale, accompanied the growth of the newer cities of the West, such as Milwaukee, where "Boss" Jackson Hadley, in the later 1850's, constructed a political machine out of the contractors and laborers engaged in paving and railroad-building enterprises.[115] So pervasive was this pattern of political practice that the editor of *The Nation* could refer in 1869 to the "state of corruption into which municipal affairs have fallen in San Francisco, in Chicago, though Chicago is only a bantling compared to New York, and also in Philadelphia, though Philadelphia is not, as New York is, the receptacle for the dregs of the European immigration." [116]

Disclosures of corrupt practices in municipal government, as early as the later 1850's, aroused increasing concern, especially in New York City. By the mid-1860's, citizens' groups such as the Citizens' Association and the Union League Club were discussing the need for reform. That corrupt practices prevailed, no one doubted, and there were rumors of the existence of "rings"; but the size of the city made it difficult to know where to place the blame. Conservatives, disturbed by the revolutionary changes in the American social scene, laid the prevalence of corruption to the

169

new elements in the electorate and officialdom of the large cities and to the opportunities for graft in municipal government arising from the competition in American cities, since the 1850's, for utility franchises and contracts for public works.

These views, as well as the feeling that the growth of large cities threatened traditional democratic government in the United States, were expressed by the historian-biographer James Parton in a much praised article on the misgovernment of New York City, which appeared in the October, 1866 issue of *The North American Review*,[117] five years before the exposure of the Tweed Ring.

JAMES PARTON ON MUNICIPAL CORRUPTION IN NEW YORK CITY: 1866

We have undertaken to write something about the government of the city of New York, and yet . . . we find that we have been employed in nothing else but discovering in how many ways, and under what a variety of names and pretexts, immature and greedy men steal from that fruitful and ill-fenced orchard, the city treasury. . . .

The twenty-four Councilmen . . . are mostly very young men — the majority appear to be under thirty. . . . There is a certain air about most of these young Councilmen, which, in the eyes of a New-Yorker, stamps them as belonging to what has been styled of late years "our ruling class," — butcher-boys who have got into politics, bar-keepers who have taken a leading part in primary ward meetings, and young fellows who hang about engine-houses and billiard-rooms. A stranger would naturally expect to find in such a board men who have shown ability and acquired distinction in private business. We say . . . that there *are* honest and estimable men in the body; but we also assert, that there is not an individual in it who has attained any considerable rank in the vocation which he professes. . . . The majority of this board are about equal, in point of experience and ability, to the management of an oyster-stand in a market. Such expressions as "them laws," "sot the table," "71st rigment," and "them arguments is played out," may be heard . . . in this sumptuous [council] chamber. . . .

Debates is a ludicrous word to apply to the proceedings of the Councilmen. . . . The most reckless haste marks every part of the performance. . . . Measures involving an expenditure of millions . . . are hurried through both boards in less time than *paterfamilias* expends in buying his Sunday dinner in the market; and, frequently, such measures are so mysteriously worded that no one outside of the Ring can understand their real object. . . . The most usual manner of stealing is to receive money for awarding or procuring contracts, appointments, donations, or increase of salaries, which money, of course, the favored person gets back, if he can, from the public treasury; and he usually can. The President of the Board of Health, last spring, when the city was threatened with cholera, had occasion to remonstrate with a person who held the contract for removing dead animals from the streets, and threatened him with the breaking of the contract if its conditions were not better complied with. "That would be rather hard, Mr. Schultz," replied the man, "for that contract cost me $60,000." . . .

The question now occurs, How was it that a city containing so many public spirited and honorable men fell into the control of a gang of thieves? It has all come about in one generation. . . . The time was when men, after a brilliant career in Congress, regarded it as promotion to be Mayor of the city; when a seat in the city legislature was the coveted reward of a lifetime of honest dealing in private business; . . . when the very ward committees were composed of eminent merchants and lawyers. . . . In other words, the time was when the city was governed by its natural chiefs, — the men who had a divine right to govern it. Nay, more: it was once a distinction to be a voter, — since none could vote who were not householders. . . . This system was changed by the Constitutional Convention of 1821, which abolished the household restriction, and admitted to the polls all citizens, native and foreign, except convicted criminals and madmen. . . .

The evil consequences did not immediately appear because the habit of selecting respectable men for the public service survived the system which had created that habit. . . . About the year 1850 . . . when street railroads . . . were projected, the Corporation conceived the fancy that they had the right to grant the privilege of laying rails in the public streets to private companies. . . . And it was in connection with those railroad grants that the corruption, on a great scale, began. It was then that the low, immature, ignorant, unprincipled, irresponsible, untaxed persons who formed the majority of the city legislature discovered that an alderman could, by a judicious use of his opportunities, . . . make his fortune, during a single term of service. "Rings" were then first formed; "agents" were then first employed, — the mysterious go-betweens who have to be "seen" before anything can be done. . . . Thus the system of spoliation began. . . . From that time to this, the ordinary New York politician has regarded public office in no other light than as a chance to steal without the risk of the penitentiary.

And let no one suppose that this is a subject which concerns the people of New York only . . . [for] the evils under which New York suffers exist, to some degree, in many other towns, and threaten *all* of them. New York . . . is a sieve which lets through the best of the emigration that comes to our shores, but catches and retains the worst; and therefore it is in that city that the system of unqualified suffrage has been *first* put to a test under which it has broken down completely and hopelessly. But in all our large cities there is of necessity an assemblage of ignorant, irresponsible, and thoughtless men, totally incapable of performing the duties of citizenship. We accordingly find in Brooklyn, Philadelphia, Boston, New Orleans, San Francisco, Chicago, Albany, Rochester, Buffalo, St. Louis, and many other cities, the insidious beginnings of that misgovernment which has made New York the by-word and despair of the nation.[118]

Limiting the suffrage ranked high in Parton's prescription for the purification of government and politics in New York City — that and the election of the city council, as well as the mayor, on a citywide basis rather than by wards, as a means of reducing the influence in the city council of the "wards and districts inhabited chiefly by ignorant foreigners and vicious natives." He proposed restricting the suffrage to persons who had paid a direct tax and denying it to anyone who could not read English of medium difficulty. He wished to reduce the number of elective officials, to give the mayor and aldermen longer terms of office, and to accord permanent tenure to appointed personnel. He took the view that municipal stealing deprived the city of funds that could be used for welfare. His ideal was a municipal legislature "composed of men eminent in business, in science, and in benevolence." [119]

Views similar to Parton's were expressed in the reform proposals of a committee of the Union League Club of New York, appointed in December, 1866, to recommend reforms that would eliminate the "corruption and inefficiency," especially in the legislative branch of the government of New York City. The committee's report recognized that the contemporary large city constituted a special environment that put a strain on traditional democratic procedures. The committee emphasized the need for a more business-minded and accountable administration of municipal government and took a remarkably forward-looking view of the services that city government should be obliged to perform.

A NEW APPROACH TO THE GOVERNMENT OF LARGE CITIES: 1867

There may be stated, as facts generally recognized in this country, that cities are worse governed than towns or small villages; that in proportion as cities increase in population their governments have become corrupt, their officers inferior, the administration of laws and ordinances lax and defective. . . . The public mind demands an efficient and appropriate system of city government, which it has not yet found. . . . To find what belongs to a city government . . . we must . . . look into those . . . peculiar inconveniences, those special claims of charity and humanity, those various demands of taste, those inevitable opportunities of vice and crime, those petty details of business and affairs, which a dense population, the close proximity of person and residence, of wealth and poverty, of refinement and vulgarity, of vice and virtue, in great cities must always create, and which are sure to be found much alike and much in the same proportion, whatever may be the form of national government under which the city exists. . . . [Thus] systems for drainage, ventilation, cleanliness and locomotion; provisions for the care of the poor, the sick, the orphans and the intemperate; rules for the raising of revenue, and the care and protection of the public moneys, and the payment of public creditors; regulations to secure the safety and regularity of buildings and conveyances; the creation of parks and the control of amusements; regulations as to the enforcement of city ordinances and the protection of city property; efficient provisions for the extinguishment of fires, and for police, and for the protection of life and health . . . constitute substantially the scope and duty of a city government. . . .

The fact is, that the duties of a city government are in much the larger part *merely executive and ministerial.* . . . The government of a city is altogether more a matter of business than of statesmanship. . . . It is to be noticed [that] these city abuses . . . are not much found where population is so small that nearly all the citizens know each other, and know all the officers, and the details of all the purposes for which money is expended, and what is being done in nearly every building. But when a population reaches the numbers of Rochester, Buffalo or Albany, and criminals begin to be organized, and citizens may be strangers to each other, and expenditures are so large and varied, as not to be generally known, then municipal politics assume the features of an occupation; the stealings of office, and not the principles of American republican government, are the object and the inspiration of political activity and organization. Bad men organize to support officers and aspirants for office, as a condition of enjoying impunity in their unlawful pursuits; primary meetings, which the best men do not attend, make all nominations, and a nomination usually secures an election; and the result of this whole false theory of party responsibility and political government in large cities is, that party caucus and drill are the strongholds and vigorous machinery through which bad men grasp all power for selfish purposes. . . . The gradual demoralization which has attended this system in New-York, has reached a stage which has appalled the city, aroused the attention of the nation, and become the public scandal of the United States on the other side of the Atlantic. . . .

If we wait till those in authority in the city governments shall mature. . . , when shall we have adequate public urinals; when bathing houses, where the poor can cheaply purify themselves; when a system of well regulated cabs, cars and omnibuses; when streets and sewers well repaired, cleaned and purified; when piers and wharves that would not disgrace the harbors of the Malay pirates; when adequately ventilated and lighted tenement houses; when well regulated evening schools, sufficient for the children of the poor; when comprehensive and economical provisions by which sickness and poverty may be alleviated at the public charge; when wise and honest provisions for the rearing and the education of vagrants and orphans . . . ? It has hardly entered into the mind of any one that such reforms are possible as shall make the city government an organization of virtue and intelligence, and an inspiration and a power in behalf of all that is wise, and pure, and humane and noble in our city life. If such be too much to hope in our day, we may at least find a brief delight in the thought of what New-York and its people would soon become, if the exercise of all its large powers of government could be placed and kept in the hands of her purest, wisest and best citizens.[120]

9. URBAN SERVICES

The Union League Club's standard of urban service, as projected in its 1866 report, went far beyond what the average city dweller expected of city government in the two generations preceding the Civil War and, indeed, for some time thereafter. As cities grew in population, their governments were forced to expand and regularize municipal services, but they did this in general within the frame of the laissez-faire attitudes of the time, which held that the individual citizen could be expected to contribute his efforts to the solution of local problems and that if private enterprise could provide adequate service it should be allowed to do so. As yet, the provision of water was the only utility in which cities made a major investment, and this was because of the recognized relationship between an adequate water supply and the threat of fire and epidemics in congested cities. Philadelphia's yellow fever epidemic in 1793 prompted the Pennsylvania city to pioneer in providing a municipal waterworks, completed as early as 1801; but it was not until the accelerated urban growth of the 1830's that agitation for municipal waterworks became widespread. By 1860, as many as 12 of the 16 largest cities of the country had municipally owned water systems.[121] On the other hand, gas lighting, introduced in Baltimore in 1817 and in other cities in the 1820's, was provided by private companies, as were urban transit facilities, such as hacks, omnibuses, and horse-drawn railways. When municipal restrictions on overloading of horsecars were proposed in Philadelphia in 1859, a local newspaper contended that this was a matter that would "regulate itself according to the public convenience. The owners of railroads are losers if they overload their horses, and they are not usually so blind to their own interests as to kill them by overloading." [122]

Street construction and cleaning, as well as waste disposal, were early viewed as joint responsibilities of the citizen and the municipality. The costs of street construction were met by charges against the abutting property and by general funds raised through taxation; but the citizens themselves were expected to assume some responsibility for cleaning and repair. The construction of public sewer systems, which were introduced in Boston as early as 1823 and in other major cities in the 1840's and 1850's, was financed in the same fashion.[123] The disposal of human and animal waste and the accumulation of garbage and trash, inevitable in congested communities, presented a problem of ever widening proportions, which, like the provision of water, was thought to affect the public health. Its solution was left at first to individual effort, to scavenging animals that were allowed to roam the streets, or to privately supported contractors. But gradually it was seen to pose a problem of community concern, which called for assumption of authority by the municipality, with assistance from the individual citizen. Mayor Ambrose Kingsland of New York City made this point in his annual message to the Board of Aldermen in 1851.

CLEAN STREETS — A MUNICIPAL OBLIGATION: 1851

Perhaps no department of the city government has received more attention at the hands of the municipal authorities than that of "cleaning streets"; nor can I recall any to which public notice has been drawn with more persevering energy. The obvious reason for this is to be found in the fact, that every member of the community has a personal interest in the matter. Many experiments have been made as to the best and most economical method of performing this important work; but I believe I echo the sentiments of every citizen, in according my commendation to the system now in operation, viz: That of having the streets cleaned by the city authorities. . . .

It has been too much the practice to cause the large thoroughfares to be scrupulously cleaned, while scarcely any attention is paid to the smaller and less frequented, but most densely populated streets in the city. The practice . . . is not only grievously wrong, and manifestly unjust to those residing therein, but is absolutely detrimental to the health of the city; for . . . the accumulation of dirt in the narrow streets, inhabited generally by the poorer class of our citizens, invariably generates disease; and during the prevalence of epidemic or contagious diseases, experience . . . demonstrated that the ratio of mortality in these locations is much greater than in any other portions of the city, no matter what may be the character of the population. . . .

But . . . the efforts [of the authorities] must be unavailing unless they are sustained by the co-operations of our citizens in observing faithfully the ordinances providing against the throwing of garbage, &c., into the street. . . . I understand that . . . parties . . . violating these ordinances, and arrested by policemen, are so frequently discharged without any punishment whatever beyond a brief reprimand, that the officers become discouraged, and hesitate to perform again the . . . duty of . . . arresting parties guilty of similar offences. If these complaints are well founded, . . . great injustice is done not only to the officers . . . but also to the city, for whose benefit these wise regulations were framed, the observance of which is so necessary to the health and comfort of our citizens.[124]

The insistent demand for the expansion and regularization of police facilities in new cities as well as old, by the 1850's, brought into focus the conflict between citizen individualism and the need for controls that conditions in large cities imposed. By custom, in the police, as in other areas of municipal officialdom, Americans favored the citizen functionary. In the early nineteenth-century city, the maintenance of order, beyond the overall obligation of the mayor, was the responsibility of constables, elected in the wards, and of an appointed night watch made up of citizens employed in other pursuits during the day. Many individuals provided their own protection; merchants and storekeepers often hired private watchmen.[125]

Efforts to strengthen and regularize police protection were triggered by the growing violence and disorder that characterized American cities in greater or less degree, beginning in the mid-1830's and reaching a peak in the draft riots in New York and Boston in 1863. Many factors contributed to the volatility of behavior in these years. Personal insecurity in a badly housed, rapidly changing, and increasingly diverse population and the urge for companionship in the impersonal city encouraged the spontaneous grouping of youths into gangs that functioned at times almost like barbarian clans. Gang feuds could keep sections of the city in a state of riotous fighting for days. The political parties were quick to use the brawn and skills of these rambunctious youths in ward politics, which frequently resulted in election riots. At the same time, the prevailing tradition of individualism and voluntarism encouraged citizens to take the law into their own hands, especially when police facilities were minimal and even unidentifiable. Race riots occurred in several cities as early as 1834, as abolitionist activity got under way. Nationality friction intensified with the upswing in immigration; parades of national groups and Catholic funeral processions set off incidents. Job competition after the panics of 1837 and 1857 led to open conflict. The speed of urban growth and industrialization and the social alienation they fostered seemed to encourage personal violence and even professional criminality.[126]

A riot in Boston in 1837, touched off by a clash between volunteer firemen and Irish mourners and put down only by intervention of the militia, led to provisions in 1838 (soon copied in other cities) for day police to supplement the constables and night watch.[127] A wave of disorders in the mid-1840's prompted New York City to institute the next major reform, which was abolition of the watch altogether and the establishment of an integrated day and night force. This reform, achieved in 1845, followed the example of London's Metropolitan Police Act of 1829 and was widely imitated in the decade of the 1850's.[128] But though the police were increased in number and improved in organization, their appointive character kept them politically involved and dependent, and their lack of professionalism hindered their efficiency.

Provisions for state-appointed commissions to supervise police activity, adopted for many cities after the 1857 disturbances, marked an attempt to correct this situation by circumventing local political influences, but such moves were themselves often politically motivated.[129] Real improvement was achieved, however, in some cities, such as in Philadelphia, where there was an accommodation to ethnic politics, and in Boston.[130] In the new cities of the Middle West, the pattern of police protection recapitulated the experience of the older cities, but in a much shorter time span. In Milwaukee, police protection went through the evolution from elected ward constables to an integrated police force in a ten-year period. "The City Attorney who drew the Ordinance of 1855," *The Milwaukee Daily Sentinel* reported, "had several copies from other cities of the best Police Regulations in the country; and after consulting the charter, common law, and common sense, wrote the ordinance as presented." [131]

Criticism of the police was especially bitter in the 1850's, a decade of disorder exacerbated by rapid urban growth. In 1853, James W. Gerard, New York lawyer and philanthropist, wrote a pamphlet, *London and New York: their Crime and Police*, comparing police protection in the two cities, to New York's disadvantage. The reforms he proposed included: 1) an increase in the number of patrolmen; 2) their nomination by the Chief of Police rather than by the aldermen, for appointment by the mayor; 3) tenure for good behavior rather than for a limited term coinciding with municipal elections; and 4) the wearing of an identifying uniform. This last recommendation, though resisted as un-American and undemocratic, was being carried out in some cities in the late 1850's. The regularizing of police procedures and the identification of policemen by uniform, by the 1860's, illustrate the extent to which the increasing size of cities led to the formalization of secondary relationships, to use a sociological term. Gerard blamed the inadequacy and anonymity of the police for the rampant disorder and personal insecurity in American cities of the 1850's.[132]

URBAN DISORDER AND THE NEED
FOR IMPROVED POLICE PROTECTION

I have traversed the highways and byways of London, at all hours of the day and night, to watch the workings of its police. I . . . knew them by their *uniform*, walking their ceaseless round, at every turn I took. There is something assuring . . . in their steady, solemn tread of two miles an hour, resounding in the quiet street — a signal to the law-breaker to beware, and to the peaceful inhabitant that the eye of the policeman is watching over his safety. You do not see there, as you will nightly in our broad thoroughfares, four or five rowdies walking arm in arm abreast, filled with liquor and deviltry, with segars in their mouths elevated at an angle of 45 deg. and their hats cocked sideways at 30 deg. cracking their coarse jokes, or singing their ribald songs, and who if you come too near them, may jostle you in the way, and if you say a word in reply, or prepare to defend yourself, if a knife is not drawn you are well off; the chances are much in favor of your being knocked down. . . .

Look any and *every* day in the week, at your morning paper, and see what a black record of crime has been committed in your public streets the day and the night before, what *stabbings*, what shootings, what knockings down, what assaults by slung shots and otherwise; insults to women and other disgusting details of violence! . . . It is very commonly answered, that these acts are done by foreigners recently come here, and not by our citizens: granted, and what is the commentary? Why do not these foreigners commit these acts of violence in their own countries? . . . The answer is . . . found in the weakness of our police. It shows that . . . they fear the police of Europe, for they know them to be efficient and numerous; they do not fear our own, because from their small number and other reasons, there is neither a physical nor a moral power about it. . . . New York is the house of refuge for a large proportion of thieves and housebreakers, as the police of London make that city too hot for them. . . .

Look also at our sister city of Philadelphia, which used to be called the city of brotherly love, from the quiet of its streets, and the order and propriety of its population. And what has Philadelphia been for the last ten years? Misrule and riot have reigned there, to the defiance of its magistrates, and have made its streets hideous. Assaults, and shootings, and murders, arising, among other causes, from the gangs of rowdies attached to, or running with their engines . . . so that the fire-alarm bell there has been, for years, a signal for a deadly fight.

Look at Baltimore, and what scenes have been presented there for the last six months? Violence of the most savage kind, so frequent, so daring, and by such powerful gangs, as to overawe, openly and publicly, the magistrates and police of the city; and the citizens, to protect themselves, go armed; and, if they are compelled to go out at night, do so with a fair chance of a personal encounter. Such was the daring of the disturbers of the public peace in Baltimore, that it was currently circulated in the papers, that the Mayor of that city had determined to resign, in despair, of being able, with all the aid of the police, to put down rowdyism. . . . If New York, Baltimore, and Philadelphia will only take a few practical hints from the experience of London, they will soon give a moral power to their police, which it does not now possess. . . .

I appeal to the experience of every man for the truth of what I say, that there is no *moral* power in our police — there is nothing in their dress that strikes any terror into the thief or felon — there is nothing in the dress of our policemen to distinguish them from the mass of people among whom they are mingling. You cannot tell them by day, unless you are near enough to see the twinkling little star; and when night comes, that little star does not shine out, but is in *total eclipse*. I ask, if you want a policeman in the night time, how are you to know him or find him? How can you tell at night whether the man whom you see standing at a corner, or walking slowly along, is a policeman or a robber? [133]

The transition from citizen responsibility to quasi-professional practice that characterized the regularization of urban services in these years is seen in the evolution of fire-protection service from a volunteer to a full-time, paid fire-fighting force, a development resulting from the growing size of cities and urban structures and from changes in the technology of fighting fires. Unpaid volunteers performed the fire-fighting function in most cities until well into the nineteenth century. In the newer cities, the substantial citizens served as volunteer firemen, encouraged by civic spirit and the exemption from such civic obligations as highway labor and militia and jury duty. In the older cities, the volunteer companies ultimately enrolled a less prestigious group, which often acquired a vested interest of group loyalty and political power. Pressure for change from a volunteer to a paid force, proposed as early as the 1830's, increased in the 1850's with the introduction of steam fire engines that required more professional handling and with the growing criticism of the volunteer companies because of their unruly behavior. Boston established a paid force in 1837; during the 1850's and 1860's most of the larger cities adopted this practice.[134] The experience of Cincinnati in the 1850's, as recounted in Charles Cist's *Sketches and Statistics of Cincinnati in 1859*, reveals the involvement of the volunteer firemen in politics, the change in the character of the citizen volunteers, and the resistance of the companies to professionalization.

EFFORTS TO ACHIEVE A PAID FIRE-FIGHTING FORCE — CINCINNATI: 1850's

Cincinnati, like her sister cities at the east, originally employed volunteer companies for the extinguishment of fires, and for several years . . . these associations . . . developed many daring and heroic deeds. But as the older members became less fit for active service, by the lapse of years and demands in other employments for their time and labors, the institution . . . , as elsewhere, gradually and silently fell into the hands of boys, comparatively, and the same scenes of strife, disorder and dissipation marked our fire department which have disgraced Baltimore, Philadelphia and other eastern cities. Fire riots, as they have been called, attended many instances in which the different engines were called into service, and in several cases violence and even murder were the result.

It was also discovered . . . that the numbers and *esprit de corps* of the fire department, made the members an element capable of being moulded by politicians to their own ends for election purposes. The engine houses became places of resort of evenings and on the Sabbath, not only of a large share of the members, but of their acquaintances, and every species of immorality was the consequences. Orderly citizens who deplored this state of things could perceive no remedy for it, while they feared it would become worse and worse in the future. . . .

Just at this juncture, the invention of the steam fire engine brought the question of reform to an issue, by affording a starting point to it. Mr. [James H.] Walker and his associates in [the city] council advocated the introduction of these engines, and the adoption of the pay system for firemen, which was its natural result. Violent was the opposition in and out of doors. All the baser passions of those interested in perpetuating the existing evils were aroused. . . . But . . . an ordinance in conformity to the proposed measure . . . after a stormy and obstinate debate [in the council] was . . . carried, and without unnecessary delay put into operation. . . . Mr. Walker personally effected a settlement between the city and each company of their respective interests, which in the main and finally proved satisfactory to both parties, and the whole community has now settled down into full acquiescence with and support of the new organization. . . . But the nature and degree of the difficulties, and the arduous labor of removing them may be inferred from the fact that to this day, at Baltimore, Philadelphia, and other places, where a kindred reform has been agitated for a length of years, the pressure in and outside the public authorities has hitherto successfully resisted the desired change.[135]

At a time when the health and welfare of the individual were assumed to be primarily his own responsibility, city governments concerned themselves only intermittently with the public health. Epidemics — cholera, smallpox, and yellow fever — continued to plague the cities of pre-Civil War America, and when they struck, the mayor and council, in their capacity as a board of health, imposed quarantines and attempted to enforce sanitary regulations. The increasing squalor of slum neighborhoods prompted misgivings respecting their relationship to the health of the city as a whole; and public-minded citizens, inspired by the passage of the English Public Health Act in 1848, began to look into conditions in the congested areas of American cities. Pressure from voluntary groups like the Association for Improving the Condition of the Poor, the Citizens' Association, the sanitarians, and the medical fraternity led to an investigation, in 1856, of slum conditions in New York, the first in an American city, and the enactment in 1867 of the first tenement house law, a half-way measure that established minimal structural and sanitary standards.[136] Wartime conditions drew attention to the unhealthful environment of American cities, with the result that by the later 1860's most large cities were subject to health regulations administered by professional boards of health, sometimes metropolitan in scope, authorized by the state legislatures and independent of the mayor and council.[137]

The editorial arguments of *The New York Evening Post* of January 22, 1866, in urging the passage of New York's metropolitan health bill, show both the prevailing desire for efficient municipal administration and the influence of unsanitary slum conditions, together with the threat of a cholera epidemic and the example of other large cities, in motivating the legislation. The emphasis of Boards of Health at this stage of scientific knowledge was upon ensuring the physical cleanliness of the city as a preventive of disease.

MUNICIPAL RESPONSIBILITY FOR
THE PUBLIC HEALTH — NEW YORK: 1860's

[The Metropolitan Health Bill] unites the territory now included in the Metropolitan Police District in a "Metropolitan Sanitary District." It constitutes four men versed in sanitary science and the four Metropolitan Police Commissioners [as] a Metropolitan Board of Health. . . . This board . . . has authority by the bill to enforce cleanliness in all parts of the city. . . . Ten of [fifteen] inspectors are to be medical men of several years' experience in the city, and the others must be specially qualified. . . . To enforce its measures, the Board of Health has the full co-operation of the police. This secures at once economy and efficiency. . . .

The bill . . . removes the care of the city's health entirely from political office-holders and places it in the hands of men of science; it does not propose an untried experiment, for in its main features advantage has been taken of the experience of London, Liverpool, Paris and Philadelphia, all which cities have boards of health similarly constituted with that proposed for New York. In London the creation of such a board of health, with adequate powers, has resulted in reducing the mortality from one in twenty to one in forty-five. In Liverpool it has been reduced from one in twenty-eight to one in forty-one; in Philadelphia from one in thirty-nine to one in fifty-seven. . . .

If we are to prepare ourselves against cholera . . . we have no time to lose. . . . The gentlemen named in the bill as commissioners of health have been chosen . . . because they have made the sanitary care of large cities a special study, and are known to be capable and distinguished in that branch of science. The co-operation of the police force is necessary to the effective cleansing of the city; it saves enormous waste, does away with a multitude of petty officeholders, who corrupt the city elections, and substitutes for these incapable persons a thoroughly disciplined sanitary force. . . . It is a reform in the right direction — towards economy and the concentration of necessary authority in the hands of competent persons.[138]

The interference with property and the regulation of living habits implied in housing and sanitary legislation posed the dilemma of how to reconcile municipal controls with the philosophy of an individualist society — more of a problem for the American city of the pre-Civil War era than for the city of colonial times. Dr. Edward B. Dalton, sanitary superintendent of New York's Metropolitan Board of Health, alluded to this dilemma in an article he wrote for the April, 1868 *North American Review*, discussing the first annual report of the New York Metropolitan Board of Health.

PRIVATE RIGHTS VS. MUNICIPAL REGULATION — HOUSING AND POLLUTION: 1868

Far more appalling than the magnitude of the material labor before the Board [of Health] was the apathy which possessed the minds of those who were the more immediate sufferers from these nuisances, and the sullen, but obstinate opposition of those to whom they had long been a source of profit. Accustomed for years to the undisturbed possession of what they considered . . . their rights, this latter class stigmatized as tyranny and usurpation every effort to abate the causes of physical disease and moral degradation; while those in whom long-continued submission had engendered a lethargic content were, in many instances, almost equally ready to join in resistance to any measure which would tend to disturb them in their habitual mode of life. . . . A people long accustomed to order their lives, each individual in his own way, without reference to those about him, cannot all at once be brought to see the benefit of a measure which shall subordinate personal advantage to the general good. . . . They must . . . discern that each individual will in the end enjoy far greater benefits when all shall so live as to contribute to the public welfare. . . .

Deference to the rights of every citizen, combined with a firm enforcement of its regulations, has been the stronghold of the [Board]. The tenement-houses, as well as other premises likely to be detrimental to the public health, remained constantly under the strict supervision of the Board, and subject to its authority, until . . . in 1867 . . . a tenement-house law was passed, which it is hoped will establish on a permanent basis improvements which might otherwise be but temporary. . . .

In several of the suits that the Board has been engaged in, having reference to the abatement of nuisances consisting of offensive odors, the question has been mooted as to what particular odors are and what are not detrimental to health. We are convinced that the only consistent and philosophical position on this question is, that all odors are detrimental to health — that is, that unadulterated atmospheric air is best adapted to preserve all the organs in a perfectly healthful condition, and that anything which impairs the absolute purity of the atmosphere must of necessity be deleterious.

When, however, we consider the conditions under which a great city exists, the multitudinous necessities which attach to its traffic and its growth, we cannot expect that the atmosphere which pervades it shall be absolutely pure; still, we must not lose sight of the principle that the odors which attend on the various life of the city are so many warnings of the danger, and that it is incumbent upon us to watch jealously these warnings, and see to it that they do not reach an intensity beyond that demanded by actual necessity.

The vast multitudes that throng the avenues of a metropolis, whose thoroughfares are bounded on either side by lofty warehouses or dwellings, whose streets are tunneled with sewers, the contents of which, made up of all the débris of the growth and decay of the community, are poured into the rivers that wash its shores, whose buildings are illumined with gas, the manufacture of which must be carried on either within or close upon the city precincts, whose wharves are crowded with vessels from every foreign port, and whose population is made up in great measure of the surplus of every country of the Old World, cannot expect to breathe the bracing air of the mountains or the sea-shore. But they can expect, and should demand, that the impurities be reduced to the minimum that unavoidably attaches to the prosperity and progress of the city. To reach this point is the aim of the Metropolitan Board of Health.[139]

If mid-nineteenth-century cities assumed only a minimal responsibility for public health, such also was their behavior with respect to the cultural, aesthetic, and recreational aspects of community life. Opera and theater, increasingly available from the 1820's onward, were commercial enterprises. New Orleans had regular seasons of French opera as early as the 1790's, but Italian opera was not introduced in the United States until 1825, with a performance of Rossini's *Barber of Seville,* in New York. Museums, like pleasure gardens, were commercial ventures or membership enterprises. Under pressure from reformers as well as urban workingmen, free public school systems were widely adopted in American cities in the 1840's in advance of provisions for statewide support, but private educational institutions, such as tuition academies, parochial schools, and mechanics' institutes also ministered to the desire for educational facilities. The subscription library, pioneered by Benjamin Franklin in the 1730's, was still the prevailing form in what was to become a basic area of urban service. Peterborough, New Hampshire, provided a municipal library as early as 1833; but no major city had a tax-supported library until the opening of the Boston Public Library in 1854.[140]

Despite the tradition of colonial practice that aspired, through planning, to achieve the green country town, practical rather than aesthetic considerations conditioned the character of urban design in the first half of the nineteenth century. L'Enfant's plan for Washington, D.C., led a few cities to adopt a radial street pattern, but the overwhelming number settled for the right-angled grid because of its utility for speedy house construction and dependable description in real estate negotiations and speculation. The premium on space, in a period of slow transportation, gave residential and commercial construction precedence over the ornamental squares and parade grounds grudgingly provided in some city plans and prevalent in European cities. The commissioners who adopted the grid plan for New York City, made public in 1811, admitted that they were leaving few open spaces. Given the high price of land, they felt they should be economical in this regard; moreover, they wrote, "strait-sided and right-angled houses are the most cheap to build and the most convenient to live in." [141]

From the Atlantic to the Pacific the grid supplied the standard pattern for the American city. Even before American occupation of Yerba Buena (later San Francisco) in 1846, the Mexican alcalde had commissioned a Swiss newcomer to superimpose a grid pattern on the meandering streets of the existing Spanish pueblo; and once the Americans were in control, landowners insisted that the grid should provide the prevailing design, despite some efforts to introduce a street plan adapted to San Francisco's hilly terrain.[142] In an account of San Francisco, written in 1854 by Frank Soulé and others, the authors deplored the expense and dislocation involved as a result of popular insistence upon perpetuating and extending the grid plan.

LOCKING SAN FRANCISCO INTO A GRIDIRON STREET PLAN: 1840's

During 1853, the population of San Francisco was considerably increased. At the close of the year, the city was estimated to contain nearly fifty thousand inhabitants, or more than a seventh part of the whole population of California. . . . [In this year, the city] was particularly improved by the erection of a large number of elegant and substantial fireproof brick and stone buildings. Some of these would be remarkable in any country for their great size, strength and beauty. . . .

While in the centre of the city these great buildings were rapidly rising, in the districts beyond and in the outskirts, other material improvements, in levelling the unequal ground and erecting additional houses, generally of frame, and in the formation of gardens, were being daily carried on. A second and a third time, new and supposed better street grades were being everywhere established. To carry out these, enormous and costly excavations had to be made at particular localities, while at others immense mounds of earth had to be thrown over deep valleys. Generally the streets in the lower part of the city were raised several feet above the former height, while on the high grounds towards the north and west, the lines of streets had to be lowered from ten to fifty feet. Although the city generally may in the end be much improved by the adoption of these grades, the necessity thereby created of excavating, or of filling up the building lots along the

artificial street line, and of raising or of lowering substantial buildings already erected, to suit the new level, has caused incalculable
injury and loss to individual citizens. Perhaps, under the existing
plan of San Francisco, which . . . is on the principle of strait
lines of street crossing at right angles, without regard to the natural inequalities of the ground, something like the existing grades
of the streets was unavoidable, if a prudent regard was to be had
to the future appearance of the city and convenient access to the
remotest parts of it. But on viewing the sad destruction of property caused to particular persons by these new grades, we are only
the more imbittered against the original designers of the town for
their absurd mathematical notions. If the great thoroughfares had
been adapted to the natural configuration of the tract of country
upon which the city stands, there might have been some apparent
irregularity in the plan, and . . . perhaps some little ground
available for building purposes lost, yet many millions of dollars
would have been saved to the community at large, which, as
matters stand, have already been unprofitably expended, while
millions more must still be spent in overcoming the obstacles wil-
fully placed in the way by the originally defective plans.[143]

Minority voices in many cities spoke for urban planning as a
means of achieving less utilitarian goals. Among them were the
park advocates, who not only related the need for open spaces to
public health but saw parks as places of amusement and recreation
where some of the virtues of the countryside could be retained or
introduced in congested cities. Parks were viewed, also, as one of
the prerequisites for the realization of a "great city." [144] Philadelphia had purchased a few acres of land for a park as early as
1812; but only in exceptional cases, as in Savannah, did cities provide new parks and squares adequate to the needs of expanding
populations. Finally, under pressure from reformers citing the example of European cities and from the municipal administration,
New York City pioneered in developing the first large public park
in America — Central Park, authorized by the state legislature in
1851. Its influential design — American in the sense that it emphasized the naturalistic rather than the formal — was the work of
Frederick Law Olmsted and Calvert Vaux. During the 1850's and
1860's nearly every major city in the United States made plans for
spacious public parks.

As early as 1830, residents of Brooklyn deplored the lack of planning and of parks and public promenades, as the village was fast being transformed into a populous and potentially congested suburb of New York City. Editor Alden Spooner of *The Long Island Star* tried to encourage his fellow Brooklynites to assume responsibility for the aesthetic improvement of the community, at least by planting trees, and to develop the emerging city according to a plan that would ensure "health, comfort, and ornament." He expressed some of these views in 1830 in a series of editorials entitled "Our Village."

TREES TO GROW IN BROOKLYN: 1830

The almost unprecedented increase of this village has been accompanied with too little reference to its future interests. . . . One may look in vain for a public square, a well shaded avenue or even a sufficient cemetery. The whole object seems to have been to cover every lot of 18 by 22 with a house, to project and open unneeded as well as unheard of streets, and to tumble the hills into the vallies. . . . We have not a single public square, and the only walk that our townsmen can enjoy, is the crumbling margin of the heights. . . . Even this promenade is totally neglected by the hand of improvement — no path is laid out, no tree planted, and no terrace regulated, either for beauty or safety. . . . The decoration of the streets by setting out shade trees, is so entirely within the compass of the most limited means, that we cannot but hope ere long to see some general movement upon the subject. If owners of lots will only consult their convenience and interest so far as to plant one tree in front of each, we shall soon have a "forest city" of surpassing beauty.[145]

A utilitarian influence leading to support for public parks was the attraction of the spacious, landscaped cemeteries that, from the 1830's forward, became one of the admired features of American cities. By that time, urban congestion affected not only the living but the dead. Burial space was at a premium, as commercial expansion enveloped the narrow churchyards in the older cities; consequently, municipalities, private organizations, and churches began to acquire cemeteries on the outskirts. The form of these cemeteries was influenced by the romantic, naturalistic landscape design then in vogue. Indeed, Boston's Mount Auburn Cemetery was originally part of the gardens of the Massachusetts Horticultural Society. In the absence of public parks, these bucolic retreats

189

became resorts for the public, a circumstance that emphasized the need for large public parks and influenced their naturalistic style.[146] The distinguished landscape gardener, Andrew Jackson Downing, cited the popular appeal of these cemeteries in arguing for the provision in American cities of parks and public gardens such as furnished "salubrious and wholesome breathing spaces" in many cities of Europe, especially Germany. He proposed that parks be subsidized by joint-stock enterprise, gifts of philanthropic citizens, fairs and tea parties, a modest tax upon the community, or a small admission fee. He expressed these views in issues of the *Horticulturist,* of which he was editor at the time of his death in 1852.[147]

A. J. DOWNING ON PUBLIC PARKS
AND GARDENS: 1848

I am fully satisfied of the benefit of [public parks and gardens] . . . and of their being most completely adapted to our institutions. But how to achieve them? What do we find among us to warrant the belief that public parks, for instance, are within the means of our people? . . .

Several things: but most of all, the condition of our public *cemeteries* at the present moment. Why, twenty years ago, such a thing as an embellished, rural cemetery was unheard of in the United States; and at the present moment, we surpass all other nations in these beautiful resting places of the dead. Greenwood, Mount Auburn, and Laurel Hill, are . . . the only places in the country that can give an untravelled American any idea of the . . . public parks and gardens abroad. Judging from the crowds of people in carriages, and on foot, which I find constantly thronging Greenwood and Mount Auburn, I think it is plain enough how much our citizens, of all classes, would enjoy public parks on a similar scale. Indeed, the only drawback to these beautiful and highly kept cemeteries, to my taste, is the gala-day air of *recreation* they present. People seem to go there to enjoy themselves, and not to indulge in any serious recollections or regrets. Can you doubt that if our large towns had suburban pleasure-grounds, like Greenwood (excepting the monuments), where the best music could be heard daily, they would become the constant resort of citizens, or that being so, they would tend to soften and allay some of the feverish unrest of business which seems to have possession of most Americans, body and soul. . . .

Let our people once see for themselves the influence for good which it would effect, no less than the healthful enjoyment it will afford, and I feel confident that the taste for public pleasure-grounds, in the United States, will spread as rapidly as that for cemeteries has done. If my own observation of the effect of these places in Germany is worth anything, you may take my word for it that they will be better preachers of temperance than any temperance societies, better refiners of national manners than dancing-schools, and better promoters of good feeling than any lectures on the philosophy of happiness ever delivered in the lecture-room.[148]

Until public parks were proposed in Atlantic coast communities, the cities of the Middle West were no more concerned than their eastern sisters with providing open spaces for ornament and recreation, despite their greater availability of land. By 1851, however, St. Louis journalists were arguing for parks as an attraction to the city, especially in the summer months; and once New York projected its Central Park, newer cities, like Milwaukee, considered it essential to follow suit.[149] "Lungs" for the city was the expression used, a term that figured in 1852 in the annual message of L. M. Kennett, mayor of St. Louis, who took the view that a public park was a municipal obligation, essential to the image of a modern city.

"LUNGS" FOR ST. LOUIS: 1852

Last year, I deemed it my duty to urge upon the Council the necessity of purchasing a suitable site and the erection of a Town Hall worthy of the city. . . . We are authorized by charter to do so, as also to purchase parks and squares (*lungs*) for the city. . . . Perhaps the want of a large park in the city (which can now only be obtained at great expense), can best be supplied by a wide avenue or drive properly located just beyond the western limit. . . . This can now be done at a comparatively trifling expense, and would afford a breathing place of vast extent, which ere long will be on the border, if not actually within the limits of the city itself. I hope an effort will be made to effect this . . . and in the meantime, would urge [you] to purchase the ground of other public squares — if they can possibly be obtained — in the very heart of our present population. Nothing can be more necessary for the health and comfort, or add more to the beauty of the city. In every large town of the old world, and in the eastern portion of our country, they are considered as indispensable as light and water, and yet St. Louis, where land was once so cheap, has failed to possess herself of a park worthy of the name, or indeed of half a dozen open squares. Let us remedy this oversight to the extent of our ability.[150]

Frederick Law Olmsted's commitment to the development of public parks and to the planning of suburbs in the naturalistic style was based, as was that of Andrew J. Downing, on the need for tempering the city with the benefits of nature. Even more than Downing and the earlier proponents of bringing nature to the city, he believed that urban living was inevitable; and he saw the "strong drift townward" of the later 1860's as heralding a permanent change in American society. Olmsted regarded parks as an antidote for the deleterious aspects of urban living; and he believed that to serve this function they must be so designed as to simulate the natural, rural atmosphere of which city dwellers were being deprived. Since tracts of adequate size for large public parks were available only on the outskirts of existing cities, the problem of access to them led Olmsted to stress the need for city planning to provide not only parks but tree-lined highways, or parkways, throughout the city.[151] Boston was one of the many cities that solicited Olmsted's advice on park planning, and one of his most comprehensive plans for parks and parkways ultimately was carried out there. In an address delivered at the Lowell Institute in Boston, February 25, 1870, Olmsted reflected a philosophy of planning that comprehended not only design but social considerations.

FREDERICK LAW OLMSTED ON PARKS AND PARKWAYS AS A PALLIATIVE FOR URBAN ILLS: 1870

There can be no doubt . . . that, in all our modern civilization, . . . there is a strong drift townward. . . . It also appears to be nearly certain that the recent rapid enlargement of towns and withdrawal of people from rural conditions of living is the result mainly of circumstances of a permanent character. . . . Now, knowing that the average length of . . . life . . . in towns has been much less than in the country, and that the average amount of disease and misery and of vice and crime has been much greater in towns, this would be a very dark prospect for civilization, if it were not that modern Science has beyond all question determined many of the causes of the special evils by which men are afflicted in towns. . . . It has shown . . . that

. . . in the interior parts of large and closely built towns, a given quantity of air contains considerably less of the elements which we require to receive through the lungs than the air of the country . . . and that . . . it carries into the lungs highly corrupt and irritating matters, the action of which tends strongly to vitiate all our sources of vigor . . . and very seriously affect the mind and the moral strength. . . . People from the country are even conscious of the effect on their nerves and minds of the street contact — often complaining that they feel confused by it; and if we had no relief from it at all during our waking hours, we should all be conscious of suffering from it. It is upon our opportunities of relief from it, therefore, that not only our comfort in town life, but our ability to maintain a temperate, good-natured, and healthy state of mind, depends. . . .

Air is disinfected by sunlight and foliage. Foliage also acts mechanically to purify the air by screening it. Opportunity and inducement to escape at frequent intervals from the confined and vitiated air of the commercial quarter, and to supply the lungs with air screened and purified by trees, and recently acted upon by sunlight, together with opportunity and inducement to escape from conditions requiring vigilance, wariness, and activity toward other men — if these could be supplied economically, our problem would be solved. . . .

What I would ask is, whether we might not with economy make special provision in some of our streets — in a twentieth or a fiftieth part, if you please, of all — for trees to remain as a permanent furniture of the city? . . . If such [tree-lined] streets were made still broader in some parts, with spacious malls, the advantage would be increased. If each of them were . . . laid out with laterals and connections . . . to serve as a convenient trunk-line of communication between two large districts of the town or the business centre and the suburbs, a very great number of people might thus be placed every day under influences counteracting those with which we desire to contend. . . .

We come then to the question: what accommodations for recreation can we provide which shall be so agreeable and so accessible as to be efficiently attractive to the great body of citizens, and . . . also cause those who resort to them for pleasure to subject themselves . . . to conditions strongly counteractive to the special enervating conditions of the town? . . . If I ask myself where I have experienced the most complete gratification of [the gregarious and neighborly instinct] in public and out of doors, among trees, I find that it has been in the promenade of the Champs Elysees. As closely following it I should name other

193

promenades of Europe, and our own . . . New York parks. . . . I have several times seen fifty thousand people participating in them; and the more I have seen of them, the more highly [do] I . . . estimate their value as means of counteracting the evils of town life. . . .

If the great city . . . is to be laid out little by little, and chiefly to suit the views of land-owners, acting only individually, and thinking only of how what they do is to affect the value in the next week or the next year of the few lots that each may hold at the time, the opportunities of so obeying this inclination as at the same time to give the lungs a bath of pure sunny air, to give the mind a suggestion of rest from the devouring eagerness and intellectual strife of town life, will always be few to any, to many will amount to nothing. . . . We want a ground to which people may easily go after their day's work is done, and where they may stroll for an hour, seeing, hearing, and feeling nothing of the bustle and jar of the streets. . . . Practically, what we most want is a simple, broad, open space of clean greensward . . . as a central feature. We want depth of wood enough about it . . . to completely shut out the city from our landscapes. The word *park*, in town nomenclature, should, I think, be reserved for grounds of the character and purpose thus described. . . .

A park fairly well managed near a large town, will surely become a new centre of that town. With the determination of location, size, and boundaries should therefore be associated the duty of arranging new trunk routes of communication between it and the distant parts of the town existing and forecasted. . . . I hope you will agree with me that . . . reserves of ground for the purposes I have referred to should be fixed upon as soon as possible, before the difficulty of arranging them, which arises from private building, shall be greatly more formidable than now . . . for want of a little comprehensive and business-like foresight and study.[152]

10. CITY VS. COUNTRY

In accepting the "drift townward" as representing a permanent change in American life and in proposing means of coping with this development, Olmsted was contributing to a debate on the implications of urban growth and on the relative merits of city and country that had found continuous expression since the 1830's. In these years of burgeoning urbanism Americans found many reasons to criticize cities, but there was more pride in the growth of cities and more willingness to accept them, even among writers and publicists, than generally has been supposed. Emerson, for example, despite his devotion to nature and his belief that cities were unduly artificial and commercial, recognized their inevitability and the contribution they made to American culture. Like many Americans, in later years, he sought to have the advantages of both city and country, opting to live outside the large city but within range of its intellectual influence and seeking for his children both "rural strength and religion" and "city facility and polish." Men of letters like Hawthorne and Melville, though they often wrote disparagingly of cities, were stimulated as well as repelled by the "entangled life of many men together" in the bustling, if often sordid, urban scene.[153] Southerners apostrophized the rural existence to rationalize their way of life, but residents of the region also saw in cities the possibility of achieving sectional self-sufficiency. Cities were criticized for their physical squalor and for the threat they posed to basic American ideals, such as the "independent spirit" that "carried man into the country"; yet they were pervasively praised as giving evidence both of the nation's progress and of its conformity to a worldwide urbanizing trend.[154]

A sampling of contemporary responses to the "rush to the city" and the "sudden growth of towns," as expressed from the 1830's through the 1860's, reveals conflicting reactions to rapid urban growth but a prevailing tendency, by the mid-century, to accept cities, despite their shortcomings, as a fact of American life. Typical of early resistance to the urbanward trend — in the spirit of the oft-made observation that "God made the country, man the town" — is an article in an 1836 issue of *Knickerbocker* magazine, which, though it condemns the consequences of city living, indirectly suggests some of the reasons for the city's contemporary appeal.

CITY LIVING CRITICIZED: 1836

. . . great cities are not, to the mass of their inhabitants, favorable to the growth of virtue, and the consequent increase of human happiness. The stir, and noise, and excitement with which they are filled — the anxiety and care with which the mind appears to be loaded — is exhausting. . . . But in all this there is something exceedingly fascinating, particularly to the juvenile

195

mind — something that addresses itself so forcibly to the external senses, that few have the moral power and courage to resist its influence. . . . So much splendor and show dazzle the mind. . . . No wonder, then, that youth from the country are generally led astray by first impressions, on entering one of our large and crowded cities, and sigh to exchange their quiet and peaceful abodes for a residence amid the bustle and noise of the town. . . .

Beside the love of gain, which predominates universally in cities, pride and vanity spring up in rank luxuriance in these hotbeds of vice and immorality. . . . A citizen feels his consequence, and is apt to institute invidious comparisons between the town and country — to speak of the latter, its intellect, attainments, and manners — with supercilious contempt. Frequently we hear them boast of the superiority of their talents, the extent of their acquirements, and the polish of their manners. . . . Having risen from the dunghill, these fellows, like chanticleer, strut and crow, as if they were the legitimate lords and sovereigns of the earth. . . . The quiet of the country speaks to my ear a language far more intelligible.[155]

Less than twenty years later, a diametrically opposite view was advanced by the editor of *Harper's New Monthly Magazine*, who wrote that the city offered real opportunities the country could not match and that the charms of the countryside were most often voiced by city dwellers. He expressed these ideas in "The Editor's Easy Chair," in the issue of July, 1855.

CITY LIVING PRAISED: 1855

. . . it is plain that the great things in history have not been done in the country. The triumphs of literature, of art, and of general affairs, have always been achieved among the multitude of men. . . . But the real denizens of the country — . . . Can we truthfully say that their lives are more lofty, more noble, and inspiring than the life of the citizen? The country is Arcadian because it is unknown. . . . The statistics of the Insane Asylum show a proportionate majority from the country. The silence, the seclusion, the drudging toil, the long monotony of the year, the mental idleness, lead gradually to such results.

It certainly is not surprising that the chances of the city tempt a youth whose life in the country has been an unintermitted toil from dawn to dark, rewarded with a slight pittance. . . . The city, by its very artificial multiplicity of luxuries, offers a thousand chances for employment and success. If he has talent and ambition, he will surely burst away from the relentless tedium of potatoes and corn, and earn more money in an hour by writing a paragraph exhorting people to go and hoe corn and potatoes, than he would by hoeing them for a day. We are far from advising country boys to come to the city. Contentment and character, which are really better than fame or fortune, are quite as attainable in the country as in the city. But, as enterprising youths always will try the town, and as many of the most successful citizens were originally country boys, it is useless to deny that here is the great arena. If they fail, they may return, but the reader of newspapers and other poetical works should understand that the poetry of the country is only visible from the city.[156]

The persistence of contrasting opinions concerning large cities, as late as 1870, when they were becoming a recognized reality of American life, is seen in the divergent views of Mark Twain and Walt Whitman. Twain, in New York in 1867 as correspondent for *The Alta California* of San Francisco, found the magnitude and excitement of the city more nerve-racking than rewarding, its anonymity and variety no substitute for the friendliness of a river town or mining camp. On the other hand, it was the vibrant, multitudinous society of the large city that provided the fulfillment that Whitman found in New York and Brooklyn, on visiting them after an absence, in 1870.

CONTRASTING VIEWS OF THE LARGE CITY: MARK TWAIN AND WALT WHITMAN

Mark Twain [1867]. The only trouble about this town is, that it is too large. You cannot accomplish anything in the way of business, you cannot even pay a friendly call, without devoting a whole day to it. . . . The distances are too great. . . . You cannot ride . . . unless you are willing to go in a packed omnibus that labors, and plunges, and struggles along at the rate of three miles in four hours and a half, always getting left behind by fast walkers, and always apparently hopelessly tangled up with vehicles that are trying to get to some place or other and can't. Or, if you can stomach it, you can ride in a horse-car and stand up for three-quarters of an hour, in the midst of a file of men that extends from front to rear (seats all crammed of course,) — or you can take one of the platforms, if you please, but they are so crowded you will have to hang on by your eye-lashes and your toe-nails. . . .

. . . I have at last, after several months' experience, made up my mind that . . . [New York] is a splendid desert — a domed and steepled solitude, where a stranger is lonely in the midst of a million of his race. A man walks his tedious miles through the same interminable street every day, elbowing his way through a buzzing multitude of men, yet never seeing a familiar face, and never seeing a strange one the second time. . . . Every man seems to feel that he has got the duties of two lifetimes to accomplish in one, and so he rushes, rushes, rushes, and never has time to be companionable — never has any time at his disposal to fool away on matters which do not involve dollars and duty and business.

All this has a tendency to make the city-bred man impatient of interruption, suspicious of strangers, and fearful of being bored, and his business interfered with. The natural result is . . . the serene indifference of the New Yorker to everybody and everything without the pale of his private and individual circle.

There is something in this ceaseless buzz, and hurry, and bustle, that keeps a stranger in a state of unwholesome excitement all the time, and makes him restless and uneasy . . . a something which impels him to try to do everything, and yet permits him to do nothing. . . . A stranger feels unsatisfied, here, a good part of the time. He starts to a library; changes, and moves toward a theatre; changes again and thinks he will visit a friend; goes within a biscuit-toss of a picture-gallery, a billiard-room, a beer-cellar and a circus, in succession, and finally drifts home and to bed, without having really done anything or gone anywhere.

Walt Whitman [1870]. The splendor, picturesqueness, and oceanic amplitude and rush of these great cities, the . . . lofty new buildings, facades of marble and iron, of original grandeur and elegance of design, with the masses of gay color, the preponderance of white and blue, the flags flying, the endless ships, the tumultuous streets, Broadway, the heavy, low, musical roar, hardly ever intermitted, even at night; the jobbers' houses, the rich shops, the wharves, the great Central Park, and the Brooklyn Park of hills, . . . the assemblages of the citizens in their groups, conversations, trades, evening amusements . . . these, I say, and the like of these, completely satisfy my senses of power, fulness, motion, &c., and give me, through such senses . . . a continued exaltation and absolute fulfilment. Always and more and more

. . . I realize . . . that not Nature alone is great in her fields of
freedom and the open air, in her storms, the shows of night and
day, the mountains, forests, seas — but in the artificial, the work
of man too is equally great — in this profusion of teeming humanity — in these ingenuities, streets, goods, houses, ships —
these hurrying, feverish, electric crowds of men, their complicated
business genius, (not least among the geniuses,) and all this
mighty, many-threaded wealth and industry concentrated here.[157]

The decade of the 1860's is a benchmark in the history of
urbanism in the United States in terms of popular recognition of
both the drift of population cityward and the inevitability of large
cities in the American economy. In the half century since 1820,
the proportion of urban dwellers had increased from less than 10
per cent to more than a quarter of the total population. In 1820,
only three cities in the United States had exceeded 50,000 in population; New York, the largest, numbered less than 125,000. Fifty
years later, the New York City-Brooklyn metropolitan complex
totaled nearly a million and a half people, and eight other cities
had populations ranging from more than 215,000 to nearly 950,000.
A network of sizable cities stretched across the continent, constituting regional centers for mobilizing the economy and growing at
a rate such as to cause unprecedented interest and concern. In 1869,
E. L. Godkin of the *Nation* spoke for many of his contemporaries
when he called the influence of cities "now almost all-pervading"
and identified the "great city" question as one of the major problems
of American life.[158]

The nation's large cities now were assuming a form and presenting problems similar to those they were to exhibit only in greater
degree in the half century to follow. Already they were surrounded
by suburbs, made possible by transportation developments that at
the same time extended the cities' regional and national influence.
New "lofty" buildings, though not yet real skyscrapers, suggested
the vertical dimension that was increasingly to differentiate city
from country.[159] In terms of the intermingling of residence and
business structures and the diffusion of ethnic and racial groups
throughout the community, the cities of pre-Civil War America
were less spatially segregated and specialized than they were to become later; but already housing conditions in congested areas of the
large cities pointed up an increasing social stratification and seg-

mentation in the urban society. The department stores, theaters, libraries, and museums, increasingly available in the large cities, showed that here one could shop better, enjoy more varied entertainment, and find more cultural resources than in rural areas. The influence of the large cities outside their borders had so much effect that one commentator could assert in 1866 that in the cities of the United States one found "the real national life." [160]

In municipal government and politics one could see a beginning of more professional approaches to providing urban services, such as police, fire, and health protection. At the same time, the intensification of machine politics and "boss" rule, in part a response to the fragmentation of the large city, had set a pattern of municipal corruption that was to assume endemic proportions in the ensuing half century; those who resisted these developments were anticipating the stance of later reformers by criticizing the large city for its lack of community and by proposing changes in the structure of municipal government to minimize the influence of the newer elements in the urban society. So far, the prevailing philosophy of municipal government stemmed from the nation's private enterprise tradition;[161] but many city dwellers were beginning to realize that the environment of large cities raised problems compelling city governments to assume some responsibility for public health, housing, recreation, and the orderly development of the physical scene. In at least some quarters it was recognized that the imperatives of life in large urban centers required reconciliation of individual liberty with "the welfare of the community." [162]

Though many Americans saw the growth of large cities as potentially antithetical to the preservation of the nation's democratic tradition, and though the dialogue between proponents of country life and city residence continued, many thoughtful citizens took the view that the trend cityward was producing a permanent change to which they must adjust, for good or ill. There were those who believed that the metropolitan spirit now becoming manifest could transform cities through comprehensive planning to the point where they would contribute in social as well as economic and cultural terms to the enlargement of American life. One such optimist was the novelist and popular writer Leonard Kip, an important member of the Albany, New York cultural community, who envisioned cities so ordered, through the operation of an enlarged metropolitan spirit, as to ensure the comfort, convenience, and happiness of the increasing urban segment of American society, a development that promised to earn cities as respected a place in the American tradition as farms. He expressed these views in an article entitled "The Building of Cities," which appeared in a family magazine, *Hours at Home*, in July, 1870.[163]

THE CITY OF THE FUTURE — AN 1870 VIEW

As a habit, we of the Western Continent have not always hitherto been accustomed to pride ourselves over much upon our cities, or upon the abstract attractions of our city life. . . . But of late years, a more metropolitan taste is evidently controlling us, and we are gradually losing that olden spirit of contempt for city life and scenes. . . . In fact, we are beginning slowly to understand . . . that uncleanliness, inordinate disproportion of crime, and a dingy absence of beauty, are not of themselves the necessary concomitants of city life, but are rather mere unholy parasites which long neglect has allowed to cluster around it; and that it is possible, with good management, to retain the advantages afforded by large massing of population, and not necessarily to assume its disadvantages also. . . . We are losing that shamefacedness with which we were wont to speak disparagingly of the city as brick and mortar, and the hypocrisy with which we affected to gloat over country freedom. . . . Men who have made fortunes and wish to retire upon them are now as prone to seek metropolitan life as formerly they were to build their country villas. . . . Yearly the [cityward] current enlarges. Some may lament the fact, and . . . undertake to prove that it is the commencement . . . of natural degeneracy and corruption. Still the great fact remains; and in view of it we must accept it cordially and look around to see how to make the most of it, — how the swelling cities . . . can be made, by fulfilling all their destiny and exerting all their capacity for improvement, to increase the comfort and happiness of those who seek their shelter, — and how, in equal measure, they can attract new crowds of willing subjects within their borders. . . .

There is indeed no policy so mistaken as that of desiring a city to be made up relentlessly of square blocks and air-line avenues. . . . Looking upon such a city as a whole, it can scarcely fail to be dispiriting with its regularity. . . . We are daily told that our streets should be better paved and our wharves improved, — our lighting conducted upon more liberal principles, — our public buildings constructed with more economy and taste. . . . [Now] we should awaken to the necessity of liberal expenditure in promoting the comfort and elegance of our cities. . . . We all know . . . to what a pitch of magnificence Paris has attained by reason of concerted effort, and how abundantly the increasing wealth of the Imperial city is sufficing to meet even the immense debt thus created. And we have evidences that the force of its example is infecting other European cities with similar zeal for improvement, so that in every direction the great capitals are laying out avenues and parks, and turning insignificant lanes into broad boulevards. Only in America does the public temper seem to falter and fail to catch the spirit of the times.

It is true that we do a little something. . . . A street is widened here, or a public park laid out there, — and so far it is all very well. But the trouble is, that these efforts are mere disorganized fragments of what should constitute a great, comprehensive design, to be prosecuted with force and energy as a whole. . . . Since calculations must be made, is there no way of causing the people to understand that a calmly digested plan and a liberal expenditure for instant, elaborate, and widespread improvement is the most far-sighted economy that could be adopted? . . .

Having our cities laid out and fully built upon, then comes the question of their beautifying and adornment. . . . To many persons the question of civic decoration is a novel one, for it seems to them that when clean, straight streets are laid out and lined with costly buildings, and all such mere matters of comfort, convenience, and easy intercourse attended to, the whole thing is finished. They cannot comprehend that in every city there are waste places which should be made pleasant, and that there must always be, here and there, quiet corners which should be turned into bowers of beauty . . . by contrast with the angular and more artificial surroundings. . . .

In some respects, indeed, we have improved upon the cities of the last generation. Looking back upon them with a critical eye, we can now see that there was little in them to attract. Even in the best streets we can remember only ill-built jumbles of shabby brick houses, with here and there one carried up to four stories to excite our complacent admiration; rough cobble-stone pavements, and clumsy wooden awning-posts lining the sidewalks. . . . In a material aspect there is a great stride in the present appearance of our cities. . . . But to the truly metropolitan spirit it is only just begun. Prophetically we can look forward and see the picture as it will be spread out twenty years hence . . . the business portions of our cities almost entirely rebuilt, and with magnificence,

— underground railways affording new facilities for intercourse, — beautiful bridges spanning the rivers, — perfectly systematized drainage, paving, and lighting, . . . galleries and museums to vie with those of Europe, — and every public square a bower of loveliness, with its wealth of flowers, statuary, and fountains. This . . . is for any city no far-off prospect . . . ; it is the natural result, to be . . . taken as a matter of right, if the true, enlarged metropolitan spirit is properly cultivated throughout the country. . . . Then perhaps, the long-standing jealousy between town and country may die out, never to be renewed; since each will be recognized as holding its separate place, to which the other should not hope to aspire.[164]

PART THREE

URBAN EXPANSION 1870-1920

In the half century between 1870 and 1920 the American city came of age in the sense that by 1920 urban dwellers constituted a majority of the population and that city governments were assuming responsibilities that connoted a social maturity rarely anticipated 50 years earlier. The intensity of urbanism was greatest in the industrial states of New England and the Middle Atlantic area. By 1920 the populations of Massachusetts and Rhode Island were more than 90 per cent urban, and in New York and New Jersey as many as eight out of every ten residents lived in communities of 2,500 or more. But by 1920 every section of the nation had a sizable urban component. In the upper Middle West the proportion of urban dwellers had increased from 20 to more than 50 per cent of the total population; on the Pacific coast, cities accounted for more than 57 per cent of the combined populations of California, Oregon, and Washington. Even in the traditionally rural South, the proportion of city dwellers increased from one-tenth to one-quarter of the total population in these years. When Oklahoma finally was opened to settlement in April, 1889, the "Sooners" raced in to create cities as well as farms, and communities like Guthrie, Oklahoma, took urban form almost overnight.

But it was the growth of large cities, especially in the more recently settled parts of the country, that seemed to symbolize the nature and magnitude of the nation's increasing urbanism by the later nineteenth century. In 1870 only New York City had a population of more than 750,000 although the combined populations of New York and Brooklyn then constituted a metropolitan unit of twice that number. The federal census used the categories of suburb and metropolitan district for the first time, in 1880, for New York City only. By 1910, however, the census identified metropolitan growth in other parts of the country. It then recognized 25 metropolitan units ranging in size from the New York metropolitan district (including Newark) of 6,500,000 people to the Portland, Oregon, metropolitan district with a population of about 215,000. By 1920, the United States had seven cities of more than 750,000 people and 11 metropolitan clusters of that size or larger. By then, New York City's metropolitan area numbered nearly 8,000,000 people; Chicago's included more than 3,000,000; Philadelphia's, nearly 2,500,000; and those of Boston, Detroit, and Pittsburgh, in excess of 1,000,000. In the Midwest and Far West, Los Angeles, Minneapolis, Seattle, Portland, Denver, Omaha, and

Oakland, California, attained big-city status; the rapid growth of Birmingham, Dallas, and Houston symbolized the proliferation of big cities in the South.

The magnetism of the large city was evident as early as 1871 to a midwestern editor who wrote that contemporaries seemed to prefer to be "the most insignificant member of some great community than a very important member of a small one. . . . Better be the 1/1,000,000,000 of New York than the 1/1 of Aroostook County." To economist Edmund J. James, writing in 1899, the increase in the number of cities with populations of 200,000 and more made the later nineteenth century "not only the age of cities, but the age of great cities." [1] Tables 3.1 and 3.2, based on census data, reveal the expansion of urbanism in all sections of the country between 1870 and 1920 and the growth of big cities not only in the Northeast and upper Middle West but in the South and Far West as well. The figures in Table 3.1 represent the percentages of urban dwellers in the total population of the States.

Table 3.1

URBAN GROWTH BY STATE AND SECTION: 1870–1920[2]

	1870	1880	1890	1900	1910	1920
United States	25.7	28.2	35.1	39.7	45.7	51.2
New England						
Maine	21.0	22.6	28.1	33.5	35.3	39.0
New Hampshire	26.2	30.0	39.3	46.7	51.8	56.2
Massachusetts	66.7	74.7	82.0	86.0	89.0	90.0
Rhode Island	74.6	82.0	85.3	88.3	91.0	91.9
Connecticut	33.0	41.9	50.9	59.9	65.6	67.8
Vermont	6.9	10.0	15.2	22.1	27.8	31.2
Middle Atlantic						
New York	50.0	56.4	65.1	72.9	78.9	82.7
New Jersey	43.7	54.4	62.6	70.6	76.4	79.9
Pennsylvania	37.3	41.6	48.6	54.7	60.4	65.1
South Atlantic						
Delaware	24.7	33.4	42.2	46.4	48.0	54.2
Maryland	37.8	40.2	47.6	49.8	50.8	60.0
District of Columbia	91.6	90.0	100.0	100.0	100.0	100.0
Virginia	11.9	12.5	17.1	18.3	23.1	29.2
West Virginia	8.1	8.7	10.7	13.1	18.7	25.2
North Carolina	3.4	3.9	7.2	9.9	14.4	19.2

Table 3.1 (Cont.)

	1870	1880	1890	1900	1910	1920
South Atlantic (cont.)						
South Carolina	8.6	7.5	10.1	12.8	14.8	17.5
Georgia	8.4	9.4	14.0	15.6	20.6	25.1
Florida	8.1	10.0	19.8	20.3	29.1	36.5
North Central						
Ohio	25.6	32.2	41.1	48.1	55.9	63.8
Indiana	14.7	19.5	26.9	34.3	42.4	50.6
Illinois	23.5	30.6	44.9	54.3	61.7	67.9
Missouri	25.0	25.2	32.0	36.3	42.3	46.6
Michigan	20.1	24.8	34.9	39.3	47.2	61.1
Wisconsin	19.6	24.1	33.2	38.2	43.0	47.3
Iowa	13.1	15.2	21.2	25.6	30.6	36.4
Minnesota	16.1	19.1	33.8	34.1	41.0	44.1
Kansas	14.2	10.5	18.9	22.4	29.1	34.8
Nebraska	18.0	13.6	27.4	23.7	26.1	31.3
North Dakota	—	a	8.2	10.2	13.1	16.0
South Dakota	—	a	5.6	7.3	11.0	13.6
South Central						
Kentucky	14.8	15.2	19.2	21.8	24.3	26.2
Tennessee	7.5	7.5	13.5	16.2	20.2	26.1
Alabama	6.3	5.4	10.1	11.9	17.3	21.7
Mississippi	4.0	3.1	5.4	7.7	11.5	13.4
Arkansas	2.6	4.0	6.5	8.5	12.9	16.6
Louisiana	27.9	25.5	25.4	26.5	30.0	34.9
Texas	6.7	9.2	15.6	17.1	24.1	32.4
Oklahoma	—	—	3.7	7.4	19.2	26.5
Mountain						
Montana	15.1	17.8	27.1	34.7	35.5	31.3
Idaho	—	—	—	6.2	21.5	27.6
Wyoming	—	29.6	34.3	28.8	29.6	29.4
Colorado	11.9	31.4	45.0	48.3	50.3	48.2
New Mexico	5.2	5.5	6.2	14.0	14.2	18.0
Arizona	33.4	17.3	9.4	15.9	31.0	36.1
Utah	18.4	23.4	35.7	38.1	46.3	48.0
Nevada	16.6	31.1	33.8	17.0	16.3	19.7
Pacific						
Washington	—	9.5	35.6	40.8	53.0	54.8
Oregon	9.1	14.8	27.9	32.2	45.6	49.8
California	37.2	42.9	48.6	52.3	61.8	67.9

a That part of Dakota Territory which later became North and South Dakota was 7.3 per cent urban in 1880.

1. FRONT RUNNERS IN URBAN GROWTH

The nation's advancing urbanism was a subject of popular interest throughout the half century from 1870 to 1920, but the growth of large cities attracted special attention in the late 1870's and 1880's, when they experienced spectacular population increases, and again around 1920, when the census disclosed that the United States had become predominantly urban. In the 1880's, attention was focused especially on cities that benefited from the settlement and exploitation of the trans-Mississippi West and from new developments in the post-Civil War South. No city had more news value, in terms of its growth, than Chicago, whose rise from the ashes of a great fire was one of the marvels of the urban development of the time. Chicago increased in population (in part through annexations) from about 300,000 in 1870 to more than 2,700,000 in 1920. A feature article on the Midwest metropolis, written by A. A. Hayes for an 1880 issue of *Harper's New Monthly Magazine,* described the vigor of its contemporary economy and stressed the bearing of contacts with a rich and rapidly developing hinterland upon its economic growth.

CHICAGO, "METROPOLIS OF THE PRAIRIES": 1880

"The metropolis of the Northwest. . . ," I hear a resident of Chicago say. . . . Call it what we may, it is assuredly one of the wonders of the world, in its rapid growth, in its recovery from disaster, in its greatness today, and in its prospects for the future. New York and Boston, about 250 years old, have respectively 1,000,000 and 350,000 inhabitants. Chicago made up her half million in little over forty years. . . .

If the fire [in October, 1871] was a remarkable episode in the history of Chicago, what shall be said of its rising from the ashes, of the marvellous rebuilding of the city, of the work of only about eight years? It is estimated that some $41,000,000 were spent in new buildings on the burned district in the twelve months after the fire. Chicago is the very phoenix of cities. . . .

On the south, near the lake shore, and again on the north side, are two distinct dwelling quarters of a very high class, and calculated to astonish all who have not seen them. The ample space secured around dwellings — so rare in Eastern cities — is of itself an immense attraction . . . [and] to the system of parks and

Table 3.2

POPULATION GROWTH OF REPRESENTATIVE CITIES
BY SECTION: 1870–1920[3]

	1870	1880	1890	1900	1910	1920
New England						
Boston	250,526	362,839	448,477	560,892	670,585	748,060
Lowell	40,928	59,475	77,696	94,969	106,294	112,759
Providence	68,904	104,857	132,146	175,597	224,326	237,595
New Haven	50,840	62,882	86,045	108,027	133,605	162,537
Worcester	41,105	58,291	84,655	118,421	145,986	179,754
Middle Atlantic						
New York	942,292	1,164,673	1,441,216	3,437,202	4,766,883	5,620,048
Brooklyn	419,921	599,495	838,547	In N.Y.C.	In N.Y.C.	In N.Y.C.
Rochester	62,386	89,366	133,896	162,608	218,149	295,750
Buffalo	117,714	155,134	255,664	352,387	423,715	506,775
Newark	105,059	136,508	181,830	246,070	347,469	414,524
Jersey City	82,546	120,722	163,003	206,433	267,779	298,103
Philadelphia	674,022	847,170	1,046,964	1,293,697	1,549,008	1,823,779
Pittsburgh	139,256	235,071	343,904	451,512	533,905	588,343
South Atlantic						
Baltimore	267,354	332,313	434,439	508,957	558,485	733,826
Washington	109,199	147,293	188,932	278,718	331,069	437,571
Richmond	51,038	63,600	81,388	85,050	127,628	171,667
Durham, N.C.	—	2,041	5,485	6,679	18,241	21,719
Charlotte, N.C.	4,473	7,094	11,557	18,091	34,014	46,338
Charleston	48,956	49,984	54,955	55,807	58,833	67,957
Savannah	28,235	30,709	43,189	54,244	65,064	83,252
Atlanta	21,789	37,409	65,533	89,872	154,839	200,616

North Central						
Cincinnati	216,239	255,139	296,908	325,902	363,591	401,247
Cleveland	92,829	160,146	261,353	381,768	560,663	796,841
Detroit	79,577	116,340	205,876	285,704	465,766	993,678
Milwaukee	71,440	115,587	204,468	285,315	373,857	457,147
Chicago	298,977	503,185	1,099,850	1,698,575	2,185,283	2,701,705
St. Louis	310,864	350,518	451,770	575,238	687,029	772,897
Kansas City, Mo.	32,260	55,785	132,716	163,752	248,381	324,410
Wichita, Kans.	—	4,911	23,853	24,671	52,450	72,217
Omaha	16,083	30,518	140,452	102,555	124,096	191,601
Minneapolis	13,066	46,887	164,738	202,718	301,408	380,582
South Central						
Mobile	32,034	29,132	31,076	38,469	51,521	60,777
Birmingham	—	3,086	26,178	38,415	132,685	178,806
New Orleans	191,418	216,090	242,039	287,104	339,075	387,219
Memphis	40,226	33,592	64,495	102,320	131,105	162,351
Nashville	25,865	43,350	76,168	80,865	110,364	118,342
Louisville	100,753	123,758	161,129	204,731	223,928	234,891
Houston	9,382	16,513	27,557	44,633	78,800	138,276
Dallas	—	10,358	38,067	42,638	92,104	158,976
Mountain						
Denver	4,759	35,629	106,713	133,859	213,381	256,491
Salt Lake City	12,854	20,768	44,843	53,531	92,777	118,110
Pacific						
Los Angeles	5,728	11,183	50,395	102,479	319,198	576,673
San Francisco	149,473	233,959	298,997	342,782	416,912	506,676
Portland, Ore.	8,293	17,577	46,385	90,426	207,214	258,288
Seattle	1,107	3,533	42,837	80,671	237,194	315,312

connecting boulevards . . . too much praise cannot be accorded. . . .

Of the strides which Chicago has made in commerce and manufactures, it is difficult to convey any idea in words. . . . Chicago is an enormous grain market. . . . In the year 1879 there were brought into the city, of flour, 3,370,000 barrels; of wheat, corn, oats, rye, and barley, 122,533,000 bushels. And it is curious to learn that all came by rail except 36,000 barrels of flour and 339,000 bushels of grain by the lake, and 42,000 barrels of flour and 6,479,000 bushels of grain by the canal, thus showing what the iron roads have done for the city.

A glance at the map will show to what dimensions has grown the system of [rail]roads connecting Chicago with the region west and north of it. . . . The ten miles built toward Elgin in 1847–48 were the beginning of the Chicago and Northwestern Railway. Its ramifications now extend to Milwaukee and Lake Superior; to Minneapolis and St. Paul, and away to Watertown, in Dakota Territory; and to the Missouri at Council Bluffs, opposite Omaha. The Illinois Central extends to Cairo, with a line thence, and practically its own, to New Orleans; also to Dubuque, Iowa, and Sioux City. The Chicago, Rock Island, and Pacific gives a line to Atchison and Leavenworth, and a second to Council Bluffs. The Chicago, Burlington, and Quincy extends to Burlington, Council Bluffs again, Plattsmouth, Kearny Junction (on the Union Pacific Railroad), and other points in Nebraska; to Quincy and Louisiana, with connection for Kansas City and Topeka; and to St. Louis. The Chicago and Alton has lines to Kansas City and St. Louis. Over the roads just mentioned, and their almost innumerable branches, come most of the cereals. In connection with the great Eastern roads, they make up a body of lines which, hardly thirty years old, is simply a marvel. . . .

It is, indeed, strange to think that Chicago — this young inland city — is the primary market for a large part of the food supply not only of this country, but also of Europe. . . . Our Western domain is so vast, our Western soil so fertile, and our Western population so industrious and enterprising, that this food can be produced there more cheaply than by the dwellers in the overcrowded countries of the Old World. . . . To receive such an incoming stream are waiting twenty elevators. . . . Their aggregate capacity is 16,840,000 bushels. . . .

Suppose that you walk down to the Board of Trade Building just before noon. There is a large room . . . quiet enough up to noon; but then — well, take the New York Stock Exchange when "the bottom is dropping out" of stocks, and a panic is impending; multiply the excitement several times, substitute the shrillest and hardest voices . . . for the more tempered ones of New York — and even then you will not have a fair idea of the hour for "dealing." Yet there is a very pronounced method in all this mid-day madness. These apparently crazy people are only buying and selling the grain which you saw in the elevator. . . . All the world are customers here. . . .

Among the great interests of Chicago the business in pine lumber occupies a prominent place. How necessary this article is in the building up of the West he knows well who has traversed it. . . . What a market for lumber this admirably situated city can command may be readily seen. . . . By sailing vessels and steamers the lumber is brought to Chicago. In this business are employed over $80,000,000 (several times the aggregate capital of all the city banks), and between 7000 and 10,000 men. . . . In the attempt to give an idea of the extent of the Chicago lumber trade . . . it may help . . . to mention that . . . if a number of canal-boats, each containing one-eighth of a million feet, were loaded with the importation of 1879, and placed in line in the Erie Canal, they would reach, touching end to end, from Albany to Rochester — three hundred miles. In early days, doors, sashes, and blinds were shipped from the East to the little town at Fort Dearborn. *Nous avons changé tout cela*, and with a vengeance! The writer saw the cars, at a large Chicago factory, loading not only for Denver, Leadville, Santa Fe, and Salt Lake City, but — tell it not in New England — for Connecticut as well.

Another enterprise which has brought wealth to Chicago is the stock business. It is of vast importance and of astounding dimensions. The Union Stock-Yards are situated near the southern limit of the city, and surpass anything of the kind elsewhere. Hither came, in 1879, 1,216,000 head of cattle, 6,539,000 hogs, 325,000 sheep. . . . The writer walked through lanes dividing up some *twelve acres* of dressed pork belonging to one firm, and standing higher than his head. . . .

. A very important . . . industry in Chicago is the manufacture of all things pertaining to the fittings of railways, and of other articles which can be made by the same machinery. . . . There are other manufacturers far too numerous to mention. There is an establishment for making soap, double the size of any in Europe, and probably the largest in the world, which sends its products over the entire globe. There are five iron and steel works; manufactories of carriages; great breweries; agricultural implement works; and very many other industrial establishments. No one can visit Chicago without being strongly impressed with the curious reversal, growing more marked every day, of the old order of things. To what extent the city will ultimately supply the rest of the country and the world with the articles formerly furnished by them to her it is quite impossible to predict.

The shops are large, and contain extensive and varied stocks. . . . Churches, institutions of learning, and libraries abound. . . . Music is much cultivated. . . . Besides the Illinois Humane Society, there are similar organizations for the prevention of cruelty to children and the suppression of vice. The Chicago Literary Club is a most useful and interesting institution. It holds regular meetings, at which papers, often learned and abstruse, are read and discussed. . . . The undertaking by busy citizens of work of this kind, the interest taken in the Historical Society, the large and increasing demand for books, and the collection of pictures and works of art, are notable and gratifying signs of the times. They show not only that progress in culture which comes with years, but an exceptional movement in that direction, due to the growing conviction among the men who have built up the city and their own fortunes at the same time that they will live longer and happier lives if they devote more of their time than in days past to other than mere material interests.[4]

The new and enterprising quality of Atlanta by 1880 made it the focus of interest as a symbol of urban development in the post-Civil War "New South." Though Atlanta in 1880 was nowhere near the size of Chicago, the speed of its recovery from destruction — in this instance the consequences of war — and its role as a railroad-implemented distribution center gave the two cities points of similarity. Though the South still lagged behind the other sections in terms of urban growth, the expansion of its railroad network and a new emphasis on manufacturing after the war encouraged the growth of the older cities and the rise of new ones like Birmingham, Alabama, and Durham and Charlotte, North Carolina. However, as late as 1920 the South had only nine cities exceeding 100,000 in population. New Orleans was still the largest, with a population of 387,219; next in size came Louisville (234,891) and Atlanta (200,616). Atlanta's approximation to the national pattern of urbanism in 1879, when its population was still under 40,000, was described by Ernest Ingersoll in *Harper's New Monthly Magazine*, for December, 1879.

ATLANTA, "CHICAGO OF THE SOUTH": 1879

Those who have spoken of [Atlanta] as the "Chicago of the South," appear to have struck not very wide of the mark. Forty years ago there was nothing at all here. . . . How, then, did Atlanta come to exist at all; and, much more, how did she succeed, like the goddess whose name she suggests, in outstripping all her older sisters, Augusta, Savannah, Macon, and the rest? The answer is found in one word — railways.

Atlanta is a "fiat" town, and was put where she is by act of Legislature rather than by the natural course of events. . . . Here [in 1835] right out in the woods, it was resolved to begin the "State" railway north to the Tennessee line, and the spot naturally came to be known as "Terminus." . . . Patience fails to recount the growth of the settlement into a village, and the expansion of the village into the city which now calls itself a metropolis. . . . It was supposed at first that the town would be built some distance west of its present position, and money was invested in that region. Then a shrewd land-owner gave the site of the present Union passenger station, which was accepted by the railroads, bringing the centre of growth in the town over to that spot. Thus money was lost and made, but the city increased in population . . . educated the country people, became enterprising, and . . . took to herself city-like ways and pride, and asserted herself to be the gate to the South, through which all commerce and emigration from the Northwest must pass. . . .

So, deriving her success from a multitude of business advantages, and from her favorable situation in point of geography and climate, Atlanta has waxed great and powerful. . . . All the evidences of busy life are around you, and only unless you are fresh from New York or Baltimore or Chicago do you notice the provincial air. The telegraph pole at your elbow bears the little red box that carries the electric fire-alarm to ever-ready steamers and ladder trucks; the lamp-post serves as standard for the mail drop-letter box; and a policeman in full uniform will assist you into a street car for any part of the city, if you need the help of the "force." There are banks, and boards of trade, and business exchanges, and all the rest of the list of "modern conveniences," from artificial ice to a Turkish bath or a complete system of telephonic communication. Yet, however comfortable this is for the citizen, it . . . makes Atlanta too much like a hundred other large towns with which we are all acquainted in the North, and leaves less that is peculiar, characteristic, and picturesque than perhaps exists in any other city in the South. . . .

To the stranger's eye the city itself presents few marks of that tide of war which . . . surged so destructively across its whole area. There are ruins in the suburbs of what were once stately mansions [but] . . . the city itself has been rebuilt, and the houses that survived the shelling are already becoming dignified with historical interest. . . . It was in 1865 that the citizens and merchants came back to their desolate homes. . . . Business had to be built up from the very foundation again, and the energy with which this task was attempted shows the strong faith Atlanta men feel in their lively town. . . . By mutual help and enterprise, together with a vast amount of personal labor, the ruins were replaced by substantial business edifices, new hotels of magnificent proportions were erected, churches more lofty in gable and spire arose upon the sites of those destroyed, and the vacant streets were refilled with people.

Atlanta became at once the distributing point for Western products, and now finds tributary to her a wide range of country. She handles a large portion of all the grain of Tennessee and Kentucky, besides much from the Upper Mississippi Valley. Much of the flour of the Northwestern mills comes into her warehouses, and thence finds its way southward and eastward. The same is true of the canned meats of Chicago, St. Louis, and Cincinnati packing houses: this is a very important item of her wholesale business. The provision men naturally were the first to obtain foothold in the new town. After them came the dry-goods people. Most of them began in a very modest way — brought their goods tied up in a blanket almost — yet now the jobbing trade in dry-goods alone amounts to some millions of dollars annually. No tobacco can be grown in the vicinity of Atlanta, hence she is without tobacco factories; but she used to handle an enormous quantity of it, and there are half a dozen firms who deal wholly in it now. . . .

Another source of prosperity to the city is cotton. The "cotton belt" of Georgia is a strip of country between here and Augusta. Years ago the land became exhausted, and the cultivation of cotton came to be of small account. Then followed the discovery of the guano islands of Peru, and the subsequent invention of artificial fertilizers. . . . It was proved that by their use the worn-out cotton belt could be made to produce as bountiful crops . . . as the Mississippi bottoms did; and, moreover, that cotton could be raised as far north as the foot of the Tennessee mountains. Atlanta, therefore, has come to be not only a great dépôt of supply for this guano, furnishing its vicinage a hundred thousand tons a year, but also the entrepôt of all the cotton produced within a circle of nearly two hundred miles. This cotton is bought mainly for foreign export, and is shipped under through bills of lading to foreign ports, thus dodging the factors at New York, Savannah, and other coast cities. . . . There are other extensive business interests. Iron is mined near by, and extensive foundries and rolling-mills manufacture it. Great crops of corn and grain are raised throughout the central part of the State, which find their way into Atlanta distilleries, while her wine-merchants are many and rich. . . .

To view the town itself, let me commend a ride along the new "boulevard" on the eastern edge [from which] the solid squares of the city's business houses, the lofty proportions of her great hostelries, the scores of spires of her handsome churches and school-houses, and the charming, foliage-hidden avenues of her dwelling-places and suburbs — all appear to the best advantage. . . . Atlanta boasts, undoubtedly upon a firm basis of facts, that she offers the best educational privileges to her citizens of any community, large or small, south of "the line." Unless Richmond, Virginia, be excepted, this is true. Atlanta has a complete system of graded and high schools, and they are fully attended. Then there are two or three commercial colleges, two "universities" for colored pupils who desire more than a common-school education, two medical colleges, and an instructive display of the geological and agricultural resources of the State at the State-house. . . . The Library is self-supporting, contains some thousands of well-selected and, what is more, well-read volumes, has chess-rooms and reading-rooms attached, and is a matter of just pride and comfort to the town.[5]

But it was the emergence of large cities as well as thriving towns and villages in the more recently settled West that, by the later 1880's, seemed the most remarkable aspect of the nation's accelerating urbanism. Contemporaries marveled at Minneapolis and St. Paul, cities of close to 150,000 people, whose location at the "gateway to an empire" helped to explain their imposing business blocks, palatial residences, impressive railway offices, towering flour mills, and "vast wholesale dry-goods and grocery houses." They praised Kansas City — "wonderful town" — for "refinements of living" that were underwritten by the city's financial and commercial relations with the "rich agricultural regions to the west and southwest." They lauded Denver — "Queen City of the Plains" — for "wide, shaded, and attractive-looking streets, handsome residences surrounded by spacious grounds, noble public buildings, and the many luxuries of city life" — excellences it had gained in less than 25 years in its role as the "natural concentrator" of economic activities in a developing "new country." [6] In the 20 years from 1870 to 1890, when farmers made their rapid occupation of the Great Plains, Kansas City grew in population from 32,260 to 132,716; Denver increased in numbers from 4,559 to 106,713; and Omaha, another "natural concentrator" in this expansive rural area, from 16,083 to 140,452.

Some commentators found the smaller cities of the plains equally impressive evidence of the pervasiveness of urban development and of the speed, often accelerated by eastern capital, with which fully implemented urbanism was emerging on the agricultural frontier in the later nineteenth century. Writing in an 1888 issue of *Harper's New Monthly Magazine*, feature writer Frank Spearman described the up-to-date urbanism of these smaller new communities that had blossomed in what was still thought of as the "Great American Desert."

URBANISM ON THE PLAINS: 1888

Reflecting more perfectly the substantial development of the new West than the great centres [like Omaha, Kansas City, and Wichita] are the well-built, bright, and attractive inland towns of Nebraska, Dakota, and Kansas, cities . . . ranging from 3000 to 15,000 inhabitants. There are so many of these in the desert that it is almost a pity to single out a few for mention; but out of many of at least equal merit let us glance at Hastings, Nebraska, a town fifteen years old, with a population of 15,000 intelligent, enterprising, and prosperous people, possessed of all the conveniences of city life, such as gas and electric light, waterworks, street-cars, and a free mail delivery; its streets lined with blocks of handsome brick structures; a centre of heavy financial and industrial interests; its homes representing all that is modern and progressive in architecture. How surprised one would be, who has not seen this country for five years, at the towns numbered by the score in Dakota, Kansas, and Nebraska which rival in every respect the most prosperous towns in New York and New England. . . . Or look at McCook, Nebraska, one of the newest and farthest west of all desert towns — an infant of five years, for there was nothing but a sod house five years ago where the town of 3000 is now, . . . possessing everything necessary in the line of churches, schools, and social advantages to make anyone content with a habitation in the desert, and whose founders had confidence enough in its future to supply it with a system of water-works equal in extent to that of Lincoln.[7]

Not all the seeds of urbanism planted in this predominantly rural region produced lasting cities. Here, as earlier in the Mississippi Valley, townsite speculation projected many an abortive urban center that failed to survive the "paper" stage; activities peculiar to the opening of this "last" West supported transient cities that flourished only until settlement and exploitation of the region entered a new phase. Such transience was typical of the construction towns associated with laying the railroad network on the plains and of the mining towns whose life span often depended on the magnitude of a "strike." Though some of these towns became permanent centers of trade and manufacturing, many disappeared once their purpose had been served. The particular qualities of such transient towns are illustrated by the experience of Benton, Nebraska, a temporary terminus of the Union Pacific, 700 miles from Omaha. J. H. Beadle, western correspondent of *The Cincinnati Commercial*, described its brief, prefabricated existence in 1868.

MUSHROOM TOWNS OF THE PLAINS AND MOUNTAIN WEST: 1868

Here had sprung up in two weeks, as if by the touch of Aladdin's Lamp, a city of three thousand people; there were regular squares arranged into five wards, a city government of mayor and aldermen, a daily paper, and a volume of ordinances for the public health. It was the end of the freight and passenger, and beginning of the construction, division; twice every day immense trains arrived and departed, and stages left for Utah, Montana, and Idaho; all the goods formerly hauled across the plains came here by rail and were reshipped, and for ten hours daily the streets were thronged with motley crowds of railroad men, Mexicans and Indians, gamblers, "cappers," and saloon-keepers, merchants, miners, and mule-whackers. . . . Twenty-three saloons paid license to the evanescent corporation, and five dance-houses amused our elegant leisure. . . .

The great institution of Benton was the "Big Tent," sometimes, with equal truth but less politeness, called the "Gamblers'

Tent." This structure was a nice frame, a hundred feet long and forty feet wide, covered with canvass and conveniently floored for dancing, to which and gambling it was entirely devoted. It was moved successively to all the mushroom terminus "cities." . . . To look on Benton, a motley collection of log and canvass tents, one would have sworn that there was no trade; but in those canvass tents, immense sums changed hands. E. Block & Co., Wholesale Dealers in Liquors and Tobacco . . . did a business of $30,000 a month. Others did far better. . . . Transactions in real estate in all these towns were, of course, most uncertain; and everything that looked solid was a sham. Red brick fronts, brown stone fronts, and stuccoed walls, were found to have been made to order and shipped in (pine) sections. Ready made houses were finally sent out in lots, boxed, marked, and numbered; half a dozen men could erect a block in a day, and two boys with screw-drivers put up a "habitable dwelling" in three hours. A very good graystone stucco front, with plain sides, twenty by forty tent, could be had for $300; and if your business happened to desert you, or the town moved on, you only had to take your store to pieces, ship it on a platform car to the next city, and set up again. . . .

An army officer told me that he went up the Platte Valley . . . and observed a piece of rising ground near the junction of the two streams, where for miles not a live shrub or a blade of grass was to be seen. Six months after he returned and the "Great and Growing City of the Platte" covered the site; three thousand people made the desert hum with business and pleasure; there were fine hotels, elegant restaurants, and billiard halls and saloons, while a hundred merchants jostled each other through banks and insurance offices. All the machinery of society was in easy operation; there were two daily papers, a Mayor and a Common Council, an aristocracy and a common people, with old settlers, new comers, and first families. Six months after he returned and hunted for the site. A few piles of straw and brick, with debris of oyster cans nearly covered by the shifting sands, alone enabled him to find it. The "city" had got up and emigrated to the next terminus.[8]

The Kansas cattle towns had an element of transience, for their prosperity often depended on a particular exploitation of the plains prevailing before establishment of farms interrupted the northward drives of Texas cattle. These cattle drives toward railhead markets or northern ranges took place from the later 1860's to the mid-1880's. Abilene, Ellsworth, Newton, and Wichita flourished successively as cattle-trading centers while they were the terminal points of railroads on which cattle could be shipped eastward. The last of the Kansas cattle towns was Dodge City, which claimed the title of "Cowboy Capital" from 1873 until a quarantine law in the mid-1880's pushed the cattle trails west to the Kansas-Colorado border. Dodge City was laid out in 1872 as the temporary terminus of the Atchison, Topeka, and Santa Fe Railroad. Its transient population, during the years of the cattle drives, gave it a reputation for lawlessness that the facts did not warrant, though it contributed to that aspect of the legend of the American West.[9] The relationship of the cattle drives to its early economy may be seen in newspaper reports for 1877, collected by Robert M. Wright, president of the company that created the town.

DODGE CITY — KANSAS CATTLE TOWN: 1877

Abilene, Ellsworth, and Hays City on the Kansas Pacific Railroad, then Newton and Wichita, and now Dodge City on the Atchison, Topeka & Santa Fe road, have all, in their turn, enjoyed the "boil and bubble, toil [and] trouble" of the Texas cattle trade. Three hundred and sixty-seven miles west from Kansas City we step off at Dodge, slumbering as yet in the tranquil stillness of a May morning. In this respect Dodge is peculiar. She awakes from her slumbers about eleven, A.M., takes her sugar and lemon at twelve M., a square meal at one P.M., commences biz at two o'clock, gets lively at four, and at ten it is hip-hip-hurrah! till five in the morning. Not being a full-fledged Dodgeite, we breakfasted . . . at nine o'clock, and meandered around until we found ourselves on top of the new and handsome courthouse. A lovely prairie landscape was here spread out before us. . . . As far as the eye could reach, for miles up the [Arkansas] river and past the city, the bright green velvety carpet was dotted by thousands of long-horns which have, in the last few days, arrived, after months of travel, some of them from beyond the Rio Grande. . . .

Dodge City has now about twelve hundred inhabitants — residents we mean, for there is a daily population of twice that many; six or seven large general stores, the largest of which, Rath and Wright, does a quarter of a million retail trade in a year; and the usual complement of drug stores, bakers, butchers, blacksmiths, etc.; and last, but not by any means the least, nineteen saloons — no little ten-by-twelves, but seventy-five to one hundred feet long, glittering with paint and mirrors, and some of them paying one hundred dollars per month for the naked room. . . .

This being my first visit to the metropolis of the West, we were very pleasantly surprised, after the cock and bull stories that lunatic correspondents had given the public. Not a man was swinging from a telegraph pole; not a pistol was fired; no disturbance of any kind was noted. . . . The Texas cattlemen and cowboys, instead of being armed to the teeth, with blood in their eye, conduct themselves with propriety, many of them being thorough gentlemen.

Dodge City is supported principally by the immense cattle trade that is carried on here. During the season that has just now fairly opened, not less than two hundred thousand head will find a market here, and there are nearly a hundred purchasers who make their headquarters here during the season. . . . From our window in the Dodge House, which by the way, is one of the best and most commodious in the west, can be seen five herds, ranging from one thousand to ten thousand each, that are awaiting transportation. The stock yards here are the largest west of St. Louis.[10]

By the late nineteenth century, urbanism was far more prevalent on the Pacific coast than in the plains and mountain West. A combination of the seaports, which early attracted traders, the urban background of many participants in the mining rushes, and the need of terminals for the transcontinental railroads encouraged the growth of sizable cities in California, Washington, and even Oregon. As early as the 1870's, San Francisco, benefiting from its connection with the first transcontinental railroad, the discovery of the Comstock Lode, the expansion of industry, and the activities of the San Francisco Stock Exchange, dominated an economic empire reaching from the Pacific Ocean to the Rocky Mountains. These developments produced a group of men who amassed large fortunes and whose ostentatious life style displayed the aspirations to urbanity of the California metropolis.[11] San Francisco doubled in population between 1870 and 1890; by 1920 it numbered half a million. The American novelist, William Henry Bishop, who visited the city in 1882, was surprised to find not a mining camp but a cosmopolitan city cut to the national mold.

COSMOPOLITAN SAN FRANCISCO: 1882

How strange it is, arriving from the other side of the world, to find the line of people waiting for us at the edge of the dock, all dressed in the usual way, and chattering in the familiar speech, even to the latest bit of current slang. . . . This remarkable young city, which had eight hundred and fifty people in 1848, twenty thousand in '49, has now, after an existence of thirty-four years, three hundred thousand. . . . We live in an age of expeditious movement and labor-saving inventions, and with unlimited means such as are here enjoyed the work of years is condensed into months. Camp it is none, but a solid luxurious city. . . .

The San Francisco householder, and the Croesus particularly, has "a station like the herald Mercury new-lighted on a heaven-kissing hill." How in the world, I have asked, does he get up there? Well, then, by the cable roads. . . . It is a peculiar kind of tramway . . . invented expressly for the purpose of overcoming steep elevations. Two cars, coupled together, are seen moving, at a high rate of speed, without . . . ostensible means of locomotion. . . . The solution of the mystery is in an endless wire cable hidden in a box in the road-bed, and turning over a great wheel in an engine-house at the top of the hill. . . .

The great houses on the hill, like almost all the residences of the city, are found to be of wood. . . . The fact is attributed to the superior warmth and dryness of wood over brick or stone in a moist, cool climate, and also to its greater security against earthquakes. Whatever the reasons, the San Francisco Croesuses have reared for themselves palaces which might be swept off by a breath. . . . They are large, rather over-ornate, and of no particular style. The Hopkins residence, which is a costly Gothic château, carried out, like the rest, in wood, may be excepted from this description. . . .

San Francisco has to offer among its other advantages that of saving a trip around the world; that is to say, whoever has seen Europe, and shirks further wanderings, may derive from the compact Chinese city of 30,000 souls, which makes a part of this, such an idea of the life and aspect of things in the Celestial Empire as will act as a considerable alleviation of curiosity. The Chinese immigrants . . . have rarely erected buildings of their own. They have fitted themselves into what they have found. . . . With all their peculiar industries, their smells of tobacco and cooking-oil, their red and yellow signs, their opium pipes, high-soled slipper shoes, sticks of India ink, silver pens, and packets of face-powder in the windows, their fruits and fish, their curious groceries and more curious butcher's-meat — they have fitted all this into the Yankee buildings, and taken such absolute possession of them that it is no longer America, but Shanghai or Hong Kong. The restaurants make the nearest approach to having a national façade, but this is brought about by adding highly decorated balconies, with lanterns and inscriptions, instead of building anew. . . .

The Italian community is numerous. The part of it which remains on shore [since many are fishermen] is largely grocers, butchers, and restaurateurs. . . . The French colony is also numerous, and their language heard upon the street continually. . . . A considerable Mexican and Spanish contingent mingles with the Italians along Upper Dupont, Vallejo, and Green streets. A Mexican military company, as at Los Angeles, marches with the red, white, and green tricolor on the anniversary of the national independence in September. . . . The Latin race especially seems to have sought the place. . . . But German and Scandinavian names upon the sign-boards, the Russian Ivanovich and Abramovich, and Hungarian Harasthy, show that no one blood or influence has exclusive sway.[12]

So great was the interest in cities by the late 1870's that the compilers of the federal census of 1880 undertook for the first time to identify the dimension of American society that was urban as distinct from rural. They classified as urban all persons living in incorporated communities of 8,000 or more people — a formula that had been used as early as 1874 by the economist and statistician Dr. Francis Walker in his *Statistical Atlas of the United States*. This formula was altered in 1906, when the minimum population for classification as urban was set at 2,500; this standard of measurement prevailed until the Census of 1940. The changes in size criteria reflect the difficulty of defining urban status and measuring the growth of urbanism. The authors of the Census of 1880 attempted to grapple with these problems in a special section on cities, the first in the history of the census.

THE DIFFICULTY OF DEFINING URBANISM: 1880

We meet . . . at the outset of this discussion with several difficulties. For instance: What constitutes a city? In most of the states there is no doubt on this point. All dense bodies of population, of any considerable magnitude, have municipal charters. The entire population of every city is urban; consequently, the line can be sharply drawn. In several of the older states, however, we find dense bodies of population combined with outlying rural settlements under one government. This is the case in several of the townships in the neighborhood of Chicago, Illinois, and around other centers in the prairie states, and in New York, New Jersey, and Pennsylvania. It is in the New England states, however, that we meet with the greatest difficulty, for here . . . a so-called "town," which is to all intents and purposes a township, may comprise a population of 10,000 or 15,000 or even more, and consist of one or more dense bodies of population, with a scattering rural population also included under the town government. . . .

Again, at several natural centers there are, or in the past have been, groups of cities, one of which is commonly much larger than any other, . . . all of which, while legally distinct, might be regarded as constituting a true unit of residence and industry. Shall these be taken separately in our account or aggregated, in disregard of merely political divisions? . . . Nor is it always clear what is to be regarded as the unit of residence and industry. While it is generally true that the small cities which surround a great one owe their importance and even existence, to it, and therefore that in annexing them it is simply claiming its own, there are instances of cities being closely coterminous, each having a clear *raison d'être* of its own; while in more than one case the limits of the modern city embrace the sites of at least two distinct centers of population and trade. . . . It will need to be borne in mind . . . that while the determination of new centers of residence and industry in the unceasing growth of population has constantly tended to increase the number of cities known to the census, there has been a movement, far less considerable and very irregular, in the other direction, viz, to a reduction of the number of cities through annexation and consolidation.[13]

The findings of the Census of 1920, the first to disclose that the United States was predominantly urban, made city growth momentarily as newsworthy as it had been in the 1880's and attracted attention to the front runners among the nation's largest cities, in percentage of population increase and absolute population growth in the decade from 1910 to 1920. The front runners in percentage of population growth were Detroit (113 per cent), Los

Angeles (80 per cent), and Cleveland (42 per cent) — all beneficiaries of the expansion of new industries — and Baltimore (31 per cent), which owed much of its increase to the annexation of neighboring territory. For absolute population increase during this decade, New York City was first, with an increase of 853,165. Together, the five cities represent the pervasiveness of large-city growth throughout the nation in the post-Civil War years.

The automobile and the motion picture were important underwriters of the phenomenal growth of Detroit and Los Angeles. Detroit could take advantage of the demand for the horseless carriage because of its proximity to the raw materials of production, its availability of labor, its good location for distribution, and the promotional expertise of its specialists in automobile construction. The growth of Los Angeles was the result of the combined influence of technology, transportation, and local promotion. The Southern Pacific Railroad arrived in 1876, induced by the community's purchase of $600,000 in railroad bonds. Promotional activities of the Chamber of Commerce after 1888 publicized an allegedly healthful climate; engineering developments ensured the city an adequate water supply; and by the early twentieth century the motion picture industry was contributing in a significant way to the city's image and economy. Los Angeles grew from a population of fewer than 6,000 in 1870 to nearly 600,000 by 1920. New York City's population increase derived from many factors, not the least of which, according to one commentator, was "the infallible law of 'them as has gits.' " In the summer of 1920, *The Sun and New York Herald* attempted to discover the reasons for the phenomenal population growth of the nation's large cities. Some of its findings were reported in *The Literary Digest* later in the year.

FRONT RUNNERS IN POPULATION GROWTH: 1920

Detroit, with a numerical increase greater than any other city except New York, claims a large portion of the census spotlight by reason of being the only city of more than a hundred thousand population that doubled in numbers during the past ten years. . . . In the last twenty years . . . Detroit has quadrupled in population. . . . Of course the festive if malodorous gasoline-car is responsible for Detroit's unprecedented leap in population from 465,766 to 993,739, or 113.4 per cent. She is said to furnish 70 per cent. of the world's motor-vehicles. . . .

Thousands of workers from all parts of the country flocked to Detroit because of the high wages her industries were paying. . . . She claims that her accessibility to the steel, copper, and coal regions by virtue of her water outlets and elaborate rail centers helped her grow. Her motor-car and allied industries absorb about half of her working men and women. . . .

An inquisitive newspaper recently wired a Los Angeles patriot and asked how it was that the population of the movie center of the world had increased from 319,198 to 575,480, or more than eighty per cent., during the last ten years. A brief reply was the result, contained in "several crimson and gold booklets, a dozen circular letters, twenty newspapers, three volumes of scenery, two city guide-books, a 200-page volume having to do with climate, twenty-seven letters from real estate firms, six motor-car catalogs, two volumes of California verse, a song-book, and a photograph of a citron-tree." There wasn't a word about the movies, but the patriot . . . summarized the situation by saying that Los Angeles's growth might be attributed to increased industries, foreign trade, the open-shop policy, development of natural resources, and the benefits of a perfect climate. . . .

Cleveland . . . reports that her growth from 560,663 to 796,836 in ten years is due to "more automobile-factories, more and larger iron and steel manufactures, and a city government willing to go all the way to get desirable businesses to Cleveland." . . . Baltimore jumped 31.4 per cent. in ten years, and were you not to investigate you might be inclined to say that Baltimore had been deceiving folk and adopting some of those crass and vulgar methods that may be quite all right for Middle-West upstarts, but not to be tolerated where dignity lives and nice decorum is its own reward. In 1910 Baltimore had 558,485, and now she contains 733,826 residents. She did most of it by annexation. By absorbing surrounding towns and manufacturing localities she gained 100,000. And a majority of these places were war-born and now have been converted into peace-products producers. The city proper added a little more than seventy thousand to herself. . . .

New York grows because it is New York — the greatest commercial center, the greatest amusement center; because of the infallible law of "them as has gits"; because, and in many cases, unfortunately, immigration arrives in New York and stays in New York, dazzled by its size and wealth and high wages; because being the great seaport, that which the rest of America produces comes to New York for distribution.

New York grows naturally because her business is vaster and

therefore presents opportunity for a greater number of persons. She is the art center of the New World, and because she is so huge, so rich, so mysterious, prospective immigrants in the darkest and furthermost pockets of the Old World know only of New York — have heard of no other place than New York, and to New York they come to take what they can get and get everything they can. And then to New York come the young folk of the small town. They come in vast numbers because the old home town is small, limited in opportunity as they see it, and because someone has told them that more money is to be made with less effort in New York.

Recall the days of your own youth. Did the magazine story with Detroit or Chicago or even San Francisco intrigue you so much as the yarn that began something like this: "Eustace stood at the window transfixt. Two hundred feet beneath him Broadway was drawing on her evening wrap. A million lights jeweled the Great White Way, and a million people were scurrying." [14]

2. WHY CITIES GREW

The increasing concentration of population in cities and especially in large cities was primarily a consequence of the industrialization of the United States, which had begun to accelerate by 1860, and of the nature of the technological changes that went along with and encouraged that industrialization. The mechanization of farming, together with the existence of railroads to move crops to distant markets, made it possible for fewer hands to feed more people. The nation's railroad network, which reached its peak of growth in this half century, became increasingly effective as iron rails were replaced by steel and as the use of more powerful locomotives and heavier stock permitted increased speed and the long haul of bulk goods. Coal could now effectively be moved to centralized manufacturing locations where its use for industrial production was supplemented, in the 1880's, by the availability of central-station electric power. This reliance on rail transport and centralized power encouraged the concentration of manufacturing in large centers with good rail connections, as did the presumed multiplier effect, in such aggregations of population and industrial activity, of a ready consumer market, an available labor pool, and the proximity of related production and servicing facilities.

To these basic economic factors were added other situations explaining city growth in this half century when the large city had a stronger appeal than at any other time in the nation's urban experience. One was the promotional activity of aggressive individuals and groups who were able, given the existence of new facilities, to reach widely beyond the city's boundaries for control of raw materials and markets, and to lure industrial enterprises from smaller centers. Another was the attraction of the city as a place to live at a time when the difference between country and city in potential standard of living was greater than ever before in American history. Significant, too, is the existence of a pool of potential city dwellers created by the phenomenal upsurge in immigration from Europe during these years.

Contemporaries, attempting to explain the magnitude of urban growth, emphasized the economic factors that encouraged this realization of what they considered a natural tendency, in society, toward urban living. As early as 1878, B. C. Magie, writing in *Scribner's Monthly*, attributed the "social revolution" implicit in contemporary urban growth to the working of a natural law, by which population concentrated in cities to the extent that farm machinery and the railroad facilitated the release of food producers from the land. "To create a larger proportion of men who *can* live in cities," he wrote, "it is only necessary to enable the producers of food to obtain a larger supply from the same land with less human labor, that is, by improved machinery." [15] A similar emphasis on material and natural factors was expressed by Josiah Strong, Congregational clergyman and exponent of the "social gospel," who, twenty years later, was attempting to explain the marked increase in city population. He stated his views in an article, "The Problem of the Twentieth Century City," which appeared in *The North American Review* in 1897, and in a book, *The Twentieth Century City*, published in 1898.

MATERIAL REASONS FOR THE URBAN DRIFT

The accelerated rate of growth of the city in modern times . . . is due primarily to three causes: 1) The application of machinery to agriculture, which enables four men to do the work formerly done by fourteen; 2) the rise of manufactures in the cities, which attracts the men released from the farms, and 3) the railway, which not only makes the transfer of population easy, but, which is more important, makes it possible to feed a massed population, no matter how vast.

There is a gregarious instinct in men, which has always made the city as large as it could well be; and these three causes have liberated and emphasized this instinct during this century. As this instinct and these causes are all permanent, it is obvious that this tendency will prove permanent.

Some have imagined that the pressure upon the city might be relieved . . . by removing families to unoccupied lands and teaching them to engage in agriculture. . . . But those who expect to solve or even to simplify the problem by this method fail to appreciate the profound change which has come over the world's industry during this century, by which it has ceased to be individual and has become organized. . . . It has separated as by an impassable gulf the simple, homespun, individualistic life of the world's past from the complex, closely associated life of the present and the world's future. . . .

The greater part of our population must live in cities — cities much greater than the world has yet seen — cities which by their preponderance of numbers and of wealth must inevitably control civilization and destiny; and we must learn — though we have not yet learned — to live in cities with safety to our health, our morals, and our liberties.[16]

To Henry J. Fletcher, writing in *The Forum* in 1895, the migration of manufacturing to populous centers of production at a time when the state of technology encouraged concentration was the key factor in fostering the accumulation of population in large cities. Though this resulted, in his opinion, in an "excessive massing of people," he admitted that there was "no resisting the trend" — it operated like a law of nature against which the country and the lesser towns "contend in vain."

CONCENTRATION OF PRODUCTION AND EXCHANGE, A CAUSE OF LARGE-CITY GROWTH

Doubtless the chief cause of this remarkable concentration is the natural superiority . . . of large centres for all the processes of production and exchange. Here the manufacturer and the jobber come into direct contact with their customers. The retailer finds all the different articles needed to replenish his stock. Competition between producers raises the quality of goods while lowering prices, buyers are attracted by the great variety offered, and thus all the makers of a given article find it to their advantage to get together, and the greater the market the more powerfully it attracts both buyer and seller. Cheap freights and passenger fares, improved postal and telegraph service, and all the devices to facilitate business between distant places, help the movement.

I have talked with many persons who, as managers or owners of manufacturing or jobbing concerns, followed the current and removed their business to larger cities. Each had a special reason, applicable either to the nature of his business or the local conditions prevailing in the town whence he came. The Western cities have not been content to await the natural process of accretion; commercial organizations and real-estate syndicates have done the most active missionary work, and a great many manufacturers have been induced to leave the country towns, tempted by large "bonuses" of cash, land, and buildings. . . . In the case of Minneapolis, the development of Minnesota and the Dakotas has induced the transfer to that city of many producers in order to be nearer to the consumers, but in nearly every case the removal has been at the expense of some smaller town. The great mills, like those of Minneapolis, can produce flour more economically than any small mill however well equipped, and can sell it at a smaller margin of profit. . . . Chicago, with its suburbs, has swallowed the factories and workshops and workpeople of villages and minor cities within a radius of many hundred miles. Multitudes flock to the cities because the drift is that way, because business is dull in the villages, often without any distinct analysis of reasons, but in reality because production and exchange, in so far as it is not by its nature local, is being rapidly removed thither.[17]

The momentum of city growth certainly was heightened by the organized efforts of promotional groups such as real estate boards, chambers of commerce, merchants' and manufacturers' associations, and boards of trade, aided and abetted by the local press. By the 1880's, the emphasis was upon attracting manufacturers. This was the aim, for example, of the Association for the Advancement of Milwaukee, organized in the late 1880's, on the pattern of a promotional agency in Kansas City. Supporting the efforts of the Milwaukee organization to induce new enterprises to settle there by the provision of free rent, free sites, and the subscription of local capital, *The Evening Wisconsin* argued: "The manufactories should be urged to come; we should go out and compel them to come in. Thus other manufacturing cities are doing with 'results profitable to themselves." [18] Typical of such promotional efforts during the 1870's and 1880's were the activities of the Manufacturers' and Real Estate Exchange of Indianapolis and the Indianapolis Board of Trade. In 1874, the Exchange distributed a 16-page brochure, that included an open letter to potential incoming industries.

PROMOTING INDIANAPOLIS: 1870's AND 1880's

Rooms of the Manufacturers' and Real Estate Exchange,
No. 92 East Market Street, Indianapolis, Ind., 1874.
Dear Sir:

Permit us to call your attention to the accompanying pamphlet, setting forth the advantages of Indianapolis as a place favorable for manufactures, commerce and business interests of all kinds. A careful perusal will, we think, convince you, that the several subjects here made prominent have been mostly hitherto overlooked by persons at a distance.

In order to promote the highest development of the whole country, it is important to disseminate a knowledge of facts, as they exist in various localities. In the more densely populated portions of the United States, it is with great difficulty that fortunes are made, and, in many cases, a bare subsistence is all that can be expected. The great West, through this little book, would utter a loud call to thousands of such persons, saying, Come out hither, and be convinced, that labor here will be rewarded with the highest success. The means and the materials are all provided. Nothing is wanting but active brains, willing hands, and, of course, sufficient capital to carry on enterprises of merit — and INDIANAPOLIS will yet take rank among the leading cities of the world.

Read for yourself, and having done so, circulate the book among your neighbors — among the young enterprising men of your acquaintance, who are just asking: Where shall we locate to commence life most advantageously?

If your impressions are favorable towards a removal to this place, please inform us by letter, as we think there are other considerations of a personal nature, which can be adduced, to bring you to an affirmative decision. . . .

G. S. Wright, Secretary
A. L. Roache, President

THE FOLLOWING POINTS OF ADVANTAGE ARE POSSESSED BY INDIANAPOLIS (1874)

1. It is the most centrally located city in the United States.
2. It is the nucleus of the greatest net-work of railroads in the world.
3. It is near the point of the funnel through which the whole west and south-west cattle trade must pass on its way east.
4. It is near the center of the corn belt of the United States.
5. This, with the climate, gives it great advantage in pork packing.
6. Through Indianapolis is the shortest route for the transportation to the eastern cities of all the agricultural products of the great Mississippi Valley.
7. The numerous competing trunk lines of railroads give superior advantages for freights, making it one of the best wholesale centers in the west.
8. Near Indianapolis are inexhaustible deposits of a superior quality of coal which can be delivered in the city for steam purposes at 6 to 8 cents per bushel, and which makes as good iron as charcoal, without coking.
9. There are vast deposits of iron within a few miles of the city, which will largely take the place of Lake Superior ore.
10. It is in the center of a timbered region which is unsurpassed in the world for quality, variety and quantity. . . .
13. Indiana has the largest school fund of any State in the Union, and Indianapolis has fully availed herself of the advantage.
14. The city debt is less than 1½ per cent. of the taxables.
15. The entire State, county, township and city tax is only $1.76 on the $100.
16. It is claimed that statistics show that Indianapolis has the lowest death rate of *any city in the United States.*

G. S. Wright, Secretary, Manufacturers' and Real Estate Exchange.

A brochure published in 1889 summarized some of the achievements of the Board of Trade's promotional effort.

The Industries of the City of Indianapolis: the Advantages Offered for Business Location and the Investment of Capital. Published under the Auspices of the Indianapolis Board of Trade (1889). . . . The growth of the [jobbing] business is attested by the rapid increase in the number of houses thus engaged. . . . Since [1876], the houses have become numerous, now numbering more than two hundred travelers and making total sales which in 1888 aggregated $38,430,000. . . . When the jobbing trade was first undertaken by merchants of Indianapolis, the business now controlled from here was in the hands of merchants of other cities, principally Chicago and Cincinnati. Much of this territory has been gradually acquired by Indianapolis. . . . Beginning with a territory of the most limited dimensions, the jobbing trade of Indianapolis now controls the State, portions of Illinois, Ohio, Michigan, Kentucky, as far south as Tennessee, besides in special lines considerable territory west of the Missouri River. . . . And . . . there are yet fields for enterprise that might be advantageously occupied. The opportunities for openings are worthy the attention and investigation of capitalists seeking investment for their money, and every encouragement and aid will be offered new comers, by citizens and the Board of Trade. . . .

The location of Indianapolis, in the center of a rich agricultural country, near to supplies of iron, wood, stone, coal, etc., possessing unsurpassed transportation accommodations, supplied with an abundance of the best quality of coal, available to consumers at the lowest prices, the distributing point for natural gas, which will be furnished to industries free, with other conveniences and appointments, make the city one of unlimited advantages for manufacturing purposes. There are still openings in this city for men of enterprise and capital to engage in the manufacture of articles, the production of which is hardly sufficient to equal the demand. . . . No city in the United States offers more flattering inducements for factory sites than Indianapolis. . . . Citizens have encouraged investment of this character, and will not only welcome the advent of manufacturing enterprises but will substantially aid all ventures proposed in such connection by the donation of land and other means at their disposal.[19]

In addition to the economic realities that encouraged urban growth, the appeal of the city as a place to live contributed significantly to its magnetism in the years from 1870 to 1920. In this half century the difference in standard of comfort and enjoyment between city and farm was greater than in any period before or since. E. L. Godkin, writing in *The Nation* in 1869, saw a puzzling phenomenon in the increasing tendency of native Americans, despite continuing praise of rural living, "to abandon the country and crowd into the towns to engage in trade and manufactures." Newspaper writers and poets were busily extolling the delights of the agricultural life, he wrote, "but the farmer, though he reads their articles and poems, quits the farm as soon as he can find any other way of making a livelihood; and if he does not, his son does." [20] Edward Everett Hale, alluding to the libraries, art galleries, and hospitals for special diseases available in big cities, asserted in 1888 that it was an "absurd mistake" to talk about cities as "great sores. . . . There is every reason to think that high civilization demands large cities, and does not exist without them." [21] Many contemporaries took the view that a life in which "both the city and the country have a part" (now possible through improved transportation) was the ideal; but the superior virtues of city living were increasingly asserted. One forum for this argument was the American Social Service Association, whose president, Frederick J. Kingsbury, Connecticut banker, industrialist, and amateur historian, expressed the case for city living in his presidential address, "The Tendency of Men to Live in Cities," delivered in 1895.

THE ADVANTAGES OF CITY LIVING: 1895

Aside from . . . industrial convenience, doubtless one of the very strongest of forces in the building of the city is the human instinct of gregariousness. . . . There is always a craving to get where there are more people. The countryman, boy or girl, longs for the village, the villager for the larger town, and the dweller in the larger town for the great city; and, having once gone, they are seldom satisfied to return to a place of less size. . . . As long ago as 1870 Mr. Frederick Law Olmsted, in a paper read before this Association, said, "There can be no doubt that in all our modern civilization . . . there is a strong drift townward"; and he quotes the language of an intelligent woman, whose early life had been spent in one of the most agreeable and convenient farming countries in the United States: "If I were offered a deed of the best farm I ever saw, on condition of going back to the country to live, I would not take it. I would rather face starvation in town." . . .

Doubtless one of the most potent factors in the modern growth of cities has been the immense improvement in the facilities for travel, which . . . make it as easy to get from city to country as from country to city; but the tide, except for temporary purposes, all sets one way. Nevertheless, there is no question that this ease of locomotion has been availed of to a surprising extent in transporting each year in the summer season a very large portion, not of the rich alone, but of nearly every class, not only from our great cities, but from our moderately large towns, to the woods and lakes and seashore for a time . . . and this fact is a great alleviation and antidote to some of the unfavorable influences of city life. . . .

If you will examine any city newspaper of fifty or sixty years ago, you will find frequent advertisements for boys as clerks in stores; and almost always they read "one from the country preferred." Now you never see this. Why is it? I think mainly because the class of boys which these advertisements were expected to attract from the country are no longer there. This was really a call for the well-educated boys of the well-to-do farmers of native stock, who thought they could better themselves by going to a city. They went, and did better themselves; and those who stayed behind fell behind. The country people deteriorated, and the country boy was no longer for business purposes the equal of the boy who had been trained in city ways. . . .

We must remember, too, that cities as places of human habitation have vastly improved within half a century. About fifty years ago neither New York nor Boston had public water, and very few of our cities had either water or gas, and horse railroads had not been thought of. When we stop to think what this really means in sanitary matters, it seems to me that the increase of cities is no longer a matter of surprise. . . . [Moreover], it must be noticed that it is always in cities that those who can afford it get the best food; and, if you are living in the country, you are largely dependent on the city for your supply. . . . It is also only in great cities, as a rule, that the best medical skill can be obtained. There we all go . . . to have our most serious diseases treated and our most critical surgical operations performed. It is almost wholly owing to the unsanitary condition among the children of the very poor that the city death-rate is so high. Mr. C. F. Wingate, in a paper read here in 1885, quotes Dr. Sargent as saying that "life in towns is, on the whole, more healthful than in the country." . . .

[In addition, citing the Reverend Dr. Greer], "There is more . . . in common village life to lower and degrade and demoralize than in the city. Take the matter of amusements in the city. There are good ones, and we can make a choice. In the country one cannot make a choice. If a theatrical company comes to a village, it is a poor company. If a concert is given, it is a poor concert. . . . Then, again, there is a loneliness, an isolation, in the country life; and this tends to lower and depreciate that life. I believe statistics show that a large contingent of the insane in our asylums come from the farms. That hard drudgery of struggle with the clod and the soil from early morning to evening twilight is a lonely and bitter struggle." . . .

The country is a good place to rest in, especially if one can control his surroundings. . . . But the tranquil appearance of a country town, the apparent simplicity and serenity of rural life, the sweet idyllic harmony of rural surroundings, are, as every one must know who has much experience, very deceptive. . . . The small jealousies and rivalries, the ambitions, bickerings and strifes of a small rural community, are greatly intensified by the circumscribed area in which they find their vent, and compared with the same human frailties in a larger sphere have all the drawbacks of temper in a cart. Mr. (Lacon) Colton says: "If you would be known, and not know, vegetate in a village. If you would know, and not be known, live in a city." [22]

The prevailing preference for city living is reflected in, as it was to some degree caused by, the concern with big cities in contemporary fiction and drama. William Dean Howells, Stephen Crane, Frank Norris, Abraham Cahan, and Theodore Dreiser found the settings and themes of their novels in the great cities of their day — evidence of the current preoccupation with the city; and their works were outnumbered by scores of books dealing in popular — even sensational — fashion with the excitement and opportunity cities offered. Who knows how many youths were lured from country homes by the attractions of the city (indeed the acquaintance they gained with it) as described and implied in the many books by Horatio Alger dealing with city themes? Ragged Dick, the prototype of Alger's youthful heroes, expressed the excitement associated in these years with life in cities and the identification of the city with a kind of opportunity and fulfillment once, but no longer, associated with the farm. Alger's *Ragged Dick; or, Street Life in New York*, published in 1868, not only provided a running description of New York City, whetting the appetite of the curious, but expressed the cocky, self-assured outlook of the city boy, schooled in the city streets, who with perseverance, hard work, and more than a little bit of luck could win "fame and fortune" in the big city.

RAGGED DICK SHOWS A COUNTRY BOY
THE BIG CITY

The boys crossed to the West side of Broadway, and walked slowly up the street. To Frank [a lad from the country] it was a very interesting spectacle. Accustomed to the quiet of the country, there was something fascinating in the crowds of people thronging the sidewalks, and the great variety of vehicles constantly passing and repassing in the street. Then again the shop-windows with their multifarious contents interested and amused him, and he was constantly checking Dick to look at some well-stocked window.

"I don't see how so many shopkeepers can find people enough to buy of them," he said. "We haven't got but two stores in our village, and Broadway seems to be full of them."

"Yes," said Dick; "and its pretty much the same in the avenoos, 'specially the Third, Sixth, and Eighth avenoos. The Bowery, too, is a great place for shoppin'. There everybody sells cheaper'n anybody else, and nobody pretends to make no profit on their goods."

"Where's Barnum's Museum?" asked Frank.

"Oh, that's down nearly opposite the Astor House," said Dick. "Didn't you see a great building with lots of flags?"

"Yes."

"Well, that's Barnum's. That's where the Happy Family live, and the lions, and bears, and curiosities generally. It's a tip-top place. . . . It's most as good as the Old Bowery, only the plays isn't quite so excitin'."

"I'll go if I get time," said Frank. "There is a boy at home who came to New York a month ago, and went to Barnum's, and has been talking about it ever since." . . .

"What building is that?" asked Frank, pointing to a structure several rods back from the street. . . .

"That is the New York Hospital," said Dick. "They're a rich institution, and take care of sick people on very reasonable terms."

"Did you ever go in there?"

"Yes," said Dick; "there was a friend of mine, Johnny Mullen, he was a newsboy, got run over by a omnibus as he was crossin' Broadway down near Park Place. He was carried to the Hospital, and me and some of his friends paid his board while he was there. It was only three dollars a week, which was very cheap, considerin' all the care they took of him." [23]

The lure of the city at another level of society, as well as the continuing dialogue on the relative merits of the big city and the small town, is brought out in Clyde Fitch's play *The City*, produced in New York in 1909. The play deals with the conflict in a small-town family, all of whose members except Rand, the father, have the "New York bee in their bonnets." Though tragedy befalls the family upon their removal to New York, George, the son, still defends the city for the challenge and the opportunities it poses.

A PLAYWRIGHT'S VIEW OF THE LURE OF THE CITY: 1909

Mrs. Rand. Well, I've done all, in a social way, a woman can in Middleburg, and I want to do more. . . .

Rand. Molly, wouldn't you rather be *it* in Middleburg — than *nit* in the City? . . .

Cicely. I don't care a darn about the position, if I can only have something to do, and something to see! Who wants to smell new-mown hay, if he can breathe in gasolene on Fifth Avenue instead! Think of the theatres! the crowds! *Think* of being able to go out on the street and *see some one you didn't know even by sight!!* . . .

George. Middleburg and her banks are just as picayune to *me*, in comparison with the *City* and a *big career there*, as *East Middleburg and real estate* were to *you* in *1860!* . . .

Rand. You've all got an exaggerated idea of the importance of the City. This country isn't *made* or run by New York or its half dozen sisters! It's in the smaller towns, — and spread all over the country, — that you find the bone and sinew of the United States! . . . Did Lincoln need New York? Did Grant? Did a metropolis turn out McKinley, or have anything to do with forming the character and career of Grover Cleveland? . . .

[Later]

Mrs. Rand. Oh, why did we ever come here! . . . I haven't had a happy moment since I left . . . my old home. . . . I'm lonesome for my church, and if I died I wouldn't have a handful of people at my funeral. . . . Oh, what the City has done for the whole of us!

Teresa. Yes, you're right, mother. I was happy too, till I came here. It was the City that taught me to make the worst of things, instead of the best of them. . . .

> *Van Vranken.* I agree with Tess! She and I, in a small town, would have been happy always! I'd not have been tempted like I am here. . . .
> *George.* . . . *No!* You're all wrong! Don't blame the City. It's not her fault! It's our own! What the City does is to bring out what's strongest in us. If at heart we're good, the good in us will win! If the bad is strongest, God help us! Don't blame the City! *She* gives the man his opportunity; it is up to *him* what he makes of it! A man can live in a small town all his life, and deceive the whole place and *himself* into thinking he's got all the virtues, when at heart he's a hypocrite! . . . *But the City!!!* A man goes to the gates of the City and knocks! New York or Chicago, Boston or San Francisco, no matter *what* city so long as it's big, and busy, and selfish, and self-centred. And she comes to her gates and takes him in, and she stands him in the middle of her market place — where Wall Street and Herald Square and Fifth Avenue and the Bowery, and Harlem, and Forty-second Street all meet, and there she strips him naked of all his disguises — and all his hypocrisies, — and she paints his ambition on her fences, and lights up her skyscrapers with it! what *he wants* to be and *what he thinks he is!* — and then she says to him, Make good if you can, or to Hell with you! And what is in him comes out to clothe his nakedness, and to the City he can't lie! I *know* because I *tried!* [24]

Opportunities to enjoy theatrical entertainment, musical performances, and exhibits of the graphic arts are traditionally important in the psychological pull of the city; and this attraction was never more important than in the years between 1870 and 1920, when such cultural facilities were greatly expanded because of the magnitude of the urban audience, the patronage of urban-industrial wealth, the mobility supplied by improved transportation, and the competitive aspirations of the nation's fast-growing cities. Many of the major cities now had permanent symphony orchestras that played extended seasons. Both New York and Chicago had as many as three opera houses in which repertory rivaling that in European houses was performed. By 1900, New York City had 45 theaters where plays enjoyed long runs and were of a diversity to suit everybody's taste. A theatrical syndicate, operating a nationwide circuit, made it possible for smaller cities to have plays for shorter runs. By 1915, the year *The Birth of a Nation* was produced, the motion picture had arrived to meet the needs of the widening urban audience for theatrical entertainment. Beginning in 1869, with the opening of Washington's Corcoran Gallery, art museums proliferated in the major cities so that fine painting and sculpture were accessible to the public to an extent not known in America before the Civil War.

The cultural resources of the nation's cities were assessed in 1904 by Hugo Münsterberg (1863–1916), a German-born psychologist who in 1892 had become professor of psychology at Harvard University. His book, *The Americans*, published in 1904, was designed to acquaint German readers with contemporary tendencies in American life.

CULTURAL ATTRACTIONS AND THE APPEAL OF THE CITY: 1904

There is certainly no lack of theatres, for almost every town has its "opera house," and the large cities have really too many. . . . The equipments of the stage . . . leave very little to be desired, and the settings sometimes surpass anything which can be seen in Europe. . . . And these . . . bring many a graceful comedy and light opera to a really artistic performance. The great public, too, is quite content, and fills the theatres to overflowing. . . . Artistic productions of the more serious sort are drowned out by a great tide of worthless entertainments; and . . . if one looks at the announcements of what is to be given in New York on any single evening, it is tremendously borne home on one by the bad practice of repeating the [good] plays night after night for many weeks, so that a person who wants to see real art has soon seen every production which is worth while. In this respect New York is distinctly behind Paris, Berlin, or Vienna, although about on a level with London; and in the other large cities of America the situation is rather worse. . . . Now, in a town of moderate size, one piece cannot be repeated many nights, so that the companies have to travel about. The best companies stay not less than a week, and if the town is large enough, they stay from four to six weeks. . . . In this way . . . the small city is able to see the best actors and the newest pieces. . . .

The history of music in America has shown what can be attained by endowment — how the public demand can be educated so that even the very best art will finally be self-supporting. The development of the Boston Symphony Orchestra . . . is thoroughly typical. It was realized that symphony concerts, like the best given in Germany, would not be self-supporting, in view of

241

the deficient musical education of the country. In 1880 Boston had two symphony orchestras, but both were of little account. They were composed of over-busied musicians, who could not spare the time needed for study and rehearsals. Then one of the most liberal and appreciative men of the country, Henry Lee Higginson, came forward and engaged the best musicians whom he could find, to give all their time and energy to an orchestra; and he himself guaranteed the expenses. During the first few years he paid out a fortune annually, but year by year the sum grew less, and to-day Boston so thoroughly enjoys its twenty-four symphony concerts, which are not surpassed by those of any European orchestra, that the large music-hall is too small to hold those who wish to attend. This example has been imitated, and now New York, Chicago, Philadelphia, and other cities have excellent and permanent orchestras.

Likewise various cities, but especially New York, enjoy a few weeks of German, French, and Italian opera which is equal to the best opera in Europe, by a company that brings together the best singers of Europe and America. . . . Extraordinarily high subscriptions for the boxes, and a reduced rental of the Metropolitan Opera House, which was erected by patrons of art, have given brilliant support to the undertaking. Without going into questions of principle, an impartial friend of music must admit that even the performances of Parsifal were artistically not inferior to those of Bayreuth, and the audience was quite as much in sympathy with the great masterpiece as are the assemblages of tourists at Bayreuth. The artistic education proceeding from these larger centres is felt through the entire country, and there is a growing desire for less ambitious but permanent opera companies. . . .

Every large city has its conservatory and its surplus of trained music teachers, and almost every city has societies which give oratorios, and innumerable singing clubs, chamber concerts, and regular musical festivals. Even the concerts by other soloists than that fashionable favourite of American ladies, Paderewski, are well attended. . . . Boston has been the great centre for oratorio. . . . And the influence of the musical Germans was strongly felt by the middle of the century. The Germania Orchestra of Boston was founded in 1848, and now all the Western cities where German influences are strong, such as Milwaukee, Cincinnati, Chicago, and St. Louis, are centres of music, with many male choruses and much private cultivation of music in the home. . . .

In former times, the true artist [painter or sculptor] had to prefer Europe to his native home, because in his home he found no congenial spirits; this is now wholly changed. There is still the complaint that the American cities are even now no Kunststädte; and, compared with Munich or with Paris, this is still true. But New York is no more and no less a Kunststädte than is Berlin. In all the large cities of America the connoisseurs and patrons of art have organized themselves in clubs . . . and the large art schools with well-known teachers and studios of private masters have become great centres for artistic endeavour. . . . Of course, the public art galleries of America are necessarily far behind those of Europe, since the art treasures of the world were for the most part distributed when America began to collect. And yet it is surprising what treasures have been secured, and in some branches of modern painting and industrial art the American collections are not to be surpassed. Thus the Japanese collection of pottery in Boston has nowhere its equal, and the Metropolitan Museum in New York leads the world in several respects.[25]

3. TECHNOLOGY

As in the pre-Civil War years, technological innovations encouraged urbanization not only by stimulating industrial development but also by enabling cities to adjust physically to large increases in population and business. Undoubtedly the most significant innovation was the development in the late 1870's and 1880's of electricity as a practical source of light and power, which added many new dimensions to urban life. Pioneers in the production of a commercially practical electric dynamo were Charles F. Brush, originator of the arc lamp for store and street illumination, and Thomas Edison, inventor of the incandescent lamp for street and home lighting. The California Electric Light Company, incorporated in San Francisco in June, 1879, pioneered in the business of producing and selling electric service to the public. By 1900, nearly 2,800 power stations were in operation in the United States.

By the 1890's electric-powered vehicles were working a revolution in urban mass transit, easing (especially in the newer cities) the threat of congestion at the central core. They moved much faster than horsecars and even than cable cars, which were introduced in San Francisco, New York, Chicago, and Philadelphia, in the 1870's and 1880's. Electric-powered vehicles were cleaner and less hazardous than the steam-propelled (later electrified) elevated trains which ran on a roadbed constructed on pillars above the streets. Elevated trains were in use in New York, by 1870, and later in Brooklyn, Kansas City, and Chicago. Electric trolleys, supplied with current from overhead wires, were introduced in Richmond, Virginia, in 1888; by 1900 they had replaced the horse-car in most American cities.[26] Subways, made practical when electric power was available, were completed in Boston in 1901 and in New York in 1904. Walter G. Marshall, a British traveler, described the New York "L" as it operated in the 1870's, when steam was still the source of propulsion.

THE OPERATION OF THE NEW YORK "L": 1879

And now how to get about in New York. There is first the elevated railway. Answering to our "underground" in London, in affording rapid conveyance through the city without interfering with the traffic, it is raised high above the streets instead of being tunnelled under them. The effect of the "elevated" — the "L," as New Yorkers generally call it — is, to my mind, anything but beautiful. . . . The tracks are lifted to a height of thirty feet (in some places higher) upon iron pillars, the up line on one side of the street and the down on the other. . . . Beneath the raised lines is the roadway for horses and carriages, and the lines of rail for the tramway cars, with the pavements beyond. As you sit in a car on the "L" and are being whirled along, you can put your head out of [the] window and salute a friend who is walking on the street pavement below. In some places, where the streets are narrow, the railway is built right over the "sidewalks" . . . close up against the walls of the houses. . . .

As might be expected, the elevated railway is immensely patronized. Trains run at frequent intervals on the several lines, from 5.30 in the morning till 12 o'clock at night, and during the crowded hours, namely from 5.30 A.M. to 7.30 A.M., and from 5 P.M. to 7 P.M., they follow each other as fast as can be managed. . . . The fare during these busy hours is five cents . . . at other times, ten cents. Of course it is needless to observe that there are no classes, as in our passenger trains, but all ride together in a long car, or carriage, the seats ranged lengthwise at the sides, with a passage down the middle and a door at each end, four cars being as many as are run at a time on the "elevated." . . . As a financial enterprise the elevated railway has turned out a success beyond even the expectations of its pro-moters. . . . As a natural consequence of the introduction of the elevated railway, property lying contiguous to the overhead lines has considerably depreciated in value. The nineteen hours and more of incessant rumbling day and night from the passing trains; the blocking out of a sufficiency of light . . . ; the full, close view passengers on the cars can have into rooms on the second and third floors; the frequent squirtings of oil from the engines . . . all these are objections that have been reasonably urged by unfortunate occupants of houses whose comfort has been so unjustly molested.[27]

To Richmond, Virginia, goes the distinction of having the first commercially successful electric traction line. An electric railway was operated in Berlin in 1879, but the preoccupation in the United States at this time with the need for improved urban transit turned experimentation here in the direction of electric traction. Though an electric streetcar was run in Cleveland in 1884, the first extended trolley service, inaugurated in 1888, resulted from a contract given by the City of Richmond to Frank J. Sprague, one of Edison's early technicians.[28] At least 25 other electric trolley lines began operation within a year. City promotion in the "New South" was in part responsible for Richmond's adoption of the new mode of urban transit. New lines were needed in connection with the Virginia Exposition, to be held there in October and November, 1888. The city's ultramodern street railways, as a Chamber of Commerce publication pointed out, were a positive symbol of its urban potential.

RICHMOND, VIRGINIA — PIONEER IN ELECTRIC TRACTION: 1888

Richmond . . . is a city keeping well abreast of the activity and progress of the age. It owns its water works and gas works and is developing both to meet the demands of the growing population. . . . It is sometimes called "the Electric City" by reason of the fact that electricity is here employed for so many purposes — for propelling street-cars; for furnishing motive power to manufactories; for unloading ships; for street and house light-ing, etc., and it is the place for the first experiments in and the first invention of electric-heating apparatuses. . . .

The street railways of Richmond and Manchester [a suburb

opposite Richmond on the James River] have a mileage of *routes* of 18 5/6 miles, most of which is laid with double track, and 6 1/2 miles of which is operated by electricity (Edison-Sprague "overhead wire"). . . . This is the longest electrical street railway in the world, and the most successful, inasmuch as it climbs steep hills, turns sharp curves and threads crowded streets with a rapidity of movement, an ease in management and an economy in expenses heretofore unknown. Our entire street-car system is to be run by electricity by the first of October — horses and mules will be utterly discarded. . . . All the lines will extend their tracks to the Exposition Grounds. . . . All this done we will have street-car *routes* twenty-five miles in length, most of them laid with double track. . . . In the utilization of electricity for street railways, Richmond leads the world.[29]

To New Yorkers, the opening of the Rapid Transit Subway, in October, 1904, was an event as significant in the history of their city as the completion of the Erie Canal in 1825 and the Croton Aqueduct in 1842, an improvement which guaranteed the city a dependable source of water, conveyed from sources nearly 40 miles to the north. They saw underground rapid transit, made possible by electric power, as a means of intracity population movement that would permit increasing numbers of people to live in large urban clusters. The magnitude of the engineering achievement impressed contemporaries with the unimagined promise of the twentieth-century city. These views were expressed in editorials in *The New York Times.*

REACTIONS TO THE OPENING
OF NEW YORK'S SUBWAY: 1904

In modern city life distance is measured in time, and time is not only money in the old sense — it is health, vigor, education, and morality. That is to say, reduction in the time of transit between home and work opens up great regions where these blessings are possible, as they are not in congested city districts. The essential advantage of the subway system is the extension of the home area. . . .

Speaking generally thirty minutes is the limit of real convenience for a journey night and morning, and an hour may be called the maximum limit within which work and business can be reached without a serious impairment of efficiency. Thirty years ago, this extreme limit was reached toward the north at

Fifty-ninth Street. By the use of the branch of the rapid transit system opened to-day and its connections, less than a half hour will take passengers at least a dozen miles from the City Hall, and an hour to the confines of Westchester County. . . .

The tunnel [now] building under the East River at the lower end of the city, the tunnel building by the Pennsylvania Station near the centre of Manhattan, with the lines already in operation or planned, will open up a region now thinly settled, stretching in a semi-circle from a dozen to a score of miles in radius. Within these limits and those extended to the north by the present lines a population of ten millions can be, and we believe will be, housed comfortably, healthfully, and relatively cheaply. That is the future which the rapid transit system has made, not the dream of visionaries, but the calculable and reasonable aim of engineers, capitalists, and the Municipal Government.[30]

The subway in every aspect will be a surprise and a delight for the observant and intelligent citizen who will see it in operation for the first time. Clean, white, well lighted, equable in temperature, free from smoke and gases usually associated with tunnel transit, well ventilated from end to end, and equipped with cars as comfortable as any run above ground, it will invite the formation of "the subway habit," to the immediate relief of the surface and elevated lines and the satisfaction of all who travel with the sole purpose of "getting there" in the least time possible.[31]

The application of electric power to the lighting of stores, theaters, and streets made the "bright lights" of the city even brighter — and their operation more dependable. The effectiveness of gas light, available by the 1820's, and provided for the streets by contract with private companies, depended on the diligence of the lamplighters; and city dwellers often complained about the frequency of unlighted lamps. In 1878, Brush's electric arc lamps were installed in the show windows of John Wanamaker's store in Philadelphia; and soon thereafter, other stores, as well as hotels, installed the new "electric lamps," and cities began to consider the possibility of electric lighting for the city streets. On March 31, 1880, Wabash, Indiana, became the first city in the United States to be entirely lighted by electricity, after agreeing with the patentees of the Brush light to test its qualities. To provide the light, four lamps, in plain glass globes, were suspended from the flagstaff of the courthouse and connected with a "Brush Dynamo Electric Machine" in the basement. One of the many outsiders who came to witness the occasion described the public reaction.[32]

WABASH, INDIANA — PIONEER IN ELECTRIC STREET LIGHTING: 1880

At 8 o'clock the ringing of the court house bell announced that the exhibition was about to commence. . . . The city, to say the least, presented a gloomy, uninviting appearance, showing an abundance of room for more light. Suddenly from the towering dome of the court house, burst a flood of light, which, under ordinary circumstances, would have caused a shout of rejoicing. . . . The people, almost with bated breath, stood overwhelmed with awe. . . . The strange, weird light, exceeded in power only by the sun, yet mild as moonlight, rendered the court house square as light as mid-day. . . . Ben Franklin . . . brought down the lightning from the heavens on a kite-string and bottled it. . . . Brush and Edison take a steam engine, belt it to a huge electro-magnetic machine, manufacture lightning and use it to light cities and hamlets, thus benefiting mankind and blessing posterity. . . . At a distance of one square [from the court house] we could very distinctly read nonpareil print. At a distance of two squares we could read brevier print; at four squares, ordinary display advertising.[33]

Just as the omnibus companies had resisted the technological innovation of the horsecar, so the gas companies resisted the competition of electricity with its lucrative franchises for street lighting and its other urban uses. Officers of the gas companies belittled "Tom Edison's promises" as a "giant humbug" and tried to discourage the use of electricity on grounds of its alleged danger. This attitude was satirized by a Milwaukee newspaper editor in a December, 1881 issue of *The Evening Wisconsin*.

GAS COMPANY DEROGATION OF ELECTRIC LIGHT — MILWAUKEE: 1881

A FRIGHTFUL INVENTION — A Fond du Lac Man Makes a Remarkable Address to the Electric Lamps on East Water Street — He Tells What Numerous Dangers Beset Those Who Use "Incandescent Carbons" —

Last evening a Wisconsin scribe saw a heavy man sturdily

braced on East Water Street, shaking his heavy hickory cane angrily at the electric lights. Being accosted by the reporter as to the cause of his violent gesticulations, he cried in a loud voice, still gesticulating with his stick at the lights:

"Why, boy, those things are murderous — murderers! If any one connects the positive and negative ends of those wires he will be killed instantly. In addition to this, the danger of fire is constant, as the incandescent carbon points may be broken or dropped; the light attracts dangerous thunder storms; it spoils food; injures iron and wooden wares; demoralizes ministers; makes hotel men charge extra; produces a disease that renders all merchants using it apt to make mistakes in their books in favor of themselves; starts school teachers to quarreling; prevents marriages; originates domestic troubles; makes the servant want to be boss; . . . fastens snow to the sidewalks; . . . gives birth to cranks; prevents poor boys from becoming president; makes bank cashiers dishonest; . . . makes dogs go mad in Winter, and increases contagious diseases; puts the sawbuck or wheel-barrow just where the man of the house will fall over it, when coming home from the "lodge"; renders lamp posts unfriendly; . . . breeds gossips; reduces the standing of boarding house hash, and shows up everybody by night."

"What is your business, sir," asked the reporter.

"I have retired from business and am now vice president of the Fond du Lac Gas Company," he replied proudly.[34]

Electric-powered elevators ultimately played a part in the technological advances in architecture that took advantage of "skyroom" for business and residential purposes and thus further facilitated the accommodation of large numbers of people in limited space. Chicago architects pioneered an architectural form in which an iron or steel skeleton or cage replaced masonry in support of the roof and walls, permitting construction to proceed to unprecedented heights. William L. Jenney's Home Insurance Building (1885) in Chicago is credited with being the first example of the skyscraper style that was perfected between 1890 and 1910 by a Chicago school of architects including Louis Sullivan, D. H. Burnham, and Dankmar Adler.[35] Soon, towering structures, suggestive of the "soaring" city of the early twentieth century, appeared in other large cities, especially New York, where a 60-story giant, the Woolworth Building, was completed in 1913. Without the availability of elevators, tall buildings would have been impractical. Steam-driven and hydraulic elevators antedated the electric elevator, which was developed in the 1880's and came into increasing use in the 1890's to accommodate the traffic demands of taller buildings. Writing in *Harper's New Monthly Magazine* of February, 1892, Julian Ralph, a New York journalist, described some details of the new urban architecture that was built according to what he called "the Chicago method."

CHICAGO'S TOWERS: 1892

I do not know how many very tall buildings Chicago contains, but they must number nearly two dozen. Some of them are artistically designed, and hide their height in well-balanced proportions. A few are mere boxes punctured with window-holes, and stand above their neighbors like great hitching-posts. The best of them are very elegantly and completely appointed, and the communities of men inside them might almost live their lives within their walls, so multifarious are the occupations and services of the tenants. The best New York office buildings are not injured by comparison with these towering structures, except that they are not so tall as the Chicago buildings, but there is not in New York any office structure that can be compared with Chicago's so-called Chamber of Commerce office building, so far as are concerned the advantages of light and air and openness and roominess which its tenants enjoy. In these respects there is only one finer building in America, and that is in Minneapolis. It is a great mistake to think that we in New York possess all the elegant, rich, and ornamental outgrowths of taste, or that we know better than the West what are the luxuries and comforts of the age. With their floors of deftly laid mosaic-work, their walls of marble and onyx, their balustrades of copper worked into arabesquerie, their artistic lanterns, elegant electric fixtures, their costly and luxurious public rooms, these Chicago office buildings force an exclamation of praise, however unwillingly it comes.

They have adopted what they call "the Chicago method" in putting up these steepling hives. This plan is to construct the actual edifice of steel framework, to which are added thin outer walls of brick, or stone masonry. . . . The exterior walls are mere envelopes. . . . The manner in which the great weight of houses so tall as to include between sixteen and twenty-four stories is distributed upon the ground beneath them is ingenious. Wherever one of the principal upright pillars is to be set up, the builders lay a pad of steel and cement of such extent that the pads for all the pillars cover all the site. . . .

I have referred to the number of these stupendous structures. Let it be known next that they are all in a very small district, that narrow area which composes Chicago's office region . . . at the edges of which one-twenty-fifth of all the railroad mileage of the world is said to terminate, though the district is but little more than half a mile square or 300 acres in extent. One of these buildings — and not the largest — has a population of 4000 persons. It was visited and its elevators were used on three days, when a count was kept, by 19,000, 18,000, and 20,000 persons. . . .

It seems to many strangers who visit Chicago that it is reasonable to prophesy a speedy end to the feverish impulse to swell the number of these giant piles, either through legislative ordinance or by the· fever running its course. . . . In the first place, the tall buildings darken the streets, and transform the lower stories of opposite houses into so many cellars or damp and dark basements. In the next place, the great number of tall and splendid office houses is depreciating the value of the humbler property in their neighborhoods. . . . One of the foremost business men in the city, [however,] asserts that he can perceive no reason why the entire business heart of the town — that square half-mile of which I have spoken — should not soon be all builded up of cloud-capped towers. . . . The only trouble he foresees will be in the solution of the problem [of] what to do with the people who will then crowd the streets as never streets were clogged before. . . .

In the tall buildings are the most modern and rapid elevators, machines that fly up through the towers like glass balls from a trap at a shooting contest. The slow-going stranger . . . feels himself loaded into one of those frail-looking baskets of steel netting, and the next instant the elevator-boy touches the trigger, and up goes the whole load as a feather is caught up by a gale. The descent is more simple. Something lets go, and you fall from ten to twenty stories as it happens.[36]

Although Chicago's dynamism produced the skyscraper style, the transformation from horizontal to vertical that this application of new technology had effected in the physical appearance of cities by 1920 was best expressed in New York City. With the multiplication and dispersed location of large cities, each of which was the economic nerve center of a metropolitan region, New York no longer held undisputed rank as the national metropolis. It nevertheless was the nation's largest city; and its fabled power as a financial center, the abundance and renown of its cultural and entertainment resources, and its unquestioned preeminence in retail merchandising made it the symbol of the city for many contemporaries who viewed the growth of large cities as testimony to the potential of American progress. This was the admiringly positive view of W. L. George, a British journalist who spent six months in the United States in 1920. George called "colossal" New York "the microcosm of the new civilization of America."

NEW YORK — "CITY OF GIANTS": 1920

I may offend a Londoner by giving this name of Megalopolis to New York. For London, with its population of seven and [a] half millions, lays claim to the title of "The Great City." It is true that New York itself has a population of little over five and a half millions, and that even if we add the surrounding territory of Yonkers, Mount Vernon, Jersey City, Newark, etc., the total might be less than that of London; but New York is a city great not only in area; it is great in height, in spirit, in emotion. . . . Magnificence is the first thing that strikes one in New York. Its great buildings, its spreading luxury, its lights, its air of skeptical pleasure, its moral anaesthesia, its cool ferocity, all that suggests republican Rome with a touch of Babylon.

I love New York. . . . It is all the cities. Where Chicago offers energy, New York offers splendor. It is the only American city where people work and play; in the others they work. I feel that inevitably in the second generation, if not in the first, the oil and cotton of the South, the wheat of the Middle West come to fuse themselves in the crucible of pleasure that lies on the Hudson.

Perhaps that is why most of the other cities call New York degenerate, because it is not so much an industrial city as a city of commerce, a city of financiers. . . . Indeed, to me, New York is . . . the microcosm of the new civilization of America, of which the Middle West is the basis and the South the memory.

The colossal scale of New York naturally makes upon the stranger his first impression. . . . Fifth Avenue, people so many, traffic so thick that one has to take one's turn at a crossing, that police control has become mechanical, beyond the power of man. . . . One goes up Broadway at night to see the crowded colored signs of the movie shows and the theaters twinkle and eddy, inviting, clamorous, Babylonian! . . . New York . . .

is the giant city grouped about its colossal forest of parallelepipeds of concrete and steel. . . .

Standing by the building plot between Vanderbilt and Park Avenues, and looking westward, you see a strange thing — an enormous office building against the back of which outlines itself the spire of a church. A big office and a little church; what a change since the Middle Ages! . . . Height is the new destination of American architecture. Even in the distant suburbs of Manhattan — at High Bridge, for instance — the twelve-floor building is there, and the cottage is not. . . . Few private buildings in New York are equal to the big apartment houses, such as those of Park Avenue and Madison Avenue which are square and logical. . . .

I wonder what would have happened to Manhattan if the building law [the zoning ordinance of 1916] had not interfered; a time would have come when from the Battery to Forty-fifth Street the whole of the island would have been covered with thirty-story buildings. . . . Now the buildings are set back in their upper floors; it is still fine, because it is big, but it is losing the nobility of the sheer facade.[37]

4. SPATIAL PATTERNS: SEGMENTATION, MOBILITY, AND SUBURBANIZATION

The availability of speedier urban transit and skyscraper architecture, together with the continued increase in population, encouraged a more specialized use of space within large cities, in the later nineteenth century, than had prevailed in the pre-Civil War city. Increasingly, the leading retail stores, business and financial houses, and theaters were concentrated, often in skyscraper structures, in the city's central core. Industrial plants that once bordered the business district now tended to be located in specialized areas at the outer limits of the city or in satellite industrial communities, like Pullman, Illinois, or Gary, Indiana, in the shadow of the metropolis. In impressive residential sections at the periphery of the city or lining fashionable streets between the core and outlying areas were the homes of the most affluent city dwellers. In the intervening space were scattered enclaves of small business and industry and residential sections differentiated according to the income level of the occupants: a slum area in the deteriorating structures on the edge of the business district, and beyond this, endless streets of nondescript housing occupied by lower and middle income groups, often sorted out by nationality background and race. By 1890, this segmentation of the urban community according to specialized areas of residence and commercial and industrial pursuits increasingly characterized the physical pattern of the large cities of the nation. The existence of such specialized residential areas did not mean, however, that city populations were static. On the contrary, studies have shown that at least from the 1830's onward, the rate of population movement into and out of cities was very high, as well as the rate of residential change within a given city or specialized areas of it.

With the electrification of mass transit facilities urban populations were increasingly dispersed beyond the corporate limits of the city into suburbs, a development contemporaries viewed not only as reducing the unhealthful congestion of the central city but as providing in a "happy union of urbanity and rusticity" the best disposition of the nation's rapidly urbanizing population. As early as the 1850's and 1860's, the steam railroad and the horsecar had permitted those who could afford it to reside at the periphery of the city or in the small villages that were developing within commuting distance of it. But the electric trolley and the efforts of railroads to improve conditions for the short-trip passenger greatly accelerated the suburban trend. For example, by 1900, largely as a result of the electric trolley, the range of residence around Boston had been widened from a distance of about two and a half miles from the city hall, in the early 1870's, to a distance of six miles from the city's center; three communities on its suburban fringe increased in population in these years from 60,000 to 227,000. Though at least half of Boston's population could not afford residential arrangements of this kind, the area attracted a considerable number of the city's lower middle class.[38]

Boston clergyman and author, Edward Everett Hale, discussing "The Congestion of Cities" in the January, 1888, issue of *Forum* magazine, pointed to the ways by which railroads were making suburban residence possible for city workers.

EDWARD EVERETT HALE ON SUBURBS: 1880's

The summer exodus from the cities is very suggestive [of the desire to escape the city's congestion], and is certainly teaching a lesson and working out conclusions which lie in the right direction. . . . Many a man now takes his family into the country for several months, whose father, doing the same business and living in the same social grade, would never have thought of doing so fifty years ago. It is quite possible to carry this same relief very much farther, so as to benefit the artisan and even the day-laborer. In Massachusetts the law now compels every railway company which runs into Boston to maintain what used to be called a "laborers' train," which shall reach Boston before seven in the morning, and which shall leave Boston after six at night, with rates so low as to meet the needs of men who receive the lower grades of wages. . . . The result is that not only merchants and their clerks, whose work begins at eight or nine in the morning, have their country residences outside of Boston, but also that those workmen live in the country whose daily work in the city begins at seven in the morning. . . .

And the result is that in the last thirty years the population of Boston proper has scarcely increased. The warehouses and shops and places of manufacture have increased, in the change which has raised the population of the whole city, including the environs. . . . But the population of the working wards is about the same as it was. For the people who do the work live, in many instances, fifteen miles away from the places of their daily duty. The result . . . has been the growth of a large number of villages where working-men can live with their families in homes of their own, where the children can have the advantages of country life, or out-of-door life, while the workman himself goes into the town for his day's work and returns in the evening. . . .

Suburban life at the present moment has a bad name. This comes from the rather curious fact that the people who first undertake the development of a suburb are people who look at their problem from the lowest point of view. They have "lots" to sell, and they are apt to wish to give the impression that their suburb is not a suburb, but that it is a part of the city, with blocks of houses, asphalt pavements and curb-stones, lamp-posts and other physical arrangements, in which they imitate, as well as they can, the dreariness of the place from which they would lure their customers away. Undoubtedly they have their reward, or they would not continue in this course. But there is arising . . . another class of speculators, who . . . see that men who leave towns want to retain the charm of the country as far as possible, while they still cling to the real conveniences of city life. Thus, the railway company which gives us a pretty garden around the station, and makes the station itself comfortable —

a club-room, in fact, for the people who gather there — does its part toward luring into the suburb the men and women whom it wishes to have as regular passengers. . . . Let [the railroad manager] make his short trips quick, comfortable, and cheap, and he will have ten passengers out from the city and in again where he now has one. He has a new bonanza waiting for his pick when he really relieves the present congestion of the cities.[39]

By the early twentieth century, the decentralizing effects of electrified mass transit had been demonstrated to the point that many contemporaries believed large-city congestion had reached its peak — or with speedier and cheaper transportation, such as could be provided with subways, would soon do so. This was the view of Adna F. Weber, one of the earliest American students of urban population trends, who saw speedy rapid transit as facilitating a kind of interaction between city and suburb that would achieve Charles Kingsley's hope for "a complete interpenetration of city and country, a complete fusion of their different modes of life," with the advantages of both.[40] Weber stressed the importance of cheap and speedy transit as a means of achieving this goal in an article on "Rapid Transit and the Housing Problem," published in *Municipal Affairs* in 1902.

ADNA WEBER ON RAPID TRANSIT AND URBAN DECONGESTION: 1902

Though population must be concentrated, it does not follow that population must be congested unless we assume that a man's abode cannot be separated from his workplace. . . . Specialization means not only the minute division of tasks, but also the . . . replacement of the home workroom or small shop by the factory. . . . With the separation of workplace and home once effected, no reason exists for overcrowding of city people in their homes. . . . All that is needed is cheap and rapid transit between the home and the workplace. Such transit has already been provided in the smaller cities of this country, by the electric trolley roads, with the result that American cities have spread out over much broader territory than have European cities. . . . In cities the size of New York and Chicago the trolley is of course entirely inadequate, for even if it were able to carry the traffic it could not make the requisite speed. So far apart are the business centre and the residential outskirts of New York that a citizen who would dwell in a cottage must spend more than an hour in going to work each morning, even on the faster trains of the elevated railroad. . . . It is unreasonable to ask the mechanic or laborer to give up more than an hour or an hour and a half a day to this part of his work, and this means in the case of New York that the cars between the outlying cottage districts and the heart of the city must make an average speed of at least 30 miles an hour.

The other requirement [is] . . . *cheap* transit. Even to the highly-paid skilled workman the five-cent fare is unduly burdensome, especially if he have a large family; to the lowly-paid day laborer or sweat-shop worker the prevailing rates are actually oppressive. Instead of expending millions through its health and police departments in the effort to make the tenement districts habitable, cities might with more judgment remit taxation of street railways and other urban transit lines and at the same time secure a reduction in the . . . fare. In fact, . . . some thinkers have advocated the virtual abolition of street railway fares through the public assumption of the expenses of operation. In England and on the Continent subsidies have been granted to railroads from the public treasury aş the price of running cheap trains for workmen morning and evening.[41]

Though contemporaries welcomed the growth of suburbs as a means of reducing the congestion of the "large city," either by drawing off existing city dwellers or attracting residents who might otherwise have moved to the central city, they nevertheless viewed the suburban communities as component parts of the larger urban unit. Thus suburban dwellers in these years acceded to the practice of the large cities of periodically annexing their suburban fringes (and making themselves larger). Philadelphia's consolidation with neighboring communities as early as 1854 increased its area from 2 to 128 square miles. Annexations by Boston (1874), New Orleans (1874), St. Louis (1876), Baltimore (1888 and 1918), and Seattle (1907) brought major increases in area. In 1889, Chicago annexed neighboring territory to increase her size from 43.8 to 169.7 square miles; the creation of Greater New York in 1898, following upon some earlier annexations, augmented the area of the Empire City from 62.5 to 413.7 square miles and the population by about 1,500,000 people.[42] Weber looked upon annexation not only as a legal confirmation of the redistribution of population within the urban unit, but as a normal result of the outward flow of residents and an affirmation of the continuing identification of suburban dwellers with the mother city. He discussed the relationship of decentralization and annexation in an article published in *The North American Review* in May, 1898.

ANNEXATION — LEGAL ADJUSTMENT
TO SUBURBAN GROWTH

Chicago was the target of every journalistic joke-maker in New York up to two years ago, when the "Greater New York" idea came to the front. . . . This gives New York the first place among the cities of the world, so far as mere extent of territory goes. . . . What . . . is the justification of this immense annexation, or is it only a land-grabbing scheme to gratify local vanity and a false municipal pride? [On the contrary, it is a means of adjusting to the tendency of] an increasing proportion of the city's population to reside at a distance from their places of business, [thus] relieving the congested districts and filling up the suburbs. As far back as 1821, the Strand, one of the central wards of London, attained its maximum population and has since declined. . . .

The larger American cities have also reached the "point of saturation," where the first settled districts have been losing their population. "Down town" New York was more populous in 1860 than in 1890. . . . The decentralizing movement has also extended to the suburbs, especially in those cities like Boston where the electric trolley has been so highly exploited. . . . It thus appears that the Borough of Manhattan comprises really less than one-half of the true metropolis. And the increase in the population of the environs far exceeded that of the city itself, the respective percentages for 1880–90 being 42.66 and 25.62.

The conclusion to be drawn from the statistics here presented is that the movement toward suburban annexation is not an artificial one, but is simply the legal recognition of new economic conditions. It is a movement confined to no one country, least of all to the United States. In Europe there have been large suburban annexations in recent years. Vienna in 1891 incorporated suburbs with a population of 464,110 (as compared with 798,719 in the old city). . . . The "rise of the suburbs" is by far the most cheering movement of modern times. It means an essential modification of the process of concentration of population that has been taking place during the last hundred years and brought with it many of the most difficult political and social problems of our day. . . . But a solution of the problem is now in sight; the suburb unites the advantages of city and country. The

country's natural surroundings, the city's social surroundings —
these are both the possession of the suburb.[43]

A basic identification with the core city also characterized the
attitude of the average "suburbanite," who was emerging, at the
turn of the twentieth century, as a newly recognized "urban type."
Suburbanites of this period apparently viewed the suburb as an
extension of the city, with its more admired characteristics, rather
than as a symbol of separation from or repudiation of it. This
identification of city and suburb is evident in an article dealing
with the pros and cons of urban living, written by Howard A.
Bridgman, managing editor of *The Congregationalist,* and published in *The Independent* in 1902.

THE SUBURBANITE — AN EMERGING TYPE: 1902

A generation ago debating societies about once in so often
threshed over the question of the relative advantages of city and
of country life. There were then two distinct human types — the
city man and the country man. To them has been added in comparatively recent years a third — the suburbanite. He emerges
into view not only at great world centers like London and New
York, but in a hundred lesser cities in Europe and America. . . .
The suburbanite is a recent growth, because cheap and rapid
transportation is a modern affair. . . .

The cities, it is true, are still the goal of the average American
heart. . . . As the city man walks briskly to his office in the
morning . . . he may be pardoned for being proudly conscious
of the fact that his daily course is not hedged about with threatening time-tables; that he has easy access to the best that the rich,
resourceful city offers in the way of music, and theaters, and
lectures, and preaching, and libraries. . . . But on the other
hand, Mr. Suburbanite . . . puts in his claim to be heard. "It's
all well enough for bachelors and elderly couples and people
who like crowds, to reside in town, but if you want to bring up
a family, to prolong your days, to cultivate the neighborly feeling,
. . . leave your city block and become like me. It may be a
little more difficult for us to attend the opera, but the robin in
my elm tree struck a higher note and a sweeter one yesterday
than any *prima donna* ever reached." . . .

We are sure to get in America, through the rise of numerous
little colonies of people who plant themselves five, ten or fifteen
miles from town, a renaissance of the old, beautiful neighborhood

life that characterized this nation before the rush to the cities began. . . . There is a Villagers' Club in one of Boston's best known suburbs, composed of prominent business and professional men of the city, that for years has maintained high intellectual standards, and in its fortnightly meetings through the winter has given serious attention to large subjects in the realm of politics, literature and religion. . . .

. . . the great danger is that the self-complacent suburbanite will ignore his obligations to the city in which he spends his working hours and earns his daily bread. These obligations continue, even tho he is no longer a citizen of the metropolis. If he evades them he exposes himself to what Rev. Dr. Horton, of London, strikingly calls the "Curse of Suburbanity." . . . What attitude, then, shall the suburbanite take to the city of which he is by necessity still a part? Shall he look upon it simply as . . . a place that he is well rid of when night comes? Shall he hurry by the slum section and never notice the bundles of rags and misery that now and then disfigure the street? Shall he consider it no concern of his whether or not the city which furnishes him and his children with a living be well governed, whether its streets are clean and its parks large enough for the thousands of people who are crowded into the tenement districts? Because he has become a suburbanite shall he cast off responsibility for the city? . . .

Our ideal suburbanite is yet in the process of evolution. When he emerges he will blend the best traits of the pure city man and the pure country man. . . . Subjected daily to the influences of both city and country, their constant play upon him will make him broad, symmetrical, responsive to life on all sides and alive to all life's obligations. His suburban home . . . will strengthen him for the daily grapple with the problems that await him yonder in the noisy town. And every evening as he returns from toil he will bring to his family and his neighborhood much of the city's inspiration, so that they, too, will feel its thrill of life, and its call to strenuous labor while the day lasts.[44]

Satellite towns in the neighborhood of the expanding large cities also furthered the trend toward decentralization, even though they were more self-sufficient economic units, providing jobs for their own residents to a degree not true of the suburb, in the most limited sense of the term. During the first two decades of the twentieth century, proponents of deconcentration and advocates of a more healthful environment for the industrial population attempted to promote the planning both of suburbs and of satellite cities. Many were attracted by the idea of the "garden city" as propounded by the English reformer Ebenezer Howard. In *Tomorrow: a Peaceful Path to Real Reform* (1898), he proposed planned communities in which human society and the beauty of nature could be enjoyed together. "Town and country *must be married*," he wrote, "and out of this joyous union will spring a new hope, a new life, a new civilization." [45] Few "garden cities," constructed according to Howard's utopian pattern, took shape in the United States, but the popularity of the idea encouraged the development of a number of planned residential suburbs, such as Garden City, Long Island, and Roland Park, near Baltimore, as well as industrial towns like Kingsport, Tennessee, and Gary, Indiana. [46] A forerunner of such industrial towns was the experimental community of George M. Pullman, the Chicago railroad car manufacturer, who in the early 1880's developed Pullman, Illinois, a model factory community eight miles south of Chicago. Though scientifically planned and admirably constructed, the town suffered from the highly paternal nature of its management and from difficulties in the economy in the 1890's. [47] However, this businessman's model industrial community, like the garden city proposals, did serve to support, as well as reflect, the rising acceptance of planned urban growth, which was to have further consideration in the ensuing century. The Suburban Planning Association of Philadelphia saw industrial satellite cities, if properly planned, as augmenting the contribution of residential suburbs in overcoming urban congestion. [48]

5. THE "NEW" IMMIGRATION

Two streams of migrants furthered large-city growth in the years from 1870 to 1920. Scholars have debated as to whether newcomers from rural America or from outside the United States contributed in greater proportion to the spiraling urbanism of the late nineteenth and early twentieth centuries. Studies made of the decade from 1900 to 1910, only, show that in these ten years the country-to-city migration was slightly more voluminous than the immigration of foreigners but that as much as 30 to 40 per cent of the increase in urban dwellers resulted from the arrival of foreign born. The tide of immigration to the United States reached unprecedented size in this half century; and by tradition, the foreign born identify with cities to a greater degree than do the native population. In the 1880's the number of immigrants exceeded five million, double the figure for the 1850's — the peak decade in the pre-Civil War period; in the first two decades of the twentieth century immigration reached an all-time high: eight and three-quarter million, from 1900 to 1910, and five and three-quarter million, from 1910 to 1920.

Now, even more than earlier, newcomers to the United States remained in the ports of entry or moved to other cities. In 1890, when only 35 per cent of the total population were urban dwellers, more than 60 per cent of the foreign born resided in cities. By 1920, more than three-fourths of the foreign born were city dwellers.[49] Many were without the resources to go beyond the ports of entry, or, lacking skills, found their best opportunities in heavy industry or street and construction work in the large cities. Many Italians and Greeks stayed in the East coast cities with a view to returning to the Old Country after they had saved some money. Russian and Polish Jews, victims of persecution, saw residence among their compatriots in the city as the surest way of preserving their religion and their way of life. For the financially insecure, relief was more available in the city than in the unfamiliar countryside; and, besides, the city connoted opportunity and excitement for the alien newcomer as it did for the native born.

A change in the predominant source of immigrants — from northern and western Europe to southern and eastern Europe — not only augmented the variety of nationalities in city populations but by the early twentieth century gave many American cities a distinctly different ethnic character from what they had had in the years before the Civil War. The increase in migration from Italy, Russia, and Austria became newsworthy by 1882; by 1896, immigrants from these countries outnumbered newcomers from Ireland and Germany. By 1920, Russians were the most numerous foreign-born element in New York, Philadelphia, and Baltimore. Italians outnumbered all other foreign-born residents in Newark, Pittsburgh, San Francisco, and New Orleans and were the second most numerous foreign-born group in New York and Philadelphia. Poles, as of 1920, were the largest foreign-born group in Chicago, Buffalo, and Cleveland and the second most numerous of the foreign born in Milwaukee, Pittsburgh, and Detroit. Given the magnitude of city growth from native as well as foreign sources, the percentage of foreign born in the populations of the major cities, especially in the Middle West, was now not as great as in the pre-Civil War period. For example, Chicago's population, 50 per cent foreign born in 1860, was only 30 per cent foreign born in 1920; and the percentage of foreign born in Milwaukee dropped from 51 per cent in 1860 to 24 per cent in 1920. At the same time, taking into account both the foreign born and their American-born offspring, the proportion of urban dwellers with recent foreign antecedents was still strikingly large — as much as 80 per cent of Manhattan's population of 1890, according to estimates.

A comparison of the population of selected cities in 1900 and in 1920, in terms of the proportion of foreign born in the total population, reveals the extent to which, by 1920, immigrants born in Russia, Poland, and Italy were replacing Irish and German natives as the predominant foreign-born elements in the nation's major cities. The changing national and ethnic pattern of American cities at the beginning of the twentieth century is shown in Tables 3.3 and 3.4. The percentages shown in these tables refer to the total population of a given city.

The tendency of the foreign born and especially the most recent immigrants to concentrate in the city contributed to contemporary anxiety over the implications of large-city growth and caused widespread apprehension as to whether immigrants could adjust to American life while they remained in large urban centers. Young John R. Commons, future labor historian, viewed with apprehension the effect of the large city on the nation's capacity to "absorb" the foreign-born. His comments, not devoid of nationality stereotyping, are based on studies of the "new" immigration he made as an employee of the United States Industrial Commission shortly before his appointment as Professor of Political Economy at the University of Wisconsin.

THE LARGE CITY AN ALLEGED DETERRENT TO ABSORPTION OF THE FOREIGN BORN: 1904

. . . while one-fifth of our entire population lives in the thirty-eight cities of 100,000 population and over, two-fifths of our foreign-born population, one-third of our native offspring of foreign parents and only one-tenth of our people of native parentage live in such cities. That is to say, the tendency of the

Table 3.3

Foreign-born Elements in Populations of Selected Cities: 1900[50]

	Total Population	Percentage FB	Most Numerous FB Element		Second Most Numerous FB Element		Third Most Numerous FB Element		Fourth Most Numerous FB Element		Fifth Most Numerous FB Element		Sixth Most Numerous FB Element	
New England														
Boston	560,892	35.1	Irish	12.5	Canadian	9.0	Russian	2.7	Italian	2.4	English	2.3	German	1.9
Lowell	94,969	43.1	Canadian	20.2	Irish	12.8	English	4.7	Greek	1.3	Scottish	1.2	Swedish	0.6
Providence	175,597	32.0	Irish	10.6	English	5.5	Canadian	4.4	Italian	3.7	Swedish	1.6	Russian	1.1
New Haven	108,027	28.5	Irish	9.7	German	4.4	Italian	4.9	Russian	3.0	English	1.8	Swedish	1.3
Worcester	118,421	31.8	Irish	9.8	Canadian	7.1	Swedish	6.4	English	2.2	Russian	1.1	Polish	1.0
Middle Atlantic														
New York	3,437,202	37.0	German	9.4	Irish	8.0	Russian	4.5	Italian	4.2	Austrian	2.1	English	2.0
Buffalo	352,387	29.6	German	10.4	Polish	5.3	Canadian	4.9	Irish	3.2	English	2.0	Italian	1.6
Newark	246,070	29.0	German	10.2	Irish	5.2	Italian	3.5	English	2.4	Russian	2.2	Austrian	1.7
Philadelphia	1,293,697	22.8	Irish	7.6	German	5.5	English	2.8	Russian	2.2	Italian	1.4	Scottish	0.66
Pittsburgh	321,616	26.4	German	6.6	Irish	5.8	Polish	3.5	English	2.8	Italian	1.8	Russian	1.3
South Atlantic														
Baltimore	508,957	13.5	German	6.5	Russian	2.1	Irish	1.9	English	0.55	Polish	0.55	Italian	0.4
Washington	278,718	7.2	Irish	2.2	German	2.1	English	0.8	Italian	0.3	Canadian	0.3	Russian	0.3
Richmond	85,050	3.4	German	1.0	Irish	0.6	English	0.4	Italian	0.3	Russian	0.3	Scottish	0.15
Charleston	55,807	4.6	German	2.0	Irish	1.0	English	0.26	Italian	0.21	Russian	0.16	Scottish	0.11
Savannah	54,244	6.3	German	1.8	Irish	1.6	English	0.58	Russian	0.51	Canadian	0.24	Greek	0.2

	Population	%											
North Central													
Cincinnati	325,902	17.8	German	11.7	Irish	2.8	English	0.7	Russian	0.6	Italian	0.28	Polish 0.14
Cleveland	381,768	32.6	German	10.6	Irish	3.4	English	2.8	Hungarian	2.5	Canadian	2.3	Polish 2.3
Detroit	285,704	33.8	German	11.2	Canadian	10.1	Polish	4.7	Irish	2.2	English	2.2	Scottish 0.9
Milwaukee	285,315	31.2	German	18.9	Polish	6.0	Irish	0.92	English	0.7	Canadian	0.7	Austrian 0.6
Chicago	1,698,575	34.6	German	10.0	Irish	4.4	Polish	3.5	Swedish	2.9	Canadian	2.0	English 1.7
St. Louis	575,238	19.4	German	10.2	Irish	3.4	English	1.0	Russian	0.83	Polish	0.5	Austrian 0.45
Minneapolis	202,718	30.1	Swedish	9.9	Norwegian	5.7	Canadian	3.6	German	3.6	Irish	1.6	English 1.1
Omaha	102,555	23.0	German	5.4	Swedish	3.9	Danish	2.4	Bohemian	2.1	Irish	2.1	English 1.5
South Central													
Atlanta	89,872	2.8	German	0.7	Russian	0.55	Irish	0.3	English	0.3	Canadian	0.2	Scottish 0.07
Birmingham	38,415	5.0	German	1.2	English	0.6	Irish	0.6	Russian	0.4	Italian	0.36	Canadian 0.25
New Orleans	287,104	10.6	German	3.0	Italian	2.0	Irish	1.9	French	1.5	English	0.4	Russian 0.15
Mountain													
Denver	133,859	19.0	German	3.8	Irish	2.6	Swedish	2.5	English	2.5	Canadian	2.1	Russian 1.0
Salt Lake City	53,531	23.8	English	9.6	Swedish	3.1	Danish	1.8	German	1.8	Scottish	1.7	Welsh 1.0
Pacific													
Los Angeles	102,479	19.5	German	3.9	English	2.9	Canadian	2.8	Chinese	1.8	Irish	1.7	Mexican 0.8
San Francisco	342,782	34.1	German	10.2	Irish	4.7	Chinese	3.1	English	2.6	Italian	2.2	Swedish 1.5
Portland	90,426	28.6	Chinese	7.7	German	4.9	Canadian	2.4	English	2.1	Greek	1.9	Swedish 1.9

Table 3.4

Foreign-born Elements in Populations of Selected Cities: 1920[51]

	Total Population	Percentage FB	Most Numerous FB Element		Second Most Numerous FB Element		Third Most Numerous FB Element		Fourth Most Numerous FB Element		Fifth Most Numerous FB Element		Sixth Most Numerous FB Element	
New England														
Boston	748,060	32.4	7.6	Irish	5.7	Canadian	5.6[a]	Russian	5.1	Italian	1.7	English	1.0	Polish
Lowell	112,759	33.8	12.2	Canadian	6.6	Irish	3.3	Greek	3.2	English	2.0	Polish	1.5[a]	Russian
Providence	237,595	29.4	8.1	Italian	5.0	Irish	3.7	English	3.0	Canadian	2.6[a]	Russian	1.1	Swedish
New Haven	162,537	28.4	9.3	Italian	5.4[a]	Russian	4.4	Irish	1.9	Polish	1.7	German	1.2	English
Worcester	179,754	29.7	5.2	Irish	5.0[a]	Russian	4.5	Canadian	4.3	Swedish	2.4	Italian	2.0	Polish
Middle Atlantic														
New York	5,620,048	36.1	8.7[a]	Russian	7.0	Italian	3.6	Irish	3.5	German	2.6	Polish	2.3	Austrian
Buffalo	506,775	24.0	6.2	Polish	4.1	German	3.2	Italian	3.1	Canadian	1.4	Irish	1.3	English
Newark	414,524	28.4	6.6	Italian	5.2[a]	Russian	3.4	German	3.3	Polish	2.1	Irish	1.9	Austrian
Philadelphia	1,823,779	22.0	5.5[a]	Russian	3.5	Irish	3.4	Italian	2.2	German	1.7	Polish	1.7	English
Pittsburgh	588,343	20.5	2.7[a]	Russian	2.7	German	2.6	Polish	2.6	Italian	2.4	Irish	1.7	Austrian
South Atlantic														
Baltimore	733,826	11.6	3.4[a]	Russian	2.4	German	1.5	Polish	1.0	Italian	0.7	Irish	0.4	English
Washington	437,571	6.7	1.2[a]	Russian	1.0	Irish	0.9	Italian	0.8	German	0.7	English	0.4	Canadian
Richmond	171,667	2.7	0.6[a]	Russian	0.4	German	0.3	Italian	0.3	English	0.15	Irish	0.15	Syrian, etc.
Charleston	67,957	3.3	0.8	German	0.6	Russian	0.3	Greek	0.3	Irish	0.2	English	0.2	Italian
Savannah	83,252	4.0	0.9	Russian	0.6	German	0.4	Irish	0.4	Greek	0.35	English	0.2	Canadian

City	Population	% Foreign	Rank 1	Rank 2	Rank 3	Rank 4	Rank 5	Rank 6
North Central								
Cincinnati	401,247	10.7	German 4.4	Russian 1.0[a]	Irish 1.0	Hungarian 0.7	Italian 0.7	English 0.4
Cleveland	796,841	30.1	Polish 4.4	Hungarian 3.7	German 3.3	Russian 3.0[a]	Czech 3.0	Italian 2.3
Detroit	993,678	29.3	Canadian 6.0	Polish 5.7	German 3.0[a]	Russian 3.0[a]	English 1.7	Italian 1.6
Milwaukee	457,147	24.1	German 8.7	Polish 5.0	Russian 1.6[a]	Austrian 1.3	Hungarian 1.0	Czech 1.0
Chicago	2,701,705	29.9	Polish 5.0	Russian 4.5	German 4.2	Italian 1.2	Swedish 2.2	Irish 2.1
St. Louis	772,897	13.4	German 3.9	Norwegian 1.7[a]	Irish 1.2	Italian 1.2	Hungarian 0.9	Austrian 0.7
Minneapolis	380,582	23.2	Swedish 7.1[a]	German 4.3	Canadian 2.0	German 1.7	Russian 1.7[a]	Polish 1.3
Omaha	191,601	18.1	Czech 2.2	German 2.2	Russian 2.0[a]	Swedish 1.9	Italian 1.6	Danish 1.5
South Central								
Atlanta	200,616	2.4	Russian 0.6[a]	Polish 0.2	English 0.2	Greek 0.2	German 0.2	Canadian 0.1
Birmingham	178,806	3.4	Italian 0.9	English 0.4	Russian 0.4[a]	German 0.3	Scottish 0.25	Greek 0.25
New Orleans	387,219	7.1	Italian 2.0	German 0.9	French 0.7	Irish 0.4	Russian 0.35[a]	Mexican 0.3
Mountain								
Denver	256,491	14.9	Russian 2.0[a]	German 1.8	Swedish 1.5	English 1.4	Irish 1.25	Canadian 1.2
Salt Lake City	118,110	16.8	English 4.7	Swedish 1.9	German 1.7	Danish 1.4	Scottish 0.8	Dutch 0.7
Pacific								
Los Angeles	576,673	21.2	Mexican 3.7	Canadian 2.4	English 2.0	German 1.8	Russian 1.7[a]	Japanese 1.5
San Francisco	506,676	29.4	Italian 4.7	German 3.7	Irish 3.6	English 2.0	Canadian 1.4	French 1.4
Portland	258,288	19.3	Canadian 2.5	German 2.0	Russian 2.0[a]	Swedish 1.95	English 1.6	Norwegian 1.1

[a] Includes Lithuanians

foreign-born toward great cities is four times as great, and the tendency of the children of foreign parents is three and one-third times as great, as that of the . . . older native stock. . . . The extreme is reached in the textile manufacturing city of Fall River, where but 14 per cent of the population is of native extraction while in the two greatest cities, New York and Chicago, the proportion is 21 per cent, and the only large cities with a predominance of the native element are St. Joseph, Columbus, Indianapolis and Kansas City, with Denver equally divided. . . .

Individual cities suggest striking comparisons. In New York the census shows 785,000 persons of German descent, a number equal to nearly one-half the population of Berlin, and larger than that of any other German city, and larger even than the native element in New York (737,477). New York has nearly twice as many Irish (710,510) as Dublin, nearly as many Jews as Warsaw, half as many Italians as Rome. . . . Chicago has more Germans than Dresden, one-third as many Bohemians as Prague, one-half as many Irish as Belfast, one-half as many Scandinavians as Stockholm. . . .

From the farms of the American stock the sons leave a humdrum existence for the uncertain but magnificent rewards of industrialism. These become the business men, the heads of great enterprises, and the millionaires whose example hypnotizes the imagination of the farm lads throughout the land. Many of them find their level in clerical and professional occupations, but they escape the manual toil which to them is the token of subordination. These manual portions are the peculiar province of the foreign immigrant, and foreign immigration is mainly a movement from the farms of Europe to the cities of America. The high wages of the American industries and occupations which radiate from American cities are to them the magnet which fortune seeking is to the American born. The cities, too, furnish that choice of employers and that easy reliance on charitable and friendly assistance which is so necessary to the indigent laborer looking for work. Thus it is that those races of immigrants the least self-reliant or forehanded, like the Irish and Italians, seek the cities in greater proportions than those sturdy races like Scandinavians, English, Scotch, and Germans. The Jew, also, coming from the cities of Europe, seeks American cities by the very reason of his racial distaste for agriculture, and he finds there in his co-religionists the necessary assistance for a beginning in American livelihood. . . .

It is mainly the immigrant and the children of the immigrant who swell the ranks of [the] indigent element in our great cities.

Those who are poverty stricken are not necessarily parasitic, but they occupy that intermediate stage between the industrial and parasitic classes from which either of these classes may be recruited. If through continued poverty they become truly parasitic, then they pass over to the ranks of the criminal, the pauper, the vicious, the indolent and the vagrant, who, like the industrial class, seek the cities.

The dangerous effects of city life on immigrants and their children cannot be too strongly emphasized. This country can absorb millions of all races from Europe and can raise them and their descendants to relatively high standards of American citizenship in so far as it can find places for them on the farms. . . . [The] amazing criminality of the children of immigrants is almost wholly a product of city life, and it follows directly upon the incapacity of immigrant parents to control their children under city conditions. The boys, especially, at an early age, lose respect for their parents, who cannot talk the language of the community, and who are ignorant and helpless in the whirl of the struggle for existence, and are shut up during the daytime in shops and factories. On the streets and alleys . . . the children evade parental discipline, and for them the home is practically non-existent. . . . Far different it is with those foreigners who settle in country districts where their children are under their constant oversight. . . . Children of such immigrants become substantial citizens, while children of the same race brought up in the cities become a recruiting constituency for hoodlums, vagabonds and criminals.[52]

A less negative view of the interaction between the city and the "new" immigrants was taken by social settlement workers who neighbored with these newcomers. They saw the immigrants as making a contribution to American life, and the city as providing the kinds of institutions that made possible their adjustment, if not their quick assimilation. These social workers expressed their opinions in such publications as *Charities* magazine or in feature articles they wrote for semipopular periodicals.[53] Typical was an article on life among the Italians in American cities, written by William E. Davenport, of the Brooklyn Italian settlement house, and published in *Outlook* magazine in 1903. By 1920, Italian-born residents of the United States, most of them from southern Italy, totaled more than 1,160,000. Nearly 85 per cent of them were now urban dwellers. When they arrived, many became migrant workers, especially in railroad construction and repair; they formed Italian communities in cities of various sizes throughout the country — often located on the fringes of town or along the railroad tracks. In the larger cities they tended to reside among the friends and relatives with whom they had lived in Italy, reproducing in these localities the social practices of the homeland. At the same time, the newspapers, mutual benefit societies, and banks, which developed to serve the Italian newcomers, gave them a kind of "community" that they had not known in Europe, where their contacts had been limited to the nuclear family. The Italian colony of the American city thus became the setting not so much for preserving Old World traits and institutions as for achieving a consciousness of Italian nationality, which constituted the first phase of New World acculturation.[54]

THE ITALIAN IMMIGRANT
IN THE AMERICAN CITY: 1903

Why do these people group themselves so closely together? One cause . . . is the dependent condition of those arriving here with no knowledge of our language. If they are to obtain work, they must be with friends and relatives who have already acquired a foothold. But perhaps a deeper reason is the strong attachment which most of them possess for the ways and customs of their own land. Whatever the reason, one often finds several adjoining houses occupied exclusively by people from the same district. Thus, in Elizabeth Street, Manhattan, . . . there is to-day a group of several hundred families from Sciacca, a Sicilian fishing town. . . . These people . . . employ the Sciaccan dialect, possess Sciaccan doctors and a Sciaccan pharmacy, and prepare resplendent festas in honor of "Maria S. S. del Soccorso Protettrice della Citta de Sciacca." Then there are over 130 Italian mutual aid societies in New York City, most of them composed mainly of natives of a single Italian province, the name of which they bear. . . .

The sons of Italy, wherever found, are fond of music and outdoor life; and in New York they enjoy both of these luxuries when the band plays in Mulberry Bend Park. Then they pour forth from a hundred tenements (owned mainly by Italian landlords), and stand listening in rapt delight by the hour to the strains of "Il Trovatore," etc. . . . Already ten daily or weekly Italian sheets are published in New York City. The most important of these are the "Il Progresso," "Il Bollettina della

Sera," and "L'Avaldo." The "Rassegna" is a high-class literary review, and the character of the "Revista Commerciale" is indicated by its name. . . .

Nearly all the Italian societies give festivals annually, generally during the summer, and these have been accompanied of late by such a racket of fireworks and bursting petards as to render them a public nuisance. Frequently great wooden and pasteboard shrines are erected on the sidewalk and the streets are arched with lines of Chinese lanterns. In a recent Elizabeth Street festa great wire brackets arched the street at intervals of one hundred feet for a quarter of a mile, and huge painted candles, eight to ten feet in height . . . were presented by the wealthier families to the Madonna. . . . The Italian churches of New York are mainly attended by women, but few of the men being enthusiastic over the work of the priests. . . .

Many boys and young men arrive at Ellis Island at an age which enables them to escape . . . school attendance in this country. Working all day among those using only their own dialect, they often go for years without acquiring more than a few English words. The brightest young men enter the public night-schools as soon as a speaking acquaintance with the language is formed. . . . But there is a large margin of uncovered territory to be occupied by settlement workers. The Children's Aid Society maintains three large and crowded Italian schools in Manhattan, of which that on Leonard Street, with 600 scholars, is the oldest. The trades and occupations of New York Italians are various; . . . to-day there are in Manhattan some 2,300 Italians devoted to the trade of St. Crispin [shoemaking]; 1,300 who deal in cheese and groceries; 1,500 tailoring-shops and 3,000 barber-shops; a total of 500 butchers and bakers, and as many more who keep saloons; 200 tobacconists; and over 600 who keep fruit-stores. . . .

The Italians of New England are quite generally engaged in factory work. Thus, the shoemakers go to Lynn, Haverhill, Brockton, and East Weymouth in Massachusetts; while the marble workers and stone-cutters throng to Quincy, Milford, and Bay View, and the silk workers to Lawrence and Fall River. The immigration to Massachusetts is more largely from Genoa and the north than is that centering in New York State. . . . Boston has an Italian population of 25,000 and New Haven a colony of 12,000, while the factory towns of the Connecticut Valley — Hartford, Waterbury, Meriden, Danbury, Derby, and Ansonia — have each permanent settlements of from 1,000 to 4,000 persons. The New Jersey colonies at Hoboken, Hackensack, Passaic, Paterson, and Jersey City are growing rapidly. In the last-named place Italians occupy several important political positions, and their Fifth Ward Republican League has an enrollment of five hundred names. . . .

Philadelphia is, after New York, the largest center of Italian population in this country. Some twelve thousand of these people occupy twenty blocks in the southern part of the city. . . . The total Italian population is estimated at 45,000. They sustain sixty-six mutual aid societies, and their chief organ is a daily newspaper, "Mastro Paolo." Other journals are, "La Liberta," "La Voce della Colonia," and "Il Vesuvio," a rather volcanic sheet. . . . Italians are numerous in Detroit, and at Denver there is a colony which sustains three Italian newspapers, while that at Pueblo publishes another. In Galveston and New Orleans are large bodies of these people. . . . Of the Italians of Chicago we need not speak, for Miss Jane Addams, of Hull House, has already pleaded their cause with ability. She says: "There are women's clubs in Chicago which study Italian history, read Dante, and go into the art of Italy, but fail to know that right at their doors is this very interesting colony of ten thousand South Italians, reproducing their country's habits and manners, carrying on their transplanted life with a great deal of charm and a great deal of beauty. . . . We change the color of our table-cloths . . . to get a variety in our social life, and yet here, [unknown], are these people full of color, charm, history, who with their new life would offer a genuine addition to our own life and give us a type of social endeavor and stimulus." [55]

Migrants from Russia — another component of the "new" immigration — became urban dwellers to an even greater degree than did those from Italy. Most of these newcomers were Jews, as were large numbers of the migrants of Polish and Austrian background. The immigration of Jews to the United States increased markedly in the 1880's; as many as a million and a half arrived between 1899 and the outbreak of World War I. For several reasons these migrants were inclined to urban living — because of their often semi-urban background in Europe; because, as victims of persecution, they saw advantage in being among their countrymen and co-religionists; and because they possessed mechanical aptitude (more than others of the "new" immigration) for which there was a market in the city. Though there were large Jewish communities in Philadelphia, Baltimore, Newark, and Rochester, and in some cities of the

Middle West, New York was "the promised city" for this Eastern European Jewish migration. By 1915, the Jewish community there numbered close to 1,400,000 — nearly 28 per cent of the city's total population. As the Irish had transformed aspects of Boston's economy in the pre-Civil War period, so Jewish workers now contributed to the transformation and growth of New York City's garment industry, facilitating its organization on a contractor-small unit basis, by which the integrity of the family could be maintained and religious practices could be observed. The garment industry was manned predominantly by Eastern European Jews. The focus of New York City's Jewish community was the Lower East Side, whose bustling "Yiddishkeit" made it the symbol of the transplantation of this particular religio-ethnic group from the Old World to the New. Life in New York's East Side ghetto at the turn of the century was described by Edward Steiner in an article published in *The Outlook* magazine in 1902.

RUSSIAN AND POLISH JEWS IN NEW YORK CITY: 1902

The express company, which carries the baggage of the immigrants from the steamer, sends ninety per cent. to . . . the Ghetto, which lies between City Hall and Fifth Street and between the Bowery and the East River. This Ghetto is twice as large as that of Warsaw . . . ; it is less dirty, less suspiciously fragrant, but has enough of all these old-country characteristics to keep the young immigrant from being homesick. . . . The language of the Ghetto is Yiddish, a mixture of German, Hebrew, and Russian, but with enough English mixed with it to make the immigrant halt before such words as "gemovet," "gejumpt," "getrusted," which sooner or later will become part of his own vocabulary.

Street signs are written in Hebrew letters, and the passer-by is invited by them to drink a glass of soda for a cent, to buy two "pananas" for the same sum, to purchase a prayer-mantle or "kosher" meat, to enter a beer-saloon or a synagogue. . . . Everything is for sale on the street, from pickled cucumbers to feather beds, and almost all the work done in this Ghetto is done by Jewish workmen. There are Jewish plumbers, locksmiths, masons, and of course tailors, and work and trade are the watchwords of the Ghetto, where, in all my wanderings through it, I have not seen that genus Americanum, the corner loafer. . . .

The newcomer moves into the home of relatives or former

townsmen, and I have counted three "greeners," as they are called, with a family which already had the blessing of five children, the oldest being eight years of age. The "greener" is treated with kindness, but is made to feel his greenness at every point. There is an unwritten law in the Ghetto that for two days he must not work, but must eat all he can, for usually he arrives hungry to the starving point. His countrymen come to see him during that time, ask all sorts of questions about the old home, give much advice, and show a great deal of superior wisdom in the use of English, upon which they pride themselves, and with which they freely sprinkle their Yiddish. . . . He is put to work after the two days are over, and this process is called "ausgreenen" — getting a chance to shed old-country clothes and habits . . . ; generally he goes into a sweat-shop as an "aprater," which means that he learns to run a sewing-machine, and for two weeks he receives no wages, but a good deal of a certain kind of training . . . ; after that time he earns from one dollar to a dollar and a quarter a day, and reaches the goal of two dollars after a long apprenticeship. . . .

The one great intellectual and ethical center of the Ghetto is the Educational Alliance building, with its various scattered branches; it is everything which a Young Men's Christian Association is to a Gentile community, only more, inasmuch as it ministers to all, from childhood to old age. Israel's intellectual hunger is as great as its proverbial greed for wealth, and this gigantic building, covering a block and containing forty-three classrooms, is entirely inadequate to meet the demand. The main entrance is always in a state of siege, and two policemen are stationed there to maintain order and keep the crowding people in line. I visited it on a hot Sunday afternoon in July, and I found the large, well-stocked reading-room uncomfortably filled by young men. . . . Many of the lectures and entertainments have to be given a number of times to give all an opportunity to hear and to see, and some of the most difficult subjects discussed find the most numerous and enthusiastic hearers.[56]

By 1880, Polish communities could be identified in several major American cities, especially those of the Great Lakes, where heavy industry provided a demand for relatively unskilled laborers. The nucleus of a Polish settlement often was a cooperative boarding house established by Polish workers. These early migrants would attract their compatriots from Europe or elsewhere in the United States, and soon a mutual aid society might be formed.

The Catholic church created parishes in neighborhoods where Poles were employed, and the church and parochial school became centers of Polish settlement, culture, and influence. The activities of Polish real estate agents and building and loan associations helped to intensify the Polish character of these neighborhoods. By the 1890's, Polish-Americans were exerting considerable political influence in some of the Great Lakes cities, such as Milwaukee; at the same time, like other newcomers, they aggravated the social problems of the city.[57] Frederick Almy, writing in *The Survey* in 1911, described living conditions among Buffalo's Poles that he thought impeded their adjustment to American life.

THE "HUDDLED POLES" OF BUFFALO: 1911

Nearly all the Poles live in small one-story and two-story wooden cottages. The new cottages are mostly two stories, with accommodations for six or more families, but the older type is a one-story cottage, so built that it is adapted to four families. . . . Today there are in Buffalo 80,000 Poles, which is one-sixth of the entire population. . . . In 1902 we found one small two-story cottage in the Polish quarter . . . which housed sixty people. . . . Nothing of this sort exists today, but . . . overcrowding is still serious and dangerous. . . . There are beds under beds . . . and mattresses piled high on one bed during the day will cover all the floors at night. Lodgers in addition to the family are in some sections almost the rule rather than the exception. Under such conditions privacy of living, privacy of sleeping, privacy of dressing, privacy of toilet, privacy for study are all impossible, especially in the winter season; and those who have nerves . . . are led near to insanity. . . . Even as it is, the Poles are climbing. They have two daily newspapers; 4,000 families, representing 20,000 people, own their own homes; 5,000 of them have deposits in the savings banks, amounting to over $2,500,-000; and they own taxable property worth $12,000,000.[58]

The confrontation with a new environment was a traumatic experience for all newcomers to America, however much this was eased by association with their own compatriots; it was especially hard for those who found themselves confined to congested urban enclaves within a larger urban community dominated by a society different in religious and philosophical outlook from their own. To a greater degree, perhaps, than other groups of newcomers, the

Jewish migrants experienced the psychological consequences of the transplantation from a semirural setting in Eastern Europe to the congested, commercial-minded city. Hutchins Hapgood, a resident at the University Settlement in New York City, caught the nature of their frustrations, as well as the variegated fabric of the community, in essays published in 1902 as *The Spirit of the Ghetto*. Less well known, but equally perceptive along these lines, are the sketches of East Side life written for *Forward* by Israel Hurwitz, under the pseudonym Z. Libin, and collected for publication as *Geklibene Skitsen* in 1902. Their point of view is reflected in a review by Charles Rice, published in *The Atlantic Monthly* in 1903.

THE MOOD OF THE GHETTO — THE IMPACT OF THE CITY ON THE JEWISH MIGRANTS: 1902

Life in the East Side, . . . this huge monster of sweat-shops and tenement-holes with their human contents, offers a mine of psychological material hardly to be found in any other variety of American life. . . . In a community uniformly composed of native elements there is something of stability in character and in habits of mind. . . . It is quite different in a community made up of emigrants in various stages of assimilation with the surrounding native element. Each emigrant, torn off from quite a different economic and social environment at home, is transplanted into new conditions, economic and social, let alone the influence of a new climate and of a new habitat in general. By this violent change of surroundings, by this clash with a new environment, the emigrant undergoes a more or less violent, because sudden, psychical change. His old habits of thinking and feeling, . . . the ideals he once cherished, . . . his estimates of moral worth, aesthetic standards, national predilections and bias — in short, his whole past personality comes into collision with the new environment. As a result of this constant friction . . . his character . . . begins to disintegrate. . . . This is especially true . . . where the clash is between older, simpler, as well as more idealistic, civilizations of Eastern Europe on the one hand, and the more complex, materialistic, industrial régime of the New World on the other. It is the clash between the contemplative, slow life, where rural conditions prevail, and the rush and turmoil of urban and industrial centres of this country. . . .

This remarkable phenomenon of psychical change is especially peculiar to the East Side, since the underlying cause, the clash between two environments, is more potent here than elsewhere; most of the East Siders are natives of Russia. . . . But what makes the East Side more challenging to literary portrayal is the fact that these emigrants are Russian Jews. . . . [The Russian Jew] is essentially different from his American neighbor. The Russian Jew not only observes, perceives, or knows an external fact; he also *feels* it, and this intensely. . . . Libin leads you into the life of the [Russian Jewish] proletaire, his tenement prison, his shop, his rare amusements, his picnic parties. The shop-hand, the "finisher," the "operator," the "peddler," the half-Americanized young "swell" of the East Side, the "missis" with all her troubles and trials, the boarder with all his vexations and comic mishaps, the little waif tramping the streets, the newsboy, the "intellectual" with all his strivings and disappointments, his internal conflicts, and his struggles with a rude environment, the budding capitalist, the boss — these and many other types [constitute the variety of New York City's Jewish East Side.] [59]

6. BLACKS

The cityward migration of southern Blacks contributed to urban population increase in these years; their exodus northward enlarged the Black communities of many northern cities. Between 1875 and 1915 this movement was part of the general drift of population from rural districts to cities, accentuated somewhat between 1890 and 1900 by economic and social disturbances in the South. The migration was greatly intensified, however, by the demand for industrial workers during World War I. Between 1900 and 1920, the Negro population in Chicago increased from 30,150 to 109,458; in New York, from 60,666 to 152,467; and in Philadelphia, from 62,613 to 134,229. The Negro communities in Baltimore and Washington increased from around 80,000 to about 110,000; and Detroit's grew from 4,111 to 40,838. By 1920 nearly 85 per cent of all Negroes in the North and West were urban dwellers.

In southern cities, in the decades following the Civil War, Blacks were increasingly the victims of segregation, the unskilled restricted to menial tasks, and the middle class limited to the economic, social, and intellectual opportunities available within the boundaries of the Black community. Their lack of financial resources and their residence in scattered enclaves prevented concerted resistance to white repression and intimidation. In northern cities, too, there was increasing pressure for residential segregation in the later years of the nineteenth century — in part a consequence of prejudice and of the more specialized patterns of urban residence that followed upon the growth of population and the break-up of the "walking city." Increasingly, Blacks of all incomes and occupations found their residence limited to the congested inner-city ghetto, and their efforts to expand it resisted by lower-income white neighbors. At the same time, population solidarity led to organizational activity among the Black bourgeoisie that contributed to race pride and influence and that resulted by 1920 in the formation of such urban-based national organizations as the National Association for the Advancement of Colored People, the National Urban League, and the National Federation of Colored Women's Clubs.

The problem the city presented to the Black newcomer had become evident as early as 1905 when *Charities* magazine devoted a full issue to articles on the Negro in the city. In this issue, Fannie Barrier Williams, of the Frederick Douglass Center, discussed the society and problems of Chicago's "Black Belt," alluding, among other things, to the depressing influence of the more recent European migrants, like that of the earlier Irish and German immigration, on the Blacks' occupational status.

THE "BLACK BELT" OF CHICAGO: 1905

The last federal census showed the Negro population of Chicago to be about 35,000. The present population is estimated to be over 50,000, an increase of about forty per cent in five years. The colored people who are thus crowding into Chicago come mostly from the states of Kentucky, Tennessee, Alabama, Mississippi, Louisiana, Arkansas, and Missouri. . . . [The] many industrial strikes . . . in the last ten years have brought thousands of colored people to Chicago, either for immediate work as strike-breakers, or with the prospect of employment for both skilled and unskilled workers . . . ; thousands of Negro men and women are now employed in the stockyards and other large industrial plants where ten years ago this would not have been thought of.

This increase of Negro population has brought with it problems that directly affect the social and economic life of the newcomers. Prevented from mingling easily and generally with the rest of the city's population, according to their needs and deservings, but with no preparation made for segregation . . . they have been subject to more social ills than any other nationality among us. . . . The real problem of the social life of the colored people in Chicago, as in all northern cities, lies in the fact of their segregation. While they do not occupy all the worst streets and live in all the unsanitary houses in Chicago, what is known as the "Black Belt" is altogether forbidding and demoralizing. . . .

The organizations created and maintained by them in Chicago are numerous and touch almost every phase of our social life. . . . First in importance is the Negro church. There are 25 regularly organized colored churches. This number includes 9 Methodist, 8 Baptist, 1 Catholic, 1 Episcopal, 1 Christian and 1 Presbyterian. In addition to these there are numerous missions in various parts of the "Black Belt." . . . Most of these churches are burdened with oppressive indebtedness, and because of this their usefulness as agents of moral up-lift is seriously handicapped. . . . Thousands of Negroes know and care for no other entertainment than that furnished by the church. . . .

Next to the Negro church, in importance, as affecting the social life of the people are the secret orders, embracing such organizations as the Masons, Odd Fellows, Knights of Pythias, True Reformers, the United Brotherhood, . . . the Ancient Order of Foresters, and the Elks. Nearly all of these secret orders have auxiliary associations composed of women. . . .

In the matter of employment, the colored people of Chicago have lost in the last ten years nearly every occupation of which they once had almost a monopoly. There is now scarcely a Negro barber left in the business district. Nearly all the janitor work in the large buildings has been taken away from them by the Swedes. White men and women as waiters have supplanted colored men in nearly all the first-class hotels and restaurants. Practically all the shoe polishing is now done by Greeks. Negro coachmen and expressmen and teamsters are seldom seen in the business districts. It scarcely need be stated that colored young men and women are almost never employed as clerks and bookkeepers in business establishments. . . .

The increase of the Negro population in Chicago . . . has not tended to liberalize public sentiment; in fact hostile sentiment has been considerably intensified by the importation from time to time of colored men as strike-breakers. Then again a marked increase of crime among the Negro population has been noted in recent years. All these things have tended to put us in a bad light, resulting in an appreciable loss of friends and well-wishers.[60]

Given the wartime demand for labor, together with a reduction in the supply of immigrants from Europe, employment in the city became less of a problem for the Black newcomer during World War I. Labor agents toured the South offering Negroes free transportation to the North and jobs in northern industrial centers. George E. Haynes, Negro economist and scholar, writing in *Survey* magazine, estimated that between 400,000 and 500,000 Negroes migrated northward from 1916 to 1918. Their housing situation, as Haynes described it, ran true to the prevailing practice for underprivileged new arrivals in the city.

NEGRO HOUSING IN NEWARK: 1918

Poor housing has been the main outstanding evil which has confronted the [Negro] newcomers to northern centers. From Chicago, Cincinnati, Cleveland, Columbus, Pittsburgh, Philadelphia, Newark and a score of lesser cities comes the information that migrants are being crowded into basements, shanties, fire traps, and other types of houses unfit for human habitation. . . . In Newark, N.J., one of the daily papers last November began a series of articles with the following headlines: "Wretched Homes for Negroes One Feature of Housing Lack. Majority of Newcomers from South Are Declared to Be Living in Quarters Unfitted for Human Habitations, Though Anxious to Pay for Better Ones." This newspaper cited numbers of cases and presented a series of photographs. . . . The chief health officer reported . . . that some of the owners of the old houses had been called to task. . . . "But," he . . . added, "What is the use? I suppose these houses are as bad as they were months ago. . . . The only sure way is to pull them down, and this is what ought to be done. But I do not see how we can take such action at the present time. . . . From a practical viewpoint, these houses must remain open because of housing congestion." [61]

Race riots in a number of cities between 1917 and 1921 reflected bad housing conditions, white resistance to the rising economic position of the Negro, and antipathies bred of interracial contacts in the closely populated urban environment. The bloodiest of the riots occurred in East St. Louis, Illinois, in 1917. Washington, Chicago, and Omaha were among the cities in which riots took place in 1919, and there was a horrible outbreak in Tulsa, Oklahoma in 1921. The Chicago riot, lasting from July 27 to August 2, 1919, grew out of accumulating tension and was triggered by an incident at a bathing beach. It took a toll of 38 dead (15 whites and 23 Negroes) and 537 injured. Ultimately more fully analyzed by the Chicago Commission on Race Relations, it was reported early in *Outlook* magazine of August 13, 1919.

RACE RIOTS IN CHICAGO: 1919

Chicago has just finished her first week of rioting between whites and Negroes. Already thirty-three people have lost their lives and more than three hundred have been injured. . . . During this wild week mobs of whites pursued and beat and killed Negroes. Other mobs of Negroes pursued and beat and killed whites. From the upper windows of tenements, when darkness came, snipers picked off pedestrians or fired into squads of police and soldiers sent to bring order to the Black Belt. Armed bands in motor trucks dashed wildly up and down the streets, firing into houses. It required the combined efforts of three thousand regular policemen and six thousand State militia to . . . establish a condition even remotely resembling order. . . . The week ended with a wholesale attempt to fire the city, more than one hundred dwellings being burned and three thousand people rendered homeless.

Complications, such as refusal of the icemen's union and the milk-drivers' union to deliver their commodities into the Black Belt and fear of delivery-men moving groceries that they would be assaulted and robbed, quickly reduced the Negro population to the verge of starvation. . . . It became necessary to establish a dead line around the Black Belt, where 125,000 Negroes live, and prohibit movements in and out of either race, except under guard. Even then patrolling was unable to prevent mob action from breaking out, and at times the Loop, Chicago's main business district, was the scene of actions that disgraced the community. . . .

The trouble in Chicago in no way resembled outbreaks which have taken place in other cities, such as those in Washington and St. Louis. The Chicago situation arose primarily out of the housing situation and racial antipathy. There was no question of the Negroes taking white men's jobs, as the Negroes were brought up to Chicago to fill positions in which there was a great scarcity of available labor. The packers were primarily responsible for importing them, and it became necessary for the Negroes to live within walking or short traveling distance of their work. Accordingly, they filled up the South Side between Forty-third Street and Seventeenth Street, taking over almost entirely the section formerly occupied by Chicago's notorious "red light" district. The high wages which they received . . . made them ambitious to improve their standards of living. Accordingly, they began to spread out into the more select residential districts and produced consternation among the white people. . . . Also, for the first time in the Negroes' lives, they were catered to in a political way, and they became a powerful element in municipal politics. . . . This treatment gave the Negro population of Chicago an extraordinary opinion of its own importance and led it to claim more than the Northern people were willing to give.[62]

7. THE TENEMENT PROBLEM

The flood of newcomers, whether native or from abroad, aggravated an already serious problem of the major cities — the congestion of population in the central core and the deteriorating living quarters of the poor. Slum dwellings took different forms in different cities: deteriorated row houses in Philadelphia and Baltimore; two- and three-decker frame structures in Boston, Newark, Chicago, and St. Louis; four- and five-story barracks-like buildings in New York City, sometimes built at the rear of already extensively occupied lots. If, in some cities, lots were not crowded, rooms were. As in the years before the Civil War, the situation was worse in New York City than elsewhere, not only because of the city's greater numbers but because New York was increasingly the major stopping place of European immigrants and because of the especially unsanitary conditions that resulted from pressing into residential use structures not designed for this purpose. No one gave a more graphic description of the slum scene in New York City than Jacob Riis, himself an immigrant, nor was anyone more influential in awakening the public to the need for tenement reform. As a police reporter for the *New York Tribune* and later the *Evening Sun,* Riis came into close contact with life in New York's squalid tenement quarters. He recorded his observations in *How the Other Half Lives,* published in 1890.

THE TENEMENT SCENE — NEW YORK: 1890

Where Mulberry Street crooks like an elbow within hail of the old depravity of the Five Points, is "the Bend," foul core of New York's slums. . . . Around "the Bend" cluster the bulk of the tenements that are stamped as altogether bad, even by the optimists of the Health Department. Incessant raids cannot keep down the crowds that make them their home. . . . The whole district is a maze of narrow, often unsuspected passageways — necessarily, for there is scarce a lot that has not two, three, or four tenements upon it, swarming with unwholesome crowds. . . .

In the street, where the city wields the broom, there is at least an effort at cleaning up. There has to be, or it would be swamped in filth overrunning from the courts and alleys. . . . It requires more than ordinary courage to explore these on a hot day. The undertaker has to do it then, the police always. . . . In . . . "the Bend" proper, the late Tenement House Commission counted 155 deaths of children [under 5] in a specimen year (1882). Their percentage of the total mortality in the block was 68.28, while for the whole city the proportion was only 46.20. . . .

What if I were to tell you that this alley, and more tenement property in "the Bend," all of it notorious for years as the vilest and worst to be found anywhere, stood associated on the tax-books . . . with the name of an honored family, one of the "oldest and best," rich in possessions and in influence, and high in the councils of the city's government? It would be but the plain truth. . . .

Look into any of these houses. . . . Here is a "flat" of "parlor" and two pitch-dark coops called bedrooms. Truly, the bed is all there is room for. The family tea-kettle is on the stove, doing duty for the time being as a wash-boiler. By night it will have returned to its proper use again, a practical illustration of how poverty in "the Bend" makes both ends meet. One, two, three beds are there, if the old boxes and heaps of foul straw can be called by that name; a broken stove with crazy pipe from which the smoke leaks at every joint, a table of rough boards propped up on boxes. . . . The closeness and smell are appalling. How many people sleep here? The woman with the red bandanna shakes her head sullenly, but the bare-legged girl with the bright face counts on her fingers — five, six! . . .

Well do I recollect the visit of a health inspector to one of these tenements on a July day when the thermometer outside was climbing high in the nineties; but inside, in that awful room, with half a dozen persons washing, cooking, and sorting rags, lay the dying baby alongside the stove, where the doctor's thermometer ran up to 115°. . . . What squalor and degradation inhabit these dens the health officers know. . . . From midnight till far into the small hours of the morning the policeman's thundering rap on closed doors is heard . . . on his rounds gathering evidence of illegal overcrowding. The doors are opened unwillingly enough . . . upon such scenes. . . . In a room not thirteen feet either way slept twelve men and women, two or three in bunks set in a sort of alcove, the rest on the floor. A kerosene lamp burned dimly in the fearful atmosphere, probably to guide other and later arrivals to their "beds," for it was only just past midnight. . . . The "apartment" was one of three in two adjoining buildings we had found, within half an hour, similarly crowded. Most of the men were lodgers, who slept there for five cents a spot.[63]

Contemporary novelists, depicting the slum environment, dealt with its influence on the personal character of the poor. Stephen Crane, in his short story, *Maggie, Girl of the Streets* (1893), described the personality deterioration and family disintegration that resulted from congested urban living. In relating Maggie's progression from normal, though slum-conditioned, girlhood to prostitution and self-destruction, he attempted "to show that environment is a tremendous thing in this world, and often shapes lives regardlessly." [64]

HUMAN BREAKDOWN IN STEPHEN CRANE'S RUM ALLEY: EARLY 1890's

Eventually they entered a dark region where, from a careening building, a dozen gruesome doorways gave up loads of babies to the street and to the gutter. A wind of early autumn raised yellow dust from cobbles and swirled it against a hundred windows. Long streamers of garments fluttered from fire-escapes. In all unhandy places there were buckets, brooms, rags, and bottles. In the street infants played or fought with other infants or sat stupidly in the way of vehicles. Formidable women, with uncombed hair and disordered dress, gossiped while leaning on railings, or screamed in frantic quarrels. . . . A thousand odours of cooking food came forth to the street. The building quivered and creaked from the weight of humanity stamping about in its bowels.

A small ragged girl dragged a red, bawling infant along the crowded ways. . . . As the sullen-eyed man, followed by the blood-covered boy, drew near, the little girl burst into reproachful cries. "Ah, Jimmie, youse bin fightin' agin."

The urchin swelled disdainfully. "Ah, what d' h--l, Mag. See?"

The little girl upbraided him. "Youse allus fightin', Jimmie, an' yeh knows it puts mudder out when yehs come home half dead, an' it's like we'll all get a poundin'." She began to weep. The babe threw back his head and roared at his prospects.

"Ah," cried Jimmie, "shut up er I'll smack yer mout'. See?" As his sister continued her lamentations, he suddenly struck her. The little girl reeled and, recovering herself, burst into tears and quaveringly cursed him. As she slowly retreated, her brother advanced, dealing her cuffs. . . .

Finally the procession plunged into one of the gruesome doorways. They crawled up dark stairways and along cold, gloomy halls. At last the father pushed open a door and they entered a lighted room in which a large woman was rampant.

She stopped in a career from a seething stove to a pan-covered table. As the father and children filed in she peered at them. "Eh, what? Been fightin' agin!" She threw herself upon Jimmie. . . .

The mother's massive shoulders heaved with anger. Grasping the urchin by the neck and shoulder she shook him until he rattled. She dragged him to an unholy sink, and, soaking a rag in water, began to scrub his lacerated face with it. Jimmie screamed in pain, and tried to twist his shoulders out of the clasp of the huge arms. . . .

The father . . . bellowed at his wife. "Let the kid alone for a minute, will yeh, Mary? Yer allus poundin' 'im. When I come nights I can't get no rest 'cause yer allus poundin' a kid. Let up, d'yeh hear? Don't be allus poundin' a kid." The woman's operations on the urchin instantly increased in violence. At last she tossed him to a corner, where he limply lay weeping. . . .

The ragged girl went stealthily over to the corner where the urchin lay. "Are yehs hurted much, Jimmie?" she whispered timidly.

"Not a little bit. See?" growled the little boy.

"Will I wash d' blood?"

"Naw!"

"Will I — "

"When I catch dat Riley kid I'll break 'is face! . . . See?" . . .

In the quarrel between husband and wife the woman was victor. The man seized his hat and rushed from the room, apparently determined upon a vengeful drunk. She followed to the door and thundered at him as he made his way downstairs.

• • •

Upon a wet evening . . . two interminable rows of cars, pulled by slipping horses, jangled along a prominent side street. A dozen cabs, with coat-enshrouded drivers, clattered to and fro. Electric lights, whirring softly, shed a blurred radiance. . . .

A girl of the painted cohorts of the city went along the street. She threw changing glances at men who passed her, giving smiling invitations to those of rural or untaught pattern and usually seeming sedately unconscious of the men with a metropolitan seal upon their faces. Crossing glittering avenues, she went into the throng emerging from the places of forgetfulness. . . .

The restless doors of saloons, clashing to and fro, disclosed animated rows of men before bars and hurrying bar-keepers. A concert hall gave to the street faint sounds of swift, machine-like music, as if a group of phantom musicians were hastening. . . .

A stout gentleman, with pompous and philanthropic whiskers, went stolidly by, the broad of his back sneering at the girl. A belated man in business clothes, and in haste to catch a car, bounced against her shoulder. "Hi, there, Mary, I beg your pardon!" . . .

The girl walked on out of the realm of restaurants and saloons. She passed more glittering avenues and went into darker blocks than those where the crowd travelled.

A young man in light overcoat and derby hat received a glance shot keenly from the eyes of the girl. He stopped and looked at her, thrusting his hands into his pockets and making a mocking smile curl his lips. "Come, now, old lady," he said, "you don't mean to tell me that you sized me up for a farmer?" . . .

She smiled squarely into the face of a boy who was hurrying by with his hands buried in his overcoat pockets, his blond locks bobbing on his youthful temples, and a cheery smile of unconcern upon his lips. He turned his head and smiled back at her, waving his hands. "Not this eve — some other eve!" . . .

The girl went into gloomy districts near the river, where the tall black factories shut in the street and only occasional broad beams of light fell across the pavements from saloons. In front of one of these places . . . there stood a man with blotched features.

Further on in the darkness she met a ragged being with shifting, bloodshot eyes and grimy hands.

She went into the blackness of the final block. The shutters of the tall buildings were closed like grim lips. The structures seemed to have eyes that looked over them, beyond them, at other things. Afar off the lights of the avenues glittered as if from an impossible distance. Street-car bells jingled with a sound of merriment.

At the feet of the tall buildings appeared the deathly black hue of the river. Some hidden factory sent up a yellow glare, that lit for a moment the waters lapping oilily against timbers. The varied sounds of life, made joyous by distance and seeming unapproachableness, came faintly and died away to a silence.[65]

Necessity made New York the first of the nation's cities to face the slum problem in serious fashion. Tenement legislation of 1867 had set minimal structural standards, in part in the interest of fire protection and public health, but with the increase in population in the late 1870's and 1880's housing conditions became notoriously worse. In 1877, Alfred T. White of Brooklyn undertook a much praised venture in privately financed model tenements for working people; other concerned citizens like Felix Adler, Jacob Riis, Robert W. De Forest, and Lawrence Veiller insisted that the chief need was more adequate regulatory legislation. Through their efforts and the work of numerous commissions, the state legislature was induced to pass the Tenement Act of 1901. This first substantially effective tenement law required builders of new structures to meet improved standards of ventilation and light, to substitute indoor toilets for privy vaults in tenement yards, and to provide stronger protection against accident and fire. Much still depended, however, on the extent of enforcement; moreover, because of the unceasing demand for housing, little could be done to eliminate or improve existing substandard housing. The New York law inspired the enactment of regulatory housing legislation in New Jersey in 1904 and ultimately in cities in other states. By 1909 and 1910, the movement for housing reform had accelerated, and the founding of the National Housing Association in 1910 stimulated action in cities throughout the nation.[66]

Theodore Roosevelt had become interested in housing reform as early as the 1890's when, as president of the police board of New York City, he had accompanied Jacob Riis on nightly excursions into the New York slums. In 1911, he visited Brooklyn's tenement neighborhoods, on a tour that led him to conclude, with the optimism characteristic of progressives of the period, that advances had been made in housing conditions and that, indeed, more was being done to better the slum environment in the city than to improve the deteriorating conditions on the nation's farms. He reported his findings in *Outlook* magazine.

THEODORE ROOSEVELT ASSESSES
TENEMENT REFORM — BROOKLYN: 1911

On February 13 I spent the afternoon . . . visiting a number of tenement-houses in Brooklyn, our purpose being to see the difference between the old tenement-houses and the new. . . . Thirty years ago, when I was a member of the Albany Legislature, hardly so much as a beginning in the movement for tenement-house reform had taken place. At that time, with considerable difficulty, we passed . . . a bill to do away with the tenement-house cigar factories, but neither public opinion nor judicial opinion had been educated up to the proper point. It was still the period when educated men prided themselves on their acceptance of the . . . *laissez-faire* school of political economy. On the whole, I think that educated public opinion approved the action of the State Court of Appeals in declaring the bill unconstitutional, and thereby delaying for twenty years the cure of the festering misery which it in part sought to prevent.

Fortunately, year by year we have grown away from the destructive system of social philosophy which found expression in this decision. What I saw on my brief trip through the tenement-houses that afternoon was enough to show the really extraordinary good that had been done by legislative interference with the conditions of tenement-house life. The struggle has been hard, because the owners of the property involved have fought the improvement laws at almost every step. . . .

We first visited a number of old tenement-houses, built before there was any thought of meeting hygienic requirements. . . . Mr. Murphy [Tenement-House Commissioner] does not have an adequate force of inspectors, but he is doing all that can be done with the force he has. His aim is to do all that the law permits in making these old tenements more habitable, by giving better opportunities for light and air, preventing overcrowding, and providing for the cutting of windows; and gradually, as from natural causes the old tenement-houses are pulled down, the new tenements, built under the new law and representing an immense improvement, will take their places.

Some of the tenement-houses we first visited showed very bad conditions. . . . In one ground floor below the level of the street we found a rear room in which thirteen people had been sleeping, in addition to a baby. . . . The authorities were already working an improvement in this room. They had cut a window through one wall and had forced a reduction by over a half of the number of people who slept there. . . . It is hard to arouse the public on a matter like this to the need of law. Without law only a few exceptional men will act. The owners of tenement-house property include some hard men who care nothing for the welfare of poor people; others are themselves unaware of how bad the conditions are; while there are small owners, themselves brought up in tenement-houses, who do not understand that the conditions really are bad. All of these fight bitterly against any legislative change which would reduce, and perhaps even do away with, their profits. Mr. Murphy mentioned also the difficulty he had with some of the magistrates in securing the punishment of offenders guilty of overcrowding and the like. . . .

Having finished our tour of the older tenement-houses, we then visited several of the newer tenement-houses. The first series . . . which we saw . . . were built by Mr. [Alfred T.] White, who has been a practical pioneer in the work of raising tenement-house conditions. When he built them, there was no law requiring him to do anything else than erect another vile rookery designed merely to get the utmost possible return for the least expenditure of money. But Mr. White, without any compulsion, built his tenements practically along the lines now demanded by enlightened legislation. They were so constructed that it was an easy matter for the persons who dwelt there to keep them clean and to lead healthy and self-respecting lives. Each set of rooms was isolated from every other set of rooms, and each room was lighted by a window opening on to the outer air. Moreover, each group of buildings opened on to a large yard. . . .

My next visit was to a row of tenement houses . . . built, not by philanthropists, but by business men who wished in good faith to meet the requirements of the new tenement-house law and at the same time to get as good a return as was possible upon their investments. . . . The first suite of rooms we entered was typical of all the rest. It was on the ground floor, and consisted of a kitchen, a living-room, two bedrooms, and a bath-room. The family included a father, mother, and, I believe, five or six children. Everything was as neat as possible, and it was a really attractive apartment; the older people prosperous and contented, the children growing up under good conditions, which represented an immeasurable advance over those in which their ancestors had lived for untold generations, and an almost equally great advance over the conditions of tenement-house life in New York a generation ago. As elsewhere, I looked carefully into the bath-room. Like every one else, I had heard many stories told to the discredit of the inmates of the new tenements by those worthy persons who always object to any effort to better conditions; and chief among these stories was the statement that wherever bath-rooms were put in, the tenants used the bath-tubs for storage of coal and other goods. In each case I found the bath-room well cared for, the bath-tub used for its normal purpose, and, as I was assured by every one, regularly used, too. Inquiry developed the fact that when bath-tubs were first put in tenement-houses a score of years ago or so the inmates at first knew nothing about them, did not use them for their legitimate purposes, and did often use them as receptacles for coal and other things. But . . . a short visit among tenement-houses of the new type shows that the movement for them has been more than abundantly justified.[67]

If Jacob Riis was the chief propagandist for housing reform, Lawrence Veiller was the technician whose studies and proposals set the pattern of housing reform that prevailed in urban America in the early twentieth century. It was Veiller who established the standard for the legislation that was adopted in many American cities between 1901 and 1920. Veiller was responsible for an influential tenement house exhibit in 1900 and was the author of the New York Tenement Act of 1901. He founded the National Housing Association, and his *Housing Reform: a Hand-Book for Practical Use in American Cities* (1910) provided a model for housing legislation. Veiller's almost exclusive emphasis on regulation through codes affecting structural and sanitary standards made him a traditionalist by contrast with another group of housing reformers who advocated increasing the supply of low-cost housing through public housing, tax exemption, low-interest loans to cooperatives, limited-dividend companies, or building and loan associations. Whatever the merit of the remedies Veiller proposed, his comments point up the dilemma of priorities for the housing reformer: whether to attempt to improve existing housing through regulation or to create new communities, implemented by rapid transit, where run-down housing presumably would not exist.[68]

LAWRENCE VEILLER AND HOUSING REFORM THROUGH REGULATORY LEGISLATION: 1913

There is a great variety of opinions on [the subject of housing reform]. . . . Some of our friends seem to believe that the housing problem is essentially the problem of cheap houses. . . . Another group believe that . . . if cheap and effective rapid transit could be once provided the housing problem would be solved. . . . Still another element believes that . . . anything which tends to encourage the building of more houses will solve the housing problem, the assumption being that there is a dearth of housing accommodations and that people live under bad conditions simply because there are not enough houses to go around. . . . The assumption that thousands of people live under conditions such as are found in our large cities throughout America because there are no other places in which they can live is . . . not borne out by the facts. . . . We may as well frankly admit that there is a considerable portion of our population who will live in any kind of abode that they can get irrespective of how unhygienic it may be.

If housing reform is not to be achieved through legislation . . . how are we . . . to remedy the main housing evils which we find in America today? Take the evil of the privy vault, for example, . . . certainly the greatest evil from a sanitary point of view. I can think of a hundred cities where privy vaults exist literally by the thousands. Each one of these . . . is a potent source of infection to the community. . . . Do [the proponents of garden cities] really believe that in a city of 500,000 people where there are 12,000 of these vaults . . . the establishment of a garden city or suburb on the outskirts in which possibly a thousand people might be housed, will get rid of the vaults?

If the establishment of garden cities would not rid the city of this plague of privy vaults, I am puzzled to see in just what way the development of better transit facilities would accomplish this result. . . . Improved transit . . . might move many of the population to the more sparsely settled sections of the city, but

291

it is also equally true that in such sections privies are apt to exist to a far greater extent than they do in the older sections. . . . The tendency of better transit then would be . . . to increase the total number of such vaults within the community.

Let us take another housing evil — the evil of cellar dwellings. . . . I am here puzzled also as to how the establishment of garden cities or improvement in our systems of transit or changes in methods of taxation or government subsidies to builders of homes will drive these people from their dismal cellars. So long as these cellar rooms stay there, so long as there are landlords to derive a profit from renting them and so long as there are people poor enough . . . to live in them, they will be occupied. There is no city in America in which it is not a common experience to find such rooms occupied in considerable number and to find in the same town a very large quantity of vacant apartments of a much more adequate and sanitary type. The only method I know of by which the occupancy of these unfit habitations can be stopped is to forbid people to live in them. This can be done only through legislation; but even then people will live there, unless the laws are enforced.

In housing reform we need especially to beware of importations from across the sea . . . because the conditions which exist in the old-world countries are so totally different from those which prevail in America. . . . The methods which have been successful in Europe have been so because they have been suited to the conditions which exist there. To be successful here we should have to engraft upon our civilization the governmental bureaucracy which we find in Europe. . . . That legislation alone will solve the housing problem is of course absurd. . . . But the point . . . is that in most cases the largest results have come from legislative action and that until certain fundamental evils have been remedied it is futile, or worse, to adopt the methods of housing reform which may be said to belong to the postgraduate period rather than to the kindergarten stage of a community's development. In other words, we must get rid of our slums before we establish garden cities. We must stop people living in cellars before we concern ourselves with changes in methods of taxation. We must make it impossible for builders to build dark rooms in new houses before we urge the government to subsidize the building of houses. We must abolish privy vaults before we build model tenements. When these things have been done there is no question but that effort can be profitably expended in the other directions mentioned.[69]

8. THE CONTRIBUTIONS OF THE
SETTLEMENTS AND THE URBAN CHURCH

No group did more to ease the lot of the slum dweller and reveal the need for more effective tenement legislation than settlement workers, who became active after the mid-1880's in the major cities, especially those of the Northeast and the upper Middle West. In the period from the 1890's to World War I, particularly, they actively encouraged reform through collecting and publicizing statistics, influencing the election of officials, and getting bills passed in state legislatures. The idea of the settlement originated in England as a social and educational institution to bridge the gap that industrialism and the large city had created between the rich and the poor; but the problem of the immigrant in the slums of the American city gave the movement here a more socially oriented and nonsectarian tone. The pioneer settlement in the United States was the Neighborhood Guild (later the University Settlement), founded by Stanton Coit in 1886 on New York's lower East Side. Other representative settlements were the College Settlement and the Henry Street Settlement in New York, Hull House and the Chicago Commons in Chicago, Andover House in Boston, and Kingsley House in Pittsburgh. By 1910 the number of settlements exceeded 400. Here, concerned men and women, many directly from college or graduate school, but increasingly from a variety of occupations, took up residence in slum environments, neighboring — in the best sense of the term — with an immigrant, sweat-shop population and engaging in activities designed to meet the physical, educational, and recreational needs of the neighborhood.[70] The philosophy and program of the nation's best-known settlement were explained by Jane Addams in 1892 in an article in *Forum* magazine.

JANE ADDAMS DESCRIBES
CHICAGO'S HULL HOUSE: 1892

Hull House, Chicago's first Social Settlement, was established in September, 1889. It . . . was opened by two women, supported by many friends, in the belief that the mere foothold of a

293

house, easily accessible, ample in space, hospitable and tolerant in spirit, situated in the midst of the large foreign colonies which so easily isolate themselves in American cities, would be in itself a serviceable thing for Chicago. . . . It was opened on the theory that the dependence of classes on each other is reciprocal; and that as "the social relation is essentially a reciprocal relation, it gave a form of expression that has peculiar value." . . .

Hull House is an ample old residence, well built and somewhat ornately decorated after the manner of its time, 1856. . . . It once stood in the suburbs, but the city has steadily grown up around it and its site now has corners on three or four distinct foreign colonies. Between Halsted Street and the river live about ten thousand Italians. . . . To the south on Twelfth Street are many Germans, and side streets are given over almost entirely to Polish and Russian Jews. Further south, these Jewish colonies merge into a huge Bohemian colony, so vast that Chicago ranks as the third Bohemian city in the world. To the northwest are many Canadian-French, . . . and to the north are many Irish and first-generation Americans. . . .

The streets are inexpressibly dirty, the number of schools inadequate, factory legislation unenforced, the street-lighting bad, the paving miserable, . . . and the stables defy all laws of sanitation. . . . The Hebrews and Italians do the finishing for the great clothing-manufacturers. . . . As the design of the sweating system is the elimination of rent from the manufacture of clothing, the "outside work" is begun after the clothing leaves the cutter. For this work no basement is too dark, no stable loft too foul, no rear shanty too provisional, no tenement room too small, as these conditions imply low rental. Hence these shops abound in the worst of the foreign districts, where the sweater easily finds his cheap basement and his home finishers. . . .

This site for a Settlement was selected . . . because of its diversity and the variety of activity for which it presented an opportunity. It has been the aim of the residents to respond to all sides of the neighborhood life. . . . One thing seemed clear in regard to entertaining these foreigners: to preserve and keep for them whatever of value their past life contained and to bring them into contact with a better type of Americans. For two years, every Saturday evening, our Italian neighbors were our guests; entire families came . . . and the house became known as a place where Italians were welcome and where national holidays were observed. They came to us with their petty lawsuits, sad relics of the *vendetta*, with their incorrigible boys, with their hospital cases, with their aspirations for American clothes, and with their needs for an interpreter. . . .

But our social evenings are by no means confined to foreigners. Our most successful clubs are entirely composed of English speaking and American-born young people. . . . The boys who are known as the Young Citizens' Club are supposed to inform themselves on municipal affairs. . . . The gymnasium is a somewhat pretentious name for a building next door which was formerly a saloon, but which we rented last fall, repaired, and fitted up with simple apparatus. . . . The more definite humanitarian effect of Hull House has taken shape in a day nursery. . . . During two months of this summer the reports sent in from Hull House to the Municipal Order League and through it to the Health Department were one thousand and thirty-seven, . . . and a marked improvement has taken place in the scavenger service and in the regulation of the small stables of the ward. . . .

Last May twenty girls from a knitting factory who struck because they were docked for loss of time when they were working by the piece, came directly from the factory to Hull House. . . . They had heard that we "stood by working people." We were able to have the strike arbitrated . . . and we had the satisfaction of putting on record one more case of arbitration in the slowly growing list. . . . It is difficult to classify the Working Peoples' Social Science Club, which meets weekly at Hull House. It is social, educational, and civic in character, the latter because it strongly connects the house with the labor problems in their political and social aspects. . . .

I am always sorry to have Hull House regarded as philanthropy, although it doubtless has strong philanthropic tendencies. . . . Working people live in the same streets with those in need of charity, but they themselves require and want none of it. As one of their number has said, they require only that their aspirations be recognized and stimulated and the means of attaining them put at their disposal. Hull House makes a constant effort to secure these means, but to call that effort philanthropy is to use the word unfairly and to underestimate the duties of good citizenship.[71]

Settlement workers soon realized that the first need of their working-class neighbors was vocational training, home and school nursing, playground and bath facilities, freedom from filthy streets, and above all else improved housing conditions. They began to document the need for these and other social improvements and to present their cases to city councils and state legislatures in ways that contributed to the achievement of reform. Jacob Riis gave settlement workers major credit for the improvements that had taken place in working-class neighborhoods by 1908.

SETTLEMENT WORKERS AND IMPROVED CONDITIONS ON NEW YORK'S EAST SIDE: 1908

Twenty years ago the East Side had a bad name and it deserved it. The slum was in unchallenged control. Ragged children played in dirty gutters. Their homes were noisome tenements. . . . Into the midst of all this came the settlements. They came to help and they told the truth. In half a dozen years the old corrupt conspiracy we called our city government had been turned out. The streets were cleaned, parks and playgrounds were made for the people. But before the whole programme of reform could be put through, the enemy came back, more defiant, more corrupt than ever. They took the people's playgrounds. . . . The tenements reverted to their evil state, and worse things happened. They were overrun with lewd women who paid blackmail to the police and defied the tenants. . . .

There was a meeting in one of the settlements on the lower East Side, and Felix Adler spoke to the young men. . . . From that meeting sprang the reform movement that elected Seth Low. It brought back to the people their playgrounds . . . and the settlements are to-day pushing for more. . . . The reform started by the settlements drafted our tenement-house law that gives light and air a legal claim in the homes of the poor, and pushed it through. . . . It cleaned the streets. It brought the mortality among the tenants' babies down to the lowest mark, and last of all it made odious the very name of slum with what it stands for. When to-day we have to fight for the things that make for the city's good, for safeguarding the home, we fight no longer for but *with* the people. And this is the settlements' doing; this is the work of their twenty years' campaign of education. Other influences helped, but back of them, back of it all, were ever the push, the enthusiasm, the undaunted hope of the settlement worker who led on in the fight for better things, for cleaner things. If to-day the East Side wears a different garb, if happy children play safe from harm, in playgrounds of their own, . . . [one] can thank these "crusaders" who came to help and who have wrought so well.[72]

The activities of the settlements provided a model of practice for the Protestant church, faced with new problems springing from the secular distractions and from the fragmentation of the family in large cities. It was faced as well with the challenge posed by the denominationally different population elements that were being added to the city in large numbers in the late nineteenth and early twentieth centuries. Many clergymen of the older Protestant sects deplored the abandonment of working-class neighborhoods as churches followed their parishioners to newer sections of the city or to the suburbs. Advocates of a more socially oriented gospel, like Washington Gladden of Columbus, Ohio, and Walter Rauschenbusch of Rochester, New York, believed that the church should serve the temporal as well as the spiritual needs of city dwellers, provide social programs to counter the temptations and frustrations of city life, and engage actively in improving the lot of the underprivileged in the city. One evidence of this concern was the development of what came to be known as the "institutional" or "open" church, where round-the-clock, seven-days-a-week activities manifested the conviction that the church should minister to all aspects of the urban society.[73] Charles Stelzle, Bowery-born Presbyterian minister, saw the institutional church as a major, if not always appreciated, response to the city's challenge to organized religion.

THE CHURCH AND THE CITY —
A "SOCIAL GOSPEL" VIEW: 1907

The growth of the city is one of the wonders of modern times . . . [yet] the Church is slowly but surely losing ground in the great centers of population. Nearly every city in America is witnessing the removal of its Churches from the densely populated sections, where the Church is most needed. . . . Within recent years, forty Protestant Churches moved out of the district below Twentieth Street in New York City, while three hundred thousand people moved in, and they were all working-people. I know it is said sometimes that the people in the lower end of New York are all foreigners. I lived there too long to be fooled by that statement. But suppose it is true. . . . God, in His providence, has sent the foreigner to our very door, He has given us the mission of evangelizing him; and it will be only as the Church is willing to lose her life that she will find it again among the masses of the people. Now, if the tendency of the population is toward the cities, and if the cities are to dominate the nation, . . . it does not require a prophet . . . to foretell the result, if this failure of the Church in meeting the city problem continues. . . .[74]

The spirit and the aim of the institutional church is expressed in the platform of the Open and Institutional Church League . . . "to save all men and all of the man by all means, abolishing, so far as possible, the distinction between the religious and secular, and sanctifying all days and all means to the great end of saving the world for Christ." [According to] Josiah Strong, . . . "The institutional church . . . succeeds because it adapts itself to changed conditions. It finds that the people living around it have in their homes no opportunity to take a bath; it therefore furnishes bathing facilities. It sees that the people have little or no healthful social life; it accordingly opens attractive social rooms, and organizes clubs for men, women, boys, and girls. The people know little of legitimate amusement; the Church, therefore, provides it. They are ignorant of household economy; the Church establishes its cooking-schools, its sewing-schools, and the like. In their homes the people have few books and papers; in the Church they find a free reading-room and library." . . .

Probably no church in the entire world is doing a greater work on social lines than that being done by St. Bartholomew's Protestant Episcopal Church in New York City. Over two hundred meetings, of various kinds, are held weekly. . . . Sunday services are held in the Parish House for Germans, Armenians, and Chinese, and there are regular services in the Swedish Chapel. Each of these nationalities has a surpliced choir which renders music in its own language. . . . The church supports one of the best equipped dispensaries in the city. Fifty-four physicians volunteer their services. Last year 15,227 new patients were treated. . . . The Loan Association . . . received during the year $101,517.59, and disbursed $91,345. Loans are made to the poor at a reasonable rate of interest. . . . Club life is prominent. There are clubs for men and women, boys and girls, with a total membership of 2,796. Membership in the Girls' Evening Club entitles the holder to the use of the clubrooms and library; access to the large hall every evening after nine o'clock, to the physical-culture classes, lectures, talks, entertainments, discussion class, glee club, literature class, English composition class, the Helping Hand Society, Penny Provident and Mutual Benefit Funds; the privilege of joining one class a week in either dressmaking, millinery, embroidery, drawn-work, system sewing or cooking; also, by paying a small fee, the privilege of entering a class in stenography, typewriting, French, or bookkeeping. . . .

For those seeking work . . . an efficient employment bureau is conducted. During the past year 2,531 situations were filled. The kindergarten enrolled 259 children, the Industrial School, 336. The Fresh Air work of the parish gave outings to thousands of mothers and their children. Garments were provided for the poor, such as were able paying a small amount for them. The Penny Provident Fund received $31,483.29 from 5,196 depositors.[75]

In the social functions of the parish and the congregation, the Catholic and the Jewish churches provided many of the services Protestants attempted to supply through the institutional church; yet in many cities there remained a segment of the population — the "submerged tenth," some called it — that challenged the attention of special groups with a religious orientation. Typical of these and probably the best known was the Salvation Army, whose activities in the United States, like many other efforts to deal with the social problems of the city, followed practices that had originated in London. By the early 1880's, representatives of the Salvation Army had organized their quasi-military corps in America and had begun to minister to "rumdom, slumdom, and bumdom" in the American city. In 1894, Maud Ballington Booth, daughter-in-law of the British founder of the organization, described the specialized role of the Slum Brigade of the Army.

THE SALVATION ARMY — EFFORTS TO REACH THE "SUBMERGED TENTH": 1894

When the Salvation Army launched out upon its work of raising and helping the outcast, it . . . reached, and is now reaching the poor, otherwise untouched by religious influence. Street loungers, drunkards, wife-beaters, wild, reckless youths, and fallen women, were attracted to its halls, by the hundreds of thousands, by the open-air procession, and through the lively and enthusiastic character of its services. . . .

It is now five years since we began the Slum Brigade work in New York City. . . . Perhaps the duty which absorbs the greatest part of their time is . . . the systematic house-to-house and room-to-room visitation of all the worst homes in their neighborhood. The visits paid in saloons and dives are naturally of a different character. There it has to be personal, dealing face to face with the people upon the danger of their wild lives, and the sorrow and misery that is coming to them. Sometimes it has to be very straight and earnest talk to some drunken man. At others gentle, affectionate pleading with some poor outcast girl, down whose painted cheeks the tears of bitter remorse fall. . . . Our women work entirely without escort, and this very fact appeals to the spark of gallantry in the hearts of those rough, hardened men, and if any one dared to lay a finger upon the "Slum Sisters," or say an insulting word to them, champions would arise on every hand to defend them. . . . These visits are often lengthened into prayer-meetings, which include singing and speaking, to a more interested audience, and certainly a more needy one, than can be found within the walls of many a church. . . .

Street work is another phase of their mission. . . . In this they deal with the people whom they have not found within the saloons . . . many of them being sailors and members of the floating population. . . . They are talked to in a friendly and yet very practical way during the evening hours, when there is a great deal of street lounging. . . .

Yet another means of reaching these people is the gathering of them into our halls or meeting places. . . . The audiences are chiefly composed of men, very often young men such as from the toughest gangs in down-town sections of the city. . . . The bright, lively songs of the Salvation Army, the ever changing phases of the meetings, and the thorough bond of sympathy between the speakers on the platform and the roughs in the hall make these meetings a source of great power and interest. Of course, there are occasionally fights among the audience, chairs are upset every now and then, windows are broken . . . and yet through it all a deep, powerful wave of influence carries into the hearts of the people the sincerity and truth of things spiritual.[76]

Social-minded clergy and settlement workers were joined by many other serious citizens in believing that if the fragmentation of society and conflict of group interest in large cities were to be overcome, the poor, and especially the immigrant newcomers, needed to be better equipped for urban living and introduced to a more elevated, more traditionally "American" life style. The social programs of the institutional churches and the settlement houses were designed to meet these needs, as were the efforts to improve the living environment of the poor through housing legislation; but other reforms were advocated for the same purposes. These included efforts to improve the skills and attitudes of the poor and the foreign born through expanded educational facilities such as preschool kindergarten training, to affect habits early; vocational programs such as manual training, domestic science, and industrial art in the public schools, as well as technical institutes, to inculcate occupational skills; and university extension programs, people's institutes, and self-culture societies to bring working men and women into contact with what was currently called "the higher life." The reformers also advocated the construction of public baths, well-run lodging houses for the transient population, and recreational facilities such as social centers and small parks and playgrounds to counter the discomforts and temptations of the city, for the poor, ignorant, and alienated. Private philanthropists often subsidized these endeavors, upon their initiation by social-minded reformers; but in time the supporters of the reforms tended to involve the city government in taking over or expanding their efforts.

Robert Woods, Boston settlement worker, was a spokesman for the view that the municipal government must supplement the contribution of private agencies in ameliorating the social problems accompanying the growth of large cities. He asserted the need for a positive, active municipal government and argued for giving slum neighborhoods a voice in decisions concerning schools, poor relief, and public welfare. Woods became head of Andover House, a settlement in Boston's South End, in the early 1890's. He expressed his views in *The City Wilderness* (1898), a work that has been called the first thoroughgoing sociological study of a depressed area in an American city.

TRANSFORMING THE "CITY WILDERNESS" — BOSTON: 1898

In its official capacity [the city] sets up standards of health, intelligence, and morality, beyond which the general level of the population cannot fall. It refuses to allow the sick or hungry to go uncared for. It insists that children shall not grow up in illiteracy. It especially guards some of the avenues of degradation. Resting back upon this rudimentary protective system, the people of the city proceed first to see that no family shall be without assistance toward recovering honorably from material disaster, and secondly to supply in general some of the means of a happier and nobler existence. By this voluntary effort additional checks are put on the encroachment of social tendencies upon personal and domestic welfare.

Moreover, some of the larger local affairs are being positively ordered and directed toward beneficent ends. . . . The municipality . . . is passing from merely guarding against evil into urging on the common good. . . . There are unmistakable signs . . . that the informal social organizations of the [South End] district, touched by the many enlightening influences about them, are learning to use their collective political power for their collective interest rather than for the aggrandizement of the boss. From this point it is not so long a step to some appreciation of the general good of the city; and the step will be taken as soon as the municipality comes to stand more obviously for the particular good of the great masses of its citizens. It has been clearly shown that the boss system has its power by holding up before people whose lives at best are meagre the alluring chance of tangible benefits. The cheat of this can all be exposed by a municipal policy which . . . undertakes to minister more largely to certain keenly felt common needs. . . .

The reserve force of the city begins to assert itself definitely against some of the rank developments associated with phenomenal growth. Gradually the incoherent masses that make up the city population are being bound together by a strong municipal government. Such a city government must undertake many new responsibilities. . . . The schools, the public library with its radiating local centres, the board of health, the water department, the police, are all entering upon aggressive methods, with the social well-being in view; instead of following the old perfunctory way of simply serving the individual needs that made themselves manifest. . . . [The city also] has a new and active department of public music, giving concerts summer and winter; the art commission is to provide for the decoration of school rooms, and will share in giving the South End Free Art Exhibition; and series of evening lectures, under municipal direction, are to be given in school halls throughout the city. The bath commission is engaged upon a programme which, taking its beginning with the municipal floating and beach baths that have existed for many years, is about to give each working-class section of the city a bath-house open the year round, a playground, to be flooded for skating in the winter, and a gymnasium, all under municipal auspices.

The South End . . . will profit most especially by this humane and realistic policy. What must further come, however, is a greater degree of local autonomy. South End people are justly proud of what the City is accomplishing in their midst. They are not slow to appreciate such efforts to improve their lot. But more of their own representatives must be taken into the confidence of the administration. They must be intrusted with some active responsibility in connection with the schools, the relief of the poor, and the general public care of the local public welfare. In due time, by making the government of the city a personal interest to many local citizens, it would be possible to develop a spirit of dissatisfaction with the men who are now sent as delegates to the City Council.

The reëstablishment of a degree of local self-government in this great district is positively necessary, not only for the political training of citizens, but for securing the local identity and local loyalty out of which the feeling of social responsibility springs. American democracy does not contemplate the formation of vast, sprawling, formless masses of population governed from a single centre. Great cities, under social as well as political necessity, must restore to their local districts some of the old village powers. In this particular district, a partial embodiment, both social and political, of this policy may soon be made in a building which it is proposed to erect on a large lot of ground close to the most crowded corner in the district and owned by the City. . . . Such a building . . . would have in it a voting place, certain City offices, headquarters for the central trade-union bodies, a branch of the public library, and a large hall for lectures, concerts, picture shows, and public meetings.[77]

9. MACHINE POLITICS

One of the admitted purposes of efforts to uplift and enlighten the poor and the immigrant newcomer was to counter the influence upon them of the city political machines. Though machine politics were evident by the 1850's and under attack by the late 1860's, the boss and the machine continued to flourish in the post-Civil War years. The ever increasing size and impersonality of the nation's large cities encouraged the continued existence of machine politics, as did the amenable electorate provided by the large number of newly arriving immigrants, willing to support the machine politician in return for services that eased their adjustment to urban life. Even more than at the mid-century, public contracts for sewers, waterworks, and street construction and the award of franchises for the operation of public utilities by private companies gave manifold opportunities for graft and boodle to mayors and city councils and to the bosses who, more often than not, controlled their actions. At a lower level of "pay-off" was the exaction of protection money by minor officials such as building inspectors and police. Though the boss and the machine often served to coordinate the fragmented government in the large city and contributed to the adjustment of the foreign born, these services were less apparent to influential segments of the citizenry than the periodic disclosures of graft and corruption, the high taxes, and the inadequacy of public servants and public services for which they were blamed, and often with reason. As a result of visits to the United States in the 1880's, Lord Bryce gained the impression that the government of its cities was "the one conspicuous failure of the United States." [78] This view was also expressed by a distinguished American, Andrew D. White, chief mover for the establishment of Cornell University and its first president, from 1868 to 1885. In an article published in *Forum* magazine in 1890, White contrasted the management of American cities with what he had observed in Europe.

THE MISMANAGEMENT OF AMERICAN CITIES: 1890

Without the slightest exaggeration we may assert that, with very few exceptions, the city governments of the United States are the worst in Christendom — the most expensive, the most inefficient, and the most corrupt. No one who has any considerable knowledge of our own country and of other countries can deny this. . . . One has but to walk along the streets of . . . great American cities, to notice at once that some evil principle is at work. Everywhere are wretched wharves, foul docks, inadequate streets, and inefficient systems of sewerage, paving, and lighting. Pavements which were fairly good at the beginning, have been taken up and replaced with utter carelessness. . . . Obstacles of all sorts are allowed; tangled networks of wires frequently exist in such masses overhead as to prevent access to buildings in case of fire, and almost to cut off the rays of the sun. . . . In wet weather many of the most important thoroughfares are covered with reeking mud; in dry weather this mud, reduced to an impalpable dust containing the germs of almost every disease, is blown into the houses and into the nostrils of the citizens.

The city halls of these larger towns are the acknowledged centers of the vilest corruption. . . . Such cities, like the decaying spots on ripe fruit, tend to corrupt the whole body politic. As a rule, the men who sit in the councils of our larger cities . . . are men who in no other country would think of aspiring to such positions. Some of them, indeed, would think themselves lucky in keeping outside the prisons. Officials intrusted with the expenditure of the vast wealth of our citizens are frequently men whom no one would think of intrusting with the management of his private affairs, or, indeed, of employing in any capacity. Few have gained their positions by fitness or by public service; many have gained them by scoundrelism; some by crime. . . .

At various times it has been my lot to sojourn in nearly every one of the greater European municipalities, from Edinburgh to Athens, from St. Petersburg to Naples, from Paris to Buda-Pesth. . . . In every respect for which a city exists, they are vastly superior to our own. . . . Take . . . as a type of administration in a great metropolitan city, the municipal system of Paris. . . . First, there was the city itself, with its perfect management above ground — every street well paved, well kept, and constantly well cleansed; every house in good repair; all lines of communication carefully studied; all obstacles removed; the system of illumination so perfect that in every important street one could read a newspaper at night; the names of all streets neatly placarded at street corners; no electric wires in sight; no buildings pushed up to such a height as to cast a shade over whole quarters of the city, and thus to depress the public health; no steam boilers in places where they could . . . do injury. Underground the system was even more striking — the sewerage as perfect as the resources of science could make it; subterranean railways and canals conducting the city's refuse to remote districts, where it becomes a blessing rather than a curse. . . .

The difference between foreign cities and ours, is that all these well-ordered cities . . . accept this principle — that cities are corporations and not political bodies; that they are not concerned with matters of national policy; that national parties as such have nothing whatever to do with city questions. . . . We, on the other hand, are putting ourselves upon a basis which has always failed . . . the idea that a city is a political body, and therefore that it is to be ruled, in the long run, by a city proletariat mob, obeying national party cries [and managed on the

305

principle that] wards largely controlled by thieves and robbers can [elect] thieves and robbers, and . . . that men who can carry their ward can control the city.[79]

The techniques of mobilizing the votes at the ward level to ensure boss rule were detailed by Rufus E. Shapley in a fictitious account of the rise to political influence of one Michael Mulhooly, an Irish immigrant. Mulhooly began his political education in his uncle's saloon, popularly known as the "Tenth Precinct House," was naturalized on affidavit after having been in the United States only two years instead of five, and by cultivation of Blossom Brick, a power in the municipal legislature, himself rose to the lucrative position of alderman and ultimately was elected to Congress. Shapley tells Mulhooly's story in *Solid for Mulhooly: a Sketch of Municipal Politics under the Leaders of the Ring and the Boss,* published in 1881.[80]

HOW TO BUILD A POLITICAL MACHINE: 1880

[Mulhooly] had now won his political spurs. . . . He had voted once before he was of age; had voted four times at the election immediately succeeding his naturalization; at the following election had led to the polls six citizens whose votes it was known would be challenged, and had succeeded in persuading the election officers to receive five of them; had twice knocked down a police officer who interfered with him while he was discharging this delicate and important public duty. . . . Such men never fail to receive that recognition from the party leaders to which such invaluable party services entitle them, and accordingly, Michael Mulhooly was immediately placed upon his Ward Committee; and, at the next election, was appointed by the court an election officer to fill a vacancy, at the instance of one of the ward leaders who was a candidate for constable. This duty he also discharged so successfully that when the returns were made up by the election officers, it was found that his candidate for constable had received nearly a hundred more votes than those who kept the lists could account for or believed had been cast. Thus he commenced to comprehend those unknown quantities in politics which so materially affect results. . . .

Blossom Brick, knowing of Michael's many talents for politics, and desiring to extend his own empire over the ward in which the Tenth Precinct House was situated, undertook, not unwillingly, the task of instructing him further in the mysteries of practical politics — a task for which he was pre-eminently qualified . . . ; for Blossom Brick had become the acknowledged leader of the Municipal Legislature. He came to look upon his ward as a property which he owned, or as an empire which he had the right to rule, as with a rod of iron. No man in it could hope for any appointment except through him, and no man in it dared be a candidate even for school director without his permission. . . . He made daily visits to each department of the city government and demanded appointments for his followers and the removal of those who disobeyed him, as though the departments had been created for his exclusive benefit. He lived but for the public. In order that the people might make no mistakes he dictated what nominations should, or should not, be made. To save the people trouble, he selected in advance their candidates for legislators, for congressmen, for judges. He did not hesitate to direct legislators, congressmen and judges how they should discharge their public duties. His devotion to his party knew no bounds. At every important election he organized a campaign club which bore his name, and paraded a thousand uniformed men, bearing torches, and marching with the precision of veterans. . . .

When one man owns and dominates four wards . . . he becomes a Leader. Half a dozen such Leaders combined constitute what is called a Ring. When one Leader is powerful enough to bring three or four such Leaders under his yoke he becomes a Boss. . . . The Leaders, the Ring and the Boss combined, constitute the modern system of American politics which has been found to work so successfully in all large cities, especially in those which are fortunate enough to have secured a working majority of Leaders from Ireland. . . . The great merit of this system is that it takes from the people all the trouble of self-government and imposes that burden upon the Leaders, the Ring and the Boss, compelling them to assume all the worriment of selecting proper public servants and all the responsibility of managing public affairs, while it preserves, in unimpaired purity, the form of a "government of the people, by the people, and for the people." . . .

Mulhooly learned many political axioms from Blossom Brick:

"It matters less how many votes you have than how many you poll; it matters less how many you poll than how many you get counted."

"One election officer well in hand is worth a score of voters on the half shell."

"The result of an election is only a question of figures. A

stroke of the pen before the figures 99 is as good as the votes of a hundred millionaire taxpayers, if you're smart enough to get away with it." . . .

In speaking of the way in which nominations are made he said: "Party rules are the reins and party spirit the bit by which We drive the people all the time." . . .

Under the tuition of such a master, Michael Mulhooly could not fail to make rapid strides in the study of practical statesmanship. As a member of the Ward Committee, as the proprietor of a saloon which was becoming the party headquarters of the Ward, as well as of the Precinct, and, as the intimate friend of so powerful a Leader as Blossom Brick, his influence grew so rapidly that in a short time he was chosen as the representative of his Ward in the City Committee. From this vantage ground he could . . . study the party organization in all its divisions and subdivisions. . . . He saw that the party organization was composed primarily of Precinct Committees, Ward Committees and the City Committee, and, secondarily, of Conventions to place in nomination candidates for various offices to be chosen at elections held by the people; and . . . that . . . this perfect party organization . . . placed the entire control of the whole machinery in a central head or master-spirit, composed of one man, or two men, or half a dozen men . . . or in other words, of the Leaders, the Ring, and the Boss. . . . He saw that by this system the Leaders, the Ring, and the Boss practically nominated all candidates, and as . . . a nomination is equivalent to an election, they, therefore, practically appointed all public officers, under the form of an election by the people. . . .

He soon saw that this whole system was founded on (a) the tendency of every voter to work in the traces, and vote for any man ostensibly nominated by the party; (b) the strict enforcement of the Party Rules; and (c) the judicious distribution of the 4,036 regularly salaried offices in the various departments of the city government . . . ; the various municipal, State and national offices . . . ; and of the various contracts for public work, involving the outlay of millions of dollars given to contractors who are willing not only to Rebate, but also to properly control at all times the thousands of workmen whom they employ in the public service.[81]

The subservience of the police to machine-dominated city governments impeded the solution of the problems of vice, crime, and public order that plagued large cities as a result of their increasing size and social complexity. Few policemen considered themselves to be, or were regarded as, professional public servants acting outside the operation of local politics. Like the average citizen, they indulged their ethnic and racial prejudices on the job and showed more interest in lining their own pocketbooks than in ensuring public morality, if, indeed, there was any consensus, in the large urban community, as to what public morality was. This state of affairs was brought out dramatically in the Lexow investigations in New York, which documented the prevalence of police brutality and the collusion between the political machine, the police, and the underworld. This state senate investigation was triggered by a crusade against vice led by the Reverend Charles Parkhurst of New York City's Madison Square Presbyterian Church. Its findings disclosed that the payoff totaled $7,000,000 annually. Monthly levies were $2 to $20 for saloons, a minimum of $5 per inmate for bawdy houses. The protection money was divided 20 per cent to the patrolman-collector, 35 to 50 per cent to the precinct commander, and the rest to the inspector. It was revealed that policemen paid from $300 to $15,000 for appointment and promotion. The Lexow Committee interviewed 678 witnesses and transmitted a five-volume report to the state legislature in January, 1895.[82]

THE LEXOW INVESTIGATION — POLICE "PAYOFFS": THE 1890's

The results of the investigation [show] . . . that in a very large number of election districts . . . almost every conceivable crime against the elective franchise was either committed or permitted by the police, invariably in the interest of the dominant Democratic organization of the city of New York, commonly called Tammany Hall. The crimes thus committed or permitted by the police may be classified as follows:

Arrest and brutal treatment of Republican voters, watchers, and workers; . . . canvassing for Tammany Hall candidates; invasion of election booths; forcing of Tammany Hall pasters upon Republican voters . . . colonization of voters, illegal registration and repeating, aided and knowingly permitted by the police . . . ; cooperation with and acquiescence in the usurpation by Tammany Hall election district captains . . . of alleged rights and privileges, in violation of law.

In fact, . . . the police themselves at the several polling

places [acted] upon the principle that they were there, not as guardians of the public peace to enforce law and order, but for the purpose of acting as agents of Tammany Hall. . . . It was conclusively shown that during each of the years 1891, 1892 and 1893, very many thousands of unlawful ballots were cast and counted by the active co-operation and connivance of the police. . . .

The testimony [concerning protection of disorderly houses] establishes conclusively the fact that this variety of vice was regularly and systematically licensed by the police of the city. The system had reached such a perfection in detail that the inmates of the several houses were numbered and classified and a ratable charge placed upon each proprietor in proportion to the number of inmates, or in cases of houses of assignation the number of rooms occupied and the prices charged, reduced to a monthly rate, which was collected within a few days of the first of each month during the year. This was true apparently with reference to all disorderly houses, except in the case of a few specially favored ones. The prices ran from $25 to $50 monthly, depending upon the considerations aforesaid, besides fixed sums for the opening of new houses or the resumption of "business" in old or temporarily abandoned houses, and for "initiation fees" designed as an additional gratuity to captains upon their transfer into new precincts. The established fee for opening and initiation appears to have been $500. . . .

The evidence, furthermore, shows, that in some of the houses . . . visitors were systematically robbed, and when they made complaint at the station-house the man detailed to examine into the charge failed to arrest the perpetrator, and frightened the victim off by threats, and then returned and received his compensation, an equal division of the plunder between the thief and the officer.

The testimony, taken as a whole, conclusively establishes that the social evil was, and probably still is, fostered and protected by the police of the city, even to the extent of inducing its votaries to continue their illegal practices, maintaining substantially a partnership with them in the traffic, absorbing the largest part of the resulting profit. . . .

Testimony of Officer Edward Shalvey, who served as wardman under Captain Webb and Captain Dougherty

Question: [by Mr. John W. Goff]. Well, now . . . during the time . . . [Captain Doherty] was commander of that police precinct, you, by his authority and approval, collected money from the keepers of houses of ill-fame, keepers of policy shops, of pool-rooms, and liquor dealers? A. Yes, sir.

Q. And you collected that money from them as a bribe to be given to the captain, so that the captain would allow them to violate the law without any interference on his part, or the part of his men in that precinct? A. That was the intention.

Q. Who was the collector — who was the representative of the liquor dealers during that time . . . ? A. Alderman Clancy. . . .

Q. The other places I presume you followed the same course? A. Yes, sir.

Q. The pool-rooms and keepers of disorderly houses? A. Yes, sir; the same course.

Q. Have you stated the average amount of money that you gave to the captain each month? . . . A. Well, it used to vary from $300, $400 to $500 a month.

Q. And during that time, and while this money was being paid to the captain every month, these several places were not interfered with by the captain or his men? A. Not unless they became obnoxious to the residents. . . .

Q. That is, unless complaint was made by some responsible citizens, or unless a robbery was committed, or some public breach was committed that attracted attention to these places, they were not interfered with? A. No, sir. . . .

Q. That would be . . . $6,800 that you paid . . . to Captain Doherty . . . ? A. Yes, sir. . . .[83]

The classic indictment of the graft-ridden city of the late nineteenth century was the series of articles by Lincoln Steffens that began to appear in *McClure's Magazine* in the fall of 1902. Steffens put the blame on a permissive public as well as on the grafters whom he found dominating the governments of the major American cities, especially St. Louis, Minneapolis, Pittsburgh, and Philadelphia. When Steffens set out to write the stories on municipal corruption, a grand jury in St. Louis had recently indicted eighteen members of the municipal legislature.

LINCOLN STEFFENS ON MUNICIPAL CORRUPTION — ST. LOUIS: 1902

The corruption of St. Louis came from the top. The best citizens — the merchants and big financiers — used to rule the town, and they ruled it well. . . . But a change occurred. Public spirit became private spirit, public enterprise became private greed.

Along about 1890, public franchises and privileges were sought not only for legitimate profit and common convenience, but for loot. Taking but slight and always selfish interest in the public councils, the big men misused politics. The riff-raff, catching the smell of corruption, rushed into the Municipal Assembly, drove out the remaining respectable men, and sold the city — its streets, its wharves, its markets, and all that it had — to the now greedy business men and bribers. In other words, when the leading men began to devour their own city, the herd rushed into the trough and fed also. . . .

[A grand jury said:] "Our investigation, covering more or less fully a period of ten years, shows that, with few exceptions, no ordinance has been passed wherein valuable privileges or franchises are granted until those interested have paid the legislators the money demanded for action in the particular case. Combines in both branches of the Municipal Assembly are formed by members sufficient in number to control legislation. . . . So long has this practice existed, that such members have come to regard the receipt of money for action on pending measures as a legitimate perquisite of a legislator."

One legislator consulted a lawyer with the intention of suing a firm to recover an unpaid balance on a fee for the grant of a switch way. . . . In order to insure a regular and indisputable revenue, the combine of each house drew up a schedule of bribery prices for all possible sorts of grants, just such a list as a commercial traveler takes out on the road with him. There was a price for a grain elevator, a price for a short switch; side tracks were charged for by the linear foot . . . ; street improvement cost so much. . . . As there was a scale for favorable legislation, so there was one for defeating bills. It made a difference in the price if there was opposition, and it made a difference whether the privilege asked was legitimate or not. But nothing was passed free of charge. Many of the legislators were saloon keepers — it was in St. Louis that a practical joker nearly emptied the House of Delegates by getting a boy to rush into a session and call out, "Mister, your saloon is on fire," — but even the saloon keepers of a neighborhood had to pay to keep in their inconvenient locality a market which public interest would have moved. . . .

The blackest years were 1898, 1899, and 1900. . . . Franchises worth millions were granted without one cent of cash to the city, and with provision for only the smallest future payment; several companies which refused to pay blackmail had to leave; citizens were robbed more and more boldly; pay-rolls were padded with the names of non-existent persons; work on public improvements was neglected, while money for them went to the boodlers.[84]

Occasionally a courageous mayor would protect the public against the "sale" of franchises by unscrupulous city councillors. One such city administrator was Hazen Pingree of Detroit, a wealthy business man who was elected as a reform mayor under Republican auspices in 1889. Detroiters wanted improved rapid transit, but the City Railway Company refused to substitute electric traction for its horse-drawn lines unless the city would extend its exclusive franchise for 30 years without what most citizens considered to be adequate compensation to the city, a more reasonable fare, and additional public control. When the company succeeded in pushing a 30-year franchise extension through the Common Council, Pingree vetoed the measure on July 7, 1891, and ultimately pressured the company into giving better service.

COUNTERING A FRANCHISE "STEAL" —
DETROIT: 1891

From His Honor the Mayor to the Honorable the Common Council. . . .

My reasons for non-approval of the ordinance are as follows:
Private ownership of natural monopolies in cities is necessarily the cause of an immense financial loss to the citizens. . . . It is generally believed that this is the chief source of corruption in city governments. . . .

It is . . . evident that the effect of the ordinance is: First. To enable the old City Railway Company to assign all its franchises and property to the new corporation; and, Second: To confer upon the new corporation a franchise embracing the right to operate a street railway upon all the thoroughfares of the city for the period of 30 years, without compensation to the city. . . .

If the Detroit City Railway Company, or the Detroit Street Railway Company, does not choose to give us rapid transit, the right to furnish the new and improved facilities for travel over the lines operated by that, or those companies, could be sold for from three to four millions of dollars.

There is no good reason why Detroit should not follow the example of other cities and relieve the burdens of the people incurred by constantly increasing rates of taxation by selling such valuable franchises for the benefit of the City Treasury. Either that or to leave the money of the people in their own pockets by reducing the fare to the minimum amount.[85]

Despite the extortion, boodle, and political manipulation indulged in by machine politicians, there was in some instances a positive side to the activities of the machine. Given the political chaos of the rapidly growing cities of the 1880's and 1890's, the ability of the boss to create a workable organization among the city's diverse social and ethnic elements sometimes provided the only means of achieving constructive action. For instance, Boss George B. Cox of Cincinnati in the mid-1890's created a political organization that reconciled the fragmented elements in the community and gave the Ohio city positive, if moderate, reform government.[86] Moreover, the services performed for new and needy city dwellers by the henchmen of the machine, in anticipation of political support, provided an essential (if socially costly) community service in large cities where welfare facilities were meager and often inaccessible. This aspect of the activities of the machine was described by journalist William L. Riordon after he had interviewed Tammany politician George Washington Plunkitt. His account, based on extracts from Plunkitt's diary, appeared in *Plunkitt of Tammany Hall*, published by McClure, Phillips and Company in 1905.

THE POLITICAL MACHINE AS WELFARE AGENCY: 1905

The life of the Tammany district leader is strenuous. . . . He plays politics every day and night in the year, and his headquarters bears the inscription, "Never closed."

Everybody in the district knows . . . where to find him, and nearly everybody goes to him for assistance of one sort or another, especially the poor of the tenements.

He is always obliging. He will go to the police courts to put in a good word for the "drunks and disorderlies" or pay their fines, if a good word is not effective. He will attend christenings, weddings, and funerals. He will feed the hungry and help bury the dead. . . .

This is a record of a day's work by Plunkitt:

2 A.M.: Aroused from sleep by the ringing of his door bell; went to the door and found a bartender, who asked him to go

to the police station and bail out a saloon-keeper who had been arrested for violating the excise law. Furnished bail and returned to bed at three o'clock.

6 A.M.: Awakened by fire engines passing his house. Hastened to the scene of the fire . . . to give assistance to the fire sufferers, if needed. . . . Found several tenants who had been burned out, took them to a hotel, supplied them with clothes, fed them, and arranged temporary quarters for them until they could rent and furnish new apartments. . . .

9 A.M.: Appeared in the Municipal District Court. Directed one of his district captains to act as counsel for a widow against whom dispossess proceedings had been instituted and obtained an extension of time. Paid the rent of a poor family about to be dispossessed and gave them a dollar for food.

11 A.M.: At home again. Found four men waiting for him. One had been discharged by the Metropolitan Railway Company for neglect of duty, and wanted the district leader to fix things. Another wanted a job on the road. The third sought a place on the Subway and the fourth, a plumber, was looking for work with the Consolidated Gas Company. The district leader spent nearly three hours fixing things for the four men, and succeeded in each case.

3 P.M.: Attended the funeral of an Italian as far as the ferry. . . .

7 P.M.: Went to district headquarters and presided over a meeting of election district captains. . . .

8 P.M.: Went to a church fair. Took chances on everything, bought ice-cream for the young girls and the children. Kissed the little ones, flattered their mothers and took their fathers out for something down at the corner.

9 P.M.: At the club-house again. Spent $10 on tickets for a church excursion and promised a subscription for a new church-bell. Bought tickets for a base-ball game to be played by two nines from his district. Listened to the complaints of a dozen push-cart peddlers who said they were persecuted by the police and assured them he would go to Police Headquarters in the morning and see about it.

10:30 P.M.: Attended a Hebrew wedding reception and dance. Had previously sent a handsome wedding present to the bride.

12 P.M.: In bed.

That is the actual record of one day in the life of Plunkitt. He does some of the same things every day, but his life is not so monotonous as to be wearisome. . . . By these means the Tammany district leader reaches out into the homes of his district, keeps watch not only on the men, but also on the women and children; knows their needs, their likes and dislikes, their troubles and their hopes, and places himself in a position to use his knowledge for the benefit of his organization and himself. Is it any wonder that scandals do not permanently disable Tammany and that it speedily recovers from what seems to be crushing defeat? [87]

10. CIVIC REFORM

The decade of the 1890's and the early years of the twentieth century saw a widespread effort to overcome the increasingly publicized evils of the nation's large cities. This crusade for improvement of both political and social conditions in the city constituted the urban manifestation of the nation's progressivism in these years. The crusade was motivated by the disclosures of graft, corruption, and protected law evasion in the management of cities; by the desire to have the urban environment less congested, more healthful, and more aesthetically attractive; and by the conviction, held by the business and professional leaders in many cities, that the existing administration of city government was inefficient and wasteful. These leaders believed that prevailing practices in municipal government denied the better elements in the city their rightful voice in determining the course of community development and aggravated the widening gap between this group and newly arrived segments of the population. The reform effort was implemented by the activities of a variety of organized groups: civic clubs, law and order leagues, antivice commissions, church organizations, taxpayers' associations, chambers of commerce, and citizens' reform parties. Reform membership was drawn predominantly from the business leaders of the community (especially those associated with the new industrial development of the later nineteenth century) and from the professions — physicians, lawyers, clergymen, architects, and teachers.[88] Although the reform activity often was opposed by labor unions as well as by the political machines, workingmen on occasion manifested their "civic interest" and played an important part in some of the political parties that advocated municipal reform.

In some measure the nature of the reform movement reflected

the force of the changes in social and residential patterns that had accompanied the growth of the industrial metropolis. The movement of the middle class to the periphery of the city weakened their identification with the society and problems of the central core, which they saw as the domain of the boss and his immigrant supporters. The leaders of the reform movement often were residents of these peripheral areas, persons whose middle-class, Yankee-Protestant background gave them a concept of politics and standards of personal behavior at variance with those of the professional politicians and many of the recently arrived residents of the central core.

Reform efforts originally arose independently at the local community level, but beginning in 1894 reformers in a number of areas of municipal improvement undertook national organization. In January of that year the National Municipal League emerged from the National Conference for Good City Government held in Philadelphia. Later that year, specialists concerned with the physical problems of city management, such as paving, lighting, street cleaning, and the like, organized the American Society of Municipal Improvements. The League of American Municipalities, made up almost exclusively of mayors and councilmen, was organized in 1897. By 1903, national organizations that appealed to other municipal improvement constituencies included the American Park and Outdoor Art Association and the American League for Civic Improvement.[89] The wide range of organizations both on the national level and in all the major cities reveals the pervasiveness as well as the vitality of this organized effort to do something about the problems — economic, political, and social — presented by large cities at the turn of the twentieth century.[90]

The civic improvement clubs exerted a more continuous force for municipal reform in these years than did the more transient citizens' reform parties. Though these groups were mobilized from only a small proportion of a city's population, the stature of the members and the interlocking membership of the clubs made them a relatively permanent base for the reform effort. In some cities the reformers actually retreated from electoral politics, realizing that since reform administrations rarely succeeded themselves, the reform effort was less subject to reversal when exercised through civic organizations.[91] The pervasiveness of civic group activity throughout the United States in the early twentieth century, as reflected in the activity of city clubs, was reported in a

1912 issue of the *National Municipal Review* by Charles A. Beard, then associate professor of politics at Columbia University. The first of these particular civic societies was the City Club of New York, incorporated in 1892.

CITY CLUBS AS GENERATORS
OF MUNICIPAL REFORM: 1912

There was a time when it was thought that the citizen's duty to his government ended at the polls. . . . In our day, however, citizens, through their special associations for labor legislation, prison reform, purification of milk supply, and a hundred other public purposes, are threatening to take possession of large fields of legislation and administration by a process of "peaceful penetration." . . . In the sphere of municipal government, city clubs have for several years taken the lead as general non-partisan associations. . . . The objects of the several clubs . . . are strikingly similar. . . . The purpose of the Milwaukee Club is "to bring together in intimate association, men, who are sincerely seeking the best interests of our city; to create within the club an ideal of civic betterment, by providing, through addresses at noonday luncheons, through ample literature and otherwise, the best thought of the day in civic matters; to disseminate civic knowledge by newspaper publicity and by bulletins to be published by the club and widely distributed; to promote a spirit of cooperation among the citizens in public matters." . . . The Los Angeles club took up such matters as the city charter, the proposed municipal newspaper, the Good Government and Socialist candidates for the school board, single tax, taxation, social hygiene, public baths, and the work of the legal aid society. . . .

Each of the clubs . . . investigates special local problems and prepares reports of immense practical value. Although non-partisan in character the clubs give a great deal of attention to immediate questions of city politics and administration, and co-operate with officials and local bodies in the execution of public programs. For example, the City Club of St. Louis, in conjunction with the Civic League has just held a civic exhibit displaying the work of the several municipal departments and civic organizations of the city which, it is hoped, may be the precursor of an annual budget exhibit conducted by the municipal authorities. . . . Chicago's City Club through its committees on parks, playgrounds, and baths, and education, has been studying the relation of the public school buildings to the recreational facilities of the parks, and has made some pertinent recommendations to the city authorities to the effect that needless duplications of facilities can be avoided, with decided economy, by the use of park lands for school purposes and the school buildings for recreational purposes. In New York City, the City Club has been specially active in the subway developments and the preservation of City Hall Park. The club strongly supported the constitutional amendments making possible the establishment of a special court for condemning private property for public use and conferring upon cities in the state the power to make excess condemnations — both of which were defeated at the election of 1911 by the vote of the up-state districts. The club secured the repassage of these amendments slightly modified at the session of 1912.[92]

The involvement of women in municipal reform through the auspices of civic clubs was a corollary of the rising influence of women in public affairs that accompanied the growth of large cities. Women's clubs, such as New York City's Sorosis Club, were being founded at the beginning of the 1870's; by 1890 a General Federation of Women's Clubs had been organized. Women exerted a prime influence in the settlement movement and in the improvement of educational and recreational facilities for children in cities. Their homekeeping instincts put them strongly on the side of movements to improve the hygienic and aesthetic aspects of the urban scene. This was one of the primary interests of the Women's Municipal League of New York, which was organized in 1894 in an effort to enlist the help of women in achieving better and more honest municipal government, not at the outset through exercise of the suffrage but through social and public influence — by means of "pen and tongue." From 1894 to 1923 it lent its support to the election of reform candidates and between mayoral elections worked vigorously to improve public health and education, further city beautification, assist in the adjustment of immigrant girls, and encourage more effective street cleaning and garbage collection.

The filthy condition of city streets posed a continuing problem in the pre-automobile era (there were 20 million horses in American cities as of 1900); and though many cities had attempted systematic programs of street cleaning by the 1880's, their implementation (often obstructed by patronage considerations) was aided by the vigilance and creative zeal of women's reform organizations.

Municipal Affairs devoted most of its September, 1898, issue to "Women's Work on City Problems," including reports of women's organizations in many of the major cities of the United States. Martha A. B. Conine's report, "Women's Work in Denver," revealed that political "housecleaning" as well as "urban homemaking" was part of women's municipal reform work in the Colorado city.

ACTIVITIES OF WOMEN IN CIVIC REFORM — DENVER: 1898

The work in municipal affairs of the women of Denver dates back only to the organization of The Woman's Club of Denver, which began its work in the autumn of 1895. It was founded upon the lines of the well-known Chicago Women's Club, and at the present time has a membership of over one thousand names. . . . On April 8th the chair appointed a committee to interview the shopkeepers on Sixteenth Street, between Curtis and Arapahoe streets, asking them to hire a man to keep that block clean. They did so. That hired man went to work with brush and dust-pan on Thursday. On the following Monday the city had six men at work in the same manner, and by the end of the month, we left the city to do the work and pay the men. That was brought about by the force of example and the hearty co-operation of the street cleaning department. . . .

Through the health commissioner, Dr. Munn, notices against expectoration on the sidewalk and in all public places have been posted wherever people would permit it. A committee was appointed to wait upon street car officials, asking them to put these notices in their cars. Col. Randolph of the Cable Line at once placed them on his line, at his own expense. The tramway lines are just now putting them in all their cars. When Mrs. Trautman of the Health Protective Association of New York, visited Denver this summer, she said to the chairman of this committee: "You have accomplished more in two years along the line of prohibiting promiscuous expectoration in Denver, than we have been able to in seven."

Two dozen rubbish cans were put upon the corners of the down-town streets. This was accomplished by a persistent visiting of the city hall. . . . During the past year, the club has worked to save Thirteenth Avenue from a proposed widening of the block between Grant and Logan avenues, thereby helping to save a fine row of trees. Our study of methods prevailing in the Eastern cities as to the care and disposal of unlicensed dogs, and our continued protests against the ineffective law of Denver, aroused such interest among city officials that an excellent ordinance was framed, and after long agitation, was passed by the council. The study of Shaw's "Municipal Government of Continental Cities," was continued through the summer. . . .

Coming now to the question of reform in municipal governments, the most palpable results in that line have been effected by the Civic Federation of Denver. This is the only political working organization of women in the state aside from partisan clubs. . . . The Civic Federation has aimed to cultivate a civic conscience, and to give an opportunity to the lay-citizen to make known his wishes and exercise his political rights in a way which could not be subverted by the schemes of interested ward heelers. It had not intended to become a political party, or to put a ticket in the field, but was forced by circumstances to do so. At the last city election, the Civic Federation, acting in conjunction with the Tax-Payers, a similar organization of men, . . . prepared a list of candidates. . . . The ticket thus nominated rolled up a majority of six thousand. . . . Not only this, but suspected ballot-box frauds were probed and their perpetrators indicted by a grand jury — an instance unheard of before.

Of course such an overwhelming defeat for the usual manipulators of the city elections awakened the most violent antagonism. Every effort of time and money was put forward to defeat the reform forces at the next — a county election, which was in many ways as important to Denver as the city election itself. Although the Federation's candidates were not elected, the . . . Federation is in no sense daunted by one defeat and is pursuing its usual course. It expects the support and confidence of the better class of citizens in the future as in the past, and will not be dismayed by defeat or calumny.[93]

Although the most active proponents of civic reform were drawn from what Mrs. Conine called the "better class of citizens," workingmen contributed to the movement for municipal improvement through labor unions, through labor party activity, and even on occasion through organized civic effort when the issues were made clear to them. Workingmen made up the bulk of the Social Democratic Party in Milwaukee, which in 1910, aided by reform elements in the old-line parties, elected the mayor and gained a working majority in the city council.[94] In New York, the People's Institute, organized in 1897, with headquarters at Cooper Union, served to mobilize civic interest among the working people of Manhattan's lower East Side by conducting a program of classes and lectures on government and social questions. Its secretary, Michael M. Davis, writing in *Charities and the Commons* in 1907, argued that civic education was all that was needed to excite the worker in organized effort for municipal improvement.

"CIVIC INTEREST" AMONG THE WORKING PEOPLE — NEW YORK: 1907

The young workingman in our large cities is far from being without a definite civic interest. . . . His civic education begins on the street, chiefly through contact with policemen, and develops into definite shape, as he grows to be a young man, mainly through the influence of local [political] clubs. Through membership in these organizations he learns the ways of local politics by the time he is old enough to vote. . . . When there comes into the life of the workingman some evil which he desires to have remedied and which he cannot remedy for himself, his probable recourse is to the district leader of his organization. The only way he knows how to get what he wants is by appealing to a particular individual. . . . His purely personal point of view prevents him from realizing that a great number of evils in his life and his environment ought to be remedied by what we would call "social action." The labor unions, . . . a spontaneous popular development, have not failed to interest themselves in civic matters. They have, for example, assisted tenement-house, child-labor, and factory legislation; they have taken their part in the fight against tuberculosis, and their sanction or co-operation is given, from time to time, to many desirable measures of progress. . . .

Voluntary civic clubs composed of workingmen have not been entirely lacking. The tenement house law in New York was assisted in its passage by the energetic work of the East Side Civic Club, which circulated petitions and secured thousands of signatures. . . . The most clear and lasting evidence of the success of attempts [such as that of the People's Institute] to direct and inform the people's civic interest will be their willingness to ally themselves for special purposes of civic

improvement with *civic organizations,* or to form *local groups.*
. . . In such a large city as New York the people generally
know little or nothing of the upper-class organizations and the
methods employed by them are not generally understood. To
make them understood is to provide an outlet for the civic
interest of countless young men, now debating the question
whether to join one or the other of the great parties, or to remain independent, and thus seemingly ineffective from the
civic standpoint. . . .

No one can witness a great gathering of workingmen, such
as assembles week after week at the Cooper Union, without realizing that the civic interest of the people is living, though
often latent. To workingmen civic problems are at bottom,
vital problems of personal life, but the issues need to be
cleared of traditional attachments, and the energies that are
freed, as this civic interest clarifies, need to be directed. The
New York subway now belongs to the city chiefly because of a
great mass meeting, held at Cooper Union in 1899. The meeting not only accomplished its purpose, but demonstrated that
systematic work for civic education will bear practical fruit.
Two years ago, a body of "grab bills," already slated for passage in the New York legislature, was withdrawn within
twenty-four hours after public opinion and the press had been
roused through a similar mass meeting. . . . No one can witness a young men's club laboring for cleaner streets, or discussing how a neglected park shall be placed in order for the people's use, without feeling how very real to working people
these civic questions can be made, or rather how real they
make themselves, once they are shown clearly.[95]

One major aspiration of civic reform was to institute changes
in the structure of municipal government to make it more efficient,
more economical, and more honest, more responsive to business
and professional elements in the local electorate, and less amenable
to manipulation by machine politicians and representatives of the
utilities "interests." The reformers proposed giving the mayor
wider powers of appointment, instituting a unicameral municipal
legislature elected from the city at large rather than from individual
wards, requiring civil service standards for municipal appointments,
expanding the areas of home rule, and separating municipal elections from state and local contests. Other innovations included the
commission and city manager patterns of government, based on a

"business" model and designed to achieve a separation of legislative and administrative functions, and initiative, referendum, and recall, proposed in some instances to appease those who opposed the citywide election of members of the council. These reforms were brought about through legislative action and charter amendments. Mayoral power was strengthened and the structure of the city council was simplified early in the new century; by 1917 more than 400 cities had adopted the commission type of government, and by 1923 more than 300 cities had city managers.

In accomplishing these reforms, local groups benefited from the guidance of the National Municipal League which set up committees of specialists to propose structural changes as guides for local adoption. In 1899 and again in 1916, the League made recommendations in the form of model charters.[96] Its prescription for "democratic" city government was the reverse of the pattern of the Jacksonian period when the checks and balances implicit in a bicameral city council and popular election of a wide range of administrative officers were considered the best method of realizing the popular will. An article in *Survey* magazine, written in 1916, attests to the influence of the League in the restructuring of city governments.

THE NATIONAL MUNICIPAL LEAGUE AND STRUCTURAL CHANGES IN CITY GOVERNMENT: 1894–1916

Shortly after the National Municipal League was founded, twenty-one years ago, it organized a strong committee of men whose names afterward became historic in municipal reform. This committee devised a model charter and municipal home rule constitutional article, having, however, no hope that any city would ever adopt the charter verbatim. No city ever did, but no charter committee could entirely ignore the document, and it had a profound influence during the next two decades. Its main message was a plea for simplicity and for freedom from checks and balances and red tape. It called for an elective mayor with complete and undivided appointive power and a small council elected at large, much like the present new governments of Boston and Cleveland.

About 1910 the short ballot movement and the top wave of commission government came along, pushing the demand for simplicity still further. The league . . . instantly accept[ed] the commission manager plan, when that appeared three years ago, and organized a new model charter committee in 1913. . . . The committee has made several partial reports and has finally produced a complete charter and a home rule article for a state constitution, embodying what it believes to be the best current experience and theory.

The new model charter is a commission manager plan and calls for the election of a city council of variable size and methods of election. This council hires, from anywhere in the country, a city manager who is their sole agent, and the chief executive of the city, with appointive power over the rest of the city's administration, except the clerk, auditor and civil service commission, whom the council chooses.

The committee has drafted three alternative election methods; there is a model non-partisan primary election procedure; another providing for preferential ballot, and a third calling for proportional representation. . . . The initiative, referendum and recall are offered, as separable items, with the approval of the majority of the committee.

This model charter demonstrates how modern municipal government has caught up with the reformers. At least a dozen cities with the commission manager form, have charters that differ from the model only in minor details and much of the draftsmanship of the model has simply been discriminating work with shears and paste.

The old model charter was a lonesome pioneer. The new model charter merely falls in line abreast of Dayton, Springfield, Niagara Falls, Cadillac and Ashtabula. It marks the close of a period in municipal reform — a period of forging good tools for democracy to work with.[97]

In proposing a strengthened mayoralty, citywide election of the council, and commission or city manager government, the reformers manifested the desire of business and professional interests to minimize ward autonomy and centralize decision making in ways that would reduce the influence of voters from lower- and middle-income groups. The reformers promoted a citywide approach to the solution of urban problems — an approach generated by improved communication within the city and also by the fact that many business and professional men now resided in outlying and often underrepresented parts of the city.[98] The centralization of decision making accorded with contemporary developments in the business world and with the trend toward the systematization of science and technology, as did the organization of municipal research bureaus, which business-minded reformers strongly supported. In *City Government by Commission* (1911), Clinton R. Woodruff, secretary of the National Municipal League, quoted the mayor of Houston to illustrate the point that commission government was the "application to city administration of that type of business organization which has been so common in the field of commerce and industry."

"BUSINESS GOVERNMENT" IN HOUSTON: 1908

In the city of Houston, with a majority of the aldermen always in session, business of the people can be, and is, attended to at a moment's notice. . . . Any citizen, or citizens, who want a street paved, taxes adjusted, nuisances abated, etc., have only to call at the mayor's office and have his or their matters promptly adjusted. After a patient hearing, the matter is decided by the council in [the] presence of the applicant. . . . To demonstrate, I will cite an incident that happened several months ago. A gentleman, a non-resident of Houston, whose home was in a Western state, owned some property in our city, and the property had recently been taken into the city limits. Investigating his assessment, he found that his property had been placed at a much higher valuation than that of his neighbors. Being a stranger, he called upon one of Houston's leading attorneys and asked his advice how to proceed for relief. The attorney suggested that they step over to the mayor's office and have the matter corrected. The owner of the land thought it would be wiser for the lawyer to get some of his friends to sign a petition to the council, so that it would have some weight with the authorities. The attorney replied that this mode of procedure was entirely unnecessary, as Houston now had a business government. They called at my office, stated their mission. I sent for the tax collector, and in an hour the stranger had his matter adjusted and his tax receipt in his pocket.[99]

The repudiation of the ideal of ward autonomy implicit in proposals for citywide election of the legislative branch of city government was extolled by Harry A. Toulmin, Jr., in *The City Manager: a New Profession*, published in 1915. In this book he argued that the city manager form of city government was superior to the commission pattern. Since the turn of the 1870's, the citywide election of council members had been one of the methods proposed by conservatives to counter the political power that universal suffrage gave to the immigrant and hence to the political machine. The shift from ward representation to citywide election of the council was less easy to achieve in the large cities where subcommunities were more populous and more dispersed.

"WARDS MUST GO" — AN ARGUMENT FOR CITY MANAGER GOVERNMENT: 1915

The spirit of sectionalism has dominated the political life of every city. Ward pitted against ward, alderman against alderman, and legislation only effected by "log-rolling" extravagant measures into operation, mulcting the city, but gratifying the greed of constituents, has too long stung the conscience of decent citizenship. This constant treaty-making of factionalism has been no less than a curse. The city manager plan proposes . . . abolishing wards. The plan is not unique in this for it has been common to many forms of commission government. . . . The abolition of wards is without doubt an innovation of profound value in cities under 150,000 population. In cities of this size and under, the evils of ward systems were most apparent. The vicious system of patronage, of "log-rolling" and of selecting officials proposed by powerful aldermen for positions in the city government are all attendant evils upon treating the city, not as a unit, but as a conglomeration of disjointed and unrelated heterogeneous parts. . . . The new city is a unit. The new officers are elected each to represent all the people. Their duties are so defined that they must administer the corporate business in its entirety, not as a hodge-podge of associated localities.[100]

The aspiration for "home rule" in the platform of municipal reform sprang from increasing awareness of the difference between city and country, in ethnic composition and life style, and from conviction that efforts to find adequate solutions to urban problems were often obstructed by the hostility of rural-dominated state legislatures. As early as 1875, Missouri permitted cities with populations of 100,000 or more to frame their own charters subject to legislative approval, but as late as 1900 most large cities were still the vassals of the state legislatures, their fate subject to the play of state (and sometimes national) politics. As proposed by Frank J. Goodnow, one of its chief advocates, home rule would be an enlargement of democracy, making possible the solution of local problems by those directly concerned. Varying degrees of home rule for cities were achieved in California, Washington, and Minnesota before 1900; between then and 1924 Colorado, Oregon, Oklahoma, Michigan, Arizona, Texas, Nebraska, Ohio, Pennsylvania, New York, Nevada, and Wisconsin followed suit.[101] In an article published in the December, 1913, issue of *The Public* E. J. Batten extended the argument for home rule to a demand that the large cities of the nation be constituted as separate states, a proposal that had been made for New York in 1861 and that would be echoed a century later. Batten's proposal was reprinted in the January, 1914 issue of *The American City*.

STATEHOOD PROPOSED FOR LARGE CITIES: 1913

The problems confronting large cities are so distinct and different from those of rural districts that there is no more reason why the rural districts should participate in the government of our large cities than that [these cities] should be under the dominion of Great Britain. The large cities, under the despotism of absentee legislators, demand home rule. The country districts refuse. New York City is even deprived of its proportionate share of representation in the state legislature.

The mutual distrust between the city and country members of our legislatures is a perennial source of trouble. Dread of the growing predominance of large cities produces and maintains a constant friction between the city and country which paralyzes the action of the state legislatures and prevents remedial legislation for either section of the state. The remedy is absolute divorce. When partners disagree they dissolve partnership. Turn the large cities into separate states and these difficulties will disappear as if by magic. . . .

By erecting the large cities into states, the country districts will be equally benefited; for they will no longer stand in dread of the political dominance of the large cities. Each section will then govern itself as it sees fit without interference by the other. . . .

Viewed from a national standpoint, Congress cannot fairly or justly refuse to make separate states of Chicago, New York and Philadelphia, adding sufficient adjacent territories to provide for future growth. Their respective populations more than justify such a course. If the three largest cities were erected into states they would have a much larger average population than that of the other states. The state of New York City would be the second state in the Union — it being only exceeded in population by Pennsylvania.

The combined population of the nine states of Montana, Vermont, Utah, New Mexico, Idaho, Delaware, Arizona, Wyoming and Nevada is less than that of Cook county, Ill. (including Chicago). The obvious injustice of these states being represented by eighteen senators, while Chicago has only a fraction of two senators, shocks every sense of fairness. The injustice to New York City is much greater, for its population is twice that of Chicago.

Here is a matter of such supreme importance to the large cities of the country that it ought to become for those cities the paramount political issue, and to its advocacy all partisan politics should be subordinated.[102]

In addition to effecting changes in the form of municipal government, the forces of reform achieved a broad expansion of municipal regulatory authority and a marked extension of government-subsidized services, to the point even of municipal ownership and operation of activities that earlier had been conceded to private enterprise. This enlargement of the positive role of the city was the result of a growing conviction that cities must ensure a physically and socially wholesome environment for their residents as well as honest and efficient administration. Accumulating advances in medical knowledge, stressing the bearing of environment on the health and welfare of the community as a whole, were in part responsible for this development; it followed also from the example of European cities, especially those of Germany, widely acclaimed for their adjustment to the problems industrialization and rapid urbanization presented; and it was abetted by the excesses in which private corporations had indulged in their relations with the city.

The expansion of municipal service and regulation was manifested in the multiplication of public educational opportunities: the increase in the number of public libraries, museums, parks, playgrounds, baths, and social centers; the enactment of more effective health and building regulations; and the increasing assumption of responsibility for the aesthetic appearance of the city. Pressure for municipal ownership of waterworks, transit facilities, and electric power plants was posited on the argument that public management not only would lower the cost of these services to the people but also would eliminate a source of corruption in city government. Though such proposals struck a socialistic note that was uncongenial to many whose concern for honest, businesslike management of the municipality had attracted them to the movement for reform, the imperatives of urban living won support for a controlled economy at the local level from many to whom the idea of socialism as a form of government was distasteful.[103]

This was the view of a group of publicists in the emerging fields of urban sociology and municipal government and administration. One of these was Frederic C. Howe, who was born in 1867, a product of urbanizing America. After studying in Germany and earning his Ph.D. degree at the Johns Hopkins University, Howe began the practice of law in Cleveland in 1894. There he came under the influence of a reform-minded mayor, Tom L. Johnson, served in the Cleveland City Council, in the Ohio Senate, and on the Cleveland Tax Commission. He moved to New York in 1910 to become director of the People's Institute and then Commissioner of Immigration of the City of New York. Howe's writing exhibits the expansive optimism that characterized the urban progressives. In his book *The City: the Hope of Democracy* (1905) he rationalized the quasi-socialistic activities of city government that the interdependence of urban life tended to foster.

AN ACTIVE CITY —
"THE HOPE OF DEMOCRACY": 1905

The modern city . . . marks a revolution — a revolution in industry, politics, society, and life itself. Its coming has destroyed a rural society, whose making has occupied mankind since the fall of Rome. . . . Man has entered on an urban age. He has become a communal being . . . and society has developed into an organism like the human body, of which the city is the head, heart, and centre of the nervous system. . . . The city is . . . constantly taking on new activities and assuming new burdens. . . . We cannot live in close association without common activities, without abandoning some of our liberties to regulation. Not only do health, comfort, and happiness demand this, self-protection necessitates it. . . . The same motives that have opened up breathing spots in the form of parks, as well as public baths and gymnasiums, in the crowded quarters will, in time, lead to the establishment of city clubhouses, winter recreation centres, where such advantages as are now found in the social settlement will be offered. . . . A sense of the city as a home, . . . a thing to be loved and cared for, will be developed. In the city club the saloon will find a rival. From such centres charity work will be carried on. . . . With reduced cost of transportation, through the public ownership of the means of transit, with free books and possibly free luncheons to school children, compulsory education will become a possibility. . . .

These reforms will be possible through home rule, through the city-republic. With the city free in these regards it will be able to raise the educational age, adopt manual-training and trades' schools, fit its instruction to local needs, and ultimately elevate the standard of life of all classes. . . . Provision for public concerts in summer as well as in winter has already found a place in many municipal budgets. With the development of the city club there will come public orchestras, art exhibitions, and the like that will brighten the life of the community. . . . Here and there the idea is taking form of utilizing the public-school buildings as local clubs. . . . [The new city] will also care for the sick . . . through district physicians or visiting nurses attached to the school departments. . . .

All these functions are, in a sense, socialistic. But it is such activities as these, it is the care and protection of the people, that inspire love and affection for the city. . . . The American feels no fear of socialism when his city assumes the disposal of garbage, the supply of water or electricity, the opening up of schools, kindergartens, lodging houses, parks, playgrounds, and bath houses. Yet his father would have rubbed his eyes in amazement at the suggestion of such undertakings being proper fields of public activity.[104] . . . Amazing progress has been made in the United States within the past ten years. The most remarkable advance is in the cities of Boston, New York, Chicago, and Cleveland, which communities have been transformed in their tendencies if not in their achievements. . . . If our own cities are to follow the tendencies in England, Germany, France, and Belgium, it is likely that such functions will be greatly extended. Foreign cities are already going in for municipal milk bureaus, the supply of coal, for savings banks, not to speak of many enterprises of a purely competitive and commercial sort.

Many who assent to our advance in educational, recreative, and charitable activities hesitate at the extension of the community into the field of business. Yet the management of certain industries seems as necessary to the city's well-being as the functions already assumed. The discussion of municipal ownership has heretofore been confined to the natural monopolies, to the franchise corporations, the street railways, gas, water, electric-lighting, telephone, power, and heating companies. These industries are inevitably monopolies. . . . The public health, our comfort and convenience demand that these services should be supplied at a minimum cost. Urban life is so dependent upon them. . . . Moreover, the value of such industries is a social one, created by the very existence of the city. . . .

It would seem to be a rule of general application that whatever is of necessity a monopoly should be a public monopoly. . . . There is abundant evidence that street-railway fares under municipal ownership could be reduced to three, possibly to two cents. In Germany they have been cut down to two and one-half cents, while in England . . . the average paid in many cities is much less. . . . What the final. municipal programme of the new city will be, one can only conjecture, but that it will be a programme making for a better civilization, a larger life, and increased comfort and opportunity, the gradual progression of society gives assurance. That these increased activities will come by gradual steps, approved in time by all, is evidenced by the sanction of experience, which accepts with approval the functions which have thus far been assumed. . . .[105]

In the discussion of municipal problems it is necessary to bear in mind that the issue of city life has become one of decent human existence. . . . Every social adjustment involves some cost. . . . But under our present adjustment the sacrifice is borne by the many for the enjoyment of the few. . . . The extension of the activities of the city and the reduction of the cost of service on municipal monopolies will do something [to lift the burden on the poor]. But the greatest gain will come through a change in our methods of taxation and the assumption of the unearned increment of the land for public uses. . . . With home rule secured, with popular control attained, with the city free to determine what activities it will undertake, and what shall be its sources of revenue, then the city will be consciously allied to definite ideals, and the new civilization, which is the hope as well as the problem of democracy, will be open to realization.[106]

A convert to municipal control of public utilities was Seth Low, whose experience as mayor of Brooklyn (1882–1886) convinced him that the citizenry would benefit from the rationalization municipal control would provide in the supply of gas. Low, wealthy heir of a New York mercantile family, was twice elected mayor of Brooklyn on an independent ticket. He became president of Columbia University in 1890 and in 1901 was elected mayor of New York City on a fusion ticket. His comments on the provision of gas in Brooklyn were delivered at a dinner meeting of the Boston Merchants Association in 1889.

SETH LOW ON MUNICIPAL CONTROL
OF PUBLIC UTILITIES: 1889

[Concerning Brooklyn's experience with private gas works], we had in the first instance, a single company — the old Brooklyn Gas Company. When it became evident that it was very profitable, another company got a charter, and the competition that was expected and anticipated resulted in the setting off by agreement of different sections of the city for each company. That was done until the whole area of the city was covered, I think, by five companies. Then there came in a threatened competition from a new company making water gas. They controlled great capital; they laid parallel mains in many of the streets, and finally they came to control, by purchase or by agreement, all of our gas companies. The consequence was that at the end of the episode the gas business in Brooklyn was immensely over-capitalized; we had parallel and unnecessary mains in many of our streets, and no relief came to the consumer of gas until the Legislature, falling back upon its reserved rights, fixed an arbitrary price for gas. Even then we found ourselves only across the river from the gas companies, an officer of one of which is said to have remarked that he did not care at what figure the Legislature fixed the price of gas, provided the gas companies could regulate the pressure!

In other words, the experience of Brooklyn with private gas works . . . bears out . . . the claim . . . that the nature of the business is such that the cities themselves would profit by controlling the supply of gas as a public monopoly. . . . I am free to say that the result of my experience in the mayor's office for four years has been to change the whole current of my thoughts, which formerly ran away from that conclusion, toward it. . . . I do believe that this is the direction in which our cities must grow, even if they have been wise in beginning upon another plan. For this is to be borne in mind about all our American cities [that] the problem of cities in America is very different from that of cities abroad. We have had to make, in many instances, a great city out of the fields, and we have had to administer rapidly growing cities all over the Union at the very same moment that we

> were heavily using our credit for the purposes of growth. This has
> made the municipal problem in the United States a problem
> the like of which, I think, the world has not seen.[107]

On occasion, citizens' reform parties were able to gain political
control and put into office mayors who stood for both honest
administration and active government — sometimes so active as to
alienate those whose interest in reform was limited to a desire for
more efficient and less costly government. Some of the reform
mayors, like New York's William L. Strong (1895–98), Seth Low
(1901–1903), and John Purroy Mitchel (1914–1917), Boston's
Josiah Quincy (1895–1899), and San Francisco's James Phelan
(1897–1902), though sensitive to such issues as municipal ownership and the expansion of urban services, nevertheless were primarily interested in achieving efficiency, economy, and honest,
technically expert city management.[108] Others, some of whom
originally had strong support from the conservative business community, became predominantly committed to benefits for the
people, not only through an increase in parks, schools, and other
public services, but also through efforts to reduce the cost of living
of the average city dweller by forcing privately owned utilities,
such as gas, telephone, and streetcar companies, to reduce their
rates and augment their services. Among the mayors who distinguished themselves along these lines were Hazen Pingree of
Detroit (1890–1897), Samuel ("Golden Rule") Jones of Toledo
(1897–1905), Tom L. Johnson (1901–1909) and Newton D. Baker
(1912–1916) of Cleveland, and Daniel W. Hoan, who in 1916
began a long term as mayor of Milwaukee, after a crusading career
as city attorney. The ability of these mayors to remain in office for
several terms suggests that reformers were not always political
"morning glories," to use Plunkett's phrase, and had the capacity to
build machine support.

Mayor Pingree, increasingly the champion of Detroiters of
poor or modest means, exposed the collusion between utilities
interests and public officials and by inducing competition and
challenging traditionally permissive franchises brought about a
reduction in utility rates and traction fares. In November, 1897,
shortly after his election as governor of Michigan, he described
the accomplishments of his eight years of mayoral service in an
address before the Nineteenth Century Club of New York City.

HAZEN PINGREE AND BENEFITS
FOR THE PEOPLE — DETROIT: 1890–1897

I take some pride in saying that at the end of nearly eight years of service as mayor of Detroit, the city . . . is no longer lighted by gas, but has its own electric lighting plant and is magnificently illuminated at less than half the old rates. The gas furnished to its citizens has been reduced at least one-third in price and much improved in quality. . . . The old paving rings have been broken up. The docks at the ends of streets, which had been farmed out for a trifle to ferry companies, have been reclaimed for the use of the people. . . . The old horse cars have disappeared and a splendid system of electric cars running over grooved rails has been established. The old companies have been forced from a straight 5-cent fare without transfers, to sell tickets at the rate of six for a quarter, with transfers. A new company carrying about 40 per cent of the whole number of passengers has been brought into the city, upon which eight tickets for a quarter, with transfers, can be obtained. All the companies have been compelled to sell workingmen's tickets, during certain hours morning and evening, at 3 cents. An opposition telephone company has been established, by which rates have been reduced to less than one-quarter of those previously paid. More than 235 miles of pavement has been laid. . . . The parks have all been improved and add immensely to the health and beauty of the city. I found that over 25 per cent of the children of the city could not attend school on account of no school buildings to accommodate them. We built, while I was mayor, 33 school houses, containing 307 rooms, including one central high school building costing about $750,000. With all this the rate of taxation in the city has not materially increased. . . .

I was first selected as a candidate by the most influential people of the city, men who had large holdings in railroads, in street railway companies, in gas companies, . . . prominent merchants, bankers, and professional men, all united in requesting me to become a candidate. I discovered very soon after my election that the railroads were paying less than their share of taxes. I said so and the railroad support immediately left me. I discovered that the gas companies were charging exorbitant rates. I said so and the owners of gas stock turned their backs upon me. . . . In short, I found that every time I attempted to correct an abuse I lost a large and influential class of supporters. In short, one by one, the influential classes of the city seemed to take offense.

I was four times elected mayor, but in each campaign was made painfully aware of the loss of old friends, although my majorities gradually crept up from about 1,500 to something more than 10,000. . . . It is something to be proud of, that when the influential classes turned their backs upon me the common people of the city, who were too poor to have axes to grind, and who were only interested in the growth and progress of the municipality, always stood by me and supported me in every forward step. When you consider this experience you will not be surprised that I have come to lean upon the common people as the real foundation upon which good government must rest. . . .

My experience has brought my mind to this conclusion: That the streets of a city belong to the people and that no mayor or common council has a right to barter them away. They belong to the living and not to the dead. The remedy against many of these evils is municipal ownership and the entire abolition of monopolies, or if monopolies must exist, which depend upon public favor, their absolute control and dependence upon the people.[109]

Cleveland's Tom Johnson, former traction manager and financier, had four terms as mayor — from 1901 to 1909. He gave the city a vigorous reform government, taking the public into his confidence and educating them on municipal issues while advocating home rule, the curtailment of exploitative traction franchises, a broad expansion of urban services, and municipal ownership of public utilities. Thanks in part to his efforts, the constitution of Ohio was amended to give cities management of their purely municipal and domestic concerns; and though he failed to bring about municipal ownership of the transit company, he made some progress in the reduction of street car fares. Johnson described his activities as mayor of Cleveland in *My Story*, published in 1911.

TOM JOHNSON, REFORM MAYOR OF CLEVELAND: 1901–1909

I found a city council of eleven holdovers and eleven newly elected members, twelve of whom were Republicans and ten Democrats. My first move was to organize those of both parties who regarded the public interest as of more importance than party, against the crooked Democrats and the crooked Republicans. . . . In less than a week after taking office I ordered uniformed policemen stationed at the doors of gambling houses and houses of prostitution having saloons in connection, and instructed them to take the names and addresses of all persons who entered. . . . This method proved so successful as to the gambling houses that in a short time public gambling in Cleveland was practically abolished. . . . I ordered a strict inspection of theatres and other public buildings, made immediate war on bill-boards and ordered old frame structures torn down, put a force of "white wings" to work cleaning up the down town streets, inaugurated steps looking towards a better lighting system, set the law department to hunting up expiring street railway franchises, moved to reduce water rents, . . . established a department examiner to keep an eye on all departments of the city government, took down the "Keep Off the Grass" signs in the parks, [and] commenced to institute people's amusements in the parks. . . .

Of course all these activities cost money and as there wasn't sufficient available money in sight, the usual howl of "extravagance" was raised. But I knew these things had to be done if we were to keep our promise to give good government and I went ahead and did them, trusting to devise a way to get the funds afterwards. Under what is called economy in city government there is much foolish holding back of necessary public improvements. If fraud and graft are kept out there is not apt to be much unwisdom in public expenditures; and from the business man's standpoint the return from the original outlay is very large — even where debt is created within reasonable limits. . . . Good sanitary conditions, public parks, pure water, playgrounds for children and well paved streets are the best kind of investments, while the absence of them entails not only heavy pecuniary loss, but operates to the moral and physical deterioration of the city's inhabitants. . . .

But to give "good government" in the ordinarily accepted sense of the term, wasn't the thing I was in public life for. . . . However desirable good government, or government by good men may be, nothing worth while will be accomplished unless we have sufficient wisdom to search for the causes that really corrupt government. I agree . . . that it is . . . the kind of big business that deals in and profits from public service grants and taxation injustices that is the real evil in our cities . . . to-day. This big business furnishes the sinews of war to corrupt bosses regardless of party affiliations. . . . I believe in municipal ownership of all public service monopolies for the same reason that I believe in the municipal ownership of waterworks, of parks, of schools. I believe in the municipal ownership of these monopolies because if you do not own them they will in time own you. They will rule your politics, corrupt your institutions and finally destroy your liberties.[110]

The crusading spirit that infused the movement for municipal reform, as well as the involvement of workingmen in the movement, is exhibited in the mayoral career of Samuel ("Golden Rule") Jones of Toledo. An enlightened industrialist, Jones was elected mayor in 1897 on a Republican reform ticket. On election night he notified Washington Gladden, "I am elected in spite of six hundred saloons, the street car company and the devil." The community benefits he endorsed as mayor and his opposition to franchise deals alienated many of his business supporters; in three succeeding elections he ran on an independent ticket, strongly supported by the poor and by organized labor. Brand Whitlock, himself a reformer, who succeeded Jones as mayor of Toledo, on a home rule, non-partisan, anti-monopoly platform (1905–1913), described Jones's campaign methods in an article he wrote for *The Commons* in 1904.

CAMPAIGNING WITH "GOLDEN RULE" JONES —
TOLEDO: 1901–1903

[The election of 1901] was . . . one of the most exciting campaigns in American municipal history. [Jones] was elected by a majority over both the Republican and Democratic candidates. . . . *The Toledo Blade* in comment the next day said: "They say the people have spoken, but they needn't have hollered so loud." In the last campaign we had the Golden Rule Band, composed of men from his shop, and that was about all we did have. Everybody seemed to be against him — all the newspapers, all the parties, all the organizations, all the churches, all the wealth — everything except the people, the great common people, whose voice he was.

He would have several meetings of an evening in different parts of the city, in halls when he could get halls, in a tent now and then, if not that, in the open air, which, he said, was the best place after all to sing the songs of freedom. Such meetings no one has ever seen. Politics were not talked much; these meetings were far above politics. Democracy, the American ideal, the people as a whole governing themselves without machine or bosses to replace the kings they thought they had got rid of a century ago — these were the subjects, and the meetings were in the truest sense of the word religious. . . .

I can see the Polish laborers dressed in the clothes they had brought from Europe, standing near the flaring lights, smoking their short pipes. I can hear the band playing and see Jones climb on the platform. One night he said to the Poles: "What's the Polish word for freedom?" They shouted something back at him. He listened attent, with a smile. "Say that again." Again they bawled the mysterious word back at him. "Well," he said, "I can't understand it, but it sounds like freedom to me — it sounds good." . . .

In the slums it was the same. Crowds of outcast men and women would listen while he talked to them of life and its real meaning. He seemed somehow to place them in touch with humanity, to connect them again with all they had lost. In all these meetings songs were sung to familiar tunes in words that Jones had written.[111]

Socialist Daniel W. Hoan was elected mayor of Milwaukee in 1916 on his alleged record, as city attorney, of having "wrested thirteen million dollars worth of concessions out of the public utilities, . . . won several track depression cases, and reduced the rates of gas, light, power, street railway, and telephone" services. When his "nonpartisan" opposition urged the voters to vote against allowing "the Red Flag to replace the Stars and Stripes on the . . . City Hall," Hoan countered by asserting that "the main issue of this campaign is whether the flag of the street car company will float over the City Hall instead of the Stars and Stripes left there by Emil Seidel, former Socialist mayor." In the first of seven inaugural addresses, the new mayor affirmed his support of tenets characteristic of the municipal reform program — a municipal lighting plant, harbor improvement, city planning, a pure water supply through construction of filtration and sewage disposal facilities, a minimum wage for city workers, full competition on city contracts, and centralized purchasing of supplies.[112] In his second inaugural address, delivered on April 16, 1918, in the midst of the nation's involvement in World War I, Hoan put a strong emphasis on the importance of both social and economic city planning, especially for housing and transit facilities.

PLANNING FOR A "BETTER, BIGGER
AND BRIGHTER MILWAUKEE": 1918

At the very basis of making this a better, bigger and brighter Milwaukee, is city planning. . . . Before the public health can be materially advanced, improved housing conditions must prevail. Ways must be found . . . by which all of our citizens can be provided with sanitary, well ventilated and sun lighted rooms in which to live. As a step in this direction the planning commission should vigorously push its work of properly platting the lands adjacent to the city, and should assist in working out a law to be submitted to the coming legislature, to more systematically encourage and control the building of homes.

Congestion of population likewise leads to the impairment of proper physical development. The spreading of our population, therefore, over a large area is necessary. Rapid transportation at a reasonable cost is the best solution of this problem. From past experiences we know that private ownership of the street railways, especially when regulated by a state commission, fails to furnish adequate service at reasonable cost. The poor character of street car service which has been supplied Milwaukee in the past has done as much as any other matter to prevent the proper expansion of our city. Private ownership and exploitation of our street railway facilities will continue to be a stone around the neck of Milwaukee's proper and healthful expansion, until we follow the lead of most older European cities and substitute municipal ownership. This has received recent emphasis by virtue of the court decision, that . . . power to order needed extension of service by virtue of the franchise, has been taken away [from the City Council] and vested in the railroad commission. . . .

The electors have long believed that better service could be obtained at less cost in electric lighting if the utility furnishing the same were municipally owned and operated. During the past 20 years they have many times overwhelmingly voted favorably on this project. It is quite unbelievable that public officials could so long defeat the will of the people. We have now constructed the first unit of the street lighting system, and demonstrated that twice as much light can be furnished at nearly one-half the cost by the city for that which is being furnished by the private company. . . . This [work] should be completed within one year. Milwaukee will then be the best lighted city at the lowest cost of any municipality of its size in America.[113]

11. CITY PLANNING

The increasing awareness of the city and its problems led, in this organization-minded era, to a new concern for comprehensive city planning, in the interest not only of improving the appearance of cities but of giving them more effective commercial facilities and making them more defensible from a social point of view. In the years between the 1890's and 1920, a number of large cities proposed and implemented elaborate city plans and appointed city planning commissions. A group of city planners emerged who were professional in their outlook, but like many of the civic reformers, not fully clear as to the goals and scope of the program they projected.

Though planning under government auspices was in some ways inconsistent with the opportunist tradition of frontier-forged America, the nation's urban experience had, from its beginnings, provided precedents for planning. These could be found in the orderly design implicit in the original plans for some of the colonial cities, in L'Enfant's farsighted proposals for the development of the national capital, and in the public street platting and municipal wharf development in which cities engaged throughout the nineteenth century. From the middle of that century onward, the public park movement stimulated discussion of the overall form of cities; as early as 1869, New York's Central Park Commissioners were given wide responsibility for the development of the upper city, providing opportunities for planned growth that might have been implemented but for the play of politics. The development of comprehensive systems of interrelated parks, parkways, and local recreation grounds, as in Boston in the 1880's, anticipated later regional planning. With the accumulating attention to the evils of city life came a concern for the aesthetic as well as other aspects of the urban scene. This concern was greatly stimulated by the Chicago World's Fair of 1893 — its presentation of a "Dream City" proffered an example of urban beauty to challenge the alleged charms of the countryside and exhibited the potential of planned design for whole cities. Moreover, the transportation needs of large urban centers convinced business leaders that government, through public service commissions and municipal officials aided by transportation experts, should have a hand in the comprehensive development of the city's system of street railways, rapid transit lines, and terminal facilities, regardless of who constructed and operated the parts.

The influence of landscape architects in the tradition of Frederick Law Olmsted, as well as the example of European cities, especially Paris, gave primacy to aesthetic considerations in this phase of planning activity. In this approach to planning a concept of the City Beautiful was coupled with a concern for the City Efficient in a way that appealed to the organized advocates of civic improvement. Charles M. Robinson and George E. Kessler were leading exponents of the City Beautiful movement, which inspired municipal art societies and civic art commissions to project impressive civic centers, broad boulevards, and sculptural embellishments that both caused and reflected a new pride in city living.[114] Kessler's plan for beautifying Kansas City, issued in 1893 and financed by a tax on the benefited property, made the Missouri city an acclaimed example of City Beautiful accomplishments. The state of the improvement, as of 1910, was described by Ray F. Weirick, in *The American City.*

ACHIEVING THE "CITY BEAUTIFUL" IN KANSAS CITY: 1892–1910

Boulevard routes were first selected. These were laid down in the parts of the city capable of development as fine residential districts. The rectangular system of streets, and the extremely wavering profile of all streets were a hindrance in the design of these drives, but gave Mr. Kessler the opportunity, after a careful study of street grades, to swing the courses of boulevards from one street to another, giving both easy travel and pleasing street vistas. . . . North Terrace furnished an excellent scenic reservation, being a jumble of precipitous limestone crags, to the face of which clung an old quarry road. This road furnished the suggestion for a Cliff Drive, which was laid out several miles long amid scenery as fine as that of the mountains. . . .

If the question were asked as to what one feature has added the most fame to the Kansas City park system, the answer would undoubtedly be: the Paseo. It derives its name from the Spanish "paseo" or promenade. To start with, a tract was discovered one-half block in width and nine blocks long, lying in the heart of the city. . . . Owing to its location this line of narrow blocks is crossed by a large per cent of the population, twice every day, as most of the people going to the business section . . . travel in car lines traversing this area. The fact that the region thereabout was settled up closely with negroes and shiftless whites made it very desirable that something be done to clean up the district and build it up with attractive residences. Mr. Kessler proposed that this tract be acquired for the full half-block in width, to give fine garden effects, a divided roadway and footwalks. . . . The separate blocks were adorned respectively with fountains, a fine pergola in three flights, an imposing architectural terrace, a sunken garden, a small lake shrouded by water shrubbery and several warm stretches of lawn. At the lower end the Paseo ran for three blocks alongside of a level tract named the Parade, which was developed as an extensive playground for both children and youths.[115]

The "City Beautiful" impulse led to the restoration and expansion of L'Enfant's plan for Washington, D.C. The project was spearheaded in 1901 by Senator James McMillan and the Senate Park Commission; it was executed by the designers of the Chicago World's Fair after they visited European capitals and studied the sources of L'Enfant's inspiration. Cities large and small began to call for city plans and to propose civic centers, a development that had its most significant expression in 1908 with the publication of Daniel H. Burnham's "Plan for Chicago." Sponsored by the merged Merchants and Commercial clubs of Chicago, it drew upon Parisian precedents and added transportational and regional features to the "City Beautiful" pattern stemming from the World's Fair of 1893. In the ensuing 15 years Chicagoans spent $300,-000,000 carrying out Burnham's proposals. Their implementation led to the creation in 1909 of one of the nation's earliest city planning commissions.[116] George Hooker, commenting on the plan in *The Survey*, in September of that year, saw it not only as embodying the contemporary interest in scientific planning but as dramatizing the urban region as an appropriate planning unit.

BURNHAM'S "CHICAGO PLAN" — LANDMARK IN COMPREHENSIVE CITY PLANNING: 1908

This report is the most comprehensive and by far the most beautifully presented of the more than two score improvement reports made within the last eight years for American cities. . . . Prepared with the refreshing confidence characteristic of the

West, the report is addressed to that general desire for a beautiful and orderly city which is undoubtedly a great latent force in the community. . . .

The need for such a study for Chicago had . . . been felt more or less clearly by a good many individuals. The Columbian Exposition of 1893 had left an eager and ineffaceable impression of the artistic possibilities of orderly architectural and landscape composition; the park movement had made a brilliant demonstration of social melioration through park and playground distribution inside the city, and had proposed an ambitious outer park scheme; extensive lake front beautification had been discussed and in part begun; the daily pressures of city life were calling for constructive enterprises of various sorts and for the elimination of waste in many directions; other American cities were making careful studies for their physical improvement, and it was also being discovered that the scientific planning of cities was an established practical art on the continent of Europe. The time was therefore ripe for a deliberate attempt to set forth the general needs and possibilities of physical Chicago. . . .

One of the most interesting features of the whole report is the study of Chicago and its fan-shaped surroundings stretching away for 50 to 60 miles. The conception that this region of more than 4,000 square miles is in a sense the real Chicago, sets a new standard of spaciousness in dealing with modern cities.[117]

By 1908 and 1909, the concern for social melioration to which Hooker alluded was beginning to give a significant new dimension to planning goals. The collection of social data, such as was supplied in the Pittsburgh Survey of 1908, emphasized the point that good housing and a wholesome residential environment were as essential to the well-ordered city as efficient transportation, well-planned streets, ample parks and playgrounds, and appropriate facilities for business and industry. Addressing the seventh annual convention of the American Civic Association in 1912, George B. Ford, city planning lecturer at Columbia University, asked, "Can we with equanimity stand by and help the city spend its money on these frills and furbelows [of the City Beautiful] when only a step away the hideous slum, reeking with filth and disease, rotten with crime, is sapping the very life blood of the city?" [118] The gradual change in emphasis from aesthetic to social considerations in planning owed much to the activities of Benjamin C. Marsh, secretary of the Committee on Congestion of Population in New

York, which was formed by a group of settlement leaders in 1907. Influenced by the example of city planning and housing in European cities, Marsh saw rational planning and the expansion of government control as the only means by which the twentieth-century industrial city could be reconciled with human values. He expressed these views in a contribution to *Charities and the Commons* in 1908.

BENJAMIN C. MARSH AND SOCIAL GOALS FOR CITY PLANNING: 1908

The creation of new congested districts without the necessaries of healthy life now going on in large cities, can only be prevented by obtaining power to forbid the erection of any new buildings except in accordance with a general plan for developing all uncovered land within the city boundaries. . . . Much of our social effort in American cities to better living conditions is aftersight instead of foresight, and we are engaged in the tremendous and impossible task of trying to end the evils we have helped to cause or to perpetuate. The German town plan contemplates a very different attitude. . . . Such rational planning is essential in order to protect those who without it must sacrifice for mere shelter so much of their income and savings as to compel them to lower their standard of living or appeal to charity.

To this end five distinct functions should be involved in the system of town planning: 1. The limitation of the area within which factories may be located . . . and the securing by the municipality of proper facilities for transportation of freight by canal, railroad, subway, etc. 2. The determination by the municipality of the districts or zones within which houses of a given height may be erected per acre, the site to be covered and consequently the density of population per acre. 3. The securing by the municipality of the proper means of transportation of the people. 4. The provision of adequate streets, open spaces, parks and playgrounds in anticipation of the needs of a growing community. 5. The right of excess condemnation, i.e., the authority to condemn more than the area to be used for the immediate purposes contemplated by the condemnation, so that ultimately the city makes no net expenditure for land to be used for public purposes.[119]

John Nolen, pioneer city planner, formulated a concept of city planning that combined both social and utilitarian considerations

as goals for planning. He expressed his views on planning in the
September, 1909, issue of *The American City.*

JOHN NOLEN ON CITY MAKING —
A SCIENTIFIC ART: 1909

City Making or City Planning is simply a recognition of the
sanitary, economic, and aesthetic laws which should govern the
original arrangement and subsequent development of our cities.
These laws, however, are not easily understood nor applied. They
are themselves complex and each must be adjusted harmoniously
to the other, so that health, utility, and beauty may each have
proper consideration. . . . In a dim sort of way . . . many persons understand that the time has come when art and skill and
foresight should control what hitherto has been left to chance to
work out; that there should be a much more orderly conception
of civic action; that there is a real art of city making, and that
it behooves this generation to master and apply it.

The interrelation and interdependence of these sanitary, economic, and aesthetic laws is a point not to be longer neglected.
Heretofore we have thought that we could follow one regardless
of the other, but experience has taught us otherwise. At last we
know, for example, that there can be no great and permanent
business success without providing convenient and sanitary surroundings; indeed not without surroundings which have the mark
of beauty, if by beauty we mean fitness and appropriateness. . . .
Intelligent city planning is one of the means toward a better
utilization of our resources, toward an application of the methods
of private business to public affairs, toward efficiency, toward a
higher individual and higher collective life. If we want such substantial things as health and wealth and joy, if we want the
equally indispensable element of beauty in our daily lives, if we
want to avoid waste of money and time, we must find ways to
avail ourselves more fully of the incalculable advantages of skillful
city planning.[120]

Both Marsh and Nolen played a prominent role in the nation's first national planning conference. Held in Washington,
D.C., in May of 1909, it demonstrated the emerging social orientation of the planning movement and the growing conviction that
planning should be professional in character and should be the
responsibility of public, not private, agencies. In the same year,
Wisconsin adopted the first state law permitting cities to establish

city planning commissions and prepare city plans. By 1920, almost 300 cities had city planning commissions.[121] To planners of this period zoning, once it was upheld as a constitutional exercise of the police power, was the most efficient method of improving the urban environment both for residential advantage and for the good of the business community. Its adoption in New York City in 1916 triggered widespread imitation in other cities. Although zoning often became a substitute for more comprehensive planning, its enactment, even when motivated by commercial considerations, showed the extent to which the force of municipal reform, by the eve of World War I, had put private property in the city under government regulation and control.[122]

By the second decade of the twentieth century, the positive achievements of civic reform attested to the efforts of city dwellers to solve the problems a generation of unprecedented urban growth had presented. The achievements were in part the result of humanitarian impulses; the proponents of reform talked about the maturing of the municipal "conscience." But the achievements came about also through the practical proposals of the business community for coping with the problems of cost, contagion, and social control, which resulted from the ever continuing accumulation of population in large metropolitan centers. Though the reformers had launched *Municipal Affairs*, a publication dealing with urban issues, as early as 1897, a more definitive symbol of the efforts of cities to adjust to the imperatives of urban society was the founding in 1909 of *The American City*, a magazine avowedly designed as "a clearing-house for the experience of cities and organizations" in their efforts "to rebuild our American cities along better lines." Its editor, Arthur H. Grant, wrote in the initial issue that its publication was one of the many evidences that American cities had come of age.

THE AMERICAN CITY "COMES OF AGE": 1909

American cities are awakening to self-consciousness and to a sense of their larger responsibilities. Hitherto they have been distinguished equally for the marvelous rapidity of their growth, for the untiring energy and vigor of their builders, and for the wanton lavishness with which they have expended, often squandered, their resources. They have shown on a grand scale the vices and virtues of youth — ignorance and irresponsibility, courage and superb faith in their destinies. They have mistaken gaudiness for beauty, bigness for greatness. They have lavished millions on luxuries, but grudged the dollars for decency.

And now these big children of Uncle Sam are beginning to realize something of the seriousness of life. They have borrowed nearly or quite to their debt limits, and it is being borne in upon them that economy is a virtue that is worth cultivating. They are learnng that there is a direct relation between crime and crowding, and that it is cheaper to help men to live decently in freedom than to force them to live idly in jail. They have found that congestion breeds consumption, and that parks are better investments than potter's fields. It has been shown that if we give boys and girls no place for whole-hearted play we need not be surprised when some of them grow up into hoodlums and prostitutes. It has dawned upon us that dirt and smoke and noise are no more necessary or decent in a city than in our homes; that beauty is not necessarily more costly than ugliness; and that it pays to look a bit ahead of present needs. The American City is outgrowing its irresponsible childishness and is coming of age.[123]

The America that went to war in 1917 was a nation that was coming to accept the idea that — for good or ill — cities were here to stay; and to many, caught up in the progressive mood, cities could be and indeed were becoming good places to live. Not only what the city could be but what it already had become, as a result of the civic renaissance of the early twentieth century, was enthusiastically proclaimed by Charles Zueblin, professor of sociology at the University of Chicago, in the second edition of his book, *American Municipal Progress*, published in 1916.[124]

THE NEW CITY AND THE NEW DEMOCRACY: 1916

American municipal progress is spectacularly evident to any doubting Thomas from achievements of the twentieth century. . . . Already this century has witnessed the first municipalized street railways and telephone in American cities; a national epidemic of street paving and cleaning; the quadrupling of electric lighting service and the national appropriation of display lighting; a successful crusade against dirt of all kinds — smoke, flies, germs — and the diffusion of constructive provisions for health like baths, laundries, comfort stations, milk stations, school nurses and open air schools; fire prevention; the humanizing of the police and the advent of the policewoman; the transforming of some municipal courts into institutions for the prevention of crime and the cure of offenders; the elaboration of the school curriculum to give every child a complete education from the kindergarten to the vocational school or university or shop; municipal reference libraries; the completion of park systems in most large cities and the acceptance of the principle that the smallest city without a park and playground is not quite civilized; the modern playground movement giving organized and directed play to young and old; the social center; the democratic art museum; municipal theaters; the commission form of government; the city manager; home rule for cities; direct legislation — a greater advance than the whole nineteenth century encompassed.

The twentieth-century city is in a class by itself. History furnishes no prototype. . . . The modern city is the offspring of the industrial revolution. It is also the parent, or at least the foster-parent, of democracy. If the people have to live together they have to work together. The meditative rustics at the general store chew their cud and discuss abstract democracy. The city dwellers collectively put water and sewerage systems under the streets that they are going to pave and they learn concrete democracy. . . . The compulsion of cooperation makes the city the laboratory of applied democracy. . . .

The evils of the city are not inherent and inevitable. They are the momentary failure to use to the best advantage the city's inexhaustible latent life. . . . When a city has secured a reasonably simple form of government and equal suffrage, or even before, if these are not immediately practicable, it must have a city plan. . . . If an architect is employed to build a house, why should amateurs try to build cities? . . . A niggardly public life that made the citizen contemptuous of public officials is yielding to a dignified and beautiful public service that inspires love for the community and respect for its servants. . . . Public office becomes more honorable and citizenship more constructive as the work of the municipality increases. The progressive satisfaction of the wants of all the people has ceased to be a utopian ideal; it is the only reasonable municipal program. A social efficiency beyond the dreams of corporate "efficiency engineers" is in sight of the democratically governed municipality.

> "Bliss was it in that dawn to be alive,
> But to be young was very heaven!" [125]

PART FOUR

THE
METROPOLITAN
ERA
1920-1970's

In the half century following World War I, cities continued to attract an ever increasing proportion of the nation's population, with results, however, that often were contrary to the progressives' hopes of what an urban civilization could be. Whereas, in 1920, only slightly more than 50 per cent of the population lived in cities, the urban proportion had increased to nearly 75 per cent by 1970; and although by this date some large cities had begun to lose population, the number of incorporated places continued to grow. The most spectacular urban increases of this half century were in the South and West. By 1960, Los Angeles had replaced Philadelphia as the nation's third largest city, and was exceeded in numbers by only New York and Chicago. Houston, a city of less than 140,000 in 1920, had more than one and a quarter million residents, 50 years later. By 1970, California's population was nearly 91 per cent urban, to New Jersey's 88.9 per cent, Rhode Island's 87.1 per cent, New York's 85.5 per cent, and Massachusetts' 84.6 per cent. In the traditionally rural South, the urban proportion leaped from 28 per cent in 1920 to nearly 65 per cent in 1970. By the mid-twentieth century, urbanism in many ways pervaded the nation as a whole; some of the major urban centers, already large by 1920, were reaching almost unmanageable proportions, in both the central cities and the metropolitan areas of which they were a part.[1]

Decentralized concentration became more and more the pattern of urbanism in the United States as the twentieth century progressed. The proportion of the total population identified with large urban clusters continued to increase, but growth was more rapid on their fringes than at the central core. Economic developments explain the continuing tendency toward population concentration. The regional orientation of the national economy, encouraged by the expansion of railroads in the later nineteenth century, had caused population to gravitate toward a limited number of focal points, and by the mid-twentieth century these urban magnets were exerting an even stronger attraction. With the automation of industry and farming, fewer workers were needed in wide-ranging extractive pursuits as well as in manufacturing, and more turned to personal and professional services that had their most dependable market in large urban areas. The expansion of air passenger transport encouraged the centralization of the national business management function in a few large centers, and this also furthered the growth of existing metropolitan clusters.

By the 1920's, however, within these growing metropolitan regions, technology — and the traditional appeal of the single-family home — encouraged the outward thrust of both industry and residence. The availability of electric power for industrial production, the space needed for the use of assembly-line techniques, the ease of telephonic communication, and the practicability of motor transport of heavy goods which resulted from the improvement of highways and bridges, led to the location of industrial sites on the outskirts of cities. The automobile, coming into general use by the 1920's, as well as other improved facilities of urban mass transit, permitted city workers to live on the fringes of the central city or in suburbs within its orbit. Radio, by the 1920's, and later television provided a suburban substitute for the entertainment attractions that formerly had encouraged residence in the central city. Beginning in the 1930's, and especially after World War II, the federal government encouraged the outward drift by credit policies that stimulated home construction and ownership, especially in the suburbs.

The chief consequence of this decentralization within metropolitan areas was the relative decline in growth and population of the central city and the expansion of the suburban dimension of urban society. Between 1900 and 1920, the population of central cities, in the total population, increased more rapidly than that of the communities surrounding them; but from the 1920's onward, suburban growth took the lead, and by the 1950's the population of the central city in many metropolitan areas actually had begun to decline. The Census of 1970 revealed, for the first time, that more Americans were living in suburbs than were dwelling in central cities, a situation that gave some promise of a gradual leveling out of population density within metropolitan areas. At the same time, the coalescence of such metropolitan areas was producing gigantic webs of urbanism in various parts of the country — continuous zones of relatively high density — that foreshadowed a new regional urban configuration in the nation. The largest of these in 1970 was the concentration of population along the Atlantic coast, a megalopolitan accumulation extending from Boston to Washington and containing more than 36,000,000 persons, more than one-sixth of the entire population of the United States. A study published in 1972 predicted that by the year 2000 eight out of every 10 Americans would be living in some 28 "urban regions," each of which would number more than a million people.[2] Table 4.1, exhibiting the growth of selected cities between 1920 and 1970, reveals the expanding urbanism of the half century, especially in the West and South, the increase in metropolitan population accumulation, and the relative, and even absolute, decline in the population of central cities.

1. SUBURBS AND NEW CITIES

The twentieth-century pattern of the nation's urbanism, with its wider diffusion of suburban residence and its increasing identification of broad metropolitan regions, was revealed in a study of the New York metropolitan area undertaken in the late 1950's by the Graduate School of Public Administration of Harvard University. The New York metropolitan area increased in population between 1920 and 1970 from slightly under 8,000,000 to more than 11,500,-000. What the Census of 1970 identified as the New York-Northeastern New Jersey "urbanized area" exceeded 16,000,000 by 1970; the next in size of the nation's huge urban agglomerations, by that date, were the Los Angeles-Long Beach urbanized area, numbering more than 8,000,000, and the Chicago-Northwestern Indiana urbanized area, totaling nearly 7,000,000. Some of the findings of the New York metropolitan area study were summarized by Edgar M. Hoover and Raymond Vernon in *The Anatomy of a Metropolis,* published in 1962.

METROPOLITANISM — THE TWENTIETH-CENTURY FEATURE OF AMERICAN URBANISM: 1960

The disposition to think of a metropolitan area as a meaningful unit for study is a comparatively recent phenomenon. Time was, only four or five decades ago, when the city — not the metropolitan area — was a sufficient unit for analysis. Though urban development sometimes wandered a little beyond the city limits, this phenomenon was far from universal. Most large cities had a "downtown" section and residential and industrial neighborhoods, all of them built up at fairly high densities. Somewhere out near the political boundaries, short of the ends of the trolley lines, city development ended rather abruptly. Just beyond were open fields, dirt roads, and occasional amusement parks, set up to generate week-end traffic on the trolleys.

Here and there, the pattern was punctured by the impact of a high-speed interurban trolley or a suburban railway; where these existed, the houses and neighborhood stores were strung out a little farther beyond the city limits or clustered tightly about the passenger stations. But the distinction beween "urban places" and "rural places" was sharp enough for most purposes.

Today, metropolitan areas spill beyond their central cities, embracing smaller cities and towns, and surrounding numerous semi-rural patches. In the New York Metropolitan Region, the development radiating outward from New York City engulfs a number of old cities which once were the business and cultural centers of the countryside surrounding them. . . . If we think of the Region as a huge conical structure, in which altitude represents the concentration of human activity, we find Newark, Jersey City, Paterson, Elizabeth, Yonkers, and Bridgeport — each with a population over 100,000 — protruding as lesser peaks from its sloping flanks. Yet by any measure one cares to devise, the apex of the whole structure is on the island of Manhattan. . . .

The most general and apparent trend of recent years is the . . . wider diffusion of residence over the New York Metropolitan Region, with a thinning-out of density where it was highest, a slower drop-off of density with increasing distance from the Region's main centers, and a more spacious and more scattered pattern of new development on the fringe.

We have found several explanations for this shift. One is the recently accelerated trend toward wider suburban dispersal of many important types of the Region's jobs. More important, however, is the increased freedom that virtually all classes of the Region's population have attained in their choice of living places, which has led many to desert older and more crowded areas in favor of newer and more spacious ones. The increased freedom of residence choice that has been attained . . . can in turn be traced to rising standards of income and leisure, the mass ownership of automobiles, and relaxation of some of the special barriers affecting the residence choice of racial and other minority groups. . . . Thus, new suburban developments have been taking advantage of a vastly widened choice of areas, and have adopted lower-density layouts, because of the latitude provided by automobile transport. This has almost explosively accelerated the expansion of the Region's developed land.

The burgeoning of the newer residential developments and

Table 4.1

POPULATION GROWTH OF REPRESENTATIVE CITIES
AND METROPOLITAN AREAS: 1920–1970[3]

| | POPULATION OF CENTRAL CITY | | | METROPOLITAN AREA | | | PERCENTAGE OF CHANGE 1960 TO 1970c | | LOCALE OF STANDARD METROPOLITAN STATISTICAL AREA[d] |
| | | | | | | | CENTRAL CITY | OUTSIDE CENTRAL CITY | |
	1920a	1940b	1970c	1920a	1940b	1970c	CITY	CITY	
New England									
Boston	748,060	770,816	641,071	1,772,254	2,209,608	2,753,700	−8.1	11.3	Boston
Lowell	112,759	101,389	94,239	313,206e	132,633	212,860	2.3	64.4	Lowell
Providence	237,595	253,504	179,213	448,228	695,253	789,186	−13.6	23.0	Providence, Pawtucket, Warwick, R.I.-Mass.
New Haven	162,537	160,605	137,707	264,829	244,294	355,538	−9.4	29.1	New Haven
Worcester	179,754	193,694	176,572	268,551	276,453	344,320	−5.4	17.9	Worcester
Middle Atlantic									
New York	5,620,048	7,454,995	7,894,862	7,910,415	8,706,917	11,571,899	1.5	26.2	New York
Rochester	295,750	324,975	296,233	320,966	438,230	882,667	−7.0	41.7	Rochester
Buffalo	506,775	575,901	462,768	602,847	958,487	1,349,211	−13.1	14.5	Buffalo
Newark	414,524	429,760	382,417	included in NYC	1,291,416	1,856,556	−5.6	14.8	Newark

Jersey City	298,103	301,173	260,545	included in NYC	652,040	609,266	−5.6	4.2	Jersey City
Philadelphia	1,823,779	1,931,334	1,948,609	2,407,234	3,199,637	4,817,914	−2.7	22.6	Philadelphia, Pa.-N.J.
Pittsburgh	588,343	671,659	520,117	1,207,504	2,082,556	2,401,245	−13.9	4.4	Pittsburgh
South Atlantic									
Baltimore	733,826	859,100	905,759	787,458	1,139,529	2,070,670	−3.5	34.7	Baltimore
Washington	437,571	663,091	756,510	506,588	967,985	2,861,123	−1.0	61.9	Washington, D.C.-Md.-Va.
Richmond	171,667	193,042	249,621	205,807	266,185	518,319	13.5	24.3	Richmond
Durham, N.C.	21,719	60,195	95,438	not listed as met. dist.	80,244	190,388	21.9	23.9	Durham
Charlotte, N.C.	46,338	100,899	241,178	not listed as met. dist.	151,826	409,370	19.7	46.0	Charlotte
Charleston, S.C.	67,957	71,275	66,945	not listed as met. dist.	121,105	303,849	1.5	25.6	Charleston
Savannah	83,252	95,996	118,349	not listed as met. dist.	117,970	187,767	−20.7	77.7	Savannah
Atlanta	200,616	302,288	496,973	249,226	558,842	1,390,164	2.0	68.6	Atlanta
Miami	29,571	172,172	334,859	not listed as met. dist.	267,739	1,267,792	14.8	45.0	Miami
North Central									
Cincinnati	401,247	455,610	452,524	606,850	787,044	1,384,851	−10.0	21.7	Cincinnati, Ohio-Ky.-Ind.
Cleveland	796,841	878,336	750,903	925,720	1,267,270	2,064,194	−14.3	27.1	Cleveland
Indianapolis	314,194	386,972	743,155	339,105	460,926	1,109,882	56.0	−21.7	Indianapolis

Table 4.1 (Cont.)

| | Population of Central City | | | Metropolitan Area | | | Percentage of Change 1960 to 1970[c] | | Locale of Standard Metropolitan Statistical Area[d] |
	1920[a]	1940[b]	1970[c]	1920[a]	1940[b]	1970[c]	Central City	Outside Central City	
North Central (Cont.)									
Detroit	993,678	1,623,452	1,511,482	1,165,153	2,377,329	4,199,931	−9.5	28.5	Detroit
Milwaukee	457,147	587,472	717,099	537,737	829,629	1,403,688	−3.3	27.7	Milwaukee
Chicago	2,701,705	3,396,808	3,366,957	3,178,924	4,569,643	6,978,947	−5.2	35.3	Chicago
St. Louis	772,897	816,048	622,236	952,012	1,464,111	2,363,017	−17.0	28.5	St. Louis, Mo.-Ill.
Kansas City, Mo.	324,410	399,178	507,409	477,354	686,643	1,256,649	5.5	21.9	Kansas City, Mo.- Kans.
Wichita, Kans.	72,217	114,966	276,554	not listed as met. dist.	143,311	389,352	8.6	−11.1	Wichita
Omaha	191,601	223,844	347,328	249,999	325,153	540,142	15.2	23.4	Omaha, Nebr.-Iowa
Minneapolis	380,582	492,370	434,400	629,216	967,367	1,813,647	−10.0	55.9	Minneapolis-St. Paul
South Central									
Mobile	60,777	78,720	190,026	not listed as met. dist.	141,974	376,690	−2.5	10.8	Mobile
Birmingham	178,806	267,583	300,910	290,884	459,930	739,274	−11.7	15.3	Birmingham
New Orleans	387,219	494,537	593,471	397,915	552,244	1,046,470	−5.7	62.5	New Orleans
Memphis	162,351	292,942	623,530	214,169	358,250	770,120	25.3	−17.2	Memphis, Tenn.-Ark.
Nashville	118,342	167,402	447,877	169,194	257,267	541,108	155.3	−64.2	Nashville-Davidson
Louisville	234,891	319,077	361,472	318,159	451,473	826,553	−7.5	39.0	Louisville, Ky.-Ind.
Houston	138,276	384,514	1,232,802	168,351	528,961	1,985,031	31.2	57.0	Houston
Dallas	158,976	294,734	844,401	184,515	527,145	1,555,950	24.2	61.8	Dallas

Mountain								
Denver	256,491	322,412	514,678	264,232	445,206	1,227,529	4.2	63.7	Denver
Salt Lake City	118,110	149,934	175,885	150,066	211,623	557,635	−7.2	47.8	Salt Lake City
Pacific								
Los Angeles	576,673	1,504,277	2,816,061	879,008	2,916,403	7,032,075	13.6	20.0	Los Angeles-Long Beach
San Francisco	506,676	634,536	715,674	891,477	1,461,804	3,109,519	−3.3	31.9	San Francisco- Oakland
Portland	258,288	305,394	382,619	299,882	501,275	1,009,129	2.7	10.9	Portland, Oreg.-Wash.
Seattle	315,312	368,302	538,831	357,950	593,734	1,421,869	−4.7	64.3	Seattle-Everett

[a] These figures are taken from U. S. Census, *Fourteenth, 1920*, I, *Population*, 63–64, 72. The Census of 1920 established two categories of metropolitan agglomerations: the "metropolitan district," composed of a central city of 200,000 or more, plus all civil divisions with a density of 150 persons per square mile within 10 miles of the city's boundaries; and the "city and adjacent territory," composed of a central city of 100,000 to 200,000, plus all cities, towns, villages, or other civil divisions located within 10 miles of the boundaries of the central city.

[b] These figures are taken from U. S. Census, *Eighteenth, 1960*, I, *Characteristics of the Population*, part I, table 33, section 1:106–11. The metropolitan figures for 1940 relate to areas defined as standard metropolitan statistical areas in 1960.

[c] Figures for 1970 are taken from U. S. Department of Commerce, Bureau of Census (Nineteenth, 1970), Publications, *Number of Inhabitants*. See reports for individual states, Table 13. See also U. S. Department of Commerce, Bureau of Census (Nineteenth, 1970), Publications, *General Demographic Trends for Metropolitan Areas*, 1960–1970, issued for individual states. Some of the figures for 1970 are undoubtedly subject to correction. Population totals for cities for 1970 sometimes differ from list to list because in some lists, in the instance of some cities, the population of the city has been reduced to exclude a small segment designated as rural.

[d] As used in the Census of 1970, a Standard Metropolitan Statistical Area, except in the New England states, is a county or group of contiguous counties which contains at least one city of 50,000 inhabitants or more, or "twin cities" with a combined population of at least 50,000. In addition to the county or counties containing such a central city or cities, contiguous counties are included in an SMSA if, according to certain criteria, they are socially and economically integrated with the central city. In the New England states, Standard Metropolitan Statistical Areas consist of towns and cities instead of counties.

[e] Includes Lawrence.

their distinctive features have helped to speed the passing-on of housing in the older suburbs to a successor group of occupants less bent on modernity, space, or isolation. In much of the Core, outward movement from middle-class areas in the cities has been accelerated partly by diminished dependence on urban mass transit to get to work, so that the desire for more space can be gratified without sacrifice of access. Here, and in fact at every stage in the procession, outward movement of specific kinds of people is impelled not only by the beckoning pull of newer areas as housing becomes available farther out, and by enhanced mobility, but also by the push of the next wave, particularly in areas facing increase in density through apartment development or down-grading. . . .

These changes are rapidly shifting more and more of the Region's population into a new suburban pattern, of a type hardly conceivable before the age of universal automobile ownership. The suburbanites will probably include a somewhat growing proportion of the people who work in the Region's major central business districts, and for that group the problem of reconciling access requirements and other residence preferences will become more rather than less acute. The upper-income members of this group are, by and large, those who already spend more time commuting than anyone else. Those who elect to solve the problem by return to a city apartment are so far a relatively tiny minority, affluent and past child-rearing. These two criteria of eligibility will continue to apply generally, and no massive "return flow" from suburbs to city can be foreseen; but on a modest scale this category of city-dwellers can be expected to grow. That trend, plus continued redevelopment of slum areas, will help set the tone for a rapid adjustment of living patterns in some of the Region's oldest residence areas.[4]

The new configuration of the expanding city, as growth at its outer fringes became predominant, resulted in significant changes in the relationship of the suburbs to the central city. New suburban communities continued to be developed, as they had since the mid-nineteenth century, to accommodate the population growth of the central city. At the same time, satellite cities were now drawn increasingly into the suburban orbit of the expanding city as a result of residential needs and industrial developments associated with the outward thrust of the metropolis. As suburbia grew — both from the creation of new suburban towns and from the identification of residents of older communities with the outreaching city — the suburban complex became increasingly self-sufficient in terms of shopping, recreational facilities, and even jobs; at the same time, growth and change made the central city less attractive. With these developments came a subtle reversal in the attitude of the suburban dweller toward the central city. Until the 1920's the average suburbanite took pride in the association and identification with the city that was made possible by residing in a suburb. Thereafter, and especially from the 1940's onward, it was the partial divorce from association with the city that gave suburban living a major attraction.

The evolution of suburbia was described by Frederick Lewis Allen in an article published in *Harper's Magazine* in 1954. Allen delineated five chapters in the story of evolving suburbia — a region he knew at first hand, for he had resided since the mid-1920's in Scarsdale, a community 19 miles north of New York City.

FREDERICK LEWIS ALLEN ON THE EVOLUTION OF SUBURBIA: 1920–1950

The first chapter . . . began late in the nineteenth century, when the number of year-round commuters first became considerable. Up to that time, many well-to-do people had had country places outside the city to which they repaired for at least part of the year . . . but it was not until the later years of the century, generally speaking, that numerous people who had lived part of the year at, let us say, Milton outside Boston, or on the Main Line outside Philadelphia, or at Lake Forest, or at Webster Groves, began to remain in such places for the winter; that, contrariwise, the sons and daughters of the outlying villages began in large numbers to take city jobs to which they traveled daily; and that the regular commuters, who chose to live "forty-five minutes from Broadway," invaded these outlying villages in such numbers as to give them a truly suburban quality. (The date was later for the younger cities than for the older ones, and in the case of both Los Angeles and Detroit the pattern — especially the subsequent pattern — was distorted: in Los Angeles several suburbs came to rival the city nucleus in importance, and in Detroit the outlying industrial areas likewise became the tail that wagged the dog.) . . .

The second chapter . . . began at about the close of World War I . . . and covered roughly the nineteen-twenties — the era of the automobile revolution, during which the number of cars registered in the United States [increased from] 2-1/2 million in 1915 . . . to 26-1/2 million in 1930. When the automobile became something that almost anybody might own, and the open car gave way to the closed one which you could leave at the station in any weather, and there was a terrific spate of road-building and road-improving, all at once large areas of previously inaccessible land were opened up for suburban living. The subdivider appeared in force; farmer Jones's pasture was crisscrossed with paved streets to become Lakehurst Gardens; the short platform at the railroad station was lengthened, and lengthened yet again, to make room for the growing army of candidates for the 8.10 train. . . . Many a town which had previously regarded itself as partly independent of the city suddenly found its original inhabitants outnumbered by the "city people," who . . . captured control of the school system and imposed new zoning regulations upon the community. Suburbia was growing at a headlong pace. . . .

Then came the period of the Great Depression and World War II, a period which we might describe as the third era of Suburbia . . . when the suburban trend was almost paralyzed for a time by dismal business conditions; then was modestly resumed as commuters sought out inexpensive little houses on the outskirts of the grander developments of the twenties, and flooded into new apartment houses wherever the zoning regulations would permit them; then was slowed again by the shortages of materials, and of gasoline, during World War II. Those fifteen years, roughly from 1930 to 1945, were not exactly a period of hiatus in the suburban drift; they might better be described as a period of developing the fringes of Suburbia and filling in the chinks. But they provided scarcely a hint of what was to come after V-J Day.

For what we have witnessed since the war has been portentous. We have seen two remarkable phenomena going on at the same time. One has been the building of the mass-produced suburbs, of which the most conspicuous examples have been Levittown on ·Long Island, Lakewood outside Los Angeles, and Park Forest outside Chicago: huge settlements housing up to 70,000 people, or more, which have been constructed on what was previously unoccupied or very thinly occupied land. And the second phenomenon has been the discovery of the suburbs by business, for branch stores, regional shopping centers, and to a limited extent . . . for business headquarters. . . . One conclusion seems inescapable. The days are passing (if indeed they are not already past) when one could think of a suburban town outside one of our great cities as a village in the country. It would be much wiser, today, to think of it as a more or less comfortably spaced residential area — or residential and business area — within the greater metropolis.[5]

Suburbia often grew by subdivision, the speculative aspects of which were the twentieth-century counterpart of the townsite promotion that had been in the American tradition since the early days of settlement. The growth of Miami, Florida, and its suburbs reveals the connection between speculation in urban property and the expansive mood of the "roaring twenties," when Miami grew from less than 30,000 to more than 110,000 people. The Florida phase of the traffic in subdivisions was described by journalist Gertrude Mathews Shelby in *Harper's Magazine* for January, 1926.

SPECULATION IN SUBDIVISIONS — FLORIDA: 1925

In June an old and trusted friend turned loose upon our family a colony of Florida boom bacilli. . . . Not soon shall I forget the enchanted evening when . . . varied . . . wonder-tales, later substantiated, were told in our quiet living room. Like finding buried treasure were the accounts of fortunes acquired by the big promoters, Fischer, Merrick, Roney, Young, and Davis. They have all sold sumptuous subdivisions for uncountable millions, in some cases before the land was improved, or drained, or even before there was any land at all. Davis, at Tampa, and others at Miami, planted real estate in the bay, banked it in by sea walls, and starred shallow harbors with entirely artificial islands. Lavishly landscaped, their lots sold fast enough largely to finance such undertakings as they progressed. . . .

The fields, the wilderness, are side-walked and handsomely lamp-posted. The main ocean boulevard of the little city in which we were staying . . . has not yet a sidewalk, yet checkerboards of cement, often approached through a showy archway, mark the strangely empty site of many a sold-out backwoods subdivision. . . . Surveyors' theodolytes are seen everywhere. Roadmaking is a great industry. The available supply of wood is used up for lot-stakes. Yet houses, usually of hollow tile, pop out like the measles — they weren't there yesterday. Florida's table, I concluded, was being spread as rapidly as possible for an immense population, in-

363

vited to occupy . . . what it is believed will be a continuous pleasure city seventy-two miles long between Palm Beach and Miami. . . .

I . . . was offered by a reputable firm a great bargain in a city lot for $1000, an unusually low price. . . . This bonanza turned out to be a hole, a rockpit — and I reflected on the credulous millions who buy lots from plats without ever visiting the land! But to set against this experience I had one of exactly the opposite sort which left me with a sharp sense of personal loss. An unimportant-looking lot several blocks from the center of Fort Lauderdale . . . had been offered me about a week before at $60,000. I didn't consider it. It now resold for $75,000.

"It doesn't matter what the price is, if your location is where the buying is lively," I was told. "You get in and get out on the binder, or earnest money. If you had paid down $2500 you would have had thirty days after the abstract was satisfactorily completed and the title was approved before the first payment was due. You turn around quickly and sell your purchase-contract for a lump sum, or advance the price per acre as much as the market dictates. Arrange terms so that your resale will bring in sufficient cash to meet the first payment, to pay the usual commission, and if possible to double your outlay, or better. In addition you will have paper profits which figure perhaps several hundred per cent — even a thousand — on the amount you put into the pot. . . ."

"But what happens if I can't resell?"

"You're out of luck unless you are prepared to dig up the required amount for the first payment. You don't get your binder back. But it's not so hazardous as it sounds, with the market in this condition."

Imagine how I felt two weeks later still when the same lot resold for $95,000. By risking $2,500 with faith I could have made $35,000 clear. . . . Right then and there I succumbed to the boom bacillus.[6]

The migration to suburbia in the 1920's, though its increase was sufficient to excite popular comment, was only a trickle beside the population flood that enveloped the fringes of large cities in the years after World War II. By the 1950's, as the nation's metropolitan regions were becoming more suburb than central city, it appeared that "suburbanization" was the dominant trend in urban America. Population pressure, in a period of expanding families, was probably the basic cause of the outward surge in these years, but it was encouraged also, as earlier, by technological factors, by the availability of financing through recourse to the Federal Housing Administration and the home-loan provisions of the "G. I. Bill of Rights," and by the seemingly unalterable appeal of the countryside in the American tradition. By the mid-1950's, the alleged vulnerability of large cities to atomic attack and their difficulties in coping with crime, welfare needs, traffic congestion, and environmental pollution supplied added arguments for abandoning the crowded central city. The proportions of the suburban revolution are indicated in the statistic that between 1950 and 1955 the population of metropolitan areas increased three times as fast as that of central cities.

By 1950, the regional shopping center was symbol as well as consequence of the deconcentrated urbanism that the flight to the suburbs was producing. As early as the 1920's, chain retailers like Sears, Roebuck, and Company and Montgomery Ward learned that outlying stores with good parking space could generate a substantial business; Boston's Filene's opened a branch in suburban Wellesley in 1923. The intensification of the suburban thrust in the late 1940's and early 1950's prompted the development of the regional shopping center and a "race for the suburbs" by the department stores of the central cities that Dero Saunders described in the December, 1951, issue of *Fortune* magazine.

SHOPPING CENTER — SYMBOL OF SUBURBIA: 1951

The new frontier of American retailing is the suburban branch department store. It is destined to change radically the merchandising and shopping habits of all the larger metropolitan areas. It has already done precisely that to the third-largest U.S. consumer market, Los Angeles, whose downtown stores last year accounted for a mere 35 per cent of the area's total department-store volume. The May Co., biggest of the traditional Los Angeles department stores, does nearly half its business in its Crenshaw and Wilshire branches; and the balance will shift decisively to the suburbs with the opening of May's third branch, a 345,000-square-foot giant in the Lakewood shopping center. Broadway Stores, whose growth in the last decade has been the competitive phenomenon of Los Angeles retailing, already gets over 60 per cent of its volume from four suburban units. . . .

B. Earl Puckett, board chairman and boss of Allied Stores, has impressive credentials in the suburban-branch field. Allied's Bon Marché has a major branch in Seattle's Northgate, first of the great "packaged" regional shopping centers; the new "Shoppers' World" center, just opened west of Boston near Framingham, is built around Allied's Jordan Marsh; and Allied's plans for ringing New York with large branches of its two units, Gertz and newly bought Stern's, could well tear the city's retailing wide open. . . . Puckett . . . says, "The dynamic growth in retailing today is in the suburbs."

The extreme development of . . . suburban growth, more automobiles, choked traffic, inadequate parking, and poor public transit [explain] the early appearance and rapid growth of the suburban branch department store in sprawling, geographically segmented Los Angeles; but every major U.S. city is travelling down the same road. . . . The term "shopping center" as used here . . . means the fully integrated regional shopping center, foreshadowed by Los Angeles' Crenshaw and currently typified by Northgate, Framingham, San Francisco's Stonestown, and Los Angeles' Lakewood Center. Such a center requires within less than thirty minutes' driving time a potential market of at least half-a-million population, most of it above the national income average. The center itself will generally be built on forty or more acres . . . housing at least one large department-store branch and perhaps forty or more satellite stores; it provides parking for several thousand cars; it generally includes special-purpose units such as movie theatres or medical-dental buildings; it is carefully designed for easy flow of auto, pedestrian, bus, and truck traffic to, into, around, and out of the center. And above all, it is planned as a unit. . . .

The threat to the character of the downtown store . . . is . . . grave. . . . "I know what's going to happen," said an executive of one of the largest eastern stores. . . . "The type of customer is going to be lower and lower as the years go on; and in twenty years — though I'm not sure of the timing — the downtown store will become a basement-and-budget type of operation only. . . . As a counterstrategy, many merchants are becoming increasingly interested in revitalizing the downtown by superhighways into the heart of the city, new downtown attractions (such as the new Los Angeles auditorium), rebuilding blighted closed-in areas, etc. . . . The department stores did not create the downtown muddle in America's large cities, and they cannot solve it singlehanded. They can and should help; but in the meantime they had best roll with the punch and head for the suburbs.[7]

Increasing discussion by the 1920's of suburban life exhibited popular concern over suburban growth and a changing attitude toward the place of the suburb in American urban civilization. Earlier the movement to suburbs had been extolled as a means of making the large urban unit socially palatable, even though suburbanites maintained close working contact with the city. Now there were assertions that the move to the suburbs was prompted by "revulsion" against the congestion of city life and increasing criticism of the "characteristic suburban splitting of daily experience into widely sundered halves — one devoted to production, the other to consumption." Clergyman-sociologist Harlan P. Douglass, writing in *The Suburban Trend* (1925), envisioned a "regenerated suburb" as the hope of city civilization — an economically integrated community "large and varied enough to supply most of the needs and afford most of the satisfactions" of its residents.[8]

The surge to the suburbs as a resolution of the living problems of an inevitably urban society inspired opposition from the 1920's onward from two groups — those who objected to suburbs because they were too much like big cities and those who criticized the suburban way of life because it was not urban enough, that is, that it lacked the best in urban values. The most outspoken opponent of suburbs as an alternative to the congested city was Lewis Mumford, the best known and most emphatic twentieth-century critic of the unmanageably large city and the suburban method of escaping it. Mumford had no faith in the capacity of suburbs to meliorate the city's evils, since suburbs, like the parent city, were subject to ungovernable growth. Writing in *The New Republic* in 1921, he asserted, with characteristic forthrightness: "Suburbia — that vast and aimless drift of human beings, spreading in every direction about our cities, large and small — demonstrates the incapacity of our civilization to foster concrete ways and means for living well. Having failed to create a common life in our modern cities, we have builded suburbia, which is a common refuge from life, and the remedy is an aggravation of the disease." [9] Rejecting superconcentration in cities, he opted for regional centers of limited size, and capable of community integration, to be made viable by modern transportation, the dispersability of electric power, and the resort to prior planning. He had been influenced in these ideas, as a youthful student of biology, by the work of Sir Patrick Geddes, a Scottish biologist and sociologist who thought of the planning of cities in terms of the planning of whole regions. In a long and distinguished career as scholar and writer, Mumford continued to advocate the planned regional city, scaled to human proportions — limited in size and integrated in culture — a utopian concept the fulfillment of which was retarded by the physical mobility of population in the United States, the imperatives of real estate promotion, and the exigencies of war and depression. Mumford gave early expression to his distaste for suburbia and his hopes for the regional city in an article, "The Intolerable City," published in *Harper's Magazine* in February, 1926. The form and spirit of his regional city, set in "a permanent green matrix," in some ways recall William Penn's plans for a "green country town."

NEW REGIONAL CITIES, NOT SUBURBS — THE HOPE OF AN URBAN SOCIETY — LEWIS MUMFORD: 1926

Manifestly, the suburb is a public acknowledgment of the fact that congestion and bad housing and blank vistas and lack of recreational opportunity and endless subway rides are not humanly endurable. . . . The suburb is an attempt to recapture the environment which the big city, in its blind and heedless growth, has wiped out within its own borders. With the aid of the suburb, business and living are divided into two compartments, intermittently connected by a strip of railroad. . . . The sort of life the suburb aims at is of course only partial: inevitably the suburbanite loses many of the cultural advantages and contacts of a complete city; but even its limited effort to obtain two essential things — a decent home for children and a comely setting for life — is thin and ephemeral in its results. The suburb is not a solution. It is merely a halting place. So long as the big city continues to grow, the suburb cannot remain suburban. . . . Sooner or later it will be swallowed up and lost in the maw of the great city. . . .

Our technicians usually accept the fact of unregulated and unbounded urban growth as "given." So instead of attempting to remove the causes that create our mangled urban environments, they attempt only to relieve a few of the intolerable effects. They exhaust the devices of mechanical engineering and finance to provide palliatives for expanding cities and expanding populations, and they flinch, most of them, from asking the one question which promises any permanent and effectual answer — how can we provide a stable environment for a stable population? . . .

How are we to obtain the physical foundations of a good life in our cities?

The problem would be utterly discouraging were it not for two conditions. One is that the growth of modern invention has diminished the necessity for urban concentration. The other is . . . that the more intelligent and sensitive part of the population is becoming a little bored by "greatness," and they are beginning to feel towards their skyscrapers the way an Egyptian slave perhaps felt towards the Pyramids. . . . During the railroad era the favored urban spots were at the terminals of trunk lines. . . . The result was vast urban agglomerations . . . at points where the traffic ended, coalesced, or crossed. Modern motor transportation and modern airplane traffic do not abet this tendency: They favor a more even distribution of population . . . ; for the net of motor roads makes it possible to serve any point in a whole area by car or truck, instead of simply those points "on the line." [10] Economically, this works towards regional rather than metropolitan development; towards industrial decentralization rather than toward further congestion. . . .

The alternative to super-congestion is not "back to the farm" or "let things go." The real alternative to unlimited metropolitan growth is limited growth, and, along with it, the deliberate planning and building up of new communities. . . . Any effective effort to provide good living conditions within our existing cities rests upon achieving a fairly stable population: this can be accomplished only by building up new communities in the hinterland, which will hold back the flood . . . but also drain off some of the surplus from existing centers. What we need is a policy of "community afforestation." . . . Our present small towns and villages are unable to retain their young people because so many of them are scrub communities. . . . If we are to prevent congestion, we must deliberately create communities which will be fully equipped for work, play, study, and "living" . . . ; in other words, they must be, in English usage, complete garden cities.[11]

How would these new communities differ from existing cities? First, in placement; they would be established in relation to the best remaining water and power resources, and in country districts where land values were still low. They would be surrounded by a permanent belt of agricultural land, to provide a continuous local food supply of green vegetables, and to preserve open spaces without taking them altogether out of productive use. Second, provisions for all the institutions necessary for a community of a given size, say ten thousand or fifty thousand, would be made from the beginning. That is, the land needed for schools, churches, libraries, theaters, hospitals, municipal buildings, associations, playgrounds, and parks would be calculated, platted, and reserved; at the same time, the land needed for shops, factories, and offices would be allocated, with due respect to convenient access, to amenity, and — in the factory district — to prevailing winds and outlooks. The residential parts of the city, instead of being intersected by innumerable streets, would be planned for quiet, safety, and beauty. . . . In general, no houses higher than three stories, and no office higher than five, would be permitted; but that would not prevent the erection of a single tall building, or a small group, as high as, say, ten stories if the height served some direct purpose, such as the grouping of municipal departments, or medical services. The high building would not, however, be permitted as a mere rent barracks. . . .

The provision of gardens and playgrounds would likewise be made on the initial plan; and since the population would be definitely limited, their adequacy would be permanently insured. The time now wasted in subway travel would, since the area of the city is limited, be available for sport, rest, education, or entertainment. Land values increase in the business district of such a city; but the increase is kept for communal purposes. . . . If some potent institution, like an expanding industry or a great center of learning, caused such a city to attract more people than originally provided for, the further extension of the city, once it had filled its sites, would be taken care of by founding another city, similarly restricted in area and population, similarly surrounded by a rural belt. . . .

Here then is the choice — between growth by the "mechanical extension" of existing urban areas, and growth by the foundation of new communities, fully equipped for working, learning, and living. In the growth by mechanical extension we move inertly towards the intolerable city. . . . With a tithe of the constructive power we now spend on palliatives, we might found a hundred fresh centers in which life would really be enjoyable, in which the full benefit of modern civilization and culture might be had.[12]

Mumford's concept of newly created cities, permanently limited in size, found partial embodiment in several planned communities in the late 1920's and in the Greenbelt towns of the New Deal — "finger exercises," Mumford called them, "preparing for symphonies that are yet to come." [13] These enterprises had their inspiration in the impulse to modern planning and housing generated during the period of World War I; in the earlier Garden City idea of Ebenezer Howard; and in the neighborhood-organization programs of the American community planner, Clarence Perry. The prime movers of the experiments of the 1920's were the Regional Planning Association of America, founded in 1923, and its dynamic president, Clarence Stein, an ardent advocate of decentralization, industrial dispersal, and regional reconstruction.

The most significant consequence of this effort was the development in the late 1920's of Radburn, New Jersey, a new town of limited size designed with an eye especially to countering the hazards of the automobile for city dwellers. Though depression conditions prevented this experiment from being fully realized, it, like the ideas of Howard and Perry, influenced the thinking of Rexford Tugwell, who, during the 1930's, saw newly created, carefully planned cities as a solution to the problem of depressed farmers and slum dwellers. These were to be complete communities, located near metropolitan centers, built by the government, and leased to local cooperatives made up of the residents. Only three materialized — Greenbelt, near Washington, D.C., Greenhills, near Cincinnati, and Greendale, outside Milwaukee — and by 1954, all three had been liquidated at a loss to the government. Like Radburn, they were the victims of economic circumstances; but they nevertheless exhibited the twentieth-century effort to find in the planned dispersal of urban centers a substitute for the superconcentration of the industrial city and the unlimited proliferation of contiguous suburbs. Stein described the Radburn experiment in an account, published in 1951, entitled *Toward New Towns for America*.

RADBURN — TWENTIETH-CENTURY EXPERIMENT
IN PLANNED URBANISM: 1928

After the First World War there was a strong surge of enthusiasm for a better world. A group of us, including Lewis Mumford, Stuart Chase, Benton MacKaye, Charles Whitaker and Henry Wright, formed the Regional Planning Association of America, to discuss regional development, geotechnics, and New Communities. . . . Up to that time in America our attack on

Housing had been regulatory — legal don'ts. I went abroad in search of more constructive action. In England "New Towns" and "New Towns after the War" were attempting to chart a new way; the second Garden City, Welwyn, was being built. I returned to America a disciple of Ebenezer Howard and Raymond Unwin.

Soon after, I walked uptown with Alexander M. Bing, the successful developer of massive apartments and skyscrapers. . . . I suggested the building of a Garden City. That is how it started. We intended to create a Garden City in America. . . .

In our minds' eye we . . . had the theme that Ebenezer Howard had created so vividly in his book "Garden Cities of Tomorrow." We believed thoroughly in green belts, and towns of a limited size planned for work as well as living. We did not fully recognize that our main interest . . . had been transferred to a more pressing need, that of a town in which people could live peacefully with the automobile — or rather in spite of it. . . .

After examining some 50 possible sites [for Radburn], a large tract of undeveloped fertile farm land in the Borough of Fairlawn, New Jersey, only sixteen miles from New York, was chosen. . . . About two square miles of . . . land . . . was ultimately secured by the City Housing Corporation [a limited-dividend private corporation]. There was an area sufficient for three neighborhoods, for a population of about 25,000. . . .

Radburn's ultimate role was quite different from our original aim. It was not to be a garden city. It did not become a complete, balanced New Town. Instead of proving the investment value of large-scale housing it became, as a result of the Depression, a financial failure. Yet Radburn demonstrated for America a new form of city and community that fits the needs of present day urban living in America. . . .

The Need for Radburn — American cities were certainly not places of security in the twenties. The automobile was a disrupting menace to city life in the U.S.A. . . . Pedestrians risked a dangerous motor street crossing 20 times a mile. The roadbed was the children's main play space. . . . The checkerboard pattern made all streets equally inviting to through traffic. Quiet and peaceful repose disappeared along with safety. Porches faced bedlams of motor throughways with blocked traffic, honking horns, noxious gases. Parked cars, hard grey roads and garages replaced gardens. . . .

"The Radburn Idea," to answer the enigma "How to live with the auto" . . . used these elements: 1. *The Superblock* in place of the characteristic narrow, rectangular block. 2. *Specialized Roads Planned and Built for One Use Instead of For All Uses.* . . . 3. *Complete Separation of Pedestrian and Automobile.* . . . For this purpose overpasses and underpasses were used. 4. *Houses Turned Around.* Living and sleeping rooms facing toward gardens and parks; service rooms toward access roads. 5. *Park as Backbone* of the neighbourhood. Large open areas in the center of superblocks, joined together as a continuous park. . . .

Neighborhoods. — At Radburn, I believe, the modern neighborhood conception was applied for the first time and, in part, realized in the form that is now generally accepted. The neighborhoods were laid out with a radius of half a mile, centering on elementary schools and playgrounds. Each was to have its own shopping center. . . . The neighborhoods were planned for 7,500 to 10,000 — this to depend on the most desirable number of pupils in a school. . . . Although a start was made in the building of two of the neighborhoods, ultimately neither was completed. . . .

The early residents, approximately 400 families during the first few years, established the character of the town. They were mostly young people of medium incomes, who came mainly because of their children. . . . The community and what happened in it was soon the chief leisure interest of Radburn people. Home and community as sources of recreation and culture became very important in America in the years 1929 to 1935, when the family allowance for these interests was practically nil. At Radburn this partially accounts for the widespread, enthusiastic participation in community life that took place. Ninety-seven per cent of the adult population joined other members of the community in some form of activity. Approximately half the community worked in the Parent-Teacher Association, in Citizens' Association committees, or the Radburn Citizens' Association. . . .

Radburn was never completed. . . . When Radburn was conceived in 1928 all the economic trends were upward — the sky was the limit. But the first inhabitants had hardly put their houses in order when . . . the depression was under way. . . . In 1933 only twelve houses were erected at Radburn. Continuous, large-scale development is essential to the financial success of a new town such as Radburn. . . . That was twenty years ago. The Radburn idea is now accepted as a fundamental basis of urban residential planning in many lands. . . . Radburn is influencing the plans for New Towns in England. Back in America, the Greenbelt Towns and wartime housing developments are direct or indirect descendants. . . . And so, though the seeds that Alexander Bing and his associates planted in the Borough of Fairlawn had a limited growth at Radburn, they are germinating, developing and flowering in varied forms throughout the world.[14]

In the late 1950's limited attempts were made to create new towns somewhat in the spirit of Mumford's regional cities but placed close enough to metropolitan centers to be what might be called planned suburbs. Unlike the new towns developed in England and the Soviet Union following World War II, which were initiated and financed by the government, these conformed to American tradition in being financed by private investment. By contrast with Mumford's proposed new towns, they were on the fringe of the metropolis, not beyond it and not separated from other communities by a green belt. Their development nevertheless reflected the prevailing belief that cities in the United States had become too large and that a more satisfying life could be achieved in communities of moderate size. Among such new towns were El Dorado Hills, 30 miles north of Sacramento, California; Irvine Ranch, at the southern end of metropolitan Los Angeles; Columbia, Maryland; and Reston, Virginia.[15] The development of Reston was described in the May, 1966, issue of *The Commonwealth, the Magazine of Virginia.*

"RESTON: A NEW TOWN FOR A NEW KIND OF LIFE": 1966

Called Reston, this new city has begun to rise from a 7,000-acre site only 18 miles from Washington and six miles from Dulles Airport. More than 1700 persons already have moved into Reston, which, by 1980, will have a population of 75,000 or more. It will not be a typical suburban community that exists primarily to provide bedrooms for commuters who work in Washington. It will be a complete city itself, featuring quiet residential areas, commercial centers and industrial sections. It will have its own schools, its own churches, its own cultural facilities and its own parks. According to Reston's planners, most of its inhabitants actually will work in the new city or nearby, not in the District of Columbia.

Nor will Reston look like the typical suburban community, with subdivisions made up of row after dreary row of uniform houses on treeless lots. Reston's developers say they are trying to create a lively community of warmth and diversity. No bulldozers rumbled wildly over the site of the new city, scarring its earth and felling its trees. . . . Eventually, Reston will consist of seven separate villages, each with a "village center" that will include shopping facilities and serve as a focal point for community life. . . . All residential units will be within walking distance of the village center, and Reston's developers are determined to make walking attractive. They are providing for complete separation of automobile and pedestrian traffic. Instead of following the traditional grid pattern, Reston's streets will curve along the periphery of the residential areas. Cars will be banned from the shopping plazas. . . .

A New York real estate man [Robert E. Simon, Jr.] . . . bought the Reston site. . . . In developing Reston, Simon borrowed the "new town" concept from England and Scandinavia, where such satellite communities have been built to relieve the population pressure on old cities. The new town concept reflects the beliefs of many planners who say that the modern city is growing too big and incomprehensible. Often its residents fail to become a part of community life or develop community pride. . . . But a new town, like Reston and about 75 similar communities being planned in this country, can offer the serenity of a small town and the sophistication of a city. . . .

A curious sightseer . . . grumbled that he didn't like "so much planning." Reston's developers counter that they're planning "land, not lives," and they insist that urbanization could be disastrous without planning. . . . The day probably will come when those who criticize Reston for featuring too much planning will be unwilling to settle for a community that offers less.[16]

While Mumford and his followers condemned suburbia because it reproduced the disadvantages of the city, others criticized suburbs and regional cities of limited size because they lacked the advantages of large cities — the diversity and dynamism deemed essential to the continued vitality of American culture. William Whyte, Jr., author of *The Organization Man*, deplored the prospects for American society if rising generations were to be deprived of association with large, dynamic cities. He expressed this view in the introduction to a series of essays entitled *The Exploding Metropolis*, in which various writers attempted to expose the "assault on urbanism" characteristic of the mid-1950's and to show "how our cities can resist it."

SUBURBIA — NEW AMERICAN NORM: 1958

The growth of the metropolis and the growth of the city are not necessarily complementary: quite the opposite; in this time of "urbanization" there seems to be a growing alienation between the city and what most people conceive of as the American way of life. . . . Between 1950 and 1955 the total number of people in the country's metropolitan areas increased by 12 million . . . ; within the city limits, however, the number increased only 2,400,000. . . . In some cities the number actually declined.

Is this "urbanization"? The term is misleading. What is taking place is a sub-urbanization, and in this centrifugal movement the city has been losing some of its traditional strength as a unifying element of the region. While suburban neighborhood newspapers are showing marked increases, big metropolitan papers are barely holding their own. On the fringes of the city, people are no longer drawn inward toward the center, but outward to the new shopping centers. Los Angeles, which has sometimes been called 100 suburbs in search of a city, shows the pattern at its most extreme; there is hardly any center at all, and what center there is seems useful to most citizens chiefly as a way to get from one freeway to another.

Clearly, the norm of American aspiration is now in suburbia. The happy family of TV commercials, of magazine covers and ads, lives in suburbia; wherever there is an identifiable background it is the land of blue jeans and shopping centers, of bright new schools, of barbecue-pit participation, garden clubs, PTA, do-it-yourself, and green lawns. Here is the place to enjoy the new leisure, and as more people make more money and spend less time making it, the middle-class identification with suburbia will be made more compelling yet. The momentum would seem irresistible. It is not merely that hundreds of thousands have been moving to suburbia, here they are breeding a whole generation that will never have known the city at all.

Nor its values. Heterogeneity, concentration, specialization, tension, drive — the characteristics of the city have often been deprecated, but rarely have they been deprecated with such unwonted vigor. "I'm getting out of your skyscraper jungle," says the hero of the typical anti-success novel, and as he tells off the boss, inevitably he tells off the city as well. "To hell with your fur-lined trap, your chrome-plated merry-go-round," he says with pious indignation, and heads for the country and peace of mind.[17]

Suburbia was criticized, too, for the alleged monotony of the large-scale, mass-produced communities that both encouraged and accommodated the mass exodus to the suburbs following World War II. Two such enterprises, on which construction was begun in 1947, were Park Forest, Illinois, developed on a 2,400-acre site 30 miles south of the Chicago loop, and Levittown on Long Island. Park Forest was designed to accommodate a population of 30,000. By late 1950, Levittown had 51,000 residents living in some 15,000 identical houses, purchasable at prices of $8,000 to $9,000. Though developments of this kind often constituted improved housing for the residents and in many instances provided a sense of community, they were criticized for the assembly-line uniformity of their construction and for an impersonality as marked as that of the city their residents had left behind. Norman Hill, a free-lance writer who moved to one of these developments shortly after the end of World War II, later contrasted his life there with his earlier, and pleasantly remembered, experiences in the central city.

THE SUBURB MONOTONOUS: 1960's

Fifteen years ago I looked forward eagerly to moving out to the suburbs and into our brand new development house in Bethpage, L.I. If walking had been a delight in the busy Bronx streets of my childhood and in the busier Manhattan streets of young married days, how much more enjoyable, I thought it would be, to be able to walk regularly in the green of the country.

That is, it would be the country once the nursery-size trees and shrubs and the grass seed matured. I pictured oak-shaded avenues and wooded hills.

My home is in a development of more than 100 similar houses — the common side-to-side split-levels. And all those hundred homes — like the hundreds of thousands all over Long Island built to identical cost-cutting architectural designs, on flat converted potato-farm land — were uniformly and drearily landscaped. . . .

Each house was surrounded by what was left of the original potato farm top-soil, much of the best part of it having been scraped up by the greedy builder and hauled away to be sold. . . . So the lush green look took a long, long time to arrive, and

377

it never really turned the subdivided tract into anything resembling my vision of what "country" should be.

During the first two or three years I went for frequent walks. I enjoyed it for a while, but I grew weary of the sameness. All the houses in my immediate area were alike — colonial split-levels. All the streets looked alike. There were no surprises. No rabbits to dart across my path. No wandering brook. No unexpectedly different tree or bush. No rare yellow bird in flight.

Walking around the neighborhood grew less enchanting as the years passed. By 10 in the evening, when dinner was over and the children in bed, and I was ready to go out for a walk, there was not a living being to be seen. There was only the eerie, bluish flickering glow in every house signifying that someone inside was alive, presumably well and watching television.

The houses came to look more like the barracks of my army days. In the company of our neighbors we tried valiantly during the early years to individualize foundation plantings and enrich lawns. But time, aging, nature's perverseness and rising taxes took their toll. Original owners began to move to greener counties or back to the city. New owners — young couples with toddlers and infants — had enough to do furnishing indoors. They had little interest, time, energy or money to tackle the job of beautifying the plots around their houses.

Finally, walking became a total bore. . . . A profound change had taken place in my life. I remember, as a young boy walking in the Bronx I loved the limitless variety of colorful sights, sounds, smells, and most important, people. Each neighborhood had distinctive ethnic qualities: Italian, Jewish, Irish, German, Polish, Greek. There were fascinating store windows in every block. . . . There were children's games to watch: punchball, stickball, rollerskate hockey, captain ball. Mothers sat in long rows of folding wooden chairs in front of the red-brick apartment buildings, gossiping and rocking babies in their carriages.

At night the Bronx streets teemed with life. The shopkeepers, fighting for Depression dollars, kept their stores open late. People came out to the streets, walked, stood about on corners.

Later on, during the early days of marriage, my wife and I used to enjoy walking around Manhattan. There were an even greater variety of neighborhoods, peoples and foods. They were all there to stare at — the glamorous, the picturesque, the buildings under construction, the store windows, the drunks, the eccentrics, the ever changing vistas in and around Central Park.

There were people doing things. There were things happening. There was always something new and different.

Now, in my suburban neighborhood, even window shopping is out of the question. There are no neighborhood stores, just scattered shopping centers, many of which are dark at night. The idea of commuting to a shopping center to take a walk seems ridiculous. Besides, there's a depressing sameness about those shopping center display windows, a modern mass-marketing uniformity. . . .

I've now given up walking in the suburbs, for good I guess. I've joined the 92d Street "Y" in Manhattan, where I run around a wooden track in the gym three or four evenings a week before I commute back to Bethpage. . . . Once in a while, when the spirit moves me, I accelerate my pace and run past another human being on the track. He doesn't seem at all frightened to see me. Not even surprised.[18]

The magnitude of the migration to the suburbs by the later 1950's was such as to prompt a reassessment of the stereotype that had come to represent suburbia. By no means all suburban communities conformed to the pattern of ranch style house, giant supermarket, hyperactive social life, ethnic and racial homogeneity, preoccupation with childrearing, Republicanism in politics, and, above all, commuting, which traditionally characterized suburbia; nor were suburbs with a lower-middle-class constituency always as impersonal and monotonous as the image presented in the popular press. The studies of sociologist Herbert J. Gans served to modify this image, as did the work of Bennett M. Berger, who exposed the "myth of suburbia" in *Working-Class Suburb*, a study of auto workers in suburbia, originally published in 1960. Here Berger made the point that suburbs differed greatly from one another and often were not unlike neighborhoods within the city, whose residents were of similar socioeconomic status.[19]

The case for the city — compact, concentrated, and exciting — as opposed to the suburbanized mix that is neither city nor country was made in forthright fashion in the early 1960's by Jane Jacobs, author, urbanologist, and critic of contemporary planning.[20] The "marriage of city and country" had no appeal for Mrs. Jacobs. In her book, *The Death and Life of Great American Cities*, published in 1963, she argued for large, densely settled cities in close proximity to real countryside as an alternative to the suburban "shadows of nature" that emerged as the metropolis decentralized.

AN ARGUMENT FOR COMPACT, CENTRALIZED CITIES — JANE JACOBS: 1963

It is no accident that we Americans, probably the world's champion sentimentalizers about nature, are at one and the same time probably the world's most voracious and disrespectful destroyers of wild and rural countryside. It is neither love for nature nor respect for nature that leads to this schizophrenic attitude. Instead, it is a sentimental desire to toy, rather patronizingly, with some insipid, standardized, suburbanized shadow of nature — apparently in sheer disbelief that we and our cities, just by virtue of being, are a legitimate part of nature too, and involved with it in much deeper and more inescapable ways than grass trimming, sunbathing, and contemplative uplift. And so, each day, several thousand more acres of our countryside are eaten up by the bulldozers, covered by pavement, dotted with suburbanites who have killed the thing they thought they came to find. Our irreplaceable heritage of Grade I agricultural land (a rare treasure of nature on this earth) is sacrificed for highways or supermarket parking lots as ruthlessly and unthinkingly as the trees in the woodlands are uprooted, the streams and rivers polluted and the air itself filled with the gasoline exhausts (products of eons of nature's manufacturing) required in this great national effort to cozy up with a fictionalized nature and flee the "unnaturalness" of the city.

The semisuburbanized and suburbanized messes we create in this way become despised by their own inhabitants tomorrow. These thin dispersions lack any reasonable degree of innate vitality, staying power, or inherent usefulness as settlements. Few of them, and these only the most expensive as a rule, hold their attraction much longer than a generation; then they begin to decay in the pattern of city gray areas. Indeed, an immense amount of today's city gray belts was yesterday's dispersion closer to "nature." Of the buildings on the thirty thousand acres of already blighted or already fast-blighting residential areas in northern New Jersey, for example, half are less than forty years old.

Thirty years from now, we shall have accumulated new problems of blight and decay over acreages so immense that in comparison the present problems of the great cities' gray belts will look piddling. . . . Big cities need real countryside close by. And countryside — from man's point of view — needs big cities, with all their diverse opportunities and productivity, so human beings can be in a position to appreciate the rest of the natural world instead of to curse it. . . . Big cities have difficulties in abundance, because they have people in abundance. But vital cities are not helpless to combat even the most difficult of problems. They are not passive victims of chains of circumstances, any more than they are the malignant opposite of nature.

Vital cities have marvelous innate abilities for understanding, communicating, contriving and inventing what is required to combat their difficulties. Perhaps the most striking example of this ability is the effect that big cities have had on disease. Cities were once the most helpless and devastated victims of disease, but they became great disease conquerors. All the apparatus of surgery, hygiene, microbiology, chemistry, telecommunications, public health measures, teaching and research hospitals, ambulances and the like, which people not only in cities but also outside them depend upon for the unending war against premature mortality, are fundamentally products of big cities and would be inconceivable without big cities. The surplus wealth, the productivity, the close-grained juxtaposition of talents that permit society to support advances such as these are themselves products of our organization into cities, and especially into big and dense cities.

It may be romantic to search for the salves of society's ills in slow-moving rustic surroundings, or among innocent, unspoiled provincials, if such exist, but it is a waste of time. Does anyone suppose that, in real life, answers to any of the great questions that worry us today are going to come out of homogeneous settlements? Dull, inert cities, it is true, do contain the seeds of their own destruction and little else. But lively, diverse, intense cities contain the seeds of their own regeneration, with energy enough to carry over for problems and needs outside themselves.[21]

Another emphatic proponent of the central city — but in this instance as the magnetic core of an inevitably spreading metropolis — was Robert Moses, who for more than a half century addressed his abundant talents to rehabilitating New York City and improving its environs in ways that, paradoxically, encouraged urban sprawl. Among his many significant services to the city was his work as Commissioner of Parks, a post that he held from 1934 to 1960. In *Working for the People,* which he wrote in 1956, he testified to his faith in large cities as indispensable to a dynamic society.

ROBERT MOSES ON THE VIRTUES
OF THE CENTRAL CITY: 1956

Academic planners and those who cannot stand urban competition or tolerate a certain amount of noise, tension, hurry, and
the anonymity of urban life, advocate decentralization of cities
and dispersion of population. But their prejudices will not materially influence the logic of the situation. There are good reasons
why most cities persist. . . . It is not to be forgotten that civilization is an outgrowth and attribute of cities. Farms produce food;
oceans support commerce; the suburbs are dormitories; the mines
teem with energy . . . but civilization flourishes only in concentrated urban communities. . . .

The trouble with the prophets of doom of cities is that they
do not think like the people who live in them. Lewis Mumford,
Frank Lloyd Wright and their followers who damn urbanization
because they cannot stand the gaff of city life no doubt honestly
believe that all city people hate their existence. They do not
realize that Brooklynites adore Brooklyn, idolize the Dodgers because they symbolize it, and cheer themselves hoarse at the mention of its name. Can Mumford and the aesthetes, and Frank
Lloyd Wright and the back-to-the-land boys be right and three
million Brooklynites be wrong? . . .

Only the city can afford the arts in their broadest and most
developed sense, because, it takes population to keep art centers
alive and flourishing. The same reasoning applies to great medical
centers which require the most nearly complete clinical facilities,
to management headquarters of banking and big business, and
to many mercantile establishments which have to be close together. The nearby country as well as the suburb is meaningless
without the city. Los Angeles supports a veritable paradise of
truck farmers and orchards almost at its borders, and New York
is the big market for the potatoes, ducks and shellfish of Long
Island. . . . Our entire economy is dependent on urban, suburban and rural integration. . . .

Our big cities must be rebuilt, not abandoned. While this is
being done the suburbs will continue to grow amazingly, and
open country previously considered beyond commuting distance
will become suburban. But let us not fool ourselves about the
spreading city. There are just as many problems involved in rapid,
uncontrolled, suburban growth as in the rebuilding of substandard
midtown urban sections.[22]

The rebuilding of the central city was often the work of

businessmen and civic leaders aiming to counter the trend toward decentralization and the competition of suburban shopping facilities. A noteworthy example was the movement, underway from the mid-1940's through the 1960's, which transformed the deteriorated central city of Pittsburgh — America's classic "Coketown" — into the impressive "Golden Triangle." This project was underwritten by a nonpartisan civic coalition that linked businessmen and politicians and enlisted the resources of the federal, state, and local governments.[23] In 1971, Henry Ford II unveiled a plan to build a $500,000,000 complex of buildings to revitalize downtown Detroit.[24] A businessman's arguments for identifying his company with the central city were expressed by Shelton Fisher, president of the McGraw-Hill publishing company, in a statement in 1967 explaining the company's decision to build a new headquarters office in New York City.

A CASE FOR THE CENTRAL CITY —
NEW YORK: 1967

The decision to build a new headquarters building for McGraw-Hill in New York City has been a long time in the making, and it came only after a comprehensive search and a careful weighing of many alternatives. . . . Ten years ago, we transferred some of our New York City operations — mainly clerical, circulation, and distribution — to Hightstown, N.J., where we own several hundred acres and have erected two office buildings and a book distribution center. Later, we built major book distribution centers near St. Louis and San Francisco. These decentralization moves turned out quite well. Yet, the more we explored the possibilities for our headquarters building, the more our thoughts seemed to turn to the advantages of remaining in New York City. Why?

The reason can be explained partly by statistics. New York is, of course, a city of superlatives — everything is the biggest, or tallest, or best. In a business sense, it simply has no rival. With Wall Street and the New York and American Stock Exchanges located here, it is the financial center of the country. It is also the corporate headquarters of the country, with some 150 of the top 500 companies located in Manhattan. The United Nations makes New York a world political center. More importantly, it is . . . the largest communication center in the world. There are 1,359 publishers of books, magazines, and newspapers located here, 146 news syndicates, and the headquarters of every national radio and television network. New York's 1,137 advertising agencies also make it the nation's advertising center — a fact not unimportant to anyone who publishes magazines.

But statistics are the smallest part of the story in making our decision. McGraw-Hill's principal assets are . . . talented, creative, imaginative people who make our books interesting, our magazines informative, and our information services useful and important. New York pulls these creative people to its core like a magnet. Part of the reason is that creative people find New York's overwhelming cultural atmosphere irresistible. As a result, a large percentage of the country's authors, editors, and artists are located here. And these are the kinds of people McGraw-Hill needs to be successful. The cultural pulls on these people abound throughout the city. The New York Public Library has 7.5-million books for research and browsing. The city has 700 art galleries to inspect, 48 classical music groups to hear, 40 museums to see, a spectacular and growing Lincoln Center, and a new "happening" almost every day. It has the excitement and environment which creative people thrive on. Whatever their needs or inclinations, they can better satisfy them in New York than anywhere else. . . .

It's true that New York has its problems. But we feel it has the strength, the permanence, and compelling desire to overcome its difficulties and keep it the Number One city of the world. So, we are betting on New York's long-term good future, and in our relatively small way, McGraw-Hill is going to stay here and help make that future.[25]

Suburbs themselves in some measure retarded the outward drift of urban residence. This obstruction took the form of restrictive zoning and building codes and other exclusionary legislation that prevented construction of kinds of housing units that would attract lower-middle-class migration from the central city. In 1970 about 90 per cent of vacant developable land in the suburbs of New York City was zoned for single-family residential use; 82 per cent of the land in eight suburban counties in New Jersey was zoned for lots of a half-acre or more. These restrictions inhibited the removal to the suburbs of potential residents employed in the many factories that increasingly were being located on the fringes of the metropolis. The consequence was a reversal of the traditional pattern of commutation, which greatly increased travel-to-work expenses, especially for residents of the inner city. Proponents of opening the suburbs to blue-collar residents pointed out in 1970 that in "bedroom" suburbs like the towns of Westchester County in New York, as many workers were commuting from the city to the county as were traveling in the customary commutation pattern from the county to the city.[26]

2. URBAN REGIONS

The unending debate over the relative merits of large cities on the one hand and suburbs or even the countryside on the other, as places of residence and as factors affecting the national culture, was continuing evidence of the ambivalence toward the city that was in the American tradition from the outset of the nation's settlement. But whatever the preferred disposition of the urban population — in compact central cities or in an urban-suburban mix, the metropolitan clusters continued to grow to such an extent, in some parts of the nation, that their semirural outskirts coalesced with those of neighboring metropolitan areas. This created the urban region, surpassing in size the metropolitan agglomerations that had become standard in the mid-twentieth century. The nature of this mixed urban-rural configuration was described by geographer Jean Gottmann, professor at the University of Paris, in his book *Megalopolis*, published in 1961.

AN EMERGING MEGALOPOLITAN
REGIONALISM: THE 1960's

As one follows the main highways or railroads between Boston and Washington, D.C., one hardly loses sight of built-up areas, tightly woven residential communities, or powerful concentrations of manufacturing plants. Flying this same route one discovers, on the other hand, that behind the ribbons of densely occupied land along the principal arteries of traffic, and in between the clusters of suburbs around the old urban centers, there still remain large areas covered with woods and brush alternating with some carefully cultivated patches of farmland. These green spaces, however, when inspected at closer range, appear stuffed with a loose but immense scattering of buildings, most of them residential but some of industrial character. That is, many of these sections that look rural actually function largely as suburbs in the orbit of some city's downtown. Even the farms, which occupy the larger tilled patches, are seldom worked by people whose only occupation and income are properly agricultural. . . .

Thus the old distinctions between rural and urban do not apply here any more. . . . Most of the people living in the so-called rural areas, and still classified as "rural population" by recent censuses, have very little, if anything, to do with agriculture. In terms of their interests and work they are what used to be classified as "city folks," but their way of life and the landscapes around their residences do not fit the old meaning of urban.

In this area, then, we must abandon the idea of the city as a tightly settled and organized unit in which people, activities, and riches are crowded into a very small area clearly separated from its nonurban surroundings. Every city in this region spreads out far and wide around its original nucleus; it grows amidst an irregularly colloidal mixture of rural and suburban landscapes; it melts on broad fronts with other mixtures . . . belonging to the suburban neighborhoods of other cities. Such coalescence can be observed, for example, along the main lines of traffic that link New York City and Philadelphia. Here there are many communities that might be classified as belonging to more than one orbit. It is hard to say whether they are suburbs, or "satellites," of Philadelphia or New York, Newark, New Brunswick, or Trenton. The latter three cities themselves have been reduced to the role of suburbs of New York City in many respects, although Trenton belongs also to the orbit of Philadelphia. . . .

Thus an almost continuous system of deeply interwoven urban and suburban areas, with a total population of about 37 million people in 1960, has been erected along the Northeastern Atlantic seaboard. It straddles state boundaries, stretches across wide estuaries and bays, and encompasses many regional differences. . . . Six of its great cities would be great individual metropolises in their own right if they were located elsewhere.

There are many other large metropolitan areas and even clusters of them in various parts of the United States, but none of them is yet comparable to [the Atlantic seaboard] Megalopolis in size of population, density of population, or density of activities, be these expressed in terms of transportation, communications, banking operations, or political conferences. Megalopolis provides the whole of America with so many essential services, of the sort a community used to obtain in its "downtown" section, that it may well deserve the nickname of "Main Street of the nation." . . . In recent times Megalopolis has had concentrated within it more of the Main Street type of functions than ever, and it does not yet seem prepared to relinquish any of them. Witness, for example, the impact of the Federal government in Washington, D.C., as it tightens up over many aspects of national life; the continued crowding of financial and managerial operations into Manhattan; New York's dominance of the national market for mass communication media . . . and the preeminent influence of the universities and cultural centers of Megalopolis on American thinking and policymaking. . . .[27]

The Commission on Population Growth and the American Future, which issued its report on March 27, 1972, saw the emergence of urban regions as the most significant demographic development of the later twentieth century. The commission, headed by John D. Rockefeller III, was appointed by President Richard M. Nixon in 1969. Its projections had been anticipated by the Hudson Institute which in 1967 had predicted that by the year 2000 more than half of the population would be living in three urban regions — "Boswash" (Boston to Washington), "Chipitts" (Chicago to Pittsburgh), and "Sansan" (San Diego to San Francisco).

URBAN REGIONS — PATTERN OF THE FUTURE

The evolution of urban communities has proceeded from farm, to small town, to city, to large metropolitan area. It is now proceeding to the urban region — areas of one million people or more comprised of a continuous zone of metropolitan areas and intervening counties within which one is never far from a city. The reach of the urban economy has so increased that the most logical scale at which to grasp the trend is at the urban region level.

There have been tremendous changes in the geographic scale at which we live. Transportation technology, particularly our extensive highway system, permits us to move great distances within a short period. Some people commute daily between New York and Boston or Washington. Urban people in search of open space and recreation travel considerable distances to enjoy a weekend camping trip. A century ago, Central Park was the city park for New York. Now the "city" is the urban region along the Atlantic seaboard and its park is the Shenandoah National Park on Sky-line Drive. It is perhaps a weekend park, not one visited daily; but, on a three-day weekend, the license plates on visiting cars will be from Pennsylvania, New York, D.C., and Virginia. The scale at which we live is expanding well beyond formal metro-politan boundaries. In the future, our daily experience may well reach out into the far corners of urban regions and beyond.

An urban region is not a single "supercity"; it is a regional constellation of urban centers and their hinterland. Although substantial portions are comprised of more or less continuous geographic settlement, the urban region offers — and continues to provide — a variety of residential settings within the func-tional sphere of a metropolitan economy. This mosaic of environ-ments ranges from rural (southern New Hampshire or Indio, California) to cosmopolitan (Chicago or Los Angeles). Such en-vironments coexist within a common functional framework with-out intruding spatially on each other. Even in the largest urban region, running along the Atlantic coast from Maine to Virginia, and westward past Chicago, it is estimated that only one-fifth of the area is currently in urban use.

These regions grow not only through the increase of popula-tion but by geographic expansion. In effect, they are a product of the automobile era and new communication technology which encouraged the outward movement of industries and residences from the city proper. Density within these regions has remained relatively constant and low, even though population size has increased.

Urban regions appear to be a prominent feature of the demo-graphic future of this country. In 1920, there were 10 urban regions with over one-third of the total population. By 1970, about three-fourths of the population of the United States lived in the urban regions which already exist or are expected to develop by 2000.

The total land area encompassed by urban regions is estimated to double in the period 1960 to 1980, while the number of such areas is expected to increase from 16 to at least 23. By 2000, urban regions will occupy one-sixth of the continental United States land area, and contain five-sixths of our nation's people. . . . If our national population distributes itself according to these projections, 54 per cent of all Americans will be living in the two largest urban regions. The metropolitan belt stretching along the Atlantic seaboard and westward past Chicago would contain 41 per cent of our total population. Another 13 per cent would be in the California region lying between San Francisco and San Diego.[28]

Motor vehicles — automobiles, buses, and trucks — together with the highways that facilitated their use — were the major factors facilitating the growth of metropolitan and regional urban clusters in twentieth-century America. Motor transportation made possible the dispersion of residence and industry into the spaces not close to railroad lines, on the periphery of cities; at the same time automobiles contributed to the physical conditions in large cities that encouraged the suburban trend. Automobiles were something of a novelty on the streets of most American cities as late as 1910. In that year the number of passenger cars registered in the United States as a whole was under 500,000, and the number of trucks hardly exceeded 10,000. By 1920 passenger cars totaled more than eight million and there were more than a million registered trucks. By 1930 the total number of registered motor vehicles had leaped to nearly 27 million — a figure that now included more than 40,000 buses.[29] By the mid-1920's the motorization of traffic was virtually complete in many cities. In Detroit and Los Angeles, for example, there were as many automobiles as families. The increasing use of motor cars led to agitation for better roads. By 1914 many states had undertaken highway improvement and stretches of concrete were being laid. With the passage of the Federal-Aid Road Act (1916) and the Federal Highway Act (1921), the national government undertook extensive cooperation in highway improvement that significantly affected metropolitan growth.

As the potential impact of the automobile became evident, popular attitudes concerning its relationship to cities reflected the traditional ambivalence of the American people toward urban growth. Many contemporaries hailed the automobile as making the city so available to farm dwellers as to stem the rural migration to the city. Its use by commuters was thought to encourage suburban residence and thus ease the pressures of urban overcrowding. At the same time the business community saw motor transportation and improved highways as a means of drawing business from greater distances, eliminating small marketing centers, and thus stimulating city growth. The president of the Birmingham, Alabama, City Commission asserted in 1922 that the completion of highways was the project that would "mean the most to our city." By the mid-1920's, however, some business leaders began to have second thoughts concerning the advantages of automotive transport, as the threat it posed to business in the central city became apparent.[30]

In November, 1924, the American Academy of Political and Social Science devoted an entire issue of its *Annals* to "The Automobile: Its Province and Its Problems." Excerpts from a number of the articles exhibit the early reaction to the way automotive transport was affecting urban growth.

THE AUTOMOBILE AND THE CITY — REACTIONS: 1920's

The automobile is revolutionizing American life and American industry. The gas-driven machine has brought an era as distinct and creative as that brought by steam. . . . We are just on the threshold of the new day. Motor use has doubled in the past five years! Not a phase of American life . . . has been untouched by the automobile.[31] . . .

[The use of automobiles gives farmers access to] the social, cultural, and religious opportunities of life, which have taken many from the farm. In addition to its economic contribution, [in the movement of produce] the automobile brings the few remaining attractions of the city [entertainment, educational opportunity, shopping facilities, etc.] within such easy reach of the farm family that all incentive to migrate city-ward will soon be gone.[32] . . .

The automobile has also had another effect. . . . As cities have become crowded there has of course been a tendency to spread. Within the past this has been stopped by the limits which one could ordinarily walk to and from the nearest means of transportation. This has meant that suburbs have grown in a thin line along the railroads and in clusters around the ends of such electric railway lines as went beyond the city limits. The growth of the automobile industry and the enormous production, which has so lessened the first cost of these machines as to tempt a large proportion of the population to invest in them, have caused an ever-increasing number of suburbs to be built, of which the principal means of communication with the towns about which they cluster . . . is the automobile.[33] . . . Growth of automobile ownership has widened municipal boundaries. The actual limits of a city are far beyond the political city line. Over night the pasture land or the potato field is becoming suburban residence property.[34] . . .

The . . . vast suburban development . . . is served by a) buses, b) steam and electric railroads, plus motor cars, and c) private motor cars on door-to-door service. For a long while the electric railroads, alarmed by the competition of the motor bus, seeing it entering outlying districts before rail lines could be laid, and knowing that the public was willing to pay twice the street car fare for buses on the city routes, tried to place every obstacle in the way of this vehicle. It became increasingly clear, however, that the public wanted bus transportation. In recent years the interurban bus business has become very popular, both in competition with existing trolley routes, and in establishing lines where there was not enough travel to support trolleys.[35]

But always and everywhere that man lives remote from his fellow man, and communities are remote from their nearest neighboring communities, the automobile and the motor truck will be the foremost agency . . . in the filling up of the interstices that shall knit communities together and bring new areas into production to meet the needs of an ever-expanding race.[36]

Although automobiles encouraged the emergence of urban regions, they also contributed to physical and commercial changes within existing cities. An early forecast of the impact of the automobile on business patterns in the central city is exhibited in the experience of an Atlanta, Georgia, businessman who found his Five Points retail store bypassed as automobile traffic changed commercial practice. His reminiscences appear in Frank M. Garrett's history of Atlanta and its environs.

THE AUTOMOBILE AND THE CENTRAL CITY — ATLANTA: 1926

An Atlanta institution disappeared on October 1, 1926, when Thomas H. Pitts closed his famous cigar store and soft drink establishment at Five Points — facing Peachtree between Decatur Street and Edgewood Avenue. When interviewed by *The Journal* several days later, Mr. Pitts . . . spoke more eloquently than he probably knew, of a city in transition. He said: "Yes, I have been there a long time, and I have had my store on three points of the star. I've seen Five Points change considerably. When I first came to Atlanta . . . horse cars ran out Edgewood Avenue. Most of the shops that were there in the early part of the century have vanished. Office buildings have taken their places. Five Points has lost its 'town pump' characteristics. It is no longer a place for people to congregate, it is a place they rush away from. . . . I remember when there used to be an artesian well in the very center of the plaza, where the flagpole now stands. . . . Well, the old well went . . . but Five Points was still the center of town life. City life, I suppose I should say, for Atlanta has always called herself a city, but it was a long time before Five Points really became Metropolitan.

"I think the real thing that did it was automobiles, and more automobiles. Traffic got so congested that the only hope was to keep it going. Hundreds used to stop; now thousands pass. Five Points has become a thoroughfare, instead of a center. New traffic rules have made it impossible to park an automobile within two or three blocks of Five Points, and the traffic signals keep everything moving. . . . For years and years Five Points was the best retail spot in the city. All hotels were in a stone's throw. Folsom's restaurant was right there and Durand's restaurant, which is nearly as famous in Atlanta history as the Kimball House itself. . . . I came to Atlanta from Thomasville in 1894, and opened my first store on . . . the old Norcross corner. . . . I think I had one of the first soda fountains in town. . . . I was on the Norcross corner seven years, then I moved to the corner of Decatur and Peachtree, across the street, and was in that location for ten years. Seventeen years ago I took over the Edgewood and Decatur streets store.

"But now instead of having one community center, Atlanta has many — Tenth Street, Pershing Point, Buckhead, Little Five Points and a number of others. Five Points has become more like a Wall Street business section. In the old days, people used to go to town in the evening. Now they take their cars and ride away from town, and at night Five Points is almost deserted. It is the same way on Sundays. People used to stroll down on Sunday morning to buy the paper and a cigar, and perhaps get a drink before going to church, but they don't do that anymore. The place where soda fountain trade is, is where automobiles go, and one must have wide spaces for curb service. A central location is no longer a good one for my sort of business." [37]

3. ETHNIC ELEMENTS

The continuing increase in the proportion of urban dwellers in the nation's population was in part the consequence, as it had been earlier, of the appeal of cities for the foreign born; but a more significant cause of city population growth after 1920 was the migration of Blacks from the American South and later of Puerto Ricans. The fact that most of these newcomers remained in the central city helped to compensate for the movement of other residents to the suburbs. Though the number of new foreign born greatly diminished after 1920 because of the restrictive legislation of the 1920's and the depression of the 1930's, the foreign born continued to identify with cities to a greater degree than the population as a whole. In 1920, when the total population of the United States was barely 50 per cent urban, more than three-fourths of all foreign-born whites were city dwellers; in succeeding decades the foreign born and foreign stock continued to be proportionately more inclined to city living than the generality of the population.

By the mid-twentieth century, in most cities, the percentage of residents born outside of American possessions was markedly smaller than in the mid-nineteenth century or even as late as 1920. As of 1970, foreign-born persons exceeded 10 per cent of the population in only eight of the large cities of the United States. The population of New York City was only 18 per cent foreign born in 1970, by contrast with 48 per cent in 1860 and 36 per cent in 1920. Milwaukee's foreign born, as of 1970, constituted less than 6 per cent of the population in 1970 to more than 50 per cent in 1860 and nearly 24 per cent in 1920. The one major exception, as of 1970, to the marked decline in percentage of foreign born in city populations was Miami, where foreign born made up nearly 42 per cent of the population of the central city. More than 75 per cent of these (nearly 110,000) were natives of Cuba. In most cities, the percentage of foreign born was greater in the central city than in the metropolitan area. Table 4.2, which lists 39 representative large cities, in order of size, reveals the marked reduction, by 1970, in the proportion of the foreign-born ingredient of the nation's large cities and the tendency of the foreign born to constitute a larger proportion of the populations of central cities than of metropolitan areas.

The spectacular increase in the number of urban dwellers of Spanish-American background was the most novel development in the ethnic pattern of many major American cities by the mid-twentieth century. These newcomers represented a broad spectrum

Table 4.2

FOREIGN BORN AND FOREIGN STOCK IN SELECTED CITIES AND METROPOLITAN AREAS: 1970[38]

CENTRAL CITY	PERCENTAGE FOREIGN BORN	PERCENTAGE NATIVES OF FOREIGN OR MIXED PARENTAGE	STANDARD METROPOLITAN STATISTICAL AREA	PERCENTAGE FOREIGN BORN	PERCENTAGE NATIVES OF FOREIGN OR MIXED PARENTAGE
New York	18.2	23.7	New York	15.2	24.2
Chicago	11.1	18.6	Chicago	8.1	18.4
Los Angeles	14.6	19.2	Los Angeles-Long Beach	11.3	17.7
Philadelphia	6.5	16.6	Philadelphia, Pa.-N.J.	5.1	15.6
Detroit	7.9	14.7	Detroit	7.0	17.3
Houston	3.0	7.1	Houston	2.5	6.4
Baltimore	3.2	7.9	Baltimore	2.8	8.5
Dallas	2.1	5.2	Dallas	1.6	4.3
Washington	4.4	5.2	Washington, D.C.-Md.-Va.	4.5	8.9
Cleveland	7.5	14.4	Cleveland	6.9	18.6
Indianapolis	1.5	4.3	Indianapolis	1.2	3.7
Milwaukee	5.5	17.3	Milwaukee	4.5	16.1
San Francisco	21.6	22.7	San Francisco-Oakland	11.2	18.2
San Diego	7.6	14.6	San Diego	6.8	14.1

City		
San Antonio	5.9	17.2
Boston	13.1	23.9
Memphis	0.8	2.4
St. Louis	2.6	7.8
New Orleans	3.1	5.5
Phoenix	3.7	11.4
Columbus	2.1	5.4
Seattle	9.1	18.8
Jacksonville	1.8	4.7
Pittsburgh	6.0	19.9
Denver	4.1	12.2
Kansas City	2.0	6.4
Atlanta	1.2	2.3
Buffalo	7.6	20.7
Cincinnati	2.7	6.5
Nashville	0.8	2.0
Minneapolis	4.8	19.1
Portland	5.5	15.0
Newark	10.5	12.4
Louisville	1.0	3.8
Omaha	3.1	12.4
Miami	41.8	12.6
Birmingham	0.7	2.4
Providence	10.2	26.4
Salt Lake City	6.3	13.6

City		
San Antonio	5.2	15.6
Boston	9.9	25.5
Memphis	0.8	2.4
St. Louis, Mo.-Ill.	2.0	7.5
New Orleans	2.5	5.4
Phoenix	3.8	12.0
Columbus	1.9	5.3
Seattle-Everett	6.1	15.8
Jacksonville	1.8	4.7
Pittsburgh	4.5	19.4
Denver	3.1	10.4
Kansas City, Mo.-Kans.	1.6	5.9
Atlanta	1.2	2.7
Buffalo	6.4	20.2
Cincinnati, Ohio-Ky.-Ind.	1.8	5.7
Nashville-Davidson	0.7	1.7
Minneapolis-St. Paul	3.0	14.7
Portland, Ore.-Wash.	4.1	12.9
Newark	9.8	21.5
Louisville, Ky.-Ind.	0.8	3.4
Omaha, Nebr.-Iowa	2.6	11.1
Miami	24.2	16.4
Birmingham	0.6	2.2
Providence, Pawtucket, Warwick, R.I.-Mass.	8.1	26.0
Salt Lake City	3.7	10.7

of persons with a heritage of Spanish culture: once affluent refugees of the Cuban revolution, airborne arrivals from Puerto Rico, and migrants from Mexico, Chicanos, whose public image and under-privileged condition in many instances made them reminiscent of the Irish immigrants a century earlier, and whose barrios — or "urban villages" — recalled the residential pattern of immigrants from Italy in an earlier period. As of 1970, Spanish-speaking residents made up one-sixth of the population of New York City; natives of Mexico were the most numerous foreign-born group in Los Angeles — more than 100,000 in the central city and twice that number in the metropolitan area; and Chicago's nearly 40,000 natives of Mexico constituted that city's second largest foreign-born group.[39] Whereas the sounds of German, Italian, and Yiddish earlier connoted the ethnic variety of large cities, it was the pervasiveness of Spanish, on signs and advertisements and in the conversation of daily urban intercourse, that imparted this quality to the mid-twentieth-century city.

Although natives of Europe were far less conspicuous in cities by the mid-twentieth century than they had been a half century earlier, the foreign born and foreign stock nevertheless continued to exert a significant influence upon the cultural and political patterns of American cities. In the large cities where the foreign-born population was still sizable, natives of southern and eastern Europe were most numerous. As of 1970, Italians constituted the largest foreign-born element in New York City, Boston, Newark, and Providence, in both the central city and the metropolitan area of which it was a part. Natives of Italy were the second most numerous foreign-born group in San Francisco and the third, in Chicago. Natives of Poland were Chicago's most numerous foreign-born element, in both the central city and the metropolitan area.

The half century following 1920 saw a decline in the homogeneity of the ethnic neighborhoods that immigrants from southern and eastern Europe had created at the turn of the century. For many of these migrants time and the prosperity of the 1920's brought upward and outward mobility. The movement out of ethnic districts was slowed somewhat by the depression of the 1930's and by housing shortages in the 1940's; but it picked up again in the 1950's with the availability of suburban housing and the movement of Blacks, Puerto Ricans, Mexicans, and southern whites into the central city.

Communication in the twentieth-century city hastened the process by which newcomers absorbed the cultural practices of the wider community, frequently by the second generation; but ethnic identification persisted with repercussions in politics and social attitudes. Representatives of the more recent immigration undertook to emphasize not only their cultural heritage but their contributions to the city; and political organizations found it expedient to accord them political office, even though the dominance of the older ethnic elements, such as the Irish, in city politics, outlasted their dominance in numbers. In New York City, where the Irish were traditionally influential, Fiorello H. La Guardia, the son of Italian parents, became mayor in 1934. Vincent Impelliteri, a native of Sicily, assumed the same office in 1950. The play of politics in Chicago brought Anton J. Cermak, a Czech, to the mayoralty there in 1931.

Prague-born Cermak owed his rise in local politics to the tutelage of Irish political leaders and to the endorsement of Irish elements among Chicago Democrats; but his power was based on the support he won from the Czechs and other Central and East Europeans of his residential neighborhood. His mayoral career was cut short in February, 1933, when an assassin's bullet, aimed at President-elect Franklin D. Roosevelt, struck Cermak instead. Mauritz Hallgren provided biographical details on Cermak for readers of *The Nation* shortly after he was elected mayor in April, 1931.

A CZECH MAYOR FOR CHICAGO: 1931

Chicago, April 8 — Cermak was merely an incident in the great crusade to kill Thompsonism. . . . Hence, Tony Cermak, the only alternative candidate available, drew the unanimous support of all the good people of Chicago. . . . Who is Cermak, and what can he do for Chicago? He was born in Prague in Bohemia fifty-eight years ago, and was brought to this country when still a child. In his early teens he worked with his father in the mines at Braidwood, Illinois, attending school about three months each year. His teacher was George E. Brennan, whom he later succeeded as boss of the Illinois Democratic machine. At sixteen he came to Chicago, worked at various odd jobs, and finally found himself in politics in the old Lawndale district of the city, then, as now, populated chiefly by Czechs and other

Central and Eastern Europeans. He started as a precinct worker, but being a born politician and understanding the value of the Tammany principle, which might best be described as "taking care of the little fellows in your own district," he rose rapidly and by the time he was thirty was sent to the State legislature from the Lawndale district. . . . Cermak later served four terms in the Chicago City Council, and in 1922 was elected president of the Cook County Board of Commissioners, to which post he was reelected in 1926 and again last year. . . . He was trained in politics by Roger Sullivan and George E. Brennan, though he had great difficulty in working in harness with the latter because he believed in "taking care of" the Czechs, Poles, and other non-Irish Democrats on the West Side to the disadvantage of the Irish who then controlled the Democratic city machine.[40]

The Polish element gained increasing recognition in traditionally German Milwaukee as the twentieth century progressed, a consequence, in part, of the Poles' effort, fostered by the press and the church, to expand the appreciation of their culture and to strengthen their political influence. Poles often held the balance of power in local politics, and hence they played a growing role in city government. At the same time, in Milwaukee, as in other cities, a developing economic stratification identified the Poles, as well as members of other ethnic groups, with organizations that cut across nationality lines. Aspects of Polish acculturation in the urban setting were revealed in a brochure entitled *We, the Milwaukee Poles, the History of Milwaukeeans of Polish Descent and a Record of their Contributions to the Greatness of Milwaukee*, published in 1946 in connection with the celebration of Milwaukee's hundredth anniversary. The book reflects the role of the city in solidifying the sense of nationality in an ethnic group as well as in facilitating its adjustment to American life.

THE POLISH-AMERICANS OF MILWAUKEE: 1946

Something is apt to happen when people of a gallant nation, held together by the ties of language, culture, and religion, all of which for a long time had been ruthlessly and systematically suppressed by a foreign force, suddenly find themselves transplanted and free to think and act as they please. Something happened to Milwaukee when Polish immigrants began moving in from their oppressed motherland. Something has continued to happen ever since. . . .

The first [important event] was the ceremony of the blessing of the first Polish church here in 1872. . . . The next was the blessing of quarters of the famed Kosciuszko Guard . . . in 1887. . . . A memorable day was the departure of the Kosciuszko Guard in 1898 for the Spanish-American War. The soldiers were bade farewell by a big crowd and pelted with flowers. . . . The great artist and spokesman for the cause of Poland, Ignace Jan Paderewski, visited Milwaukee on a number of occasions, and each visit was turned into a national manifestation by local Polish residents. . . . Memorable was the first "Polish Day," arranged by Pulaski Council . . . in 1930. . . . In 1931 . . . the second Polish hero of the American Revolutionary war, Gen. Casimir Pulaski, was honored here by the unveiling of a monument to him in Pulaski park. . . .

Americans of Polish descent in Milwaukee have given ample evidence of their interest in the governmental affairs of their city. . . . If Milwaukee. . . has been a consistent leader in traffic safety, in health, in law enforcement and in fire protection, it is because people formulating plans and later carrying out the program, included Americans of Polish origin. As far as can be ascertained, the first person of Polish descent to hold municipal office in Milwaukee was Theodore Rudzinski, who was elected alderman in 1882. . . . The office of city comptroller has held great lure for Polish Americans. First to serve in that post was Roman Czerwinski, who was elected for two two-year terms, 1890–1892 and 1892–1894. . . . Louis M. Kotecki . . . served as city comptroller from 1912 to 1933. . . . Milwaukee's nationally famous police department [was] headed [in the 1940's] by Chief of Police John W. Polcyn, who was born of Polish parents.[41]

The persistence of ethnic identification among second-generation national groups in the urban setting — despite outward manifestations of acculturation — is illustrated in the mid-twentieth-century experience of Italian-Americans in many cities. Studies by sociologists William F. Whyte and Herbert Gans of two working-class Italian communities in Boston showed that while second-generation Italian-Americans had little concern for or knowledge of Italian culture, other than to use the language and maintain an Italian cuisine, they retained a pronounced Italian-American group identification that led them to support spokesmen of their group values and to resist policies that seemed to threaten those values.

This ethnic identification often persisted even after city dwellers moved from the locale of the original group settlement. In general the nationality enclaves that city life makes possible have tended to retard assimilation and to encourage the rise and retention of ethnic group attitudes, despite acculturation to the American scene. Gans labeled these communities "urban villages," seeing in their society a means of group communication that not only helped newcomers "adapt their nonurban institutions and cultures to the urban milieu" but helped to forge a group identification that transcended neighborhood as a force in the American political and social scene.[42] One such "urban village" was Boston's West End, which Gans described in his book, *The Urban Villagers*, after residing in the neighborhood from October, 1957 to May, 1958.

ETHNIC ENCLAVES AS "URBAN VILLAGES" — BOSTON'S WEST END: 1958

The West End was an urban village, located next to Boston's original and once largest skid row area, Scollay Square. . . . Several times during its existence, the population of the West End has changed in a pattern typical of other urban villages. The North and the South End were the primary areas of first settlement for Irish, Jewish, and Italian peoples, in that order. The South End also served the other ethnic groups that settled in Boston, especially Chinese, Greek, and Syrian. . . . In the late nineteenth century, [the West End] was primarily an Irish area, with Yankees scattered through the upper end. Then, around the turn of the century, the Irish were replaced by the Jews, who dominated the West End until about 1930. During this era, the West End sometimes was called the Lower East Side of Boston. In the late twenties, Italians and Poles began to arrive, the former from the North End, and they joined a small Italian settlement that had existed in the lower end of the area since the beginning of the century. Throughout the 1930's and early 1940's, the Italian influx continued until eventually they became the largest ethnic group in both the upper and lower portions of the West End. . . .

A Polish church that had been established in 1930 quickly enrolled 250 families. Although it later lost some of these, the congregation was replenished by displaced persons who came into the West End after World War II. Also there were small Greek, Albanian, and Ukrainian settlements, the latter served by a Ukrainian church located in a tenement. Consequently, proud

West Enders were able to claim that twenty-three nationalities could be found in the area. In recent years, small groups of students, artists, and Negroes had come into the West End. . . . Numerically, the West End was at its height around 1910, when it had 23,000 inhabitants. In 1920, it had 18,500 residents; in 1930 and 1940, 13,000; and, in 1950, 12,000. . . . Between 1930 and 1950, the population remained constant, at least in total number. After that time, it decreased, partially because young families moved out to raise their children in lower density urban and suburban areas, and because of the announcement in 1951 that the area would be redeveloped. . . .

Everyday life in the West End was not much different from that in other neighborhoods, urban or suburban. The men went to work in the morning, and, for most of the day, the area was occupied largely by women and children — just as in the suburbs. There were some men on the street: the older, retired ones, as well as the young and middle-aged ones who either were unemployed, worked on night shifts, or made their living as gamblers. In the afternoon, younger women could be seen pushing baby carriages. Children of all ages played on the street, and teenagers would "hang" on the corner, or play ball in the school yard. . . . Many women went shopping every day, partly to meet neighbors and to catch up on area news in the small grocery stores, and partly to buy foods that could not be obtained in the weekly excursion to the supermarket. On Sunday mornings, the streets were filled with people who were visiting with neighbors and friends before and after church.

The average West End resident had a choice between anonymity and total immersion in sociability. . . . The sharing of values was . . . encouraged by the residential stability of much of the population. Many West Enders had known each other for years, if only as acquaintances who greeted each other on the street. Everyone might not know everyone else; but, as they did know something about everyone, the net effect was the same, especially within each ethnic group. Between groups, common residence and sharing of facilities — as well as the constant struggle against absentee landlords — created enough solidarity to maintain a friendly spirit. Moreover, for many families, problems were never far away. . . . If they did not take place in one's immediate family, they . . . happened at some time to a relative or a neighbor. Thus when emergencies occurred, neighbors helped each other readily; other problems were solved within each ethnic group. For most West Enders . . . life in the area resembled that found in the village or small town, and even in the suburb.

401

Indeed, if differences of age and economic level among the residents were eliminated, many similarities between the life of the urban neighborhood and the suburb would become visible. . . .

[Whether] the second-generation Italian-Americans who lived in the West End . . . are typical of all second-generation Italians in America is difficult to say without comparative studies in other communities. Some second-generation Italians, having moved far from downtown tenement districts, working-class jobs, and Italian culture, are now living almost like their neighbors in the lower-middle-class suburbias that surround the cities. Others, who have remained in the neighborhoods in which their parents settled after they landed, are more Italian than the West Enders. The majority, who probably have a higher proportion of skilled blue-collar jobs than do the West Enders, have moved to somewhat newer areas further from the center of the city. In social structure and culture, however, I suspect that they are much like . . . the West Enders [who] are almost, but not entirely, representative of the mainstream of second-generation Italian life in America.

To most of the West Enders, the area had been home either since birth or marriage. Some were born in the West End because this was where their parents had settled when they first came to America or where they had moved later in life. Others came as adults in the Italian "invasion" of the West End during the 1930's. Many of them had grown up in the North End and had moved at the time of marriage in order to take advantage of better and larger apartments in the West End. In any case, almost all of the West Enders came to the area as a part of a group. Even their movements within the West End — that is, from the lower end to the upper — had been made together with other Italians at about the same time. . . .

Many West Enders impressed me as being true urbanites, with an empathy for the pace, crowding, and excitement of city life that one finds only in upper-middle-class cosmopolites. They are not cosmopolites, however; the parts of the city that they use and enjoy are socially, culturally, and physically far different from those frequented by the upper-middle class. And . . . the West Ender would gladly exchange his apartment for a detached house, as long as it cost no more, was located near the center of the city, and allowed his relatives, friends, and present neighbors — or similar ones — to live near him. . . .

Generally speaking, the Italian and Sicilian cultures that the immigrants brought with them to America have not been maintained by the second generation. Their over-all culture is that of

Americans. A number of Italian patterns, however, have survived, the most visible ones being food habits. In all European ethnic groups, traditional foods and cooking methods are retained long after other aspects of the immigrant culture are given up. This is true also among West Enders. . . . Another pattern that has persisted into the second generation is language. Most of the West Enders I met could speak Italian — or, more correctly, the special patois of their locality — because they had learned it from their parents, and had to use it to communicate with them. Their children — that is, the third generation — are not being taught the language, however. Also, Italian names are slowly being Anglicized. . . . There is little, if any, identification either with Italy or with the local areas from which the immigrants came originally, . . .

Acculturation thus has almost completely eroded Italian culture patterns among the second generation, and is likely to erase the rest in the third generation. In fact, the process seems to have begun soon after the arrival of the immigrants. One West Ender told me that his Italian-born mother had saved for years for a visit to Italy, but that when she was finally able to go, came back after a month, saying that she could not live among these people because she was not like any of them. The woman, even though she had never learned to speak English properly, had become Americanized in the West End. Such rapid acculturation is not surprising, for the Italians who came to America were farm laborers whose life had been an unending round of much work and little leisure. As the patterns associated with rural poverty that they brought to America were jettisoned quickly, the ensuing vacuum was filled by things American.

Assimilation, however — the disappearance of the Italian social system — has proceeded much more slowly. Indeed, the social structure of the West End . . . is still quite similar to that of the first generation. Social relationships are almost entirely limited to other Italians, because much sociability is based on kinship, and because most friendships are made in childhood, and are thus influenced by residential propinquity. Intermarriage with non-Italians is unusual among the second generation, and is not favored for the third. . . . Relationships with members of other ethnic groups are friendly but infrequent.[43]

The most portentous change in the population ingredients of American cities in the half century following World War I was the dramatic increase in the number of Black urban dwellers throughout the nation and the advent of Puerto Ricans in large numbers in several cities. Though Blacks were no new element in American cities by 1920, the novelty of Black urbanization in the succeeding years was the rapidity of it in the South and its magnitude in the North and West. By 1960 close to 60 per cent of southern Blacks were city dwellers; and by the close of the 1960's, the Black population of the North and West was more than 95 per cent urban. In 1970 in the nation as a whole, 16 cities with a population of 25,000 or over had more Negro residents than whites. These included Washington, D.C. (71 per cent Black), Newark (54 per cent), Gary (53 per cent), Atlanta (51 per cent), and East St. Louis (69.1 per cent). By 1970 the Negro populations of New York and Chicago numbered more than one million, and there were more than half a million Blacks in Detroit, in Philadelphia, in Washington, and in Los Angeles.

In the years following World War I, and especially during the 1940's, three great streams of Negro migrants moved out of the South to northern cities: the first, along the Atlantic coast to Washington, Baltimore, Philadelphia, and New York; the second, from the Gulf region to St. Louis and the cities of the Great Lakes, such as Cleveland, Detroit, and Chicago; and the third, from Texas and Oklahoma to the cities of the Pacific coast, especially Los Angeles. By the 1960's, however, the northward migration from southern farms was basically over, and most Negro movement in the North was from one large city to another.[44] Table 4.3 reveals the growth in the number of Blacks in selected central cities between 1900 and 1970 and demonstrates the pronounced increases in the Black populations of the cities of the North and West by contrast to the relatively stable growth patterns in the cities of the South.

The Negro population of New York City more than doubled during the 1920's — from 153,000 to more than 327,000; Harlem, developing into a Negro "city within a city," came to symbolize the postwar urban migration of southern Blacks. This once upper- and middle-class neighborhood became available to Black residents as its earlier occupants, many of them Italians and Russian Jews, left Manhattan for other sections of the city. By 1930, about 72 per cent of Manhattan's Blacks were living in Harlem.[45] For the moment, many Negro intellectuals saw the urban concentrations of Blacks as promoting a kind of race pride and race consciousness that held promise for their people. This was the view of Alain Locke, Harvard-educated professor of philosophy at Howard University, who in the mid-1920's regarded the urbanization of the Negro as conducive to a Black renaissance.

THE CITY AND THE "NEW" NEGRO —
ALAIN LOCKE: 1925

The tide of Negro migration, northward and city-ward, is not to be fully explained as a blind flood started by the demands of war industry coupled with the shutting off of foreign migration, or by the pressure of poor crops coupled with increased social terrorism in certain sections of the South and Southwest. Neither labor demand, the boll-weevil nor the Ku Klux Klan is a basic factor, however contributory any or all of them may have been. The wash and rush of this human tide on the beach line of the northern city centers is to be explained primarily in terms of a new vision of opportunity, of social and economic freedom, of a spirit to seize, even in the face of an extortionate and heavy toll, a chance for the improvement of conditions. With each successive wave of it, the movement of the Negro becomes more and more a mass movement toward the larger and the more democratic chance — in the Negro's case a deliberate flight not only from countryside to city, but from medieval America to modern.

Take Harlem as an instance of this. Here in Manhattan is not merely the largest Negro community in the world, but the first concentration in history of so many diverse elements of Negro life. It has attracted the African, the West Indian, the Negro American; has brought together the Negro of the North and the Negro of the South; the man from the city and the man from the town and village; the peasant, the student, the business man, the professional man, artist, poet, musician, adventurer and worker, preacher and criminal, exploiter and social outcast. Each group has come with its own separate motives and for its own special ends, but their greatest experience has been the finding of one another. Proscription and prejudice have thrown these dissimilar elements into a common area of contact and interaction. Within this area, race sympathy and unity have determined a further fusing of sentiment and experience. So what began in terms of segregation becomes more and more, as its elements mix and react, the laboratory of a great race-welding. Hitherto, it must be admitted that American Negroes have been a race more in name than in fact, or to be exact, more in sentiment than in experience. The chief bond between them has been

Table 4.3

Number and Percentage of Blacks in Selected Central Cities: 1900–1970[46]

	1900		1910		1920		1930		1940		1950		1960		1970	
	Total Black	Percentage	Total Black	Percentage	Total Black	Percentage	Total Black	Percentage	Total Black	Percentage	Total Black	Percentage	Total Black	Percentage	Total Black	Percentage
New England																
Boston	11,591	2.1	13,564	2.0	16,350	2.2	20,574	2.6	23,679	3.1	40,057	5.0	63,165	9.0	104,707	16.3
Lowell	136	0.1	133	0.1	170	0.2	126	0.1	94	0.1	157	0.2	390	0.4	786	0.8
Providence	4,817	2.7	5,316	2.4	5,655	2.4	5,473	2.2	6,388	2.5	8,304	3.3	11,153	5.4	15,875	8.9
New Haven	2,887	2.7	3,561	2.7	4,573	2.8	5,302	3.3	6,235	3.9	9,605	5.8	22,113	14.5	36,158	26.3
Worcester	1,104	0.9	1,241	0.9	1,258	0.7	1,378	0.7	1,353	0.7	1,568	0.8	2,013	1.1	3,294	1.9
Middle Atlantic																
New York	60,666	1.8	91,709	1.9	152,467	2.7	327,706	4.7	458,444	6.1	747,610	9.5	1,087,931	14.0	1,668,115	21.1
Rochester	601	0.4	879	0.4	1,579	0.5	2,679	0.8	3,262	1.0	7,590	2.3	23,586	7.4	49,647	16.8
Buffalo	1,698	0.5	1,773	0.4	4,511	0.9	13,563	2.4	17,694	3.1	36,645	6.3	70,904	13.3	94,329	20.4
Newark	6,694	2.7	9,475	2.7	16,977	4.1	38,880	8.8	45,760	10.6	74,965	17.1	138,035	34.1	207,458	54.2
Jersey City	3,704	1.8	5,960	2.2	8,000	2.7	12,575	4.0	13,416	4.5	20,758	6.9	36,692	13.3	54,595	21.0
Philadelphia	62,613	4.8	84,459	5.5	134,229	7.4	219,599	11.3	250,880	13.0	376,041	18.2	529,240	26.4	653,791	33.6
Pittsburgh	20,355	4.5	25,623	4.8	37,725	6.4	54,983	8.2	62,216	9.3	82,453	12.2	100,692	16.7	104,904	20.2
South Atlantic																
Baltimore	79,258	15.6	84,749	15.2	108,322	14.8	142,106	17.7	165,843	19.3	225,099	23.7	325,589	34.7	420,210	46.4
Washington	86,702	31.1	94,446	28.5	109,966	25.1	132,068	27.1	187,266	28.2	280,803	35.0	411,737	53.9	537,712	71.1
Richmond	32,230	37.9	46,733	36.6	54,041	31.5	52,988	29.0	61,251	31.7	72,996	31.7	91,972	41.8	104,766	42.0
Durham	2,241	33.6	6,869	37.7	7,654	31.2	18,717	36.0	23,347	38.8	26,095	36.6	28,258	36.1	37,022	38.8
Charlotte	7,151	39.5	11,752	34.6	14,641	31.6	25,163	30.4	31,403	31.1	37,481	28.0	56,248	28.0	72,972	30.3
Charleston	31,522	56.5	31,056	52.8	32,326	47.6	28,062	45.1	31,765	44.6	30,854	44.0	33,522	50.8	30,251	45.2
Savannah	28,090	51.8	33,246	51.1	39,179	47.1	38,896	45.7	43,237	45.0	48,282	40.4	53,035	35.5	53,111	44.9
Atlanta	35,727	39.8	51,902	33.5	62,796	31.3	90,075	33.3	104,533	34.6	121,285	36.6	186,464	38.2	255,051	51.3
Jacksonville	16,236	57.1	29,293	50.8	41,520	45.3	48,196	37.2	61,782	35.7	72,450	35.4	82,525	41.0	118,158	22.3
Miami	a	—	2,258	41.3	9,270	31.3	25,116	22.7	36,857	21.4	40,262	16.2	65,213	22.3	76,156	22.7
North Central																
Cincinnati	14,482	4.4	19,639	5.4	30,079	7.5	47,818	10.6	55,593	12.2	78,196	15.5	108,754	21.6	125,000	27.6
Cleveland	5,988	1.6	8,448	1.5	34,451	4.3	71,899	8.0	84,504	9.6	147,847	16.1	250,818	28.6	287,841	38.3
Detroit	4,111	1.4	5,741	1.2	40,838	4.1	120,066	7.7	149,119	9.2	300,506	16.2	482,223	41.3	660,428	43.7

Milwaukee	0.3	862	0.3	980	0.5	2,229	1.3	7,501	1.5	8,821	3.4	21,772	8.5	63,170	14.7	105,088
Chicago	1.8	30,150	2.0	44,103	4.1	109,458	6.9	233,903	8.2	277,731	13.6	492,265	22.9	812,637	32.7	1,102,620
Indianapolis	9.4	15,931	9.3	21,816	11.0	34,678	12.1	43,967	13.2	51,142	15.0	63,867	20.6	98,049	18.0	134,320
Gary	—	b	2.3	383	9.6	5,299	17.8	17,922	18.3	20,394	29.3	39,253	38.8	69,123	52.8	92,695
St. Louis	6.2	35,516	6.4	43,960	9.0	69,854	11.4	93,580	13.3	108,765	17.9	153,766	28.6	214,377	40.9	254,191
East St. Louis	6.0	1,799	10.0	5,882	11.1	7,437	15.5	11,536	22.2	16,798	33.5	27,555	44.4	36,338	69.1	48,368
Kansas City, Mo.	10.7	17,567	9.5	23,566	9.5	30,719	9.6	38,574	10.4	41,574	12.2	55,682	17.5	83,146	22.1	112,005
Wichita	5.6	1,389	4.7	2,457	4.9	3,545	5.1	5,623	4.9	5,686	4.8	8,082	7.8	19,861	9.7	26,841
Omaha	3.4	3,443	3.6	4,426	5.4	10,315	5.2	11,123	5.4	12,015	6.5	16,311	8.3	25,155	9.9	34,431
Minneapolis	0.8	1,548	0.9	2,592	1.0	3,927	0.9	4,176	0.9	4,646	1.3	6,807	2.4	11,785	4.4	19,005
South Central																
Mobile	44.3	17,045	44.2	22,763	39.3	23,906	35.9	24,514	36.9	29,046	35.5	45,819	32.4	65,619	35.4	67,356
Birmingham	43.1	16,575	39.4	53,305	39.3	70,230	38.2	99,077	40.7	108,938	39.9	130,025	39.6	135,113	42.0	126,388
New Orleans	27.1	77,714	26.3	89,262	26.1	100,930	28.3	129,632	30.1	149,034	31.9	181,775	37.2	233,514	45.0	267,308
Jackson, Miss.	56.9	4,447	49.6	10,554	43.5	9,936	40.2	19,423	39.1	24,256	40.8	40,168	35.7	51,556	39.7	61,063
Memphis	48.8	49,910	40.0	52,441	37.7	61,181	38.1	96,550	41.5	121,498	37.2	147,141	37.0	184,320	38.9	242,513
Nashville	37.2	30,044	33.1	36,523	30.1	35,633	27.8	42,836	28.3	47,318	31.4	54,696	37.8	64,570	19.6	87,576
Louisville	19.1	39,139	18.1	40,522	17.1	40,087	15.4	47,354	14.8	47,158	15.6	57,657	17.9	70,075	23.8	86,040
Houston	32.7	14,608	30.4	23,929	24.6	33,960	21.7	63,337	22.4	86,302	20.9	124,766	22.9	215,037	25.7	316,551
Dallas	21.2	9,035	19.6	18,024	15.1	24,023	14.9	38,742	17.1	50,407	13.1	56,958	19.0	129,242	24.9	210,238
Fort Worth	15.9	4,249	18.1	13,280	14.9	15,896	13.6	2,360	14.2	25,254	13.2	36,933	15.8	56,440	19.9	78,324
Mountain																
Denver	2.9	3,923	2.5	5,426	2.4	6,075	2.5	7,204	2.4	7,836	3.6	15,059	6.0	29,651	9.1	47,011
Salt Lake City	0.5	278	0.8	737	0.6	718	0.5	681	0.5	694	0.6	1,127	0.8	1,560	1.2	2,135
Pacific																
Los Angeles	2.1	2,131	2.4	7,599	2.7	15,579	3.1	38,894	4.2	63,774	8.7	171,209	13.5	334,916	17.9	503,606
Compton	c	c						1		—	4.5	2,180	39.4	28,265	71.0	55,781
Oakland	1.5	1,026	2.0	3,055	2.5	5,489	2.6	7,503	2.8	8,462	12.4	47,562	22.8	83,618	34.5	124,710
San Francisco	0.5	1,654	0.4	1,642	0.5	2,414	0.6	3,803	0.8	4,846	5.6	43,502	10.0	74,383	13.4	96,078
Portland	0.9	775	0.5	1,045	0.6	1,556	0.5	1,559	0.6	1,931	2.5	9,529	4.2	15,637	5.6	21,572
Seattle	0.5	406	1.0	2,296	0.9	2,894	0.9	3,303	1.0	3,789	3.3	15,666	4.8	26,901	7.1	37,868

a Total population less than 2,500 in 1900.
b Not listed.
c Total population less than 2,500 through 1920; in 1930 total population was 12,516, of which one person was reported as Negro; total population in 1940 was 16,198, but none was reported as Negro.

> . . . a problem in common rather than a life in common. In Harlem, Negro life is seizing upon its first chance for group expression and self-determination. It is — or promises at least to be — a race capital. That is why our comparison is taken with those nascent centers of folk-expression and self-determination which are playing a creative part in the world to-day. Without pretense to their political significance, Harlem has the same role to play for the New Negro as Dublin has had for the New Ireland or Prague for the New Czechoslovakia.[47]

By the 1930's it was already apparent that urban concentration brought little improvement in the lot of many Negroes and no guarantee of the resolution of racial tension. For the great majority, the Black ghetto proved to be a dead-end existence, blighted by progressively deteriorating housing, inadequate municipal services, and widespread crime and disorder. More than in the case of earlier migrant groups, Black newcomers were confined to the inner city, prevented by both poverty and discrimination from easy outward movement. The poverty that locked the great majority in the central city ghetto was in part a consequence of conditions in the mid-twentieth-century urban environment that were different from those of the era when European migrants were adjusting to the city: the scarcity of jobs for unskilled workers, membership restrictions imposed by unions, and the existence of maximum-hour legislation. Resistance to color, as seen in restrictive covenants and economic zoning in the suburbs, posed another obstacle. In the 1960's the movement of Blacks, especially those of higher economic status, to suburbia accelerated; but as late as 1970, when about 12 per cent of the total population of the United States was Black, the population of central cities was 21 per cent Black and suburban population only 5 per cent Negro.[48]

In the 1940's, as Negro participation in World War II brought race discrimination under attack, Black leaders, like the publisher of the *Chicago Defender,* were arguing that "restrictive covenant agreements and the iron ring creating a Negro ghetto must be smashed." [49] In 1944 and periodically thereafter, the Chicago Commission on Human Relations held conferences dealing with the problems peculiar to Chicago's Black "city within a city." One area of discussion at the conference held in May, 1957 was Black segregation and the difficulties, by contrast with the experience of other migrant groups, of escaping from the ghetto.

THE IRON RING OF THE BLACK GHETTO —
CHICAGO: 1957

A *"new"* segregation — *comment of James C. Downs, Chairman, Real Estate Research Corporation:* When the . . . migration of the non-white started we had a new element enter the picture. . . . The assimilation [such as achieved by earlier migrant groups] was not as easily accomplished. . . . As we view the population growth of the future, THE single highest percentage of ethnicity will be of non-white people. . . . This brings me to the patterns of segregation. Most people think of segregation as being applied to peoples of a different color. This is not at all true, nor is it true in the history of Chicago's society. We have had segregated groups, minority groups, identifiable by territory of occupancy ever since this city was started. . . .

Segregation appears to exist in all minority groups when there are certain separative common factors exhibited publicly by a group. For example, in the days of language barriers we had very clearly identifiable ghettos, if you want to use the term, although most people . . . think of a ghetto as some kind of a slum area. It hasn't anything to do with slums. The meaning of "ghetto" is that people within the ghetto live there because of some ethnic or nationalist characteristic. And where there was a language barrier, people of common language sought common residence for their greater convenience.

Where there is a strong religious, identifiable and congealing element, we have had segregated areas based on religious as well as nationalist backgrounds. I am delighted that the nationalist churches, particularly in my own church, the Roman Catholic Church, are disappearing from the scene. You no longer live in the area of the Polish Catholic, or the Czech Catholic, or the German Catholic, where the sermon on Sunday is preached in that language, and where everybody gathers around the church out of a nationalist origin. These are now disappearing. As the language barrier has disappeared, so are those neighborhoods disappearing.

There is still, however, skin color which operates as a segregating factor. . . . I feel that it is a great tragedy that within the City of Chicago we have one of the largest non-white cities of the world which, in many ways, is a separate city. This city is now growing very rapidly. It is growing by peripheral expansion, and by the increased homogeneous occupancy of areas adjacent to those areas already homogeneous. If this practice . . . continues to operate to the . . . perpetuation and strengthening of the completely segregated community, let me say that this city is in trouble. It is in trouble politically; it is in trouble economically; it is in trouble socially; it is in trouble culturally.

Actually . . . we have very little race trouble in peripheral expansion. Where we have had our trouble in expansion of occupancy is in what is known as "hedge-hopping;" that is, where there is a substantial distance over which a new group moves into an area. This was the background of the trouble at Cicero. This was the background of the trouble at Trumbull Park. . . .

Yet, in my opinion, the existence of this homogeneous community is the major problem which we face. For a long time there were a number of limitations with respect to circulation. These limitations still exist to a great degree, but they operated all that time in peripheral expansion. That is, if you would have gone down Cottage Grove Avenue in 1935, you would have thought that you were seeing things. You looked to the left, and there was a white city. You looked to the right, and there was a Negro city.

This line was maintained by restrictive covenants. It was also maintained, let me say, by economic limitations in the non-white group. Prior to 1935, there were a very limited number of non-whites in this community who had sufficiently substantial purchasing power to purchase what we then called "standard housing."

The disappearance of the legal restrictive covenant did not bring the disappearance of restrictions. There [are] still maintained in Chicago and elsewhere, in my opinion, covenants of violence. People hoping to restrict a certain area do not have a legal covenant; they do not have any agreement; they do not have any rights in court. They do not have any effective operation, except the threat of violence. . . . And the threat of violence still exists in our own community. . . .

The economic limitations are . . . disappearing, but they have not disappeared. A man owns an apartment building. . . . And suppose he decided that he was going to take in so many Negro families — there would be sanctions operated against that man. He would have difficulties. He would be sniped at from here and from there. He would have problems. These hostile reactions are and will be less as times goes on, but they still exist.

"Covenants of violence" — *comment of Nissen N. Gross, Midwest Director, Civil Rights Division, Anti-Defamation League:* I have been in the field for the past seventeen years out in the

very tension situations themselves at Airport Homes, Fernwood, Park Manor, Peoria Street, and Trumbull Park, trying to determine what was taking place. . . . I have seen many situations where special police guards had to be placed in front and in back of individual homes in area after area in the City of Chicago where you have had the move-in of non-whites into an otherwise previously white area. I have seen policemen take their lives into their hands and dash into a mob to try to arrest the instigators of the mob. I have also seen an individual instance of a policeman turning his back when such mob violence is taking place. . . .

I can recall when Trumbull Park was at the height of tension, when the Negro families literally took their lives in their hands if they desired to walk along certain streets out there and when in order to make certain that their lives were protected, the police had to give them an escort down one or two streets. We had people crying out, "Why aren't the tenants allowed to use the swimming pool?" "Why aren't the tenants allowed to use Trumbull Park for recreational facilities?" "Why can't they move in any direction they desire to?" I wish the critics could be in those situations to see and hear the ugly tones of mob violence and then they'd understand that though everyone is entitled to the total enforcement of every civil right, sometimes to insist . . . is to lose your life in the process.[50]

During the 1940's and 1950's, resentment against Negroes who moved into all-white neighborhoods precipitated more than a hundred incidents. The racial tension of the mid-1960's was of different origin. In these uprisings Negroes gave vent to anger aggravated by conditions in their urban environment and inflicted damage upon their own ghetto neighborhoods, which they viewed not as symbolic of opportunity for a Black renaissance but as manifestations of their repressive, circumscribed world. Rioting, beginning in Harlem in 1964, exploded in the Black ghettos of the major cities and lasted into 1968, with a heavy toll of deaths, thousands of arrests, and property damage totaling hundreds of millions of dollars.[51] Urban riots were so widespread in the summer of 1967 as to prompt President Lyndon B. Johnson to appoint the National Advisory Commission on Civil Disorders. Its report, issued in 1968, revealed the pervasiveness of racial tension (and its ominous potential), as well as some of the basic reasons for such tension.

411

"BURN, BABY, BURN!" — BLACK PROTEST IN AMERICAN CITIES: 1967

The civil disorders of 1967 involved Negroes acting against local symbols of white American society, authority, and property in Negro neighborhoods — rather than against white persons. . . . In the 75 disorders studied by a Senate subcommittee, 83 deaths were reported. Eighty-two per cent of the deaths and more than half the injuries occurred in Newark and Detroit. About 10 per cent of the dead and 36 per cent of the injured were public employees, primarily law officers and firemen. The overwhelming majority of the persons killed or injured in all the disorders were Negro civilians. . . . In Detroit, . . . the highest recent estimate [of damage] is $45 million. In Newark, . . . damage was estimated at $10.2 million, 80 per cent in inventory losses.

In the 24 disorders in 23 cities. . . , disorder did not erupt as a result of a single "triggering" or "precipitating" incident. Instead, it was generated out of an increasingly disturbed social atmosphere, in which typically a series of tension-heightening incidents over a period of weeks or months became linked in the minds of many in the Negro community with a reservoir of underlying grievances. At some point in the mounting tension, a further incident — in itself often routine or trivial — became the breaking point and the tension spilled over into violence. . . .

The typical rioter was a teenager or young adult, a lifelong resident of the city in which he rioted, a high school dropout; he was, nevertheless, somewhat better educated than his nonrioting Negro neighbor, and was usually underemployed or employed in a menial job. He was proud of his race, extremely hostile to both whites and middle-class Negroes and, although informed about politics, highly distrustful of the political system. . . . The proportion of Negroes in local government was substantially smaller than the Negro proportion of population. Only three of the 20 cities studied had more than one Negro legislator; none had ever had a Negro mayor or city manager. In only four cities did Negroes hold other important policy-making positions or serve as heads of municipal departments. . . .

Social and economic conditions in the riot cities constituted a clear pattern of severe disadvantage for Negroes compared with whites. . . . Negroes had completed fewer years of education and fewer had attended high school. Negroes were twice as likely to be unemployed and three times as likely to be in unskilled and service jobs. Negroes averaged 70 per cent of the income earned by whites and were more than twice as likely to be living in poverty. Although housing cost Negroes relatively more, they had worse housing — three times as likely to be overcrowded and substandard. When compared to white suburbs, the relative disadvantage was even more pronounced. . . .

White racism is essentially responsible for the explosive mixture which has been accumulating in our cities since the end of World War II. Among the ingredients of this mixture are: *Pervasive discrimination and segregation* in employment, education, and housing, which have resulted in the continuing exclusion of great numbers of Negroes from the benefits of economic progress. *Black in-migration and white exodus,* which have produced the massive and growing concentrations of impoverished Negroes in our major cities, creating a growing crisis of deteriorating facilities and services and unmet human needs. *The black ghettos,* where segregation and poverty converge on the young to destroy opportunity and enforce failure. Crime, drug addiction, dependency on welfare, and bitterness and resentment against society in general and white society in particular are the result. . . .

A striking difference in environment from that of white, middle-class Americans profoundly influences the lives of residents of the ghetto. Crime rates, consistently higher than in other areas, create a pronounced sense of insecurity. For example, in one city one low-income Negro district had 35 times as many serious crimes against persons as a high-income white district. . . . Poor health and sanitation conditions in the ghetto result in higher mortality rates, a higher incidence of major diseases, and lower availability and utilization of medical services. . . . Garbage collection is often inadequate. Of an estimated 14,000 cases of rat bite in the United States in 1965, most were in ghetto neighborhoods. Ghetto residents believe they are exploited by local merchants; and evidence substantiates some of these beliefs. A study conducted in one city by the Federal Trade Commission showed that higher prices were charged for goods sold in ghetto stores than in other areas. . . .

By 1985, the Negro population in central cities is expected to increase by 68 per cent to approximately 20.3 million. Coupled with the continued exodus of white families to the suburbs, this growth will produce majority Negro populations in many of the Nation's largest cities. The future of these cities, and of their burgeoning Negro populations, is grim. Most new employment opportunities are being created in suburbs and outlying areas. . . . In prospect, therefore, is further deterioration of already inadequate municipal tax bases in the face of increasing demands

413

for public services, and continuing unemployment and poverty among the urban Negro population. . . .

The share of the nation's resources now allocated to programs for the disadvantaged is insufficient to arrest the deterioration of life in central-city ghettos. Under such conditions, a rising proportion of Negroes may come to see in the deprivation and segregation they experience, a justification for violent protest, or for extending support to now isolated extremists who advocate civil disruption. Large-scale and continuing violence could result, followed by white retaliation, and, ultimately, the separation of the two communities in a garrison state. . . .

We believe that the only possible choice for America is . . . a policy which combines ghetto enrichment with programs designed to encourage integration of substantial numbers of Negroes into the society outside the ghetto. Enrichment must be an important adjunct to integration, for no matter how ambitious or energetic the program, few Negroes now living in central cities can be quickly integrated. In the meantime, large-scale improvement in the quality of ghetto life is essential. But this can be no more than an interim strategy. Programs must be developed which will permit substantial Negro movement out of the ghettos. The primary goal must be a single society, in which every citizen will be free to live and work according to his capabilities and desires, not his color.[52]

By the late 1960's the new aggressiveness of "Black Power" had triggered a white reaction in many cities, especially in working-class, ethnic-group neighborhoods. Factors contributing to this white resistance were the physical insecurity of big-city living, as symbolized by "crime in the streets"; the bearing of both busing and the movement of Blacks into white neighborhoods upon the aspirations for social mobility of recently arrived ethnic groups; and the growing feeling among "Middle Americans," especially those of the more recent immigration, that the operation of urban welfare programs constituted preferential treatment of Black and Puerto Rican minorities. According to a study published by the National Urban Coalition in 1972, many of Detroit's Polish-Americans or Newark's Italian-Americans saw their neighborhoods as the areas that got "block busted," the schools their children attended the ones most likely to be affected by attempts to achieve racial integration. They regarded themselves as caught in the middle between a system of "rich and powerful" that "blocks them from moving more than a little ahead" and the Blacks and Chicanos, who are "pushing them hard from behind." [53] Tension between Jews and Blacks figured in a teachers' strike in New York City during the fall of 1968. The protagonists were the residents of the Ocean Hill-Brownsville school district of Brooklyn, predominantly Negro, with a sizable Puerto Rican minority, and the teachers' union, with a large Jewish membership. *Time* magazine suggested the causes of Jewish-Black tension in reporting the controversy.

THE BLACK AND THE JEW —
NEW YORK CITY: 1969

New York City has become the center of black anti-Semitism, although it exists in almost every urban center where large communities of Negroes and Jews intermingle. New York has more Jews (1.8 million) and more blacks (1.5 million) than any other city in the world. The predominantly Negro areas of Harlem and Brooklyn's Ocean Hill-Brownsville were once solidly Jewish: now the Jewish presence is signified by absentee storekeepers and landlords who, fairly or not, are regarded by the Negro as colonial exploiters. More often than not, the black child is taught — in a crumbling, inadequate public school — by a Jewish teacher. More often than not, the hated neighborhood welfare center, to the black a symbol of indifferent, domineering white bureaucracy, is staffed by Jewish social workers. "If you happen to be an uneducated, poorly trained Negro living in the ghetto," says Bayard Rustin, executive director of the A. Philip Randolph Institute, "you see only four kinds of white people — the policeman, the businessman, the teacher and the welfare worker. In many cities, three of these four are Jewish."

Tensions between blacks and Jews have simmered under the surface for years, but they broke into the open with the recent battle over the decentralization project in the Ocean Hill-Brownsville school district. Financed in part by the Ford Foundation, the experiment gave a community-elected neighborhood board and its Negro administrator, Rhody McCoy, a measure of local control over policies in the area's eight schools. The project was opposed by the predominantly Jewish United Federation of Teachers, which feared that decentralization, if applied to the entire system, would destroy the union's bargaining power.

After the black local governing board ousted ten teachers accused of sabotaging the project, the U.F.T. stayed out of the schools for 36 days in three separate city-wide walkouts. What began as a contest for power ended in an exchange of racist epithets. Negro parents denounced the striking teachers as "Jew pigs." The teachers' union charged that Ocean Hill-Brownsville militants were "black Nazis" [who] printed anti-Semitic materials that were supposedly being distributed in the area's schools.[54]

A confrontation of Italian-Americans and Blacks occurred, in 1970, in the campaign for the mayoralty in Newark.[55] In this election, Kenneth A. Gibson, the Black candidate, defeated the incumbent, Hugh J. Addonizio. Strong opposition to Gibson came from the North Ward Citizens Committee, an urban vigilance group allegedly organized out of fear of Black disorder. Newark's North Ward is a predominantly Italian-American neighborhood with a growing Black population, in a city whose Black population increased from 17 per cent of the total in 1950 to more than 54 per cent in 1970.[56] The details of the campaign, reported in *The New York Times*, reveal the polarization on the basis of race.

ITALIANS AND BLACKS — MAYORAL POLITICS IN NEWARK: 1970

Newark, June 13, 1970. The bitterly contested mayoral campaign reached a climax here this weekend in the heavily black wards and the white ethnic neighborhoods where the election will be decided. . . . Addonizio . . . somberly warned audiences in predominantly white neighborhoods . . . : "You all know what is involved here. Everything you hold sacred — your home, your families and your jobs. We cannot let the leaders of race hatred take control of our city." . . . In turn, Mr. Gibson warned that an Addonizio victory . . . could leave the city . . . in a racial "shambles." "No one can rule a divided city," he contended. . . .

Arm in arm with the Rev. Ralph David Abernathy, the Negro civil rights leader, Mr. Gibson campaigned in every ward today along with black members of the New York Mets, Jets and Knicks, and Dick Gregory, the black comedian and civil rights activist. In addition, several hundred students — both blacks and whites — from Eastern universities began an intensive three-day drive to get out the vote in every ward. . . .

In the Addonizio camp, the stated objective was to polarize the vote. To this end, the Mayor seized upon the specter of black militancy and warned white audiences that his loss on Tuesday could precipitate a chaotic and even black revolution in the city.[57]

Migrants from Puerto Rico gave added variety to the population mix in the twentieth-century city, bringing problems somewhat similar, in many instances, to those that followed the mounting migration of Blacks. The Puerto Rican migration — novel because it was so largely airborne — became newsworthy in New York City as early as the mid-1940's, and New York continued to be the major magnet; but by 1970 Chicago had upwards of 100,000, Boston had 25,000 (an increase from 800 in less than a decade), and there were sizable Puerto Rican communities in many cities in the Middle Atlantic states and New England. At the census of 1970, in which a special interest was taken in enumerating Americans of Spanish heritage, it was found that nearly 88 per cent of this ethnic group were city dwellers, more likely to be residents of central cities than suburbs.

In metropolitan New York City, as of 1970, residents of Puerto Rican birth or parentage numbered more than 845,000, nearly 812,000 of whom resided in the central city. Here they inhabited several densely occupied enclaves where the Spanish language was spoken and Puerto Rican customs were practiced. Poverty, the language barrier, and a minimal educational background, together with the constancy of their contacts with the homeland, were major impediments to the adjustment of Puerto Rican newcomers to the American city. A 1970 study showed their median income in New York City to be considerably less than that of nonwhites as a group. As many as 57 per cent of the residents of Boston's South End *barrio* were receiving some sort of public assistance. The volatility of the color question in American cities, by the 1960's, also complicated the problem of adjustment. Light-skinned Puerto Ricans tended to be assimilated into white society, while those with darker skins found themselves treated as Negroes. This triggered serious racial tension between Puerto Ricans and Blacks, a variant on the ethnic animosities often encountered among recent arrivals in urban communities.[58]

As with urban Blacks and perhaps because of their behavior, the Puerto Ricans developed a movement for group identity in the 1960's, making a mounting demand for political recognition and the opportunity to run their own affairs. Also, as with the Blacks, this took two forms: militant reformism, on the one hand, and revolutionary violence, on the other. The Young Lords were in

417

many ways the Puerto Rican counterpart of the Black Panthers. Puerto Rican newcomers usually stayed with relatives on arrival, where their housing often was dilapidated and rat-infested. The marginal existence of many of them, their response to the city, and their exploitation by landlords and employers (sometimes their own compatriots) were revealed in studies made in 1964–1965 by Oscar Lewis, distinguished anthropologist and author of *La Vida: A Puerto Rican Family in the Culture of Poverty — San Juan and New York*. Excerpts from some of the interviews he conducted reveal the influence of the urban environment on the attitudes of this migrant group.

PUERTO RICANS AND THE AMERICAN CITY: 1964

I didn't have any relatives in New York, but I had a girl friend who worked there in a factory. She used to write me and tell me that she earned more money than in Puerto Rico and lived more comfortably. She also said that because she was earning her own money she didn't have to put up with men who wanted to dominate her. She aroused my interest by telling me these things, especially about not having to be a slave to your husband. So when she sent me money for the fare and offered me hospitality in New York, I left that very month.

Many of the people who come here feel that it's safe to cheat someone else or play any dirty trick because they figure out this place is so big can simply move away and no one is ever going to find them. In Puerto Rico you can't get lost like that. Suppose you move to Santurce. All anyone has to do is go ask in your old neighborhood and in five minutes they know where to find you. Everybody in the barrio knows who you are and where you went. Then he takes a bus and in fifteen minutes he is at your house. But here, you may move into the apartment next to mine and it will be ten years before I find out you are there.

I stayed with my *compadres* for about two months when I came and then I wanted to be alone with my little boy, so I went to live as a boarder in the home of a family from Mayagüez. They had a very large apartment with eight rooms which they rented out. They leased one to me for $10 a week with meals. I had to pay for Jimmy's meals myself.

The room was small and I slept in the same bed with my boy. They really took advantage of me. I had just arrived from Puerto Rico and didn't know my way around and they played me for a sucker. On my days off I had to clean the whole apartment. After I had paid rent and everything! . . . When they sent one of us boarders out for something, the husband went along. We couldn't leave the house alone because the people on the street might make us catch on to what was going on.

I lived with those people for a year and a half because I was afraid to move to another place. They told me, "Ah, if you go to a furnished room with your child they'll probably break in on you. They kill women here when they live alone." So I stayed out of fear. Later on, though, when I began to know my way around, I began to wake up and see that it was nonsense.[59]

By the 1970's, the dichotomy between Blacks and whites, made increasingly evident by the tendency of the population to dispose itself in large metropolitan clusters, had become the most potentially explosive feature of the nation's urban culture. This situation resulted in part from the economic conditions and social attitudes that kept most Blacks and Puerto Ricans confined to the central cities where, in an increasing number, they were becoming numerically dominant. But it was the result, too, of the development of a more unified socio-religious outlook on the part of the white society — Catholic, Jewish, and Protestant — as it experienced economic advancement and no longer was fragmented by continuing waves of European immigrants. The cleavage between Black and white followed also from the high rate of physical mobility — especially to the suburbs — on the part of white urban dwellers and from the organization of white ethnic groups as a reaction to the more aggressive activities of Blacks that their concentration in the central city encouraged. Some contemporaries argued that time would resolve these tensions as it had other group conflicts in the history of the nation's urbanism; but others saw, in the fact of color and in the realities of the mid-twentieth-century economy, conditions that made it essential for government — both federal and local — to find innovative solutions if harmony and public order were to prevail.

4. FEDERAL INVOLVEMENT: RELIEF

The heightened involvement of the federal government in urban matters differentiated the nation's urbanism in the twentieth

century from that of earlier years. This came about largely as a result of problems presented by dependent segments of the population of the large cities. The depression of the 1930's first involved
the federal government in local welfare — an area traditionally left
to the municipality, the county, and the state. The stock market
crash of 1929, to which excesses of urban promotion had contributed, spotlighted many intensifying problems of the twentieth-
century city: the increasing cost of expanded urban services; the
decline in the tax base with the movement of the middle class to
the suburbs; the dislocations resulting from speculative investment
in urban real estate; the financial instability of many of the newcomers who had been lured to the city in the prosperous 1920's;
and the dependence, more clearly exhibited than ever before, of
the large industrial city upon the health of the national economy.
Mounting unemployment, demonstrations at city halls, and looting
of food stores in the major cities challenged the effectiveness of the
traditional solutions to the endemic problem of urban poverty,
such as organized and unorganized private charity and local public
relief. By January, 1931, more than 85,000 New Yorkers were depending on daily breadlines for subsistence. Six months later, municipal resources for relief were exhausted in virtually every city of
the nation.[60] An article written by Frank Bane of the American
Public Welfare Association revealed the pervasiveness of unemployment in the nation's cities and the inadequacy of local governments to cope with the problem. The article was published in the
November, 1932 issue of *The National Municipal Review.*

HOW TO FEED THE HUNGRY? 1931–1932

Many cities have reached or are reaching the limit of their
ability to handle the fast mounting relief load that has accumulated during this long continued depression. . . . Cities of varying sizes located in different sections of the country all . . . tell
the same tragic story of increasing relief loads, families with
resources completely exhausted and standards of relief declining. . . .

Conditions in Chicago have been steadily growing worse. . . .
The unemployed number between 600,000 and 700,000 or about
40 per cent of the employable workers with more and more of
these being forced to ask for relief. . . . In Detroit the public
welfare department has been operating on credit since March,

1932, with current bills unpaid totaling $2,650,000. . . . In January, 1932, the city was caring for 48,000 families. By August this number had been reduced to 21,500 families with relief given at the rate of 15 cents per day per person. Part of this lowered case load in the fourth year of the depression is accounted for by the fact that about 200,000 people have left Detroit within the past eighteen months. . . .

The situation in July, 1932, in Philadelphia was described by the Community Council as one of "Slow Starvation and Progressive Disintegration of Family Life." . . . In June the governor of Pennsylvania estimated that 250,000 persons in Philadelphia "faced actual starvation." . . . Pittsburgh likewise has an increasingly serious problem with 178,000 unemployed and 30,000 on parttime work, and relief expenditures for 1932 about three times that of 1931. . . . In Boston the amount spent on relief almost doubled this last year. . . . New York City has a huge relief program with 1,000,000 of the city's 3,200,000 working population unemployed. Relief has been given on a "Disaster Basis" with disastrous effects on the population. Expenditures are running about $6,000,000 per month. . . .

In Cincinnati . . . standards of relief have been radically reduced so that the average relief given is only about $5.00 per week per family. In April the city had over 700 evictions. The May census shows that only one half of the working population is employed on a full-time basis. Some idea of the decline in living standards can be guessed by the fact that payrolls declined about $96,000,000 during the last year and only about $2,000,000 was given for relief. . . . Cleveland has had great difficulty in balancing its budget during the past year. . . . On September 24 the R.F.C. made $2,807,000 available for Cuyahoga County and the city of Cleveland to meet their emergency relief needs until the end of the year. . . . In Toledo . . . the city has resorted to a commissary distribution of the cheapest grade of foods at a cost of 6 cents per person per day. . . .

St. Louis, Missouri, is having an unusually bad time. . . . The city can assume no more obligations against municipal revenue and has also reached the limit of its taxing power. . . . In Birmingham, Alabama, there were 12,000 tax delinquencies and there had been 6,000 tax sales by the first of the year. . . . In Denver the . . . special unemployment fund of $452,700 which was raised by private subscription last November was exhausted by spring and the committee $100,000 in debt by the time an additional $175,000 was raised. . . . Portland, Oregon, has nearly 40,000 unemployed and over 13,000 families on relief. . . . Last winter Los Angeles had more than 150,000 unemployed, of whom 60,000 were heads of families. . . .

It has been demonstrated that national assistance on an increasing scale is a necessity if the financial integrity of municipalities is to be safeguarded and if relief is to be "furnished for needy and distressed people." [61]

Testimony at Congressional hearings concerning conditions in Philadelphia in the early 1930's documents both the human dimension of relief needs and the growing conviction, by 1932, that the federal government must help shoulder the relief program of the municipalities. The Quaker City had a strong tradition of private philanthropy, and as its first response to the depression a Committee of One Hundred organized a private agency, the Committee for Unemployment Relief. Although the Committee raised $4,000,-000 in private donations, the events of 1930–1932 convinced it that the magnitude of the relief problem called not for more charity in the Hoover tradition "but for government action to save the health and indeed the lives of a large portion of the citizenry." [62] In May, 1932, Karl de Schweinitz, testifying before a Senate committee, described what happened in Philadelphia in the spring of 1932 when local relief funds had been exhausted.

WHEN LOCAL RELIEF DRIED UP — PHILADELPHIA: 1932

Mr. de Schweinitz. On April 11 we mailed to families the last food orders they received from private funds. It was not until April 22 that the giving of aid to [more than 43,000] families from public funds began, so that there was a period of about 11 days when many families received nothing. We have received reports from workers as to how these families managed. The material I am about to give you is typical, although it is based on a small sample. We made an intensive study of 91 families. . . . In a little less than 9 per cent of these families there were pregnant mothers and in a little more than one-third of the families children of nursing age. This is how some of these families managed.

One woman said she borrowed 50 cents from a friend and bought stale bread for 3-1/2 cents per loaf, and that is all they had for eleven days except for one or two meals. . . . One woman went along the docks and picked up vegetables that fell from the wagons. Sometimes the fish vendors gave her fish at the end of the day. On two different occasions this family was without food for a day and a half. . . . Here is another family which for two days had nothing to eat but bread, and during most of the rest of the time they had only two meals a day. Their meals consisted of bread and coffee for breakfast, and bread and raw or cooked carrots for dinner. . . . Another family did not have food for two days. Then the husband went out and gathered dandelions and the family lived on them. Here is another family which for two and a half days went without food. . . .

Actually, death from starvation is not a frequent occurrence. You do not often hear about casualties of that sort. This is because people live in just the way that I have described. They live on inadequacies, and because they live on inadequacies the thing does not become dramatic and we do not hear about it. Yet the cost in human suffering is just as great as if they starved to death overnight.

Senator Costigan. What you say is not only shockingly true but Senator Copeland, of New York, has recently reported cases of known starvation this past winter.

Mr. de Schweinitz. The hospitals have had definite cases of starvation. . . . A great many people raise the question as to whether the unemployed . . . are out of work because of their own fault. They are not. We have definite studies to show that they had had long and good work records and that they are active, earnest human beings. All they want is a job.[63]

As the sources of state and local relief dried up, the plight of the cities seemed to call for more positive action by the federal government than was traditional in its relations with municipalities. As late as the mid-1920's most federal administrators saw the involvement of the federal government in municipal matters as limited to supplying guidance and coordination of local efforts. Herbert Hoover, speaking in 1927 of his activities as Secretary of Commerce, took pride in the role the Department of Commerce had played in coordinating federal-city relations. The editors of *The American City* praised his statement as "an inspiring outline of some of the aids which the National Government can give to its local units, not by paternalism and compulsion, but by leadership and cooperation."

WHAT WASHINGTON DOES FOR CITIES — HERBERT HOOVER: 1927

Within the past six years the Department of Commerce has largely increased its [contacts with the nation's cities]. The Advisory Committee on Building Codes . . . serves as a disinterested national clearing-house between interested municipal officials, national trade associations, and professional societies. . . . Since the committee's first reports were published they have been consulted by practically everybody undertaking revision of municipal building codes. . . . Local officials, individuals and groups throughout the country have likewise contributed to the work of our Advisory Committee on City Planning and Zoning, and have applied its general conclusions to local situations. Even more recently another contact has been established through our Aeronautics Branch, whose services are sought in connection with the establishment of airport facilities by hundreds of cities and towns. . . . The National Conference on Street and Highway Safety . . . has furnished a meeting-ground for many different local and national groups.

In this field of joint study of ways and means of handling administrative problems, the drafting of uniform laws and ordinances has revealed many advantages. . . . It insures systematic discussion. . . . It brings out clearly the type of problems which can be handled through reliance on local authority, and also those which can be handled best by voluntary cooperation with citizens and groups. . . . Uniformity is promoted where it is desirable, while on the other hand the way is left entirely free for the local experimentation and progressive development which are so fruitful, and so firmly engrained in our American tradition.[64]

By the early 1930's the mayors of the depression-beleaguered cities wanted something more than coordination from Washington, and they played an important role in goading the national government into assuming positive responsibility for the well-being of city dwellers. In May, 1932, at the instigation of Mayor Frank Murphy of Detroit, the mayors of 67 large cities drafted an appeal for federal help. The United States Conference of Mayors, organized early in 1933, continued to press for national action. High on the list of the mayors' requests was federal assistance in the areas of unemployment relief and urban housing. At the instigation of President Franklin D. Roosevelt, who believed that the crisis called for energetic action by the federal government, Congress created the Public Works Administration (PWA) and the Works Progress Administration (WPA), which directly and indirectly provided work for the unemployed; the Home Owners Loan Corporation (HOLC), which reduced foreclosures; and the Federal Housing Authority (FHA), which insured loans for housing construction. The resolutions adopted at the 1936 meeting of the Conference of Mayors stated the mayors' immediate priorities and anticipated later developments in federal-city relations. These resolutions were reported in the January, 1937, issue of *The American City*.

WHAT THE CITIES WANT FROM WASHINGTON: 1937

The Executives of the principal cities of the United States, as represented in the U.S. Conference of Mayors, . . . feel that the Federal Government is responsible for the relief of "the unemployables" and that work relief is the American way. Consequently, heading the list of resolutions adopted at their recent Annual Conference in Washington, D.C., we find the determination to petition Congress . . . to provide adequate funds to carry the work program forward, on the basis of providing jobs to all employable persons. . . . A second resolution concerns the authorization of sufficient funds to complete the present PWA program, and recommends the establishment of PWA as a permanent agency of the Federal Government, with such powers and duties as may make it possible for the Federal Government, when economic conditions so demand, to be prepared to provide substantial stimulus to employment on public works throughout the country. Third, the cities feel that the relief of the transient unemployed is a peculiarly national problem, and that Congress should enact a transient relief program. The fourth resolution calls for the enactment of housing legislation . . . to help the cities meet the responsibility of providing decent, cheap and healthful houses for those unable to secure such housing, and to eliminate slum areas. Number five will take the form of a petition to the President and Congress to give consideration to the consolidation of all present welfare activities of the Federal Government into a Department of Public Welfare.[65]

Although Frank Murphy of Detroit and Daniel W. Hoan of Milwaukee played leading roles in the work of the U.S. Conference of Mayors, no municipal executive was more influential in enlisting the aid of the federal government for cities than New York's bouncing Fiorello H. La Guardia, elected mayor in 1933 on a platform promising public housing, more playgrounds, and relief, education, and health care for the poor. President of the Conference of Mayors in 1936, he was frequently its spokesman in Washington, urging Congressional support for programs such as PWA and WPA. New York City received substantial sums of federal money, not only because of La Guardia's aggressiveness and his rapport with New Deal administrators but also because his efforts to improve the city's finances helped it to qualify for aid and because he encouraged having projects ready when federal money became available. In 1939, looking back on the New Deal period in an address delivered at the National Conference of Social Work, he testified to the contributions the federal government had made, often at the insistence of the mayors, in helping cities with their problems during the depression.

LA GUARDIA ON FEDERAL AID
FOR DISTRESSED CITIES: 1939

I have been told that my subject has to do with making democracy work in a large city. Well, as mayor of one of the large cities, my main occupation just now is getting work for a great many of the unemployed. Times are changing; and what used to be the functions of a municipality are greatly enlarged . . . from what they were a quarter of a century ago. . . . The problem that confronts us is economic, and we have yet to solve it. . . . I speak from actual experience. . . . We are not theorizing when we see this one city alone faced with 300,000 unemployed, when in the country, as a whole, there are from eight to ten million unemployed. . . . I believe the American way of giving aid to the unemployed is to provide work for them so that they can earn enough to support their families and maintain the dignity and self-respect of citizens of our democracy. . . .

I know the jokes, the sneers, and the jeers, that are directed against the W.P.A. But I call as witness New Yorkers who can tell of the playgrounds and park layouts we have built in these years, the repaving, the fire houses, the sanitary plants. We have billions of dollars of permanent public works to show for it, which would not exist if these men had not been put to work. . . . I would like to take some of these people who disparage the W.P.A. and show them some of the sewer construction that is going on where men who never had a pick and shovel in their hands before, are down there digging because they want to earn the allowance the Government gives them. I wish those critics could see our great swimming pools, built in the sweat of the brow by men who were unemployed and found their way to the W.P.A. . . .

The most hopeful policy that has come out of our entire depression has been that in a time of great distress, the mighty arm of Uncle Sam reached out, and he said to his sons: "Come on, we will give you jobs." That is what W.P.A. is. Oh, I know what they say about mayors. They will tell you that mayors go to Washington just to get funds. I would not think much of a mayor who would not exert himself to his weary utmost if he knew that otherwise thousands of people in his city must remain in want. ·. . . The American people will refuse and refuse and refuse to return to bread lines and soup kitchens, and we cannot blame them.⁶⁶

The rationale for the new involvement of the federal government with urban problems was spelled out in the mid-1930's in a report sponsored by the National Resources Committee, whose previous reports, significantly, had been concerned primarily with the problems of rural America. This statement of the implications of urban problems for the national economy (Secretary of the Interior Harold Ickes called it "the first major national study of cities in the United States") gave perceptive expression to most of the issues that were to make the city the number-one problem of the United States for the remainder of the twentieth century — especially the relationship of the well-being of city dwellers to the health of the national economy and the inability of state legislatures to cope with the administrative problems of urban communities that transcend state lines.

A CREDO OF FEDERAL RESPONSIBILITY FOR THE CITY: 1937

The modern nation finds in its cities the focal point of much that is threatening and much that is promising in the life of its people. Scanning the troubled horizons of the past few years for these symptoms of national strength and national strain, we find first of all that the city has become not only one of the fundamental supports but also one of the primary problems of the Nation's economy.

As America pitches back and forth between alternate depression and recurrent prosperity, it is in the Nation's cities that the shadow of economic insecurity is darkest. For in the city will be found the workshop of our industrial society and the nerve center of our vast and delicate commercial mechanism. In 1935 one-fifth of all the employable persons on relief in the country were to be found in our 10 largest cities. Subject to continuing unemployment, lacking the rural reserves of shelter and subsistence, the city worker is seriously handicapped in the struggle for existence.

In time of national stress the task of relief and recovery falls not merely upon a single community or segment of the Nation, but upon the Nation as a whole. It is the Federal Government that has had to assume the major burdens of providing emergency relief for the city as well as the farm, of stimulating public works in the Nation's urban centers, and even of reviving insolvent municipal finances. Of the billions of dollars devoted to public emergency relief during the period 1933 to 1936, a large percent was contributed by the Federal Government. . . .

In looking at the urban problem, therefore, we consider it not as the concern of the city alone, but as a problem of the farmer as well, in that it is a problem of all the American Nation. From the point of view of the highest and best use of our national resources, our urban communities are potential assets of great value, and we must consider from the point of view of the national welfare how they may be most effectively aided in their development. . . .

The city has seemed at times the despair of America, but at others to be the Nation's hope, the battleground of democracy. Surely in the long run, the Nation's destiny will be profoundly affected by the cities which have two-thirds of its population and its wealth. There is liberty of development in isolation and wide spaces, but there is also freedom in the many-sided life of the city where each may find his own kind. There is democracy in the scattered few, but there is also democracy in the thick crowd with its vital impulse and its insistent demand for a just participation in the gains of our civilization. There is fertility and creation in the rich soil of the broad countryside, but there is also fertility and creativeness in forms of industry, art, personality, emerging even from the city streets and reaching toward the sky. . . .

It may be questioned . . . whether the National Government has given sufficient attention to some of the specific and common problems of urban dwellers as it has for farmers through the

Department of Agriculture, and it is the purpose of this inquiry to indicate some of the emerging city problems in which the Nation as a whole has an interest and in which the National Government may be helpful. It is not the business of the United States Government to assume responsibility for the solution of purely local problems any more than it is the business of local governments to assume primary responsibility for the settlement of national problems. Yet, the United States Government cannot properly remain indifferent to the common life of American citizens simply because they happen to be found in what we call "cities." The sanitation, the education, the housing, the working and living conditions, the economic security — in brief, the general welfare of all its citizens — are American concerns, insofar as they are within the range of Federal power and responsibility under the Constitution. . . .

Urban housing is one of the most burdensome problems the country now has to face and it calls for the Nation's most serious consideration. A real property inventory of 64 cities . . . showed that more than one-sixth of 1,500,000 residential dwellings were substandard. . . . Urban public health is endangered particularly in blighted areas and among low income groups. . . . Dirt, smoke, waste, soot, grime, and the reckless pollution of water are still among the noxious enemies of city life despite valiant official attempts to regulate these evils. . . . Juvenile delinquency, organized crime, and commercial rackets are among the . . . persistent urban problems. . . . Urban public finance is another emerging problem of vast proportions. In the recent depression, urban areas pouring millions into the national treasury were forced to pass the hat, begging for financial support. . . .

The concrete facts of our urban and administrative life frequently defy State lines and local control. Twenty-two of our 96 metropolitan districts containing . . . one-fifth of all our inhabitants, straddle State lines and call for a larger measure of interstate, and Federal cooperation in certain fields than is now found. . . . All in all there has been more widespread national neglect of our cities than of any other major segment of our national existence. Whether this is to be attributed to the absorption of our best efforts by the demands of our commercial and industrial system, or by other pressing claims of national policy, it is evident that America must now set out to overcome the continual and cumulative disregard of urban policies and administration and to take into account the place of the urban community in the national economy.[67]

5. HOUSING AND URBAN REHABILITATION

Housing and urban renewal, more than unemployment, were the areas in which the federal government was to have its chief continuing involvement in the affairs of the nation's cities. Public housing had been discussed at the turn of the century, but it was not until World War I that federal construction of housing was authorized as a means of attracting skilled workers to defense industries and this subject to the provision that all such housing would be sold to private purchasers at the end of the war. The responsibility of the federal government for housing was greatly expanded in the 1930's, when Congress authorized federal guarantees of home mortgages, construction of low-rent housing projects under the PWA, and, in the Housing Act of 1937, federal loans and subsidies for locally approved housing construction. The rapid expansion of urban populations during and following World War II not only aggravated the housing shortage but called attention to the deteriorated housing conditions in the slums of most large cities. Improved housing was seen as a significant part of post-war adjustment; consequently, the Housing Act of 1949 empowered the federal government to underwrite slum clearance and urban redevelopment and to provide for the construction of 810,000 units of public housing over a six-year period.

This legislation received strong support from cities that expected increased tax revenues from new building programs and was favored by downtown businessmen who saw slum clearance as a method of bringing more affluent customers into the inner city. When it became evident that the implementation of this legislation often reduced available dwelling facilities for the poor, new legislation in 1954 made obligatory the provision of workable arrangements for the relocation of persons (they were most often Blacks) displaced by redevelopment projects and authorized federal support for urban renewal — the upgrading of sound existing housing. Both urban redevelopment and urban renewal (expanded in the Housing Act of 1961) were designed in part to slow down the exodus to suburbia that was causing increasing concern in these years, as well as to increase the supply of improved housing. The socially defensible implementation of federal housing and urban renewal policy was to suffer, over the years, from a lack of clarity on the part of federal officialdom concerning the goals to be achieved and from the conflicting, contradictory, and often self-serving motivation of groups responsible for decision making at the local level.

The debate over public housing, as authorized in the Housing Act of 1949, arrayed two broad coalitions against one another: on the one hand, business groups, such as the National Association of Real Estate Brokers and the National Association of Home Builders, and on the other, public interest groups, such as the National Housing Conference, the United States Conference of Mayors, the AFL, the CIO, the NAACP, the Urban League, and the League of Women Voters. Passage of the measure, after the public housing feature was sustained by a narrow margin, was influenced by President Harry Truman's support and by the strength of the urban electorate shown in the presidential election of 1948.[68] Hearings in 1945 before the Senate subcommittee on housing and urban redevelopment, chaired by Senator Robert Taft, had brought into focus the conflicting attitudes, in terms of social and political philosophy, on this urban-motivated policy.

THE PROS AND CONS OF PUBLIC HOUSING —
SENATE HEARINGS: 1945

Mr. La Guardia. I understand, Mr. Chairman, that this is a hearing on the question of public housing and slum clearance.

Senator Taft. That is the post-war aspect of the plan for the next 10 years.

Mr. La Guardia. At this point . . . I would like permission to insert a prepared statement from the United States Conference of Mayors. . . .

Of all groups interested in housing and in the clearance and redevelopment of slum areas, the executives of American cities, speaking through the United States Conference of Mayors, are beyond question — except perhaps for the people who themselves live in slums — the most vitally concerned. To us, housing and slum clearance are not just questions of social reform, but concrete and practical matters of good municipal housekeeping. . . . We want to make it clear that . . . every possible attempt should be made to solve the housing problems of our people through the operation of private enterprise. . . . It must be admitted, however, that after every attempt has been made, there will undoubtedly be a very substantial number of families who cannot afford even the lowest-cost houses of adequate standards produced by private enterprise. For these people the only answer is public housing. . . .

The cities of the country have had a visible demonstration of the benefits which can be achieved under the low-rent public housing program authorized by the United States Housing Act. This program . . . has taken families from the slums, and it has made decent housing available to those who would otherwise have to live out their lives in the slums. . . . We believe that the various localities should determine the extent and nature of the programs which they are to undertake. . . . We believe that the role of the Federal Government should be restricted to that of giving financial aid and technical assistance. . . . Our cities must begin as soon as possible to make plans for their postwar projects of low-rent housing and slum clearance. Not only will these projects be of immeasurable benefit to the communities themselves, but they will form a vast reservoir of work for men and women when they are released from the armed services or are no longer needed in war industries. At one and the same time we can provide jobs to tide the Nation over a difficult reconversion period and correct one of the principal dislocations in our national life. . . . We respectfully urge this committee . . . to produce a bold plan . . . which will make certain the right of every American family to a decent home.[69]

• • •

Senator Taft. . . . you may proceed, Mr. Merrion. . . .

Mr. Merrion. I am Joseph E. Merrion, president of the National Association of Home Builders of the United States. . . . I am a practical home builder. I come before you as the president of my group, which is composed of thousands of small businessmen like myself who have been building the great bulk of housing units in this country. . . . It is estimated that at least 80 percent of the individuals and firms that are engaged in the private-home building business are included in our membership. . . . Because we initiate to a great extent the home building of the country . . . we feel that a large part of the responsibility for the future housing of America is ours. . . .

During the depression years proponents of socialized housing in this country were successful in persuading the Congress to pass the United States Housing Act. . . . Examination of public housing discloses the fact that the cost of construction has often been exorbitant; the "one for one" demolition requirement has not been met; much of the housing has been built on the peripheries of cities while slums remained; and those who lived in the slums and on relief have not generally been permitted to occupy the housing. Instead, a favored few, skimmed from the top of the low-income group, have been housed at the expense of all others. Less needy families have occupied the new shelter, paying approximately half of the property's rental value. We do not concede the need nor the right of the Federal Government, either directly or by subsidy to local housing authorities, to enter the housing field by building, owning, or operating permanent housing projects. We feel that in so doing the Government is invading the field of private enterprise, setting itself up in business in competition with citizens and taxpayers. . . .

Our association is opposed to public housing not only because it will eventually destroy the entire building industry — dealers, financing institutions, and builders, but because it is the first step in the socialization of our country — the destruction of our democratic free-enterprise system. Like many evils, a first step . . . is appealing and popular. Only by fully recognizing the social, political, and industrial disaster which will come with its growth can one properly gauge the eventual result. Obviously, it is ridiculous to construct new housing for the very lowest income group. There are great quantities of structurally sound but blighted housing which can be rehabilitated for those of our people who cannot earn sufficient income to acquire new shelter. . . . As in the case of providing the other two essentials of life — clothing and food — there is no reason for the Government to subsidize the housing itself. The individuals must be given relief in the same fashion as in these other necessities of life.

We, therefore, will resist legislation which seeks to promote and expand public housing. Beyond this, we will recommend legislation which will permit private enterprise to gradually supply the low-cost housing need. There is no simple method of solving this problem of clearing slums and decently housing the lowest-income group. The answer lies in a healthy, expanding economy, an improved educational system, a social consciousness in each community which will demand the enforcement of safety and sanitation codes and the provision of welfare activities which will gradually raise the level of the slum-dwellers' condition.[70]

Housing — both as fulfilling a social need and as a means of stimulating the national economy — was central to the arguments that led to the creation of a cabinet-level Department of Housing and Urban Development. President John F. Kennedy stressed both of these points in arguing for the new department, which was not authorized until September, 1965, during the administration of Lyndon B. Johnson, his successor.

JOHN F. KENNEDY ON THE CHALLENGE OF THE CITY: 1962

In my special message on housing of March 9, 1961, and again in my message on the state of the Union earlier this year, I recommended the establishment . . . of a new Department of Urban Affairs and Housing, of Cabinet rank. . . . The times we live in urgently call for this action. In a few short decades . . . we shall be . . . living in expanded urban areas in housing that does not now exist, served by community facilities that do not now exist, moving about by means of systems of urban transportation that do not now exist. The challenge is great, and the time is short. I propose to act now to strengthen and improve the machinery through which, in large part, the Federal Government must act to carry out its proper role of encouragement and assistance to States and local governments, to voluntary efforts and to private enterprise, in the solution of these problems.

The present and future problems of our cities are as complex as they are manifold. There must be expansion: but orderly and planned expansion, not explosion and sprawl. Basic public facilities must be extended ever further into the areas surrounding urban centers; but they must be planned and coordinated so as to favor rather than hamper the sound growth of our communities. The scourge of blight must be overcome, and the central core areas of our cities, with all their great richness of economic and cultural wealth, must be restored to lasting vitality. New values must be created to provide a more efficient local economy and provide revenues to support essential local services. Sound old housing must be conserved and improved, and new housing created, to serve better all income groups in our population and to move ever closer to the goal of a decent home in a suitable living environment for every American family. We will neglect our cities at our peril, for in neglecting them we neglect the Nation.[71]

The emphasis on federal housing policy in the later 1960's was upon neighborhood rehabilitation — a response to criticism of urban renewal for underwriting the improvement of central business districts and the construction of luxury apartments at the expense of the needs of slum dwellers. Studies showed that the majority of the persons dislocated by slum clearance were merely relocated in other slums where they often suffered the social and psychological consequences of being uprooted from familiar surroundings.[72] The Model Cities program, authorized in the Demonstration Cities Act of October, 1966, sought to attack urban blight on a massive scale by providing for special supplementary grants to cities that would attempt, by a combined housing and social effort, to renovate whole neighborhoods. The Housing and Urban Development Act (signed August 1, 1968) carried this program even further by authorizing expenditures of more than $5,000,000,000 for urban renewal, model cities programs, rent subsidies, and guarantees of privately financed housing construction. The increasingly social focus of federal housing policy in the 1960's, as well as the coordinated effort involved in its implementation, was discussed in 1968 by Robert C. Weaver, the first Secretary of Housing and Urban Development. Following are brief excerpts from his article, "Rebuilding American Cities: an Overview," which was published in the December, 1968 issue of *Current History*.

SECRETARY WEAVER ON THE FEDERAL COMMITMENT TO URBAN REHABILITATION: 1968

It was not until the 1960's that Americans began to recognize . . . that the great city was a reality and that all the critical variables of urbanization were interrelated and must be considered in federal responses. So a whole new family of urban programs was born: open space land, urban mass transportation, rehabilitation, grants for urban beautification and neighborhood centers. Planning aids were greatly expanded and increasing emphasis was given to the planning process.

It became clear, however, that these solutions . . . were not enough. What was needed was a coordinated effort that involved not only the building and rebuilding of physical facilities, but a simultaneous attack on the human problems — of poverty, of unemployment, of education, of health deficiencies. . . . So the Model Cities Program was developed. This is a national effort to give cities the financial and technical aid they need to plan and carry out far-reaching programs to solve the social, economic and physical problems of large slum neighborhoods. This program gives cities planning funds as well as additional money to carry out special and innovative projects in the neighborhoods. . . .

435

For the first time, many of the cities will be dealing simultaneously with all the problems of a slum area and concentrating their resources to solve these problems. For example, the problem of unemployment cannot be solved just by creating jobs. There must be education and job training to prepare people for those jobs; there must be transportation, so people can get to their jobs; and in the case of working mothers, day-care facilities may be needed for their children.

Seventy-five cities have already received Model Cities planning grants and will start the action phases of their program this year. Planning grants will be made to an additional 70 to 80 cities.

There will be two major benefits from this program: first, the United States will have developed a practical operating mechanism in which all urban and social specialists will come together — architects and planners, health and welfare authorities and educators, builders and transportation experts. The people of the area must, by law, be heavily involved in the planning and the implementing of these programs. This is extremely important. It is the only way to end the feeling of isolation and alienation that is so crippling to those who are poor and ignored in any society. Second, the program will operate on a large scale. Unless a major impact is made on large neighborhoods, we will be back where we started.

And that brings Americans to the next long step forward they should be taking as a nation. In 1968, recognizing that housing was a basic requirement to all our other efforts, President Johnson set the United States on the pathway of a national building and rebuilding program on a scale unprecedented in this nation. The administration has given us these goals: The construction of 26.2 million new housing units, by both private and public means, in the next ten years. This can be compared to 14.4 million units built in the past decade. Public assistance for 4 million of these units, as compared with one-half million in the last ten years. Public assistance to rebuild 2 million existing units which are sound but dilapidated. This compares to 25,000 units in the last decade.

If the United States is to meet this schedule, new mechanisms and techniques must be created and applied on a giant scale. There must be technological advances. There must be innovations in housing finance. There must be methods of bringing private financial resources and industrial and management methods into low-income housing. There must be advances in ways of keeping utilities and public services abreast of our building efforts. In many ways, the United States is embarked on a whole new era of experimentation in urban concerns and in the mass production of housing. It has come late. But at least Americans are now aware of the extent of their problems, and are consciously preparing to meet them on a national level.[73]

The Model Cities program represented the peak of concern on the part of the federal government for the problems of the inner city. In the early 1970's, the administration of President Richard M. Nixon sought to curtail funds for urban renewal and Model Cities programs and to substitute a policy of federal revenue sharing that was as likely to channel funds to suburban communities as to support specific projects to improve conditions among the inner city poor. The ideal, under the Model Cities Act, of involving the people of the area in programs to rehabilitate depressed neighborhoods generated a number of problems. Conflicts developed among contending groups in given communities, especially on questions of design and on decisions as to whether subsidized housing units should be grouped together or scattered throughout the development. Professional planners objected to having their role taken over by amateurs. Local politicians and city officials regretted their loss of control over federal funds. The mood of the Nixon administration was to reduce federal involvement and to criticize specific programs as costly and inefficient. Despite these difficulties, work on large-scale urban renewal projects continued to advance, if slowly, and some of the Model Cities programs gave proof that federal funds could be used effectively to help meet the pressing problems of central cities, as identified by local residents. One example was the experience of Atlanta, Georgia, described in *The New York Times* in November, 1969.

"MODEL CITIES" ACCOMPLISHMENTS IN ATLANTA: 1969

Atlanta was the first city in the nation to get a Model Cities grant. By pushing for speed, cutting red tape and preparing the groundwork early, it obtained its grant May 20. . . . Atlanta implemented its first project under the $7,175,000 Federal grant on June 4. This is a shuttle bus program, contracted with the Atlanta Transit Company, providing bus service in the area for a dime and a transfer to the outside system for 15 cents more. The area contains 45,000 people, which would make it the seventh largest city in Georgia if it were incorporated. A day-care program has been established to handle 350 children daily. It is supervised by Senior Citizens of Atlanta, and 165 elderly persons have enrolled. Construction has just begun on an educational complex that eventually will cost more than $30-million. The Atomic Energy Commission has already provided $1.3-million for a science center. The plan is to acquire 65 acres eventually for schools. Other accomplishments of Model Cities of Atlanta include the resurfacing of 22 streets; and consumer buying assistance programs, and a liaison with the Alliance Theatre, a part of the city's cultural center.[74]

The philosophy underlying the model cities program reflected a new concept of city planning — one that put greater emphasis on improving social conditions than upon transforming the physical environment. Though thought had been given to rational social planning for cities as early as 1908 and 1909, most planning activities in the era of World War I and its aftermath reflected the progressives' conviction that improvements in the physical environment constituted the major solution to the problems of city life. Thus quasi-independent planning commissions, operating under municipal auspices but with strong support from the business community, conceived master plans for cities as early as 1914 and regional plans for metropolitan areas by the 1920's. These blueprints emphasized spatial considerations in providing for improved transportation systems and zoning regulations that would realize the aspirations of municipal reformers for public order, civic beauty, and efficient and profitable land use.

The federal programs of the 1930's and later encouraged planning to achieve social goals, and once the planning profession could look to the federal government as well as to local business interests for support, social scientists making use of computers, simulation models, and systems analysis joined the architects and engineers in the planning fraternity and began to influence community planning activities. To this group, poverty, unemployment, and racial and class discrimination were crucial problems of the city that needed correction before the attractive, efficient, slumless city could be realized. "Even urban design, traditionally based primarily on aesthetic considerations," was now "paying attention to the social processes that shape . . . urban form," said Herbert Gans, an exponent of the new goal-oriented rational planning.[75] Thus planning, which in early America was aimed primarily at producing an orderly commercial community, was responding by the mid-twentieth century to the social realities of the large and socially heterogeneous city.

The complexities of city planning with an eye to racial integration and the relief of poverty as well as to appropriate design were exhibited in the reactions in the early 1970's to a federally aided low-income project in the Forest Hills section of Queens, in New York City. The location of the project resulted from the "scatter-site" approach to racial integration. As originally approved, it embodied a forward-looking design, including low structures as well as towers. Changes in the plan projected three monumental 23-story buildings. Large segments of the community resisted, not only because of the size of the design but also because of the implications of the injection of low-income residents in such large numbers into a middle-class neighborhood. The local reaction was reported in Michael Tabor's eye-witness account, which originally appeared in *Genesis 2*, a Cambridge, Massachusetts publication.

THE COMPLICATIONS OF CITY PLANNING WITH SOCIAL GOALS — FOREST HILLS: 1971

On November 22, 1971, excavation began for construction of a federally aided low-income housing project in Forest Hills, New York. The residents, or at least the vocal ones, do not want that housing to be in their neighborhood, and have been demonstrating almost daily since November to let the city know precisely that. The public housing is part of the Lindsay Administration's "scatter-site" program, which is designed to insure that "the goal of racial and economic integrated housing would not be abandoned." Forest Hills is a Jewish neighborhood in residential, largely middle-class Queens. . . . I went to Forest Hills for a week . . . to try to find out what has happened. Here is what I found:

First, there are all sorts of excuses people give for not wanting the housing project, but the main reason is fear — perhaps even justifiable fear. They have moved out of two, three, four or more neighborhoods before coming to Forest Hills. They have watched blacks, Puerto Ricans, and welfare families move in and seen their neighborhoods deteriorate. . . . They also equate low-income housing with rape, murder, muggings and robbery.

439

They read about crime in and near other public housing projects, like those in former Jewish Rockaway, and fear it will happen in their neighborhood.

Second, the Forest Hills people you read about are not all rich or even upper "middle class" at all. Many hold down two and three jobs to be able to afford to live there. Most live in garden apartments and high-rises. They are relatively comfortable, living in a safe area. Eighty-five to ninety per cent of the 150,000 to 200,000 residents are Jewish. Ten to fifteen per cent of these are Orthodox.

Third, the American Jewish Congress, the Union of American Hebrew Congregations (Reform), the Anti-Defamation League of B'nai B'rith, and some other national Jewish organizations are in favor of the project. They have supported the concepts of scatter-site and public housing in the past. . . . These liberal Jewish groups have hedged a bit because of the reaction. They're starting to qualify their support. But they'll stand firm.

Fourth, the NAACP, the Urban League, and other civil rights groups condemn the resident reaction as a racist exclusion of non-whites. A few residents (perhaps 100) have joined as many as 400 others in a "Vigil of Welcome" sponsored by 41 community, religious, civil rights, and union organizations. Radical groups also attack those opposing the project as rascists. These radicals march with the "Vigil" group, sponsor their own demonstrations at the building site (at which they wave red flags), and picket the office of the militantly anti-project Forest Hills Residents Association. . . .

Fifth, NEGRO, a black capitalist group, is opposed to the development. Why isn't some of that money going toward rehabilitating neighborhoods in black communities, they ask. CORE sees the move as a general trend to remove the poor from valuable real estate in Manhattan and put them in walled ghettos elsewhere, thus defusing the political power of the black masses. . . .

So you see, this is a complicated issue. If the buildings go up, residents insist that they will move out. There will be plenty of room in Forest Hills for low-income and welfare people then.[76]

By the early 1970's, the social tensions precipitated by federal housing programs were only one dimension of the dilemma federal housing presented. Staggering costs resulted from an acceleration of construction beginning in the 1960's, as well as from federal subsidies authorized by legislation passed in 1969 which limited rents in public housing to 25 per cent of a tenant's income. Tenants were blamed for the rapid deterioration of public housing, and grand jury indictments began to disclose corruption on the part of real estate, building, and banking interests, in collusion with officials of the Federal Housing Administration. As the mood of the nation became more critical of vesting wide powers in the national government and of subsidizing the poor at the expense of middle-income Americans, the involvement of the federal government in housing came under increasing scrutiny and criticism.

Meanwhile, despite augmented federal support for urban programs in the later 1960's, the fiscal difficulties of the nation's large cities were so critical that many mayors urged new forms of federal assistance — in this instance direct financial aid. Proposals included federal revenue sharing, the assumption of welfare costs by the federal government, and an increase in federally financed city jobs of the Neighborhood Youth Corps type. Revenue sharing was achieved in October, 1972, with the passage of the State and Local Fiscal Assistance Act of 1972. This measure provided for the disbursement of $30,100,000,000 over a five-year period, to the states and to local governments, to be used by localities as they saw fit — even for the reduction of taxes. The United States Conference of Mayors was one of the most vigorous proponents of federal revenue sharing. The need for direct federal support was expressed in April, 1971 by several members of its Legislative Action Committee.

A CALL FOR FISCAL AID
FROM THE FEDERAL GOVERNMENT: 1971

Henry W. Maier (Milwaukee): "The cities are financing education, police and health — the social overhead of poverty — with the property tax, a tax that was designed only to finance fire, sewer and garbage costs. The Federal income tax should be financing social overhead costs."

Peter F. Flaherty (Pittsburgh): "If we get revenue sharing, I'll use it to stop tax increases, to keep people from jumping into the suburbs."

Roman S. Gribbs (Detroit): "Unemployment is at the doorsteps of the Mayors. In the inner city we have 25 per cent unemployment, and among young people it's 48 per cent. . . . I

441

have a disaster plan budget cutting city employees if we don't get more money. I'm going into every city service. I'll close 15 to 31 recreation centers and six firehouses . . . and if you see services cut back, you'll see blowups of some kind."

Moon Landrieu (New Orleans): "Our population is 593,000, but we provide the transportation facilities, every major park, the zoo, cultural facilities and the airport for a metropolitan area of 1.1 million. And we get nothing back from the suburbs; they contribute nothing. We don't even get the sales tax, because of shopping centers in the suburbs. All we get is the poor and an eroding tax base. . . . The trend is frightening."

James H. J. Tate (Philadelphia): "It's the same every place — that's what we're trying to tell Congress. Let me start by saying that we will lock up 26 playgrounds this summer because we don't have the funds for people to run them. . . . We're in trouble, and we need help." [77]

6. CAPITAL CITY

The spectacular growth of Washington, D.C., beginning especially in the 1930's, was an urban manifestation of the expanding activities of the national government in the twentieth century of which aid to cities was only one element. In the 1930's, when most cities were stagnating, the population of the capital city grew from less than 487,000 to more than 663,000 — an increase of 36 per cent. By 1970, its population stood at more than 750,000 within a metropolitan cluster of nearly 3,000,000. The expansion of government during World War I had given an initial stimulus to accelerated growth, but it was the proliferation of federal activity during the New Deal that made Washington the nation's "boom town" of the 1930's. The hectic consequences of this extraordinary growth were described by Oliver McKee, Jr., in *The North American Review* of February, 1935.

NEW DEAL WASHINGTON — BOOM TOWN OF THE 1930's: 1935

The New Deal has made the capital a boom town. A bonanza prosperity sets its population apart from those of other American cities. . . . If the easy money and the fat payrolls of Washington are those of a boom town, so too is the carefree spirit, the mood of adventure, the exhilaration of exciting living which the humblest office-holders share with the Brain Trust as co-workers in the great experimental laboratory set up in their city. . . .

The impact of the New Deal on Washington has done more than create a fermentation of ideas. It has had important physical effects as well. A serious housing shortage is one of these. People in the medium income group find it increasingly difficult to rent a decent house or apartment within their means. . . . The repeal of Prohibition and the huge additions to the population of Washington after many lean years, have again brought cheer to the hotels of Washington. The tourist trade continues to fill sight-seeing places with rubbernecks, but business men, to a greater extent than ever before, swell the throngs that daily detrain at the Union Station. Government control over business brings representatives of industry to the capital, in large numbers, to attend NRA code hearings or to become acquainted with other New Deal units. . . .

Notwithstanding the big Federal payroll and increased population, the capital nevertheless has a real relief problem on its hands. . . . Washington is easily accessible to most of the South, and thousands of Southern Negroes have come to the city in the hope that Uncle Sam would provide them with a present-day equivalent of "forty dollars [sic] and a mule." The New Deal . . . has encouraged millions to look on the Federal Government as a universal provider. So the capital, as the point of origin for the distribution of the New Deal billions, has exercised a potent appeal to the footloose and the nomads. Additional thousands have journeyed to the city in the hope of landing Federal jobs. Those without sufficient political pull to land a government billet have been added to the city's unemployed. . . .

A city more beautiful in its external features year by year, Washington has become the focal point for a centralization of governmental authority that goes far beyond anything the country has previously seen. That centralization made boom conditions inevitable. For when government attempts a big job, whether it be conducting a war or fighting a depression by priming the pump, a vast expansion in its organization always follows.[78]

What the war on the depression had done to increase the growth of the "headquarters" city was repeated under the stimulus of World War II. Washington's population increased to more than 800,000 by 1950, within a metropolitan area that numbered nearly one and a half million. Housing and office space were at a greater premium than during the 1930's, as Washington, with the nearby mighty Pentagon, became the focal center of the international war effort. Wartime gas rationing complicated life for the city's transient population; government workers jammed the street cars, and bicycle riders glutted the streets. Donald Wilhelm, writing in the September, 1941, issue of *The American Mercury*, described the pressures on housing and urban services in the initial months of Washington's adjustment to a wartime life style.

WARTIME WASHINGTON — BOOM TOWN OF THE 1940's: 1941

America's feverish preparations for war have set off booms in the industrial centers, [and] have left no town untouched in some degree. But the place where it all starts is Boom Town No. 1 — Washington, D.C. Washington never before was such a spectacle, not in the previous World War, not even in the frenetic days when Gen. Hugh (Ironpants) Johnson whooped it up for the NRA Blue Eagle.

Hotel clerks smile superciliously when you ask for a room. . . . Many a businessman flies back to New York for the night, flies down again next morning. Restaurants are packed and their prices inch relentlessly upward. . . . The airport is the busiest in the United States . . . save La Guardia Field, New York. . . . The government employes are crowded and uncomfortable both in their offices and in their living quarters, working long hours with no overtime pay, worried over the impact of rising rents and the rising cost of living, on their average $1500 salaries.

There are 240,000 men and women on one or another public payroll in Washington now and they are increasing at the rate of 5000 a month. . . . The horde of government employes go to work in all kinds of places. The government has taken over 200-odd mansions, hotels and apartment houses to use as offices. It is a bit startling to find the official with whom you have business sitting amid the shiny tiles of what last week, or yesterday, was obviously a bathroom. Sometimes the fixtures have been decently boxed in to serve as chairs or tables; sometimes not. . . .

Housing is as scarce as office space. Washington has, in a decade, more than doubled in population. It had 700,000 residents in 1940, and had spilled another 300,000 across District lines into its suburbs. . . . The latest figures of the Bureau of Labor Statistics indicate rents have risen to the highest level of any American city. . . . Still, the job-seekers swarm in. . . . Some of these hopefuls help fill the great government automobile camp for 1000 cars in East Potomac Park; but no one stays there more than two weeks. . . . A good many workers commute from Baltimore. Some are living in houseboats on the Potomac.

Of all the cities hit by the defense boom, Washington was perhaps the least ready to cope with the problems entailed. The telephone company is struggling fairly successfully with its impossible task. . . . The streetcar and bus system is doing the best it can to handle 4,200,000 passengers a week, which is 1,000,000 more than last year. Other services aren't rising to the emergency so well. Educators do not like even to imagine what the school situation will be this fall. Hospitals are overcrowded and are ejecting chronic sufferers to make beds available for other patients. Many physicians and dentists announce that they cannot serve newcomers; their established practice is already too large. The capital has been shocked by a series of crimes, including attacks on women. Inevitably the boom has attracted thousands of floaters to the city, and the great growth in population has spread the police department very thin.[79]

By the 1960's, Washington, though still not the "national city" in the sense that this was true of such capital cities as London, Paris, and Rome, nevertheless conformed increasingly to the pattern of other American metropolitan centers. Following the national trend, the central city actually decreased in population between 1960 and 1970 while the metropolitan area of which it was a part increased from 2,001,897 to 2,861,123. By 1970, its Black population, numbering more than half a million, constituted 71 per cent of the population of the central city, a development that brought more into the open the "secret city" of Blacks that had existed in the nation's capital since before the Civil War. In 1967, the structure of its municipal government was made more like that of other American cities, as Congress brought to an end government by commission and inaugurated an era of modified home rule under a mayor and city council — appointed, however, rather than elected. Of the new officials, appointed by President Lyndon B. Johnson and approved by the Senate, the mayor and five of the nine council members were Blacks. The opening in September, 1971, of the John F. Kennedy Center for the Performing Arts manifested an effort to bring the cultural resources of the city more into line with those of other leading cities in the United States.

By the 1960's Washington was experiencing, too, many of the social problems that plagued other large American cities. Several of these — crime, racial tension, fiscal shortages, and the flight to the suburbs — were discussed in the July 29, 1968, issue of *U.S. News and World Report.*

WASHINGTON — AMERICAN CITY: 1968

"Tragic" is the word that is beginning to be used to describe conditions in Washington, D.C. . . . Fear has become a real element in Washington life. Crime is rising at a rate higher than in any other of the nation's large cities. . . . Racial tensions are high in spite of all-out efforts for integration. Negroes make up more than 65 per cent of the city's population of about 800,000. . . . Barely a year ago, a white superintendent of the city schools who once had been acclaimed for desegregating the school system was forced to quit under fire from Negroes. His white successor is threatened with dismissal six months after taking office. The school population is more than 92 per cent Negroes. The superintendent who was forced out last year describes the situation in the schools as "chaotic." . . .

The city has an integrated government under a Negro mayor, Walter E. Washington. Mayor Washington told Congress recently that the capital . . . is "in desperate need of money." The Federal Government supplied 70 million dollars in funds for running the city in the year that ended June 30 [1968]. For the current year, Mayor Washington asks for a formula that would set the federal payment at 30 per cent of what the city collects in taxes. This would boost the federal contribution to 99.1 million. The mayor also is seeking additional taxes. Mr. Washington says: "It would be difficult to overstate the city's needs for a sharp and immediate increase in revenues."

The problem of crime keeps growing even though Washington has more police per 1,000 inhabitants than any other large city in the United States. . . . Retailers say that many people apparently are afraid to shop downtown because of the crime rate. . . . A leading downtown merchant reported that he had been compelled to build up his security force to the point where his store now has "more protection than some small cities." . . . Washington's climate of crime affects the lives of many thousands of people. For instance, nighttime bus service was discontinued for a time earlier this year after more than 200 holdups between January and May of bus drivers and, finally, the murder of a driver by a robber. Busmen refused to work after dark until a plan was devised for riders without the exact fare to be given redeemable scrip instead of change. . . .

Officials analyzing the crime problem point out that the largest increase in the city's population is among young Negroes, a large percentage of whom are unemployed. The President's Commission on Crime in the District of Columbia reported in December, 1966: "The perpetrators of serious crime in the District are most often young male Negroes. In the 1950–65 period, 80 per cent of all persons arrested for serious offenses were Negroes and 31 per cent were juveniles." The Commission also noted: "One third of the city's population exists at little more than a subsistence level. One half of all large families are partially or completely indigent, one fourth of its adult Negro population is functionally illiterate, one fourth of all live births are illegitimate, one sixth of all housing units are overcrowded, and 25,000 housing units are in sufficiently bad condition to warrant removal." . . .

Flight of businesses to the suburbs, going on for years, was accelerated by the April [1968] riots and the subsequent increase in crime. Wallace B. Agnew, a real estate man, observes: "Not a day passes that some merchant doesn't call and ask if I have any vacancies in a suburban shopping center." [80]

7. CITY MANAGEMENT: NEW STYLE

The concern, on the part of the nation's cities, for eliciting federal aid focused attention on the mayor as the spokesman for the city's needs and on the new breed of chief executive who was inhabiting the city hall. The emergence of the new style of mayor — often similar in personality to the chief executive of a large corporation — was in part the result of the declining influence of the boss and the machine, a development encouraged by the immigration restrictions of the 1920's, the availability of social security and unemployment insurance, and the use of the nonpartisan ballot, which weakened party organization in many cities.

The mid-twentieth-century mayor was a combination of administrator, politician, and public relations man, sensitive to the growing magnitude of the services city dwellers expected of municipal governments in the areas of professionally administered fire and police protection, garbage collection, sewage disposal, traffic engineering, pollution control, health services, city planning, and the like, and capable of negotiating both with the state and federal governments and with the many interest groups within the city.

Charter changes strengthened the mayoral office by giving the mayor wider powers with respect to appointments and budget control and by limiting the size and authority of the city council. At the same time, the mayors' capacity to govern was adversely affected not only by the growing complexity of the city's problems and the need for dealing with state and federal agencies in their solution, but also by the activities of autonomous agencies such as the Port of New York Authority and by the independence and inflexibility of the municipal bureaucracy, bolstered by civil service protection and employee unionization. Critics of the increasingly professionalized and bureaucratized municipal governments contended that large cities were better run but less well governed in the mid-twentieth century than in the days of the boss and the machine when a mayor could count on the political loyalty of bureau chiefs and department commissioners in the implementation of comprehensive programs.[81]

By the early 1970's, racial tension and fiscal difficulties aggravated by inflation, the movement of the middle class to the suburbs, and the tendency of the poor to concentrate in the central city were in the forefront of the problems of the big-city mayors, and in some major cities, such as Los Angeles, Cleveland, Gary, and Newark, Blacks were being elected to the mayoral office. The complexity and variety of mayoral activities in the mid-twentieth-century city and the magnitude of the problems involved are reflected in journalist Richard Reeves's characterization of the mayoralty of New York City's John V. Lindsay, in an article that appeared in *The New York Times Magazine* in January, 1968.

LINDSAY — MID-TWENTIETH-CENTURY MAYOR: 1968

Lindsay moves at the pace of the great city. His red-carpeted corner office at City Hall is a nice place to visit, but he doesn't live there. One night early last September, for example, the city was being run instead from Rosario's Pizzeria on East Houston Street on the Lower East Side. There was the Mayor of New

York leaning against a wall decorated with the telephone numbers of girls named Angela and Maria. He had the pay phone in one hand and a lemon ice in the other. "O. K., Fred," he said. "How much?"

"Fred" was Frederick O'Reilly Hayes, the young Budget Director whom Lindsay had recruited from a top job in the Federal Office of Economic Opportunity. "How much?" meant "How many million dollars do the teachers want?" Hayes and other city officials were at Gracie Mansion trying to end the strike of 55,000 teachers against city schools. The Mayor was on one of his summer walks and was checking on the progress of negotiations.

His walk that hot night had taken him all around the town. To the Puerto Rican barrio — "*Viva Linzee!*" from the dark faces in the windows above the boarded-up storefronts. To Harlem — "Hi, Mayor," from a kid kicking a Rheingold can. . . . To Little Italy on the Lower East Side — . . . .

The walks had started quietly enough, but by the end of the summer they were drawing almost as much national attention as the American League pennant race. Chasing along behind Lindsay that night in Harlem were gangs of laughing Negro children, a dozen reporters and photographers, a Congressman from Michigan, columnist Art Buchwald and William Attwood, editor in chief of Look magazine and other Cowles publications. . . .

Lindsay does not claim credit for the cool summer — a cool which almost exploded when hundreds of East Harlem teen-agers ran wild for three August nights. "We were lucky," he says. "There was a lot of rain and a lot of people in the ghetto communities worked very, very hard."

But Lindsay cared; he worked hard to pacify the ghettos. The Mayor's Summer Task Force, financed with $700,000 donated by private companies, organized neighborhood task forces that searched out natural young leaders to work in the streets. There were slum teen-agers who got their kicks out of talking their friends into cooling it, instead of leading those same friends into riot. The task force also paid for the free plane rides, boat rides, movies and jazz concerts that kept kids off the hot junkyard streets. And Lindsay also put up city money to supplement the Federal anti-poverty funds used to pay 42,000 members of the Neighborhood Youth Corps $1.50 an hour to clean out vacant lots and work in hospitals. . . .

Then Lindsay helped organize and became the spokesman for the Urban Coalition, a national group which hopes to bring the nation's private power into the fight to save the cities. The combined political power of the individual coalition members — men like Walter Reuther and Henry Ford II — is enormous. . . .

Lindsay has balanced the city's $5-billion operating budget for two years . . . by begging and bludgeoning the State Legislature for new taxing powers. But now he may need new taxes for the second time in three years and he will travel to Albany to plead for a tax-sharing plan called "Urbanaid." Under his plan, municipalities would receive a portion of the state income tax proportionate to local expenses. Urbanaid will die amid the laughter of upstate legislators who have no intention of giving the city a fair share of the taxes paid by its residents.

The Federal Government will someday take over welfare payments . . . but until that day the hopes of New York Mayors will sink in a welfare budget that will reach $1.4-billion this year. . . . Lindsay did win one big gamble last year in Washington. He bet $25-million of city money on the Federal Model Cities program and won at least $30-million back. The Democratic City Council had not wanted to appropriate Model Cities money for redeveloping three slum areas — Harlem, Central Brooklyn and the South Bronx — because everyone thought Washington would approve only one area. Everyone but Lindsay. He thought the Federal Government would have to come into all three if city funds were already committed. He was right.

Model Cities was one of the Mayor's most substantial achievements during 1967. Perhaps the most important decision he made was approving a school decentralization plan recommended by a mayoral committee headed by McGeorge Bundy, president of the Ford Foundation. If the Legislature also approves the plan, the school system will be broken up into 30 to 60 autonomous districts.

The new districts would also break the power of the Board of Education, which functions independently of City Hall: "No matter how many asbestos walls are put up between me and the Board of Education," Lindsay said, "at the end I get the blame if there's trouble, and I bloody well ought to have something to say about what's going on." . . .

Lindsay . . . knows what he wants to do, but he has not mastered the bureaucracy and he has not been able to attract or keep men who can do it for him. Lindsay is . . . challenging the city unions for the right to promote talented young employes over senior bureaucrats, battling the Patrolmen's Benevolent Association to modernize the Police Department, hiring the thinkers of the RAND Corporation to take a new look at municipal government. But is he winning, or will the clerks outlast him? . . .

There are as many as 300 separate operations involved in getting a city job started. . . . His critics say he is not interested in the nitty-gritty of pushing what he wants past the 312,000 anonymous men and women of the city's bureaucracy. In fact, he has concentrated on trying to reorganize the bureaucracy, an emphasis that has probably slowed it down even more.

He feels that a Federal-type structure — with 10 administrations replacing 49 city agencies — will eventually streamline city government so that it will respond to the chief executive. But change comes slowly and the City Council has approved only three of the administrations — Housing and Development, Health Services and Environmental Protection. . . .

"You can just about get things started in four years," he said the other day. "You can just about get them going down the track. But that's not such a small accomplishment — not in this city."

Survival is an accomplishment. Lindsay likes to say that history has proved the Mayor of New York *can* go somewhere: "Look, Jimmy Walker went to Europe; Bill O'Dwyer went to Mexico."

"You have to be a little crazy to take this job." [82]

Big-city mayors were occasionally still products of old-fashioned machine politics. This was exhibited in the career of Chicago's Mayor Richard J. Daley, who owed his election in 1955 and on four successive occasions to his one-man domination of a tightly articulated and controlled political machine. Daley followed the traditional path to boss control, working his way up from neighborhood club member to precinct captain to committeeman to state legislator to chairman of the Cook County Democratic Central Committee. Along the way he gained a reputation for intelligence, hard work, and expertise in the art of government finance. With the kind of influence in national politics that could win concessions for the city, he sponsored construction projects that not only produced patronage but gained him the support of the city's business leaders and minimized the force of the Republican opposition. Much of his political clout depended upon his mastery of the details of machine politics and his ability to foster his image as an invincible leader who could "get things done." [83] Some of the techniques he employed are revealed in this excerpt from journalist Mike Royko's biography of Daley, entitled *Boss*.

CHICAGO'S DALEY — MID-TWENTIETH-CENTURY BOSS AND MAYOR

From where Daley sits, alone atop the Machine, he sees all the parts, and his job is to keep them functioning properly. One part that has been brought into perfect synchronization is organized labor — perhaps the single biggest factor in the unique survival of the big city organization in Chicago. Labor provides Daley with his strongest personal support and contributes great sums to his campaigns. Daley's roots are deep in organized labor. His father was an organizer of his sheet-metal workers' local. . . . Daley grew up with Steve Bailey, who became head of the Plumbers' Union, and as Daley developed politically, Bailey brought him into contact with other labor leaders.

Thousands of trade union men are employed by local government. Unlike the federal government and many other cities, Chicago always pays the top construction rate, rather than the lower maintenance scale, although most of the work is maintenance. Daley's massive public works projects, gilded with overtime pay in his rush to cut ribbons before elections, are another major source of union jobs.

His policy is that a labor leader be appointed to every policy-making city board or committee. In recent years, it has worked out this way: the head of the Janitors' Union was on the police board, the park board, the Public Buildings Commission, and several others. The head of the Plumbers' Union was on the Board of Health and ran the St. Patrick's Day parade. The head of the Electricians' Union was vice-president of the Board of Education. The Clothing Workers' Union had a man on the library board. . . .

[Another] part of the Machine is money. Once again, only Daley knows how much it has and how it is spent. As party chairman, he controls its treasury. The spending is lavish. . . . The amount used for "precinct money," which is handed out to the precinct captains and used in any way that helps bring out the Democratic vote, can exceed the entire Republican campaign outlay. This can mean paying out a couple of dollars or a couple of chickens to voters in poor neighborhoods, or bottles of cheap wine in the Skid Row areas. . . . The money comes from countless sources. From the patronage army, it goes into the ward offices as dues, and part of it is turned over to party headquarters. Every ward leader throws his annual $25-a-head golf days, corned beef dinners, and picnics. The ticket books are thrust at the patronage workers and they either sell them or, as they say, "eat them," bearing the cost themselves. . . .

Contractors may be the biggest of all contributors. Daley's public works program has poured billions into their pockets, and they in turn have given millions back to the party in contributions. Much of it comes from contractors who are favored, despite the seemingly fair system of competitive bidding. In some fields, only a handful of contractors ever bid, and they manage to arrange things so that at the end of the year each has received about the same amount of work and the same profit. A contractor who is not part of this "brotherhood" refrains from bidding on governmental work. If he tries to push his way in by submitting a reasonable bid, which would assure him of being the successful low bidder, he may suddenly find that the unions are unable to supply him with the workers he needs. Even Republican businessmen contribute money to the Machine, more than they give to Republican candidates. Republicans can't do anything for them, but Daley can. . . .

If Daley's one-man rule bothers the men who sit on the [Cook County Democratic] Central Committee, they are careful to keep it to themselves. The meetings take on the mood of a religious service, with the committeemen chanting their praise of his leadership. . . . Only once in recent years has anybody stood up and talked back, and he was one of the suburban committeemen. . . . Lynn Williams, a wealthy manufacturer and probably the most liberal member of the Central Committee, had been angered by Daley's attacks on liberals after the 1968 Democratic Convention. Daley had been making speeches lambasting pseudoliberals, liberal-intellectuals, suburban liberals, suburban-liberal-intellectuals, and pseudoliberal-intellectual suburbanites. . . .

Williams, a strong supporter of young Adlai Stevenson, who had angered Daley with an attack on "feudal" politics, stood up, finally, at a Central Committee meeting and delivered a scathing rebuttal to Daley, saying that without liberal participation the party would be nothing but a skeleton, its only goal, power.

As he talked, the committeemen's heads swiveled as if they were watching a tennis game, wonder and fear on their faces. They had never heard such talk, and wondered what Chairman Daley would do. Strike him with lightning. Throw the bum out?

When Williams finished, Daley, in a surprisingly soft voice, said, "I've always been a liberal myself." Other committeemen joined in his defense, recalling countless liberal acts by Daley. . . . The shock of the committeemen at the sound of somebody criticizing Daley didn't surprise Williams. He has said: "Most of them are mediocrities at best, and not very intelligent. . . . Most are in need of slavery — their own — and they want to follow a strong leader."

In March 1970, the committeemen met for the purpose of re-electing Daley chairman. Alderman Keane nominated him and eighteen other committeemen made lengthy speeches seconding the nomination. One of them recited, "R, you're rare; I, you're important; C, you're courageous; H, you're heavenly; A, you're able; R, you're renowned; D, you're Democratic; J, is for your being a joy to know; D, you're diligent; A, you're adorable; L, you're loyal; E, you're energetic; and Y, you're youthful."

Once again Lynn Williams stood, but not to criticize. He, too, joined in the praise and made one of the seconding speeches. Daley had since slated young Adlai Stevenson III, whom Williams had supported, for the U.S. Senate. Daley and Williams even exchanged handshakes. In a way, Williams seemed to emphasize his own point about the committee's need to follow a strong leader.[84]

By the 1920's, effective municipal administration demanded the professional application of highly specialized mechanical techniques. The provision of urban services, already greatly broadened as a result of the progressives' expanded concept of municipal responsibility, was affected by the automotive and electronic revolution of the twentieth century. Just as technology, in producing the electric trolley, the subway, and the skyscraper, had promoted an adjustment to urban concentration by the turn of the twentieth century, so technology and engineering continued to devise methods of coping with the problems the increasing concentration of population presented. In Milwaukee, for example, a motorcycle police patrol had been adopted as early as 1910, and electric police and fire alarm systems were installed a year later. Motorized fire engines were in use by 1914, as was motorized street sweeping. Radio control of the motorized police was an innovation of 1930, with radio service to suburban police added in 1931. Water purification, using chlorine, was begun in 1910; after 1939, all water furnished by the city was subjected to complete filtration treatment.[85]

Electronic devices became important to another basic urban

problem — traffic control — as early as 1920, when automobiles already were numerous enough in cities to raise fears that "uncontrolled vehicles" might form "a mob . . . even more formidable than a mob of human beings." [86] In spring, 1920, New York City inaugurated an experimental system of traffic towers in the center of Fifth Avenue whose lights regulated the alternation of north-south and east-west traffic.[87] With the advent of television, by the 1950's, traffic engineers, using closed circuit TV and electronic communication, could control the flow of traffic on the throughways to and from a city's suburbs.[88]

8. METROPOLITAN GOVERNMENT

Big city management had become so complex and so frustrating by the mid-twentieth century as to give rise to a variety of proposals for restructuring urban government. Some municipalities were now so large that their government as single units seemed no longer possible; yet the proliferation of suburbs around the central cities further obstructed effective administration. The rise of these independent units not only deprived the core city of tax resources for facilities suburbanites used but also duplicated costs and hindered a unified approach to common problems of land use, traffic regulation, air pollution, and social engineering. Though the suburbs increasingly resisted annexation by the central city, this method of promoting administrative integration was sometimes used, as were city-county consolidation and voluntary agreements between the governments of central cities and those of the suburbs on such matters as the sharing of hospitals, fire and police protection, and the provision of water and gas. But efforts to organize viable metropolitan governments met with scant success, despite the intensification of interest by the 1950's in metropolitan regional planning.[89] The 1965 report of the Advisory Commission on Intergovernmental Relations, appointed by Congress in 1959 and made up of governors, congressmen, and mayors, blamed the fragmentation of government within metropolitan areas for the nation's failure to cope more effectively with the problems of its large cities.

METROPOLITAN GOVERNMENT —
CHALLENGE OF THE 1960's

Underlying many metropolitan problems is the failure of governmental institutions to come to grips with the growing interdependence of people and communities within metropolitan areas. As urban settlement spreads across lines of local jurisdiction, the cities and suburbs together come to comprise a single integrated area for living and working. People look for housing and employment within a broad region circumscribed more by the convenience of commuting and by personal preferences than by local government boundaries. . . . Local communities share many kinds of natural resources used for urban living: water supplies, drainage basins, recreation areas. They also share many manmade facilities that cut across local boundaries, such as highway and utility systems, and many other facilities that serve large segments of the metropolitan population, such as airports and commercial centers. These forms of interaction, together with the metropolitan character of housing and employment markets, create a broad area of common interest. The optimum use of shared facilities and resources calls for a high level of cooperation and for coordinated action by interdependent communities.

The policies of any one community typically have considerable impact in other parts of the metropolitan area. If one locality fails to control air or water pollution, its neighbors suffer. . . . Metropolitan service needs also provide compelling arguments for joint action. In such fields as water supply and sewage disposal, the cost of service per household can be reduced dramatically in large-scale operations by joint agreement of local governments. Similarly, areawide transportation systems — highways, public transit — require joint planning if they are to provide needed service at reasonable cost.

Despite the evident and important benefits of cooperative action in metropolitan areas, many local governments continue to go it alone. The realities of functional interdependence in metropolitan areas are in conflict with concepts of home rule that predate the age of metropolitan growth. Home rule in the contemporary metropolitan setting has often led to local isolation and conflict, to the detriment of the metropolitan population at large. . . . A major task for government in metropolitan areas is to develop policies consistent with the integrated character of the modern metropolitan community. . . .

Metropolitan areas are governed not only by traditional cities, towns, and counties, but also by a wide variety of special districts that overlap other boundaries. The complexity of local government can be illustrated by listing the array of local jurisdictions responsible for Park Forest, a suburb of Chicago, as of 1956: Cook County, Will County, Cook County Forest Preserve District, village of Park Forest, Rich Township, Bloom Township, Monee Township, Suburban Tuberculosis Sanitarium District, Bloom Township Sanitary District, Non-High School District 216, Non-High School District 213, Rich Township High School District 227, Elementary School District 163, South Cook County Mosquito Abatement District. . . . Public control of government policies tends to break down when citizens have to deal with a network of independent governments, each responsible for highly specialized activities. Even where good channels are developed for registering public concern, each government is so circumscribed in its powers and in the area of its jurisdiction that important metropolitan action is virtually impossible for local governments to undertake.[90]

Efforts to create a workable kind of municipal government coterminous with the metropolitan area were encouraged by the example of Toronto where a "metro" government was authorized in 1953. After a number of attempts, Dade County, Florida, which includes the flourishing city of Miami, achieved a comprehensive metropolitan government in 1957; Nashville, Tennessee, consolidated five counties under one jurisdiction in 1962; and in late 1969 a streamlined "Unigov" was authorized for the Indianapolis metropolitan area. By the move Marion County's wealthy suburbanites were absorbed into the Indianapolis tax base, and the city's boundaries were increased from 82 square miles to more than 400. Businessmen exerted a strong influence in achieving these "metro" governments; and that of Indianapolis owed its realization in considerable measure to the dynamism of its 37-year-old mayor, Richard Lugar.[91] The pioneering efforts of the proponents of metro government in Dade County brought the problem of metropolitan fragmentation into focus in the mid-1950's. These efforts were described in *Business Week* in November, 1956.

METRO GOVERNMENT FOR GREATER MIAMI: 1956

Greater Miami . . . , a concentration of 26 municipalities and thickly settled unincorporated areas in Dade County, last week moved a long step nearer to something no other U.S. metropolitan region has — an over-all government with power that crosses city and village lines. . . .

Few regions have grown so spectacularly as Metropolitan Miami in the postwar years. The growth, to a population estimated at more than 650,000, has been largely outside Miami itself. With one county government and 26 municipal governments, Greater Miami has been suffering from an anomaly: too many governments, not enough government. There has been no one body responsible for meeting the challenge of the area's rapid growth, and no one body able to do so if it chose. Sewage disposal in the area as a whole has been neglected to the point where Biscayne Bay, a scenic and recreational area, has been polluted. There isn't an expressway in the area, there's no arterial highway system, and traffic is badly congested. In the rush of expansion, the absence of a regional master plan has allowed vacant land to be passed over or developed for the wrong purposes. Communities buy and sell water among themselves. . . .

Dade County's interest in doing something about a unified attack on metropolitan problems goes back to the 1940's. The legislature approved a plan to form a single countywide school system; public health services, and Miami's Jackson Memorial Hospital, were transferred to the county. But the voters drew the line at city-county consolidation, put up for referendum in 1945 and 1947. Meanwhile, local governments continued to multiply. New residential areas — veterans' homes on the one extreme and the plushest winter estates on the other — incorporated as fast as they grew up. "Liquor license towns" were created — towns that wanted to regulate their own saloon hours and license fees. Other areas incorporated because they wanted to set their own zoning and building regulations — they found the county's code either too stiff or too lax for their own taste. Some areas incorporated as a defense against annexation by adjoining municipalities.

In the end it was the pollution problem that brought the issue to a head. The first step in 1950 was a recommendation of William L. Pallot, chairman of the Miami Public Works Board, for creation of a metropolitan sanitary district. State Sen. R. B. Gautier . . . began fighting for a metropolitan government. . . . In 1953, the third and last try was made to consolidate the government of Dade County and, this time, only the city of Miami. It lost in the city by only 980 votes. Pallot then published an open letter calling for concerted action along other lines, and the Miami City Commission created the Metropolitan Miami Municipal Board to study the whole situation.

In 1954, the new study group contracted with the University of Miami to oversee a survey of possible plans, and the university engaged the Public Administration Service of Chicago as consultant. The PAS report at the end of 1954 recommended a federation of governments, with modifications from the Toronto plan. The Dade County delegation, led by Sen. Gautier, opened a fight in the legislature for approval of a constitutional amendment granting home rule to Dade County and a bill permitting a charter to be drafted for metropolitan Miami.

What came out of the 1955 session of the legislature, however, was not what PAS had suggested. . . . As in many other states, the legislature is dominated by men from rural areas, where the county is the preeminent unit of government. The legislature wouldn't go along with the abolition of the county government, as proposed in the PAS plan. Instead the legislature approved a compromise that preserved the Board of County Commissioners and gave it . . . power to "do everything necessary to carry on a central metropolitan government." . . .

"We're living in a paradise on top of septic tanks," said one Miamian in commenting on the new approach to areawide problems. "There's not a mile of freeway or limited-access road. A dozen bridges must open every time a sailboat comes along, while we argue over whether to build tunnels or bridges. Nothing much has been done about downtown parking. You wouldn't expect a resort to be much concerned about government, but we do have new blood down here. You can see how the area is changing when the legislature lets us have home rule and the state goes for Eisenhower." [92]

"Metro" had its troubles from the outset, difficulties that sprang from the problem of reconciling the localism of the suburban units with the goal of achieving common metropolitan policies and regulation. Although the metropolitan government was given wide powers to solve traffic, sanitation, tax, and zoning problems, the means of their implementation was not made sufficiently clear, and positive action triggered resistance from the suburbs. The election of the county commissioners since 1963 on a countywide basis, in addition to the diffused and somewhat rootless nature of the population, prevented strong leadership from

459

developing. When the county manager attempted to be a policy maker, he found himself gagged by the commissioners, who symbolized the opposition to "metro" encroachment in local affairs.[93] The original city manager, who ultimately resigned under fire, foresaw the difficulties that continued to plague Miami's pioneering metropolitan government. His reactions shortly after he took office were reported by John Kay Adams in *The Rotarian* for April, 1959.

MIAMI'S "METRO" HAS ITS DIFFICULTIES: 1959

Orvin W. Campbell . . . was city manager of San Diego, California . . . when he was hired to take over the $35,000-a-year administration job in Dade County. The suburbs had been in open revolt for two months when Campbell sat down at his desk in the Dade County Court House. "There was a 'typhoon' around here when I arrived," said Campbell. "For six months the most constructive thing I could do was sit here and be calm." . . . He brushes aside most talk of a polite, go-slow approach that will protect the imaginary rights of every little bootleg village. "I don't think our cities have a choice," he said. "You can't handle this piecemeal. If you have critical problems, you have to build a whole structure, not just a chimney. You can't close your eyes to metropolitan problems. Perhaps you can proceed more slowly in some areas, but Miami can't wait. Dade County doesn't have one mile of freeway, despite the heavy demands of tourist traffic. Only one of three houses is connected to a sewer. Miami can't go any further unless it corrects these things." . . .

The first order of business for Campbell was to ease the fears of the municipalities that they would be summarily abolished. . . . "As long as a town or city doesn't have problems, we don't want to bother it," Campbell said. "But it must meet standards. If a police department does not provide law enforcement — if, for example, it permits vice — we intend to go in and police the area. We won't take over the department. We'll just do its job. We can do a city's work, but we can't abolish the city. This can be done only by a vote of the residents. When the people talk about suburban cities, most of them think about big entities. They forget about little towns of a few hundred or less which provide no service. They are set up to get around zoning controls or to obtain liquor licenses. We had one town with a population of 75 and a police force of 25. It was nothing but a speed trap."

Campbell is pressing hard for coordinated policing, zoning, and sewer and water improvements. . . . A uniform county-wide building code, the first, has been established. There is now county-wide licensing of building trades, better welfare services, and a reduction of county departments from 35 to 17. . . . "We won't have metropolitan government in Miami in a polished form for a decade," says Campbell. "But that doesn't mean we wait that long to begin." [94]

While some mid-century reformers were arguing for the extension of unified authority over an entire metropolitan area, others, especially in the nation's largest cities, were emphasizing the need for more neighborhood autonomy — "face-to-face government" — within the central city. Pressure for this change was encouraged by the widely held conviction that a sense of community was one of the chief casualties of large city growth. It was felt that some cities had become so unwieldy in size and so bureaucratized in administration as to prevent adequate citizen influence in connection with local services such as education, welfare, sanitation, and police. The desire for more community participation — even to the point of community "control" — was also a corollary of the growing assertion of Black and Puerto Rican identities in many large cities by the 1960's and of the resistance of white ethnic groups, especially in lower-middle- and middle-income neighborhoods, to citywide policies designed to achieve racial integration.

From the mid-1960's onward, a broad variety of proposals were advanced for decentralizing city government. These included such devices as neighborhood corporations, little city halls, and community districts with representation on city-wide boards or with responsibility, as in the case of decentralized education units, for decisions on local matters under the guidelines set up by central agencies. Proponents of neighborhood government differed on such matters as the appropriate size of the district, the methods of electing officers, and the extent of autonomy that should prevail. They agreed, however, that the size of a district should not be such as to preclude effective planning of community life and that cohesive neighborhoods should not be separated. At the same time, specialists in municipal administration saw no inconsistency in having decentralization within the central city and centralization at the regional level. Thus they advocated "metro" governments that would make possible a wider tax base and areawide controls, but at the same time neighborhood units sufficiently autonomous to guarantee a wider participation of the citizenry, and especially minorities, in the decision making process.[95]

A pioneer neighborhood corporation that by 1969 had served as a model for some 70 others was the East Central Citizens Organization of Columbus, Ohio, founded in 1965 in an area near the central business district and comprising about 6,500 residents, mostly Blacks. Its early activities were described by Milton Kotler of the Institute for Policy Studies in Washington, who served as its adviser.[96]

A NEIGHBORHOOD IN CHARGE OF ITS DESTINY — COLUMBUS, OHIO'S ECCO: 1969

The formal legal organization of ECCO is set forth in a democratic constitution. Under the bylaws . . . any resident at least sixteen years old who lives within the boundaries of the corporate territory can sign the roster and become a member. The fundamental authority of the corporation is derived from its membership, which meets in assembly to elect the council members and chairman, and to transact legislative business over the laws, programs, and budget of ECCO. Its assemblies require a quorum of 10 percent of the members; they have been legally convened nine times in the past three years. The Executive Council now has thirty members, elected both from the four neighborhood clubs (which existed before ECCO, and were re-formed to comprise four ECCO districts) and at large in an annual assembly. . . . The council has executive authority, and legislative power is vested in the assembly.

The current annual budget of ECCO is approximately $202,-947, consisting mainly of a grant from the U.S. Office of Economic Opportunity. A major program is the Youth Civic Center of ECCO, offering many youth activities in delinquency prevention, education, recreation, and job placement, and training in typing, shorthand, and crafts such as upholstering. The youth programs are governed by a youth committee of ECCO which has independence in the programming, management, and budgeting of their center. . . . Many other programs are now offered in ECCO, and the organization has a large full- and part-time staff. The programs of ECCO include educational projects, such as tutoring, nurseries for retarded children, day care, adult education, and community drives for greater local control of administration and management of the local public school in the ECCO territory. In the area of housing, ECCO has a co-operative code-enforcement program with the city government, and is purchasing houses for rehabilitation and leasing to the Metropolitan Housing Agency. In employment, it successfully demonstrated a new plan for operating the state employment service office locally. It is also employing residents in a new sewing center, which is already marketing products. In the field of health, it operates a program with the Public Health Service, and has developed a plan for its own twenty-four hour Health Clinic, emphasizing night service to meet the needs of residents who work during the day. . . . In the field of economic development, the organization has a credit union and has scheduled the opening of a supermarket. It also works closely with the federal Small Business Administration to finance local enterprise. . . .

For the first time, the residents legally decide certain matters of community life. They are steadily practicing the art of political decision-making and living with and learning from the consequences of their decisions. . . . The continuing strategy of ECCO is to develop new, independent programs and to reach agreement with the city for territorial jurisdiction over these public activities. Thus, it succeeded in becoming the exclusive antipoverty authority in its territory. . . . ECCO has also jurisdiction over the neighborhood public library, appointing the librarian and selecting books, while the city carries its costs. . . . ECCO residents are now orators and officials, and practical political wisdom is developing in a community where earlier the only expressions were frustration and escape.[97]

One of the many big-city plans for formalizing and legalizing neighborhood government was devised by the Citizens League (Twin Cities, Minnesota) in 1970. Its counterpart in New York City was a plan for neighborhood government of New York City, proposed at about the same time by the office of the mayor.[98] Excerpts from the Minnesota plan reveal the concern for minority representation that constituted a significant ingredient of the proposals for neighborhood governance.

"SUB-URBS" IN THE CITY —
TWIN CITIES, MINNESOTA: 1970

We recommend a double approach to the problem of citizen participation and minority representation by [urging] the Minneapolis City Council to support establishment of Community councils and amendment of the City Charter to provide for election of at-large aldermen. . . . Community councils should have the following powers: 1. *Appointment* of their own people to serve on citywide agencies. . . . 2. *Review and comment:* Community councils should be notified of all spot zoning changes, variances, permits, licenses and public improvements requested or proposed within their boundaries for their review, comment and recommendation within a reasonable period of time. 3. *Planning and resolutions:* Community councils . . . should initiate plans for the development of their areas and should hold public meetings for discussion of issues, and they may pass resolutions to be forwarded to the appropriate agency or governing body. . . . *Setting of boundaries.* A boundary commission, consisting of the chairmen of the City Council, School Board, Park Board, City Planning Commission, and Human Relations Commission, the Mayor, and a member of the County Board who is a resident of Minneapolis, should be established for the purposes of developing and setting boundaries for each Community council and its election districts. Suggested boundaries should reflect areas identified as communities, while election districts should be developed which will maximize the opportunity for election of minorities. The commission should act to fix the boundaries only after holding public hearings. . . .

Community councils should be made up of residents elected from small geographic districts and residents elected by a proportional vote from a combination of districts within the community. Aldermen and district-elected Park Board members should be ex-officio, non-voting members. . . . Members of the Community council should serve two-year terms and be elected in elections jointly with the city general election. . . . Each Community council should appoint an executive secretary who would be exempt from civil service and paid a salary not less than assistants to the City Council. The executive secretary should work under the direction of the Community council to represent it at public hearings, committee meetings of legislative bodies and act as the advocate for citizens of the community. He should consider citizen complaints and seek their resolution with appropriate public officials and agencies.[99]

The desire for regional and neighborhood government within the same area led to suggestions for two- or three-tier government that were being discussed in the early 1970's.[100] Alan K. Campbell, dean of the Maxwell Graduate School of Syracuse University, proposed a two-tier solution for the New York City metropolitan region in an article published in *The New York Times* in February, 1972.

TWO-TIER GOVERNMENT—"METRO" AND NEIGHBORHOOD RECONCILED — NEW YORK: 1972

The evident legitimacy of arguments for both centralization and decentralization underscores our need for a system which recognizes the validity of each. The present system denies both, particularly as they apply to the nation's largest urban areas. Metropolitan government without a second-tier, community level, deserves the criticism heaped upon it by advocates of community control. Critics of metro offer New York City as proof of the failure of this governmental form [a reference to the creation in 1898 of Greater New York, through adding Brooklyn and other neighboring communities to New York City].

New York metro is in trouble because, first, it has ceased being metropolitan. Its creation also destroyed smaller, well-knit communities within the boroughs. Complete restructuring of the New York system on a two-tier model would provide a system which, region-wide, would recognize the realities of fiscal disparities and technological imperatives alike. Certain services would be regionalized, while, simultaneously, communities with real power would be recreated within the city. Such a system could overcome functional and jurisdictional fragmentation, and open the entire region's tax base as a resource to meet needs that are concentrated in the region's disadvantaged areas. At the same time, a revised sense of local community identity and power could flourish without becoming the nostalgia for a romanticized small-town past which occasionally afflicts radical decentralizers.

Gathered within city boundaries are Gulliverian social problems that must be fought from a Lilliputian tax-base — a base at best staying level, at worst declining absolutely. A system embracing the entire metropolitan area, underpinned by community governments, will offer much greater potential political power to minority communities than our present system does. New coalitions across the region will become possible. Everyone in the region will share access to a growing tax base. The possibility of overcoming the present mismatch of resources to needs — a mismatch between city and suburbia as well as between high and low income suburbs will then be possible.[101]

The case against decentralization, either as implemented by neighborhood control or in conjunction with area-wide government, found expression in opposition to the proposed multi-tier rule for New York City. The opposition was stated in an open letter from ex-Mayor Robert F. Wagner and a group of businessmen, political leaders, and labor spokesmen, addressed in March, 1972, to Governor Nelson Rockefeller, Mayor John V. Lindsay, and the New York City Council. Excerpts from the letter follow.

THE DANGERS OF DECENTRALIZATION —
NEW YORK: 1972

The press has reported proposals to fragment the existing New York City government into several layers. One plan calls for a central city upper tier, five borough governments as a middle tier, and a "local" tier of 30 mini-governments. Any plan must be judged against the crying need for more and better city services for all its citizens and for more responsible government, not less. In our view this plan is a prescription for regression to days of ward rule and boss rule, of fragmentation and corruption. . . . Such a dismantling of the New York City government, and the efforts to reassemble it in a number of separate governments, . . . could probably before long amount to $1 billion annually in additional administrative costs. Further, to date, no proof has been adduced that all this additional cost and confusion would improve the delivery of services in any way. Without careful planning and testing, the new system would undoubtedly reduce the quality while increasing the costs of services. . . .

The weakening of the central authority which now rests in the office of the Mayor — who can be removed by the electorate if he fails to fulfill his function — would be a backward step which would wipe out not only all the gains of the charters of 1936 and 1961, but also practically every other improvement in city government during the past four decades. Domination of government by regionally parochial interests will result in "log-rolling" politics for the expense budget, the capital budget, the city plan, and other major functions. . . . Our City's critical need is for additional resources. This need will only be increased by the demands of decentralization. What is required is greater unity, not polarization and fragmentation. Dispersed city government, hastily created, will increase cost, cut services, and eliminate political responsibility and accountability.[102]

9. URBAN PROBLEMS

By the 1970's, when three out of every four Americans were city dwellers, increasingly identified with large cities and their environs, the conditions of city life had become virtually everyone's concern, and the alleged "crisis of the city" was a commonplace of popular discussion. In many ways, "crisis" has been an endemic condition of the nation's urbanism. No period in the nation's urban experience has lacked the "problem of the city," either in real or imagined form. Yet by the mid-twentieth century, the magnitude of many of the cities gave increased visibility and urgency to the situation.

Noise and congestion — traditional grounds for criticizing cities — were aggravated by the widespread use of the automobile. The era of predominant urbanism coincided with the automobile age; and by the early 1920's Americans were expressing concern over the problem of motor vehicles in cities. To a greater degree than earlier means of urban transit, the automobile demanded space for itself. Hence parking needs, traffic congestion, and the greater incidence of accidents because of speed and amateur operation of the vehicle were early a primary consideration in efforts to cope with the effect of the automobile on the city. Community planners, seeing in the automobile a potential means of dispersing population and thus relieving the residential crowding of the central city, nevertheless were concerned about its effect on congestion there. As early as the 1920's they talked in terms of widening streets, designating one-way thoroughfares, imposing zoning regulations to reduce traffic in business areas, and providing arterial highways to channel the flow of motor traffic to and from the suburbs. City dwellers had been subject to traffic regulation of a sort since colonial times; but parking ordinances and other proposals for coping with parking problems provided further examples of how the imperatives of city living led to encroachments on individual liberty and inspired municipal undertakings that competed with private enterprise.[103] The evolution of these developments in Baltimore from the early 1920's to 1940 was described in *The American City* by Wallace L. Braun, traffic engineer of the Baltimore Police Department.

467

PARKING — EARLY PROBLEM OF THE
"AUTOMOBILE AGE" — BALTIMORE: 1920–1940

As in most other cities in the United States, the streets in Baltimore were planned long before the advent of the motor car. These streets are as they were, no wider except in instances where some sidewalk width has been added to the street bed. Only in rare cases did such reconstruction add a full traffic lane in each direction. . . . Immediately after the first World War it was not unusual for a motorist to drive to his office or some store in the business district and find a place to park his car adjacent to his destination. After the day's work or after the longest shopping spree, the car was waiting unticketed where it had been left. What convenience! It probably never occurred to any of these early drivers that a time would come when he would be restrained by law from indulging in such practices.

As automobiles became more numerous, the demand for places to park along the curbs of the streets increased until it was not long before the available space within the business district was filled early each day. The overflow either had to park farther away, making it less convenient to drive one's car, or park double, thereby encroaching upon the moving traffic lanes and thus adding to the general traffic congestion. There can be no doubt that these conditions were a contributing factor in the decentralization of business activity experienced in the early 1920's.

The first attempt to control parking in Baltimore was to limit the time any vehicle was allowed to remain in a particular place. This limit was in most cases two hours. It is probable that the greatest benefits derived by such regulations accrued to the merchants, in that a greater turnover in the available spaces was accomplished. This provided an opportunity for more customers to park. It is doubtful that traffic congestion was improved by these regulations. On the contrary, it is probable that it suffered an increase in severity due to those drivers who, for one reason or another, were staying in the business district for a longer period than two hours, leaving one parking space after staying their time limit and driving around looking for another.

Prior to 1926 the Police Commissioner of Baltimore had assumed the authority to designate where and for what period of time parking was to be allowed. In that year, however, this authority was questioned by appeal to a higher court in the case of a conviction in the traffic court for a parking violation. It was found that such authority was unconstitutional and that parking regulations and the designation of one-way streets should be a function of the legislative body of the city. Immediately thereafter the City Council passed an ordinance embodying essentially all the regulations previously invoked by the Police Commissioner. Included in the ordinance then passed was the designation of that area of the city now known as the central business district. . . . The ordinance prohibited the parking of vehicles on 14 of the streets in the central business district between 7:30 A.M. and 9:30 A.M., and 4:30 P.M. and 6 P.M. In addition, parking was limited to two hours in any one block of the streets mentioned therein between the hours of 9:30 A.M. and 4:30 P.M. . . .

The business depression period beginning with 1930 caused quite a few buildings in the central business district to become vacant. When it was seen that there was no prospect of ever renting them again, the owners of many of the older ones had them razed in order to save taxes. Though the city has thus lost considerable income, it has relieved the parking problem, for in nearly every case the land was converted into parking lots. . . .

[The continuing enactment of parking ordinances since 1926] shows a definite trend towards the general elimination of parking in the central business district. But the elimination of parking is only a part of the solution. Mr. Motorist would still like to go from his home to the business area in the shortest possible time and find a place to park his car convenient to his destination for as long as necessary. . . . The provision of adequate terminal facilities should be a municipal function. It is probable that these facilities could be more efficiently located to the profit of both the motorist and the city government. The fee should be nominal, yet ample to defray the cost of operation and at the same time reimburse the city for loss in tax revenue resulting from the razing of the buildings occupying the sites required for these off-street parking facilities.[104]

By the 1960's, automobile traffic, like many cities, had got out of hand in terms of magnitude and manageability. Automobiles constituted the major mode of urban transportation, as early as the mid-century; by 1970 nearly two-thirds of all commuter work trips were made in private autos and 14 per cent by buses on highways.[105] The bumper-to-bumper congestion at rush hours and the carbon monoxide fumes that motor vehicles exude made the automobile one of the major aggravations of life in large cities. The seriousness of the problem and some of the solutions proposed for coping with it were discussed by Francis Bello in *The Exploding Metropolis,* a collection of essays compiled by the editors of *Fortune* magazine in 1958.

THE AUTOMOBILE AND THE CITY: LATE 1950's

Residents of New York City, Chicago, and Philadelphia — where downtown travel is overwhelmingly by public transit — may find it hard to appreciate how heavily most other American cities are dominated by the automobile. . . . In fifteen of the nation's twenty-five largest cities, 60 per cent or more of all riders entering the downtown business district arrive by automobile. In . . . Houston, Cincinnati, Kansas City, Dallas, and San Antonio — automobiles carry more than 70 per cent of all those riding into the heart of town. In New York City, by contrast, a scant 17 per cent use automobiles; 83 per cent use public transit. . . . [In the Los Angeles metropolitan area] about 95 per cent of all travel is by automobile — a figure unequaled in any other large city. . . .

As in Los Angeles, traffic engineers in practically every large city have found ways to move more vehicles through their city's streets than they had believed possible in the past. And all agree that much more can still be done. It may be possible to reserve certain streets exclusively for trucks, buses, or even pedestrians, and perhaps the use should vary with the time of day. . . .

Then there is the question of parking. No city ever seems to have enough. A number of big cities — among them San Francisco, Chicago, and Pittsburgh — have floated bond issues to finance large parking garages, which are usually privately operated. Many cities have also held stormy public hearings over proposed ordinances that would require builders to provide a prescribed amount of parking space with all new buildings. . . . The fact is that it will never be possible to provide parking space in the largest cities for all the motorists who want to come to them. There wouldn't be anything left worth coming to. If all of New York's transit riders drove in by automobile, for example, all of Manhattan below Fiftieth Street would have to be converted to multiple-deck parking garages.

There is one radical solution that is beginning to get a good deal of attention. Keep the cars out. Turn the central city into a pedestrian mall. Probably the boldest scheme built around this principle is one put forward recently by architect Victor Gruen, who is famous for proposing and designing J. L. Hudson's great shopping center, Northland, ten miles north of Detroit. Asked to prepare a redevelopment plan for downtown Fort Worth, Gruen proposed that the city should counterattack by adopting the most popular features of the suburban shopping center. His plan: let people drive up to the edge of the business center on spacious perimeter expressways, give them plenty of parking space, then make them get out and walk. Allow no cars at all in the central area — and endow it with so many eye-filling, imaginative, and compelling features that workers and shoppers would rather head for the heart of Fort Worth than anywhere else in Texas.

The area that would be closed off and redeveloped — preserving all important buildings — would embrace practically all of the present center of Forth Worth . . . roughly fifteen blocks square. Six large parking garages would thrust into the redeveloped area so that no garage would be more than three or four minutes' walk from the center. For those unable or unwilling to walk, Gruen proposes small, slow-moving electric shuttle cars; others have suggested moving sidewalks. All delivery trucks would be banished underground. Aboveground, there would be no exhaust fumes, honking horns, squealing brakes, or traffic lights — just throngs of happy people, making and spending money.[106]

Air pollution, to which the automobile was only one contributor, was another of the hazards of the industrial city that was reaching critical proportions by the mid-twentieth century. The image of Los Angeles had long been clouded by its smog-bound atmosphere; but by 1970, in other cities — especially New York — the combustion of sulfur-bearing fuels created admittedly unhealthful conditions during periods of poor air circulation. On Thanksgiving week-end in 1966, approximately 80 deaths in New York were attributed to the high levels of sulfur dioxide and other pollutants hovering over the city. Added to air pollution, as a count against the physical viability of large cities, was the increased accumulation of solid wastes — a result, in part, of the popular fascination with packaging. A study published in 1973 predicted that within five years nearly half of the nation's urban centers would run out of places in which to dump the 250 million tons of trash and garbage that annually accumulate in American cities.[107] Norman Mailer called New York's atrocious air "the first problem of our city," when, in a moment of exasperation with life in the metropolis, he raised the question, "Why are we in New York?" He made this query in an article that appeared in May, 1969, in *The New York Times Magazine.*

NORMAN MAILER ON AIR POLLUTION —
NEW YORK CITY "ETHERIZED": 1969

How is one to speak of the illness of a city? A clear day can come, a morning in early May like the pride of June. . . . It is hard on such mornings to believe that New York is the victim "etherized upon a table." Yet by afternoon the city is incarcerated once more. Haze covers the sky, a grim, formless glare blazes back from the horizon. The city has become unbalanced again. By the time work is done, New Yorkers push through the acrid, lung-rotting air and work their way home, avoiding each other's eyes in the subway. . . .

Recollect: When we were children, we were told air was invisible, and it was. Now we see it shift and thicken, move in gray depression over a stricken sky. Now we grow used to living with colds all year, and viruses suggestive of plague. Tempers shorten in our hideous air. The sick get sicker, the violent more violent. . . . It is the first problem of the city, our atrocious air. People do not die dramatically like the one-day victims of Donora, rather they dwindle imperceptibly, die five years before their time, 10 years before, cough or sneeze helplessly into the middle of someone else's good mood, stroll about with the hot iron of future asthma manacled to their lungs. The air pollution in New York is so bad, and gives so much promise of getting worse, that there is no solution to any other problem until the air is relieved of its poisonous ingestions. New York has conceivably the worst air of any city in the universe today — certainly it is the worst air in the most technologically developed nation in the world, which is to say it is the air of the future if the future is not shifted from its program. Once Los Angeles was famous for the liver-yellow of its smog; we have surpassed her.

That is our pervasive ill. It is fed by a host of tributary ills which flow into the air, fed first by our traffic, renowned through the world for its incapacity to move. Midtown Manhattan is next to impenetrable by vehicle from midday to evening — the average rate of advance is, in fact, 6 miles an hour, about the speed of a horse at a walk. Once free of the center, there is the threat of hour-long tie-ups at every bridge, tunnel, and expressway if even a single car breaks down in a lane. . . . All the while stalled cars gun their motors while waiting in place, pumping carbon monoxide into air already laden with caustic sulphur-oxide from fuel oil we burn to make electricity.

Given this daily burden, this air pollution, noise pollution, stagnant transport, all-but-crippled subways . . . every New Yorker sallies forth into an environment which strips him before noon of his good cheer, his charity, his calm nerve, and his ability to discipline his anger.[108]

The sounds of the city always differentiated it from the countryside; and though "city cries" and the rumble of traffic intrigued Americans of the early nineteenth century, the bearing of urban noise on the health of city dwellers was questioned as early as the 1890's. By the mid-twentieth century, the din of large cities had become so pronounced as to prompt the organization of pressure groups like Citizens for a Quieter City, Inc., and the appointment in New York City of a Task Force on Noise Control. Its report, published early in 1970, cited construction air-compressors and subways as "top noisemakers" that could produce "permanent hearing damage."[109]

Annoying as were the noise, traffic congestion, and air pollution that beset mid-twentieth-century urban dwellers, it was poverty and its consequences, especially crime, that increasingly were recognized to be the basic problem of the nation's big-city civilization. Poverty always was a fact of American urban communities; but it was not until the later nineteenth century that environment rather than human frailty was seen to be its major cause. Moreover, poverty often is not as pervasively visible as the manifestations of some of the other problems of life in large cities. It took until the mid-twentieth century for urbanization to produce in cities so manifest a segment of disadvantaged as to dramatize the close connection between poverty and the great urban dilemmas of crime in the streets, drugs, racial tension, run-down housing, lack of sanitation, and heavy welfare costs. By the 1960's, the War on Poverty, as conceived by President Kennedy and implemented by his successor, Lyndon B. Johnson, was based on the assumption that poverty — whatever its cause — was at the heart of the problem of the large city. The differences between the new urban poor and their nineteenth-century predecessors were described from this point of view by Michael Harrington in *The Other America*. This mid-twentieth-century counterpart of Jacob Riis's *How the Other Half Lives* (1890) was originally published in 1962.

MICHAEL HARRINGTON ON THE CITY AND THE "OTHER AMERICANS": 1960's

Where the ethnic slum once stood, in the "old" slum neighborhood, there is a new type of slum. Its citizens are the internal migrants, the Negroes, the poor whites from the farms, the Puerto Ricans. They join the failures from the old ethnic culture and form an entirely different kind of neighborhood. For many of them, the crucial problem is color, and this makes the ghetto walls higher than they have ever been. All of them arrive at a time of housing shortage . . . and thus it is harder to escape even when income rises. But, above all, these people do not participate in the culture of aspiration that was the vitality of the ethnic slum. . . .

In Chicago, an important element is the Negro; in St. Louis, the white sharecropper; in Los Angeles, the Mexican-American. . . . In New York City the minorities form an important part of the slum population. The Public Assistance recipients in the fifties included 31.3 per cent whites, 40.0 per cent Negroes, and 28.7 per cent Puerto Ricans. New York, with an estimated two million Negroes and Puerto Ricans in the metropolitan area, would show minority participation in the slum culture more dramatically than most cities. Yet, the Northern migration of Negroes is affecting almost every city outside the South (and the poor white farmers . . . are a major factor in many Midwestern and border-state cities).

There is a wall around these slums that did not exist before: the suburbs. The President's Civil Rights Commission in 1959 reported that the suburban zoning laws keep out low-income housing and force the poor to remain in the decaying, central area of the cities. The very development of the metropolitan areas thus has the tendency to lock the door on the poor. This becomes even more of a factor when one realizes how important color is in the new form of the old slums. . . . In this context, the decline of aspiration is partly a function of [the fact that] there *is* less opportunity than there was in the days of the huge ethnic slums. The people understand this even if they do not articulate it precisely.

Then, the ethnic slum usually centered upon a stable family life. The pattern of the slums of the sixties is "serial monogamy" where a woman lives with one man for a considerable period of time, bears his children, and then moves on to another man. . . . To be sure, the older ethnic slums produced their share of violence and gangsterism. Yet their family patterns, their value systems, their very access to the outside world provided a strong counterforce to the degradation of environment. In the new form of the slum, these checks are not so strong, and the culture of poverty becomes all the more powerful for that fact.

Lastly, the inhabitants of the slums of the sixties are regularly the victims of a bureaucratically enforced rootlessness. . . . The housing programs, and particularly the Urban Renewal activities of the mid- and late fifties, set off a migration within the cities. In 1959, for instance, the Mill Creek area of St. Louis was cleared as part of an urban renewal effort. In the place of a Negro slum there arose a middle-income housing development. Typically, the majority of those evicted were forced to find housing within the existing, and contracted, Negro ghetto. (In St. Louis 50 per cent of the families displaced disappeared from sight of the authorities altogether; of those whose movements are known, only 14 per cent found their way into low-cost projects.)

This constant movement makes it impossible for a community to develop in these slums. In 1958 a study in New York carried the poignant cry of an old resident in one of these transitional areas: "Nobody, not even an angel, can avoid trouble here! Too many people with no investment and no pride in the neighborhood! Too many just passing through! I feel sorriest for the kids — they've never known what a decent neighborhood is like!" [110]

The provision of work relief and a guaranteed minimum income were among the mid-century solutions proposed for countering the persistence of poverty in American cities. Proponents argued for government financing of permanent job programs, of the type that were regarded as temporary during the depression of the 1930's, suited to the great number of poor able to function only at the unskilled and semi-skilled levels. Wages for these jobs would have to be such as to provide incomes approximating the American standard. Proponents argued, too, for some method of providing a guaranteed minimum income (through a negative income tax or family allowance) to families in which the potential wage earner is incapable of earning an adequate income. These proposals posed the dilemma of how to provide "a reasonable income floor without at the same time significantly reducing the incentive of able-bodied persons to work." [111]

The close association between poverty and crime was demonstrated in mid-twentieth-century studies showing that the highest rates of crime and delinquency occurred in urban areas where incomes were lowest, houses most deteriorated, and families most disorganized, regardless of the ethnic and racial character of the inhabitants. In 1960 a slum area in Cleveland produced 22 major crimes per 1,000 population, whereas there were less than 10 per 1,000 in the city as a whole. In 1957 the inner core of Milwaukee, comprising fewer than 14 per cent of the city's population, produced 60 per cent of the adult arrests for murder, 48 per cent for rape, and 69 per cent for aggravated assault in the city as a whole.[112] Though American cities probably were less crime-ridden in the twentieth century than a century earlier, the decade of the 1960's saw a newsworthy upsurge in big-city crime rates. This resulted in part from the increasing size of large cities, the fluctuating populations of their inner core, temptations induced by the prevailing affluence in the economy, and the expanded use of drugs, especially among the disadvantaged elements in the population. As a consequence, there developed throughout the United States an unprecedented fear of crime on the streets of the nation's large cities.[113] Whether or not this fear was justified, it so damaged the image of the city as to augment the movement of middle-class city dwellers to the suburbs and to reduce the patronage of and support for many of the cultural institutions that traditionally contributed to the attraction of city living. Newspaper columnist Jimmy Breslin gave compelling expression to this feeling of insecurity and to the relationship of drugs to city crime in a political advertisement that appeared in *The New York Daily News* during the mayoral campaign of 1969, when he was running for president of the City Council.

JIMMY BRESLIN ON DRUGS
AND THE INSECURITY OF CITY LIFE: 1969

Like everybody else in the city of New York, I'm afraid of crime, and I hate what it has done to the life of the city. I still remember the night a junk pusher with a shotgun caught a detective named Pollins in a dark hallway and fired a couple of feet away. They took Pollins to the Hospital for Joint Diseases and this one little nurse tried so hard to help save him, but it was useless. At the end, exhausted, she stood in the doorway leading to the street and she refused to go home unless somebody drove her. She said a nurse could not go through the small park across the street from the hospital and come out alive.

This kind of feeling is everywhere in New York. The woman around the corner from me came home from shopping the other afternoon and a prowler was at her the moment she closed the front door and tried to kill her with a tire iron. A day later, my friend Mabel came home from scrubbing somebody else's floors all day and three of them pulled her into a doorway on Franklin Avenue in Brooklyn, took her purse, and then started punching. One of the punches left Mabel's ear damaged. Mabel is black. About 70 per cent of the crimes in this city are committed by minority people against other minority people. . . .

But it is either enormous ignorance or an enormous lie to tell people that 5,500 more policemen, strategically placed, will stop the crime in New York. For we in this city grow, in the soot and chipped plaster and spilled garbage of the ghetto, a breed of kids who have so much to give us, but are given so little of life to lead that some of them give up. They have nothing at home, and they sit in schools where white teachers don't know how to teach them, and when they think ahead, they see nothing. . . .

The trouble for the city of New York starts when these kids give up. Mindless, desperate, often deranged for want of heroin, they are the ones who are out stealing all over this city. . . . Narcotics is at the bottom of 60 per cent of the crime in this city. . . . Any man who claims he has an immediate, outright solution to the crime problem is a liar. Mention jail to these young people we worry about; particularly mention jail to the youngest of them; and they look at you and they laugh. Jail is a place they want to be able to say they come from.

And so they steal, these young guys do. Steal cars and purses and they steal in the daytime and they steal at night and they steal on the street or they come into your apartment and they use a knife or a lead pipe or even a gun. . . . And then these kids step out, which is street talk for going on a holdup, and they come into drugstores and liquor stores with pistols shaking in their wet hands and the clerks behind the counters have heart attacks and enough of them get slugged and shot to keep a city of eight million living in degrees of fear.[114]

The prevalence of crime and unruly behavior in American cities in the 1960's raised controversial questions, as they always had, concerning the maintenance of "law and order" and the role of the police. No longer adjuncts of political party organization, as they were in the nineteenth century, the twentieth-century police, like most other municipal servants in this "era of administration," were the products of special training and civil service appointment. The disorders of the 1960's emphasized the gap in background and temperament that existed between most policemen and those segments of the urban society in which difficulties were most likely to arise. In many instances the police, like other elements in large-city society, lacked a sense of community and found themselves alienated both from the city dwellers they were obliged to discipline and those they were supposed to serve.[115] The dilemma of the mid-twentieth-century police was discussed by Hallock Hoffman in *The Center Magazine*, a publication of the Center for the Study of Democratic Institutions, in Santa Barbara, California.

"LAW AND ORDER" IN THE CITY — THE DILEMMA OF THE POLICE: 1968

More and more Americans, white and black, have come to look on policemen as potential enemies. More and more policemen have come to feel that they work in hostile territory, surrounded by citizens on whom they dare not count for neutrality, let alone support. Efforts by policemen to do their jobs, as they understand them, precipitate riots; efforts by citizens to express opposition to public policies bring them too often under police violence. We have to ask whether the warfare between the citizens and the police results from the "system" — from the whole social arrangement of our society, of which the police are a part — or whether it is something that may be ameliorated by reforms of police regulations, training, recruiting, and administration. . . .

Policemen are agents for maintaining external order. . . . The evidence of good police work . . . is that no property is being damaged, and the people who count are not being hurt. To achieve this result, the policeman seeks signs of incipient violence to persons and property *before* the violence begins. He does this by looking for anything out of the ordinary — he is suspicious of the unusual, the out-of-the-way, and the extraordinary. This makes the policeman enforce the community "mores" as well as its laws. . . . The policeman identifies his work and his interests with those of the owners or controllers of property. They are usually the dominant persons in his community. They can cause him trouble, and get him advantage. This is only to say that the policeman fits into the American class system. In general, he is a lower-middle-class person; and his aspiring upward mobility appears to him to depend upon pleasing the upper-middle-class people for whom, in the main, he works.

Because of this identification, many ghetto crimes against persons are tolerantly dismissed by policemen as "that's the way *they* are," while damage of the ghetto property of non-ghetto landlords is treated as grave disorder. . . . But the forces of segregation and . . . economic privation have crammed minority populations into crowded and circumscribed areas of the major cities. They have made these areas explosive; they have also made the areas — from a police point of view — enclaves within which misbehavior and violence may be confined. . . . How can the policemen of our larger cities be equipped to meet these potential calamities? The easy answer, the one being given, is that they should have all the technically sophisticated arms now available in order to fight a major war — the kinds of arms that stun and sicken and incapacitate, rather than kill. . . .

Another kind of equipment would be possible. It would depend less on arms and more on moral power and better training and new policies. 1) Police departments could recruit large numbers of young men and women from among the deprived, and deploy them to protect each other and the ghettos. . . . Self-determination requires self-policing. 2) The police could be trained in nonviolence, and relieved of guns in connection with riot control. So far, guns have only started or escalated violence — they have not suppressed it. 3) Police could be specialized. Most of the center-city battles have been set off by arrests for minor offenses, including traffic offenses. . . . 4) Some policemen should be commissioned to buy or rent residences in troublesome districts and to become "neighborhood constables" there. They would aim to become integrated members of the community rather than to exist as "the authority." They would not replace other specialists — patrols in cars, detectives, narcotics agents, etc. — but would give local residents police support against those who would take advantage of them. . . . Police departments ought to be decentralized, both in operation and in control. . . . Communities should be encouraged to develop committees of oversight to see that the police are doing their jobs well. Such civilian oversight could do much to reduce the feeling that the police are brutal and abrasive. . . . Crowd- and riot-control squads could be specially trained, and policemen without this training should not be assigned to such work.

These suggestions may be useful for stirring up discussion. They are not "answers." . . . If we can keep an experimental turn of mind, and aim at de-escalating violence rather than at containing or preventing conflict . . . we will get to community-police relations that work.[116]

10. THE URBAN PROSPECT

Whatever the validity of contemporary police practice, police protection was only one of many urban services, coupled with mounting welfare expenditures, presenting costs which, as never before, threatened the fiscal stability of many of the nation's large cities. High taxes, as well as noise, traffic congestion, air pollution, racial tension, and physical insecurity, figured in the deteriorating image of the large city by the 1970's.[117] Yet most Americans did not want to reside far from sizable urban centers, and the long-lived debate concerning the relative merits of city and country went on. By the 1970's most Americans viewed conditions in large cities, not as contrary to nature (the view of opponents of cities in the early nineteenth century) but rather as a crime against nature. At the start of the twentieth century, most thoughtful Americans had accepted the city with all its faults, confident in the hope that these faults could be corrected. By the mid-century, they were less optimistic; some cities seemingly had become too large to make their redemption possible.[118]

There was hope for the city, nevertheless, in the persistence of the city-country debate and the continuing recognition of society's dependence on what cities traditionally had to offer. The debate was joined, in a 1971 version, by Eugene Raskin, adjunct professor of architecture at Columbia University, Samuel Tenenbaum, of Long Island University, and Richard Reeves, chief metropolitan urban affairs correspondent of *The New York Times.*

ARE OUR CITIES DOOMED?
"YES," SAYS RASKIN

It does not take 20–20 vision to see that our big cities are not merely in a state of crisis. They are dying. Inevitably. They are physically obsolete, financially unworkable, crime-ridden, garbage-strewn, polluted, torn by racial conflicts, wallowing in welfare, unemployment, despair and official corruption. . . . Urban planners and others who come up with temporary patchwork schemes . . . to keep the cities going another year or two or three are as pathetic as the officers of the Titantic charting tomorrow's course while the water rises above their ears. . . .

What were the needs that gave birth to cities? In admittedly oversimplified terms they were three: Defense — stout walls. . . ; Commerce — the exchange of goods, the gathering of artisans and professionals, the growth of industry; Excitement — the stimulation of varied contacts, new people and experiences, the lure of the bright lights. . . . Today, in the final decades of the twentieth century, it is abundantly clear that cities can no longer meet these needs. . . . On the contrary, it is exactly in these main areas that the city fails most conspicuously.

Defense? A farce. In the era of intercontinental missiles defense is the last thing a city is good for. A city is a prime target, as was made entirely evident during World War II. . . . Commerce? Laughter from the wings. It is hardly a secret that businesses and industries by the dozens are moving out of town as fast as they can go. . . . Excitement? Too much, and of the wrong kind. The average city dweller hurries from his job . . . or from his rich, full day on the welfare line, happy if he makes it home to his police lock without being mugged and without finding his flat burglarized. . . . Even the non-average person (the one with lots of money) is finding the city less rewarding each year. His limousine can't get through the clogged streets; the once chic restaurants are deteriorating or closing; the nightclubs are practically all gone. . . .

The finest values of the urban center are just beginning to be seen . . . the place of Culture, of concerts, ballet, opera, museums, film festivals, of conventions and expositions, and of governmental facilities. . . . But "Exposition City" as one might name the urban center of the future . . . can be manned by a small fraction of the present teeming and miserable millions. Where will the rest go? They will go where they are going already — those who can, that is, . . . out of town, to live near their Industrial Parks, in their Adult Villages, their Young Ideas Towns, their Smoky Hills, their Retirement Communities, their Resorts, their Farms, and don't look now, yes, their Communes.[119]

ARE OUR CITIES DOOMED?
"NO," SAYS TENENBAUM

From the outset, it should be said that the city and civilization go together, that cities are the breeding places of civilization. . . . Talk about depopulated cities is idle and without foundation. Cities are increasing at enormous bounds, and the present movement to cities is as strong as it ever was. . . . By and large, in cities man lives with more ease, with more comfort, and probably with greater physical safety. Where can one duplicate the variety of foods available to him, or the purity of the city's milk and water supply; or the professional skills of its hospitals; or the multiplicity of institutions to serve his spiritual and cultural needs? . . .

Where can he achieve better? What better place for the panoply of ceremony and high emotion? Where else can man better find congenial spirits to meet his social needs? Where else can he find more varied markets for his talents and abilities? Where else can he have such freedom to differ and not be a pariah? . . . Where else can he better obtain the encouragement and the sense of personal triumph that come with success? Where else can he better find others to join him in common enterprise but in a city, built by man for man, the product of his intelligence, in which every part displays man's intelligence? [120]

ARE OUR CITIES DOOMED?
"NOT NECESSARILY," SAYS REEVES

The cities *are* dying, but somehow it is hard to visualize parents leading their children up the Empire State Building like the Sun Pyramid of Teotihuacán. It is easier, but not much, to imagine families searching for bits of pottery — or plastic and aluminum — after paying their $1 to a National Park Service man to wander through the grassy ruins of Detroit or Newark. Cities are dying of neglect, . . . the neglect of 200 celebrated years of American heritage and history. . . .

"I think our governments will remain virtuous for centuries as long as they are chiefly agricultural," Jefferson wrote. "When they get piled upon one another in large cities, as in Europe, they will become as corrupt as in Europe." . . . Skip 150 years to the New Deal agricultural recovery acts of the nineteen-thirties, which led to consolidation and mechanization of the farms, which led to the migration northward of field hands and share-croppers, black and white, unskilled, uneducated, unable to cope with an urban society.

The nineteen-forties brought the Federal Housing Administration, which subsidized the flight to the suburbs by the urban middle class and eroded the cities' tax base. The nineteen-fifties produced the National Defense Highway Act — heaven knows what it was defending — which made it so much easier for factories and shopping centers to desert downtown. I am not saying that these things were not necessary, perhaps desirable. But someone in Washington might have noticed what they were doing to the cities. Perhaps the Congressman from northern California might have noticed, the one who asked me recently: "Whatever happened to Harlem? Boy, I can remember when you used to go up there for a good time, the dancing and all."

All this is prologue to saying that there is a solution, that Professor Raskin goes too far in pronouncing the patient dead — although Professor Tenenbaum probably oversteps a bit in comparing Detroit with Athens. The solution is in Washington. The nation must notice its cities — and it *will* notice because a city or two will go bankrupt and there will be more welfare, more drugs, more crime, more riots. It's a trite solution: more money. I like the way it was put by Arthur Natfalin, the former Mayor of Minneapolis who now teaches at the University of Minnesota. He suggested that the cities just surrender — "We've lost the war, now rebuild us like Germany and Japan."

That's it. We were beaten by a great strategy. Washington and the state capitols decreed long ago that the cities would raise money by property taxes and would have to provide a few essential property services . . . pick up the garbage and put out the fires. Then the cities were left to educate the children, build hospitals, shelter, clothe and feed the poor, stop crime and deal with new problems, such as drugs. . . . The cities *are* dying. And they will go on dying until the Federal income tax is used to pay for the solutions to national problems. . . .

How much Federal money is needed? Not $11-billion, the amount proposed by President Nixon. No, we are talking about a Government that subsidized 10 million F.H.A. homes, that spent $60-billion on those defense highways. The daily costs of Vietnam, Cambodia and Laos hardly need to be mentioned. Most of the money will have to go for education and easing the cities' welfare burden. More than money is needed, however. The creativity of the nation is necessary — the United States has to figure out how to make an urban society work. . . .

The solutions to the cities' ailments are available, both at home and in Washington. It is inconceivable that they will not be found although the cure will change the cities and their functions. . . . Some day the people in the cities and Washington are going to get together to diagnose the ailment. And some day the people of New York, Detroit and Newark may get together to march on Washington. If enough of them do, a certain Congressman from California may be able to figure out what happened to Harlem.[121]

As of the early 1970's, the city constituted the nation's major domestic problem. The size of many of the largest cities was at the heart of the difficulty, in terms both of their governance and of the costs of management; and population specialists continued to argue for channeling migration or relocating population in ways that would keep urban communities within population limits conducive to democratic control and efficient administration.[122] A hard reality was the need for money to meet the social imperatives of urban societies, such as housing and welfare, as well as the costs of urban services, at a time when much was expected of local government and when inflation plagued the economy. The continuing flight to the suburbs deprived the central city of potential tax revenue and sharpened the distinctions between the society of the inner city and that of the suburban ring, though by 1970 the suburbs were growing so fast that they threatened soon to recapitulate many of the problems of the central city.

The subordination of cities in the nation's federal-state structure (despite the magnitude of urbanism) affected the speed with which national solutions could be found for the problems of the city, as did the play of politics and the prevailing attitude toward city dwellers of administrations in power at the federal and state levels.[123] The war in Vietnam took precedence over the "war" on poverty. In the face of both inflation and recession, joblessness increased; yet in part because of inflation President Nixon was constrained to veto legislation that might have coped with the situation. Public willingness to face up to urban problems was affected also by the paradox of large-scale urbanism, with its need for collective and associative regulatory action, in a society that customarily has put a strong premium upon individual and family autonomy, at least in times of security, and which traditionally has been fragmented by the physical mobility and the ethnic and racial variety of its population.

Nevertheless, by the second half of the twentieth century, the American public seemed to be increasingly convinced of the inevitability of the continuing urbanization of American society and increasingly sensitive to the importance of the central city and its problems to the welfare of the metropolitan cluster, however wide the dispersal of population to its fringes. There was increasing evidence, too, of a growing conviction that the federal government should assume broader responsibility for the problems of urban America, by supplying fiscal assistance to central cities, in view of the concentration of dependent elements there; by encouraging experimentation with methods of insuring clean air, pure water, more open space, residential integration, and adequate police protection in large cities; and by undertaking to enforce the implementation of these goals, once such methods were settled upon. Hopeful signs were the enactment of federal revenue sharing, in 1972, the smog-fighting transportation controls proposed in 1973 as a means of implementing the Clean Air Act of 1970, and the recommendation in 1973, by a New York State commission, of zoning standards that would, in effect, make it impossible for suburban communities to impose zoning barriers against the in-migration of members of minority groups, desirous of leaving the central city.[124]

By 1970 specialists in urban affairs were stressing the need for a national urban policy within the context of which the federal, state, and local governments could attempt to cope with the economic and social realities of the contemporary urban scene. One policy statement was formulated by Daniel P. Moynihan, professor of education and urban politics at Harvard University and former director of the Urban Affairs Council in the administration of President Richard M. Nixon. Moynihan presented this proposal in an article entitled "Toward a National Urban Policy," originally published in the Fall, 1969, issue of *The Public Interest*. His ten points, scaled, he said, "roughly to correspond to a combined measure of urgency and importance," reflect the wide dimensions of the nation's contemporary urban problems and its broadened expectations concerning the role of the federal government in urban affairs.

"TOWARD A NATIONAL URBAN POLICY": 1969

1. The poverty and social isolation of minority groups in central cities is the single most serious problem of the American city today. It must be attacked with urgency, with a greater commitment of resources than has heretofore been the case, and with programs designed especially for this purpose. . . .

2. Economic and social forces in urban areas are not self-balancing. Imbalances in industry, transportation, housing, social services, and similar elements of urban life frequently tend to become more rather than less pronounced, and this tendency is often abetted by public policies. A concept of urban balance may be tentatively set forth: a social condition in which forces tending to produce imbalance induce counterforces that simultaneously admit change while maintaining equilibrium. It must be the constant object of federal officials whose programs affect urban areas — and there are few whose do not — to seek such equilibrium. . . .

3. At least part of the relative ineffectiveness of the efforts of urban government to respond to urban problems derives from the fragmented and obsolescent structure of urban government itself. The federal government should constantly encourage and provide initiatives for the reorganization of local government in response to the reality of metropolitan conditions. The objective of the federal government should be that local government be stronger and more effective, more visible, accessible, and meaningful to local inhabitants. To this end the federal government should discourage the creation of paragovernments designed to deal with special problems by evading or avoiding the jurisdiction of established local authorities, and should encourage effective decentralization. . . .

4. A primary object of federal urban policy must be to restore the fiscal vitality of urban government, with the particular object of ensuring that local governments normally have enough resources on hand or available to make local initiative in public affairs a reality. . . .

5. Federal urban policy should seek to equalize the provision of public services as among different jurisdictions in metropolitan areas. . . .

6. The federal government must assert a specific interest in the movement of people, displaced by technology or driven by poverty, from rural to urban areas, and also in the movement from densely populated central cities to suburban areas. . . .

7. State government has an indispensable role in the manage-

ment of urban affairs, and must be supported and encouraged by the federal government in the performance of this role. . . .

8. The federal government must develop and put into practice far more effective incentive systems than now exist whereby state and local governments, and private interests too, can be led to achieve the goals of federal programs. . . .

9. The federal government must provide more and better information concerning urban affairs, and should sponsor extensive and sustained research into urban problems. . . .

10. The federal government, by its own example, and by incentives, should seek the development of a far heightened sense of the finite resources of the natural environment, and the fundamental importance of aesthetics in successful urban growth.[125]

NOTES

PART ONE

1. The determination. of the degree to which New England towns were "urban" depends on how one defines "urban." For example, Gerard Warden questions whether Boston should be called "urban" in the later seventeenth-century in view of the fact that its population hardly exceeded 6,000. He suggests that as late as 1776 it could more appropriately be called "a large town than . . . a modern city." Gerard B. Warden, *Boston, 1689–1776* (Boston: Little, Brown, 1970), 15–17. See Conrad M. Arensberg, "American Communities," *American Anthropologist,* LVII (December, 1955), 1148–51; Michael Zuckerman, *Peaceable Kingdoms: New England Towns in the Eighteenth Century* (New York: Alfred Knopf, 1970), 4, 8, 12, 35, 47, 71, 116; Kenneth A. Lockridge and Alan Kreider, "The Evolution of Massachusetts Town Government, 1640 to 1740," *William and Mary Quarterly,* Third series, XXIII (October, 1966), 555–56, 569–70; Carl Bridenbaugh, "The New England Town: A Way of Life," American Antiquarian Society, *Proceedings,* LVI (1946), 19–48; Sumner C. Powell, *Puritan Village: The Formation of a New England Town* (Garden City, N.Y.: Doubleday, 1965); Edward M. Cook, "Local Leadership and the Typology of New England Towns, 1700–1785," *Political Science Quarterly,* LXXXVI (December, 1971), 586–608; William Haller, Jr., *The Puritan Frontier, Town-Planting in New England Colonial Development, 1630–1660* (New York: Columbia University Press, 1951); Philip J. Greven, Jr., *Four Generations: Population, Land, and Family in Colonial Andover, Massachusetts* (Ithaca: Cornell University Press, 1970); Sam Bass Warner, Jr., *The Urban Wilderness: a History of the American City* (New York: Harper and Row, 1972), 8–14.

2. Carl Bridenbaugh, *Cities in the Wilderness: The First Century of Urban Life in America, 1625–1742* (New York: Ronald Press, 1938), 6n, 143n, 303n; Carl Bridenbaugh, *Cities in Revolt: Urban Life in America, 1743–1776* (New York: Alfred Knopf, 1955), 5, 216–17. For fuller statistics on the population of colonial towns and cities, see Evarts Greene and Virginia D. Harrington, *American Population before the Federal Census of 1790* (New York: Columbia University Press, 1932) and Stella H. Sutherland, *Population Distribution in Colonial America* (New York: Columbia University Press, 1936).

3. Darrett B. Rutman, *Winthrop's Boston: Portrait of a Puritan Town, 1630–1649* (Chapel Hill: University of North Carolina Press), 4, 68; Rollin G. Osterweis, *Three Centuries of New Haven, 1638–1938* (New Haven: Yale University Press, 1953), 12. For the characteristics of a town that remained primarily agricultural, see Kenneth A. Lockridge, *A New England Town: The First Hundred Years: Dedham, Mass., 1636–1736* (New York:

489

Norton, 1970). The nature of the covenanted community and its relationship to the multiplication of towns in the United States are well developed in Page Smith, *As A City Upon A Hill: The Town in American History* (New York: Alfred Knopf, 1966). For the pattern of the New England village, see John W. Reps, *Town Planning in Frontier America* (Princeton: Princeton University Press, 1969), 145–62. Reps writes: "As in other New England communities the village of New Haven formed one part of a rural-urban community unit." p. 159. See also Anthony N. B. Garvan, *Architecture and Town Planning in Colonial Connecticut* (New Haven: Yale University Press, 1951).

4. Samuel Maverick, "A Briefe Discription of New England and the Severall Townes therein, together with the Present Government thereof," Massachusetts Historical Society, *Proceedings*, second series, I (1884–1885), 235–38, 245.

5. *Ibid.*, 235–36, 238–39, 245. Benjamin Labaree, in *Patriots and Partisans: The Merchants of Newburyport, 1764–1815* (Cambridge: Harvard University Press, 1962), pp. 1–5, describes the way the town of Newburyport was differentiated, as a result of urban activities, from the town of Newbury. John Josselyn, an English traveler, describing the New England of 1663, remarked upon the many "Sea-Towns twenty and thirty miles distant from one another," eastward from what is now New York: "*Westchester . . . Greenwich . . . Chichester, Fairfield, Stratford, Milford . . .* Newhaven the Metropolis of the [Connecticut] Colony." John Josselyn, *An Account of Two Voyages to New-England* (London: G. Widdowes, 1675), reprinted in Massachusetts Historical Society, *Collections*, third series, III (Cambridge: E. W. Melcalf, 1833), 314–15.

6. Rutman, *Winthrop's Boston*, 200; [Edward] *Johnson's Wonder-working Providence, 1628–1651*, ed. by J. Franklin Jameson (New York: Scribner's Sons, 1910), 71. Johnson describes the founding of many New England towns; his description of the establishment of the town and church of Woburn provides full detail on the way towns were authorized and laid out and on the nature of the covenant on which they were based. *Ibid.*, 212–16.

7. "Description of the Towne of Mannadens, 1661," in *Narratives of New Netherland*, ed. by J. Franklin Jameson (New York: Scribner's Sons, 1909), 421–23. See also Daniel Denton, *A Brief Description of New-York: Formerly Called New-Netherlands. With the Places thereunto Adjoyning* (London, 1670: Facsimile Text edition, ed. by Victor Paltsits); Wayne Andrews, ed., "A Glance at New York in 1697: The Travel Diary of Dr. Benjamin Bullivant," *New-York Historical Society Quarterly*, XL (January, 1956), 55–73; Bayrd Still, *Mirror for Gotham: New York as seen by contemporaries from Dutch days to the present* (New York: New York University Press, 1956), Chaps. 1 and 2.

8. Samuel Hazard, *Annals of Pennsylvania from the Discovery of the Delaware* (Philadelphia: Hazard and Mitchell, 1850), 516–17.

9. Reps, *Town Planning in Frontier America*, 204–13. As in the pattern for the New England town, each settler was entitled to a farm in the "liberty lands" outside the city, as well as to one or more lots within the city boundaries.

10. *Ibid.*, 211. See Hannah B. Roach, "The Planting of Philadelphia, a Seventeenth-Century Real Estate Development," *Pennsylvania Magazine of History and Biography*, XCII (1968), 3–47, 143–94.

11. William Penn, *A Further Account of the Province of Pennsylvania*

(London, 1685), in Albert C. Myers, ed., *Narratives of Early Pennsylvania, West New Jersey and Delaware, 1630–1707,* (New York: Scribner's Sons, 1912), 260–62.

12. Sam Bass Warner, Jr., *The Private City: Philadelphia in Three Periods of Its Growth* (Philadelphia: University of Pennsylvania Press, 1968), 11; James T. Lemon, "Urbanization and the Development of Eighteenth-Century Southeastern Pennsylvania and Adjacent Delaware," in *William and Mary Quarterly,* Third series, XXIV (October, 1967), 504–508, 510–12, 528–33; James T. Lemon, *The Best Poor Man's Country* (Baltimore: Johns Hopkins Press, 1972), 118–49; Clarence P. Gould, "The Economic Causes of the Rise of Baltimore," in Anon., *Essays in Colonial History Presented to Charles McLean Andrews by His Students* (Freeport, N.Y.: Books for Libraries Press, 1966; first published, 1931), 225–51.

13. "Instructions . . . for the intended voyage to Virginia," as quoted in Reps, *Town Planning in Frontier America,* 108; *ibid.,* 107–29; John C. Rainbolt, "The Absence of Towns in Seventeenth-Century Virginia," *Journal of Southern History,* XXXV (August, 1969), 350–56, 360; Edward M. Riley, "The Town Acts of Colonial Virginia," *Journal of Southern History,* XVI (August, 1950), 306–23; Carl Bridenbaugh, *Seat of Empire* (Williamsburg: Colonial Williamsburg [1950]); Jane Carson, *We Were There: Descriptions of Williamsburg, 1699–1859, Compiled from Contemporary Sources . . .* (Williamsburg: Colonial Williamsburg, 1965).

14. "An Account of the Present State and Government of Virginia," Massachusetts Historical Society, *Collections,* first series, V (1798), 124–25, 128, 129–30. The authors were Henry Hartwell, James Blair, and Edward Chilton. The more accurate title for this work, discovered after publication by the Massachusetts Historical Society, is *Large and True Account of the Present State of Virginia.*

15. [Francis Makemie], *A Plain & Friendly Perswasive to the Inhabitants of Virginia and Maryland For Promoting Towns & Cohabitation. By a Well-Wisher to Both Governments* (London: John Humfreys, 1705), reprinted in *The Virginia Magazine of History and Biography,* IV (1896–97), 261–64, 271.

16. Reps, *Town Planning in Frontier America,* 141. The law establishing Williamsburg was "the most detailed town planning law yet adopted in the colonies. . . . The principal street, Duke of Gloucester Street, was named in the act. All houses built on this street were to be set back six feet and to 'front alike.' For other streets the directors of the town were authorized to adopt rules and orders governing dwelling size and setbacks." *Ibid.,* 139.

17. Hugh Jones, *The Present State of Virginia* (New York: Reprinted for Joseph Sabin, 1865), 25–26, 35.

18. Maurice Mathews, "A Contemporary View of Carolina in 1680," *South Carolina Historical Magazine,* LV (July, 1954), 154.

19. Reps, *Town Planning in Frontier America,* 238–60.

20. Francis Moore, *A Voyage to Georgia, Begun in the Year 1735* (London: Printed for Jacob Robinson, 1744), 24–25, 28–31.

21. "New-Jersey Reader," in *The New-York Gazette: or, The Weekly Post-Boy,* March 19, 1753.

22. "A brief Consideration of NEW-YORK, with respect to its natural Advantages: Its Superiority in several Instances, over some of the neighbouring Colonies," *The Independent Reflector,* January 18, 1753. For detail on this publication, see Milton M. Klein, ed., *The Independent Reflector or*

Weekly Essays on Sundry Important Subjects More particularly adapted to the Province of New-York (Cambridge, Mass.: Belknap Press, 1963).

23. L. H. Butterfield, ed., *Diary and Autobiography of John Adams* (Cambridge, Mass.: Belknap Press, 1961), I, 54, 80–81.

24. L. H. Butterfield, ed., *The Earliest Diary of John Adams* (Cambridge, Mass.: Belknap Press, 1966), 99. The editor remarks that the word "pretty," as inserted in the last line, is a matter of the "merest guess" inasmuch as "this word is almost entirely worn away in the margin of the MS. *Ibid.,* 100.

25. Sam Bass Warner, Jr., "If All the World Were Philadelphia," *American Historical Review,* LXXIV (October, 1968), 30.

26. Bernard Bailyn, *The New England Merchants in the Seventeenth Century* (Cambridge: Harvard University Press, 1955), 36–37, 105–8, 139–42.

27. Adolph B. Benson, *The America of 1750: Peter Kalm's Travels in North America* (New York: Dover Publications, 1964), I, 134–36. See also I, 18, 20, 25, 27–28, 30, 33, 130–32.

28. Stuart Bruchey, ed., *The Colonial Merchant* (New York: Harcourt, Brace and World, 1966), 172.

29. W. T. Baxter, *The House of Hancock: Business in Boston* (Cambridge: Harvard University Press, 1945), 86–87.

30. Carl Bridenbaugh, *The Colonial Craftsman* (New York: New York University Press, 1950), *passim.*

31. The advertising pages of *The New-York Gazette* for the mid-1750's contain many notices of the sale of Negro slaves; rewards for runaway servants of Irish, Scottish, or German birth; rooms for rent and houses and stores for rent or sale in New York City and farm lands for sale in neighboring New Jersey; artisans' services, especially tailors'; sales, by vendue or at stores, of grain, pork, and tar, and of imports, such as European and India dry goods, books, and West Indies sugar and molasses. A "snow" was a square-rigged vessel differing from a brig only in having a trysail toward the stern from the mainmast. "Ducap" is a heavy corded silk.

32. *The American Weekly Mercury* (Philadelphia), October 10–17, 1734, carried the following advertisement, printed in German: "This is to inform Germans who live here and in the country nearby that opposite the jail in Market Street in the pharmacy called Paracelsis-Kopf, where the pharmacist Mr. Evan Jones formerly resided, all chemical preparations will henceforth be available, as well as Galenish medicines, court plaster, salves, powders, and similar items. Prices are very reasonable. Dispensed by William Shippen, chemist."

33. Bridenbaugh, *Cities in the Wilderness,* 408–10; Bridenbaugh, *Cities in Revolt,* 333–34. In a diary entry for September 3, 1729, Newport clergyman John Comer reported the existence of a night watch in Boston, set up "because in ye last week in July a mob rose to prevent ye landing of Irish." *The Diary of John Comer,* ed. by C. Edwin Barrows, Rhode Island Historical Society, *Collections,* VIII (1893), 78.

34. *Records of Boston Selectmen, 1716 to 1736,* in *A Report of the Record Commissioners of the City of Boston* (Boston: Rockwell and Churchill, 1885), 29, 200, 312–13, 318; *Boston Records from 1700 to 1728,* in *A Report of the Record Commissioners of the City of Boston* (Boston: Rockwell and Churchill, 1883), 176–77.

35. The records of the Boston town government, especially during the 1720's, contain many evidences of proscriptive legislation concerning Indians,

Negroes, and mulattoes, such as special regulations concerning burial, provisions for street work in lieu of jury duty, restraints on carrying sticks or canes, day or night, and limitations on freedom of contact between free Blacks and slaves. *Ibid.*, 115, 173 ff., 223.

36. Bridenbaugh, *Cities in the Wilderness*, 48, 163, 249, 411; Bridenbaugh, *Cities in Revolt*, 88; Jackson T. Main, *The Social Structure of Revolutionary America* (Princeton: Princeton University Press, 1965), 36, 41, 60, 185–89, 195, 282; Bailyn, *The New England Merchants in the Seventeenth Century*, 194–95; James A. Henretta, "Economic Development and Social Structure in Colonial Boston," *William and Mary Quarterly*, Third series, XXII (January, 1965), 75–92; Raymond A. Mohl, "Poverty in Early America, A Reappraisal: The Case of Eighteenth-Century New York City," *New York History*, L (January, 1969), 5–27. Henretta writes: "By the third quarter of the 18th century, an integrated economic and political hierarchy based on mercantile wealth had emerged in Boston to replace the lack of social stratification of the early part of the century and the archaic distinctions of power and prestige of the religious community of the seventeenth century. All the important offices of the town government, those with functions vital to the existence and prosperity of the town, were lodged firmly in the hands of a broad elite, entry into which was conditioned by commercial achievement and family background. The representatives to the General Court and the selectmen were the leaders of the town in economic endeavor as well as in political acumen." 89–90. In spite of the differences in economic status of Bostonians by the mid-eighteenth century, they "still retained a remarkable sense of community spirit, a familiarity with one another that transcended the class or economic lines which divided larger European towns. There were very rich people and very poor people in Boston, but very few insuperable barriers between them." Warden, *Boston, 1689–1776*, p. 25.

37. John Adams, visiting Philadelphia in 1774, reported: "The Regularity and Elegance of this City are very striking." *Diary and Autobiography*, II, 116. Of New York City he wrote in the same year: "With all the Opulence and Splendor of this City, there is very little good Breeding to be found. We have been treated with an assiduous Respect. But I have not seen one real Gentleman, one well bred Man since I came to Town. At their Entertainments there is no Conversation that is agreable. There is no Modesty — No attention to one another. They talk very loud, very fast, and alltogether. If they ask you a Question, before you can utter 3 Words of your Answer, they will break out upon you, again — and talk away." *Ibid.*, II, 109. For further references to distinctions in urban personality see Carl Bridenbaugh, ed., *Gentleman's Progress: The Itinerarium of Dr. Alexander Hamilton* (Chapel Hill: University of North Carolina Press, 1948), 23, 43–44, 146, 192–93.

38. [Josiah Quincy, Junior], "Journal of Josiah Quincy, Junior, 1773," Massachusetts Historical Society, *Proceedings*, XLIX (1915–1916), 441–42, 444–45, 447, 450–51, 477–80.

39. *The Independent Reflector*, January 18, 1753.

40. Sumner C. Powell, in discussing the history of Sudbury, Massachusetts, contends that the town as a political entity was distinctly different from any English political institution the settlers had known, though the practices of the town governments were in some ways similar to those of English boroughs. Powell, *Puritan Village: the Formation of a New England Town*, 111, 178–79.

41. Warner, *The Private City*, 10.

42. *Minutes of the Common Council of the City of New York: 1675–1776* (New York: Dodd, Mead, 1905), IV, 77–86, 90–93, 95–97, 101–105, 107–109, 122–27. For detail on city government in the colonial period see Ernest S. Griffith, *History of American City Government: the Colonial Period* (New York: Oxford, 1938).

43. [Benjamin Franklin] *The Autobiography of Benjamin Franklin*, ed. by Leonard W. Labaree, Ralph L. Ketcham, Helen C. Boatfield, and Helene H. Fineman (New Haven: Yale University Press, 1964), 116, 130.

44. *Ibid.*, 173–75, 202–204.

45. On the nature and implications of town and city government in colonial America see Lockridge and Kreider, "The Evolution of Massachusetts Town Government, 1640–1740," 549–74; Michael Zuckerman, "The Social Context of Democracy in Massachusetts," in Stanley N. Katz, ed., *Essays in Politics and Social Development in Colonial America* (Boston: Little, Brown, 1971), 226–45; Gary B. Nash, "The Rattle of Rights and Privileges: Pennsylvania Politics, 1701–1709," *ibid.*, 246–67; Judith M. Diamondstone, "Philadelphia's Municipal Corporation, 1701–1776," *Pennsylvania Magazine*, XC (April, 1966), 183–201.

46. George W. Edwards, "New York City Politics Before the American Revolution," *Political Science Quarterly*, XXXVI (December, 1921), 590.

47. Broadside, Timothy Wheelwright to J. P. Zenger, September 12, 1734, in New York Public Library, "Broadsides, 1734."

48. *New-York Weekly Journal*, September 27, 1735.

49. Bridenbaugh, *Cities in Revolt: Urban Life in America, 1743–1776*, 422–25.

50. Merrill Jensen, *The Founding of a Nation: a History of the American Revolution* (New York: Oxford, 1968), 99, 111, 119–22, 130, 146–49. See also Jesse Lemisch, "Jack Tar in the Streets: Merchant Seamen in the Politics of Revolutionary America," *William and Mary Quarterly*, Third series, XXV (July, 1968), 370–407; Gordon S. Wood, "A Note on Mobs in the American Revolution," *ibid.*, XXIII (October, 1966), 635–42; Pauline Maier, "Popular Uprisings and Civil Authority in Eighteenth-Century America," *ibid.*, XXVII (1970), 3–35. See also Pauline Maier, *From Resistance to Revolution: Colonial Radicals and the Development of American Opposition to Britain* (New York: Alfred Knopf, 1972).

51. "The Montresor Journals," ed. by G. D. Scull, New-York Historical Society, *Collections*, XIV (1881), 336–39.

52. [John Boyle], "Boyle's Journal of Occurrences in Boston, 1759–1778," *The New England Historical and Genealogical Register*, LXXXIV (October, 1930), 369–72.

53. Richard Walsh, "The Charleston Mechanics: A Brief Study, 1760–1776," *The South Carolina Historical Magazine*, LX (July, 1959), 123–44; Pauline Maier, "The Charleston Mob and the Evolution of Popular Politics in Revolutionary South Carolina, 1765–1784," *Perspectives in American History*, IV (1970), 182–85; Jensen, *The Founding of a Nation*, 146; Gouverneur Morris to Mr. Penn, May 20, 1774, in Jared Sparks, *The Life of Gouverneur Morris, with Selections from his Correspondence and Miscellaneous Papers. . . .* (Boston: Gray and Bowen, 1832), I, 25; Max Mintz, *Gouverneur Morris and the American Revolution* (Norman: University of Oklahoma Press, 1970), Chap. 3.

54. Probus to the Printer, *New-York Journal, Or General Advertiser*,

November 19, 1767. The role of urban laborers, artisans, and tradesmen in the Revolutionary movement is discussed in Bernard Mason, "The Heritage of Carl Becker: the Historiography of the Revolution in New York," *New-York Historical Society Quarterly*, LIII (April, 1969), 145–46, and Marc Egnal and Joseph A. Ernst, "An Economic Interpretation of the American Revolution," *William and Mary Quarterly*, Third series, XXIX (January, 1972), 3–32. Egnal and Ernst conclude: "Apart from the area of tobacco cultivation, the protests against Britain centered in the cities. Any recounting of the Revolutionary movement must necessarily focus on these centers and recognize the significance of the urban classes, merchant and laborer alike, which went beyond the weight of their numbers," p. 30. See also L. Jesse Lemisch, "New York's Petitions and Resolves," *New-York Historical Society Quarterly*, XLIX (October, 1965), 313–26.

55. Lieutenant-Governor Colden to the Earl of Dartmouth, June 1, July 6, 1774, in E. B. O'Callaghan, *Documents Relative to the Colonial History of the State of New-York* (Albany: Weed, Parsons, 1857), VIII, 433, 470.

56. Ewald G. Schaukirk, "Diary," published as *Occupation of New York City by the British*, a reprint from *Pennsylvania Magazine of History and Biography*, I (January, 1877), 1–4, 8, 10, 16–17, 23, 28. See also Still, *Mirror for Gotham*, Chap. 3.

57. See David T. Gilchrist, ed., *The Growth of the Seaport Cities, 1790–1825* (Charlottesville: University Press of Virginia, 1967); George Rogers Taylor, "American Urban Growth Preceding the Railway Age," *Journal of Economic History*, XXVII (September, 1967), 309–39.

58. See Richard C. Wade, *The Urban Frontier: the Rise of Western Cities* (Cambridge: Harvard University Press, 1959). Evidence of the contemporary rating of city size is seen in an article, "Changes in the Population of Cities," that appeared in *Hunt's Merchants' Magazine*, VIII (January, 1843), 102: "In 1790, when the first census was taken, Philadelphia was the largest city in America, its population being over 42,000, while New York had but 33,000. . . . In 1810, Philadelphia was ahead of New York by only about 300 inhabitants. . . . In 1820, New York had overreached Philadelphia by more than 15,000 inhabitants." For more precise figures, see Still, *Mirror for Gotham*, 345, fn. 2.

59. Still, *Mirror for Gotham*, 54–77, 345, fn. 2.

60. See Robert G. Albion, *The Rise of New York Port [1815–1860]* (New York: Scribner's Sons, 1939). On the role of the seaports as an economic hinge in this period, see Jean Gottmann, *Megalopolis* (Cambridge: M.I.T. Press, 1961), 102–38.

61. Allan Pred, "Manufacturing in the American Mercantile City: 1800–1840," *Annals of the Association of American Geographers*, LVI (June, 1966), 309–10, 337.

62. *Carey's American Pocket Atlas* (Philadelphia: Lang and Ustick, 1796), 92; Constance M. Green, *The Rise of Urban America* (New York: Harper and Row, 1965), 58–59; Raphael Semmes, *Baltimore as seen by visitors, 1783–1860* (Baltimore: Maryland Historical Society, 1953); Auguste Levasseur, *Lafayette in America in 1824 and 1825; or, Journal of a Voyage to the United States* (Philadelphia: Carey and Lea, 1829), I, 163–70. The Scottish reformer Frances Wright visited Baltimore during her first sojourn in the United States, from 1818 to 1820. Baltimore symbolized to her one "wonderful evidence of the amazing and almost inconceivable growth" of the

country. Frances Wright D'Arusmont, *Views of Society and Manners in America . . . during the Years 1818, 1819, and 1820. By an Englishwoman* (London: Longman, Hurst, Rees, Orme, and Brown, 1821), 487.

63. Francois A. F., duc de La Rochefoucauld-Liancourt, *Travels through the United States of North America . . . in the Years 1795, 1796, and 1797* (London: R. Phillips, 1799), II, 129–30.

64. Richard C. Wade, "Urban Life in Western America, 1790–1830," *American Historical Review,* LXIV (October, 1958), 14–30; Wade, *Urban Frontier, passim.*

65. George Flower, *History of the English Settlement in Edwards County, Illinois, founded in 1817 and 1818 by Morris Birkbeck and George Flower,* with preface and footnotes by E. B. Washburne, in Chicago Historical Society, *Collections,* I (1882), 94, 99, 125–29.

66. Wade, "Urban Life in Western America," 21; James Mease, *The Picture of Philadelphia* (Philadelphia: B. and T. Kite, 1811).

67. Daniel Drake, *Natural and Statistical View, or Picture of Cincinnati and the Miami Country* (Cincinnati: Looker and Wallack, 1815), 130, 142, 147, 170, 228–30, 232. Daniel Drake (1785–1852) was taken to Kentucky when his parents migrated there in 1788. After studying medicine with a Cincinnati physician, he attended the Medical School at the University of Pennsylvania. He became the leading physician of his time in the West, as well as editor, writer, and teacher in the medical field. His *Picture of Cincinnati* was widely circulated and translated abroad. In addition he was involved in a wide variety of public enterprises in Cincinnati. Albert P. Mathews, "Daniel Drake," *Dictionary of American Biography,* V, 426–27.

68. Constance McLaughlin Green, *American Cities in the Growth of the Nation* (London: John De Graf, 1957), 66–75.

69. Timothy Flint, *Recollections of the Last Ten Years, Passed in Occasional Residences and Journeyings in the Valley of the Mississippi . . .* (Boston: Cummings, Hilliard, 1826), 301–303, 308.

70. Pred, "Manufacturing in the American Mercantile City: 1800–1840," 325, 332, 336–37.

71. Blake McKelvey, "A History of Urban Government in America," *Recueils de la Société Jean Bodin,* VI, 638–39. See Roger J. Champagne, "Liberty Boys and Mechanics of New York City, 1764–1774," *Labor History,* VIII (Spring, 1967), 115–35; Staughton Lynd, "The Mechanics in New York Politics, 1774–1788," *ibid.,* V (Fall, 1964), 225–46; Alfred Young, "The Mechanics and the Jeffersonians: New York, 1789–1801," *ibid.,* 247–76; Staughton Lynd and Alfred Young, "After Carl Becker: The Mechanics and New York City Politics, 1774–1801," *ibid.,* 215–24; Raymond A. Mohl, "Poverty, Politics, and the City Mechanics of New York City," *ibid.,* XII (Winter, 1971), 38–51.

72. See Kenneth R. Nodyne, "The Role of De Witt Clinton and the Municipal Government in the Development of Cultural Organizations in New York City, 1803–1817," unpublished doctoral dissertation, New York University, 1969. In Clinton's *Introductory Discourse Delivered Before the Literary and Philosophical Society of New York,* in May, 1814, Clinton stressed New York City's potential for cultural leadership in the nation because of the size of its population, its extensive commerce, the number of its manufacturers, its affluence, and its geographical location. Nodyne, "The Role of De Witt Clinton," 79.

73. *Minutes of the Common Council of the City of New York* (New York: City of New York, M. B. Brown Printing & Binding, 1917), VIII

(July 6, 1814–Jan. 27, 1817), 177–78. I am indebted to Dr. Kenneth Nodyne for calling this item to my attention.

74. J. H. Powell, *Bring Out Your Dead: the Great Plague of Yellow Fever in Philadelphia in 1793* (Philadelphia: University of Pennsylvania Press, 1949), v, *passim*. For the impact of the epidemic of 1822 on New York City, see Peter Neilson, *Recollections of a Six Years' Residence in the United States of America* (Glasgow: D. Robertson, 1830), 5–7.

75. Mathew Carey, *A Short Account of the Malignant Fever, lately prevalent in Philadelphia . . . 4th ed., improved* (Philadelphia: Carey, 1794), 16–17, 21–22, 61–62.

76. The annual report of the Society for the Prevention of Pauperism for 1819 expressed "astonishment and apprehension" at the recent increase in arrivals of immigrants from Europe to the United States. Whereas the total had been only 4,000 in 1806, the annual number had increased to 22,240 in 1817. In the 20 months preceding December, 1819, the New York port alone had seen the arrival of 28,000. "Many of them arrive here destitute of everything," the report asserted. "When they do arrive, instead of seeking the interior, they cluster in our cities or sojourn along our seaboard, depending on the incidents of time, charity, or depredation, for subsistence." According to the statement of Mayor Cadwallader Colden, the arrivals in New York City from March 2, 1818 to December 11, 1819 included 7,539 English, 6,062 Irish, 1,942 Scots, 922 French, 590 Welsh, 499 Germans, 372 Swiss, 255 Hollanders, 217 Spanish, and 103 Italians. *Second Annual Report of the Managers of the Society for the Prevention of Pauperism in the City of New-York* (New York: E. Conrad, 1820), 18–20, 67, fn. 20.

77. Raymond A. Mohl, "Humanitarianism in the Preindustrial City: The New York Society for the Prevention of Pauperism, 1817–1823," *Journal of American History*, LVII (December, 1970), 577; "Report on the Subject of Pauperism," in *First Annual Report of the Managers of the Society for the Prevention of Pauperism in the City of New-York* (New-York: J. Seymour, 1818), 12. On the relationship of efforts to do away with pauperism and a concern for maintaining order in a changing society, see Raymond A. Mohl, "Poverty, Pauperism, and Social Order in the Preindustrial American City, 1780–1840," *Social Science Quarterly*, LII (March, 1972), 936–48. The Pennsylvania Society for the Promotion of Public Economy (1817) and the Baltimore Society for the Prevention of Pauperism (1820) had programs similar to those of the New York society. See Blanche D. Coll, "The Baltimore Society for the Prevention of Pauperism," *American Historical Review*, LXI (October, 1955), 77–87; Benjamin J. Klebaner, "Poverty and Its Relief in American Thought, 1815–61," *Social Service Review*, XXXVIII (December, 1964), 382, 387–88.

78. New York Society for the Prevention of Pauperism, "Report on the Subject of Pauperism," 13–24. For a full discussion of this and other programs for dealing with poverty, see Raymond A. Mohl, *Poverty in New York, 1783–1825* (New York: Oxford, 1971).

79. *Fifth Annual Report of the Society for the Prevention of Pauperism in the City of New-York* (New York: J. Seymour, 1821), 8, 13.

80. Jefferson to David Williams, November 14, 1803, in *The Writings of Thomas Jefferson, Library Edition* (Washington, D.C.: Thomas Jefferson Memorial Association, 1903), X, 431. He added, "The general desire of men to live by their heads rather than by their hands, and the strong allurements of great cities to those who have any turn for dissipation, threaten to make

them here, as in Europe, the sinks of voluntary misery." On September 23, 1800, Jefferson had written Dr. Benjamin Rush, "The yellow fever will discourage the growth of great cities in our nation, & I view great cities as pestilential to the morals, the health, and the liberties of man," in *The Writings of Thomas Jefferson*, collected and edited by P. L. Ford (New York: G. P. Putnam's Sons, 1894), VII, 459. On September 8, 1823, Jefferson wrote William Short: "A city life offers you indeed more means of dissipating time, but more frequent, also, and more painful objects of vice and wretchedness. New York, for example, like London, seems to be a Cloacina of all the depravities of human nature. Philadelphia doubtless has its share. Here [at Monticello], on the contrary, crime is scarcely heard of, breaches of order rare, and our societies, if not refined, are rational, moral, and affectionate at least." *Writings of Thomas Jefferson, Library Edition*, XV, 468–69.

81. Alexander Hamilton, "Report on the Subject of Manufactures," in Harold C. Syrett, ed., *The Papers of Alexander Hamilton* (New York: Columbia University Press, 1966), X, 253; [George Tucker], "On the Future Destiny of the United States," in *Essays on Various Subjects of Taste, Morals, and National Policy, by a Citizen of Virginia* (Georgetown, D.C.: Milligan, 1822), 19. Tucker argues that though cities make poverty more evident, they are conducive to developments in the arts and sciences that produce a more attractive way of life for those who are exempt from this evil. *Ibid.*, 76–77, 84–85. For a discussion of "thinking on economic growth that prevailed in the leading urban centers of the northeastern seaboard for the first fifty years of the Republic under the Constitution," see Joseph Dorfman, "Economic Thought," in Gilchrist, ed., *The Growth of the Seaport Cities*, 151–77.

82. Isaac Holmes, *An Account of the United States of America, derived from actual observation, during a residence of four years in that republic* (London: Caxton Press, 1823), 262–88. Holmes describes, in order, Washington, New York, Philadelphia, Baltimore, Boston, Charleston, Savannah, New Orleans, Louisville, Cincinnati, St. Louis, and Pittsburgh.

83. William Tudor, *Letters on the Eastern States* (Boston: Wells and Lilly, 1821), 121–22, 253, 261, 263.

PART TWO

1. *The New York Tribune*, February 5, 1867.

2. U.S. Census, *Fourth, 1820, Census for 1820* (Washington, D.C.: Gales & Seaton, 1821), *passim;* U.S. Census, *Ninth, 1870*, I, *The Statistics of the Population of the United States* (Washington: Government Printing Office, 1872), Table III, "Population of Civil Divisions less than Counties," 77–296, *passim*. In the Ninth Census the population is given for counties, townships, and what are identified as cities, towns, and villages. In the instance of New England towns, I have identified the community as urban if the population of the town exceeded 4,500.

3. U.S. Census, *Sixteenth, 1940, Population,* I, *Number of Inhabitants* (Washington: Government Printing Office, 1942), 32–33.

4. See George Rogers Taylor, "American Urban Growth Preceding the Railway Age," *Journal of Economic History,* XXVII (September, 1967), 309–39; Blake McKelvey, "The Erie Canal: Mother of Cities," *New-York Historical Society Quarterly,* XXXV (January, 1951), 55–80; Blake McKelvey, *Rochester: The Water-Power City: 1815–1854* (Cambridge: Harvard University Press, 1945); John T. Horton, "Old Erie — the Growth of an Ameri-

can Community [Buffalo]," in John T. Horton, Edward T. Williams, and Harry S. Douglass, *History of Northwestern New York* (New York: Lewis Historical Publishing Co., [1947?]), I, 4–492; Robert W. Bingham, *The Cradle of the Queen City* (Buffalo: Buffalo Historical Society, 1931).

5. [Anon.], "The Railroad System," *The North American Review*, CIV (April, 1867), 490–91; James W. Livingood, *The Philadelphia-Baltimore Trade Rivalry* (Harrisburg: Pennsylvania Historical and Museum Commission, 1947); Harry N. Scheiber, "Urban Rivalry and Internal Improvements in the Old Northwest," *Ohio History*, LXXI (October, 1962), 227–39; Robert G. Albion, *Rise of New York Port* (New York: Scribner's Sons, 1939); John R. Borchert, "American Metropolitan Evolution," *Geographical Review*, LVII (July, 1967), 303, 319.

6. Document no. 42, *Documents of the Board of Aldermen of the City of New York*, IX (July, 1842–May, 1843), 353.

7. "Report of the President of the New-York and Albany Railroad Company, made in pursuance of resolutions of the Senate, dated February 3, 1842," Document no. 28, February 8, 1842, New York State, *Senate Documents*, 65th Session, 1842, II, 19–21. For earlier tabled recommendations to the Board of Aldermen, see Document no. 10, July 24, 1840, "Report of the Joint Special Committee on the Communication from the Mayor, relative to the New-York and Albany Railroad," *Documents of the Board of Aldermen of the City of New York*, VII (May 1840–May, 1841), 109–17. See also Joseph E. Bloomfield, "The Influence of Internal Improvements on the Growth of Commercial Cities," *Hunt's Merchants' Magazine*, XIII (September, 1845), 259–63.

8. Blake McKelvey, *The Urbanization of America: 1860–1915* (New Brunswick, N.J.: Rutgers University Press, 1963), 4–6.

9. Isaac C. Kendall [?], *The Growth of New York* (New York: George W. Wood, 1865), 10–11, 15–18.

10. For an extensive discussion of the beginnings of urban mass transit, see George Rogers Taylor, "The Beginnings of Mass Transportation in Urban America," I, *Smithsonian Journal of History*, I (Summer, 1966), 35–50; (Autumn, 1966), 31–54.

11. [Thomas P. Kettell], "Internal Transportation," *Democratic Review*, XXVII (August, 1850), 148–52.

12. [Anon.], "City Population," *Hunt's Merchants' Magazine*, XLIV (January, 1861), 66–68; [Anon.], "Street Railways of New York and Brooklyn," *American Railroad Journal*, XXXII (October 8, 1859), 648–49.

13. Alexander Easton, *A Practical Treatise on Street or Horse-power Railways* . . . (Philadelphia: Crissey and Markley, 1859), 3–7.

14. *The Missouri Reporter*, December 23, 1841. See Elliot Rosen, "The Growth of the American City, 1830 to 1860: Economic Foundations of Urban Growth in the Pre-Civil War Period," unpublished doctoral dissertation, New York University, 1954; Blake McKelvey, *The City in American History* (London: Allen and Unwin, 1969), 46–49.

15. See Constance M. Green, *Holyoke, Massachusetts* (New Haven: Yale University Press, 1939); Constance M. Green, *American Cities in the Growth of the Nation* (London: John De Graf, 1957), Chap. IV ("New England Manufacturing Cities: Holyoke and Naugatuck"). For a consideration of locational matters, see Jeffrey G. Williamson and Joseph A. Swanson, "The Growth of Cities in the American Northeast, 1820–1870," *Explorations in Entrepreneurial History*, 2d series, IV, no. 1; supplement, 3–101; Borchert, 304.

16. Michael Chevalier, *Society, Manners, and Politics in the United States: Being a Series of Letters on North America* (Boston: Weeks, Jordan, 1839), 128–32, 136–37, 140–42.

17. Taylor, "Beginnings of Mass Transportation in America," I, 39; Sam B. Warner, Jr., *The Private City* (Philadelphia: University of Pennsylvania Press), 70–71. See Edwin T. Freedley, *Philadelphia and Its Manufactures, A Handbook Exhibiting the Development, Variety, and Statistics of the Manufacturing Industry of Philadelphia in 1857* (Philadelphia: E. Young, 1858), *passim.*

18. Leland D. Baldwin, *Pittsburgh, The Story of a City* (Pittsburgh: University of Pittsburgh Press, 1937), 222. See also Tyrone Power, *Impressions of America, during the Years 1833, 1834, and 1835* (London: R. Bentley, 1836), II, 310–11, and Alexander Mackay, *The Western World; or Travels in the United States in 1846–1847* (London: R. Bentley, 1850), 86.

19. Anthony Trollope, *North America* (New York: Harper and Brothers, 1862), 364–67.

20. *De Bow's Review,* I (February, 1846), 145. See also Bayrd Still, "Patterns of Mid-Nineteenth Century Urbanization in the Middle West," *Mississippi Valley Historical Review,* XXVIII (September, 1941), 187–206.

21. J. W. S. [Jesup W. Scott], "Westward the Star of Empire: the Great Western Valley — Its Growth of Population and of Cities," *De Bow's Review,* XXVII (August, 1859), 125–36; Charles N. Glaab and A. Theodore Brown, *A History of Urban America* (New York: Macmillan, 1967), 78–80. See also John S. Wright, *Chicago: Past, Present, Future. Relations to the Great Interior and to the Continent* (Chicago: Horton and Leonard, 1870).

22. J. W. S. [Jesup W. Scott], "The Great West," *De Bow's Review,* XV (July, 1853), 50–52.

23. James Fenimore Cooper, *Home As Found* (New York: D. Appleton and Co., 1873), 31–32, 119–21. For an extended description of town site speculation, see [Anon.], "Commercial Delusions," *The American Review: A Whig Journal of Politics, Literature, Art and Science,* II (October, 1845), 341–57. See also John L. Peyton, *Over the Alleghenies and Across the Prairies* (London: Simpkin, Marshall & Co., 1848), 330–36.

24. Major Walter Wilkey [pseud.], *Western Emigration. Narrative of a Tour to, & One Year's Residence in "Edensburgh" (Illinois)* (New-York: G. Clairborne, and Others, 1839), reprinted in *The Magazine of History with Notes and Queries,* no. 28 (New York: William Abbatt, 1914), 856.

25. *Ibid.,* 872–74. See also James B. Walker, *Experiences of Pioneer Life in the Early Settlements and Cities of the West* (Chicago: Sumner, 1881), 155–57; Michael Chevalier, *Society, Manners, and Politics in the United States: Letters on North America,* ed. by John W. Ward (New York: Doubleday, 1961), 295–97.

26. [Anon.], "The Progress of the Northwest," *Merchants' Magazine and Commercial Review,* III (July, 1840), 39–40.

27. Daniel J. Boorstin, *The Americans: the National Experience* (New York: Random House, 1965), 118–19.

28. *Atchison* (Kansas) *Free Press,* quoted in Wright, *Chicago: Past, Present, Future,* 347–48. For fuller development of this theme, see Wyatt W. Belcher, *The Economic Rivalry between St. Louis and Chicago, 1850–1880* (New York: Columbia University Press, 1947). St. Louis grew from 160,773 in 1860 to 310,864 in 1870; Chicago grew in the same years from 112,172 to 298,977. Charles Francis Adams, Jr., writing in 1868, cited the fact that in 33 years Chicago had grown from nothing to a population larger

than Boston's. As late as 1840, he said, Boston was the "best balanced commercial city in America," but now, like St. Louis, it "reposed, though not in content, in the laurels of earlier days" and had let New York wrest commercial advantages. By taking advantage of steam power, Chicago was doing to St. Louis what New York had done to Boston. It is not natural advantage, he wrote, "which designates centres of trade and influence, but local energy and enterprise. . . . This fact Boston ignored, and Chicago realized, about the year 1840." Charles F. Adams, Jr., "Boston," *The North American Review*, CVI (January, 1868), 6, 10, 14.

29. James Parton, "The City of St. Louis," *The Atlantic Monthly*, XIX (June, 1867), 655, 657–59, 672.

30. See Table 2.2.

31. See Eugene Genovese, *The Political Economy of Slavery: Studies in the Economy and Society of the Slave South* (New York: Pantheon, 1961–65), 24–25, 136, 171–73, 186–87, 234, 236. Here Genovese makes points implicit in the advice Francis Makemie gave the southern colonies in 1705. See also Julius Rubin, "Urban Growth and Regional Development," in Gilchrist, ed., *The Growth of the Seaport Cities, 1790–1825*, 14–21. The British journalist, Charles Mackay, contrasted urban development in the North and South after a visit in 1857 and 1858: "In the southern States . . . there is nothing like the same social, commercial, and literary energy that exists in the north. . . . The cities in the free 'Far West' double, treble, and quadruple their population in twenty, sometimes in ten years. The cities of the Slave States . . . either remain stationary or increase disproportionately. . . . The railways in the North are well conducted. Populous towns, villages, and manufactories swarm and glitter along the line; but in the South the railways are for the most part ill-served and ill-regulated." Charles Mackay, *Life and Liberty in America: or Sketches of a Tour in the United States and Canada, in 1857–8* (2 vols., London: Smith, Elder, 1859), II, 35–36.

32. Ellwood Fisher, "The North and the South," *De Bow's Review*, VII (August, 1849), 134, 137, 140–42; (September, 1849), 263–66; (October, 1849), 306–307. Fisher's article was published in pamphlet form in various parts of the country in 1849: by *The Daily Chronicle*, Cincinnati, 1849; by John T. Towers, Washington, D.C., 1849; by J. B. Colin, Richmond, Va., 1849 (the title page was headed, "Read and Circulate"); and in two editions by A. J. Burke, Charleston, S.C. It was reprinted, with some additional material from the 1850 Census, in *De Bow's Review*, XXIII (August, 1857), 194–201; (September, 1857), 272–82; (October, 1857), 377–85. In a favorable review of the article, printed in *De Bow's Review*, VIII (January, 1850), 47, the author refers to "Mr. Ellwood Fisher, of Cincinnati," who "gallantly threw down the gauntlet" to the North. The city directories of Cincinnati for 1849–1851 do not list an Ellwood Fisher. For a rebuttal of Fisher's arguments, see Osgood Mussey, *Review of Ellwood Fisher's Lecture on the North and South* (Cincinnati: Wright, Fisher, 1849).

33. "Python," "The Relative Political Status of the North and South," *De°Bow's Review*, XXII (February, 1857), 113–32; (March, 1857), 225–48. Another article in the February, 1857, issue of *De Bow's Review* argued: "Freedom from dependence, the self-reliance, necessarily resulting from the isolation of country life, and the absence of most of the temptations to which men are exposed in their daily intercourse and constant traffic with each other, develop many of the more striking traits and ennobling virtues of the planter life. It was probably knowledge of these virtues, resulting from similar causes in his own times, which led Cicero to estimate so highly the ad-

vantages of this pursuit, for he had abundant opportunity to contrast them with their opposite vices in the crowded capital of the Roman Republic. He probably saw, that the tendency of society to congregate into masses . . . was only counteracted by the sterner virtues of the agricultural life, and the conservative influence of the institution of slavery. . . . What a spectacle do we behold in the Northern states of this Confederacy? Not only agrarianism, communism, spiritualism, and Mormonism, but infidelity, opposition to parental control, to the marriage tie, to law, and all the usages which time has consecrated as the necessary cement of society." [Anon.], "The Prospects of Southern Agriculture," *De Bow's Review*, XX (February, 1857), 181, 192.

34. Daniel R. Hundley, *Social Relations in Our Southern States* (New-York: Henry B. Price, 1860), 24–26, 55–56, 74, 164, 258.

35. [Anon.], "Contests for the Trade of the Mississippi Valley," *De Bow's Review*, III (February, 1847), 98; [Anon.], "Virginia and the Chesapeake Bay," *ibid.*, XXIV (May, 1858), 436–37.

36. [Anon.], "Contests for the Trade of the Mississippi Valley," *De Bow's Review*, III (February, 1847), 98, 100, 103, 105–108.

37. Hinton R. Helper, *Compendium of The Impending Crisis of the South* (New York: Burdick, 1859), 195.

38. *Ibid.*, 195–96, 198–99.

39. [Anon.], "Baltimore — Her Past and Present," *De Bow's Review*, XXIX (September, 1860), 291–93. See also [Anon.], "Who Profits by Our Commerce?" *ibid.*, XXIV (June, 1858), 449–50; [Anon.], "The Cities of Georgia — Savannah," *ibid.*, XXVIII (January, 1860), 20–28; [Anon.], "Cities of the South — Richmond," *ibid.*, XXVIII (February, 1860), 187–201; [Anon.], "Mobile — Its Past and Present," *ibid.*, XXVIII (March, 1860), 305; [Anon.], "Commercial, Agricultural, and Intellectual Independence of the South," *ibid.*, XXIX (September, 1860), 466–88; W. M. Burwell, "The Commercial Future of the South. Theory of Trade Lines, or Commercial Magnetism Applied to a Direct Intercourse between the City of Memphis and the Market Cities of Europe," *ibid.*, XXX (February, 1861), 129–56.

40. See Ollinger Crenshaw, "Urban and Rural Voting in the Election of 1860," in Eric Goldman, ed., *Historiography and Urbanization* (Baltimore: Johns Hopkins Press, 1941), 43–63.

41. *Buffalo Republic*, quoted in *The Milwaukee Daily Sentinel*, May 24, 1856.

42. The New York City position was expressed in *The New York Herald* (November 4, 1860): "Let us not be too confident that nothing can destroy our prosperity. If we fulfill our obligations to the Southern States it cannot be destroyed; but if we fail to do so and throw away the advantages of our position, which makes New York the Constantinople of the New World, we ought not and cannot with reason expect any other result than that which is foreshadowed in the article from *The Charleston Mercury*. . . . There is a terrible reckoning . . . in store for those who are now busy loosing the ties and alignments which bind the North and South."

43. Charleston, S.C. *Mercury*, October 27, 1860, quoted in *The New York Herald*, November 4, 1860.

44. Oscar Handlin, *Boston's Immigrants, 1790–1865: A Study in Acculturation* (Cambridge: Harvard University Press, 1941), 79–82.

45. Bayrd Still, *Milwaukee: The History of a City* (Madison: State Historical Society of Wisconsin, 1948, 1965), 72–81, 111–32.

46. *Population of the United States in 1860; compiled from the Original*

Returns of the Eighth Census (Washington: Government Printing Office, 1864), xiii, xxxi–xxxii, 608–15, *passim; Statistics of the United States . . . in 1860; compiled from the original returns and being the final exhibit of the Eighth Census* (Washington: Government Printing Office, 1866), lvii–lviii.

47. *Report of the* [Massachusetts] *Bureau of Statistics of Labor . . . from August 2, 1869, to March 1, 1870, inclusive, being the first seven months since its organization* (Boston: Wright and Potter, 1870), 174–76. See also Handlin, *Boston's Immigrants,* 93–127.

48. Fredrika Bremer, *The Homes of the New World; Impressions of America,* tr. by Mary Howitt (2 vols., New York: Harper and Brothers, 1853), I, 606–607, 609–10, 614–16; II, 91, 165–66. On the Germanism of Milwaukee and its appeal for migrants, see John Kerler, Jr., to August Frank in Reutlingen, Wurttemberg, March 27, 1850: ". . . my preference was for Wisconsin, namely Milwaukee, because my father was mainly looking for a place in which Germans had settled and where one could manage better with his own language. . . . Milwaukee . . . is first among the places partly inhabited by Germans. Taking language and climate into consideration, this includes Cincinnati, St. Louis, Chicago, Detroit, Buffalo and New York. . . . Milwaukee is the only place in which I found that the Americans concern themselves with learning German, and where the German language and German ways are bold enough to take a foothold. You will find inns, beer cellars and billiard and bowling alleys, as well as German beer. . . . The Dutchman (the Americans call the Germans this name by way of derision) plays a more independent role — has balls, concerts and theaters — naturally not to be compared to those in Germany and has even managed to get laws printed in German. . . . I would not recommend land farther than ten miles from [Milwaukee]. . . . When living nearer to the city one can go there at any time and thus cultivate those products that are worth more." Harry H. Anderson, ed., *German-American Pioneers in Wisconsin and Michigan: The Frank-Kerler Letters, 1848–1864* (Milwaukee: Milwaukee County Historical Association, 1971), 76–77.

49. Karl T. Griesinger, *Land und Leute in Amerika: Skizzen aus dem amerikanischen Leben* (2 vols., Stuttgart: A. Kröner, 1863), quoted in Bayrd Still, *Mirror for Gotham* (New York: New York University Press, 1956), 161–63. See Clyde Griffen, "Workers Divided: The Effect of Craft and Ethnic Differences in Poughkeepsie, New York, 1850–1880," in Stephan Thernstrom and Richard Sennett, eds., *Nineteenth-Century Cities* (New Haven: Yale University Press, 1969), 49–93.

50. Still, *Mirror for Gotham,* 189.

51. *The Diary of George Templeton Strong,* ed. by Allan Nevins and Milton H. Thomas (4 vols., New York: Macmillan Co., 1952), I, 94, 177–78, 318; II, 197, 348.

52. Frederick Douglass to Harriet Beecher Stowe, March 8, 1853, in *Proceedings of the Colored National Convention, held in Rochester, July 6th, 7th, and 8th, 1853* (Rochester: Office of Frederick Douglass' Paper, 1853), 35; Still, *Mirror for Gotham,* 89.

53. See Table 2.3 on ethnic ingredients of population.

54. Still, *Mirror for Gotham,* 89.

55. *Frederick Douglass' Paper,* March 4, 1853.

56. Leon F. Litwack, *North of Slavery: the Negro in the Free States, 1790–1860* (Chicago: University of Chicago Press, 1961), 100–102.

57. Karl Bernhard, Duke of Saxe-Weimar, *Travels through North America, during the years 1825 and 1826* (2 vols., Philadelphia: Carey, Lea

and Carey, 1828), I, 126, 133; Mrs. [Frances] Trollope, *Domestic Manners of the Americans* (London: Whittaker, Treacher, 1832), II, 178–79.

58. Leslie H. Fishel, Jr., and Benjamin Quarles, *The Negro American: A Documentary History* (Glenview, Ill.: Scott, Foresman, 1967), 141, 155, 159–60.

59. Litwack, *North of Slavery*, 102.

60. [Society of Friends], *A Statistical Inquiry into the Condition of the People of Colour of the City and Districts of Philadelphia* (Philadelphia: Kite and Walton, 1849), 5–7, 9–10, 17–18, 22, 30–32.

61. Litwack, *North of Slavery*, 97, 110–12, 114–15, 132–33, 142–49, 179–80.

62. On this topic see Richard Wade, *Slavery in the Cities* (New York: Oxford, 1964), *passim*. Useful population figures will be found in the Appendix, 325–30. See also Genovese, *The Political Economy of Slavery*, 224–26.

63. Frederick Law Olmsted, *A Journey in the Seaboard Slave States* (New York: Dix and Edwards, 1856), 14–15, 102–103, 591–92.

64. Constance M. Green, *Washington, Village and Capital, 1800–1878* (Princeton: Princeton University Press, 1962), 272–84.

65. J. T. Trowbridge, *The South: A Tour of its Battlefields and Ruined Cities, A Journey through the Desolated States, and Talks with the People* (Hartford: L. Stebbins, 1886), 453–55, 460.

66. "Our Negro Population," in *The New York World*, March 16, 1867. See David P. Thelen and Leslie H. Fishel, Jr., "Reconstruction in the North: The *World* Looks at New York," *New York History*, XLIX (October, 1968), 405–12.

67. See, for examples, Mrs. Ann S. Stephens, *High Life in New York. By Jonathan Slick, Esq.* [pseud.] (New York: Edward Stephens, 1843); [Anon.], *Easy Nat; or, Boston Bars and Boston Boys* (Boston: Redding, 1844); Osgood Bradbury, *The Mysteries of Boston: or, Woman's Temptation. By a Member of the Suffolk Bar* [anon.] (Boston: J. N. Bradley, 1844); Edward H. Durell, *New Orleans As I Found It. By H. Didimus* [pseud.] (New York: Harper and Brothers, 1845); Justin Jones, *Big Dick, the King of the Negroes; or, Virtue and Vice Contrasted. A Romance of High and Low Life in Boston. By Harry Hazel* [pseud.] (Boston: Star Spangled Banner Office, 1846); Edward Z. C. Judson, *The Mysteries and Miseries of New York: A Story of Real Life. By Ned Buntline* [pseud.] (New York: Bedford, 1848); Charles E. Averill, *The Secrets of the Twin Cities; or, The Great Metropolis Unmasked. A Startling Story of City Scenes in Boston and New York* (Boston: G. H. Williams, 1849); Boz, Jr. [pseud.], *The Moral City! or, Glances at Social Life in Boston* (Boston: John A. French, 1849); James Rees, *Mysteries of City Life; or, Stray Leaves from the World's Book, being a series of tales, sketches, incidents, and scenes founded upon the notes of a home missionary* (Philadelphia: J. W. Moore, 1849); Asmodeus [pseud.], *Sharps and Flats; or, The Perils of City Life. Being the Adventures of One Who Lived by His Wits* (Boston: William Berry, [1850]); George G. Foster, *Celio: or, New York above ground and under-ground* (New York: De Witt and Davenport [1850]); George G. Foster, *New York Naked* (New York: De Witt and Davenport, [185–]); Edward Z. C. Judson, *The Mysteries and Miseries of New Orleans. By Ned Buntline* [pseud.] (New York: L. Ormsby [1851]); [Anon.], *The Mysteries and Miseries of San Francisco. By a Californian* (New York: Garrett [1853]); Osgood Bradbury, *Louise Martin, the Village Maiden; or, the Dangers of City Life; a Story of*

City Scenes and Thrilling Adventures (Boston: G. H. Williams, 1853). See also Adrienne Siegel, "The Image of the American City in Popular Fiction, 1840–1870," unpublished doctoral dissertation, New York University, 1973.

68. [Anon.], *City Cries: or, A Peep at Scenes in Town. By an Observer* (Philadelphia: G. S. Appleton, 1850), 3. See Louis Bader, "Gas Illumination in New York City, 1823–1863," unpublished doctoral dissertation, New York University, 1970.

69. [Anon.], *City Characters: or, Familiar Scenes in Town* (Philadelphia: G. S. Appleton, 1851), 5.

70. Matthew H. Smith, *Sunshine and Shadow in New York* (Hartford: J. B. Burr and Co., 1868); James D. McCabe [Edward W. Martin, pseud.], *The Secrets of the Great City* (Philadelphia: Jones, Brothers, 1868); James D. McCabe, Jr., *Lights and Shadows of New York Life; or, the Sights and Sensations of the Great City* . . . (Philadelphia: National Publishing, 1872).

71. Junius H. Browne, *The Great Metropolis; a Mirror of New-York* (Hartford: American Publishing Co., 1869), 137. See also Mackay, *Life and Liberty in America*, II, 163–64.

72. [George G. Foster], *New York by Gas-light: with here and there a streak of sunshine* (New York: Dewitt and Davenport, 1850), 101, 105–108. See [George G. Foster], *New York in Slices, by an experienced carver; being the original slices published in The New York Tribune* (New York: W. F. Burgess, 1849), 43–47. Foster's *New York in Slices* originally appeared in *The New York Tribune* between July and November, 1848. A similar series, attributed to him and entitled *Philadelphia in Slices*, was published in *The Tribune* between October, 1848, and February, 1849. The author is more critical of the "b'hoys" of Philadelphia than of those described in *New York in Slices:* "That most odious and disgusting of all characters, the B'hoy, . . . has actually a lower and more thorough development of debasement in Philadelphia than in New-York." George R. Taylor, " 'Philadelphia in Slices' by George G. Foster," *Pennsylvania Magazine of History and Biography*, XCIII (January, 1969), 35. See also Edward Z. C. Judson, *The G'hals of New York: A Novel* By Ned Buntline [pseud.] (New York: R. M. DeWitt, 1850); Edward Z. C. Judson, *The B'hoys of New York: A Sequel to the Mysteries and Miseries of New York* By Ned Buntline [pseud.] (New York: W. F. Burgess, 1850); Justin Jones, *Tom, Dick, & Harry: or, The Boys and Girls of Boston. A Tale Founded on Metropolitan Adventures by Moonlight! Starlight!! Gaslight!!! Lamplight!!!! Electric Light!!!!! Northern Lights!!!!!! and Total Darkness* By Harry Hazel [pseud.] (Boston: Star Spangled Banner Office, 1849).

73. *Dictionary of American Biography*, X, 237–38; I, 515–16. See Judson, *The Mysteries and Miseries of New York: A Story of Real Life*, 9–12; Glenn H. Blayney, "City Life in American Drama, 1825–1860," in A. Dayle Wallace and Woodburn O. Ross, *Studies in Honor of John Wilcox* (Detroit: Wayne University Press, 1958), 102–103, 123.

74. [Benjamin A. Baker], *A Glance at New York* (New York: S. French and Son [189–?], 3–7.

75. Stephen F. Ginsberg, "Above the Law: Volunteer Firemen in New York City," *New York History*, L (April, 1969), 165–68. See also Stephen F. Ginsberg, "The History of Fire Protection in New York City, 1800–1842," unpublished doctoral dissertation, New York University, 1968; Alexander J. Wall, "The Great Fire of 1835," *New-York Historical Society Quarterly*, XX (January, 1936), 3–22.

76. Mackay, *Life and Liberty in America*, I, 48–51, 54–55. The author

of "Philadelphia in Slices" (October 30, 1848) attempted to rescue the firemen from the reputation the rowdies gave them. He wrote: "The Firemen . . . have acquired a reputation for rowdyism and brutality, altogether undeserved, simply from the atrocities of gangs of ruffians and rowdy apprentices, who do not regularly belong to the Fire Companies at all, and for the most part are not citizens of Philadelphia. Nine-tenths of those whose rascalities have made Philadelphia so unjustly notorious live in the dens and shanties of the suburbs, and are as much detested by the Firemen as by all other good citizens. . . . One of their favorite tricks is to raise a false alarm of fire and then make a rush for the engine-houses, pushing aside the regular firemen and assuming their places at the ropes. In this way they gradually usurped control of two or three engines and apparatuses, and finally drove away the respectable members of the companies, who chose rather to give up their property than to incur the disgrace of such ruffianly association." Taylor, " 'Philadelphia in Slices' by George G. Foster," 34–36. See also James D. Burn, *Three Years Among the Working-Classes in the United States during the War* (London: Smith, Elder, 1865), 108–112.

77. [Anon.], *Boston Illustrated* (Boston: James P. Osgood, 1872), 72–73. James D. McCabe wrote, in his *The Secrets of the Great City: a Work Descriptive of the Virtues and the Vices, the Mysteries, Miseries and Crimes of New York City* (Philadelphia: Jones, Brothers, 1868), 169: "No one cares to come to New York without seeing Stewart's, and all go away satisfied that the immense establishment is one of the sights of the metropolis."

78. *The New York Times*, August 29, 1859; George T. Borrett, *Letters from Canada and the United States* (London, 1865), quoted in Still, *Mirror for Gotham*, 190–91.

79. [Anon.], *Chicago As It Is: a Strangers' and Tourists' Guide to the City of Chicago* (Chicago: Religious and Philosophical Publication Association, 1866), 111. See also Joel H. Ross, *What I Saw in New-York; or a Bird's Eye View of City Life* (Auburn, N.Y.: Derby and Miller, 1851), 177 (reference to department stores).

80. Edwin T. Freedley, *Philadelphia, and its Manufactures; a Hand-book of the Great Manufactories and Representative Mercantile Houses of Philadelphia in 1867* (Philadelphia: Edward Young, 1867), 612, 616.

81. *Ibid.*, 616–20.

82. Boorstin, *The Americans: the National Experience*, 136–37; Isabella Lucy Bird Bishop, *The Englishwoman in America*, quoted in Still, *Mirror for Gotham*, 155; [Anon.], *New Orleans and Environs . . . a Complete Guide to all Subjects of General Interest in the Southern Metropolis* (New Orleans: B. M. Norman, 1845), 141. See Ivan D. Steen, "The British Traveler and the American City, 1850–1860," unpublished doctoral dissertation, New York University, 1962, pp. 12–76; Mackay, *Life and Liberty in America*, I, 39–46.

83. Anthony Trollope, *North America* (New York: Harper and Brothers, 1862), 552, 555–57, 560.

84. Boorstin, *The Americans: the National Experience*, 147.

85. W. H. G. Kingston, *Western Wanderings or, a Pleasure Tour in the Canadas* (2 vols., London: Chapman and Hall, 1856), II, 276–77.

86. *The New York Times*, August 23, 1859.

87. [Anon.], *A Traveler's Sketch* (Philadelphia: McLaughlin Brothers, 1861), 4. This brochure, put out to advertise the Continental Hotel, stressed Philadelphia's location between New York and Washington as a meeting place and emphasized the attractions of the city served by this centrally lo-

cated, ultramodern hotel. The "perpendicular railway" was soon adopted in the Sherman House in Chicago. [Anon.], *A Guide to the City of Chicago* (Chicago: T. Ellwood Zell, 1868), 135.

88. *The New York Times*, April 26, 1872 (obituary); *The New York Herald*, April 4, 1895.

89. [Anon.], "Palace Homes for the Traveller," *Godey's Lady's Book and Magazine*, LX (May, 1860), 465–66.

90. [Anon.], *The Stranger in Baltimore: a New Hand Book, containing Sketches of the Early History and Present Condition of Baltimore, with a Description of Its Notable Localities, and Other Information Useful to both Citizens and Strangers* (Baltimore: J. F. Weishampel, Jr., 1866), 14; Bessie L. Pierce, *A History of Chicago* (New York: Alfred Knopf, 1940), II, 476.

91. *Twenty-seventh Annual Report of the New York Association for Improving the Condition of the Poor, for the Year 1870* (New York: Trow and Smith, 1870), 46.

92. *Frank Leslie's Illustrated Newspaper*, XXI (December 2, 1865), 162. The author reported that almost all of the houses on the avenue were occupied by their owners; the few that might be for rent commanded sums ranging "from $4,000 per annum (never less) up to the gentle and genial rental of $12,000." *Ibid.*, 162–63.

93. *Miller's New York As It Is or Stranger's Guide-Book to the Cities of New York, Brooklyn, and Adjacent Places* (New York: James Miller, 1860), 22, 73. See Leon Moses and Harold F. Williamson, "The Location of Economic Activities in Cities," *American Economic Review*, LVII (May, 1967), 211–22.

94. *Frank Leslie's Illustrated Newspaper*, XXI (November 18, 1865), 134. Though travelers expanded on the extravagance of fashionable society in New York (especially the "shoddy aristocracy"), some contended that this lavish spending occurred in New York City only. See Edward Dicey, who wrote, after visiting the United States in 1862, "Money is spent freely, just as it is made; but, with the exception of New York, I was never in any American city where the style of living could compare for extravagance with that of the wealthy classes of the Old World." *Six Months in the Federal States* (London and Cambridge: Macmillan, 1863), I, 305.

95. *Frank Leslie's Illustrated Newspaper*, XXI (November 18, 1865), 134. According to Dixon Wecter, some 600 balls, "more or less public," were given in New York City in 1865–1866, representing a total expenditure of $7,000,000. *The Saga of American Society* (New York: Scribner's Sons, 1937), 106.

96. *The Nation*, I (July 6, 1865), 12.

97. Smith, *Sunshine and Shadow in New York*, 40–41.

98. Christopher Tunnard and Henry Hope Reed, *American Skyline* (Boston: Houghton Mifflin, 1955), 96–99, 102, 130. The New York City press described the design of the John Jacob Astor house, built in 1859, as "quite a relief to the monotonous view presented by a vast range on either side of the avenue, of brownstone fronts which, although stately and spacious, so closely resemble each other as to easily pass for duplicates of the same original." *The New York Tribune*, November 28, 1859.

99. *The Cleveland Leader*, January 28, 1858, as quoted in Edmund H. Chapman, *Cleveland: Village to Metropolis* (Cleveland: Western Reserve Historical Society and Press of Western Reserve University, 1964), 143.

100. [Anon.], "First-Class Tenement-Houses," in *Frank Leslie's Illus-*

trated Newspaper, IX (March 10, 1860), 224. For references to boarding, see Joseph J. Rubin and Charles H. Brown, eds., *Walt Whitman of the New York Aurora* (State College, Pa.: Bald Eagle Press, 1950), 22–23; McCabe, *The Secrets of the Great City*, 40. See also P. B. Wight, "Apartment Houses Practically Considered," *Putnam's Magazine*, VI (September, 1870), 306–13.

101. McCabe, *The Secrets of the Great City*, 38–40.

102. "The Diary of Sidney George Fisher, 1859–1860," *Pennsylvania Magazine of History*, LXXXVII (April, 1963), 206–207.

103. Tunnard and Reed, *American Skyline*, 101–104; John W. Reps, *The Making of Urban America: A History of City Planning in the United States* (Princeton: Princeton University Press, 1965), 339–44. See Olmsted, Vaux & Co., *Preliminary Report upon the Proposed Suburban Village at Riverside, Near Chicago* (New York: Sutton, Bowne, 1868); Albert Fein, *Frederick Law Olmsted and the American Environmental Tradition* (New York: Braziller, 1972), 32, 33.

104. [Anon.], *Out of Town: Being a Descriptive, Historical and Statistical Account of the Suburban Towns and Residences of Chicago* (Chicago: Western News, 1869), 4.

105. Taylor, "The Beginnings of Mass Transportation in Urban America," part I, 37. In 1850, population density for New York's fully settled area was 135.6 to the acre. Comparable figures for London were 116.9; Boston, 82.7; Philadelphia, 80.

106. Association for Improving the Condition of the Poor, *First Report of a Committee on the Sanitary Condition of the Laboring Classes in the City of New York with Remedial Suggestions* (New York: John F. Trow, 1853), 7–9, 20–22. See also *Twenty-sixth Annual Report of the New York Association for Improving the Condition of the Poor for the Year 1869* (New York: Trow and Smith, 1869), 73; Robert H. Bremner, *From the Depths: The Discovery of Poverty in the United States* (New York: New York University Press, 1956), 33–38. See Edward Lubitz, "The Tenement Problem in New York City and the Movement for its Reform, 1856–1867," unpublished doctoral dissertation, New York University, 1970.

107. McCabe, *The Secrets of the Great City*, 245–48. "New York, like all other large cities both in the Old and New World, has its poles of social life," wrote an Englishman who resided in the United States in the early 1860's. "The region which skirts the wharves with its seething purlieus, dens, and stinking stews, is the antipodes of the flowery land of the Fifth Avenue and its borders." Burn, *Three Years Among the Working Classes*, 120. See also Samuel B. Halliday, *The Lost and Found; or Life among the Poor* (New York: Blakeman and Mason, 1859).

108. Charles Loring Brace, *The Dangerous Classes of New York and Twenty Years' Work Among Them* (New York: Wynkoop and Hallenbeck, 1880), 317–19; *Twenty-fifth Annual Report of the New York Association for Improving the Condition of the Poor for the Year 1868* (New York: Trow and Smith, 1868), 72.

109. *The New York Evening Post*, June 18, 1827. See Joseph M. Hawes, *Children in Urban Society: Juvenile Delinquency in Nineteenth-Century America* (New York: Oxford, 1971).

110. John A. Fairlie, *Municipal Administration* (New York: Macmillan, 1910), 82.

111. Official transcription of statement made by William M. Tweed before the Aldermanic Committee investigating the Tweed Ring, after the exposure of the ring. Denis T. Lynch, *"Boss" Tweed* (New York: Boni and

Liveright, 1927), 50. See Seymour Mandelbaum, *Boss Tweed's New York* (New York: John Wiley and Sons, 1965), Chap. 6.

112. *The Milwaukee Sentinel*, November 26, 1852, quoted in James S. Buck, *Milwaukee under the Charter*, III (Milwaukee: Symes, Swain, 1884), 410–11.

113. A Philadelphia editor expressed sympathy for the mayor's position in commenting on the 1859 annual message of Mayor Daniel F. Tiemann of New York: "The Mayor of New York complains that he has so little authority he cannot make reforms. 'The Mayoralty should be invested with larger powers.' The executive departments are not responsible to him, he says; and without this responsibility, unity and efficiency of action cannot be expected. In only one department, that of the streets, has he had the appointment of its head. He wishes to have the power of removal. The city of New York raises, in the shape of taxes, eight millions of dollars; a larger sum than any one State of the Union. . . . If it has . . . the collection and disbursement of revenues so important, the forms of its government ought to be . . . balanced with as much nicety as those of the State governments which are in some respects far less influential and important. As it is, when a bad or unpopular Mayor, or one opposite to the party ruling the State, gets into office, the people find that he has too much power, and run up to the Legislature . . . and have a large slice taken off his prerogatives. When, afterwards, an efficient officer comes into power, he finds it impossible to prevent the most flagrant abuses. . . . One of the great causes of the success of the ancient free cities, was the fact that . . . each developed its own institutions as best adapted to its own wants. It might not be amiss for the State Governments to interfere less, and leave each city to develope itself and try experiment in its own way." *The Dollar Newspaper* (Philadelphia), February 16, 1859. This article refers to "Communication from His Honor the Mayor, Daniel F. Tiemann, Jan. 3, 1859," Document no. 1, *Documents of the Board of Aldermen of the City of New York*, XXVI, part 1 (New York, 1859).

114. [Fernando Wood], "Annual Message," Document no. 1, *Documents of the Board of Aldermen of the City of New York*, XXIII (1856), 1–4, 6, 10, 13, 16.

115. Warner, *The Private City*, 88; Alexander B. Callow, Jr., *The Tweed Ring* (New York: Oxford, 1966), 13–14; Still, *Milwaukee: the History of a City*, 144–45.

116. [Anon.], "Our Great Cities," *The Nation*, IX (November 11, 1869), 404.

117. Articles by Parton describing Chicago, St. Louis, Cincinnati, and Pittsburgh appeared in *The Atlantic Monthly* in 1867 and 1868. He found much to praise in these western cities, in contrast to his attitude toward New York City. He admired the "public spirit and energy" that had created "furious and thundering Chicago." Life in St. Louis was serene, comfortable, cheering, and expansive. He found Pittsburgh's business leaders desirous of making a stronger commitment to the development of what promised to be a great city; and in Cincinnati he was impressed not only with the frugality exhibited in the city's governance but with the industry and probity of an officialdom drawn from the city's leading business men. He wrote: "It was like going back to the primitive ages — to that remote period when Benjamin Franklin was printer and public servant, and when Samuel Adams served the State — to see the Mayor of Cincinnati performing his full share of the labor of conducting a business . . . and yet punctual at his office in the City Hall, and strictly attentive to its duties during five of the best hours of the day."

James Parton, "Chicago," *The Atlantic Monthly*, XIX (March, 1867), 339; "The City of St. Louis," *ibid.*, XIX (June, 1867), 655; "Pittsburgh," *ibid.*, XXI (January, 1868), 32; "Cincinnati," *ibid.*, XX (August, 1867), 233.

118. James Parton, "The Government of the City of New York," *The North American Review*, CIII (October, 1866), 415, 419–20, 428, 433–34, 445–48, 463–64. Parton wanted to "give the city back to its legitimate owners, the virtuous and industrious portion of its inhabitants." *Ibid.*, 460. The *Nation* praised Parton's article, taking the view that all the growing cities of the Union were "moving toward the pit of corruption" in which New York was "wallowing." *The Nation's* articles proposed educational tests for the suffrage, which would halt the trend (aggravated by immigration) as a result of which the "purses of the rich cities are passing into the hands of the ignorant." [Anon.], "The Government of Our Great Cities," *The Nation*, III (October 18, 1866), 312–13.

119. Parton, "The Government of the City of New York," 459, 463.

120. Union League Club, *The Report of the Committee on Municipal Reform especially in the City of New York* (New York: John W. Amerman, 1867), 3–4, 12, 15–19, 31–32. Throughout 1867, *The Nation* published articles proposing reforms in the structure of government "in our large cities." [Anon.], "Municipal Government," *The Nation*, IV (May 30, 1867), 434–35. An article in *The North American Review* asserted that the judiciary had deteriorated, along with municipal officials, ever since the state had had an elected judiciary. The author wrote: "The disgraceful character of the municipal government of New York is notorious. The absolute exclusion of all honest men from any practical control of affairs in that city and the supremacy in the Common Council, of pickpockets, prizefighters, emigrant runners, pimps, and the lowest class of liquor dealers, are facts which admit of no question. . . . The present Mayor is a gentleman of high character; but he is comparatively powerless. . . . a few members of the Common Council are honest and unpurchasable; but they are too few to constitute any check upon the majority, even when a three-fourths vote is required." [Anon.], "The Judiciary of New York City," *The North American Review*, CV (July, 1867), 148. Views similar to those expressed in the Union League Club report were asserted by Charles Nordhoff in "The Misgovernment of New York," *The North American Review*, CXIII (1871), 321–43. "Great cities are, so far, the curse and the puzzle of our civilization," he wrote. "Neither here nor in Europe has any ruler discovered how to rule them." He blamed the Irish immigrants for the city's misgovernment. *Ibid.*, 321.

121. Nelson Blake, *Water for the Cities: A History of the Urban Water Supply Problem in the United States* (Syracuse: Syracuse University Press, 1956), 267.

122. *The Dollar Newspaper* (Philadelphia), February 9, 1859.

123. Fairlie, *Municipal Administration*, 247–48.

124. [Ambrose Kingsland], "Annual Message," Document no. 1, *Documents of the Board of Aldermen of the City of New York*, XVIII, part 1 (January–May, 1851), 21–23.

125. Still, *Milwaukee: the History of a City*, 230–32.

126. Warner, *The Private City*, 129, 140, 151; Roger Lane, *Policing the City: Boston, 1822–1885* (Cambridge: Harvard University Press, 1967), 31, 33; Linda K. Kerber, "Abolitionists and Amalgamators: The New York City Race Riots of 1834," *New York History*, XLVIII (January, 1967), 28–39.

127. Lane, *Policing the City*, 37; Pierce, *A History of Chicago*, II, 309–10.

128. James F. Richardson, *The New York Police* (New York: Oxford, 1970), Chaps. 2–7; Raymond B. Fosdick, *American Police Systems* (New York: Century, 1921), 62–67.

129. *Ibid.*, 78, 89–92. Boston was one of the last large cities to provide for a state-appointed police commission.

130. Warner, *The Private City*, 156; Lane, *Policing the City*, 95–96, 117.

131. *The Milwaukee Daily Sentinel*, September 10, 1855. See Still, "Patterns of Mid-Nineteenth-Century Urbanization," 187–206.

132. James W. Gerard, *London and New York: their Crime and Police* (New York: Bryant, 1853), 12–18.

133. *Ibid.*, 6–9, 17.

134. Lane, *Policing the City: Boston, 1822–1885*, 34. For involvement of the firemen in city politics, see Ginsberg, "Above the Law: Volunteer Firemen in New York City, 1836–1837," 165–86.

135. Charles Cist, *Sketches and Statistics of Cincinnati in 1859* (preface dated June 1, 1859), 355–57 .

136. See Lubitz, "The Tenement Problem in New York City and the Movement for its Reform, 1856–1867."

137. Charles E. Rosenberg, *The Cholera Years: The United States in 1832, 1849, and 1866* (Chicago: University of Chicago Press, 1962), 226–33; Howard D. Kramer, "Effect of the Civil War on the Public Health Movement," *Mississippi Valley Historical Review*, XXXV (December, 1948), 449, 461–62.

138. *The New York Evening Post*, January 26, 1866.

139. Edward B. Dalton, "The Metropolitan Board of Health of New York," *The North American Review*, CCXIX (April, 1868), 362–63, 369, 374–75.

140. Carl Wittke, *We Who Built America: the Saga of the Immigrant* (New York: Prentice-Hall, 1939), 375. See Stanley K. Schultz, *The Culture Factory: Boston Public Schools 1789–1860* (New York: Oxford, 1973).

141. Reps, *The Making of Urban America*, 297, 299.

142. Mel Scott, *The San Francisco Bay Area: a Metropolis in Perspective* (Berkeley and Los Angeles: University of California Press, 1959), 19–20, 24–26, 29–37; Reps, *The Making of Urban America*, 294–324.

143. Frank Soulé, John H. Gihon, M.D., and James Nisbet, *The Annals of San Francisco* (New York: D. Appleton and Co., 1855), 488–90.

144. Fairlie, *Municipal Administration*, 262–63. See also [Anon.], *Sketch of Fairmount, Lemon Hill, and the Adjoining Grounds as a Public Park* (Philadelphia, 1855). In his annual message, delivered May 7, 1860, Mayor Samuel S. Powell wrote: "If it is desirable to increase the boundaries of the city, and to attract a large population, it is indispensable that something else should be provided than interminable rows of brick houses along lines of dusty streets, for these alone can never constitute a great city. The people require something more than these, and hence the necessities for institutions for educational purposes and places of amusement and relaxation, spacious parks and drives for the benefit of all classes; and it is to be hoped that the time will come when the people will require that these shall be ornamented with statuary and works of art, when we may properly claim to represent a great city."

145. *The Long Island Star*, April 29, May 5, 1830; September 25, 1834. I am indebted to Dr. Donald E. Simon for calling these editorials to my attention. See Donald E. Simon, "The Public Park Movement in Brooklyn, 1824–1873," unpublished doctoral dissertation, New York University, 1972.

146. See Reps, *The Making of Urban America*, Chap. 12, and Peter J. Schmitt, *Back to Nature: The Arcadian Myth in Urban America* (New York: Oxford, 1970), *passim*. Among the best known cemeteries conforming to the rural style in the major cities were Mount Auburn (Boston), Laurel Hill (Philadelphia), Greenwood (Brooklyn), Wood Lawn (New York), Allegheny (Pittsburgh), Spring Grove (Cincinnati), Forest Lawn (Buffalo), Rose Hill, Graceland, and Oakwood (Chicago), Crown Hill (Indianapolis), Mt. Olivet (Nashville), Bellefontaine (St. Louis), Mountain View (Oakland, Cal.), Glenwood (Washington, D.C.). [Anon.], *Spring Grove Cemetery: Its History and Improvements* . . . (Cincinnati: Robert Clarke, 1869), 2–3, 130–33.

147. Andrew J. Downing, "A Talk about Public Parks and Gardens," from *Horticulturist*, October, 1848, in *Rural Essays* (New York: George P. Putnam, 1853), 140–46; "Public Cemeteries and Public Gardens," from *Horticulturist*, July, 1849, *ibid.*, 154–58; "Cockneyism in the Country," from *Horticulturist*, September, 1849, *ibid.*, 239–42; "The New-York Park," from *Horticulturist*, September, 1849, *ibid.*, 239–42.

148. Downing, "A Talk about Public Parks and Gardens," from *Horticulturist*, October, 1848, *ibid.*, 144, 146.

149. [Anon.], "Civic and Rural Embellishment," *Western Journal*, VII (1851), 78; James S. Buck, *Milwaukee under the Charter*, IV (Milwaukee: Swain and Tait, 1886), 368–69.

150. *Western Journal*, VIII (1852), 194.

151. Albert Fein, ed., *Landscape into Cityscape: Frederick Law Olmsted's Plans for a Greater New York City* (Ithaca: Cornell University Press, 1967), 63–88; Fein, *Frederick Law Olmsted and the American Environmental Tradition*, 18–22. Downing argued in 1851, in *Horticulturist*, that "half a million people have a *right* to ask for . . . parks and pleasure-grounds, as well as for paving stones and gas-lights." Andrew J. Downing, *Rural Essays* (New York: R. Worthington, 1881), 148.

152. Frederick L. Olmsted, *Public Parks and the Enlargement of Towns* (Printed for the American Social Science Association, Cambridge, Mass.: Riverside Press, 1870), 4, 10–11, 15–18, 21–25.

153. Bliss Perry, ed., *The Heart of Emerson's Journals* (Boston: Houghton Mifflin, 1937), 208. In a lecture on "Culture," delivered in the early 1850's, Emerson said: ". . . the aesthetic value of railroads is to unite the advantages of town and country life, neither of which we can spare. A man should live in or near a large town, because . . . in a city, the total attraction of all the citizens is sure to conquer, first or last, every repulsion, and drag the most improbable hermit within its walls some day in the year. In town he can find the swimming-school, the gymnasium, the dancing-master, the shooting-gallery, opera, theatre and panorama; the chemist's shop, the museum of natural history; the gallery of fine arts; the national orators, in their turn; foreign travellers, the libraries and his clubs." Ralph W. Emerson, *The Conduct of Life* (Boston: Houghton Mifflin, 1904), 148. Lecturing on Boston in 1861, he said: "Of great cities you cannot compute the influences. . . . Each great city gathers these values and delights for mankind, and comes to be the brag of its age and population." R. W. Emerson, *Complete Works*, Centenary ed. (Boston: Houghton Mifflin), XII, 187. For an extensive treatment of Emerson's views on the city, see Michael H. Cowan, *City of the West: Emerson, America, and the Urban Metaphor* (New Haven: Yale University Press, 1967), 154, 182, 192, 225, 245, 261, 275. For a somewhat different interpretation see Morton and Lucia White, *The Intellectual versus the City: From Thomas Jefferson to Frank Lloyd Wright* (Cambridge:

Harvard University Press and M.I.T. Press, 1962), Chaps. 3 and 4. For the reaction of some outstanding men of letters to the American city of the 1840's and 1850's, see Edgar Allan Poe, *Doings of Gotham . . . as described in a series of letters to the Editors of The Columbia Spy, now first collected by Jacob E. Spannuth* (Pottsville, Pa.: Jacob E. Spannuth, Publisher, 1929), *passim*; Nathaniel Hawthorne, *The Blithedale Romance* (1852), Chap. 17; Herman Melville, *Pierre, or, the Ambiguities* (1852), Book 16.

154. *The New York Daily Tribune*, January 25, 1869. The surge of popular interest in cities may have been stimulated in part by the publication of the Census of 1840, which revealed the rapid growth of cities in the United States. This coincided with the publication in England of Robert Vaughan's *The Age of Great Cities; or Modern Civilization Viewed in its Relation to Intelligence, Morals, and Religion* (London: Jackson and Walford, 1843). Vaughan wrote: "Our age is pre-eminently the age of great cities. Babylon and Thebes, Carthage and Rome, were great cities, but the world has never been so covered with cities as at the present time, and society generally has never been so leavened with the spirit natural to cities." (p. 1). A similar view was expressed by Jesup W. Scott in issues of *Hunt's Merchants' Magazine* for 1843. In the August, 1843 issue he wrote: "The increasing tendency to reside in towns and cities which is manifested by the inhabitants of all countries, as they make progress in the arts and refinements of civilization, is sufficiently obvious to most men who think on the subject. But it is not so apparent to those whose attention has not been particularly turned to the matter, that the improvements of the last century have so much strengthened that tendency as almost to make it seem like a new principle of society, growing out of the combined agency of steam power and machinery." "Internal Trade of the United States," *Hunt's Merchants' Magazine*, IX (August, 1843), 31. See also [Anon.], "Changes in the Population of Cities," *Hunt's Merchants' Magazine*, VIII (January, 1843), 102–103. For a reference to city growth as a symbol of progress, see Benjamin J. Lossing, "Growth of Cities in the United States," *Harper's New Monthly Magazine*, VII (June–November, 1853), 171: "We have many startling data with which to illustrate the wonderful progress of our country in industrial pursuits, social refinement, and true national greatness; but there is none more tangible than the growth of our cities."

155. [Anon.] "Town and Country," *The Knickerbocker*, VIII (November, 1836), 537–39. See also [Anon.], "Our Village," *ibid.*, XV (May, 1840), 387.

156. "Editor's Easy Chair," *Harper's New Monthly Magazine*, LXII (July, 1855), 271–72.

157. Walt Whitman, *Democratic Vistas*, in *Complete Poetry and Prose*, Cowley ed. (New York: Pelligrini and Cudahy, 1948), II, 215; Franklin Walker and G. Ezra Dane, *Mark Twain's Travels with Mr. Brown* (New York: Alfred Knopf, 1940), 82–83, 259–61, 278.

158. E. L. Godkin, "Our Great Cities," *The Nation*, IX (November 11, 1869), 404. Though the nation as a whole was only 26 per cent urban in 1870, Rhode Island was 75 per cent urban; Massachusetts, 67 per cent; New York, 50 per cent; New Jersey, 44 per cent; Maryland, 39 per cent; and Pennsylvania, 37 per cent. The population of the ten largest cities was as follows: New York, 942,292; Philadelphia, 674,022; Brooklyn, 419,921; St. Louis, 310,864; Chicago, 298,977; Baltimore, 267,354; Boston, 250,526; Cincinnati, 216,239; New Orleans, 191,418; Pittsburgh, 139,256. See Diana Klebanow, "E. L. Godkin, the City, and Civic Responsibility," *New-York Historical Society Quarterly*, LV (January, 1971), 55–57, and "Edwin L.

Godkin and the American City,"unpublished doctoral dissertation, New York University, 1968.

159. George W. Curtis, *Harper's New Monthly Magazine*, IX (July, 1854), 261.

160. [Anon.], "Town and Country Abroad and at Home," *The Nation*, II (May 15, 1866), 618: ". . . here, as on the Continent, the real national life is in the cities. The highest activity of the people is displayed in them, and away from them is to be out of the world." E. L. Godkin wrote in 1869: "The influence of cities is now almost all-pervading. They draw to them the most energetic and enterprising of the population, the greatest talent as well as the greatest wealth, the soberest and steadiest and most intelligent, as well as the most ignorant and vicious. City ideas and city standards of morality spread through the country as surely, though perhaps not as rapidly, as city fashions in dress. The closeness with which farmers' daughters now copy the cut of city women's clothes is but one symptom of the process of moral and intellectual assimilation which is going on, and which is rapidly transforming vast tracts of our territory into mere suburbs of great towns." Godkin, "Our Great Cities," 404.

161. Sam B. Warner, Jr. views the years 1830 to 1860 as the period when the need for urban services, in connection with the growth of large cities, first brought the city into conflict with the tradition of individual or private enterprise that prevailed in the United States. This was the era, he writes, "when the big city and the tradition of privatism first confronted each other. In these years, the basic American municipal relationships between public and private functions were set, and the communitarian limits of a city of private money makers were reached, and passed. This was the turning point in American urban history when tradition failed to adapt itself to modern urban and industrial life." *The Private City*, xi.

162. "Marcel," "Town Meetings for our Great Cities," *The Nation*, II (May 29, 1866), 685. In 1868, Andrew H. Green, comptroller of Central Park, urged the adoption of planning in Westchester County for the purpose of its better coordination with New York City. See *Twelfth Annual Report of the Board of Commissioners of the Central Park for the Year ending December 31, 1868* (New York: *Evening Post*, n.d.), 149–50.

163. Leonard Kip, "The Building of Our Cities," *Hours at Home*, XI (July, 1870), 206–12. Kip was born in New York City in 1826, graduated from Trinity College in 1846, and went to Albany, where he was admitted to the bar. He wrote numerous books and novels between 1850 and 1889. A member of several literary and scientific societies, he was elected president of the Albany Institute in 1885. He died in Albany in 1906. *National Cyclopaedia of American Biography* (New York: White, 1909), XI, 439–40.

164. Kip, "The Building of Our Cities," 206–12.

PART THREE

1. *The Milwaukee Daily Sentinel*, March 18, 1871; Edmund J. James, "The Growth of Great Cities in Area and Population," in The American Academy of Political and Social Science, *The Annals*, XIII (1899), 8; Blake McKelvey, *The Urbanization of America [1865–1915]* (New Brunswick, N.J.: Rutgers University Press, 1963), 51.

2. U.S. Census, *Sixteenth, 1940, Population*, I, *Number of Inhabitants*, 20–24.

3. *Ibid.*, 32–33.

4. A. A. Hayes, Jr., "The Metropolis of the Prairies," *Harper's New Monthly Magazine*, LXI (October, 1880), 711, 719–23, 725, 727, 729–31. Calling Chicago a "magnificent city," in 1888, Charles Dudley Warner contended that its "metropolitan character and appearance" had taken shape since the mid-1870's. "There is in history no parallel to this product of a freely acting democracy: not St. Petersburg, rising out of the marshes at an imperial edict, nor Berlin, the magic creation of a consolidated empire and a Caesar's power." Charles Dudley Warner, "Studies of the Great West," *Harper's New Monthly Magazine*, LXXVI (1887–1888), 872. See Bessie L. Pierce, *A History of Chicago*, III: *The Rise of a Modern City, 1871–1893* (New York: Alfred Knopf, 1957), Chaps. 3–6.

5. Ernest Ingersoll, "Atlanta," *ibid.*, LX (December, 1879), 30–33, 37–39, 42.

6. Warner, "Studies of the Great West," *Harper's New Monthly Magazine*, LXXVI (1887–1888), 559–60; LXXVII (1888), 759–61; Edwards Roberts, "The City of Denver," *ibid.*, LXXVI (1887–1888), 944–57.

7. Frank H. Spearman, "The Great American Desert," *ibid.*, LXXVII (July, 1888), 245.

8. J. H. Beadle, *The Undeveloped West; or, Five Years in the Territories* . . . (Philadelphia: National Publishing Company, 1873), 87–90, 92, 99–100. See W. E. Webb, "Air Towns and Their Inhabitants," *Harper's New Monthly Magazine*, LI (1875), 828–35. On mining towns, see Duane A. Smith, *Rocky Mountain Mining Camps* (Bloomington: Indiana University Press, 1967); Rodman W. Paul, *Mining Frontiers of the Far West* (New York: Holt, Rinehart and Winston, 1963).

9. For extensive coverage of the cattle towns, see Robert R. Dykstra, *The Cattle Towns* (New York: Alfred Knopf, 1968).

10. Robert M. Wright, *Dodge City — The Cowboy Capital* (pub. ? 1913?), 258–61.

11. Mel Scott, *The San Francisco Bay Area: a Metropolis in Perspective* (Berkeley and Los Angeles: University of California Press, 1959), 51. See Earle Pomeroy, *The Pacific Slope* (New York: Alfred Knopf, 1965).

12. William Henry Bishop, "San Francisco," *Harper's New Monthly Magazine*, LXVI (1882–1883), 815, 819, 824–25, 827, 829.

13. *Statistics of the Population of the United States at the Tenth Census (June 1, 1880)*, xxix–xxx. The Census of 1880 devoted two full volumes to a report on the social statistics of cities, which included for all the major cities a historical sketch of the city, a map of the city, statistics on its population growth from 1790 to 1880, and commentary on railroad facilities, topography, climate, streets and street paving, public buildings, public parks and pleasure grounds, places of amusement, cemeteries, markets, drainage, sanitary authority, street cleaning, city government, gas and waterworks, police, public schools, horse-railways, fire department, manufactures, provision for infectious diseases. U.S. Census, *Tenth, 1880, Report of the Statistics of Cities*, . . . *by George E. Waring*, parts I and II, *passim*. The authors of the Census of 1850 listed all cities of 4,000 or over, but expressed regret at their inability to derive the proportion of urban dwellers in the total population.

14. *The Literary Digest*, LVI (1920), July 3, 1920, p. 27; August 21, 1920, pp. 71, 74–75, 78.

15. Magie's article, based on the findings of the Census of 1870, represents an early effort to study comparative urban-rural growth by section. In constructing his statistics, he uses a community of 10,000 as the criterion for establishing urban status. He saw the city as "scarcely second even to the steam-engine" in being productive of savings in time and labor. "It becomes the chief instrumentality in the promotion of civilization — at least in the movement which we call social progress. It is the principle of association carried to its fullest extent." B. C. Magie, "The Growth of Cities in the United States," *Scribner's Monthly*, XV (1877–78), 418–24. For a sophisticated analysis of the locational aspects of city growth in these years, see Eric Lampard, "The Evolving System of Cities in the United States: Urbanization and Economic Development," in Harvey S. Perloff and Lowdon Wingo, eds., *Issues in Urban Economics* (Baltimore: Johns Hopkins Press, 1968), 81–139. See also Allan R. Pred, *The Spatial Dynamics of U.S. Urban Industrial Growth, 1800–1914* (Cambridge: M.I.T. Press, 1966); Allan R. Pred, "Industrialization, Initial Advantage, and American Metropolitan Growth," *Geographical Review*, LV (April, 1965), 158–85; Robert Higgs, "The Growth of Cities in a Midwestern Region, 1870–1900," *Journal of Regional Science*, IX (1969), 369–75.

16. Josiah Strong, "The Problem of the Twentieth Century City," *The North American Review*, CLXV (September, 1897), 343–44, 348.

17. Henry J. Fletcher, "The Drift of Population to Cities: Remedies," *Forum*, XIX (August, 1895), 740–41. See also "Why Cities Grow," *The Literary Digest*, August 17, 1918, p. 22, where the author, arguing for city specialization, contends that "any amount of effort put into [industrial specialization] . . . is well invested" because of "the wonderful prestige which a city gains through specialization. Consider for a moment the advertising which the rubber-plants have brought to Akron, the automobile to Detroit, the milling industry to Minneapolis and St. Paul, steel to Chattanooga, shoes to Brockton and St. Louis."

18. Bayrd Still, *Milwaukee: the History of a City* (Madison: State Historical Society of Wisconsin, 1948, 1965), 348–53. William W. Howard, writing in *Harper's Weekly Magazine*, XXXV (July 18, 1891), 538, praised the efforts of the Association for the Advancement of Milwaukee in advertising the city's advantages as a manufacturing and distributing center. These were expansively pointed out in [A. Cressy Morrison, ed.], *Milwaukee Illustrated, Photogravures of All the Important Public and Private Buildings, Monuments and Scenes in the Cream City* (Milwaukee: C. N. Caspar, 1901).

19. [G. S. Wright], *Indianapolis: Its Advantages for Commerce and Manufactures. Published and Compiled by the Manufacturers and Real Estate Exchange* (Indianapolis: Wright, Baker & Co., 1874); *The Industries of the City of Indianapolis: the Advantages Offered for Business Location and the Investment of Capital. Published under the Auspices of the Indianapolis Board of Trade* (Chicago and Indianapolis: A. N. Marquis, 1889), 16, 44, 91.

20. E. L. Godkin, "The Coming of the Barbarian," *The Nation*, IX (July 15, 1869), 45.

21. Edward Everett Hale, "The Congestion of Cities," *Forum*, IV (January, 1888), 527.

22. Frederick J. Kingsbury, "The Tendency of Men to Live in Cities," *Journal of Social Science*, XXXIII (1895), 8–11, 14–18.

23. Horatio Alger, *Ragged Dick; or, Street Life in New York with the Bootblacks* (Boston: Loring, 1868), 54–55, 57.

24. Clyde Fitch, *The City*, in *Plays by Clyde Fitch*, ed. by Montrose J. Moses and Virginia Gerson (4 vols., Boston: Little, Brown, 1915), IV, 458–59, 466–67, 470–71, 625–29.

25. Hugo Munsterberg, *The Americans* (New York: McClure, Phillips, 1905), 473–78, 490–91.

26. *Dictionary of American History* (New York: Scribner's Sons, 1946), II, 194–200.

27. Walter G. Marshall, *Through America, or Nine Months in the United States* (London: S. Low, Marston, Searle & Rivington, 1882), 24–28.

28. *Dictionary of American History*, II, 199; McKelvey, *The Urbanization of America*, 179.

29. W. D. Chesterton, *Richmond, Virginia: an Outline of Its Attractions and Industries*. Prepared by order of the Chamber of Commerce and published under the direction of its Committee on Information and Statistics (Richmond: William E. Jones, 1888), 3–4, 12.

30. *The New York Times*, October 27, 1904.

31. *Ibid.*, July 17, 1904.

32. *Dictionary of American History*, II, 197; Still, *Milwaukee: the History of a City*, 366.

33. [Thomas B. Helm], *History of Wabash County, Indiana* (Chicago: John Morris, 1884), 241.

34. (Milwaukee) *The Evening Wisconsin*, December 21, 1881.

35. *Dictionary of American History*, II, 201; W. Sloane Kennedy, "The Vertical Railway," *Harper's New Monthly Magazine*, LXV (November, 1882), 889–94; Carl W. Condit, *The Chicago School of Architecture* (Chicago: University of Chicago Press, 1964), *passim*.

36. Julian Ralph, "Chicago — the Main Exhibit," *Harper's New Monthly Magazine*, LXXXIV (February, 1892), 426–28.

37. W. L. George, *Hail Columbia! Random Impressions of a Conservative English Radical* (New York: Harper and Bros., 1921), 153–55, 157–61.

38. Sam B. Warner, Jr., *Streetcar Suburbs* (Cambridge: Harvard University and M.I.T. Press, 1962), 15–45. See also "Editorial," *Lend a Hand*, I (May, 1886), 253. For a discussion of physical mobility in the nineteenth-century city see Stephan Thernstrom and Peter R. Knights, "Men in Motion: Some Data and Speculations about Urban Population Mobility in Nineteenth-Century America," *The Journal of Interdisciplinary History*, I (Autumn, 1970), 7–35.

39. Hale, "The Congestion of Cities," *Forum*, IV (January, 1888), 531–33, 535; Charles Zueblin, *A Decade of Civic Development* (Chicago: University of Chicago Press, 1905), 169–70; Homer Hoyt, ed., U.S. Federal Housing Administration, *The Structure and Growth of Residential Neighborhoods in American Cities* (Washington: Government Printing Office, 1939).

40. Adna F. Weber, *The Growth of Cities in the Nineteenth Century: a Study in Statistics* (New York: Macmillan, 1899), 475. See Scott Donaldson, "City and Country: Marriage Proposals," *American Quarterly*, XX (Fall, 1968), 547–52. An anonymous commentator on the findings of the Census of 1900 interpreted it as signifying "a halt in the set toward the cities," a change resulting from "the latest advance in facilities of communication," the "telephone, the trolley-car and the bicycle, or, to be strictly 'up-to-date,' the automobile." He attributed this, too, to the 50 per cent decline in railroad commutation fares, during the past ten years, as a consequence of the competition posed by trolley extension. [Anon.], "A Sign of the Census," *Scribner's Magazine*, XXVIII (1900), 634–35. Frank Carlton, writing in *Popular Science*

Monthly (1906) contended that the "flood tide of city migration is near; an ebb toward the rural districts may be anticipated. . . . The age of decentralization is just ahead." He laid this development to the replacement of steam power with electric power, as a result of which manufacturing was moving to the suburbs, and country and suburban homes could be "equipped with many city conveniences and advantages." Frank J. Carlton, "Urban and Rural Life," *Popular Science Monthly*, LXVIII (1906), 255–56. See also Adna F. Weber, "Growth of Cities in the United States: 1890–1900," *Municipal Affairs*, V (1901), 367–75. For statistics on the deconcentration of city populations see Taylor, "Beginnings of Mass Transportation in Urban America," and Kenneth T. Jackson, "Metropolitan Government versus Suburban Autonomy," in Kenneth T. Jackson and Stanley K. Schultz, eds., *Cities in American History* (New York: Alfred Knopf, 1972), 442–62. See also Leo F. Schnore, "Satellites and Suburbs," in William M. Dobriner, ed., *The Suburban Community* (New York: G. P. Putnam's Sons, 1958), 109–19.

41. Adna F. Weber, "Rapid Transit and the Housing Problem," *Municipal Affairs*, VI (1902), 411–12, 414–15.

42. National Municipal League Committee on Metropolitan Government, *The Government of Metropolitan Areas in the United States* (New York: National Municipal League, 1930), 68.

43. Adna F. Weber, "Suburban Annexations," *The North American Review*, CLXVI (May, 1898), 612, 614–16.

44. Howard A. Bridgman, "The Suburbanite," *The Independent*, LIV (1902), 862–64. Magazine articles on suburban living and architecture increased in number at the turn of the century. See Waldon Fawcett, "Suburban Life in America," *Cosmopolitan*, XXXV (1903), 308–16.

45. Ebenezer Howard, *Tomorrow: A Peaceful Path to Real Reform*, quoted in David R. Weimer, ed., *City and Country in America* (New York: Appleton-Century-Crofts, 1962), 122.

46. The Garden City Association of America was formed in 1906 by Ebenezer Howard and a group of American churchmen and financiers, including Bishop Henry C. Potter of the Episcopal Church; W. D. P. Bliss, Episcopal minister and Christian Socialist; August Belmont; and E. R. L. Gould, president of the City and Suburban Homes Co. It intended to build no model towns, itself, but to advise industrialists on how to plan garden cities on Howard's principles. Towns, projected under the guidance of this group, were not built because of the panic of 1907. [Anon.], "Garden Cities Association of America," *Charities*, XVII (November 17, 1907), 286. Adna Weber admired the garden city as a means of "combining the advantages of city and country." "The Significance of Recent City Growth: the Era of Small Industrial Centers," in The American Academy of Political and Social Science, *The Annals*, XXIII (January–June, 1904), 236. See also [Anon.], Editorial, "Suburban Cottages Versus Flats," *The Independent*, LXII (1907), 749; Graham R. Taylor, *Satellite Cities: A Study of Industrial Suburbs* (New York: Appleton-Century-Crofts, 1915).

47. For a discussion of Pullman, see Stanley Buder, *Pullman, an Experiment in Industrial Order and Community Planning* (New York: Oxford, 1967).

48. Carol Aronovici, "Suburban Development," in *Housing and Town Planning*, The American Academy of Political and Social Science, *The Annals*, LI (January, 1914), 234–35.

49. In 1920, when 51.4 per cent of the total population was urban, the percentage of the total foreign-born population living in cities was 75.4. The

most highly urbanized foreign-born groups came from the following countries: Albania, 91.9 per cent; Turkey 91.3 per cent; Rumania, 90.9 per cent; Russia, 88.6 per cent; Lithuania, 87.8 per cent; Greece, 87.5 per cent; Ireland, 86.9 per cent; Italy, 84.4 per cent; Poland, 84.4 per cent; Hungary, 80 per cent. The German born were 67.5 per cent urban. U.S. Census, *Fourteenth, 1920, II, Population, 1920,* pp. 737–68.

50. U.S. Census, *Twelfth, 1900, I, Population,* pt. 1, pp. 796–803.

51. U.S. Census, *Fourteenth, 1920, II, Population, 1920, General Report and Analytical Tables,* 737–67.

52. John R. Commons, "City Life, Crime and Poverty," *The Chautauquan,* XXXIX (April, 1904), 115–19. For an example of outspoken criticism of the foreign born, see [Anon.], "Pests Imported from Europe," *The Illustrated American,* XV (April 7, 1894), 373.

53. In 1904, *Charities* magazine inaugurated a series of articles on "strangers within our gates," the work, not of "unfriendly outsiders" but of "people who know them through contact with their colonies in the city." The first in the series was an issue on the Italians, often at this time the object of outspoken criticism by opponents of the "new" immigration. *Charities,* XII (May 7, 1904), 443. See Robert A. Woods, "South End House, Notes on the Italians in Boston," *ibid.,* 451–52; Eliot Norton, "The Need of a General Plan for Settling Immigrants Outside the Great Cities," *ibid.,* 152–54; Antonio Mangano, "The Associated Life of the Italians in New York City," *ibid.,* 476–82; Kate H. Claghorn, "The Changing Character of Immigration," *The World's Work,* I (November, 1900–April, 1901), 385.

54. See Humbert S. Nelli, "Italians in Urban America: A Study in Ethnic Adjustment," *International Migration Review,* New Series, I (Summer, 1967), 38–55; Humbert S. Nelli, *The Italians in Chicago, 1880–1930: a Study in Ethnic Mobility* (New York: Oxford, 1970); Luciano J. Iorizzo and Salvatore Mondello, *The Italian Americans* (New York: Twayne Publishers, 1971), Chaps. III–VI; and Phyllis H. Williams, *South Italian Folkways in Europe and America* (London: Oxford, 1938).

55. William E. Davenport, "The Italian Immigrant in America," *The Outlook,* LXXIII (January–April, 1903), 31–32, 34, 36–37.

56. Edward A. Steiner, "The Russian and Polish Jew in New York," *The Outlook,* LXXII (September–December, 1902), 529–30, 534. For a contemporaneous description of the sweatshop system in Chicago, see Florence Kelley, "The Sweating System," in *Hull-House Maps and Papers* (New York: Thomas Y. Crowell, 1895), 33. See also, Oscar Handlin, *Adventure in Freedom* (New York: McGraw-Hill, 1954).

57. Still, *Milwaukee: the History of a City,* 268–72; Michael Kruszka, "Forty Thousand Polanders," *The Milwaukee Sentinel,* October 16, 1895. See William I. Thomas and Florian Znaniecki, *The Polish Peasant in Europe and America* (New York: Dover Publications, 1958); Paul Fox, *The Poles in America* (New York, George H. Doran, [1922?]); Donald B. Cole, *Immigrant City: Lawrence, Massachusetts, 1845–1921* (Chapel Hill: University of North Carolina Press, 1963).

58. Frederic Almy, "The Housing Awakening: V. The Huddled Poles of Buffalo," *Survey,* XXV (February, 1911), 767–68, 771.

59. Charles Rice, "Libin, A New Interpreter of East Side Life," *The Atlantic Monthly,* XCI (February, 1903), 256–59. See also Hutchins Hapgood, *The Spirit of the Ghetto,* ed. by Moses Rischin (Cambridge, Mass.: Belknap Press, 1967). For a perceptive contemporary review of Hapgood by Grace I. Colbran, *see Bookman,* XVII (March, 1903), 97–98. For an

evaluation of Hurwitz [Libin], see Hillel Rogoff, *Nine Yiddish Writers* (New York: Forward, 1931), 63–69.

60. Fannie Barrier Williams, "Social Bonds in the 'Black Belt' of Chicago: Negro organizations and the new spirit pervading them," *Charities*, XV (October 7, 1905), 40–44. See also Lillian Brandt, "The Make-Up of New York Groups," *ibid.*, 7–11; Frances A. Kellor, "Assisted Emigration from the South: the Women," *ibid.*, 11–14; Carl Kelsey, "Some Causes of Negro Emigration: the Men," *ibid.*, 15–17; Mary White Ovington, "The Negro Home in New York," *ibid.*, 27; George E. Haynes, "Negroes Move North: Their Departure from the South," *Survey*, XL (May 4, 1918), 115–22; Louise V. Kennedy, *The Negro Peasant Turns Cityward* (New York: Columbia University Press, 1930); Reynolds Farley, "The Urbanization of Negroes in the United States," *Journal of Social History*, I (Spring, 1968), 241–58; John Hope Franklin, *From Slavery to Freedom* (New York: Alfred Knopf, 1967), *passim*; Zane Miller, "The Black Experience in the Modern American City," in Mohl and Richardson, *The Urban Experience*, 44–60; William M. Welty, "Black Shepherds: A Study of the Leading Negro Clergymen in New York City, 1900–1940," unpublished doctoral dissertation, New York University, 1969.

61. George E. Haynes, "Negroes Move North: Their Arrival in the North," *Survey*, XLI (January 4, 1919), 459–60.

62. Charles W. Holman, "Race Riots in Chicago," *The Outlook*, CXXII (August 13, 1919), 566–67. See also "Racial Tension and Race Riots," *ibid.*, 532–34; William M. Tuttle, Jr., *Race Riot: Chicago in the Red Summer of 1919* (New York: Atheneum, 1970); Chicago Commission on Race Relations, *The Negro in Chicago: A Study of Race Relations and a Race Riot* (Chicago: University of Chicago Press, 1922); Elliott M. Rudwick, *Race Riot at East St. Louis, July 2, 1917* (New York: Atheneum, 1972).

63. Jacob A. Riis, *How the Other Half Lives: Studies Among the Tenements of New York* (New York: Scribner's Sons, 1890), 55–56, 61, 64–65, 68, 70. For a corroboration of these observations see William Dean Howells, *Impressions and Experiences* (New York: Harper and Bros., 1896), 129–31, 134. See also Jacob A. Riis, *The Battle with the Slums* (New York: Macmillan, 1902); *Encyclopaedia Britannica* (11th edition: London, 1910), XIII, 827.

64. Robert H. Bremner, *From the Depths: the Discovery of Poverty in the United States* (New York: New York University Press, 1956), 104–105.

65. Stephen Crane, *Maggie A Girl of the Streets* (New York: D. Appleton and Co., 1896), 9–13, 15, 139–44.

66. Robert W. De Forest, "A Brief History of the Housing Movement in America," in *Housing and Town Planning*, The American Academy of Political and Social Science, *The Annals*, LI (January, 1914), 8–16. Writing in 1913, De Forest pointed out that since the passage of the 1901 law the number of privy vaults located in tenement house yards had been reduced from 9,000 to 375.

67. Theodore Roosevelt, "The American Worker in Country and Town: I — A Visit to the Tenements," *The Outlook*, XCVII (April, 1911), 934–37.

68. Roy Lubove, *The Urban Community: Housing and Planning in the Progressive Era* (Englewood Cliffs, N.J.: Prentice-Hall, 1967), 6–8, 55; Roy Lubove, *The Progressives and the Slums. Tenement House Reform in New York City, 1890–1917* (Pittsburgh: University of Pittsburgh Press, 1962).

69. Lawrence Veiller, "Housing Reform through Legislation," *Housing and Town Planning*, The American Academy of Political and Social Science, *The Annals*, LI (January, 1914), 70–74, 76–77.

70. Allen F. Davis, *Spearheads for Reform* (New York: Oxford, 1967);

Bremner, *The Discovery of Poverty in the United States;* Clarke Chambers, *Seedtime of Reform: American Social Service and Social Action* (Minneapolis: University of Minnesota Press, 1963); Harry Kraus, "The Settlement House Movement in New York City, 1880–1914," unpublished doctoral dissertation, New York University, 1970.

71. Jane Addams, "Hull House, Chicago: An Effort Toward Social Democracy," *Forum,* XIV (October, 1892), 226–30, 232, 237–39, 241. In slightly expanded form this material appeared in two lectures delivered by Jane Addams before the School of Applied Ethics at Plymouth, Massachusetts, in 1892. In the first lecture, entitled, "The Subjective Necessity for Social Settlements," Miss Addams wrote: "The Settlement . . . is an experimental effort to aid in the solution of the social and industrial problems which are engendered by the modern conditions of life in a great city. It insists that these problems are not confined to any one portion of a city. It is an attempt to relieve, at the same time, the overaccumulation at one end of society and the destitution at the other; but it assumes that this overaccumulation and destitution is most sorely felt in the things that pertain to social and educational advantage." *Philanthropy and Social Progress: Seven Essays by Miss Jane Addams, Robert A. Woods, et al., delivered before the School of Applied Ethics at Plymouth, Mass. . . . 1892* (New York: Thomas Y. Crowell, 1893), 22. Graham Taylor, resident warden of another well-known Chicago settlement, described the origins of the settlements as follows: ". . . more by an instinctive impulse than by any concerted movement, groups of men and women, at first only from the universities, but more and more from other and equally adequate sources of supply, took up their residence among and became a part of the residential population in the industrial districts of the cities. Thus social settlements arose almost spontaneously. . . . We who are at Chicago Commons . . . choose to live . . . where we seem to be most needed. . . . We are here to be all we can to the people and to receive all they are to us as friends and neighbors." "A Social Center for Civic Cooperation: Chicago Commons," *The Commons,* IX (1904), 587. See also Nicholas Kelley, "Early Days at Hull House," *Social Service Review* (Chicago), XXVIII (1954), 424–29.

72. Jacob Riis, "What Settlements Stand For," *The Outlook,* LXXXIX (1908), 71–72.

73. On this theme, see Robert D. Cross, *The Church and the City* (Indianapolis: Bobbs-Merrill, 1967); Aaron I. Abell, *The Urban Impact on American Protestantism* (Cambridge: Harvard University Press, 1943); Charles H. Hopkins, *The Rise of the Social Gospel in American Protestantism* (New Haven: Yale University Press, 1940); Henry F. May, *Protestant Churches and Industrial America* (New York: Harper and Brothers, 1949).

74. Charles Stelzle, "The Spirit of Social Unrest," in Charles Stelzle et al., *The Social Application of Religion* (Cincinnati: Jennings & Graham, 1908), 13, 25–26.

75. Charles Stelzle, *Christianity's Storm Center: A Study of the Modern City* (New York: Fleming H. Revell, 1907), 176–79, 180.

76. Maud Ballington Booth, "Salvation Army Work in the Slums," *Scribner's Magazine,* XVII (January, 1895), 103, 110–12. See also Aaron I. Abell, *The Urban Impact on American Protestantism, 1865–1900* (Cambridge: Harvard University Press, 1943).

77. Robert A. Woods, ed., *The City Wilderness: a Settlement Study by Residents and Associates of the South End House* (Boston: Houghton Mifflin, 1898), 290–91, 304–308. See also Robert A. Woods, "The Univer-

sity Settlement Idea," in *Philanthropy and Social Progress: Seven Essays* . . . *Delivered before the School of Applied Ethics at Plymouth, Mass., during the Session of 1892* (New York: T. Y. Crowell, 1893); Robert A. Woods, ed., *Americans in Process: a Settlement Study* (Boston: Houghton Mifflin, 1902); and Jane A. Shikoh, "The 'Higher Life' in the American City of the 1890s: a Study of its Leaders and their Activities in New York, Chicago, Philadelphia, St. Louis, Boston, and Buffalo," unpublished doctoral dissertation, New York University, 1972; Lucille O'Connell, "Public and Philanthropic Facilities for the Adjustment of Immigrants in New York City, 1900–1920, as Illustrated in the Polish Experience," unpublished doctoral dissertation, New York University, 1973.

78. James Bryce, *The American Commonwealth* (London: Macmillan, 1891, I, 608.

79. Andrew D. White, "The Government of American Cities," *Forum*, X (December, 1890), 357–58, 361–62, 369–70.

80. David M. Means, writing under the pseudonym Henry Champernowne, contended in 1894 that boss rule was a factor of city size (*The Boss: An Essay upon the Art of Governing American Cities* (New York: George Richmond, 1894): "Every city where all the inhabitants have an equal voice in the election, when it becomes great, is ruled by a boss; for the inhabitants, being generally engaged in necessary work, have little time to consult as to the manner after which, or the men by whom, they desire to be governed; moreover their numbers are so great that they cannot know one another, and it is impossible for them all, or for any great part of them, to meet together in one place for deliberation. . . . But some sharp-sighted men . . . combine secretly with one another, and put forth before the time of the election the names of such men as they desire for rulers. By combining in this way they generally make sure of success, for the rest of the inhabitants, having no organization, must, if they vote at all, vote for such rulers as are thus offered them. . . . Now in the American city this leader of the men who make it their business to determine who the rulers shall be is called a boss. The apparent rulers are indeed chosen by the people, but the boss is the true ruler, by virtue of his courage and ability, and he governs through the apparent rulers." He exhorted the boss to govern in a benevolent fashion, being constantly concerned "to make the life of the citizens more and more agreeable to them." 8–12, 243. For a profile of city bosses, see Harold Zink, *City Bosses in the United States: A Study of Twenty Municipal Bosses* (Durham, N.C.: Duke University Press, 1930), *passim*.

81. [Rufus E. Shapley], *Solid for Mulhooly: a Sketch of Municipal Politics under the Leaders of the Ring and the Boss* (New York: G. W. Carleton, 1881), 22–23, 30, 35–36, 38–39, 45–47, 50–54.

82. James F. Richardson, *The New York Police: Colonial Times to 1901* (New York: Oxford, 1970), 234–38, 284–89; J. T. Adams, ed., *Dictionary of American History* (New York: Scribner's Sons, 1946), III, 267–68.

83. *Report and Proceedings of the Senate Committee appointed to investigate the Police Department of the City of New York* (5 vols. Transmitted to the Legislature, January 18, 1895), I, 15–17, 33–36; V, 5399–5401.

84. Claude H. Wetmore and Lincoln Steffens, "Tweed Days in St. Louis: Joseph W. Folk's Single-handed Exposure of Corruption, High and Low," *McClure's Magazine*, XIX (October, 1902), 577–79.

85. Veto message of Hazen Pingree, July 7, 1891, *Journal of the* [Detroit] *Common Council*, 1891, p. 553. I am indebted to Dr. Ashod Apraha-

mian for supplying me with this quotation. See Melvin G. Holli, *Reform in Detroit: Hazen S. Pingree and Urban Politics* (New York: Oxford, 1969).

86. Zane L. Miller, *Boss Cox's Cincinnati: Urban Politics in the Progressive Era* (New York: Oxford, 1968), 239–41.

87. William L. Riordon, *Plunkitt of Tammany Hall* (New York: McClure, Phillips and Co., 1905), 167–68, 170–74, 183. See also Robert K. Merton, "Latent Functions of the Machine," in Alexander B. Callow, Jr., *American Urban History* (New York: Oxford, 1969), 291–300.

88. See Samuel P. Hays, "The Politics of Reform in Municipal Government in the Progressive Era," *Pacific Northwest Quarterly*, LV (October, 1964), 157–69; Bruce M. Stave, "Urban Bosses and Reform," in Mohl and Richardson, *The Urban Experience*, 185–95; Joel A. Tarr, *A Study in Boss Politics: William Lorimer of Chicago* (Urbana, Ill.: University of Illinois Press, 1971).

89. Clinton R. Woodruff, "The Nationalization of Municipal Movements," in The American Academy of Political and Social Science, *The Annals*, XXI (January–June, 1903), 252–60.

90. Delos Wilcox, *The American City: A Problem in Democracy* (New York: Macmillan, 1904), 407–408, 410–13.

91. See Richard Skolnik, "Civic Group Progressivism in New York City," *New York History*, LI (July, 1970), 411–39; James B. Crooks, *Politics and Progress: The Rise of Urban Progressivism in Baltimore, 1895 to 1911* (Baton Rouge: Louisiana State University Press, 1968).

92. Charles A. Beard, "Recent Activities of City Clubs," *National Municipal Review*, I (1912), 431–34.

93. Martha A. B. Conine, "Women's Work in Denver," *Municipal Affairs*, II (September, 1898), 527–31. See also Neva R. Deardorff, in "Women in Municipal Activities," The American Academy of Political and Social Science, *The Annals*, LVI (November, 1914), 71–77; Mary I. Wood, "Civic Activities of Women's Clubs," *ibid.*, 78–87; Joyce Smith, "The Woman's Municipal League of New York City: Municipal Housekeeping, 1894–1923," unpublished seminar paper, History Department, New York University; Lawrence H. Larsen, "Nineteenth-Century Street Sanitation: A Study in Filth and Frustration," *Wisconsin Magazine of History*, LII (Spring, 1969), 239–47.

94. Still, *Milwaukee: the History of a City*, 316–17. See Joseph Huthmacher, "Urban Liberalism and the Age of Reform," *Mississippi Valley Historical Review*, XLIX (September, 1962), 231–41.

95. Michael M. Davis, "Civic Interest Among the People," *Charities and the Commons*, XVII (October, 1906–April, 1907), 257–60. See also Charles Sprague Smith, *Working with the People* (New York: A. Wessels, 1904); Robert Fisher, "The People's Institute of New York City, 1897–1934: Culture, Progressive Democracy, and the People," unpublished doctoral dissertation, New York University, 1974.

96. Frank M. Stewart, *A Half Century of Municipal Reform: the History of the Municipal Reform League* (Berkeley: University of California Press, 1950), Chaps. 3 and 4.

97. [Anon.], "A New 'Model' for City Charters," *Survey*, XXXVI (May 27, 1916), 225. See also review by Robert C. Brooks, of Cornell University, of *A Municipal Program* (1900), *Municipal Affairs*, IV (March, 1900), 235–39.

98. On the point that the business community, represented largely by chambers of commerce, was the major force promoting the movements for

commission and city manager government, see James Weinstein, "Organized Business and the City Commission and Manager Movements," *Journal of Southern History*, XXVIII (1962), 166–82.

99. Mayor H. B. Rice, speech at Charlotte, North Carolina, November 18, 1908, quoted in Clinton R. Woodruff, *City Government by Commission* (New York: D. Appleton and Co., 1911), 30–31.

100. Harry A. Toulmin, Jr., *The City Manager: a New Profession* (New York: D. Appleton and Co., 1915), 42–43.

101. Charles M. Kneier, *City Government in the United States* (New York: Harper and Brothers, 1957), 71–72.

102. [Anon.], "Editorial Comment: Why Not Make States Out of Our Large Cities?" *The American City*, X (January, 1914), 1–2; see also [Anon.], "Shall Our Great Cities Be Made States?" *ibid.*, X (February, 1914), 142–44. See Lurton W. Blassingame, "Frank J. Goodnow and the American City," unpublished doctoral dissertation, New York University, 1968.

103. Municipal electric light plants increased from 386 in 1896 to 2,318 in 1917. As early as 1893, *The Review of Reviews* reported that the mayors of the nation's largest cities were discussing "the advisability of the assumption by the municipal government of these quasipublic works." *The Review of Reviews*, VII (February, 1893), 68. Of the 36 largest cities in 1915, all but Indianapolis had municipal waterworks. Charles N. Glaab, *The American City: A Documentary History* (Homewood, Ill.: Dorsey Press, 1963), 372. See Marilyn T. Williams, "The Municipal Bath Movement in the United States, 1890–1915," unpublished doctoral dissertation, New York University, 1972.

104. Frederic C. Howe, *The City: the Hope of Democracy* (New York: Scribner's Sons, 1906), 9, 22, 281–84, 286–87, 304.

105. *Ibid.*, 287–90, 305.

106. *Ibid.*, 291–92, 297, 313.

107. Seth Low, "The Work of Cities," *Lend A Hand*, IV (April, 1889), 255–57.

108. See Gerald Kurland, *Seth Low: The Reformer in an Urban and Industrial Age* (New York: Twayne Publishers, 1971); Seth Low, "The Government of Cities in the United States," *The Century Magazine*, XLII (September, 1891), 730–36; Seth Low, "The Problem of City Government in the United States," *The Outlook*, LIII (April, 1896), 624–26; George F. Knerr, "The Mayoral Administration of William L. Strong, New York City, 1895 to 1897," unpublished doctoral dissertation, New York University, 1957; Edwin R. Lewinson, *John Purroy Mitchel: The Boy Mayor of New York* (New York: Astra Books, 1965); Josiah Quincy, "The Development of American Cities," *The Arena*, XVII (March, 1897), 529–37, and "Municipal Progress in Boston," *Independent*, LII (February 15, 1900); James D. Phelan, "Municipal Conditions and the New Charter," *The Overland Monthly*, XXVII (1896), 104–11; Jack Tager, *The Intellectual as Urban Reformer: Brand Whitlock and the Progressive Movement* (Cleveland: The Press of Case Western Reserve University, 1968).

109. Reprint of newspaper article in *The Detroit Tribune*, November 12, 1897, reporting speech of Hazen Pingree to Nineteenth Century Club (Lansing, Mich.: Robert Smith, [1898?]), 5–8. Pingree refers to his concern for "the poor and the humble" in *Facts and Opinions* (Detroit: F. B. Dickerson, 1895), 90, and to competition as a means of forcing a reduction in rates and fares, in "The Problem of Municipal Reform: Contract by Referendum," in *Arena*, XVII (April, 1897), 710. See also Hazen Pingree, "Detroit: A Municipal Study," *The Outlook*, LV (February 6, 1897), 437–42,

and "Municipal Ownership of Street Railways," *Munsey's Magazine*, XXII (November, 1899), 220–25; Holli, *Reform in Detroit*, 74, 157–181.

110. Tom L. Johnson, *My Story*, ed. by Elizabeth Hauser (New York: B. H. Huebsch, 1911), 121–25, 148–49, 194. See Robert H. Bremner, "The Civic Revival in Ohio: The Fight against Privilege in Cleveland and Toledo," unpublished doctoral dissertation, Ohio State University, 1943; Hoyt L. Warner, *Progressivism in Ohio, 1897–1917* (Columbus: Ohio State University Press, 1964); Eugene C. Murdoch, "Cleveland's Johnson: First Term," *Ohio Historical Quarterly*, LXVII (January, 1958), 39–48, and "Life of Tom L. Johnson," unpublished doctoral dissertation, Columbia University, 1951; Clarence H. Cramer, *Newton D. Baker: A Biography* (Cleveland: World Publishing, 1961). For progressivism in other cities, see Louis G. Geiger, *Joseph W. Folk of Missouri* (Columbia: Curators of the University of Missouri, 1953); Ransom E. Noble, *New Jersey Progressivism before Wilson* (Princeton: Princeton University Press, 1946); George E. Mowry, *The California Progressives* (Berkeley: University of California Press, 1963); William D. Miller, *Memphis during the Progressive Era, 1900–1917* (Memphis: Memphis State University Press, 1957).

111. Brand Whitlock, "Campaigning with 'Sam Jones,'" *The Commons*, IX (August, 1904), 355–56. Writing in 1899, Jones declared: ". . . the hope of American municipalities to-day lies in augmenting the ranks of the independent, or better, the non-partisan voter. . . . The growth of the sentiment favoring municipal socialism in the cities of America is one of the promising signs of the better day. Hundreds of thousands of dollars have been appropriated within the last few years to such humanizing and educating influences as children's playgrounds, free baths, free music in the parks for the people, and in some instances our municipalities have provided free lectures and free concerts for the winter evenings. . . . Our cities are to be saved by the development of the collective idea. We are coming to understand that every public utility and necessity to the public welfare should be publicly owned, publicly operated, and publicly paid for. Among the properties that according to any scientific conception of the purpose of government should be so owned are water works, heating and lighting plants, street railways, telephones, fire alarms, telegraphs, parks, playgrounds, baths, wash-houses, printing establishments." Samuel M. Jones, "The New Patriotism: a Golden Rule Government for Cities," *Municipal Affairs*, III (September, 1899), quoted in Glaab, *The American City: A Documentary History*, 409, 411–12.

112. Still, *Milwaukee: the History of a City*, 515–23. See also Marvin Wachman, *History of the Social Democratic Party of Milwaukee, 1897–1910* (*Illinois Studies in the Social Sciences*, vol. 28, no. 1, Urbana, 1945); Frederick I. Olson, "The Milwaukee Socialist Party, 1897–1941," unpublished doctoral dissertation, Harvard University.

113. Daniel W. Hoan, *Inaugural Address*, delivered to the Common Council of Milwaukee, Wis., April 16, 1918 (Milwaukee: Phoenix Printing Co.).

114. Mel Scott, *American City Planning since 1890* (Berkeley: University of California Press, 1969), 26–46; Frederick Law Olmsted, "The Town-Planning Movement in America," in *Housing and Planning*, The American Academy of Political and Social Science, *The Annals*, LI (January, 1914), 172–79; Charles M. Robinson, "Improvement in City Life, III. Aesthetic Progress," *The Atlantic Monthly*, LXXXIII (June, 1899), 771–85. For a reaction to the Chicago World's Fair, see Candace Wheeler, "A Dream City," *Harper's New Monthly Magazine*, LXXXVI (May, 1893), 830–31, 833.

See also Harvey A. Kantor, "The City Beautiful in New York," *New-York Historical Society Quarterly*, LVII (April, 1973), 149–71.

115. Ray F. Weirick, "The Park and Boulevard System of Kansas City, Mo.," *The American City*, III (July–December, 1910), 213–14.

116. Scott, *American City Planning*, 47–71, 100–109; Daniel H. Burnham and Edward H. Bennett, *The Plan of Chicago* (Chicago: The Commercial Club, 1909).

117. George E. Hooker, "A Plan for Chicago," *Survey*, XXII (September 4, 1909), 778–80.

118. George B. Ford, "Digging Deeper into City Planning," *The American City*, VI (March, 1912), 559; Scott, *American City Planning*, 83–100.

119. Benjamin C. Marsh, "City Planning in Justice to the Working Population," *Charities and the Commons*, XIX (February 1, 1908), 1515. See also Benjamin C. Marsh, *An Introduction to City Planning: Democracy's Challenge to the American City* (New York: [pub.?], 1909). Marsh wrote in 1912: "Individualism has been the basic difficulty in securing proper city planning in American cities; the unwillingness of people to subordinate themselves to control which will secure the normal and economic development of the city as a whole — such necessary control including determination by the governments as to which districts shall be devoted to home, which to commercial and which to manufacturing purposes. The state must assume its function and control and regulate the use of land. A beginning has been made naturally in tenement house laws, inadequate as they are in every American city, and in building laws." *The American City*, VI (March, 1912), 556.

120. John Nolen, "City Making," *The American City*, I (September, 1909), 15, 19. See Scott, *American City Planning since 1890*, 127.

121. *Ibid.*, 101, 182. Cities that early established city planning commissions are Hartford (1907), Chicago (1909), Baltimore and Detroit (1910), Jersey City, Newark, St. Louis, Pittsburgh, Philadelphia, Salem, Mass., and Lincoln, Neb. (1911). Olmsted, "Town-Planning Movement in America," 181.

122. Scott, *American City Planning since 1890*, 133, 152–63.

123. Arthur H. Grant, "The Conning Tower," *The American City*, I (September, 1909), 20. Senator Theodore H. Burton of Ohio, writing in the same issue, attributed the problems of American cities to the speed of their growth and to the attitude of privatism in American life: "The primal source of these problems is to be found in the intense egotism of urban life. In the cities the competition between individuals is so keen, the ambition for individual advancement along every line is so torturing, that the individual is inclined to lose sight of the general welfare in the dynamic contest for personal aggrandizement. The marvelous growth of our cities, the almost instantaneous transition of small villages into flourishing centers of trade and population has intensified these problems. In Europe the great cities have been, to a greater extent, the development of centuries of conservative accretion and expansion. Their civic problems have thus been less acute since they have been of gradual development." *Ibid.*, 14.

124. Frequently the municipal reform movement took on the tone of a revival campaign; and Professor Zueblin was often imported as a speaker. A "civic revival" in Fort Wayne, Indiana, was described by Charles M. Robinson: "Large white cards, with the words, 'All for One and One for All,' were in the show windows of the stores. . . . Beneath, it was stated that the phrase was the 'slogan of the civic revival,' and there followed the explanation that a civic revival is 'a mass movement by all the people to beautify and

"betterfy" their home town.' . . . The movement was started by the Commercial Club, but it did not stay long at the point of starting. A large civic revival committee, representative of many interests, was appointed, and thereafter it could be truthfully said . . . that the revival was under the auspices 'of the people of Ft. Wayne.' The first thing required was a civic revivalist, or civic evangelist, and Professor Charles Zueblin, who had stirred Grand Rapids in a somewhat similar movement a year before, was sent for. From June 2 to June 6 inclusive, he delivered each afternoon and every evening a different illustrated lecture on some phase of municipal betterment. The lectures were given in the largest theater of the city, but toward the end almost as many persons were turned away because of lack of room as were admitted." *The Survey*, XXII (August 14, 1909), 687–88. See a series of nine articles entitled "The Civic Renascence," written by Zueblin for *The Chautauquan*, XXXVIII, beginning in September, 1903. See also Howard R. Weiner, "The Response to the American City, 1885–1915, as Reflected in Writings Dealing with the City in Scholarly and Professional Serial Publications," unpublished doctoral dissertation, New York University, 1972.

125. Charles Zueblin, *American Municipal Progress* (New York: Macmillan, 1916), xi–xii, 1–2, 4, 398–401.

PART FOUR

1. U.S. Department of Commerce, *1970 Census of Population*, "United States, Final Population Counts, Advanced Report," February, 1971. Urban proportions for 1960 and 1970, by section, were as follows: Northeast — 80.2 per cent (1960), 80.4 per cent (1970); North Central — 68.7 per cent (1960), 71.5 per cent (1970); South — 58.5 per cent (1960), 64.6 per cent (1970); West — 77.7 per cent (1960), 82.9 per cent (1970). For a more comprehensive summary of urban developments in the metropolitan era, see Blake McKelvey, *The Emergence of Metropolitan America: 1915–1966* (New Brunswick, N.J.: Rutgers University Press, 1968).

2. Advisory Commission on Intergovernmental Relations, *Urban and Rural America: Policies for Future Growth* (Washington: Government Printing Office, 1968); *U.S. Department of Commerce News*, release of Monday, September 28, 1970; *The New York Times*, February 6, 1972. According to the Census of 1970, the combined population of the suburban rings totaled some 74,000,000, whereas the combined populations of central cities totaled 62,000,000 and the region outside standard metropolitan statistical areas, 64,000,000. Hans Blumenfeld's study of population development in the Philadelphia metropolitan area revealed that the spread of the metropolitan population from the center to the periphery progressed with great regularity, with density decreasing consistently from the center to the periphery. During the first half of the twentieth century "the crest of the wave of metropolitan expansion moved outward at the rate of one mile per decade." Hans Blumenfeld, "The Tidal Wave of Metropolitan Expansion," *Journal of the American Institute of Planners*, XX (Winter, 1954), 3–14.

3. U.S. Census, *Fourteenth*, 1920, I, *Population*, 63–64, 72; U.S. Census, *Eighteenth*, 1960, I, *Characteristics of the Population*, part I, table 33, section 1: 106–11; U.S. Department of Commerce, Bureau of Census [Nineteenth, 1970], Publications, *Number of Inhabitants*, table 13 of reports for individual states.

4. Edgar M. Hoover and Raymond Vernon, *Anatomy of a Metropolis*

(New York: Doubleday, 1962), 1–2, 227–29. See Kenneth T. Jackson, "The Crabgrass Frontier: 150 Years of Suburban Growth in America," in Mohl and Richardson, *The Urban Experience*, 208–20.

5. Frederick Lewis Allen, "The Big Change in Suburbia," *Harper's Magazine*, CCVIII (June, 1954), 24, *ibid.*, CCIX (July, 1954), 47–48. As early as 1925, Allen had described the contemporary trend to the suburbs in "Suburban Nightmare," *The Independent*, CXIV (1925), 670–72.

6. Gertrude M. Shelby, "Florida Frenzy," *Harper's Magazine*, CLII (January, 1926), 178, 180–81. See also Frederick Lewis Allen, *Only Yesterday* (New York: Harper and Brothers, 1957), 270–79.

7. Dero A. Saunders, "Race for the Suburbs," *Fortune*, XLIV (December, 1951), 99, 101–102, 173.

8. Harlan Paul Douglass, *The Suburban Trend* (New York: Century Co., 1925), 3–4, 36–37, 229, 301–302, 304.

9. Lewis Mumford, "The Wilderness of Suburbia," *The New Republic*, XXVIII (August–November, 1921), 45. See also Lewis Mumford, "The City," in Harold E. Stearns, ed., *Civilization in the United States, an Inquiry by Thirty Americans* (New York: Harcourt, Brace and Co., 1922), 3–20. In 1945, Mumford wrote he believed this to be "the first historic analysis" of American urban development published in the United States. Lewis Mumford, *City Development: Studies in Disintegration and Renewal* (New York: Harcourt, Brace and Co., 1945), 3, 23–25.

10. In commenting on this article in 1970, Mr. Mumford pointed out: "This was a legitimate hope still in the nineteen twenties; no one could then foresee that the airplane would increase metropolitan congestion and that the highway engineers would in their expressways duplicate and magnify all the errors made by the railroad era in ruining and blighting the existing cities."

11. Mr. Mumford writes, "Now called New Towns."

12. Lewis Mumford, "The Intolerable City: Must It Keep On Growing?" *Harper's Magazine*, CLII (February, 1926), 287–93. See also Lewis Mumford, "Regions to Live In," *Survey*, LIV (May 1, 1925), 151–52, and "What Is a City?" *Architectural Record*, LXXXII (November, 1937), 59–62. See also "Statement of Lewis Mumford," in *Federal Role in Urban Affairs* (Hearings before the Subcommittee on Executive Reorganization of the Committee on Government Operations, United States Senate, April 21, 1967), part 17, pp. 3395–3607.

13. Lewis Mumford, "Introduction," in Clarence S. Stein, *Toward New Towns for America* (Liverpool: University Press of Liverpool, Eaton Press, Ltd., 1951), 20. On the Greenbelt towns, see Joseph L. Arnold, *The New Deal in the Suburbs: A History of the Greenbelt Town Program, 1935–1954* (Columbus: Ohio State University Press, 1971).

14. Stein, *Toward New Towns for America*, 21, 38–39, 41–42, 44, 47, 49–50, 56–57, 64, 66–67.

15. Edward P. Eichler and Bernard Norwitch, "New Towns," in *Toward a National Urban Policy*, ed. by Daniel P. Moynihan (New York: Basic Books, 1970), 306–10. Robert E. Simon paid $30,000,000 for the Reston site and undertook its development with the backing of the Gulf Oil Company. Richard Atcheson, "Creating a New Town," in *Holiday* (February, 1966), 121, 123. Columbia, Maryland, is described in Jack Rosenthal, "A Tale of One City," *The New York Times Magazine*, December 26, 1971, pp. 4, 16–18, 23, 26. Bernard Weissbourd and Herbert Channick proposed the development of "a massive ten-year program of development of new towns in outlying areas" to draw off the Negro population from city ghettos. The proposed strategy en-

tailed the construction in these new towns of 350,000 subsidized housing units each year and the withdrawal of public subsidies for housing, sewers, water, roads, and mass transportation from ordinary subdivision development for re-channeling into the new towns, thus eliminating the competition of segregated housing development. "An Urban Strategy," *The Center Magazine*, I (September, 1968), 57–58. See also "New Communities in America and their Objectives," in Advisory Committee on Intergovernmental Relations, *Urban and Rural America: Policies for Future Growth*, 62-106.

16. Ed Grimsley, "Reston: a new town for a new kind of life," offprint from *The Commonwealth: the Magazine of Virginia*, May, 1966.

17. William H. Whyte, Jr., "Introduction," in *The Exploding Metropolis* (Garden City, N.Y.: Doubleday, Inc., 1958), viii–x.

18. Norman Hill, "Ah, For Those Walks in the Bronx," *The New York Times*, June 7, 1970, Section VIII, 1, 7. See also Penn Kimball, "Dream Town — Large Economy Size," *The New York Times Magazine*, December 14, 1952, pp. 12, 36, 43; Mel Scott, *American City Planning since 1890* (Berkeley: University of California Press, 1969), 456–57; Herbert J. Gans, *The Levittowners* (New York: Pantheon Books, 1967).

19. Bennett M. Berger, *Working-Class Suburb* (Berkeley: University of California Press, 1968), 8–10; Herbert J. Gans, "Urbanism and Suburbanism as Ways of Life: a Re-evaluation of Definitions," in Arnold Rose, ed., *Human Behavior and Social Processes* (Boston: Houghton Mifflin, 1962), 625–48, and Herbert J. Gans, *People and Plans: Essays on Urban Problems and Solutions* (New York: Basic Books, 1968), 127–201 (planning for the suburbs and new towns).

20. Jane Jacobs, "Downtown Is for People," in *The Exploding Metropolis*, 146.

21. Jane Jacobs, *The Death and Life of Great American Cities* (New York: Vintage Books, 1963), 445–48. See also Letitia Kent, "Jane Jacobs: Against Urban Renewal, for Urban Life," *The New York Times Magazine*, May 25, 1969, pp. 34 ff.

22. Robert Moses, *Working for the People* (New York: Harper and Brothers, 1956), 85–89.

23. Roy Lubove, *Twentieth-Century Pittsburgh* (New York: John Wiley and Sons, Inc., 1969), 106–41.

24. *The New York Times*, November 25, 1971.

25. Shelton Fisher, "Why Build in New York," *McGraw-Hill News*, November 30, 1967.

26. Linda and Paul Davidoff and Neil M. Gold, "The Suburbs Have to Open Their Gates," *The New York Times Magazine*, November 7, 1971, p. 44. For a discussion of the continued appeal of suburbia in the late 1960's and early 1970's, as well as its implications for racial tension, see Herbert J. Gans, "The White Exodus to Suburbia Steps Up," *The New York Times Magazine*, January 7, 1968.

27. Jean Gottmann, *Megalopolis: The Urbanized Northeastern Seaboard of the United States* (Cambridge: M.I.T. Press, 1961), 5–8.

28. United States Commission on Population Growth and the American Future, *Population and the American Future: The Report of the Commission on Population Growth and the American Future* (Washington: Government Printing Office, 1972), 36–37; Frederick Gutheim, "The Institutional Setting of Urban Affairs," in *Urban America: Goals and Problems* (Washington: Government Printing Office, 1967), 128 fn. The Urban Land Institute predicted in 1967 that by the year 2000 as much as 77 per cent of the popula-

tion would be concentrated in four megalopolitan corridors (one in California, one along the east coast of Florida, one around the rim of the Great Lakes, and one along the Atlantic seaboard), thirteen "outlying urban regions," and six free-standing metropolitan areas with a population of a million or more each. Lyle C. Fitch, "Goals for Urban Development," *ibid.*, 19.

29. U.S. Bureau of the Census, *Historical Statistics of the United States, Colonial Times to 1957* (Washington: Government Printing Office, 1960), 462.

30. Blaine A. Brownell, "A Symbol of Modernity: Attitudes Toward the Automobile in Southern Cities in the 1920s," *American Quarterly*, XXIV (March, 1972), 22, 24–25, 29, 43.

31. Clyde L. King, "Foreword," in *The Automobile: Its Province and Its Problems*, The American Academy of Political and Social Science, *The Annals*, CXVI (November, 1924), vii.

32. John M. McKee, "The Automobile and American Agriculture," *ibid.*, 17.

33. John F. Harbeson, "The Automobile and the 'Home' of the Future," *ibid.*, 59.

34. M. H. James, "The Automobile and Recreation," *ibid.*, 33–34.

35. Roy D. Chapin, "The Motor's Part in Transportation," *ibid.*, 3–4.

36. William J. Showalter, "The Automobile and the Pioneer," *ibid.*, 25.

37. Franklin M. Garrett, *Atlanta and Environs* (New York: Lewis Historical Publishing Company, 1954), II, 821–22.

38. The statistics in this chart are drawn from U.S. Department of Commerce, Bureau of the Census, *1970 Census of Population: General Social and Economic Statistics*. In the volumes for pertinent states, see Table 40 (Summary of Social Characteristics) and Table 81 (Ethnic Characteristics for Areas and Places). See also U.S. Census of Population: Final Report PC (2) — IA, Nativity and Parentage: Social and Economic Characteristics of the Foreign Stock by Country of Origin (Washington: Government Printing Office, 1965), 24–32.

39. For Cuban migration, see "Latinization of Miami Area," *The New York Times*, April 18, 1973. For Chicanos, see John H. Burma, *Mexican Americans in the United States* (Cambridge, Mass.: Schenkman, 1970); Carey McWilliams, *North from Mexico* (Philadelphia: Lippincott, 1949); Stan Steiner, *La Raza: the Mexican Americans* (New York: Harper and Row, 1969), Chap. 11 (Los Angeles barrios).

40. Mauritz A. Hallgren, "Chicago Goes Tammany," *The Nation*, CXXXII (April 22, 1931), 446–48.

41. Excerpts from Wallace E. Maciejewski, "Our Role in Municipal Affairs," 71; Edward S. Kerstein, "Milwaukeeans of Polish Extraction Serving on the Police Department," 73; and John Rapala, "Some Highlights in the History of Milwaukee Poles," 131, in Thaddeus Borun, compiler, *We, the Milwaukee Poles* (Milwaukee: Nowiny Publishing Co., 1946). See Bayrd Still, *Milwaukee: The History of a City* (Madison: State Historical Society of Wisconsin, 1965), 467–68.

42. On this theme see William F. Whyte, *Street Corner Society* (Chicago: University of Chicago Press, 1943); Herbert J. Gans, *The Urban Villagers: Group and Class in the Life of Italian Americans* (New York: Free Press, 1962); Robert E. Lane, *Political Life: Why People Get Involved in Politics* (New York: Free Press, 1961); Robert A. Dahl, *Who Governs: Democracy and Power in an American City* (New Haven: Yale University

Press, 1961); Edgar Litt, *Ethnic Politics in the United States* (Glenview, Ill.: Scott, Foresman, 1970); David Ward, *Cities and Immigrants: A Geography of Change in Nineteenth-Century America* (New York: Oxford, 1971).

43. Gans, *The Urban Villagers*, 4–8, 14–16, 18–19, 23–24, 33–36.

44. Reynolds Farley, "The Urbanization of Negroes in the United States," *Journal of Social History*, I (Spring, 1968), 255; *Congressional Quarterly*, Weekly Report, No. 36 (September 8, 1967), 1758–60; "Details of Negro Population Growth in Urban Areas Shown in Census Report," *United States Department of Commerce News*, release of July 6, 1971. See Charles Tilly, "Migration to American Cities," in Moynihan, ed., *Toward a National Urban Policy*, 160–66.

45. Gilbert Osofsky, *Harlem: The Making of a Ghetto: Negro New York, 1890–1930* (New York: Harper and Row, 1963), 127–30. See also Seth Scheiner, *Negro Mecca: A History of the Negro in New York City, 1865–1920* (New York: New York University Press, 1965); Allen H. Spear, *Black Chicago: The Making of a Negro Ghetto, 1890–1920* (Chicago: University of Chicago Press, 1967); Constance M. Green, *The Secret City: A History of Race Relations in the Nation's Capital* (Princeton: Princeton University Press, 1967); Horace Cayton and St. Clair Drake, *Black Metropolis* (New York: Harper and Row, 1962); Kenneth B. Clark, *Dark Ghetto: Dilemmas of Social Power* (New York: Harper and Row, 1965); New York State, *Second Report of the New York State Temporary Commission on the Condition of the Colored Urban Population* (Albany, 1939).

46. U.S. Census, *Twelfth*, 1900, *Abstract of the Twelfth Census of the United States*, 1900, tables 81, 91; U.S. Bureau of the Census, *Negro Population, 1790–1915* (Washington: Government Printing Office, 1918), table 12 (for 1910); U.S. Census, *Fourteenth*, 1920, *Abstract of the Fourteenth Census of the United States*, 1920, tables 80, 81, 91; U.S. Bureau of the Census, *Negroes in the United States, 1920–1932* (Washington: Government Printing Office, 1935), Chap. V, tables 9, 10, 11; U.S. Census, *Sixteenth*, 1940, *Population*, II, *Characteristics of the Population*, tables 41, 51, 52 (in U.S. summary), table 31 (for individual states); U.S. Census, *Seventeenth*, 1950, *Population*, II, *Characteristics of the Population*, parts 1–50, table 38, Chap. B; *Population*, III, *Census Tract Statistics: Selected Population and Housing Characteristics*, part 1, table 1; U.S. Census, *Eighteenth*, 1960, *Population*, I, *Characteristics of the Population*, parts 1–50, table 21, Chap. B; *U.S. Department of Commerce News*, release by Henry H. Smith, Feb. 10, 1971 (CB71–72); *The New York Times*, May 19, 1971.

47. Alain Locke, *The New Negro: an Interpretation* (New York: Albert and Charles Boni, 1925), 6–7.

48. These figures are taken from a report in *The New York Times* (July 12, 1970), 22, based on a study, "The Economic Future of City and Suburbs," made by David L. Birch of the Harvard Business School, and commissioned by the Committee for Economic Development. Recent studies show that there always have been suburban communities of Blacks, generally of three types (older suburbs experiencing population succession, new developments designed for Negro occupancy, and some suburban enclaves). In the past, Blacks in suburbs were generally of lower socioeconomic status than Blacks in central cities. The recent migration of Blacks to suburbs is of Blacks of higher economic status, and it was predicted that by 1970 the socioeconomic status of suburban Blacks would exceed that of central city Blacks. Comment of Reynolds Farley, in Office of Population Research, Princeton, N.J., *Population Index*, XXXV, no. 3 (July–September, 1969), 236.

49. *The Chicago Defender,* editorial, July 22, 1944.

50. James C. Downs, "Chicago's Ethnic Composition and Attitudes," in Chicago Commission on Human Relations, *Solving the Problems of Chicago's Population Growth,* May 29, 1957 (n.p., n.d.), 11–13; Nissen M. Gross, "Civil Rights Violations and Housing," *ibid.,* 151–52. See also Charles S. Johnson, "Backgrounds of the Negro Migrant Population," in Mayor's Committee on Race Relations, *City Planning in Race Relations,* proceedings of the Mayor's Conference on Race Relations, February, 1944 (published by Mayor's Committee on Race Relations, 134 N. LaSalle St., Chicago), 11–14.

51. Joseph Boskin, "The Revolt of the Urban Ghettoes, 1964–1967," in The American Academy of Political and Social Science, *The Annals,* CCCLXXXII (March, 1969), 1–14.

52. *Report of the National Advisory Commission on Civil Disorders* (Washington: Government Printing Office, 1968), 3–5, 7, 10–11.

53. Jerome H. Skolnick, *The Politics of Protest* (New York: Simon and Schuster, 1969), 149–75; Murray Friedman, "Introduction: Middle America and the 'New Pluralism,'" in *Overcoming Middle Class Rage,* ed. by Murray Friedman (Philadelphia: Westminster Press, 1971), 15–53; *The State of the Cities: Report of the Commission on the Cities in the '70's,* Senator Fred R. Harris and Mayor John V. Lindsay, co-chairmen (New York: Praeger Publishers, 1972), 20–22.

54. *Time,* January 31, 1969, p. 55. See also Martin Mayer, *The Teachers Strike: New York, 1968* (New York: Harper and Row, 1969); Naomi Levine, *Ocean Hill-Brownsville: A Case History of Schools in Crisis* (New York: Popular Library, 1969); Earl Raab, "The Black Revolution and the Jewish Question," *Commentary,* XLVII (January, 1969), 23–33; Steven Bloom, "Interactions between Blacks and Jews in New York City, 1900–1930, as Reflected in the Black Press," unpublished doctoral dissertation, New York University, 1973.

55. One member of a Newark Italian social club asserted, "I don't like Addonizio. . . . But I'm voting for him, because it's white against Black now." *The New York Times,* June 13, 1970.

56. *U.S. Department of Commerce News,* release for July 6, 1971, p 2.

57. *The New York Times,* June 14, 1970.

58. "The Puerto Ricans," *Newsweek,* June 15, 1970; *U.S. Department of Commerce News Release,* Oct. 15, 1972. See also Joseph P. Fitzpatrick, "Puerto Ricans in Perspective: The Meaning of Migration to the Mainland," *International Migration Review,* New Series, II (Spring, 1968), 7–19; Nathan Glazer and Daniel P. Moynihan, *Beyond the Melting Pot; the Negroes, Puerto Ricans, Jews, Italians and Irish of New York City* (Cambridge: M.I.T. Press, 1970), 86–136. Air service between San Juan and New York was introduced in 1945. The first year of heavy migration was 1944. *Ibid.,* 93.

59. Oscar Lewis, *A Study of Slum Culture: Backgrounds for La Vida* (New York: Random House, 1968), 124, 128, 141–42.

60. Bernard Sternsher, ed., *Hitting Home: The Great Depression in Town and Country* (Chicago: Quadrangle Books, 1970), 9–16, 31–36. See also Studs Terkel, *Hard Times: An Oral History of the Great Depression* (New York: Pantheon Books, 1970); Milton Meltzer, *Brother, Can You Spare a Dime?: The Great Depression, 1929–1933* (New York: Alfred Knopf, 1969).

61. Frank Bane, "Feeding the Hungry," *National Municipal Review,* XXI (November, 1932), 628–33. See also Irving Bernstein, *The Lean Years:*

A *History of the American Worker, 1920–1933* (Boston: Houghton Mifflin, 1960), 291–302.

62. Bonnie Fox Schwartz, "Unemployment Relief in Philadelphia, 1930–1932: A Study of the Depression's Impact on Voluntarism," *Pennsylvania Magazine of History and Biography*, XCII (January, 1969), 86–108. See also Raymond L. Koch, "Politics and Relief in Minneapolis During the 1930's," *Minnesota History*, XLI (Winter, 1968), 153–70; Roman Heleniak, "Local Reaction to the Great Depression in New Orleans, 1929–1933," *Louisiana History*, X (Fall, 1969), 289–306.

63. *Federal Cooperation in Unemployment Relief.* Hearings before a Subcommittee of the Committee on Manufactures, United States Senate, 72nd Congress, 1st session, on S. 4592 (Washington: Government Printing Office, 1932), 20–26. For a vivid description of life in Chicago's Hoovervilles, in late 1932, see Edmund Wilson, *The American Earthquake: a Documentary of the Twenties and Thirties* (London: W. H. Allen, 1958), especially pp. 457, 462–63.

64. [Herbert Hoover], "A Statement from Secretary Hoover to Readers of the American City," *The American City*, XXXVII (November, 1927), 575–76.

65. "What the Cities Want from Washington," *The American City*, LII (January, 1937), 69. See also "Federal Aid for Public Works and Utilities," *ibid.*, 5. The mayors insisted that the responsibility for "direct relief" lay with the localities and the states.

66. Fiorello H. La Guardia, "Making Democracy Work in the Modern Industrial City," *Proceedings of the National Conference of Social Work: Selected Papers, Sixty-sixth Annual Conference, Buffalo, N.Y., June 18–24, 1939* (New York: Columbia University Press, 1939), 159–60, 164–65, 167. See Charles Garrett, *The La Guardia Years* (New Brunswick, N.J.: Rutgers University Press, 1961), 178–84. Garrett writes: "No administration in the city's history built as many public projects or projects of such importance as did La Guardia's. . . . Mainly it was the result of New Deal expenditures for recovery and relief . . . ; by June, 1940, when 94 per cent of the PWA program in New York City had been completed (105 out of 116 projects), the city had received outright PWA grants of $115,938,000 and had borrowed an additional $136,086,000 under the program, acquiring in all more than $250,000,000 of construction funds; WPA money, including a relatively small appropriation made by the city, ran to about $145,000,000 a year, at least until 1938." Garrett, 179. For La Guardia's appearance before the House Committee on Appropriations, in support of WPA, see *Congressional Digest*, XVIII.

67. *Our Cities: Their Role in the National Economy* (June, 1937), report of the Urbanism Committee to the National Resources Committee (Washington: Government Printing Office, 1937), v–vii, ix–x. An early statement of the new assumption by the federal government of responsibility for cities is found in Charles E. Merriam, "The Federal Government Recognizes the Cities," in *National Municipal Review*, XXIII (February, 1934), 107–9, 116. See also Martin Meyerson, Barbara Terjett, and William L. C. Wheaton, *Housing, People, and Cities* (New York: McGraw-Hill, 1962), Chap. 13. By 1966 there were more than 70 federal-aid programs directly supporting urban development, as well as a number of other kinds of federal aid available to local governments in metropolitan areas. United States, Advisory Commission on Intergovernmental Relations, *Metropolitan America: Challenge to Federalism* (Washington: Government Printing Office, 1966), 8.

68. Meyerson, Terrett, and Wheaton, *Housing, People, and Cities,* 269–87; Richard O. Davies, *Housing Reform during the Truman Administration* (Columbia: University of Missouri Press, 1966), Chaps. 2, 3, 7, 8. Although the Housing Act of 1949 called for the construction of 810,000 units of public housing over a six-year period, less than 360,000 units had been built by July 1, 1964, although 15 years had elapsed since the passage of the law. *Ibid.,* 136.

69. "Statement of Hon. Fiorello H. La Guardia," January 16, 1945, in *Hearings before the Subcommittee on Housing and Urban Redevelopment of the Special Committee on Post-War Economic Policy and Planning,* U.S. Senate, 79th Congress, 1st session, part 11, *Housing and Urban Redevelopment* (Washington: Government Printing Office, 1945), 1707–9.

70. "Statement of Joseph E. Merrion," *ibid.,* part 13, pp. 2075–76, 2080, 2084–85.

71. Reorganization Plan No. 1 of 1962 — Message from the President of the United States (House Document No. 320), in *Congressional Record: Proceedings and Debates of the 87th Congress: Second Session,* Volume 108, part I (January 10, 1962, to February 1, 1962) (Washington: Government Printing Office, 1962), 1137–38. In his earlier Special Message to Congress on Housing, as reported in *The New York Times,* March 3, 1961, Kennedy asserted that construction to meet the social goals of housing would "contribute to the nation's economic recovery and its long-term economic growth." James Reston, reacting to Kennedy's message of January 30, 1962, pointed out that urban communities were turning to the federal government to deal with their rising problems related to population, transportation, and housing "because unrepresentative State Legislatures have increasingly favored rural interests to the detriment of urban interests." *The New York Times,* January 31, 1962. The *Times* attributed the continuing opposition to the creation of a Department of Housing and Urban Affairs to "an almost traditional Congressional reluctance to recognize city problems and authorize Federal participation in solving them." *The New York Times,* September 12, 1965. A cabinet-level department to deal with urban matters had been proposed as early as the 1940's.

72. See Herbert J. Gans, "The Failure of Urban Renewal, a Critique and Some Proposals," *Commentary,* XXXIX (April, 1965), 29–37; Martin Anderson, *The Federal Bulldozer: a Critical Analysis of Urban Renewal, 1949–62* (Cambridge: M.I.T. Press [1964?].

73. Robert C. Weaver, "Rebuilding American Cities: an Overview," *Current History,* LV (December, 1968), 324, 326, 364–65. See also Robert C. Weaver, *The Urban Complex* (Garden City, N.Y.: Anchor Books, 1966) and *Dilemmas of Urban America* (New York: Atheneum, 1967).

74. *The New York Times,* November 23, 1969. See also *The Model Cities Program: the Planning Process in Atlanta, Seattle, and Dayton, prepared by the firm of Marshall Kaplan, Gans, and Kahn* (New York: Praeger, 1970); Howard W. Hallman, *Neighborhood Control of Public Programs: Case Studies of Community Corporations and Neighborhood Boards* (New York: Praeger, 1970); and Edward M. Kaitz and Herbert H. Hyman, *Urban Planning for Social Welfare: a Model Cities Approach* (New York: Praeger, 1970).

75. Gans, "City Planning in America: A Sociological Analysis," in *People and Plans, Essays on Urban Problems and Solutions,* 60, 65, 68–74. See Harvey S. Perloff, "New Directions in Social Planning," *Journal of the American Institute of Planners,* XXXI (1965), 297–303; Melvin M. Web-

ber, "Comprehensive Planning and Social Responsibility," *ibid.*, XXIX (1963), 232–41; Robert C. Weaver, "Major Factors in Urban Planning," in *The Urban Condition*, ed. by Leonard J. Duhl (New York: Basic Books, 1963). For the approach of the regional planner at the mid-century, see William B. Shore, "An Alternative to 'Spread City,'" *The New York Times*, June 27, 1971.

76. Mike Tabor, "Forest Hills Report," reprinted from *Genesis 2*, Boston, in *Te'chiyat Hanefesh*, February 23, 1972.

77. *The New York Times*, April 22, 1971; *National Journal*, IV (July 1, 1972), 1075–76, 1083; (July 15, 1972), 1145–47; (October 7, 1972), 1554.

78. Oliver McKee, Jr., "Washington as a Boom Town," *The North American Review*, CCXXXIX (February, 1935), 177–79, 182–83. See also Constance M. Green, *Washington, Capital City, 1879–1950* (Princeton: Princeton University Press, 1963).

79. Donald Wilhelm, "America's Biggest Boom Town," *The American Mercury*, LIII (September, 1941), 338–39, 341–42. See also Marvin W. Schlegel, *Conscripted City: Norfolk in World War II* (Norfolk, Va.: Norfolk War History Commission, 1951).

80. *U.S. News & World Report*, LXV (July 29, 1968), 46–48. See also Green, *The Secret City: A History of Race Relations in the Nation's Capital*.

81. See Leonard I. Ruchelman, ed., *Big City Mayors: the Crisis in Urban Politics* (Bloomington: Indiana University Press, 1970); James Q. Wilson, "The Mayors vs. the Cities," *The Public Interest*, no. 16 (Summer, 1969), 25–37; "The Mood of the Mayors," *The New York Times*, June 29, 1970; Seymour Freedgood, "New Strength in City Hall," in *The Exploding Metropolis*, 62–91; Ralph Whitehead, Jr., "Milwaukee's Mercurial Henry Maier," *City*, VI (March–April, 1972), 12–20.

82. Richard Reeves, "The Impossible Takes a Little Longer," *The New York Times Magazine*, January 28, 1968, pp. 22–25, 76, 79.

83. [Anon.], "A City Run by a 'Machine,'" *U.S. News & World Report*, LXIV (February 12, 1968), 47; [Anon.], "Troubled Cities and Their Mayors," *Newsweek*, LXIX (March 13, 1967), 41; David Halberstam, "Daley of Chicago," *Harper's Magazine*, CCXXXVII (August, 1968), 25–36. In an article entitled "It's Not a Bad Crisis to Live in," published in *The New York Times Magazine*, January 22, 1967, p. 70, Irving Kristol wrote: "The greatest single disaster in the history of American big city government, during these past decades, has been the decline of the 'machine' and of the political boss. Yes, the machine and the boss were more often than not corrupt, and the present administrations of our big cities are indubitably far more honest. Unfortunately, our new breed of incorruptible and progressive mayors is deficient in one not unimportant respect: they seem unable to govern."

84. Mike Royko, *Boss: Richard J. Daley of Chicago* (New York: E. P. Dutton, 1971), 67–69, 78–80.

85. Still, *Milwaukee: the History of a City*, 545–48, 551–58, 587–90.

86. [Anon.], "The Problem of the City Auto," *The Literary Digest*, LXVI (September 4, 1920), 30.

87. Amos Schaeffer, "Discussion of the Urban Auto Problem," *National Municipal Review*, IX (July, 1920), 448.

88. Lloyd Stouffer, "Breaking Traffic Jam," *National Civic Review*, LI (October, 1962), 482–85. See also "They Are Taking the Jam Out of Traffic," *Reader's Digest* (December, 1962), 125–28.

89. Thomas H. Reed, "A Call for Plain Talk," *National Civic Review*, LI (March, 1962), 126, 128; McKelvey, *The Emergence of Metropolitan*

America, 200–214; Robert C. Wood, *Metropolis Against Itself* (New York: Committee for Economic Development, 1959); Robert C. Wood, *Suburbia: Its People and their Politics* (Boston: Houghton Mifflin, 1958); Edward C. Banfield and Morton Grodzins, *Government and Housing in Metropolitan Areas* (New York: McGraw-Hill, 1958); Roscoe C. Martin, *Metropolis in Transition: Local Government Adaptation to Changing Urban Needs* (Washington: Government Printing Office, 1963); Joseph S. Clark, "The New Urbanism," in *Goals for Urban America*, ed. by Brian J. L. Berry and Jack Meltzer (Englewood Cliffs, N.J.: Prentice-Hall, Inc., 1967), 38–51; Kenneth T. Jackson, "Metropolitan Government versus Suburban Autonomy: Politics on the Crabgrass Frontier," in *Cities in American History*, ed. by Kenneth T. Jackson and Stanley K. Schultz (New York: Alfred Knopf, 1972), 442–62. In an article published in *The Atlantic Monthly*, CXC (July, 1952), 24, William Zeckendorf, president of Webb & Knapp, real estate developers, wrote: "Satellite towns, which are the product of decentralization, are parasites. . . . Every satellite town saps off the buying power, the taxing power, and the vital factors that make for a cohesive, comprehensive, healthy city. This is just as though the United States suddenly lost the taxing power of California and New York through their setting up independent operation, but continued with the central bureaucracy and cost of maintenance of the Army and Navy, and so on. It wouldn't take very long for the U.S. to go broke on such a basis, and as long as this sort of thing can be done by the satellite towns around the mother city, we are jeopardizing the entire fiscal and political future of our great municipalities. . . . The satellite communities should be forced into the large city and taxed to make them a contributing part of the whole community."

90. Advisory Commission on Intergovernmental Relations, *Metropolitan America: Challenge to Federalism*, 1, 5–7. This book is based on various reports that were issued by the Commission between 1961 and 1965.

91. The government of Metropolitan Toronto, patterned upon the Greater London Charter, provided for a metropolitan legislature for Toronto and its 12 suburbs with jurisdiction over such regional functions as water, roads, sewers, and land-use planning. Blake McKelvey, *The City in American History* (New York: Barnes and Noble, 1969), 99; "Nashville: A Story of Progress," *Forbes Magazine*, CI (May 15, 1968), 51–52; *The American City*, LXXV (January, 1970), 76; Reed, "A Call for Plain Talk," 119–25; Brett W. Hawkins, *Nashville Metro: The Politics of City-County Consolidation* (Nashville: Vanderbilt University Press, 1966). See also "Hoosier Hotshot," *Newsweek*, January 5, 1970, pp. 32–33; "A Brash Young Mayor Stirs Indianapolis," *Business Week*, October 3, 1970, pp. 84–85. An article in the *Wall Street Journal*, December 6, 1972, praised Mayor Lugar's "regional approach" as "the most appropriate method for dealing with urban problems"; but it quoted Mayor Alioto of San Francisco as saying, "Regionalism in the mouths of many is simply a device to return political control of the cities to those who have fled the cities" — Republican-inclined suburbanites.

92. "Greater-Miami Gets a Chance," *Business Week*, November 17, 1956, pp. 176, 178, 181. In May, 1957, the voters of Dade County by a narrow majority approved the charter for the new metropolitan government. It provided for a county manager government with administration to be put in the hands of career specialists. Strong opposition came from the elected officeholders and the employees of the existing county and municipal governments. *Business Week*, May 25, 1957, p. 52.

93. [Anon.], "26 Towns, 1 Government — A Model for Big-City Areas?" *U.S. News & World Report*, February 27, 1959, pp. 82–83; [Anon.], "Blow at Miami's Metro," *Business Week*, September 1, 1962; Thomas J. Wood, "Dade County: Unbossed, Erratically Led," *Annals of the American Academy of Political and Social Science*, CCCLIII (May, 1964), 65–71.

94. John Kay Adams, "Miami's Mighty Metro," *The Rotarian* (April, 1959), 18–19.

95. The pressure for neighborhood control reverses the trend of the last half century in the direction of centralization in city government. For a general discussion of the problem and proposed patterns of neighborhood governance, see Donna E. Shalala, *Neighborhood Governance: Issues and Proposals* (New York: The American Jewish Committee, 1971), *passim.*

96. Milton Kotler argues strongly for the neighborhood corporation as a necessary response to the demand for community control. See his "Two Essays on the Neighborhood Corporation," in *Urban America: Goals and Problems* (Washington: Government Printing Office, 1967), 186–87, and "How Brooklyn Grew," *The New York Times*, February 1, 1972. See also Leo Levy and Harold M. Visotsky, "The Quality of Urban Life: an Analysis from the Perspective of Mental Health," in *Urban America*, 106–107.

97. Milton Kotler, *Neighborhood Government: the Local Foundations of Political Life* (Indianapolis: Bobbs-Merrill, 1969), 46–49. See also Hallman, *Neighborhood Control of Public Programs*, 65–73. A more critical evaluation of ECCO, denying that it has caused community morale to grow, is found in *Social Innovation in the City: New Enterprises for Community Development*, ed. by Richard S. Rosenbloom and Robin Marris (Cambridge: Harvard University Press, 1969), 100–104. For a criticism of the educational accomplishments of Ocean Hill-Brownsville, see Diane Ravitch, "Community Control Revisited," *Commentary*, LIII (February, 1972), 69–70ff.

98. John V. Lindsay, "A Plan for Neighborhood Government for New York City," New York, Office of the Mayor, June, 1970, summarized in Shalala, *Neighborhood Governance*, 37–39.

99. *Citizens League Report, Sub-urbs in The City*, Minneapolis, May 13, 1970, *ibid.*, 28–31.

100. The Committee for Economic Development, *Reshaping Government in Metropolitan Areas* (New York: Committee for Economic Development, 1970), *ibid.*, 24–27. Under a two-tier system, functions such as planning, zoning, and transportation would be transferred upward to the regional level, while street and sewer repairs and garbage pickup would be vested in the neighborhood governments. Opponents argued that decentralization would reintroduce an obstructive localism and that its motivation often was political. Criticizing city governments in 1967, Frederick Gutheim wrote: "One can glimpse in the future a possible governmental structure in which large metropolitan regional cities . . . would be mainly concerned with natural resources and the landscape, rather as can be seen emerging in the Atlantic seaboard and the San Francisco Bay region. One can further perceive, as strongly rooted in human desires and behavior, a small-scale unit of government in which the traditional face-to-face political transactions of local democracy will take place and the requirements of democratic participation and leadership [will be] sustained. Allocated between the two, or perhaps assigned to still a third level of government, would be the remaining functions of local governments, predominantly comprising services, many of them essentially economic in their nature." *Urban America*, 140.

101. Alan K. Campbell, "How to Decentralize Intelligently and Painlessly," *The New York Times*, February 3, 1972. In a letter to *The New York Times*, March 1, 1972,. Joan Aron, assistant professor of public administration, New York University, argues that if metro government for New York City is to be extended to encompass the entire metropolitan area, it might be as practical to reconstitute this "tristate regional tier as a new Federal-multistate government or even as a new metropolitan state."

102. Open Letter to Governor Rockefeller and Mayor Lindsay. See Martin Tolchin, "Wagner Leads Opposition to Three-Tier City Rule," *The New York Times*, March 11, 1972. Different three-tier proposals had been offered by two of the city's borough presidents, Percy E. Sutton (Manhattan) and Robert Abrams (Bronx). Joining Mayor Wagner in the movement of opposition were Robert Moses, Representative Herman Badillo, former deputy mayor Robert D. Sweet, Rexford E. Tompkins, chairman of the Real Estate Board of New York, Michael Maye, president of the Uniformed Fire Fighters Association, Victor Gotbaum, executive director of District Council 37 of the American Federation of State, County, and Municipal Employees, Lewis Rudin, chairman of the Association for a Better New York, Richard Ravitch, president of the H. R. H. Construction Corporation, Whitney North Seymour, U.S. Attorney for the Southern District, Herbert Brownell, former U.S. Attorney General, Bayard Rustin, civil rights leader, Bethuel M. Webster, lawyer, Dr. Kenneth B. Clark, psychologist, Thomas P. F. Hoving, Lawrence Buttenweiser, Wallace Sayre, chairman of the Government Department, Columbia University, Edward J. Kiernan, president of the Patrolmen's Benefit Association, Bruce Bromley, chairman, City Board of Ethics, Albert Shanker, president of the United Federation of Teachers, and Assemblyman Albert B. Blumenthal, deputy minority leader. See "Decentralizing the City," *The New York Times*, February 22, 1972, and Martin Tolchin, "Decentralization, a Contemporary Proposal, Is Found to be an Old Republican Stratagem," *ibid.*, February 7, 1972.

103. John Ihlder, "The Automobile and Community Planning," in *The Automobile: Its Province and Its Problems*, 199–205.

104. Wallace L. Braun, "Are Business Streets for Parking — or Motoring?" *The American City*, LV (August, 1940), 85, 87–88.

105. John R. Meyer, "Urban Transportation," in Moynihan, ed., *Toward a National Urban Policy*, 66; John R. Meyer, "Urban Transportation," in *The Metropolitan Enigma: Inquiries into the Nature and Dimensions of America's "Urban Crisis,"* ed. by James Q. Wilson (Cambridge: Harvard University Press, 1968), 42–69; Wilfred Owen, *Cities in the Motor Age* (New York: Viking Press, 1969).

106. Francis Bello, "The City and the Car," in *The Exploding Metropolis*, 37–38, 44–47. An allegedly practical moving sidewalk was proposed early in 1972. This "people mover" entailed a system of belts traveling through tubes with a controlled environment. It would take passengers aboard at two miles an hour and accelerate them until they were moving at 10 miles per hour. At this point they would move safely onto a belt moving at the same speed. For getting off, a reverse pattern would operate. *The New York Times*, March 9, 1972. See also Norman Klein and Walter Arensberg, "Auto-Free Zones: Giving Cities Back to People," *City*, VI (March–April, 1972), 45–52.

107. Glenn R. Hilst, "Pollution: Another Dimension of Urbanization," in Moynihan, ed., *Toward a National Urban Policy*, 99. See also Roger Revelle, "Pollution and Cities," in Wilson, ed., *The Metropolitan Enigma*, 92–133, and *Restoring the Quality of Our Environment*. Report of the En-

vironmental Pollution Panel of the President's Science Advisory Committee (Washington, D.C., 1965). For comment on the study, "Cities and the Nation's Disposal Crisis," see *The New York Times*, June 10, 1973.

108. Norman Mailer, "Why Are We In New York?" *The New York Times Magazine*, May 18, 1969, p. 30. For a reference to the pollution and noise of the city in 1925, see Harlan P. Douglass, *The Suburban Trend*, 306–307: "In the nation's thirty-two largest cities more than twenty-two millions of people inhabit an area which would suffice for only 10,000 American farm families on farms of average size. Even though every one of them were asleep and with no conscious contacts going on, the unsettled dust of the day and the effluvium of their lungs would go on polluting the common air. . . . Sunshine which might destroy or neutralize it cannot penetrate into dark rooms or scant air shafts. The noise of the city is nerve-racking."

109. *The New York Times*, January 13, 1970.

110. Michael Harrington, *The Other America: Poverty in the United States* (New York: Macmillan, 1962), 143, 145–47.

111. Lee Rainwater, "Poverty in the United States," in Moynihan, ed., *Toward a National Urban Policy*, 201–204. See also Daniel P. Moynihan, "Poverty in Cities," in Wilson, ed., *The Metropolitan Enigma*, 336–49. Moynihan asserts that poverty in the United States, as of 1965, was "largely an urban phenomenon." Only 6 per cent of all poor households were located on farms. More than half of the poor households were living within metropolitan areas.

112. David R. Hunter, *The Slums: Challenge and Response* (New York: Free Press, 1968), 72.

113. James Q. Wilson, "Crime," in Moynihan, ed., *Toward a National Urban Policy*, 147–51; Marvin E. Wolfgang, "Urban Crime," in Wilson, ed., *The Metropolitan Enigma*, 246, 265.

114. Jimmy Breslin, "Paying Our Dues," *The Daily News*, June 16, 1969. See Jane Everhart, "White Side, Black Side, All Around The Town," *The New York Times*, October 28, 1971. Professor Gilbert Highet, Columbia University scholar, was quoted as having taken up residence in East Hampton, Long Island, in 1970, because "he was 'frightened' by a lack of safety in the city." *The New York Times*, June 30, 1972.

115. James F. Richardson, "To Control the City: the New York Police in Historical Perspective," in Jackson and Schultz, ed., *Cities in American History*, 285–88. See also *The Police: Six Sociological Essays*, ed. by David J. Bordua (New York: John Wiley and Sons, 1967); Jerome H. Skolnick, *Justice Without Trial: Law Enforcement in a Democratic Society* (New York: John Wiley and Sons, 1966); Bruce Smith, *Police Systems in the United States* (New York: Harper and Row, 1949); James Q. Wilson, *Varieties of Police Behavior: The Management of Law and Order in Eight Communities* (Cambridge: Harvard University Press, 1968); Skolnick, ed., *The Politics of Protest*.

116. Hallock Hoffman, "Policing the Police," in *The Center Magazine*, I (May, 1968), 60–64. Some policemen took an innovative view of the drug problem, like that of Albert J. Carhart, a police lieutenant in the Linden, New Jersey, police force. Lieutenant Carhart argued that the crux of the drug problem was not so much the "junkies using heroin but the demand and supply problem." He recommended that the profit be taken out of heroin, by having a qualified physician in a government clinic give injections of heroin free of charge to any addict that walks in and asks for one." The heroin confiscated from pushers could be used in these clinics. Coupled with this

program would be civilian conservation corps where addicts could get away from addicts. "Better a supervised work camp, doing constructive work for the betterment of the country, than a guarded prison camp at the expense of the taxpayers." Albert J. Carhart, "Maybe the Answer to the Crime Rate Is This: Free Heroin Clinics," *The New York Times*, March 25, 1972.

117. Mayor John V. Lindsay's expense budget for 1972–73 totaled just under $10,000,000,000. Expenditures for welfare (the Human Resources Administration) constituted the largest item: $2,474,500. In presenting the budget, Lindsay wrote: "The actions of Albany and Washington leave us no choice but to frame a rigorously tight budget for the coming year. New York City, like every other American city, faces an annual fiscal crisis because its revenues are insufficient even to maintain existing municipal services. Until the state and Federal governments recognize their proper responsibilities in the financing of national programs, such as welfare and medical assistance, and agree to share their revenues equitably with already over-taxed localities it is the cities of America who must bear the burden." *The New York Times*, March 3, 1972.

118. In August, 1970, after a period of smog and breathless air, an editorial in *The New York Times* raised the question, "Is the City Livable?" and in taking a negative stand suggested that New York was "not really different from other cities, only larger and earlier in having to confront problems associated with metropolitan congestion [that], unattended, threaten the survival of urban life everywhere." *The New York Times*, August 4, 1970. At the same time, some urban specialists contended that the critical nature of urban problems was being exaggerated. In 1967, Daniel J. Elazar warned against imputing the evils of large cities like New York to medium-sized cities and interpreted the movement to the suburbs as evidence that the growth of cities was on the decline. He deplored the trend of reformers to transform urban America into a "citified" America, "hallowing the city as the only key to the civilized life, much as the early agrarians hallowed ruralism as the only key to a moral life." Daniel J. Elazar, "Urbanization and Federalism in the United States," in *Urban America: Goals and Problems*, 195, 202, 208. Edward C. Banfield took the view that technological, economic, demographic, and population changes, over time, would solve many of the current problems of cities and that undue alarm was causing the federal government to engage in ill-considered programs, such as subsidizing home ownership for the well-to-do and truck and automobile transportation through highway expansion, which were doing more harm than good. He saw a potential resolution of racial tension in the prevailing improvement in the economic status of many Blacks and in the increase in residential facilities, outside the slums, that would permit Blacks to leave the slum environment without losing the society of other Blacks. Edward C. Banfield, *The Unheavenly City: The Nature and Future of Our Urban Crisis* (Boston: Little, Brown, 1968), 81–87, 204–7, 255–63. See also Irving Kristol, "It's Not a Bad Crisis to Live in," *The New York Times Magazine*, January 22, 1967, p. 23ff. For an assertion of the continuing ambivalence toward the city, see Brooks Atkinson, who admitted that when he was in the country his day did not begin until the New York newspapers had arrived; at the same time he found the mood of the country more satisfying than that of the city, where people were so "preoccupied with their own miseries they hardly knew that other people existed." *Ibid.*, March 15 and December 6, 1970. See also Everett K. Wilson, "Some Notes on the Pains and Prospects of American Cities," *Confluence, An International Forum*, VII (1958), 1–15; William H. Whyte, *The Anti-City*, in Elizabeth Geen *et*

al., eds., *Man and the Modern City* (Pittsburgh: University of Pittsburgh Press, 1963), 45–58.

119. Eugene Raskin, "Are Our Cities Doomed? Yes," *The New York Times*, May 12, 1971, Section VIII, 1, 12.

120. Samuel Tenenbaum, "Are Our Cities Doomed? No," *ibid.*, 1, 11.

121. Richard Reeves, "What Can Be Done?" *ibid.*, 1, 12.

122. The Commission on Population Growth and the Future, reporting in March, 1972, recommended alternate growth centers, and urged the federal government to develop national population guidelines for regional, state, and local governments. They also recommended that limitations be imposed on immigration into cities. *The New York Times*, March 26, 1972. Students of the city were considering optimum size early in the 1950's. See James Dahir, "What Is the Best Size for a City?" *The American City*, LXVI (August, 1951), 104–5, and Otis D. Duncan, "Optimum Size of Cities," in Paul Hatt and Albert Reiss, eds., *Reader in Urban Sociology* (Glencoe, Ill.: Free Press, 1951). Robert A. Dahl, writing on "The City in the Future of Democracy," expressed the view that "optimum size for a contemporary American city is probably somewhere between 50,000 and 200,000 (which may be the threshold for wide civic participation)." He doubts that there are any economies of scale in cities over 50,000. He writes: ". . . we have barely begun to explore the ways in which small cities by federating together for specific purposes might enjoy all the cultural advantages of the large city, yet retain their individual identities, the pleasures of living in communities of lower densities and more open spaces, and relatively greater opportunities for political participation." *American Political Science Review*, LXI (December, 1967), 966.

123. In 1958, John F. Kennedy, then senator from Massachusetts, contended that cities were receiving "all too little help and encouragement from Washington and the state legislatures." The "failure of our governments to respond to the problems of the cities," he wrote, resulted from the fact that though the "majority of Americans . . . live in the metropolitan areas . . . the rural minority dominates the polls." He laid this situation to the "apportionment of representation in our Legislatures and (to a lesser extent) in Congress," which "has been either deliberately rigged or shamefully ignored so as to deny the cities and their voters that full and proportionate voice in government to which they are entitled." John F. Kennedy, "The Shame of the States," reprinted from *The New York Times Magazine*, May 18, 1958, in Ray Ginger, ed., *Modern American Cities* (Chicago: Quadrangle Books, 1969), 201–208. Though apportionment was in some measure reformed, in succeeding years, the dichotomy between suburb and inner city minimized the influence of urban dwellers at the polls. For comment on the urban program of the Nixon administration, see *The New York Times*, March 29, 1972.

124. Some of the methods of reducing smog, as proposed to implement the Clean Air Act of 1970, were enforced auto inspection, limitations on gasoline sales, prohibitions on the building of additional parking lots, installation of anti-pollution devices on cars, prohibitions on taxi cruising, bridge tolls, and bans on the use of cars in the city, one day per week. See *The New York Times*, June 16, 1973. See also *ibid.*, June 15, 1973, for references to curbs on zoning.

125. Daniel P. Moynihan, "Toward a National Urban Policy," *The Public Interest*, no. 17 (Fall, 1969), 8–10, 12–17, 19. See also, on Moynihan, *The New York Times*, July 2, December 23, 1970. Another statement of recommendations for coping with the nation's urban problems is that of the panel

convened by the National Urban Coalition and chaired by Senator Fred R. Harris and Mayor John V. Lindsay to examine the condition of American cities three years after the Kerner Commission report. See *The State of the Cities: Report of the Commission on the Cities in the '70's,* 97–110.

SUGGESTIONS FOR FURTHER READING

Popular concern with the problems of cities, especially since the 1950's, together with scholars' heightened interest in urban development, has resulted in the publication of hundreds of books and articles dealing with urban growth in the United States and with the nature and problems of the American urban scene. Fortunately, many of the best of these are now in paperbound editions, making them more accessible. Those listed below amplify discussions in the text; many of them are available in paperback. Rarely have I cited articles. An asterisk indicates that there is a paperback edition; these are not always produced by the publisher of the original work. Data on publishers and prices of paperbound books can be found in *Paperbound Books in Print* (New York: Bowker Publishing Co.).

There are, as yet, few comprehensive histories of the urban side of the American experience, despite the fact that as early as 1932 a committee of the American Historical Association cited the history of cities and urbanism as one of the areas of American history most in need of study. The first response of professional historians was to undertake comprehensive histories of individual cities or comparative studies of groups of cities for more limited periods. Arthur M. Schlesinger, Sr. made a pioneering attempt to summarize the historical impact of the city in an article published in 1940, "The City in American History," *Mississippi Valley Historical Review*, XXVII (June, 1940), 43–66; and some of the volumes of the series *A History of American Life* (New York: Macmillan, 1927–1948), which he edited in association with Dixon Ryan Fox, gave more than customary attention to the details of urban growth and urban life (cf. *John A. Krout and Dixon R. Fox, *The Completion of Independence, 1790–1830* [1944], *Allan Nevins, *The Emergence of Modern America, 1865–1878* [1927], and *Arthur M. Schlesinger, *The Rise of the City, 1878–1898* [1933]. An alternative to the comprehensive survey has been found in anthologies of significant articles from professional journals or collections of documents arranged to reveal the evolution of the nation's urban society. However, most of the output in the urban field continues to be special studies on aspects of the history of individual cities or groups of cities. These works reflect increasingly the interdisciplinary nature of the study of urban history — exhibited also in the currently expanding body of writing posing new questions about urban history and employing new methodology for describing patterns of urban growth and for measuring the effect of urbanism on American attitudes, status, and behavior.

COMPREHENSIVE SURVEYS: *Charles N. Glaab and A. Theodore Brown, *A History of Urban America* (New York: Macmillan, 1967); *Constance M. Green, *American Cities in the Growth of the Nation* (London: John De Graf, 1957); *Constance M. Green, *The Rise of Urban America* (New York: Harper and Row, 1965); Blake McKelvey, *The Urbanization of America: 1860–1915* (New Brunswick, N.J.: Rutgers University Press, 1963); Blake McKelvey, *The Emergence of Metropolitan America: 1915–1966* (New Brunswick, N.J.: Rutgers University Press, 1968).

COMPREHENSIVE WORKS WITH SPECIALIZED OR TOPICAL EMPHASES: *Blake McKelvey, *American Urbanization: A Comparative History* (Glenview, Ill.: Scott, Foresman, 1973); *Zane Miller, *The Urbanization of Modern America: A Brief History* (New York: Harcourt, Brace, Jovanovich, 1973); *Raymond A. Mohl and James F. Richardson, eds., *The Urban Experience: Themes in American History* (Belmont, Cal.: Wadsworth Publishing Co., 1973); *Ruth E. Sutter, *The Next Place You Come To* (Englewood Cliffs, N.J.: Prentice-Hall, 1973); *Sam Bass Warner, Jr., *The Urban Wilderness: A History of the American City* (New York: Harper and Row, 1973); *Adna Ferrin Weber, *The Growth of Cities in the Nineteenth Century: A Study in Statistics* (Ithaca, N.Y.: Cornell University Press, 1963 [first published in 1899]).

ANTHOLOGIES OF INTERPRETATIVE ARTICLES: *Alexander B. Callow, ed., *American Urban History: An Interpretive Reader with Commentaries* (New York: Oxford, 1969, revised ed., 1973); *Kenneth Jackson and Stanley K. Schultz, eds., *Cities in American History* (New York: Alfred Knopf, 1972); *Paul Kramer and Frederick L. Holborn, eds., *The City in American Life: A Historical Anthology* (New York: G. P. Putnam's Sons, 1970); Raymond Mohl and Neil Betten, eds., *Urban America in Historical Perspective* (New York: Weybright and Talley, 1970); *James F. Richardson, ed., *The American City: Historical Studies* (Waltham, Mass.: Xerox College Publishing Co., 1972); *Allen Wakstein, ed., *The Urbanization of America: A Reader* (Boston: Houghton Mifflin, 1970).

EDITED COLLECTIONS OF CONTEMPORARY WRITING DESCRIBING CITIES: *Charles N. Glaab, *The American City: A Documentary History* (Homewood, Ill.: Dorsey Press, 1963); Blake McKelvey, *The City in American History* (New York: Barnes and Noble, 1969) —

contains an extensive introduction; Bessie L. Pierce, ed., *As Others See Chicago: Impressions of Visitors, 1673–1933* (Chicago: University of Chicago Press, 1933); *Wilson Smith, ed., *Cities of Our Past and Present* (New York: John Wiley and Sons, 1964); *David R. Weimer, ed., *City and Country in America* (New York: Appleton-Century-Crofts, 1962); *David R. Weimer, *The City as Metaphor* (New York: Random House, 1966).

COMPREHENSIVE HISTORIES OF INDIVIDUAL CITIES OR OF SUBSTANTIAL SEGMENTS OF THEIR HISTORY: [Boston] Walter Firey, *Land Use in Central Boston* (Cambridge: Harvard University Press, 1947); Walter M. Whitehill, *Boston: A Topographical History* (Cambridge: Harvard University Press, 1959); [Baltimore] Raphael Semmes, *Baltimore as Seen by Visitors, 1783–1860* (Baltimore: Maryland Historical Society, 1953); [Buffalo] Robert W. Bingham, *The Cradle of the Queen City* (Buffalo: Buffalo Historical Society, 1931); [Chicago] Homer Hoyt, *One Hundred Years of Land Values in Chicago: The Relationship of the Growth of Chicago to the Rise in its Land Values, 1830–1933* (Chicago: University of Chicago Press, 1933); Bessie L. Pierce, *A History of Chicago* [I, *The Beginning of a City, 1673–1848*; II, *From Town to City, 1848–1871*; III, *The Rise of a Modern City, 1871–1893*] (New York: Alfred Knopf, 1937–1957); [Chicopee, Mass.] Vera Shlakman, *Economic History of a Factory Town: A Study of Chicopee, Massachusetts* (Northampton, Mass.: Department of History of Smith College, 1935); [Cincinnati] Clara Chambrun, *Cincinnati: Story of the Queen City* (New York: Scribner's Sons, 1939); [Cleveland] Edmund H. Chapman, *Cleveland: Village to Metropolis: A Case Study of Problems of Urban Development in Nineteenth-Century America* (Cleveland: Western Reserve Historical Society and Press of Western Reserve University, 1964); [Detroit] Sidney Glazer, *Detroit: A Study in Urban Development* (New York: Twayne Publishers, 1965); Arthur Pound, *Detroit: Dynamic Detroit* (New York: D. Appleton-Century, 1940); [Durham, N.C.] William K. Boyd, *The Story of Durham, City of the New South* (Durham, N.C.: Duke University Press, 1937); [Holyoke, Mass.] Constance M. Green, *Holyoke, Massachusetts: A Case History of the Industrial Revolution in America* (New Haven: Yale University Press, 1939); [Kansas City, Mo.] A. Theodore Brown, *Frontier Community: Kansas City to 1870* (Columbia: University of Missouri Press, 1963); [Lawrence, Mass.] Donald B. Cole, *Immigrant City: Lawrence, Massachusetts, 1845–1921* (Chapel Hill: University of North Carolina Press, 1963); [Los Angeles] Robert M. Fogelson, *The Fragmented Metropolis: Los Angeles, 1850–1930* (Cambridge: Harvard University Press, 1967); [Memphis] Gerald Capers, *The Biography of a River Town; Memphis: Its Heroic Age* (Chapel Hill:

University of North Carolina Press, 1939); [Milwaukee] Bayrd Still, *Milwaukee: The History of a City* (Madison: State Historical Society of Wisconsin, 1948, revised ed., 1965); [Minneapolis and St. Paul] Mildred Hartsough, *The Twin Cities as a Metropolitan Market: A Regional Study of the Economic Development of Minneapolis and St. Paul* (Minneapolis: University of Minnesota, 1925); Calvin F. Schmid, *Social Saga of Two Cities: An Ecological and Statistical Study of Social Trends in Minneapolis and St. Paul* (Minneapolis: Minnesota Council of Social Agencies, 1937); [Naugatuck, Conn.] Constance M. Green, *History of Naugatuck, Connecticut* (New Haven: Yale University Press, 1948); [New Haven] Rollin G. Osterweis, *Three Centuries of New Haven, 1638–1938* (New Haven: Yale University Press, 1953); [New York] Bayrd Still, *Mirror for Gotham: New York as Seen by Contemporaries from Dutch Days to the Present* (New York: New York University Press, 1956); [Philadelphia] *Sam Bass Warner, Jr., *The Private City: Philadelphia in Three Periods of Its Growth* (Philadelphia: University of Pennsylvania Press, 1968); [Pittsburgh] *Leland Baldwin, *Pittsburgh, the Story of a City* (Pittsburgh: University of Pittsburgh Press, 1937); *Roy Lubove, *Twentieth-Century Pittsburgh* (New York: John Wiley and Sons, 1969); [Rochester, N.Y.] Blake McKelvey, *Rochester: The Water-Power City, 1812–1854; Rochester: The Flower City, 1855–1890; Rochester: The Quest for Quality, 1890–1925* (Cambridge: Harvard University Press, 1945–1956); *Rochester: An Emerging Metropolis, 1925–1961* (Rochester: Christopher Press, 1961); [San Francisco] Mel Scott, *The San Francisco Bay Area: A Metropolis in Perspective* (Berkeley and Los Angeles: University of California Press, 1959); [Washington, D.C.] Constance M. Green, *Washington, Village and Capital, 1800–1878; Washington, Capital City, 1879–1950* (Princeton: Princeton University Press, 1962–1963).

PICTORIAL HISTORIES: [Baltimore] Francis F. Beirne, *Baltimore — A Picture History, 1858–1958* (New York: Hastings House, 1957); [Chicago] Harold Mayer and Richard C. Wade, with the assistance of Glen E. Holt, *Chicago: Growth of a Metropolis* (Chicago: University of Chicago Press, 1969); [Detroit] Milo M. Quaife, *This Is Detroit* (Detroit: Wayne University Press, 1951); [New York] *John A. Kouwenhoven, *The Columbia Historical Portrait of New York* (Garden City, N.Y.: Doubleday, 1953).

SPECIAL STUDIES CONTRIBUTING TO AN UNDERSTANDING OF URBAN DEVELOPMENT FROM COLONIAL BEGINNINGS TO 1820: *Bernard Bailyn, *The New England Merchants in the Seventeenth Century* (Cambridge: Harvard University Press, 1955); William T. Baxter, *The House of Hancock: Business in Boston, 1724–1775* (Cambridge: Harvard University Press, 1945); John B. Blake, *Public Health in the*

Town of Boston, 1630–1822 (Cambridge: Harvard University Press, 1959); *Carl Bridenbaugh, *Cities in the Wilderness: The First Century of Urban Life in America, 1625–1742* (New York: Ronald Press, 1938); *Carl Bridenbaugh, *Cities in Revolt: Urban Life in America, 1743–1776* (New York: Alfred Knopf, 1955); *Carl Bridenbaugh, *The Colonial Craftsman* (New York: New York University Press, 1950); *Carl Bridenbaugh, *Seat of Empire* [Williamsburg] (Williamsburg: Colonial Williamsburg, 1950); *Carl Bridenbaugh and Jessica Bridenbaugh, *Rebels and Gentlemen: Philadelphia in the Age of Franklin* (New York: Oxford, 1942); *John Demos, *A Little Commonwealth: Family Life in Plymouth Colony* (New York: Oxford University Press, 1970); Anthony N. B. Garvan, *Architecture and Town Planning in Colonial Connecticut* (New Haven: Yale University Press, 1951); David T. Gilchrist, ed., *The Growth of the Seaport Cities, 1790–1825* (Charlottesville: University Press of Virginia, 1967); *Philip J. Greven, Jr., *Four Generations: Population, Land, and Family in Colonial Andover, Massachusetts* (Ithaca: Cornell University Press, 1970); Ernest S. Griffith, *History of American City Government: The Colonial Period* (New York: Oxford, 1938); William Haller, *The Puritan Frontier: Town Planning in New England Colonial Development, 1630–1660* (New York: Columbia University Press, 1951); James A. Henretta, "Economic Development and Social Structure in Colonial Boston," *William and Mary Quarterly*, 3rd. ser., XXII (January, 1965), 75–92; Arthur L. Jensen, *The Maritime Commerce of Colonial Philadelphia* (Madison: State Historical Society of Wisconsin, 1963); Harold Kirker and James Kirker, *Bulfinch's Boston, 1787–1817* (New York: Oxford, 1964); Benjamin Labaree, *Patriots and Partisans: The Merchants of Newburyport, 1764–1815* (Cambridge: Harvard University Press, 1962); *Kenneth A. Lockridge, *A New England Town: The First Hundred Years: Dedham, Massachusetts, 1636–1736* (New York: Norton, 1970); Pauline Maier, *From Resistance to Revolution: Colonial Radicals and the Development of American Opposition to Britain* (New York: Alfred Knopf, 1972); *Jackson T. Main, *The Social Structure of Revolutionary America* (Princeton: Princeton University Press, 1965); Bernard Mayo, "Lexington [Kentucky]: Frontier Metropolis," in Eric Goldman, ed., *Historiography and Urbanization* (Baltimore: Johns Hopkins Press, 1941), 21–42; Raymond A. Mohl, *Poverty in New York, 1783–1825* (New York: Oxford, 1971); Sidney I. Pomerantz, *New York: An American City, 1783–1803: A Study of Urban Life* (New York: Columbia University Press, 1938, revised ed., 1965); *Sumner C. Powell, *Puritan Village: The Formation of a New England Town* (Garden City, N.Y.: Doubleday, 1965); John C. Rainbolt, "The Absence of Towns in Seventeenth-Century

Virginia," *Journal of Southern History*, XXXV (August, 1969), 343–60; John W. Reps, *Tidewater Towns: City Planning in Colonial Virginia and Maryland* (Charlottesville: University Press of Virginia, 1972); Julius Rubin, "Urban Growth and Regional Development," in David T. Gilchrist, ed., *The Growth of the Seaport Cities, 1790–1825* (Charlottesville: University Press of Virginia, 1967), 3–21; *Darrett B. Rutman, *Winthrop's Boston: Portrait of a Puritan Town, 1630–1649* (Chapel Hill: University of North Carolina Press, 1965); *Frederick B. Tolles, *Meeting House and Counting House: The Quaker Merchants of Colonial Philadelphia, 1682–1763* (New York: Norton, 1948); *Richard C. Wade, *The Urban Frontier: The Rise of Western Cities, 1790–1830* (Cambridge: Harvard University Press, 1959); *Richard Walsh, *Charleston's Sons of Liberty: A Study of the Artisans, 1763–1789* (Charleston: University of South Carolina Press, 1959); Gerard B. Warden, *Boston, 1689–1776* (Boston: Little, Brown, 1970); Thomas J. Wertenbaker, *Father Knickerbocker Rebels: New York during the Revolution* (New York: Scribner's Sons, 1948); *Thomas J. Wertenbaker, *The Golden Age of Colonial Culture* (New York: New York University Press, 1942); Thomas J. Wertenbaker, *Norfolk: Historic Southern Port*, revised ed. by Marvin W. Schlegel (Durham, N.C.: Duke University Press, 1962); *Michael Zuckerman, *Peaceable Kingdoms: New England Towns in the Eighteenth Century* (New York: Alfred Knopf, 1970).

SPECIAL STUDIES BEARING ON URBAN DEVELOPMENT, 1820 TO 1870: Robert G. Albion, *The Rise of New York Port: 1815–1860* (New York: Scribner's Sons, 1939); *Herbert Asbury, *The Gangs of New York: An Informal History of the Underworld* (New York: G. P. Putnam's Sons, 1927); Wyatt W. Belcher, *The Economic Rivalry between St. Louis and Chicago, 1850–1880* (New York: Columbia University Press, 1947); Nelson M. Blake, *Water for the Cities: A History of the Urban Water Supply Problem in the United States* (Syracuse: Syracuse University Press, 1956); *Alexander Callow, *The Tweed Ring* (New York: Oxford, 1966); Gerald M. Capers, *Occupied City: New Orleans under the Federals, 1862–1865* (Lexington: University of Kentucky Press, 1965); John Coolidge, *Mill and Mansion: A Study of Architecture and Society in Lowell, Massachusetts, 1820–1865* (New York: Columbia University Press, 1942); *Kenneth Coleman, ed., *Athens, 1861–65: As Seen through Letters in the University of Georgia Libraries* (Athens: University of Georgia Press, 1967); John Duffy, *A History of Public Health in New York City, 1625–1866* (New York: Russell Sage Foundation, 1968); Robert Ernst, *Immigrant Life in New York City, 1825–1863* (New York: King's Crown Press, 1949); Michael H. Frisch, *Town into City: Springfield, Massachusetts and the Meaning of Community, 1840–*

1880 (Cambridge: Harvard University Press, 1972); Paul W. Gates, *The Illinois Central Railroad and Its Colonization Work* (Cambridge: Harvard University Press, 1934); *Eugene Genovese, *The Political Economy of Slavery: Studies in the Economy and Society of the Slave South* (New York: Pantheon Books, 1965); Carter Goodrich, *Government Promotion of Canals and Railroads, 1800–1890* (New York: Columbia University Press, 1960); *Walter Hugins, *Jacksonian Democracy and the Working Class* (Stanford: Stanford University Press, 1960); Clayton James, *Antebellum Natchez* (Baton Rouge: Louisiana State University Press, 1968); Edward C. Kirkland, *Men, Cities and Transportation: A Study in New England History, 1820–1900* (Cambridge: Harvard University Press, 1948); Peter S. Knights, *The Plain People of Boston, 1830–1860: A Study in City Growth* (New York: Oxford, 1971); *Roger C. Lane, *Policing the City: Boston, 1822–1885* (Cambridge: Harvard University Press, 1967); Lawrence H. Larsen, "Nineteenth-Century Street Sanitation: A Study in Filth and Frustration," *Wisconsin Magazine of History*, LII (1969), 239–47; James W. Livingood, *The Philadelphia-Baltimore Trade Rivalry, 1780–1860* (Harrisburg: Pennsylvania Historical and Museum Commission, 1947); *Seymour Mandelbaum, *Boss Tweed's New York* (New York: John Wiley and Sons, 1965); Jerome Mushkat, *Tammany: The Evolution of a Political Machine: 1789–1865* (Syracuse: Syracuse University Press, 1971); Earl F. Niehaus, *The Irish in New Orleans, 1800–1860* (Baton Rouge: Louisiana State University Press, 1965); Allan Pred, "Manufacturing in the American Mercantile City: 1800–1840," *Annals of the Association of American Geographers*, LVI (June, 1966), 307–25; Merl E. Reed, *New Orleans and the Railroads: The Struggle for Commercial Empire, 1830–1860* (Baton Rouge: Louisiana State University Press, 1966); Robert C. Reinders, *End of an Era: New Orleans, 1850–1860* (New Orleans: Pelican Publishing Co., 1965); *Leonard L. Richards, "*Gentlemen of Property and Standing*": Anti-Abolitionist Mobs in Jacksonian America* (New York: Oxford, 1969); James F. Richardson, *The New York Police: Colonial Times to 1901* (New York: Oxford, 1970); Carroll S. Rosenberg, *Religion and the Rise of the American City: The New York City Mission Movement, 1812–1870* (Ithaca: Cornell University Press, 1971); *Charles E. Rosenberg, *The Cholera Years: The United States in 1832, 1849, and 1866* (Chicago: University of Chicago Press, 1962); *David J. Rothman, *The Discovery of the Asylum: Social Order and Disorder in the New Republic* (Boston: Little, Brown, 1971); Julius Rubin, *Canal or Railroad? Imitation and Innovation in the Response to the Erie Canal in Philadelphia, Baltimore, and Boston* (Philadelphia: American Philosophical Society, 1961); Peter J. Schmitt, *Back to Nature: The Arcadian Myth in*

Urban America (New York: Oxford, 1970); Stanley K. Schultz, *The Culture Factory: Boston Public Schools, 1789–1860* (New York: Oxford, 1973); George R. Taylor, "American Urban Growth Preceding the Railway Age," *Journal of Economic History*, XXVII (September, 1967), 309–39; George R. Taylor, "The Beginnings of Mass Transportation in Urban America," *Smithsonian Journal of History*, I (Summer, 1966), 35–50; (Autumn, 1966), 31–54; *Stephan Thernstrom, *Poverty and Progress: Social Mobility in a Nineteenth-Century City* (Cambridge: Harvard University Press, 1964); *Stephan Thernstrom and Richard Sennett, *Nineteenth-Century Cities: Essays in the New Urban History* (New Haven: Yale University Press, 1969); *Norman Ware, *The Industrial Worker, 1840–1860: The Reaction of American Industrial Society to the Advance of the Industrial Revolution* (Boston: Houghton Mifflin, 1924); Kenneth Wheeler, *To Wear a City's Crown: The Beginnings of Urban Growth in Texas, 1836–1865* (Cambridge: Harvard University Press, 1968); Jeffrey G. Williamson and Joseph A. Swanson, "The Growth of Cities in the American Northeast, 1820–1870," *Explorations in Entrepreneurial History*, 2d series, IV, no. 1 (1966), supplement, 3–10; Jeffrey G. Williamson, "Ante-Bellum Urbanization in the American Northeast," *Journal of Economic History*, XXV (December, 1965), 592–608.

SPECIAL STUDIES HELPFUL FOR AN UNDERSTANDING OF URBAN GROWTH AND SOCIETY, 1870 TO 1920: Aaron I. Abell, *The Urban Impact on American Protestantism, 1865–1900* (Cambridge: Harvard University Press, 1943); James B. Allen, *The Company Town in the American West* (Norman: University of Oklahoma Press, 1966); John Alley, *City Beginnings in Oklahoma Territory* (Norman: University of Oklahoma Press, 1939); *Walton Bean, *Boss Ruef's San Francisco* (Berkeley: University of California Press, 1952); *Stanley Buder, *Pullman: An Experiment in Industrial Order and Community Planning, 1880–1930* (New York: Oxford, 1967); Howard P. Chudacoff, *Mobile Americans: Residential and Social Mobility in Omaha, 1880–1920* (New York: Oxford, 1973); Thomas D. Clark and Albert D. Kirwan, *The South since Appomattox: A Century of Regional Change* (New York: Oxford, 1967), Chap. 15; James B. Crooks, *Politics and Progress: The Rise of Urban Progressivism in Baltimore, 1895 to 1911* (Baton Rouge: Louisiana State University Press, 1968); Robert D. Cross, *The Emergence of Liberal Catholicism in America* (Cambridge: Harvard University Press, 1958); *Robert D. Cross, ed., *The Church and the City, 1865–1910* (Indianapolis: Bobbs-Merrill, 1967); *Allen F. Davis, *Spearheads for Reform: The Social Settlements and the Progressive Movement, 1890–1914* (New York: Oxford, 1967); *Lyle Dorsett, *The Prendergast Machine* (New York:

Oxford, 1968); *Robert R. Dykstra, *The Cattle Towns* (New York: Alfred Knopf, 1968); *Louis G. Geiger, *Joseph W. Folk of Missouri* (Columbia: University of Missouri Press, 1953); Ray Ginger, *Altgeld's America* [Chicago] (New York: Funk and Wagnalls, 1958); Charles N. Glaab, *Kansas City and the Railroads: Community Policy in the Growth of a Regional Metropolis* (Madison: State Historical Society of Wisconsin, 1962); Joseph M. Hawes, *Children in Urban Society: Juvenile Delinquency in Nineteenth-Century America* (New York: Oxford, 1971); Samuel P. Hays, "The Politics of Reform in Municipal Government in the Progressive Era," *Pacific Northwest Historical Quarterly*, LV (October, 1964), 157–69; Robert Higgs, "The Growth of Cities in a Midwestern Region, 1870–1900," *Journal of Regional Science*, IX (1969), 369–75; *Melvin G. Holli, *Reform in Detroit: Hazen S. Pingree and Urban Politics* (New York: Oxford, 1969); *Charles H. Hopkins, *The Rise of the Social Gospel in American Protestantism, 1865–1915* (New Haven: Yale University Press, 1940); Nathan I. Huggins, *Protestants against Poverty: Boston's Charities, 1870–1900* (Westport, Conn.: Greenwood, 1970); Joseph J. Huthmacher, "Urban Liberalism and the Age of Reform," *Mississippi Valley Historical Review*, XLIX (September, 1962), 231–41; Joy J. Jackson, *New Orleans in the Gilded Age: Politics and Urban Progress, 1880–1896* (Baton Rouge: Louisiana State University Press, 1970); *Kenneth T. Jackson, *The Ku Klux Klan in the City, 1915–1930* (New York: Oxford, 1967); *Edward C. Kirkland, *Industry Comes of Age: Business, Labor and Public Policy, 1860–1897* (New York: Holt, Rinehart and Winston, 1961); Gerd Korman, *Industrialization, Immigrants and Americanizers: The View from Milwaukee, 1866–1921* (Madison: State Historical Society of Wisconsin, 1967); Roy Lubove, *The Progressives and the Slums: Tenement House Reform in New York City, 1890–1917* (Pittsburgh: University of Pittsburgh Press, 1962); *Arthur Mann, *Yankee Reformers in the Urban Age: Social Reform in Boston, 1880–1900* (New York: Harper and Row, 1954); *Henry F. May, *Protestant Churches and Industrial America* (New York: Harper and Brothers, 1949); Robert K. Merton, "The Latent Functions of the Machine," in *Social Theory and Social Structure* (New York: Free Press, 1957), 71–82; William D. Miller, *Memphis during the Progressive Era, 1900–1917* (Memphis: Memphis State University Press, 1957); *Zane Miller, *Boss Cox's Cincinnati: Urban Politics in the Progressive Era* (New York: Oxford, 1968); Remi A. Nadeau, *The City Makers: the Story of Southern California's First Boom, 1868–76* (Los Angeles: Trans-Angelo Books, 1965); Humbert S. Nelli, *The Italians in Chicago, 1880–1930: A Study in Ethnic Mobility* (New York: Oxford, 1970); Ransom E. Noble, *New Jersey Progressivism before Wilson* (Princeton: Princeton University Press,

1946); Richard C. Overton, *Burlington West: A Colonization History of the Burlington Railroad* (Cambridge: Harvard University Press, 1941); Clifford W. Patton, *The Battle for Municipal Reform* (College Park, Md.: McGrath Publishing Co., 1970; reprint of 1940 edition); *Rodman W. Paul, *Mining Frontiers of the Far West* (New York: Holt, Rinehart and Winston, 1963); Earl Pomeroy, *The Pacific Slope* (New York: Alfred Knopf, 1965); Glen C. Quiett, *They Built the West; an Epic of Rails and Cities* (New York: D. Appleton-Century, 1934); *Moses Rischin, *The Promised City: New York's Jews, 1870–1914* (Cambridge: Harvard University Press, 1962); Duane A. Smith, *Rocky Mountain Mining Camps: The Urban Frontier* (Bloomington: Indiana University Press, 1967); Frank Stewart, *A Half Century of Municipal Reform: The History of the Municipal Reform League* (Berkeley: University of California Press, 1950); Harold C. Syrett, *The City of Brooklyn, 1865–1898; a Political History* (New York: Columbia University Press, 1944); Jack Tager, *The Intellectual as Urban Reformer: Brand Whitlock and the Progressive Movement* (Cleveland: Press of Case Western Reserve University, 1968); *James H. Timberlake, *Prohibition and the Progressive Movement, 1900–1920* (Cambridge: Harvard University Press, 1963); *Stephan Thernstrom, "Urbanization, Migration, and Social Mobility in Late Nineteenth Century America," in *Towards a New Past*, ed. by Barton Bernstein (New York: Pantheon Books, 1968), 158–75; Rupert B. Vance and Nicholas J. Demerath, eds., *The Urban South* (Chapel Hill: University of North Carolina Press, 1954); Marvin Wachman, *History of the Social Democratic Party of Milwaukee, 1897–1910* (Urbana: *Illinois Studies in the Social Sciences*, XXVIII (1945); Louise Wade, *Graham Taylor: Pioneer for Social Justice, 1851–1898* (Chicago: University of Chicago Press, 1964); Hoyt L. Warner, *Progressivism in Ohio, 1897–1917* (Columbus: Ohio State University Press, 1964); *Sam B. Warner, Jr., *Streetcar Suburbs: The Process of Growth in Boston, 1870–1900* (Cambridge: Harvard University Press and M.I.T. Press, 1962); James Weinstein, "Organized Business and the City Commission and Manager Movements," *Journal of Southern History*, XXVIII (May, 1962), 167–81; *Robert H. Wiebe, *The Search for Order, 1877–1920* (New York: Hill and Wang, 1967); Oscar O. Winther, "The Rise of Metropolitan Los Angeles, 1870–1910," *Huntington Library Quarterly*, X (August, 1947), 391–405; C. Vann Woodward, *The Origins of the New South* (New Orleans: Louisiana State University Press, 1951).

BOOKS OF SPECIAL INTEREST FOR THE PERIOD SINCE 1920: *Charles Abrams, *The City Is the Frontier* (New York: Harper and Row, 1965); *Martin Anderson, *The Federal Bulldozer: A Critical Analysis of Urban Renewal, 1949–1962* (Cambridge: M.I.T. Press, 1964);

Joseph L. Arnold, *The New Deal in the Suburbs: A History of the Greenbelt Town Program, 1935–1954* (Columbus: Ohio State University Press, 1971); *Edward C. Banfield, *Big City Politics: A Comparative Guide to the Political Systems of Nine American Cities* (New York: Random House, 1965); *Edward C. Banfield, *The Unheavenly City: The Nature and Future of Our Urban Crisis* (Boston: Little, Brown, 1968); Edward C. Banfield and Morton Grodzins, *Government and Housing in Metropolitan Areas* (New York: McGraw-Hill, 1958); *Edward C. Banfield and James Q. Wilson, *City Politics* (Cambridge: Harvard University Press and M.I.T. Press, 1963); *Bennett M. Berger, *Working-Class Suburb: A Study of Auto Workers in Suburbia* (Berkeley: University of California Press, 1968); *Brian J. L. Berry and Jack Meltzer, eds., *Goals for Urban America* (Englewood Cliffs, N.J.: Prentice-Hall, 1967); *Hans Blumenfeld, *The Modern Metropolis: Its Origins, Growth, Characteristics, and Planning*, ed. by Paul D. Spreiregen (Cambridge: M.I.T. Press, 1967); *Alan K. Campbell, ed., *The States and the Urban Crisis* (Englewood Cliffs, N.J.: Prentice-Hall, 1970); *Clarke A. Chambers, *Seedtime of Reform: American Social Service and Social Action* (Minneapolis: University of Minnesota Press, 1963); *Jim Chard and Jon York, *Urban America: Crisis and Opportunity* (Belmont, Calif.: Dickenson, 1969); Paul Conkin, *Tomorrow a New World: The New Deal Community Program* (Ithaca: Cornell University Press, 1959); *Robert E. Dahl, *Who Governs: Democracy and Power in an American City* (New Haven: Yale University Press, 1961); *William E. Dobriner, ed., *The Suburban Community* (New York: G. P. Putnam's Sons, 1958); *Scott Donaldson, *The Suburban Myth* (New York: Columbia University Press, 1969); Harlan P. Douglass, *The Suburban Trend* (New York: Century, 1925); *Anthony Downs, *Urban Problems and Prospects* (Chicago: Markham Publishing Co., 1970); *Leonard J. Duhl, ed., *The Urban Condition* (New York: Basic Books, 1963); Beverly Duncan and Stanley Lieberson, *Metropolis and Region in Transition* (Beverly Hills: Sage Publications, 1970); *Lawrence M. Friedman, *Government and Slum Housing: A Century of Frustration* (Chicago: Rand McNally, 1968); *Herbert J. Gans, *The Levittowners* (New York: Pantheon Books, 1967); *Herbert J. Gans, *People and Plans: Essays on Urban Problems and Solutions* (New York: Basic Books, 1968); *Herbert J. Gans, *The Urban Villagers: Group and Class in the Life of Italian-Americans* (New York: Free Press, 1962); Charles Garrett, *The La Guardia Years: Machine and Reform Politics in New York City* (New Brunswick, N.J.: Rutgers University Press, 1961); *Ray Ginger, ed., *Modern American Cities* (Chicago: Quadrangle Books, 1969); *Nathan Glazer, ed., *Cities in Trouble* (Chicago: Quadrangle Books, 1970); *Jean Gottmann, *Megalopolis: The*

Urbanized Northeastern Seaboard of the United States (Cambridge: M.I.T. Press, 1961); *Scott Greer, *Urban Renewal and American Cities: The Dilemma of Democratic Institutions* (Indianapolis: Bobbs-Merrill, 1965); Scott Greer, *The Urbane View: Life and Politics in Metropolitan America* (New York: Oxford University Press, 1972); Howard W. Hallman, *Neighborhood Control of Public Programs: Case Studies of Community Corporations and Neighborhood Boards* (New York: Praeger, 1970); Brett W. Hawkins, *Nashville Metro: The Politics of City-County Consolidation* (Nashville: Vanderbilt University Press, 1966); *Brett W. Hawkins, *Politics and Urban Policies* (Indianapolis: Bobbs-Merrill, 1971); A. H. Hawley, *The Changing Shape of Metropolitan America: Deconcentration since 1920* (Glencoe, Ill.: Free Press, 1956); *Edgar M. Hoover and Raymond Vernon, *Anatomy of a Metropolis* (New York: Doubleday, 1962); *Werner Z. Hirsch, ed., *Urban Life and Form* (New York: Holt, Rinehart and Winston, 1963); *Jane Jacobs, *The Death and Life of Great American Cities* (New York: Vintage Books, 1963); *Jane Jacobs, *The Economy of Cities* (New York: Random House, 1969); *Paul Jacobs, *Prelude to Riot: The Urban Condition from the Bottom Up* (New York: Random House, 1968); Edward M. Kaitz and Herbert H. Hyman, *Urban Planning for Social Welfare: A Model Cities Approach* (New York: Praeger, 1970); Don S. Kirschner, *City and Country: Rural Responses to Urbanization in the 1920's* (Westport, Conn.: Greenwood, 1970); *Milton Kotler, *Neighborhood Government: The Local Foundations of Political Life* (Indianapolis: Bobbs-Merrill Co., 1969); *Jeanne Lowe, *Cities in a Race with Time: Progress and Poverty in America's Growing Cities* (New York: Random House, 1967); Theodore J. Lowi, *At the Pleasure of the Mayor: Patronage and Power in New York City, 1898–1958* (New York, Free Press, 1964); *Roy Lubove, *The Urban Community: Housing and Planning in the Progressive Era* (Englewood Cliffs, N.J.: Prentice-Hall, 1967); *Arthur Mann, *La Guardia Comes to Power: 1933* (Chicago: University of Chicago Press, 1965); *Martin Meyerson and Edward C. Banfield, *Politics, Planning and the Public Interest: The Case of Public Housing in Chicago* (Glencoe, Ill.: Free Press, 1964; earlier edition, 1955); Martin Meyerson, Barbara Terrett, and William L. C. Wheaton, *Housing, People, and Cities* (New York: McGraw-Hill Book Co., 1962); Daniel P. Moynihan, ed., *Toward a National Urban Policy* (New York: Basic Books, 1970); *George E. Mowry, *The Urban Nation, 1920–1960* (New York: Hill and Wang, 1965); Lewis Mumford, *City Development: Studies in Disintegration and Renewal* (New York: Harcourt, Brace, 1945); *Lewis Mumford, *From the Ground Up: Observations on Contemporary Architecture, Housing, Highway Building, and Civic Design* (New York: Harcourt,

Brace, 1956); *Lewis Mumford, *The Highway and the City* (New York: Harcourt, Brace, and World, 1953); *Lewis Mumford, *The Urban Prospect* (New York: Harcourt, Brace, and World, 1968); *Wilfred Owen, *Cities in the Motor Age* (New York: Viking Press, 1959); *Frances Fox Piven and Richard A. Cloward, *Regulating the Poor: The Functions of Public Welfare* (New York: Random House, 1971); Lloyd Rodwin, *Housing and Economic Progress: A Study of the Housing Experience of Boston's Middle Income Families* (Cambridge: M.I.T. Press, 1961); *Leonard I. Ruchelman, ed., *Big City Mayors: The Crisis in Urban Politics* (Bloomington: Indiana University Press, 1970); *Donna E. Shalala, *Neighborhood Governance: Issues and Proposals* (New York: The American Jewish Committee, 1971); Auguste C. Spectorsky, *The Exurbanites* (Philadelphia: Lippincott, 1955); Bruce M. Stave, *The New Deal and the Last Hurrah: Pittsburgh Machine Politics* (Pittsburgh: University of Pittsburgh Press, 1970); *Clarence S. Stein, *Toward New Towns for America* (Liverpool: University Press of Liverpool, Eaton Press, Ltd., 1951); *Frank L. Sweetser, ed., *Studies in American Urban Society* (New York: Crowell, 1970); *Jack Tager and Park D. Goist, eds., *The Urban Vision: Selected Interpretations of the Modern American City* (Homewood, Ill.: Dorsey Press, 1970); Seymour I. Toll, *The Zoned American* (New York: Grossman Publishers, 1969); *Robert C. Weaver, *Dilemmas of Urban America* (New York: Atheneum, 1967); *Robert C. Weaver, *The Urban Complex* (Garden City, N.Y.: Anchor Books, 1966); *William H. Whyte et al., eds., *The Exploding Metropolis* (Garden City, N.Y.: Doubleday, 1958); William F. Whyte, *Street Corner Society* (Chicago: University of Chicago Press, 1943, 1955); *James Q. Wilson, ed., *The Metropolitan Enigma: Inquiries into the Nature and Dimensions of America's "Urban Crisis"* (Cambridge: Harvard University Press, 1968); *James Q. Wilson, *Varieties of Police Behavior: The Management of Law and Order in Eight Communities* (Cambridge: Harvard University Press, 1968); Robert C. Wood, *Metropolis Against Itself* (New York: Committee for Economic Development, 1959); Robert C. Wood, *The Necessary Majority: Middle America and the Urban Crisis* (New York: Columbia University Press, 1972); *Robert C. Wood, *Suburbia: Its People and their Politics* (Boston: Houghton Mifflin, 1958).

A SELECTION OF BOOKS DEALING WITH BLACKS AND FOREIGN BORN IN AMERICAN CITIES: Rowland T. Berthoff, *British Immigrants in Industrial America, 1790–1950* (Cambridge: Harvard University Press, 1953); *Andrew Billingsley, *Black Families in White America* (Englewood Cliffs, N.J.: Prentice-Hall, 1968); Joseph Boskin, "The Revolt of the Urban Ghettoes," *The Annals of the American Academy of Political and Social Science*, CCCLXXXII (March, 1969), 1–14;

*Joseph Boskin, *Urban Racial Violence in the Twentieth Century* (Beverly Hills, Calif.: Glencoe Press, 1969); Letitia W. Brown, *Free Negroes in the District of Columbia, 1790–1946* (New York: Oxford, 1972); Lawrence R. Chenault, *The Puerto Rican Migrant in New York* (Columbia University Press, 1938); *Kenneth B. Clark, *Dark Ghetto: Dilemmas of Social Power* (New York: Harper and Row, 1965); Nathan Cohen, *The Los Angeles Riots: A Socio-Psychological Study* (New York: Praeger, 1970); *St. Clair Drake and Horace Cayton, *Black Metropolis: A Study of Negro Life in a Northern City* (Harper and Row, 1962); *W. E. B. DuBois, *The Philadelphia Negro: A Social Study.* Introduction by E. Digby Baltzell (New York: Schocken Books, 1967 [first published, 1899]); Robert Ernst, *Immigrant Life in New York City, 1825–1863* (New York: King's Crown Press, 1949); Farley Reynolds, "The Urbanization of Negroes in the United States," *Journal of Social History,* I (Spring, 1968), 241–58; Isaac M. Fein, *The Making of an American Jewish Community: A History of Baltimore Jewry from 1773 to 1920* (Philadelphia: Jewish Publication Society of America, 1971); *Robert M. Fogelson, *Violence as Protest: A Study of Riots and Ghettos* (Garden City, N.Y.: Doubleday, 1971); *E. Franklin Frazier, *The Negro Family in the United States* (New York: Dryden Press, 1948); *Herbert J. Gans, *The Urban Villagers: Group and Class in the Life of Italian-Americans* (New York: Free Press, 1962); Rudolph Glanz, *Jew and Italian — Historic Group Relations and the New Immigration (1881–1924)* (New York: Ktav Publishing House, 1970); *Nathan Glazer and Daniel P. Moynihan, *Beyond the Melting Pot: The Negroes, Puerto Ricans, Jews, Italians, and Irish of New York City* (Cambridge: M.I.T. Press, 1970); Milton Gordon, "Assimilation in America: Theory and Reality," *Daedalus,* XC (Spring, 1961), 263–85; *Milton Gordon, *Assimilation in American Life: The Role of Race, Religion, and National Origins* (New York: Oxford, 1964); Leo Grebler, Joan W. Moore, and Ralph Guzman, *The Mexican-American People* (New York, 1970); *Constance M. Green, *The Secret City: A History of Race Relations in the Nation's Capital* (Princeton: Princeton University Press, 1967); Oscar Handlin, *Adventure in Freedom* (New York: McGraw-Hill, 1954); *Oscar Handlin, *Boston's Immigrants, 1790–1865: A Study in Acculturation* (Cambridge: Harvard University Press, 1941, 1959); *Oscar Handlin, *The Newcomers: Negroes and Puerto Ricans in a Changing Metropolis* (Cambridge: Harvard University Press, 1959); *Oscar Handlin, *The Uprooted* (Boston: Little, Brown, 1951); Hutchins Hapgood, *The Spirit of the Ghetto,* ed. by Moses Rischin (Cambridge, Mass.: Belknap Press, 1967); *Will Herberg, *Protestant-Catholic-Jew: An Essay in American Religious Sociology* (Garden City, N.Y.: Anchor Books, 1960); *John Higham,

Strangers in the Land: Patterns of American Nativism, 1860–1925 (New York: Atheneum, 1963); Nathan I. Huggins, *Harlem Renaissance* (New York: Oxford, 1971); E. P. Hutchinson, *Immigrants and their Children, 1850–1950* (New York: John Wiley and Sons, 1965); Luciano J. Iorizzo and Salvatore Mondello, *The Italian-Americans* (New York: Twayne Publishers, 1971); *Maldwyn A. Jones, American Immigration* (Chicago: University of Chicago Press, 1960); David M. Katzman, *Before the Ghetto: Black Detroit in the Nineteenth Century* (Urbana: University of Illinois Press, 1972); Judith Kramer and Seymour Leventman, *Children of the Gilded Ghetto* (New Haven: Yale University Press, 1961); Kenneth L. Kusmer, *A Ghetto Takes Shape: Black Cleveland, 1890–1930* (Urbana: University of Illinois Press, 1973); Stanley Lieberson, *Ethnic Patterns in American Cities* (New York: Free Press, 1963); *Leon F. Litwack, North of Slavery: The Negro in the Free States, 1790–1860* (Chicago: University of Chicago Press, 1961); *Edgar Litt, Ethnic Politics in the United States* (Glenview, Ill.: Scott, Foresman, 1970); *August Meier and Elliott Rudwick, From Plantation to Ghetto* (New York: Hill and Wang, 1966); C. Wright Mills, Clarence Senior, and Rose K. Goldsen, *Puerto Rican Journey* (New York: Harper and Row, 1950); *The Negro Family: The Case for National Action* (Washington: Office of Policy Planning and Research, U.S. Department of Labor, 1965); Humbert S. Nelli, *The Italians in Chicago, 1880–1930: A Study in Ethnic Mobility* (New York: Oxford, 1970); Earl F. Niehaus, *The Irish in New Orleans, 1800–1860* (Baton Rouge: Louisiana State University Press, 1965); *Gilbert Osofsky, Harlem: The Making of a Ghetto: Negro New York, 1890–1930* (New York: Harper and Row, 1966); Roi Ottley and William J. Weatherby, eds., *The Negro in New York: An Informal Social History* (New York: New York Public Library and Oceana Publications, 1967); *Talcott Parsons and Kenneth B. Clark, eds., The Negro American* (Boston: Houghton Mifflin, 1966); *Thomas F. Pettigrew, A Profile of the Negro American* (Princeton: Van Nostrand, 1964); Lee Rainwater, *Behind Ghetto Walls: Black Families in a Federal Slum* (Chicago: Aldine, 1970); *Lee Rainwater and William Yancey, eds., The Moynihan Report and the Politics of Controversy* (Cambridge: M.I.T. Press, 1967); *Moses Rischin, The Promised City: New York's Jews, 1870–1914* (Cambridge: Harvard University Press, 1962); *Elliott M. Rudwick, Race Riot at East St. Louis, July 2, 1917* (New York: Atheneum, 1964); *Seth M. Scheiner, Negro Mecca: A History of the Negro in New York City, 1865–1920* (New York: New York University Press, 1965); William Shannon, *The American Irish* (New York: Macmillan, 1963); *Richard B. Sherman, ed., The Negro and the City* (Englewood Cliffs, N.J.: Prentice-Hall, 1970); Robert Shogan and Tom

Craig, *The Detroit Race Riot: A Study in Violence* (Philadelphia: Chilton Books, 1964); *Allen H. Spear, *Black Chicago: The Making of a Negro Ghetto, 1890–1920* (Chicago: University of Chicago Press, 1967); *Robert S. Starobin, *Industrial Slavery in the Old South* (New York: Oxford, 1969); Arvarh E. Strickland, *History of the Chicago Urban League* (Urbana: University of Illinois Press, 1973); Louis J. Swichkow and Lloyd P. Gartner, *The History of the Jews of Milwaukee* (Philadelphia: Jewish Publication Society of America, 1963); *Karl E. Taeuber and Alma F. Taeuber, *Negroes in Cities: Residential Segregation and Neighborhood Change* (New York: Atheneum, 1969); William I. Thomas and Florian Znaniecki, *The Polish Peasant in Europe and America* (New York: Dover Publications, 1958, revised ed., 1971); William Tuttle, Jr., *Race Riot: Chicago in the Red Summer of 1919* (New York: Atheneum, 1970); *Richard C. Wade, *Slavery in the Cities: The South, 1820–1860* (New York: Oxford, 1964); *David Ward, *Cities and Immigrants: A Geography of Change in Nineteenth-Century America* (New York: Oxford, 1971); *W. Lloyd Warner et al., *Color and Human Nature: Negro Personality Development in a Northern City* (New York: American Council on Education, 1941); W. Lloyd Warner and Leo Srole, *The Social Systems of American Ethnic Groups* (New York: Yale University Press, 1945); William F. Whyte, *Street Corner Society* (Chicago: University of Chicago Press, 1943, 1955); Phyllis H. Williams, *South Italian Folkways in Europe and America* (London: Oxford, 1938); *Louis Wirth, *The Ghetto* (Chicago: University of Chicago Press, 1928); Carl Wittke, *We Who Built America: The Saga of the Immigrant* (New York: Prentice-Hall, 1939).

A SELECTION OF BOOKS ON URBAN ARCHITECTURE AND CITY PLAN-NING: [*Architecture*] *Wayne Andrews, *Architecture, Ambition and Americans: A Social History of American Architecture* (New York: The Free Press, 1964); *John Burchard and Albert Bush-Brown, *The Architecture of America: A Social and Cultural History* (Boston: Little, Brown, 1961); Carl Condit, *American Building Art: The Nineteenth Century* (New York: Oxford, 1960); *Carl Condit, *American Building: Materials and Techniques from the Beginning of the Colonial Period to the Present* (Chicago: University of Chicago Press, 1968); *Carl Condit, *The Chicago School of Architecture: A History of Commercial and Public Building in the Chicago Area, 1875–1925* (Chicago: University of Chicago Press, 1964); *Carl Condit, *The Rise of the Skyscraper* (Chicago: University of Chicago Press, 1952); *John Coolidge, *Mill and Mansion: A Study of Architecture and Society in Lowell, Massachusetts, 1820–1865* (New York: Columbia University Press, 1942); *Theodore Crosby, *Architecture: City Sense* (New York: Reinhold, 1965); W. Hawkins Ferry, *The Buildings of*

Detroit (Detroit: Wayne State University Press, 1968); James M. Fitch, *Architecture and the Esthetics of Plenty* (New York: Columbia University Press, 1961); [Anon.], *A History of Real Estate, Building and Architecture in New York City* (New York: Arno Press, 1971; originally published in 1898); Lewis Mumford, *The Brown Decades* (New York: Dover, 1955); *Lewis Mumford, *From the Ground Up: Observations on Contemporary Architecture, Housing, Highway Building, and Civic Design* (New York: Harcourt, Brace, 1956); *Vincent Scully, *American Architecture and Urbanism* (New York: Praeger, 1969); Donald R. Torbert, *Significant Architecture in the History of Minneapolis* (Minneapolis: City Planning Department, 1969); *Christopher Tunnard and Henry Hope Reed, *American Skyline* (Boston: Houghton Mifflin, 1955); Winston Weisman, "A New View of the Skyscraper," in *The Rise of an American Architecture*, ed. by Edgar Kaufmann, Jr. (New York: Praeger, 1970), 115–60; [*Planning*] Walter L. Creese, *The Search for Environment: The Garden City Before and After* (New Haven: Yale University Press, 1966); George F. Chadwick, *The Park and the Town* (New York: Praeger, 1966); Albert Fein, "The American City: The Ideal and the Real," in *The Rise of an American Architecture*, ed. by Edgar Kaufmann, Jr. (New York: Praeger, 1970), 51–112; *Albert Fein, *Frederick Law Olmsted and the American Environmental Tradition* (New York: Braziller, 1972); Albert Fein, ed., *Landscape into Cityscape: Frederick Law Olmsted's Plans for a Greater New York City* (Ithaca: Cornell University Press, 1967); Arthur B. Gallion and Simon Eisner, *The Urban Pattern: City Planning and Design* (New York: Van Nostrand, 1950); *Herbert J. Gans, *People and Plans: Essays on Urban Problems and Solutions* (New York: Basic Books, 1968); Anthony N. B. Garvan, *Architecture and Town Planning in Colonial Connecticut* (New Haven: Yale University Press, 1951); William Haller, *The Puritan Frontier: Town Planning in New England Colonial Development, 1630–1660* (New York: Columbia University Press, 1951); *Roy Lubove, *Community Planning in the 1920's: The Regional Planning Association of America* (Pittsburgh: University of Pittsburgh Press, 1963); John W. Reps, *The Making of Urban America: A History of City Planning in the United States* (Princeton: Princeton University Press, 1965); John W. Reps, *Monumental Washington: The Planning and Development of the Capital Center* (Princeton: Princeton University Press, 1966); John W. Reps, *Tidewater Towns: City Planning in Colonial Virginia and Maryland* (Charlottesville: University Press of Virginia, 1972); *John W. Reps, *Town Planning in Frontier America* (Princeton: Princeton University Press, 1969); *Mel Scott, *American City Planning since 1890* (Berkeley: University of Califorina Press, 1969); Mel Scott, *The San Francisco Bay Area: A Metropolis in*

Perspective (Berkeley and Los Angeles: University of California Press, 1959); *Sam Bass Warner, Jr., ed., *Planning for a Nation of Cities* (Cambridge: M.I.T. Press, 1966); William H. Wilson, *The City Beautiful Movement in Kansas City* (Columbia: University of Missouri Press, 1964).

A SELECTION OF READINGS DEALING WITH THE NATURE OF URBAN HISTORY AND THE INTERPRETATION OF THE AMERICAN URBAN EXPERIENCE: [Historiography] Asa Briggs, "The Study of Cities," *Confluence*, VII (Summer, 1958), 107–14; *John Burchard and Oscar Handlin, eds., *The Historian and the City* (Cambridge: Harvard University Press and M.I.T. Press, 1963); Allen F. Davis, "The American Historian vs. the City," parts 1 and 2, *Social Studies*, LVI (1965), 91–96, 127–35; H. J. Dyos, ed., *The Study of Urban History* (London: Edward Arnold, 1968); *Oscar Handlin, "The Modern City as a Field of Historical Study," in *The Historian and the City, op. cit.*, 1–26; Philip M. Hauser and Leo F. Schnore, *The Study of Urbanization* (New York: John Wiley and Sons, 1965); Mark D. Hirsch, "Reflections on Urban History and Urban Reform, 1856–1915," in Donald Sheehan and Harold Syrett, eds., *Essays in American Historiography* (New York: Columbia University Press, 1960), 109–37; Dwight W. Hoover, "The Diverging Paths of American Urban History," *American Quarterly*, XX (Summer, 1968), 296–317; Dwight W. Hoover, *A Teachers' Guide to American Urban History* (Chicago: Quadrangle Books, 1971); Eric E. Lampard, "American Historians and the Study of Urbanization," *American Historical Review*, LXVII (October, 1961), 49–61; Eric E. Lampard, "The Dimensions of Urban History: A Footnote to the 'Urban Crisis,' " *Pacific Historical Review*, XXXIX (August, 1970), 261–78; Roy Lubove, "The Urbanization Process: An Approach to Historical Research," *Journal of the American Institute of Planners*, XXXIII (January, 1967), 33–39; Blake McKelvey, "American Urban History Today," *American Historical Review*, LVII (July, 1952), 919–29; *Leo F. Schnore, ed., *Social Science and the City: A Survey of Urban Research* (New York: Praeger, 1968); Stephan Thernstrom, "Reflections on the New Urban History," *Daedalus* (Spring, 1971), 359–72; Richard C. Wade, "An Agenda for Urban History," in Herbert J. Bass, ed., *The State of American History* (Chicago: Quadrangle, 1970), 43–69; Sam Bass Warner, Jr., "If All the World Were Philadelphia: A Scaffolding for Urban History, 1774–1930," *American Historical Review*, LXXIV (October, 1968), 26–43; Dana F. White, "The Underdeveloped Discipline: Interdisciplinary Directions in American Urban History," *American Studies: An Interdisciplinary Newsletter*, IX (1971), 3–16; R. Richard Wohl, "Urbanism, Urbanity, and the Historian," *University of Kansas City Review*, XXII (Autumn, 1955), 53–61. [Theory and Interpretation] Gunnar Alexandersson, *The In-*

dustrial Structure of American Cities: A Geographic Study of Urban Economy in the United States (Lincoln: University of Nebraska Press, 1956); Harlan Gilmore, *Transportation and the Growth of Cities* (Glencoe, Ill.: Free Press, 1953); Bert F. Hoselitz, "The City, the Factory, and Economic Growth," *American Economic Review,* XLV (May, 1955), 166–84; Homer Hoyt, *The Structure and Growth of Residential Neighborhoods in American Cities* (Washington: Government Printing Office, 1939); *Eric E. Lampard, "The Evolving System of Cities in the United States: Urbanization and Economic Developments," in Harvey S. Perloff and Loudon Wingo, Jr., eds., *Issues in Urban Economics* (Baltimore, 1968), 81–139; Eric E. Lampard, "The History of Cities in the Economically Advanced Areas," *Economic Development and Cultural Change,* III (1955), 81–136; Richard L. Meier, *A Communications Theory of Urban Growth* (Cambridge: M.I.T. Press, 1962); Allan R. Pred, *The Spatial Dynamics of U.S. Urban-Industrial Growth, 1800–1914* (Cambridge: M.I.T. Press, 1966); *Leonard Reissman, *The Urban Process: Cities in Industrial Society* (New York: Free Press, 1964); *Lloyd Rodwin, *Nations and Cities: A Comparison of Strategies for Urban Growth* (Boston: Houghton Mifflin, 1970); Leo F. Schnore, *The Urban Scene: Human Ecology and Demography* (New York: Free Press, 1965); Stephan Thernstrom and Peter R. Knights, "Men in Motion: Some Data and Speculation about Urban Population Mobility in Nineteenth-Century America," *Journal of Interdisciplinary History,* I (1971); *Stephan Thernstrom and Richard Sennett, eds., *Nineteenth-Century Cities: Essays in the New Urban History* (New Haven: Yale University Press, 1969); *Adna F. Weber, *The Growth of Cities in the Nineteenth Century: A Study in Statistics* (New York: Macmillan, 1899) — a pioneering study in the use of comparative statistics, reprinted, 1969 (New York: Greenwood); *[Louis Wirth], *Louis Wirth on Cities and Social Life: Selected Papers,* ed. by Albert J. Reiss, Jr. (Chicago: University of Chicago Press); *Lewis Mumford, *The Culture of Cities* (New York: Harcourt, Brace, and World, 1938); *Lewis Mumford, *The City in History: Its Origins, Its Transformations, and Its Prospects* (New York: Harcourt, Brace, and World, 1961); Page Smith, *As A City Upon a Hill: The Town in American History* (New York: Alfred Knopf, 1966); Arthur M. Schlesinger, Sr., "The City in American History," *Mississippi Valley Historical Review,* XXVII (June, 1940), 43–66; Bayrd Still, "The History of the City in American Life," *American Review,* II (1962), 20–34; *Richard C. Wade, "The City in History — Some American Perspectives," in Werner Z. Hirsch, ed., *Urban Life and Form* (New York: Holt, Rinehart, and Winston, 1963); *Robert H. Bremner, *From the Depths: The Discovery of Poverty in the United States*

(New York: New York University Press, 1956); Michael H. Cowan, *City of the West: Emerson, America, and the Urban Metaphor* (New Haven: Yale University Press, 1967); Scott Donaldson, "City and Country: Marriage Proposals," *American Quarterly*, XX (Fall, 1968), 547–66; George A. Dunlap, *The City in the American Novel, 1789– 1900* (Philadelphia: Russell and Russell, 1934); Blanche H. Gelfant, *The American City Novel, 1900–1940* (Norman: University of Oklahoma Press, 1954); Charles N. Glaab, "The Historian and the American Urban Tradition," *Wisconsin Magazine of History*, XLVII (Autumn, 1963), 12–25; *Scott Greer, *The Emerging City: Myth and Reality* (New York: Free Press, 1962); W. Stull Holt, "Some Consequences of the Urban Movement in American History," *Pacific Historical Review*, XXII (November, 1953), 337–51; *Daniel Levine, *Varieties of Reform Thought* (Madison: State Historical Society of Wisconsin, 1964); *Kevin Lynch, *The Image of the City* (Cambridge: M.I.T. Press, 1960); Kevin Lynch, "The Pattern of the Metropolis," in Kevin Lynch and Lloyd Rodwin, eds., "The Future Metropolis," *Daedalus* (Winter, 1961), 79–98; *Leo Marx, *The Machine in the Garden* (New York: Oxford, 1964); Lloyd Rodwin, ed., *The Future Metropolis* (New York: Braziller, 1960); Anselm Strauss, *Images of the American City* (Glencoe, Ill.: Free Press, 1961); *Morton White and Lucia White, *The Intellectual versus the City: From Thomas Jefferson to Frank Lloyd Wright* (Cambridge: Harvard University Press, 1962).

INDEX TO SPECIAL TOPICS
AND SELECTED CITIES

Air pollution, 185–86, 193, 429, 456, 471–73, 538, 540

American Revolution, 28, 49–57, 494

Annexation, 225–27, 257–58

Architecture: commercial, 148–50, 249–52; residential, 36, 65, 102, 154, 156–58, 160, 223, 506

Atlanta, Ga., 135–36, 214–17, 391–92, 437–38

Automobiles, 226–27, 355, 360–62, 372–73, 375, 389–92, 467–72

Baltimore, Md., 17, 57–60, 81, 112–14, 132, 180, 182, 226–27, 468–69, 494

Blacks: in city populations, 33, 102, 117, 127, 130, 132–37, 277–80, 401, 403–4, 413, 443, 445–46, 539; living conditions, 131–32, 408–14; occupations, social life, status, 32–35, 40–41, 127–39, 278–80, 405–8, 461–62, 474, 491–92, 530, 539; tension with other groups, 124–25, 134, 279–82, 410–17, 419, 439–41, 449, 531. See also Slaves; Mob activity.

Bosses. See Machine politics.

Boston, Mass., 13–14, 27–30, 33–36, 50–53, 57–59, 80–83, 86, 117, 120–21, 146–47, 178, 181, 186, 189, 241–42, 255, 271, 341, 365–66, 399–403, 488, 499–500

Brooklyn, N.Y., 86, 188–89, 206, 333

Buffalo, N.Y., 82, 114–15, 174, 275

Catholics, 102, 124–26, 178, 271, 275, 299, 409, 419

Cemeteries, rural-style, 189–90, 511

Charleston, S.C., 21–22, 33, 35–37, 39, 53, 56, 80, 113, 115–16

Chicago, Ill., 93, 98–101, 121–22, 148, 209–14, 249–51, 258, 272, 278–82, 169, 293–95, 318–19, 341, 343–44, 397–98, 408–11, 420–21, 451–54, 514

Chicanos. See Mexicans.

Chinese, 223–24

Churches, 129, 165, 253, 279, 297–300. See also Catholics, Jews, Salvation Army.

Cincinnati, Ohio, 62–64, 117, 122–23, 181–82, 314

Cities: arguments for, 19–21, 25–26, 112, 196–99, 234–37, 239, 259, 379–84, 482; criticism of, 18, 26–27, 71–73, 104–8, 160, 193–98, 269, 367–71, 376, 481, 500–1; personalities of, 27, 36–37, 65, 101–3, 252, 262, 492, 508; social responsibility of, 174–75, 191, 200, 292, 296, 301–2, 329–32, 345, 348–49, 426, 469, 511, 524. See also Urbanism, attitude toward.

Citizen associations, 169, 172–74, 183, 317–24; city clubs, 317–19

City beautification, 202, 319, 341–44, 510

City growth, causes, 10, 60–65, 80–84, 86, 88–89, 92–93, 116–17, 215, 228–43, 261–62, 277, 333–34, 352–53, 389, 393, 481, 496

City promotion, speculation, 16, 62, 64, 81–83, 94–100, 109, 160–1, 227–29, 231–34, 362–64, 515

Civil War, urbanism and, 104–16, 168

Class structure, 34–35, 53–55, 66, 138, 153–57, 159, 492, 507

Cleveland, Ohio, 153, 157, 226–27, 245, 336–38, 421, 476

Commerce. See Trade, commerce.

Crafts and craftsmen. See Labor.

Crime, vice, 179, 286–87, 308–11, 413, 446–47, 476–77, 497, 538–39
Cubans, 393
Czechs, 397–98

Denver, Colo., 217–18, 272, 320–21, 421
Detroit, Mich., 225–27, 272, 313–14, 334–36, 383, 412, 414, 421
Drugs. *See* Crime, vice.

Education, 35, 124, 131, 137, 186, 217, 301, 450, 461–63
Elevated railways, 244–45
Elevators, 153, 249–51, 505–6
Entertainment, public, 35–37, 102, 124, 138–39, 142, 186, 236, 241
Epidemics, 68, 184
European cities, size, example of, 10, 15, 24, 79, 165, 178–80, 182–84, 190–91, 193, 202, 257–58, 292–93, 299, 305, 329, 331–34, 340, 342–45

Family, impact of city on, 108, 156, 162–64, 255, 259, 273, 275, 283–86, 353, 401–3, 418–19, 447, 474–75
Federal aid to cities, 353, 365, 389, 419–42, 483–87, 532–33, 539
Fiction, drama, city in, 140–46, 237–40; 284–87, 306–8, 503–4
Fire protection, 40–41, 45, 141, 146–48, 181–82, 454, 505
Foreign born: in cities, 33, 116–24, 261–75, 392–96, 517–18; living conditions, 120–24, 275, 283–85; opposition to, 33, 124–26, 172, 491; role of city in acculturation and assimilation, 33, 122–23, 130, 263, 268–77, 294–95, 297–98, 397–403, 409, 502
French element, 65, 102, 122, 224
Frontier, cities on. *See* West.

Gangs, 140–41, 177, 180, 475, 505
Garden cities, new towns, 260–61, 291–92, 368–75, 517, 527–28
Gary, Ind., 253, 261
Gas lights, 108, 175, 247
Germans, 32–33, 59–60, 102–3, 117–19, 122–24, 241–42, 491, 502
Government, municipal, 39–49, 56,

66, 110, 165–86, 303–16, 323–40, 447–66, 509, 521, 534

Health protection, 40, 68–69, 176, 182–86, 331, 381, 463
Home rule, 168, 327–29, 331
Horsecars, 84–88, 160, 171, 197–98, 244
Hotels, boarding houses, 108, 150–53, 158
Housing, 162–64, 280, 282–92, 340, 344–45, 413, 424–41, 474, 533
Houston, Tex., 326

Immigration, 17, 33–34, 61–62, 116, 261–63, 496. *See also* Foreign born.
Indianapolis, Ind., 232–34, 457
Industry, 17, 28, 58–59, 63–64, 71–73, 88–92, 104, 117, 212–14, 228–31, 234
Institutional church, 297–99
Irish, 33–34, 65, 117–21, 125–26, 178, 284–87, 306–8, 397–98, 491, 509
Italians, 125, 224, 269–72, 294–95, 397, 399–403, 416, 531

Jefferson on cities, 71, 482–83, 496–97
Jews, 262, 268, 272–74, 276–77, 299, 415–16, 419, 439–40

Kansas City, Mo., 217–18, 231, 342–43

Labor, 17, 30–33, 47, 53–54, 66, 68, 89–91, 116, 121, 123, 126, 142, 255, 277–78, 294, 322–23, 452
Large cities, awareness of, 73, 173, 179, 194, 197, 199, 206–9, 230–31, 328, 375, 484, 512, 539–40
Leadership, in cities, 46–49, 66–67, 99, 166, 170–72, 305, 311–12, 314, 316–22, 325–27, 335–36, 492, 508–9
Levittown, N.Y., 362, 377
Libraries, 35–37, 48, 186, 217, 463
Los Angeles, Cal., 225–27, 318, 361, 365–66, 376, 422, 471–72
Lowell, Mass., 59, 89–91, 120

Machine politics, 167–69, 171–72,

302–4, 306–8, 314–16, 321, 334, 336, 338–39, 397–98, 447–48, 451–54, 521, 534

Manufacturing. *See* Industry.

Mayoralty, 39, 49, 66, 166, 168–69, 172, 182, 313, 324, 334–40, 424–27, 431, 441–42, 447–54, 466, 508

Metropolitan government, 168, 183, 429, 455–62, 535–36; Toronto, 535

Metropolitan growth, 4, 83, 202, 206, 258, 352–60, 429, 526, 528–29

Mexicans, 219, 224, 396, 415, 474

Miami, Fla., 363–64, 393, 457–61

Milwaukee, Wis., 117, 122–23, 167, 169, 178, 231–32, 248–49, 318, 339–40, 398–99, 454, 476, 502

Minneapolis, Minn., 217, 231, 250, 463–64

Mob activity, riots, 50–53, 108, 124–26, 128–30, 177–80, 280–82, 411–13, 491

Mobility, physical, social, 35, 122, 156, 158, 181, 254, 396, 408–11, 414–15, 419, 475, 485

Model cities program, 435–38, 450

Municipal corruption. *See* Government, municipal; Machine politics.

Municipal ownership, 331–40, 523–24. *See also* Cities, social responsibility of.

Music, 35–36, 139, 186, 240–42

Nashville, Tenn., 102, 457

Negroes. *See* Blacks.

Neighborhood, concern for, 259–60, 303, 373, 400–3, 414–15, 434–38, 461–66, 479, 536

New Haven, Conn., 13–14, 489

New Orleans, La., 64–65, 73, 109–11, 133–34, 157, 272

New towns. *See* Garden cities.

New York, N.Y., 15, 28–29, 31–33, 35–43, 47–51, 54–59, 69–71, 73, 80–87, 106, 123–26, 137–39, 154–56, 158, 162–65, 168–72, 176–80, 188, 226–28, 244–47, 251–53, 270–71, 273–77, 296–300, 309–11, 319, 341, 383–84, 386–87, 404–6, 417–21, 426, 448–50, 455, 465–66, 470–3, 476–77, 494, 506, 532

Newark, N.J., 280, 412, 414, 416

Noise, 27, 140, 198, 467, 473

Omnibuses, 84–88, 197

Park Forest, Ill., 362, 377

Parks, gardens, 16, 23–24, 188–94, 202, 335

Philadelphia, Pa., 15–18, 28–29, 33–37, 39, 44–46, 53, 57, 62, 68–69, 73, 86–88, 91, 101–2, 125, 129–31, 159–60, 169, 178, 180, 182, 188, 247, 272, 386, 421–23, 494

Pittsburgh, Pa., 63–64, 80, 91–92, 311, 383, 421

Planning, city, regional, 15–16, 18, 21–24, 160, 186–88, 202, 339–49, 370–75, 424, 435–40, 490

Poles, 272–75, 339, 398–99

Police, 17, 39–40, 43–44, 48, 56, 177–80, 309–11, 411, 446, 454, 460–61, 478–80

Poverty, poor relief, 35, 38, 69–71, 162-65, 420–27, 473–76, 496, 538–39

Puerto Ricans, 417–19, 449, 474

Pullman, Ill., 253, 261

Radburn, N.J., 371–74

Railroads and urban growth, 80–84, 89, 93–94, 99–101, 113, 210, 212, 215, 219–20, 222, 228–30, 369

Reform, civic, 172–74, 300–1, 316–40, 344–49, 525–26

Regulation, municipal, 17, 34, 39–43, 176–77, 184–86, 288–92, 329, 347, 467–69, 525

Reston, Va., 374–75

Retail stores, 149–50, 155–56, 365–66, 505

Revenue sharing, 441, 539

Richmond, Va., 113, 133, 244–46

Riots. *See* Mob activity.

Rochester, N.Y., 174, 272

Russians, 272–74

St. Louis, Mo., 99–103, 112, 122, 191–92, 311–13, 318, 421, 475

Salvation Army, 299–300

San Francisco, Cal., 187–88, 222–24

Savannah, Ga., 21–24, 56, 113, 188

Settlement houses, 293–96, 301, 520

Shopping centers, 365–66

Skyscrapers. *See* Architecture.

Slaves, slavery, in cities, 32, 34–35, 40–41, 111–12, 132–34, 491

Slums. *See* Tenements.
Social life, 27, 35–37, 155–56
Social mobility. *See* Mobility.
South, urbanism in, 18–24, 78, 103–16, 214, 216, 500–1
Spatial patterns, 11, 13, 16, 22, 63, 65–66, 85, 91, 154, 161–62, 199, 202, 209, 247, 253–54, 278, 352, 384–88, 413
State legislatures, relations with, 39, 66, 166–68, 178, 309, 327–28, 459, 508, 533, 540
Statehood for cities, 168, 328–29, 537
Streetcars, electric, 245–46, 254
Streets (cleaning, lighting, paving), 40, 42, 45–46; 68, 167, 175–77, 187, 247–49, 304–5, 316, 319–20
Suburbanization, 83, 85–86, 159–61, 254–61, 353–67, 390, 408, 442, 447, 474, 484, 516–17, 530; reaction to, 160–161, 254–60, 360–67, 375–80, 516–17, 526, 530
Subways, 246–47, 256
Swedes, 121–22, 279

Technological change: resistance to, 87, 248–49, 391; role in city growth, 84–86, 157, 243–53, 454–55
Tenements, tenement reform, regulation, 154, 162–64, 182–83, 185, 282–92, 296, 519
Theater, 35, 37, 138–39, 240–41
Toledo, Ohio, 338–39, 421
Towns, colonial, 11, 13–14, 17–19, 26, 489, 492
Trade, commerce, 13–15, 17–18, 28–32, 57–60, 64–65, 73, 100–1, 213–22, 234
Traffic regulation, 41, 454–55

Transit facilities, 66, 84–88, 243–47, 313–14, 335, 391, 445, 469–71, 537

Urban amenities, 63, 67, 148–58, 198–200, 214–15, 218, 235–36, 240–43, 353, 382, 384, 482, 497, 510–11, 540
Urban regions, 343–44, 353, 385–88, 528–29
Urban renewal, 382–83, 475
Urban rivalry, 80–83, 99–101, 108–9, 113–16, 499–500
Urbanism: attitude toward, 3–6, 13, 22, 27, 71–73, 76, 93–94, 98–99, 104–12, 139, 143, 152, 159–60, 192, 194–203, 230–31, 235–40, 252, 258–59, 330, 347–49, 376, 379–82, 427–29, 480–87, 512–14, 539; criteria for identifying, 2–3, 78, 206, 224–25, 488, 515
Urbanization, nature and extent of, 2–5, 10–13, 57–58, 103, 199, 206–7, 352, 387–89, 428, 525–26. *See also* City growth.

Washington, D.C., 132–33, 135, 343, 442–47
Waste removal, 40, 42, 176–77, 471
Water, provision of, 40, 175, 454
Welfare. *See* Poverty, poor relief.
West, cities in settlement of, 58, 60–65, 72, 76, 92–103, 151, 212–13, 217–24, 232
Women, in city, 89–91, 138, 141–44, 295, 299–300, 319–21

Youth, in city, 11, 140–48, 162–65, 284–87, 412, 447, 462, 477

Zoning, 253, 345, 347, 384